Christian Theology

Advance praise for *Christian Theology*

"*Christian Theology: An Introduction* is a work of prodigious learning and notable clarity. Alister McGrath here combines a mastery of the history of doctrine with his gift of communication to produce the finest university textbook available in this field. The author introduces the reader to the major Christian teachings, surveys their historical development, examines the landmark disputes, and explores myriad interpretative traditions. McGrath demonstrates throughout a knowledge of classical and contemporary material – from patristics to postmodernism – that matches his well-known expertise in Reformation studies. A glossary of key theological terms further enriches the work as a resource for private study as well as the classroom."

Professor Gabriel Fackre, Abbot Professor of Christian Theology, Andover Newton Theological School

"Dr McGrath appreciates the importance of the diversity of Christianity as well as the excitement and relevance of the key issues today. He has produced a work that can help in teaching yourself theology or can act as a valuable reference work for students in particular courses. It is a genuine introduction, with clear explanations, a full glossary and index, good recommendations for further reading, and also questions for discussion. Above all, the whole range of major doctrines is taken seriously and the reader is introduced to some of the ways they are being thought about today."

Professor David F. Ford, Regius Professor of Divinity, University of Cambridge

"This comprehensive and up-to-date training manual on theologizing as a Christian is outstanding of its kind. Dr McGrath's confident clarity, open orthodoxy, shrewd judgment, and didactic flair should secure for so user-friendly a textbook a long and fruitful life."

Professor James Packer, Sangwoo Youtong Chee Professor of Theology, Regent College, Vancouver

"Dr McGrath's *Christian Theology: An Introduction* admirably provides exactly what its title promises. It offers a clear, eminently readable and perceptive introduction to a vast range of issues and thinkers in historical theology, as well as incorporating a basic philosophical and systematic theology. It judiciously places thinkers and issues in a broad historical and theological context, achieving a due sense of historical perspective as well as theological information. It will kindle engagement on the part of the reader, and I warmly commend it to all students who are beginning a serious study of Christian theology."

Professor Anthony Thiselton, Professor of Christian Theology and Head of Department, University of Nottingham

"This is an excellent introduction to theology. It is very clearly set out and carefully planned to be an educational resource. It provides extremely helpful grounding for any student of theology. It will be invaluable as a clear and unprejudiced guide to the whole discipline of theology."

Revd. Professor J. S. K. Ward, Regius Professor of Divinity, University of Oxford

"Alister McGrath's book is a delight to read and immensely instructing. It is well-ordered, systematic, and lucid in its presentation – clearly the work of someone well attuned to the needs of students. It presents insightful analysis of a range of theological opinions without being prescriptive or overly dogmatic. We are introduced to an impressive array of theologians: classical and modern; eastern and western; 'liberal' and 'conservative'; male and female – and yet without being overwhelmed by them all . . . I recommend this book without reservation and am confident that it will become the standard textbook for a generation of theological students."

Revd. Dr John W. Pryor, Australian College of Theology, New South Wales

Also by Alister E. McGrath from Blackwell

Reformation Thought, 2nd edn (1993)
The Genesis of Doctrine (1990)
A Life of John Calvin (1990)
Luther's Theology of the Cross (1987)
The Intellectual Origins of the European Reformation (1987)
The Blackwell Encyclopedia of Modern Christian Thought (editor; 1993)

Christian Theology

An Introduction

Alister E. McGrath

BLACKWELL
Oxford UK & Cambridge USA

First published 1994
Reprinted 1994

Blackwell Publishers
108 Cowley Road
Oxford OX4 1JF
UK

238 Main Street
Cambridge, Massachusetts 02142
USA

British Library Cataloguing in Publication Data
A CIP catalogue record for this book is available from
the British Library.

Library of Congress Cataloging-in-Publication Data
McGrath, Alister E., 1953–
Christian theology: an introduction/Alister E. McGrath.
p.   cm.
Includes bibliographical references and index.
ISBN 0-631-16078-7 (alk. paper). – ISBN 0-631-16079-5 (pbk.:
alk. paper)
1. Theology, Doctrinal – Introductions. I. Title.
BT65.M34   1994
230—dc20   93-18797
                                                   CIP

Typeset in 10½ on 12½pt Palatino
by Best-set Typesetter Ltd., Hong Kong
Printed in the USA

This book is printed on acid-free paper

Contents

Part III   Christian Theology

List of Illustrations

Preface

The Swiss theologian Karl Barth offers us a vision of Christian theology at its finest. It is, he suggests, like Tuscan or Umbrian landscapes, which hold us in awe on account of the breathtaking views which they offer. Even the most distant perspectives seem so clear. Barth is but one of many theologians to have stressed the sheer excitement that the study of Christian theology can bring. This book is written in the conviction that theology is one of the most fascinating subjects anyone can hope to study. As Christianity enters into a new phase of expansion, especially in the Pacific Rim, the study of Christian theology will continue to have a key role to play in modern intellectual culture. It also remains of seminal importance to any concerned to understand the central issues of the European Reformation, as well as many other periods in human history.

Yet one major American religious publication noted recently that "most clergy, never mind lay people, have given up reading theology." As a professional teacher of theology at Oxford University, I am painfully aware that this sense of enthusiasm and excitement is rare among university and seminary students of theology. They are more often baffled and bewildered by the frequently confusing vocabulary of Christian theology, the apparent unintelligibility of much recent writing in the field, and its seeming irrelevance to the practical issues of Christian living and ministry. As someone who believes that Christian theology is amongst the most rewarding, fulfilling, and genuinely *exciting* subjects anyone can ever hope to study, I have often been depressed by this situation, and wondered if anything could be done about it. This book, which arises out of a decade of teaching theology to undergraduates and seminarians at Oxford University, is a response to that concern.

There is an obvious need for an entry-level introduction to Christian theology. Too many existing introductions make what experience shows to be hopelessly optimistic assumptions about how much their readers already know. In part, this reflects a major religious shift within western culture. Many students now wishing to study Christian theology are recent converts. Unlike their predecessors in past generations, they possess little inherited understanding of the nature of Christianity, its technical vocabulary, or the structure of its thought. Everything has to be introduced and explained. The present volume therefore assumes that its readers know nothing about Christian theology. Everything is set out as simply and clearly as possible.

For some, this will mean that the resulting work lacks sophistication and originality. Those qualities are valuable in other contexts. They are not appropriate to a book of this kind. Simplicity of expression and clarity of exposition are the virtues which have been pursued in writing this work. Equally, whilst originality has its merits, in a work of this kind it is potentially a liability. Originality implies novelty and development; in writing this book, I have deliberately avoided presenting my own ideas, as if these were of any interest or importance. In short, educational considerations have been given priority over everything else.

Inevitably, this approach means that the discussion of many major questions of Christian theology – especially questions of method – is somewhat limited. If my own notes are anything to go by, it would take a volume nearly five times the size of this one to do anything even approaching justice to the complexities of many of the issues raised. What is being offered, however, is an introduction, a sketch map, in order that the reader can pursue the questions in greater detail, having at least gained some understanding of what is at stake. My own experience strongly suggests that students stand a far better chance of understanding and appreciating seminal issues if someone is prepared to take the trouble to explain the background to the discussion, the questions at stake, and the terminology being used. I have assumed that the reader knows no language other than English, and have explained and provided a translation of every Latin, Greek, or German word or phrase that has become an accepted part of the theologian's vocabulary.

This book is not prescriptive. It does not seek to tell its readers what to believe, but rather aims to explain to them what has been believed, and to equip them to make up their minds for themselves, by describing the options available to them and their historical origins, and enabling them to understand their strengths and weaknesses.

Sadly, there is not space to discuss every theological development, movement, or writer which one might hope to include in a work of this sort. Time and time again, pressure on space has forced me to omit matters which many readers will feel ought to have been included, or to give a less full account of some questions than I would have liked. I can do no more than apologize for these shortcomings, of which I am only too painfully aware. The selection of matters to be discussed – and the manner in which they have been discussed – is based upon first-hand recent experience of teaching, and careful surveys of student opinion, in Britain, the United States, Canada, and Australia, to discover both what students think ought to be included in this volume, and what they find difficult to understand, and hence requiring extended explanation.

I owe especial thanks to the following for invaluable assistance. To my students at Wycliffe Hall, Oxford, and Oxford University in general, to whom I taught systematic theology over the period 1983–93, who brought out the need for this textbook, and helped to shape its form. To students at Princeton Theological Seminary, McGill University, Wheaton College, Drew University, Westminster Theological Seminary, Regent College (Vancouver), and Ridley College (Melbourne), on whom I tried out vast tracts of this volume in my efforts to ensure its intelligibility and applicability across the English-language world. To Professors David F. Ford (Cambridge), Gabriel Fackre (Andover Newton), and Keith Ward (Oxford), who cast a critical eye over early drafts of the work, and ensured a balanced coverage of material. To Jennifer Day, Elspeth McCullagh, and especially Julia Pryor, for reading through the material, and preventing me from lapsing into scholarly obscurantism. And finally, I owe an immeasurable debt to Blackwell Publishers, especially Stephan Chambers, for inviting me to write this work, and encouraging me throughout the long process of writing, testing, and rewriting. It has taken far longer to write this book than I care to think; I only hope that it will encourage a new generation of students to discover the fascination of Christian theology, and communicate that to others.

To the Reader:
How to Use this Work

Christian theology is one of the most fascinating subjects it is possible to study. This book aims to make that study as simple and rewarding as possible. It has been written assuming that you know nothing about Christian theology. Obviously, the more you already know, the easier you will find this volume to handle. By the time you have finished this work, you will know enough to be able to follow most technical theological discussions and arguments, benefit from specialist lectures, and get the most from further reading.

Precisely because this book is comprehensive, it includes a lot of material – considerably more than is included in most introductions of this kind. You must not be frightened by the amount of material the volume includes; you do not need to master it all. Considerable thought has been given to the best way of organizing the material. Grasping the structure of the work – which is quite simple – will allow it to be used more effectively by both teachers and students.

The book is divided into three major sections. The first section, on "landmarks," deals with the historical development of Christian theology. These four chapters give historical information which introduces key terms and ideas, some of which will not be explained again later. This volume works on the basis of "explain it the first time round." To understand fully the key theological issues you will encounter later in the work, you need to know a little about their historical background.

You also need to know something about the debates over the sources and methods of Christian theology – in short, where Christianity gets its ideas from. The second part of the work introduces you to a discussion of these issues, and will equip you to deal with the material covered in the third part, which deals with the major doctrinal issues of Christian theology. This material is organized thematically, and you should have little difficulty in finding your way to the material appropriate to your needs. If you do have any difficulties, use the index.

However, there is no need to read every chapter in this book, nor need you read them in the order in which they are set out. Each chapter can be treated as a more or less self-contained unit. The book includes copious cross-references, which will ensure that you can follow up related matters which arise in the course of each and every chapter. Once more, it must be stressed that you must not let the sheer length of the book intimidate you; it is *long* because it is *comprehensive*, and gives you access to all the information that you will need. It aims to be a one-stop freestanding reference book, which will cover all the material that you are likely to need to know about.

If you are using the book to teach yourself theology, it is recommended that you read the chapters in the order in which they are presented. However, if you are using the book in conjunction with a taught course, you can easily work out which sections of the book relate to the ordering of material used by your teacher. If in doubt, ask for guidance.

If you come across terms which you don't understand, you have two options. First, try the glossary at the end of the work, which may give you a brief definition of the term, and refer you to a discussion of the relevant material in the text. Second, try the index, which will provide you with a more extensive survey of where key discussions are located within the volume.

Finally, be assured that everything in this book – including the contents and the arrangement of the material – has been checked out at first hand with student audiences and readers in Australia, Canada, the United Kingdom, and the United States. The work is probably about as user-friendly as you can get. But both the author and the publisher welcome suggestions from teachers and students for further improvement, which will be included in later editions of the work.

Part I

Landmarks: Periods, Themes, and Personalities of Christian Theology

Introduction

Anyone who thinks about the great questions of Christian theology soon discovers that many of them have already been addressed. It is virtually impossible to do theology as if it had never been done before. There is always an element of looking over one's shoulder, to see how things were done in the past, and what answers were then given. Part of the notion of "tradition" is a willingness to take seriously the theological heritage of the past. Karl Barth expresses this idea in a pointed form:

> We cannot be in the church without taking as much responsibility for the theology of the past as for the theology of the present. Augustine, Thomas Aquinas, Luther, Schleiermacher and all the rest are not dead but living. They still speak and demand a hearing as living voices, as surely as we know that they and we belong together in the church.

It is therefore of importance that the reader becomes familiar with the Christian past, which provides vital reference points for the modern debate.

Part I of this work aims to provide an overview of the development of Christian theology, identifying the key periods, themes, and personalities which have shaped that process of evolution. Particular attention will be paid to developments since the Renaissance, in that these have had the greatest impact upon modern western theology. Nevertheless, an appreciation of at least some aspects of the development of theology during the patristic and medieval periods is essential background material to the informed study of modern theology. The present work thus aims to survey some of the most important developments associated with these eras, including the following:

- the geographical location of centers of Christian thought;
- the theological issues under debate;
- the schools of thought associated with theological issues;
- the leading theologians of the periods, and their particular concerns.

The following formative periods are considered in this brief survey of the development of Christian theology:

- the patristic period, *c.*100–451 (chapter 1);
- the Middle Ages and Renaissance, *c.*1000–*c.*1500 (chapter 2);
- the Reformation and post-Reformation periods, *c.*1500–*c.*1700 (chapter 3);
- the modern period, *c.*1700 to the present day (chapter 4).

It will be clear that it is difficult to draw firm dividing lines between many of these periods; for example, the relationships between the Middle Ages, the Renaissance, and the Reformation are controversial, with some scholars seeing the latter two as the continuation of the first, and others seeing them as distinct movements in their own right. The reader should appreciate that all divisions of history are prone to a degree of arbitrariness!

1

The Patristic Period, c.100–451

Christianity had its origins in Palestine – more specifically, the region of Judea, especially the city of Jerusalem. Christianity regarded itself as a continuation and development of Judaism, and initially flourished in regions with which Judaism was traditionally associated, supremely Palestine. However, it rapidly spread to neighboring regions, partially through the efforts of early Christian evangelists such as Paul of Tarsus. By the end of the first century, Christianity appears to have become established throughout the eastern Mediterranean world, and even to have gained a significant presence in the city of Rome, the capital of the Roman Empire. As the church at Rome became increasingly powerful, tensions began to develop between the Christian leadership at Rome and at Constantinople, foreshadowing the later schism between the western and eastern churches, centered on these respective seats of power.

In the course of this expansion, a number of regions emerged as significant centers of theological debate. Three may be singled out as having especial importance, the first two of which were Greek-speaking, and the third Latin-speaking.

1 The city of Alexandria, in modern-day Egypt, which emerged as a center of Christian theological education. A distinctive style of theology came to be associated with this city, reflecting its long-standing association with the Platonic tradition. The student will find reference to "Alexandrian" approaches in areas such as Christology and biblical interpretation (see pp. 18–19; 287–9), reflecting both the importance and the distinctiveness of the style of Christianity associated with the area.

2 The city of Antioch and the surrounding region of Cappadocia,

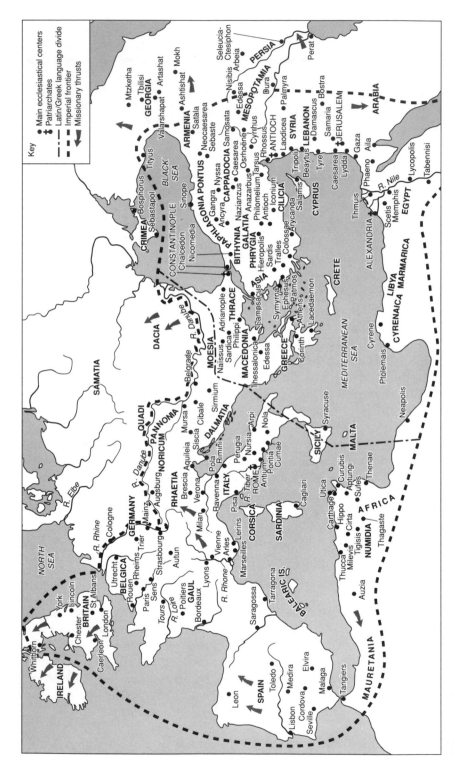

Map 1   The Roman Empire and the church in the fourth century (note that modern rather than ancient place names are used)

in modern-day Turkey. A strong Christian presence came to be established in this northern region of the eastern Mediterranean at an early stage. Some of Paul's missionary journeys took him into this region, and Antioch features significantly at several points in the history of the very early church, as recorded in the Acts of the Apostles. Antioch itself soon became a leading center of Christian thought. Like Alexandria, it became associated with particular approaches to Christology and biblical interpretation. The term "Antiochene" is often used to designate this distinct theological style (see pp. 175–6; 289–91). The "Cappadocian fathers" were also an important theological presence in this region in the fourth century, notable especially for their contribution to the doctrine of the Trinity.

3 Western north Africa, especially the area of modern-day Algeria. In the late classical period, this was the site of Carthage, a major Mediterranean city and at one time a political rival to Rome for dominance in the region. During the period when Christianity expanded in this region, it was a Roman colony. Major writers of the region include Tertullian, Cyprian of Carthage, and Augustine of Hippo.

This is not to say that other cities in the Mediterranean were devoid of significance. Rome, Constantinople, Milan, and Jerusalem were also centers of Christian theological reflection, even if none was destined to achieve quite the significance of their rivals.

A Clarification of Terms

The term "patristic" comes from the Latin word *pater*, "father," and designates both the period of the church fathers, and the distinctive ideas which came to develop within this period. The term is non-inclusive; no generally acceptable inclusive term has yet to emerge in the literature. The following related terms are frequently encountered, and should be noted.

- *The patristic period* This is a vaguely defined entity, which is often taken to be the period from the closing of the New Testament writings (*c*.100) to the definitive Council of Chalcedon (451).
- *Patristics* This term is usually understood to mean the branch of theological study which deals with the study of "the fathers" (*patres*).
- *Patrology* This term once literally meant "the study of the fathers," in much the same way as "theology" meant

study of God" (*theos*). In recent years, however, the word has shifted its meaning. It now refers to a manual of patristic literature, such as that of the noted German scholar Johannes Quasten, which allows its readers easy access to the leading ideas of patristic writers, and some of the problems of interpretation associated with them.

An Overview of the Patristic Period

The patristic period is one of the most exciting and creative periods in the history of Christian thought. This feature alone is enough to ensure that it will continue to be the subject of study for many years to come. The period is also of importance for theological reasons. Every mainstream Christian body – including the Anglican, Eastern Orthodox, Lutheran, Reformed, and Roman Catholic churches – regards the patristic period as a definitive landmark in the development of Christian doctrine. Each of these churches regards itself as continuing, extending, and, where necessary, criticizing the views of the early church writers. For example, the leading seventeenth-century Anglican writer Lancelot Andrewes (1555–1626) declared that orthodox Christianity was based upon two testaments, three creeds, four gospels, and the first five centuries of Christian history.

The period was of major importance in clarifying a number of issues. A primary task was sorting out the relationship between Christianity and Judaism. The letters of Paul in the New Testament bear witness to the importance of this issue in the first century of Christian history, as a series of doctrinal and practical issues came under consideration. Should Gentile (that is, non-Jewish) Christians be obliged to be circumcised? And how was the Old Testament to be correctly interpreted?

However, other issues soon came to the fore. One which was of especial importance in the second century is that of *apologetics* – the reasoned defense and justification of the Christian faith against its critics. During the first period of Christian history, the church was often persecuted by the state. Its agenda was that of survival; there was limited room for theological disputes when the very existence of the Christian church could not be taken for granted. This observation helps us to understand why apologetics came to be of such importance to the early church, through writers such as Justin Martyr (*c*.100–*c*.165), concerned to explain and defend the beliefs and practices of Christianity to a hostile pagan public. Although this early period produced some outstanding theologians – such as Irenaeus of Lyons (*c*.130–*c*.200) in the west, and Origen (*c*.185–*c*.254) in the east – theological debate could only begin in earnest once the church had ceased to be persecuted.

These conditions became possible during the fourth century, with the conversion of the emperor Constantine. During his period as emperor (306–37), Constantine succeeded in reconciling church and empire, with the result that the church no longer existed under a siege mentality. In 321, he decreed that Sundays should become public holidays. As a result of Constantine's influence on the empire, constructive theological debate became a public affair. Apart from a brief period of uncertainty during the reign of Julian the Apostate (361–3), the church could now count upon the support of the state. Theology thus emerged from the hidden world of secret church meetings, to become a matter of public interest and concern throughout the Roman Empire. Increasingly, doctrinal debates became a matter of both political and theological importance. Constantine wished to have a united church throughout his empire, and was thus concerned that doctrinal differences should be debated and settled as a matter of priority.

As a result, the later patristic period (from about 310 to 451) may be regarded as a high-water mark in the history of Christian theology. Theologians now enjoyed the freedom to work without the threat of persecution, and were able to address a series of issues of major importance to the consolidation of the emerging theological consensus within the churches. Establishing that consensus involved extensive debate, and a painful learning process in which the church discovered that it had to come to terms with disagreements and continuing tensions. Nonetheless, a significant degree of consensus, eventually to be enshrined in the ecumenical creeds, can be discerned as evolving within this formative period.

The patristic period is obviously of considerable importance to Christian theology. It is, however, found to be very difficult by many modern students of theology. Four main reasons can be given for this experience.

1 Some of the debates of the period seem hopelessly irrelevant to the modern world. Although they were viewed as intensely important at the time, it is often very difficult for the modern reader to empathize with the issues and to understand why they attracted such attention. It is interesting to contrast the patristic period in this respect with the Reformation era, during which many issues were addressed which are of continuing concern for the modern church; many teachers of theology find that their students are able to relate to the concerns of this later period much more easily.

2   Many of the patristic debates hinge upon philosophical issues, and only make sense if the reader has some familiarity with the philosophical debates of the period. Whereas at least some students of Christian theology have some familiarity with the ideas found in Plato's dialogues, these ideas were subject to considerable development and criticism in the Mediterranean world during the patristic period. Middle Platonism and neo-Platonism differ significantly from one another, and from Plato's original ideas. The strangeness of many of the philosophical ideas of the period acts as another barrier to the study of it, making it difficult for students beginning in theology to fully appreciate what is going on in some of the patristic debates.

3   The patristic period is characterized by immense doctrinal diversity. It was an age of flux, during which landmarks and standards – including documents such as the Nicene creed and dogmas such as the two natures of Christ – emerged gradually. Students familiar with the relative stability of other periods in Christian doctrine (such as the Reformation, in which the person of Christ was not a major issue) often find this feature of the patristic period disconcerting.

4   The period saw a major division arise, for both political and linguistic reasons, between the eastern Greek-speaking and the western Latin-speaking church. Many scholars discern a marked difference in theological temperament between theologians of the east and west: the former are often philosophically inclined and given to theological speculation, whereas the latter are often hostile to the intrusion of philosophy into theology, and regard theology as the exploration of the doctrines set out in Scripture. The famous rhetorical question of the western theologian Tertullian (c.160–c.225), "What has Athens to do with Jerusalem? Or the Academy with the church?," illustrates this point.

Key Theologians

During the course of this work, reference will be made to a significant number of theologians from the patristic period. The following six writers, however, are of especial importance, and deserve to be singled out for special mention.

Justin Martyr (c.100–c.165)

Justin is perhaps the greatest of the Apologists – the Christian writers of the second century who were concerned to defend Christianity in the face of intense criticism from pagan sources. In his "First Apology," Justin argued that traces of Christian truth were to be found in the great pagan writers. His doctrine of the *logos spermatikos* ("seed-bearing word") allowed him to affirm that God had prepared the way for his final revelation in Christ through hints of its truth in classical philosophy. Justin provides us with an important early example of a theologian who attempts to relate the gospel to the outlook of Greek philosophy, a trend especially associated with the eastern church.

Irenaeus of Lyons (*c.*130–*c.*200)

Irenaeus is believed to have been born in Smyrna (in modern-day Turkey), although he subsequently settled in Rome. He became Bishop of Lyons around 178, a position which he held until his death two decades later. Irenaeus is noted especially for his vigorous defense of Christian orthodoxy in the face of a challenge from Gnosticism (see p. 16). His most significant work, "Against all Heresies" (*Adversus omnes Haereses*) represents a major defense of the Christian understanding of salvation, and especially of the role of tradition in remaining faithful to the apostolic witness in the face of non-Christian interpretations.

Origen (*c.*185–*c.*254)

One of the most important defenders of Christianity in the third century, Origen provided an important foundation for the development of eastern Christian thought. His major contributions to the development of Christian theology can be seen in two general areas. In the field of biblical interpretation, Origen developed the notion of allegorical interpretation, arguing that the surface meaning of Scripture was to be distinguished from its deeper spiritual meaning. In the field of Christology, Origen established a tradition of distinguishing between the full divinity of the Father, and a lesser divinity of the Son. Some scholars see Arianism as a natural consequence of this approach. Origen also adopted with some enthusiasm the idea of *apocatastasis*, according to which every creature – including both humanity and Satan – will be saved (see pp. 364–5).

Tertullian (*c.*160–*c.*225)

Tertullian was originally a pagan from the north African city of Carthage, who converted to Christianity in his thirties. He is often regarded as the father of Latin theology, on account of the major impact which he had upon the western church. He defended the unity of the Old and New Testaments against Marcion, who had argued that they related to different gods. In doing so, he laid the foundations for a doctrine of the Trinity. Tertullian was strongly opposed to making Christian theology or apologetics dependent upon extra-scriptural sources. He is amongst the most forceful early exponents of the principle of the sufficiency of Scripture, denouncing those who appeal to secular philosophies (such as those of the Athenian Academy) for a true knowledge of God.

Athanasius (c.296–c.373)

Athanasius' significance relates primarily to Christological issues, which became of major importance during the fourth century. Possibly while still in his twenties, Athanasius wrote the treatise *De incarnatione* ("On the incarnation"), a powerful defense of the idea that God assumed human nature in the person of Jesus Christ. This issue proved to be of central importance in the Arian controversy (see pp. 283–7), to which Athanasius made a major contribution. Athanasius pointed out that if, as Arius argued, Christ was not fully God, a series of devastating implications followed. First, it was impossible for God to redeem humanity, as no creature could redeem another creature. And second, it followed that the Christian church was guilty of idolatry, as Christians regularly worshipped and prayed to Christ. As "idolatry" can be defined as "worship of a human construction or creation," it followed that this worship was idolatrous. Such arguments eventually carried the day, and led to the rejection of Arianism.

Augustine of Hippo (354–430)

In turning to deal with Aurelius Augustinus, usually known as "Augustine of Hippo" – or just plain "Augustine" – we encounter what is probably the greatest and most influential mind of the Christian church throughout its long history. Attracted to the Christian faith by the preaching of Bishop Ambrose of Milan, Augustine underwent a dramatic conversion experience. Having reached the age of 32 without satisfying his burning wish to know the truth, Augustine was agonizing over the great questions of human nature and destiny in a garden in Milan. He thought he heard some children singing *Tolle, lege* ("take up and read") nearby. Feeling that this was divine guidance, he found the New Testament document nearest to hand – Paul's letter to the Romans, as it happened – and read the fateful words "clothe yourselves with the Lord Jesus Christ" (Romans 13: 14). This was the final straw for Augustine, whose paganism had become increasingly difficult to maintain. As he later recalled, "a light of certainty entered my heart, and every shadow of doubt vanished." From that moment onward, Augustine dedicated his enormous intellectual abilities to the defense and consolidation of the Christian faith, writing in a style which was both passionate and intelligent, appealing to both heart and mind.

Possibly suffering from some form of asthma, Augustine left Italy to return to north Africa, and was made bishop of Hippo (in modern Algeria) in 395. The remaining thirty-five years of his life witnessed numerous controversies of major importance to the future of the Christian church in the west, and Augustine's contribution to the resolution of each of these was decisive. His careful exposition of the New Testament, particularly the letters of Paul, gained him a reputation which continues today, as the "second founder of the Christian faith" (Jerome). When the Dark Ages finally lifted over western Europe, Augustine's substantial body of theological writings would form the basis of a major program of theological renewal and development, consolidating his influence over the western church.

A major part of Augustine's contribution lies in the development of theology as an academic discipline. The early church cannot really be said to have developed any "systematic theology." Its primary concern was to defend Christianity against its critics (as in the apologetic works of Justin Martyr), and to clarify central aspects of its thinking against heresy (as in the anti-Gnostic writings of Irenaeus). Nevertheless, major doctrinal development took place during the first four centuries, especially in relation to the doctrine of the person of Christ and the doctrine of the Trinity.

Augustine's contribution was to achieve a synthesis of Christian thought, supremely in his major treatise *De civitate Dei*, "On the City of God." Like Charles Dickens's famous novel, Augustine's "City of God" is a tale of two cities – the city of the world, and the city of God (see pp. 467–8). The work is apologetic in tone: Augustine is sensitive to the charge that the fall of Rome was due to its having abandoned classic paganism in favor of Christianity. Yet as he defended Christianity against such charges, he inevitably ended up by giving a systematic presentation and exposition of the main lines of Christian belief.

However, in addition, Augustine may also be argued to have made key contributions to three major areas of Christian theology: the doctrine of the church and sacraments, arising from the Donatist controversy (see pp. 407–10); the doctrine of grace, arising from the

Pelagian controversy (see pp. 371–7); and the doctrine of the Trinity
(see pp. 257–60). Interestingly, Augustine never really explored the
area of Christology (that is, the doctrine of the person of Christ),
which would unquestionably have benefited from his considerable
wisdom and acumen.

Key Theological Developments

The following areas of theology were explored with particular vigor
during the patristic period.

The Extent of the New Testament Canon

From its outset, Christian theology recognized itself to be grounded in
Scripture. There was, however, some uncertainty as to what the term
"Scripture" actually designated. The patristic period witnessed a process of decision-making, in which limits were laid down to the New
Testament – a process usually known as "the fixing of the canon."
The word "canon" needs explanation. It derives from the Greek word
kanon meaning "a rule" or "a fixed reference point." The "canon
of Scripture" refers to a limited and defined group of writings, which
are accepted as authoritative within the Christian church. The term
"canonical" is used to refer to scriptural writings accepted to be within
the canon. Thus the Gospel of Luke is referred to as "canonical,"
whereas the Gospel of Thomas is "extra-canonical" (that is, lying
outside the canon of Scripture).

For the writers of the New Testament, the term "Scripture" meant
primarily *a writing of the Old Testament*. However, within a short
period, early Christian writers (such as Justin Martyr) were referring
to the "New Testament" (to be contrasted with the "Old Testament"),
and insisting that both were to be treated with equal authority. By
the time of Irenaeus, it was generally accepted that there were four
gospels; by the late second century, there was a consensus that the
gospels, Acts, and letters had the status of inspired Scripture. Thus
Clement of Alexandria recognized four gospels, the Acts, fourteen
letters of Paul (the letter to the Hebrews being regarded as Pauline),
and Revelation. Tertullian declared that alongside the "law and the
prophets" were the "evangelical and apostolic writings" (*evangelicae et
apostolicae litterae*), which were both to be regarded as authoritative
within the church. Gradually, agreement was reached on the list of
books which were recognized as inspired Scripture, and the order in

which they were to be arranged. In 367, Athanasius circulated his thirty-ninth Festal Letter, which identifies the twenty-seven books of the New Testament, as we now know it, as being canonical.

Debate centered especially on a number of books. The western church had hesitations about including Hebrews, in that it was not specifically attributed to an apostle; the eastern church had reservations about Revelation. Four of the smaller books (2 Peter, 2 and 3 John, and Jude) were often omitted from early lists of New Testament writings. Some writings now outside the canon were regarded with favor in parts of the church, although they ultimately failed to gain universal acceptance as canonical. Examples of this include the first letter of Clement (an early bishop of Rome, who wrote around 96) and the *Didache*, a short early Christian manual on morals and church practices, probably dating from the first quarter of the second century.

The arrangement of the material was also subject to considerable variation. Agreement was reached at an early stage that the gospels should have the place of honor within the canon, followed by the Acts of the Apostles. The eastern church tended to place the seven "catholic letters" (that is, James, 1 and 2 Peter, 1, 2 and 3 John, and Jude) before the fourteen Pauline letters (Hebrews being accepted as Pauline), whereas the western church placed Paul's letters immediately after Acts, and followed them with the catholic letters. Revelation ended the canon in both east and west, although its status was subject to debate for some time within the eastern church.

What criteria were used in drawing up the canon? The basic principle appears to have been that of the *recognition* rather than the *imposition* of authority. In other words, the works in question were recognized as already possessing authority, rather than having an arbitrary authority imposed upon them. For Irenaeus, the church does not *create* the canon; it *acknowledges*, *conserves*, and *receives* canonical Scripture on the basis of the authority which is already inherent to it. Some early Christians appear to have regarded apostolic authorship as of decisive importance; others were prepared to accept books which did not appear to have apostolic credentials. However, although the precise details of how the selection was made remain unclear, it is certain that the canon was closed within the western church by the beginning of the fifth century. The issue of the canon would not be raised again until the time of the Reformation.

The Role of Tradition

The early church was confronted with a major challenge from a movement known as Gnosticism. This diverse and complex movement, not dissimilar to the modern New Age phenomenon, achieved considerable influence in the late Roman Empire. The basic ideas of Gnosticism do not concern us at this point; what is of relevance here is that Gnosticism appeared very similar to Christianity at many points. For this reason, it was viewed as a major challenge by many early Christian writers, especially Irenaeus. Furthermore, Gnostic writers had a tendency to interpret New Testament passages in a manner which dismayed Christian leaders, and prompted questions about the correct manner of interpretation of Scripture.

In such a context, an appeal to tradition became of major importance. The word "tradition" literally means "that which has been handed down or over," although it can also refer to "the act of handing down or over." Irenaeus insisted that the "rule of faith" (*regula fidei*) was faithfully preserved by the apostolic church, and that it had found its expression in the canonical books of Scripture. The church had faithfully proclaimed the same gospel from the time of the Apostles until the present day. The Gnostics had no such claim to continuity with the early church. They had merely invented new ideas, and were improperly suggesting that these were "Christian." Irenaeus thus emphasized the continuity of the teaching and preaching office of the church and its officials (especially its bishops). Tradition came to mean "a traditional interpretation of Scripture" or "a traditional presentation of the Christian faith," which is reflected in the creeds of the church and its public doctrinal pronouncements. This fixing of the creeds as a public expression of the teaching of the church is of major importance, as will become clear in the following section.

Tertullian adopted a related approach. Scripture, he argued, is capable of being understood clearly, provided that it is read as a whole. However, he conceded that controversy over the interpretation of certain passages was inevitable. Heretics, he observed gloomily, can make Scripture say more or less anything that they like. For this reason, the tradition of the church was of considerable importance, as it indicated the manner in which Scripture had been received and interpreted within the church. The right interpretation of Scripture was thus to be found where true Christian faith and discipline had been maintained. A similar view was taken by Athanasius, who argued that Arius' Christological mistakes would never have arisen if he had remained faithful to the church's interpretation of Scripture.

Tradition was thus seen as a legacy from the Apostles, by which the church was guided and directed toward a correct interpretation of Scripture. It was not seen as a "secret source of revelation" in addition to Scripture, an idea which Irenaeus dismissed as "Gnostic." Rather, it was seen as a means of ensuring that the church remained faithful to the teaching of the Apostles, instead of adopting idiosyncratic interpretations of Scripture.

The Fixing of the Ecumenical Creeds

The English word "creed" derives from the Latin word *credo*, "I believe," with which the Apostles' creed – probably the most familiar of all the creeds – begins: "I believe in God. . . ." It has come to refer to a statement of faith, summarizing the main points of Christian belief, which is common to all Christians. For this reason, the term "creed" is never applied to statements of faith associated with specific denominations. These latter are often referred to as "confessions" (such as the Lutheran *Augsburg Confession* or the Reformed *Westminster Confession of Faith*). A "confession" pertains to a denomination, and includes specific beliefs and emphases relating to that denomination; a "creed" pertains to the entire Christian church, and includes nothing more and nothing less than a statement of beliefs which every Christian ought to be able to accept and be bound by. A "creed" has come to be recognized as a concise, formal, and universally accepted and authorized statement of the main points of Christian faith.

The patristic period saw two creeds coming to be treated with authority and respect throughout the church. The stimulus to their development appears to have been the felt need to provide a convenient summary of Christian faith suitable for public occasions, of which perhaps the most important was baptism. The early church tended to baptize its converts on Easter Day, using the period of Lent as a time of preparation and instruction for this moment of public declaration of faith and commitment. An essential requirement was that each convert who wished to be baptized should declare his or her faith in public. It seems that creeds began to emerge as a uniform declaration of faith which converts could use on such occasions.

The *Apostles' creed* is probably the most familiar form of the creed known to western Christians. It falls into three main sections, dealing with God, Jesus Christ, and the Holy Spirit. There is also material relating to the church, judgment, and resurrection.

The *Nicene creed* is the longer version of the creed (more strictly known as the "Niceno-Constantinopolitan creed") which includes additional material relating to the person of Christ and the work of the Holy Spirit. In response to the controversies concerning the divinity of Christ, this creed includes strong affirmations of his unity with God, including the expressions "God from God" and "being of one substance with the Father."

The development of the creeds was an important element in the move toward achieving a doctrinal consensus within the early church. One area of doctrine which witnessed considerable development and controversy related to the person of Christ, to which we may now turn.

The Two Natures of Jesus Christ

The two doctrines to which the patristic period may be argued to have made a decisive contribution relate to the person of Christ (an area of theology which, as we noted, is generally designated "Christology") and the nature of the Godhead. These two developments are organically related to one another. By 325, the early church had come to the conclusion that Jesus was "of one substance" (*homoousios*) with God. (The term *homoousios* can also be translated as "one in being" or "consubstantial".) The implications of this Christological statement were twofold: In the first place, it consolidated at the intellectual level the spiritual importance of Jesus Christ to Christians; in the second, however, it posed a powerful challenge to simplistic conceptions of God. For if Jesus *is* recognized as "being of the same substance" as God, then the entire doctrine of God has to be reconsidered in the light of this belief. For this reason, the historical development of the doctrine of the Trinity dates from after the emergence of a Christological consensus within the church. Only when the divinity of Christ could be treated as an agreed and assured starting point could theological speculation on the nature of God begin.

It may be noted that the Christological debates of the early church took place largely in the eastern Mediterranean world, and were conducted in the Greek language, and often in the light of the presuppositions of major Greek schools of philosophy. In practical terms, this means that many of the central terms of the Christological debates of the early church are Greek, often with a history of use within the Greek philosophical tradition.

The main features of patristic Christology will be considered in some detail at pp. 270–87, to which the reader is referred. At this early stage, however, we may summarize the main landmarks of the patristic Christological debate in terms of two schools, two debates, and two councils, as follows.

1 *Schools* The *Alexandrian school* tended to place emphasis upon the divinity of Christ, and interpret that divinity in terms of "the word becoming incarnate." A scriptural text which was of central importance to this school is John 1: 14, "the word became flesh, and dwelt among us." This emphasis upon the idea of incarnation led to the festival of Christmas being seen as especially important. The *Antiochene school*, however, placed a corresponding emphasis upon the humanity of Christ, and attached especial importance to his moral example (see pp. 287–91).

2 *Debates* The *Arian* controversy of the fourth century is widely regarded as one of the most significant in the history of the Christian church. Arius (*c*.250–*c*.336) argued that the scriptural titles for Christ, which appeared to point to his being of equal status with God, were merely courtesy titles. Christ was to be regarded as a creature, although nevertheless as pre-eminent amongst other creatures. This provoked a hostile response from Athanasius, who argued that the divinity of Christ was of central importance to the Christian understanding of salvation (an area of theology known as "soteriology"). Arius' Christology was, he declared, inadequate soteriologically. Arius' Christ could not redeem fallen humanity. In the end, Arianism (the movement associated with Arius) was declared to be heretical. This was followed by the *Apollinarian* debate, which centered on Apollinarius the Younger (*c*.310–*c*.390). A vigorous opponent of Arius, Apollinarius argued that Christ could not be regarded as being totally human. In Christ's case, the human spirit was replaced by the divine *logos*. As a result, Christ did not possess full humanity. This position was regarded as severely deficient by writers such as Gregory of Nazianzen, in that it implied that Christ could not fully redeem human nature (see pp. 288–9).

3 *Councils* The *Council of Nicea* (325) was convened by Constantine, the first Christian emperor, with a view to sorting out the destabilizing Christological disagreements within his empire. This was the first "ecumenical council" (that is, an assembly of Christians drawn from the entire Christian world, whose decisions are regarded as normative for the churches). Nicea (now the city of Iznik in modern-day Turkey) settled the Arian controversy by affirming that Jesus was *homoousios* ("one in being" or "of one substance") with the Father, thus rejecting the Arian position in favor of a vigorous assertion of the divinity of Christ. The *Council of Chalcedon* (451), the fourth ecumenical council, confirmed the decisions of Nicea, and responded to new debates which had subsequently erupted over the humanity of Christ.

The Doctrine of the Trinity

Once the Christological debates of the early church had been settled, the consequences of those decisions were explored. In this intensely creative and interesting period of Christian theology, the doctrine of the Trinity began to emerge in a recognizable form. The basic feature of this doctrine is that there are three persons within the Godhead – Father, Son, and Holy Spirit – and that these are to be regarded as equally divine and of equal status. The co-equality of Father and Son was established through the Christological debates leading up to the Council of Nicea; the divinity of the Spirit was established in the aftermath of this, especially through the writings of Athanasius and Basil of Caesarea.

The main thrust of the Trinitarian debates increasingly came to concern the manner in which the Trinity was to be understood, rather than its fundamental validity. Two quite distinct approaches gradually emerged, one associated with the eastern, and the other with the western, churches.

The *eastern* position, which continues to be of major importance within the Greek and Russian Orthodox churches of today, was developed especially by a group of three writers, based in modern-day Turkey. Basil of Caesarea (*c*.330–79), Gregory of Nazianzen (329–89), and Gregory of Nyssa (*c*.330–*c*.395), known as the *Cappadocian fathers*, began their reflections on the Trinity by considering the different ways in which the Father, Son, and Spirit are experienced. The *western* position, especially associated with Augustine of Hippo, began from the unity of God, and proceeded to explore the implications of the love of God for our understanding of the nature of the Godhead. These positions will be explored in greater detail at the appropriate point in this work (see pp. 247–60).

The doctrine of the Trinity represents a rare instance of a theological issue of concern to both the eastern and western churches. Our attention now shifts to two theological debates which were specifically linked with the western church, and have both come to be particularly associated with Augustine of Hippo.

The Doctrine of the Church

A major controversy within the western church centered on the question of the holiness of the church. The Donatists were a group of native African Christians, based in modern-day Algeria, who resented the growing influence of the Roman church in northern Africa. The Donatists argued that the church was a body of saints, within which sinners had no place. The issue became of especial importance on account of the persecution undertaken by the emperor Diocletian in 303, which persisted until the conversion of Constantine in 313. During this persecution, in which the possession of Scripture was illegal, a number of Christians handed their copies of Scripture in to the authorities. These were immediately condemned by others who had refused to cave in under such pressure. After the persecution died down, many of these *traditores* – literally, "those who handed over [their Scriptures]" – rejoined the church. The Donatists argued for their exclusion.

Augustine argued otherwise, declaring that the church must expect to remain a "mixed body" of saints and sinners, refusing to weed out those who had lapsed under persecution or for other reasons. The validity of the church's ministry and preaching did not depend upon the holiness of its ministers, but upon the person of Jesus Christ. The personal unworthiness of a minister did not compromise the validity of the sacraments. This view, which rapidly became normative within the church, has had a deep impact upon Christian thinking about the nature of the church and its ministers.

The Donatist debate, which will be explored in greater detail elsewhere (see pp. 407–10), was the first to center on the question of the doctrine of the church (known as "ecclesiology"), and related questions, such as the way in which sacraments function. Many of the issues raised by the controversy would surface again at the time of the Reformation, when ecclesiological issues would once more come to the fore (see pp. 410–15). The same may be said of the doctrine of grace, to which we now turn.

The Doctrine of Grace

The doctrine of grace had not been an issue of significance in the development of theology in the Greek-speaking eastern church. However, an intense controversy broke out over this question in the second decade of the fifth century. Pelagius, a British ascetic monk based at Rome, argued forcefully for the need for human moral responsibility. Alarmed at the moral laxity of the Roman church, he insisted upon the need for constant self-improvement, in the light of the Old Testament law and the example of Christ. In doing so, he seemed to his opponents – chief among whom was Augustine – to deny any real place to divine grace in the beginning or continuation of the Christian life. Pelagianism came to be seen as a religion of human autonomy, which held that human beings are able to take the initiative in their own salvation.

Augustine reacted forcefully against Pelagianism, insisting upon the priority of the grace of God at every stage in the Christian life, from its beginning to its end. Human beings did not, according to Augustine, possess the necessary freedom to take the initial steps toward salvation. Far from possessing "freedom of the will," humans were in possession of a will that was corrupted and tainted by sin, and which biased them toward evil and away from God. Only the grace of God could counteract this bias toward sin. So forceful was Augustine's defense of grace that he later became known as "the doctor of grace" (*doctor gratiae*).

A central theme of Augustine's thought is the *fallenness* of human nature. The imagery of "the Fall" derives from Genesis 3, and expresses the idea that human nature has "fallen" from its original pristine state. The present state of human nature is thus not what it is intended to be by God. The created order no longer directly corresponds to the "goodness" of its original integrity. It has lapsed. It has been spoiled or ruined – but not irredeemably, as the doctrines of salvation and justification affirm. The image of a "Fall" conveys the idea that creation now exists at a lower level than that intended for it by God.

According to Augustine, it follows that all human beings are now contaminated by sin from the moment of their birth. In contrast to many twentieth-century existentialist philosophies (such as that of Martin Heidegger), which affirm that "fallenness" (*Verfallenheit*) is an option which we choose (rather than something which is chosen for us), Augustine portrays sin as inherent to human nature. It is an integral, not an optional, aspect of our being. This insight, which is given more rigorous expression in Augustine's doctrine of original sin, is of central importance to his doctrines of sin and salvation. In that all are sinners, all require redemption. In that all have fallen short of the glory of God, all require to be redeemed.

For Augustine, humanity, left to its own devices and resources, could never enter into a relationship with God. Nothing that a man or woman could do was sufficient to break the stranglehold of sin. To use an image which Augustine was fortunate enough never to have encountered, it is like a narcotic addict trying to break free from the grip of heroin or cocaine. The situation cannot be transformed from within – and so, if transformation is to take place, it must come from outside the human situation. According to Augustine, God intervenes in the human dilemma. He need not have done so, but out of his love for fallen humanity, he entered into the human situation in the person of Jesus Christ in order to redeem it.

Augustine held "grace" to be the unmerited or undeserved gift of God, by which God voluntarily breaks the hold of sin upon humanity. Redemption is possible only as a divine gift. It is not something which we can achieve ourselves, but is something which has to be done for us. Augustine thus emphasizes that the resources of salvation are located outside of humanity, in God himself. It is God who initiates the process of salvation, not men or women.

For Pelagius, however, the situation looked very different. Pelagius taught that the resources of salvation are located within humanity. Individual human beings have the capacity to save themselves. They are not trapped by sin, but have the ability to do all that is necessary to be saved. Salvation is something which is earned through good works, which place God under an obligation to humanity. Pelagius marginalizes the idea of grace, understanding it in terms of demands made of humanity by God in order that salvation may be achieved – such as the Ten Commandments, or the moral example of Christ. The ethos of Pelagianism could be summed up as "salvation by merit," whereas Augustine taught "salvation by grace."

It will be obvious that these two different theologies involve very different understandings of human nature. For Augustine, human nature is weak, fallen, and powerless; for Pelagius, it is autonomous and self-sufficient. For Augustine, humanity must depend upon God for salvation; for Pelagius, God merely indicates what has to be done if salvation is to be attained, and then leaves men and women to meet those conditions unaided. For Augustine, salvation is an unmerited gift; for Pelagius, salvation is a justly earned reward.

One aspect of Augustine's understanding of grace needs further comment. As human beings were incapable of saving themselves, and as God gave his gift of grace to some (but not all), it followed that God had "preselected" those who would be saved. Developing hints of this idea to be found in the New Testament, Augustine developed a doctrine of predestination. The term "predestination" refers to God's original or eternal decision to save some, and not others. It was this aspect of Augustine's thought which many of his contemporaries, not to mention his successors, found unacceptable. It need hardly be said that there is no direct equivalent in Pelagius' thought.

The Council of Carthage (418) decided for Augustine's views on grace and sin, and condemned Pelagianism in uncompromising terms. However, Pelagianism, in various forms, continued to be a point of contention for some time to come. As the patristic era came to its close, with the Dark Ages settling over western Europe, many of the issues remained unresolved. They would be taken up again during the Middle Ages, and supremely at the time of the Reformation (see pp. 382–7).

Key Names, Words, and Phrases

By the end of this chapter, you will have encountered the following terms, which will recur during the work. Ensure that you are familiar with them! They have been capitalized as you are likely to encounter them in normal use.

*Apollinarianism
*Arianism
Augustinianism
canon
canonical
Cappadocian fathers
*Christological
*Christology
creed
*Donatist
*Donatism
*ecclesiological
*ecclesiology
ecumenical council
extra-canonical
*incarnation
patristic
patrology
*Pelagian
*Pelagianism
*soteriology
*Trinity
*Trinitarian

Those terms marked with an asterisk will be explored in greater detail later in this work.

Questions for Chapter 1

1 Locate the following cities or regions on map 1 (p. 6):
   Alexandria;   Antioch;   Cappadocia;   Constantinople;
   Hippo; Jerusalem; Rome.

2 Now find the Latin/Greek dividing line on the same
   map. Latin was the main language west of that line, and
   Greek east of it. Identify the predominant language in
   each of the cities mentioned in question 1.

3 Which language would you associate with the following writers: Athanasius; Augustine of Hippo; Origen;
   Tertullian?

4 The following movements were of major importance
   during the patristic period: Arianism; Donatism; Gnosticism; Pelagianism. Associate the controversies centering
   on each of these movements with one of the following
   theologians: Athanasius; Augustine of Hippo; Irenaeus
   of Lyons. (Note that one of these theologians is associated
   with more than one controversy.)

5 Why was there relatively little interest in the doctrine of
   the church in this early period?

2

The Middle Ages and the Renaissance, *c.*1050–*c.*1500

The patristic period centered on the Mediterranean world, and on seats of power such as Rome and Constantinople. The fall of Rome to invading forces from the north threw the western Mediterranean world into confusion. Instability was widespread throughout the region. Historians still refer to the period from the fall of Rome to about the year 1000 as the "Dark Ages," to indicate that culture and learning were relatively hard to come by during these centuries of instability and insecurity. Although theological discussion continued in the western church during this period, it was set against the context of a survival mentality. There was relatively little public interest in such theological debates. In the eastern Mediterranean, instability also came to develop as Islam began to spread throughout the region. Although Christianity was never displaced totally, it soon found itself with the status of a minority religion.

During this period in European history, the center of Christian theological reflection shifted from the Mediterranean world to western Europe. In 410, Rome was finally conquered by Alaric, an event which is often regarded as marking the beginning of the "Dark Ages" in western Europe. The expansion of Islam around the Mediterranean in the seventh century led to widespread political destabilization and further structural changes in the region. By the eleventh century, a degree of stability had settled upon the area, three major power groupings having emerged to take the place of the former Roman Empire.

1 Byzantium, centered on the city of Constantinople (now Istanbul, in modern-day Turkey). The form of Christianity which predominated in this region was based on the Greek language, and was deeply

rooted in the writings of patristic scholars of the eastern Mediterranean region, such as Athanasius, the Cappadocians, and John of Damascus. A full discussion of Byzantine theology lies beyond the scope of this book, which focuses upon the western theological tradition.

2   Western Europe, mainly regions such as France, Germany, the Low Countries, and northern Italy. The form of Christianity which came to dominate this region was centered on the city of Rome, and its bishop, known as "the Pope." (However, for the period known as the "Great Schism," some confusion developed: there were two rival claimants for the papacy, one based at Rome, the other at the southern French city of Avignon.) Here, theology came to be concentrated in the great cathedral and university schools of Paris and elsewhere, based largely on the Latin writings of Augustine, Ambrose, and Hilary of Poitiers.

3   The Caliphate, an Islamic region embracing much of the extreme eastern and southern parts of the Mediterranean. The expansion of Islam continued, with the fall of Constantinople in 1453 sending shock waves throughout much of Europe. By the end of the fifteenth century, Islam had established a significant presence in two regions of the continent of Europe: Spain and the Balkans. This advance was eventually halted by the defeat of the Moors in Spain in the final decade of the fifteenth century, and the defeat of Islamic armies outside Vienna in 1523.

An event of fundamental importance to the history of the church took place during this period. For a variety of reasons, relations between the eastern church, based at Constantinople, and the western, based at Rome, became increasingly strained during the ninth and tenth centuries. Growing disagreement over the *filioque* clause in the Nicene creed (see pp. 266–9) was of no small importance to this increasingly sour atmosphere. Other factors also contributed, including the political rivalry between Latin-speaking Rome and Greek-speaking Constantinople, and the increasing claims to authority of the Roman Pope. The final break between the Catholic west and Orthodox east is usually dated to 1054, although this date is slightly arbitrary.

One major result of this tension was that there was little theological interaction between east and west. Although western theologians such as Thomas Aquinas felt free to draw on the writings of Greek fathers, these works tended to antedate this period. The works of later Orthodox theologians, such as the noted writer Gregory Palamas, attracted little attention in the west. It is only in the twentieth century that western theology may really be said to have begun to rediscover the riches of the Orthodox tradition.

Our concern in this volume is primarily with western European

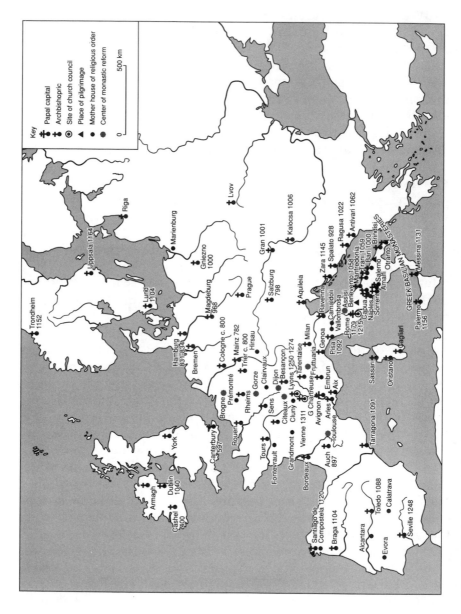

Map 2 *Main theological and ecclesiastical centers in western Europe during the Middle Ages*

theology, which has had a deep impact upon modern Christian thought. The term "medieval theology" is often used to refer to western theology during this era, whereas the term "Byzantine theology" is used to refer to the theology of the eastern church over roughly the same period, prior to the fall of Constantinople in 1453. During this period in western European history, the centers of Christian theology gradually moved northward, to central France and Germany. Although Rome remained a center of Christian power in the region, intellectual activity gradually came to migrate to the monasteries of France, such as Chartres, Reims, and Bec. With the foundation of the medieval universities, theology rapidly established itself as a central area of academic study. A typical medieval university possessed four faculties: the lower faculty of arts, and the three higher faculties of theology, medicine, and law.

A Clarification of Terms

Defining periods in history is notoriously difficult. Part of the problem lies in the absence of universal agreement on the defining characteristics of eras. This is especially the case with the "Middle Ages," the "Renaissance," and the "modern period." There are also major difficulties in defining some of the intellectual movements of the period, especially humanism.

The period under consideration in this chapter gave rise to two of the most important intellectual movements in the history of thought: *scholasticism* and *humanism*. Scholasticism and humanism dominated the intellectual world – including the theological world – between 1300 and 1500. Although it could be argued that scholasticism was on the wane by the year 1500, it still exerted immense influence in many European universities, such as the University of Paris. An understanding of the nature of both these movements is essential to any attempt to make sense of the development of Christian theology during the period, or to understand the religious and intellectual pressures which eventually gave rise to the Reformation. The two movements are related, in that the latter is generally regarded as being a response to the cultural poverty and theological overprecision of the former. In what follows, we shall attempt to clarify some of the terms used in the literature relating to this major period of Christian theology.

The Middle Ages

The term "the Middle Ages" was invented by writers of the Renaissance, and seems to have come into general use toward the end of the sixteenth century. The writers of the Renaissance were anxious to discredit the period intervening between the glories of classical antiquity and their own time. They thus invented the term "the Middle Ages" to refer to an uninteresting and stagnant phase separating two important and creative periods. The adjective "medieval" means "relating to the Middle Ages." The term "medieval theology" has passed into general use, and can generally be interpreted to mean "western European theology in the period between the end of the Dark Ages and the sixteenth century." It must, however, be appreciated that the term is imprecise, disputed, and open to various interpretations.

When the so-called Dark Ages finally lifted from western Europe, giving birth to the Middle Ages, the scene was set for revival in every field of academic work. The restoration of some degree of political stability in France in the late eleventh century encouraged the re-emergence of the University of Paris, which rapidly became recognized as the intellectual center of Europe. A number of theological "schools" were established on the Left Bank of the Seine, and on the Île de la Cité, in the shadow of the newly built cathedral of Notre Dame de Paris.

One such school was the Collège de la Sorbonne, which eventually achieved such fame that "the Sorbonne" eventually came to be a shorthand way of referring to the University of Paris. Even in the sixteenth century, Paris was widely recognized as a leading center for theological and philosophical study, including amongst its students such prominent individuals as Erasmus of Rotterdam and John Calvin. Other such centers of study were soon established elsewhere in Europe. A new program of theological development began, concerned with consolidating the intellectual, legal, and spiritual aspects of the life of the Christian church.

The early part of the medieval period is dominated by developments in France. Several monasteries produced outstanding Christian writers and thinkers, for example, Lanfranc (c.1010–89) and Anselm (c.1033–1109), both from the monastery at Bec, in Normandy. The University of Paris soon established itself as a leading center of theological speculation, with such scholars as Peter Abelard (1079–1142), Albert the Great (c.1200–80), Thomas Aquinas (c.1225–74), and Bonaventure (c.1217–74). The fourteenth and fifteenth centuries witnessed a considerable expansion of the university sector in western

Europe, with major new universities being founded in Germany and elsewhere.

A central resource to the new medieval interest in theology is also linked with Paris. At some point shortly before 1140, Peter Lombard arrived at the university to teach. One of his primary concerns was to get his students to wrestle with the thorny issues of theology. His contribution was a textbook – perhaps one of the most boring books that has ever been written. The *Sententiarum libri quattuor* or *Four Books of the Sentences* bring together quotations from Scripture and the patristic writers, arranged topically. The task Peter set his students was simple: Make sense of the quotes. The book proved to be of major importance in developing the Augustinian heritage, in that students were obliged to wrestle with the ideas of Augustine, and reconcile apparently contradictory texts by devising suitable theological explanations of the inconsistencies.

Some writers attempted to have the book banned, noting its occasional incautious statements (such as the opinion that Christ did not exist as a person, a view which came to be known as "Christological nihilism"). However, by 1215 the work was firmly established as the most important textbook of the age. It became obligatory for theologians to comment on Lombard's work. The resulting writings, known as *Commentaries on the Sentences*, became one of the most familiar theological genres of the Middle Ages. Outstanding examples include those of Thomas Aquinas, Bonaventure, and Duns Scotus.

The Renaissance

The French term "Renaissance" is now universally used to designate the literary and artistic revival in fourteenth- and fifteenth-century Italy. In 1546 Paolo Giovio referred to the fourteenth century as "that happy century in which Latin letters are conceived to have been reborn" (*renatae*), anticipating this nomenclature. Certain historians, most notably Jacob Burckhardt, argued that the Renaissance gave birth to the modern era. It was in this era, Burckhardt claimed, that human beings first began to think of themselves as *individuals*. In many ways, Burckhardt's definition of the Renaissance in purely individualist terms is highly questionable. But in one sense, he is unquestionably correct: *something* novel and exciting developed in Renaissance Italy, which proved capable of exercising a fascination over generations of thinkers.

It is not entirely clear why Italy became the cradle of this brilliant new movement in the history of ideas. A number of factors have been identified as having some bearing on the question.

1 Scholastic theology – the major intellectual force of the medieval period – was never particularly influential in Italy. Although many Italians achieved fame as theologians (including Thomas Aquinas and Gregory of Rimini), they generally lived and worked in northern Europe. There was thus an intellectual vacuum in Italy during the fourteenth century. Vacuums tend to be filled – and Renaissance humanism filled this particular gap.

2 Italy was saturated with visible and tangible reminders of the greatness of antiquity. The ruins of ancient Roman buildings and monuments were scattered throughout the land, and appear to have aroused interest in the civilization of ancient Rome at the time of the Renaissance, acting as a stimulus to its thinkers to recover the vitality of classical Roman culture at a time which was culturally arid and barren.

3 As Byzantium began to crumble – Constantinople finally fell in 1453 – there was an exodus of Greek-speaking intellectuals westward. Italy happened to be conveniently close to Constantinople, with the result that many such emigrés settled in Italian cities. A revival of the Greek language was thus inevitable, and with it a revival of interest in the Greek classics.

It will be clear that a central component of the worldview of the Italian Renaissance is a return to the cultural glories of antiquity, and a marginalization of the intellectual achievements of the Middle Ages. Renaissance writers had scant regard for the latter, regarding them as outweighed by the greater achievements of antiquity. What was true of culture in general was also true of theology: They regarded the late classical period as totally overshadowing the theological writings of the Middle Ages, both in substance and in style. Indeed, the Renaissance may partly be seen as a reaction against the type of approach increasingly associated with the faculties of arts and theology of northern European universities. Irritated by the technical nature of the language and discussions of the scholastics, the writers of the Renaissance by-passed them altogether. In the case of Christian theology, the key to the future lay in a direct engagement with the text of Scripture and the writings of the patristic period. We shall explore this matter further shortly (see pp. 51–2).

Scholasticism

Scholasticism is probably one of the most despised intellectual movements in human history. Thus the English word "dunce" (fool) derives from the name of one of the greatest scholastic writers, Duns

Scotus. Scholastic thinkers – the "schoolmen" – are often represented as debating earnestly, if pointlessly, over how many angels could dance on the head of a pin. Although this particular debate never actually took place, intriguing though its outcome would unquestionably have been, it summarizes precisely the way in which scholasticism was regarded by most people, especially the humanists, at the beginning of the sixteenth century: it was futile, arid intellectual speculation over trivia. Erasmus of Rotterdam, a gentleman whom we shall consider in more detail shortly, spent a few semesters toward the end of the fifteenth century at the scholasticism-dominated University of Paris. He wrote at length of the many things he detested about Paris: the lice, the poor food, the stinking latrines, and the utterly tedious debates which vexed the schoolmen. Could God have become a cucumber instead of a human being? Could he undo the past, by making a prostitute into a virgin? Although serious questions lay behind these debates, Erasmus' waspish wit diverted attention from those questions themselves to the frivolous and ridiculous way in which they were debated.

The very word "scholasticism" could be argued to be the invention of humanist writers, anxious to discredit the movement which it represented. We have already noted that the phrase "the Middle Ages" was largely a humanist invention, coined by sixteenth-century humanist writers to refer disparagingly to an uninteresting period of stagnation between antiquity (the classical period) and modernity (the Renaissance). The "Middle Ages" were seen as little more than an intermezzo between the cultural magnificence of antiquity and its revival during the Renaissance. Similarly, the term "scholastics" (*scholastici*) was used by humanists to refer, equally disparagingly, to the ideas of the Middle Ages. In their concern to discredit the ideas of the medieval period, in order to enhance the attractions of the classical period, the humanists had little interest in drawing distinctions between the various types of "scholastics" – such as Thomists and Scotists. The word "scholasticism" is thus both pejorative and imprecise – yet the historian cannot avoid using it.

How may scholasticism be defined? Like many other significant cultural terms, such as "humanism" and "Enlightenment" it is difficult to offer a precise definition, capable of doing justice to all the distinctive positions of the major schools within the Middle Ages. Perhaps the following working definition may be helpful: Scholasticism is best regarded as the medieval movement, flourishing in the period 1200–1500, which placed emphasis upon the rational justification of religious belief, and the systematic presentation of those beliefs. "Scholasticism" thus does not refer to a *specific system of beliefs*, but to a *particular way of organizing theology* – a highly developed method of presenting material, making fine distinctions, and attempting to achieve a comprehensive view of theology. It is perhaps understandable why, to its humanist critics, scholasticism seemed to degenerate into little more than logical nit-picking.

However, scholasticism may be argued to have produced vitally important work in a number of key areas of Christian theology, especially in relation to the role of reason and logic in theology. The writings of Thomas Aquinas, Duns Scotus, and William of Ockham – often singled out as the three most influential of all scholastic writers – make massive contributions to this area of theology, which have served as landmarks ever since.

So what types of scholasticism were there? Like "humanism," the term "scholasticism" defines an approach or method, rather than a specific set of doctrines which result from the application of this method. There are thus several different types of scholasticism. This section will explore briefly some of the main types, or "schools," paying particular attention to those of relevance to the development of theology during the medieval period. We begin by drawing a distinction between "realism" and "nominalism," two very different theories of knowledge which both had a major impact upon the development of scholasticism.

Realism and nominalism

The distinction between "realism" and "nominalism" is of considerable importance to an understanding of medieval theology, thus obliging us to explore it in a little detail. The early part of the scholastic period (c.1200–c.1350) was dominated by realism, whereas the later part (c.1350–c.1500) was dominated by nominalism. The difference between the two systems may be described as follows. Consider two white stones. Realism affirms that there is a universal concept of "whiteness" which these two stones embody. These particular stones possess the universal characteristic of "whiteness." While the white stones exist in time and space, the universal of "whiteness" exists on a different metaphysical plane. Nominalism, however, asserts that the universal concept of "whiteness" is unnecessary, and instead argues that we should concentrate on particulars. There are these two white stones – and there is no need to start talking about "a universal concept of whiteness."

The idea of a "universal," used here without definition, needs to be explored further. Consider Socrates. He is a human being, and is an example of humanity. Now consider Plato and Aristotle. They are also human beings, and examples of humanity. We could go on doing this for some time, naming as many individuals as we liked, but the same basic pattern emerges: Individual named people are examples of humanity. Realism argues that the abstract idea of "humanity" has a real existence of its own. It is the universal; particular people – such as Socrates, Plato, and Aristotle – are individual examples of this universal. The common feature of humanity which unites these three individuals has a real existence of its own.

Two major scholastic "schools" influenced by realism dominate the earlier medieval period. These are *Thomism* and *Scotism*, derived from the writings of Thomas Aquinas and Duns Scotus respectively. Late scholasticism, however, came to be dominated by two other schools, both committed to nominalism, rather than realism. These are generally known as the "modern way" (*via moderna*) and the "modern Augustinian school" (*schola Augustiniana moderna*).

The modern way

The term *via moderna* – "the modern way" – is now becoming generally accepted as the best way of referring to the movement once known as "nominalism," including amongst its adherents such fourteenth- and fifteenth-century thinkers as William of Ockham, Pierre d'Ailly, Robert Holcot, and Gabriel Biel. During the fifteenth century, the "modern way" began to make significant inroads into many northern European universities – for example, at Paris, Heidelberg, and Erfurt. In addition to its philosophical nominalism, the movement adopted a doctrine of justification which many of its critics branded as "Pelagian." It is against this background that Luther's theology is set.

The modern Augustinian school

One of the strongholds of the "modern way" in the early fourteenth century was the University of Oxford. It was here also that the first major negative reaction against the movement occurred. The individual responsible for this backlash was Thomas Bradwardine, later to become Archbishop of Canterbury. Bradwardine wrote a furious attack on the ideas of the Oxford "modern way," entitled *The Case of God against Pelagius*. In this book, he developed a theory of justification which represents a return to the views of Augustine, as they are found in the latter's anti-Pelagian writings.

Important though Oxford was as a theological center, the Hundred Years War of 1337–1453 led to its becoming increasingly isolated from the continent of Europe. Whereas Bradwardine's ideas would be developed in England by John Wycliffe, they were taken up on the mainland of Europe by Gregory of Rimini at the University of Paris. Gregory had one particularly significant advantage over Bradwardine: He was a member of a religious order (the Order of the Hermits of St Augustine, generally referred to as the "Augustinian order"). And just as the Dominicans propagated the views of Thomas Aquinas and the Franciscans those of Duns Scotus, so the Augustinians would promote the ideas of Gregory of Rimini. It is this transmission of an Augustinian tradition, deriving from Gregory of Rimini, within the Augustinian order which is increasingly referred to as the *schola Augustiniana moderna*, the "modern Augustinian school." What were these views?

First, Gregory adopted a nominalist view on the question of universals. Like many thinkers of his time, he had little use for the realism of Thomas Aquinas or Duns Scotus. In this respect, he has much in common with thinkers of the "modern way," such as Robert Holcot or Gabriel Biel. Second, Gregory developed a soteriology, or doctrine of salvation, which reflects the influence of Augustine. We find an emphasis upon the need for grace, upon the fallenness and sinfulness of humanity, upon the divine initiative in justification, and upon divine predestination. Salvation is understood to be *totally* a work of God, from its beginning to its end. Where the proponents of the "modern way" held that humans could initiate their justification by "doing their best," Gregory insisted that only God could initiate justification.

The "modern way" held that most (but not all) necessary soteriological resources were located *within* human nature. The merits of Christ are an example of a resource lying *outside* humanity; the ability to desist from sin and turn to righteousness is, for a writer such as Biel, an example of a vital soteriological resource located within humanity. In marked contrast, Gregory of Rimini argued that these resources were located exclusively outside human nature. Even the ability to desist from sin and turn to righteousness arose through the action of God, not through human action.

It is obvious that these two approaches represent two totally different ways of understanding the human and divine roles in justification. Although Gregory's academic Augustinianism was particularly associated with the Augustinian order, not every Augustinian monastery or university school seems to have adopted its ideas. Nevertheless, it seems that a school of thought which was strongly Augustinian in cast was in existence in the late Middle Ages on the eve of the Reformation. In many ways, the Wittenberg reformers, with their particular emphasis upon the anti-Pelagian writings of Augustine, may be regarded as having rediscovered and revitalized this tradition.

Humanism

The term "humanism" has now come to mean a worldview which denies the existence or relevance of God, or which is committed to a purely secular outlook. This is not what the word meant at the time of the Renaissance. Most humanists of the period were religious, and concerned to purify and renew Christianity, rather than eliminate it. The term "humanism" actually turns out to be quite difficult to define. In the recent past, two major lines of interpretation of the movement were predominant. According to the first, humanism was a movement devoted to the study of classical languages and literature; according to the second, humanism was basically a set of ideas, comprising the new philosophy of the Renaissance.

As will become clear, both these interpretations of humanism have serious shortcomings. For example, it is beyond doubt that the Renaissance witnessed the rise of classical scholarship. The Greek and Latin classics were widely studied in their original languages. It might therefore seem that humanism was essentially a scholarly movement devoted to the study of the classical period. This is to overlook, however, the question of *why* the humanists wished to study the classics in the first place. The evidence available unquestionably indicates that such study was regarded as a means to an end, rather than an end in itself. That end was the promotion of contemporary written and spoken eloquence. In other words, the humanists studied the classics as models of written eloquence, in order to gain inspiration and instruction. Classical learning and philological competence were simply the tools used to exploit the resources of antiquity. As has often been pointed out, the writings of the humanists devoted to the promotion of eloquence, written or spoken, far exceed those devoted to classical scholarship or philology.

According to several other recent interpreters of humanism, the movement embodied the new philosophy of the Renaissance, which arose as a reaction to scholasticism. Thus it was argued that the Renaissance was an age of Platonism, whereas scholasticism was a period of Aristotelianism. Others argued that the Renaissance was essentially an anti-religious phenomenon, foreshadowing the secularism of the eighteenth-century Enlightenment.

Two major difficulties confronted this rather ambitious interpretation of humanism. First, as we have seen, humanists appear to have been primarily concerned with the promotion of eloquence. While it is not true to say that humanists made no significant contribution to philosophy, the fact remains that they were primarily interested in the world of letters. Thus, in comparison with those devoted to the "pursuit of eloquence," there are remarkably few humanist writings devoted to philosophy – and these are generally somewhat amateurish.

Second, intensive study of humanist writings uncovered the disquieting fact that "humanism" was remarkably heterogeneous. For example, many humanist writers did indeed favor Platonism – but others favored Aristotelianism. Some Italian humanists did indeed display what seemed to be anti-religious attitudes – but most Italian humanists were profoundly religious. Some humanists were indeed republicans – but others adopted different political attitudes. Recent studies have also drawn attention to a less attractive side of humanism – the obsession of some humanists with magic and superstition – which is difficult to harmonize with the conventional view of the movement. In short, it became increasingly clear that "humanism" seemed to lack any coherent philosophy. No single philosophical or political idea dominated or characterized the movement. It seemed to many that the term "humanism" would have to be dropped from the vocabulary of historians, because it had no meaningful content. Designating a writer as a "humanist" actually conveys little hard information concerning his or her philosophical, political, or religious views.

A more realistic approach, which has gained widespread acceptance in scholarly circles, is to view humanism as a cultural and educational movement, primarily concerned with the promotion of eloquence in its various forms. Its interests in morals, philosophy, and politics are of secondary importance. To be a humanist is to be concerned with eloquence first and foremost, and with other matters incidentally. Humanism was essentially a cultural program, which appealed to classical antiquity as a model of eloquence. In art and architecture, as in the written and spoken word, antiquity was seen as a cultural resource, which could be appropriated by the Renaissance. Humanism was thus concerned with *how ideas were obtained and expressed*, rather than with *the actual substance of those ideas*. A humanist might be a Platonist or an Aristotelian – but in both cases, the ideas involved derived from antiquity. A humanist might be a skeptic or a believer – but both attitudes could be defended from antiquity.

Northern European humanism

The form of "humanism" which proved to be of especial importance theologically is primarily northern European humanism, rather than Italian humanism. We must therefore consider what form this northern European movement took.

It is becoming increasingly clear that northern European humanism was decisively influenced by Italian humanism at every stage of its development. Three main channels for the diffusion of the methods and ideals of the Italian Renaissance into northern Europe have been identified:

1 Through northern European scholars moving south to Italy, perhaps to study at an Italian university or as part of a diplomatic mission. On returning to their homeland, they brought the spirit of the Renaissance back with them.

2 Through the foreign correspondence of the Italian humanists. Humanism was concerned with the promotion of written eloquence, and the writing of letters was seen as a means of embodying and spreading the ideals of the Renaissance. The foreign correspondence of Italian humanists was considerable, extending to most parts of northern Europe.

3 Through printed books, originating from sources such as the Aldine Press in Venice. These works were often reprinted by northern European presses, particularly those at Basel in Switzerland. Italian humanists often dedicated their works to northern European patrons, thus ensuring that they were taken notice of in potentially influential quarters.

Although there are major variations within northern European humanism, two ideals seem to have achieved widespread acceptance throughout the movement. First, we find the same concern for written and spoken eloquence, after the fashion of the classical period, as in the Italian Reformation. Second, we find a religious program directed toward the corporate revival of the Christian church. The Latin slogan *Christianismus renascens*, "Christianity being born again," summarizes the aims of this program, and indicates its relation to the "rebirth" of letters associated with the Renaissance.

In view of the importance of humanism to the Reformation in Europe, we shall consider some of its local variants, with particular reference to Switzerland, France, and England.

Swiss humanism

Perhaps on account of its geographical position, Switzerland proved especially receptive to the ideas of the Italian Renaissance. The University of Vienna attracted large numbers of students from this region. A palace revolution within the faculty of arts, engineered largely through the influence of Konrad Celtis, ensured that Vienna became a center of humanist learning in the final years of the fifteenth century, attracting individuals such as the great humanist writer Joachim von Watt, alias Vadian. Vadian, having gained every academic honor possible at Vienna, returned to his native town of St Gallen,

becoming its leading citizen (Burgomeister) in 1529. The University of
Basel also achieved a similar reputation in the 1510s, and became the
center of a humanist group (usually known as a "sodality"), focusing
on such individuals as Thomas Wyttenbach.

Swiss humanism has been the subject of intensive study, and its
basic ethos is fairly well understood. For its leading representatives,
Christianity was primarily a way of life, rather than a set of doctrines.
Reform was indeed needed – but that reform related primarily to the
morality of the church, and the need for personal moral renewal of
individual believers. There was no pressure for a reform of church
doctrine.

The ethos of Swiss humanism was strongly moralistic, with Scripture
being regarded as prescribing correct moral behavior for Christians,
rather than narrating the promises of God. This ethos has a number
of significant implications, especially in relation to the doctrine of
justification. In the first place, the questions which stimulated Luther's
concern for the doctrine were quite absent from Swiss circles. Justification was something of a non-issue. Second, as it became an issue in
Germany, a certain degree of anxiety became evident within Swiss
humanist circles in the 1520s about Luther's doctrine of justification.
To the Swiss humanists, Luther seemed to be developing ideas which
were a radical threat to morality, and thus to the distinctive ethos of
their movement.

The importance of these observations relates to Huldrych Zwingli,
educated at the universities of Vienna (1498–1502) and Basel (1502–6).
Zwingli's program of reform at Zurich, initiated in 1519, bears the
hallmark of Swiss humanist moralism. Augustine, the "doctor of
grace," does not appear to figure prominently in Zwingli's thought
until the 1520s (and even then, his influence relates primarily to
Zwingli's sacramental thinking). Zwingli finally broke with the moralism of Swiss humanism (probably around 1523, certainly by 1525),
but until this point his program of reform was based upon the moralist
educational outlook so characteristic of Swiss humanist sodalities of
this period.

French humanism

In early sixteenth-century France, the study of law was in the process
of radical revision. The absolutist French monarchy under Francis I,
with its increasing trend toward administrative centralization, regarded
legal reform as essential to the modernization of France. In order to
speed up the process of reform, with its goal of formulating a legal
system universally valid throughout France, it patronized a group of

scholars, centered on the Universities of Bourges and Orléans, who were engaged on the theoretical aspects of general codes of law founded on universal principles. A pioneer amongst these latter was Guillaume Budé, who argued for a direct return to Roman law as a means of meeting the new legal needs of France which was both eloquent and economic. In contrast with the Italian custom (*mos italicus*) of reading classical legal texts in the light of the glosses and commentaries of medieval jurists, the French developed the procedure (*mos gallicus*) of appealing directly to the original classical legal sources in their original languages.

One direct result of the French humanist program of proceeding directly *ad fontes* was a marked impatience with glosses (annotations to the text) and commentaries. Far from being viewed as useful study tools, these became increasingly regarded as obstacles to engagement with the original text. The interpretations of classical Roman legal texts by writers such as Bartholus and Accursius came to be regarded as irrelevant. They were like distorting filters placed between the reader and the text. As humanist scholarship became more confident in its assertions, the reliability of Accursius and others was increasingly called into question. The great Spanish scholar Antonio Nebrija published a detailed account of errors he had detected in Accursius' glosses, while Rabelais wrote scornfully of "the inept opinions of Accursius."

The importance of this development to the Reformation must be noted. One student at Bourges and Orléans during the heyday of this French legal humanism was the future church reformer, John Calvin, who probably arrived at Orléans in 1528. In studying civil law at Orléans and Bourges, Calvin came into first-hand contact with a major constituent element of the humanist movement. This encounter at least turned Calvin into a competent lawyer: When he was subsequently called upon to assist with the codification of the "laws and edicts" of Geneva, he was able to draw on his knowledge of the *corpus iuris civilis* for models of contract, property law, and judicial procedure. But Calvin learned more than this from French humanism.

The origins of Calvin's methods as perhaps the greatest biblical commentator and preacher of his age may be argued to lie in his study of law in the advanced atmosphere of Orléans and Bourges. There is every indication that Calvin learned from Budé the need to be a competent philologist, to approach a foundational text directly, to interpret it within the linguistic and historical parameters of its context, and apply it to the needs of his own day. It is precisely this attitude which undergirds Calvin's exposition of Scripture, especially in his sermons, in which he aims to fuse the horizons of Scripture and the context of his audience. French humanism gave Calvin both the incentive and the tools to enable the documents of yesteryear to interact with the situation of the city of Geneva in the 1550s.

English humanism

Perhaps the most important center of humanism in early sixteenth-century England was located at the University of Cambridge, although the importance of Oxford and London must not be understated. Cambridge was the home of the early English Reformation, centering on the "White Horse Circle" (named after a now-demolished tavern close to Queens' College), where individuals such as Robert Barnes met to devour and discuss the latest writings of Martin Luther during the early 1520s. It was only to be expected that the tavern should soon be nicknamed "little Germany," just as later the King Street area – once home of Cambridge's Communist Party – would be known as "little Moscow" during the 1930s.

Key Theologians

Of the many theologians of importance to have emerged during this period of enormous creativity, the following are of especial interest and importance.

Anselm of Canterbury (c. 1033–1109)

Anselm was born in northern Italy, but soon moved to France, then establishing a reputation as a center for learning. He quickly mastered the arts of logic and grammar, and acquired a formidable reputation as a teacher at the Norman abbey of Bec. Standing at the dawn of the theological renaissance of the twelfth century, Anselm made decisive contributions in two areas of discussion: proofs for the existence of God, and the rational interpretation of Christ's death upon the cross.

The *Proslogion* (the word is virtually untranslatable) was written around 1079. It is a remarkable work, in which Anselm sets himself the task of formulating an argument which will lead to belief in the existence and character of God as highest good. The resulting analysis, often known as the "ontological argument," leads to the derivation of the existence of God from an affirmation of his being "that than which nothing greater can be conceived." Although the argument has been contested since its inception, it has remained one of the most intriguing components of philosophical theology to this day. The *Proslogion* is also of importance on account of its clear appeal to reason in matters of theology, and its appreciation of the role of logic. In many ways, the work anticipates the best aspects of scholastic theology. Anselm's phrase *fides quaerens intellectum* ("faith seeking understanding") has passed into widespread use.

Following the Norman invasion of England (1066), Anselm was invited to become Archbishop of Canterbury in 1093, thus ensuring the consolidation of Norman influence over the English church. It was not an entirely happy period of his life, due to a series of violent disputes between the church and the monarchy over land rights. During one period spent working away from England in Italy, Anselm penned perhaps his most important work, *Cur Deus homo* ("Why God became man"). In this work, Anselm seeks to set out a rational demonstration of the necessity of God becoming man, and an analysis of the benefits which accrue to humanity as a result of the incarnation and obedience of the Son of God. This argument, to be considered at length later in this work, remains of foundational importance to any discussion of "theories of the atonement" – in other words, under-standings of the meaning of the death and resurrection of Christ, and its significance for humanity. Once more, the work exhibits the characteristics which are typical of scholasticism at its best: The appeal to reason, the logical marshaling of arguments, the relent-less exploration of the implications of ideas, and the fundamental conviction that, at its heart, the Christian gospel *is* rational, and can be *shown* to be rational.

Thomas Aquinas (*c*.1225–74)

Aquinas was born at the castle of Roccasecca in Italy, the youngest son of Count Landulf of Aquino. To judge by his nickname – "the dumb ox" – he was rather portly. In 1244, while in his late teens, Aquinas decided to join the Dominican order, also known as the "Order of Preachers." His parents were hostile to this idea: they rather hoped he would become a Benedictine, and perhaps end up as abbot of Monte Cassino, one of the most prestigious positions in the medieval church. His brothers forcibly imprisoned him in one of the family's castles for a year to encourage him to change his mind. Despite this intense opposition from his family, Aquinas eventually got his way, and ended up becoming one of the most important religious thinkers of the Middle Ages. One of his teachers is reported to have said that "the bellowing of that ox will be heard throughout the world."

Aquinas began his studies at Paris, before moving to Cologne in 1248. In 1252 he returned to Paris to study theology. Four years later, he was granted permission to teach theology at the university. For the next three years he lectured on Matthew's Gospel and began to write the *Summa contra Gentiles*, "Summary against the Gentiles." In this major work, Aquinas provided important arguments in favor of the Christian faith for the benefit of missionaries working amongst Moslems and Jews. In 1266, he began the most famous of his many writings, usually known by its Latin title, *Summa Theologiae*. In this work, Thomas developed a detailed study of key aspects of Christian theology (such as the role of reason and faith), as well as a detailed analysis of key doctrinal questions (such as the divinity of Christ). The work is divided into three parts, with each of the first two parts subdivided into two. Part I deals chiefly with God the creator; Part II with the restoration of humanity to God; and Part III with the manner in which the person and work of Christ bring about the salvation of humanity.

On December 6, 1273, Aquinas declared that he could write no longer. "All that I have written seems like straw to me," he said. It is possible that he may have had some sort of breakdown, perhaps brought on by overwork. He died on March 7, 1274.

Amongst Aquinas' key contributions to theology, the following are of especial importance, and are discussed elsewhere in this volume:

- the "Five Ways" (arguments for the existence of God) (see pp. 132–5);
- the principle of analogy, which provides a theological foundation for knowing God through the creation (see pp. 135–6);
- the relation between faith and reason (see pp. 48–50).

Duns Scotus (*c.*1265–1308)

Scotus was unquestionably one of the finest minds of the Middle Ages. In his short life, he taught at Cambridge, Oxford, and Paris, and produced three versions of a *Commentary on the Sentences*. Known as the "subtle doctor" on account of the very fine distinctions which he frequently drew between the possible meaning of terms, he was responsible for a number of developments of considerable significance to Christian theology. Only three can be noted here.

1 Scotus was a champion of the theory of knowledge associated with Aristotle. The earlier Middle Ages were dominated by a different theory of knowledge, going back to Augustine of Hippo, known as "illuminationism," in which knowledge was understood to arise from the illumination of the human intellect by God. This view, which was championed by writers such as Henry of Ghent, was subjected to devastating criticism by Scotus.

2 Scotus regarded the divine will as taking precedent over the divine intellect, a doctrine often referred to as *voluntarism*. Thomas Aquinas had argued for the primacy of the divine intellect; Scotus opened the way to new approaches to theology, based on the assumption of the priority of the divine will. An example illustrates the point. Consider the idea of merit – that is to say, a human moral action which is deemed worthy of reward by God. What is the basis of this decision? Aquinas argued that the divine intellect recognized the inherent worth of the human moral act. It then informed the will to reward it appropriately. Scotus argued along very different lines. The divine will to reward the moral action came before any evaluation of its inherent worth. This approach is of considerable importance in relation to the doctrines of justification and predestination, and will be considered in more detail later.

3 Scotus was a champion of the doctrine of the immaculate conception of Mary, the mother of Jesus. Thomas Aquinas had taught that Mary shared the common sinful condition of humanity. She was tainted by sin (Latin: *macula*), like everyone else, apart from Christ. Scotus, however, argued that Christ, by virtue of his perfect work of redemption, was able to keep Mary free from the taint of original sin. Such was the influence of Scotus that the "immaculate position" (from the Latin *immacula*, "free of sin") became dominant by the end of the Middle Ages.

William of Ockham (*c.*1285–1347)

In many ways, Ockham may be regarded as developing some of the lines of argument associated with Scotus. Of particular importance is his consistent defense of a voluntarist position, giving priority to the divine will over the divine intellect. It is, however, probably his philosophical position which has ensured his permanent place of note in the history of Christian theology. Two major elements of his teaching may be noted.

1 Ockham's Razor, often referred to as "the principle of parsimony." Ockham insisted that simplicity was both a theological and a philosophical virtue. His "razor" eliminated all hypotheses which were not absolutely essential. This had major implications for his theology of

justification. Earlier medieval theologians (including Thomas Aquinas) had argued that God was obliged to justify sinful humanity by means of a "created habit of grace" – in other words, an intermediate supernatural entity, infused by God into the human soul, which permitted the sinner to be pronounced justified. Ockham dismissed this notion as an unnecessary irrelevance, and declared that justification was the direct acceptance of a sinner by God. The way was thus opened to the more personalist approach to justification associated with the early Reformation.

2   Ockham was a vigorous defender of nominalism. In part, this resulted from his use of the razor: Universals were declared to be a totally unnecessary hypothesis, and were thus eliminated. The growing impact of the "modern way" in western Europe owes a considerable debt to him. One aspect of his thought which proved to be of especial importance is the "dialectic between the two powers of God." This device allowed Ockham to contrast the way things are with the way things could have been. A full discussion of this follows later; for the moment, it is enough to note that Ockham made a decisive contribution to discussions of divine omnipotence, which are of continuing importance today.

Erasmus of Rotterdam (*c.*1469–1536)

Desiderius Erasmus is generally regarded as the most important humanist writer of the Renaissance, and had a profound impact upon Christian theology during the first half of the sixteenth century. Although not a Protestant in any sense of the term, Erasmus did much to lay the intellectual foundations of the Reformation, not least through his extensive editorial undertakings, including the production of the first printed text of the Greek New Testament (see pp. 52–3). His *Enchiridion militis Christiani* ("Handbook of the Christian Soldier"), was a landmark in religious publishing. Although the work was first published in 1503, and then reprinted in 1509, its real impact dates from its third printing in 1515. From that moment onward it became a cult work, apparently going through twenty-three editions in the next six years. Its appeal was to educated lay men and women, whom Erasmus regarded as the most importance resource that the church possessed. Its amazing popularity in the years after 1515 makes it possible to suggest that it brought about a radical alteration in lay self-perception – and it can hardly be overlooked that the reforming rumbles at Zurich and Wittenberg date from soon after the *Enchiridion* became a best-seller.

The *Enchiridion* developed the revolutionary thesis that the church of the day could be reformed by a collective return to the writings of the fathers and Scripture. The regular reading of Scripture is put forward as the key to a new lay piety, on the basis of which the church may be renewed and reformed. Erasmus conceived of his work as a lay person's guide to Scripture, providing a simple yet learned exposition of the "philosophy of Christ." This "philosophy" is really a form of practical morality, rather than an academic philosophy: The New Testament concerns the knowledge of good and evil, in order that its readers may eschew the latter and love the former. The New Testament is the *lex Christi*, "the law of Christ," which Christians are called to obey. Christ is the example whom Christians are called to imitate. Yet Erasmus does not understand Christian faith to be a mere external observance of a moral code. His characteristically humanist emphasis upon inner religion leads him to suggest that reading of Scripture *transforms* its readers, giving them a new motivation to love God and their neighbors.

A number of features of this book are of particular importance. First, Erasmus understands the future vitality of Christianity to lie with the laity, not the clergy. The clergy are seen as educators, whose function is to allow the laity to achieve the same level of understanding as themselves. There is no room for any superstitions which give the clergy a permanent status superior to their lay charges. Second, Erasmus' strong emphasis upon the "inner religion" results in an understanding of Christianity which makes no reference to the church – its rites, priests, or institutions. Why bother confessing sins to another human, asks Erasmus, just because he's a priest, when you can confess them directly to God?

In addition to these radical suggestions, Erasmus undertook extensive scholarly projects. Two of these are of especial importance to the development of Christian theology:

1 The production of the first Greek New Testament. As noted earlier, this allowed theologians direct access to the original text of the New Testament, with explosive results.
2 The production of reliable editions of patristic works, including the writings of Augustine. Theologians thus had access to the full text of such major works, instead of having to rely upon second-hand quotations, often taken out of context. A new understanding of Augustine's theology began to develop as a result, with significant implications for the theological development of the period.

Key Theological Developments

The major renaissance in theology which took place during the period under consideration focused on a number of issues, of which the following are of especial importance. They are simply noted at this point; detailed discussion of most of them will take place later in this work. The first six such developments are associated with scholasticism (see pp. 32–6), the last two with humanism (see pp. 37–42).

The Consolidation of the Patristic Heritage

When the Dark Ages lifted, Christian theologians tended to pick up where the great patristic writers had left off. In that the western church was Latin-speaking, it was natural that its theologians should turn to the substantial collection of works by Augustine of Hippo, and take this as a starting point for their own theological speculations. Peter Lombard's *Sentences* may be regarded as a critical compilation of quotations ("Sentences") drawn largely from the writings of Augustine, upon which medieval theologians were required to comment.

The Exploration of the Role of Reason in Theology

The new concern to establish Christian theology upon a totally reliable foundation led to a considered exploration of the role of reason in theology, a central and defining characteristic of scholasticism (see p. 33). As the theological renaissance of the early Middle Ages proceeded, two themes began to dominate theological debate: The need to *systematize* and *expand* Christian theology; and the need to *demonstrate the inherent rationality* of that theology. Although most early medieval theology was little more than a replay of the views of Augustine, there was growing pressure to systematize Augustine's ideas, and take them further. But how could this be done? A "theory of method" was urgently needed. And on the basis of what philosophical system could the rationality of Christian theology be demonstrated?

The eleventh-century writer Anselm of Canterbury gave expression to this basic belief of the rationality of the Christian faith in two phrases which have come to be linked with his name: *fides quaerens intellectum* ("faith seeking understanding"), and *credo ut intellegam* ("I believe, in order that I may understand"). His basic insight was that, while faith came before understanding, the content of that faith was nevertheless rational. These definitive formulae established the priority of faith over reason, just as they asserted the entire reasonableness of faith. In the preface to his *Monologium*, Anselm stated explicitly that he would establish nothing in Scripture on the basis of Scripture itself; instead, he would establish everything that he could on the basis of "rational evidence and the natural light of truth." Nevertheless, Anselm is no rationalist; reason has its limits!

The eleventh and early twelfth centuries saw a growing conviction that philosophy could be an invaluable asset to Christian theology at two different levels. In the first place, it could demonstrate the reasonableness of faith, and thus defend it against non-Christian critics. In the second, it offered ways of systematically exploring and arranging the articles of faith, so that they could be better understood. But which philosophy? The answer to this question came through the rediscovery of the writings of Aristotle, in the late twelfth and early thirteenth centuries. By about 1270, Aristotle had become established as "the Philosopher." His ideas came to dominate theological thinking, despite fierce opposition from more conservative quarters.

Through the influence of writers such as Thomas Aquinas and Duns Scotus, Aristotle's ideas became established as the best means of consolidating and developing Christian theology. The ideas of Christian theology were thus arranged and correlated systematically, on the basis of Aristotelian presuppositions. Equally, the rationality of Christian faith was demonstrated on the basis of Aristotelian ideas. Thus some of Thomas Aquinas' famous "proofs" for the existence of God actually rely on principles of Aristotelian physics, rather than on any distinctively Christian insights.

Initially, this development was welcomed by many, who saw it as providing important ways of defending the rationality of the Christian faith – a discipline which has since come to be known as "apologetics," from the Greek word *apologia* (defense). Thomas Aquinas' *Summa contra Gentiles* is an excellent example of a work of theology which draws on Aristotelianism. At points, the argument seems to work like this: If you can agree with the Aristotelian ideas presented in this writing, then you ought to become a Christian. As Aristotle was highly regarded by many Moslem academics of the period, Thomas can be seen as exploiting the apologetic potential of this philosopher.

This development came to be viewed with concern by some later medieval writers, such as Hugolino of Orvieto. A number of central Christian insights seemed to have been lost, as a result of a growing reliance upon the ideas and methods of a pagan philosopher. Particular concern centered on the doctrine of justification. The idea of the "righteousness of God" came to be discussed in terms of the Aristotelian idea of "distributive justice." Here, "righteousness" (*iustitia*) was defined in terms of "giving someone what they were entitled to." This seemed to lead to a doctrine of justification by merit. In other words, justification takes place on the basis of entitlement, rather than grace. It can be shown without difficulty that this concern lies behind Martin Luther's growing dislike of Aristotle, and his eventual break with scholastic doctrines of justification.

The Development of Theological Systems

We have already noted the pressure to consolidate the patristic, and especially the Augustinian, heritage (p. 48). This pressure to system-atize, which is integral to scholasticism, led to the development of sophisticated theological systems, which Etienne Gilson, a noted historian of the period, has described as "cathedrals of the mind" (see p. 182). This development is perhaps best seen in Thomas Aquinas' *Summa Theologiae*, which represents one of the most forceful statements of the comprehensive and all-embracing character of this approach to Christian theology.

The Development of Sacramental Theology

The early church had been somewhat imprecise in its discussion of the sacraments. There was little general agreement concerning either how a sacrament was to be defined, or what items were to be included in a list of the sacraments (see pp. 428–31). Baptism and eucharist were generally agreed to be sacramental; there was relatively little agree-ment on anything else. However, with the theological renaissance of the Middle Ages, the church was coming to play an increasingly important role in society. There was new pressure for the church to place its acts of public worship on a secure intellectual footing, and to consolidate the theoretical aspects of its worship. As a result, sacramental theology developed considerably during the period. Agreement was reached on the definition of a sacrament, the number of the sacraments, and the precise identity of these sacraments.

The Development of the Theology of Grace

A central element of the Augustinian heritage was a theology of grace. However, Augustine's theology of grace had been stated in a polemical context. In other words, Augustine had been obliged to state his theology of grace in the heat of a controversy, often in response to the challenges and provocations of his opponents. As a result, his writings on the subject were often unsystematic. Occasionally, Augustine developed distinctions in response to the needs of the moment, and failed to lay an adequate theological foundation for them. The theologians of the Middle Ages saw themselves as charged with the task of consolidating Augustine's doctrine of grace, placing it upon a more reliable foundation, and exploring its consequences. As a result, the doctrines of grace and justification were developed considerably during the period, laying the foundation for the Reformation debates over these central issues.

The Role of Mary in the Scheme of Salvation

This new interest in grace and justification led to a new concern to understand the role of Mary, the mother of Jesus Christ, in salvation. Growing interest in devotion to Mary, linked with intense theological speculation concerning the nature of original sin and redemption, led to a series of developments relating to Mary. Many of these are linked with Duns Scotus, who placed Mariology (that is, the area of theology dealing with Mary) on a considerably more developed foundation than hitherto. Intense debate broke out between "maculists" (who held that Mary was subject to original sin, like everyone else) and "immaculists" (who held that she was preserved from the taint of original sin). There was also considerable discussion over whether Mary could be said to be "co-redemptrix" (that is to say, whether she was to be regarded as a figure of redemption, in a manner similar to Jesus Christ).

Returning Directly to the Sources of Christian Theology

A central element of the humanist agenda was the return to the original sources of western European culture in classical Rome and Athens. The theological counterpart to this element was the direct return to the foundational resources of Christian theology, above all in the New Testament. This agenda proved to be of major significance, as will be seen later (see p. 53). One of its most important consequences was a new appreciation of the foundational importance of Scripture as a theological resource. As interest in Scripture developed, it became increasingly clear that existing Latin translations of this source were inadequate. Supreme among these was the "Vulgate," a Latin translation of the Bible which achieved widespread influence during the Middle Ages. As revision of translations, especially the Vulgate, proceeded, it became clear that theological revision was inevitable.

The rise of humanist textual and philological techniques was to expose distressing discrepancies between the Vulgate and the texts it purported to translate – and thus open the way to doctrinal reform as a consequence. It is for this reason that humanism is of decisive importance to the development of medieval theology: It demonstrated the total unreliability of this translation of the Bible – and hence, it seemed, of theologies based upon it. The biblical basis of scholasticism seemed to collapse, as humanism uncovered error after error in its translation. We shall explore this point further in what follows; it is unquestionably one of the most significant developments in the history of Christian theology at this time.

The Critique of the Vulgate Translation of Scripture

The literary and cultural program of humanism can be summarized in the slogan *ad fontes* – "back to the original sources." The "filter" of medieval commentaries – whether on legal texts or on the Bible – is abandoned, in order to engage directly with the original texts. Applied to the Christian church, the slogan *ad fontes* meant a direct return to the title-deeds of Christianity – to the patristic writers, and supremely to the Bible, studied in its original languages. This necessitated direct access to the Greek text of the New Testament.

The first printed Greek New Testament was produced by Erasmus in 1516. Erasmus' text was not as reliable as it ought to have been: He had access to a mere four manuscripts for most of the New Testament, and only one for its final part, the Book of Revelation. As it happened, that manuscript left out five verses, which Erasmus himself had to translate into Greek from the Latin of the Vulgate. Nevertheless, it proved to be a literary milestone. For the first time, theologians had the opportunity of comparing the original Greek text of the New Testament with the later Vulgate translation into Latin.

Drawing on work carried out earlier by the Italian humanist Lorenzo Valla, Erasmus showed that the Vulgate translation of several major New Testament texts could not be justified. As a number of medieval church practices and beliefs were based upon these texts, Erasmus' allegations were viewed with consternation by many conservative Catholics (who wanted to retain these practices and beliefs) and with equally great delight by the reformers (who wanted to eliminate them). Three classic examples of translation errors will indicate the relevance of Erasmus' biblical scholarship.

1 Much medieval theology justified the inclusion of matrimony in the list of sacraments on the basis of a New Testament text which – at least, in the Vulgate translation – spoke of marriage being a *sacramentum* (Ephesians 5: 31–2). Erasmus pointed out that the Greek word (*musterion*) here translated as "sacrament" simply meant "mystery." There was no reference whatsoever to marriage being a "sacrament." One of the classic proof texts used by medieval theologians to justify the inclusion of matrimony in the list of sacraments was thus rendered virtually useless.

2 The Vulgate translated the opening words of Jesus' ministry (Matthew 4: 17) as "*do penance*, for the kingdom of heaven is at hand." This translation suggested that the coming of the kingdom of heaven had a direct connection with the sacrament of penance. Erasmus, again following Valla, pointed out that the Greek should be translated as "*repent*, for the Kingdom of heaven is at hand." In other words, where the Vulgate seemed to refer to an outward practice (the sacrament of penance), Erasmus insisted that the reference was to an inward psychological attitude – that of "being repentant." Once more, an important justification of the sacramental system of the medieval church was challenged.

3 According to the Vulgate, Gabriel greeted Mary as "the one who is full of grace" (*gratia plena*) (Luke 1: 28), thus suggesting the image of a reservoir full of grace, which could be drawn upon at time of need. But, as Erasmus pointed out, the Greek simply meant "favored one," or "one who has found favor." Once more, an important feature of medieval theology seemed to be contradicted by humanist New Testament scholarship.

These developments undermined the credibility of the Vulgate translation, opening the way to theological revision on the basis of a better understanding of the biblical text. They also demonstrated the importance of biblical scholarship in relation to theology. Theology could not be permitted to base itself upon translation mistakes! The recognition of the vitally important role of biblical scholarship to Christian theology thus dates from the second decade of the sixteenth century. It also led to the theological concerns of the Reformation, to which we shall now turn.

Key Names, Words, and Phrases

By the end of this chapter, you will have encountered the following terms, some of which will recur during the work. Ensure that you are familiar with them! They have been capitalized as you are likely to encounter them in normal use.

ad fontes
*apologetics
*Five Ways
humanism
immaculate conception
medieval
Middle Ages
*ontological argument
Renaissance
scholasticism
*theories of the atonement
*voluntarism
Vulgate

Those terms marked with an asterisk will be explored in greater detail later in this work.

Questions for Chapter 2

1 What was the language spoken by most western theologians during this period?

2 "Humanists were people who were interested in studying classical Rome." How helpful is this definition of the term?

3 What were the major themes of scholastic theology?

4 Why was there such interest in the theology of the sacraments during the Middle Ages?

5 What is meant by the slogan *ad fontes*?

3

The Reformation and Post-Reformation Periods, *c*.1500–*c*.1700

The term "Reformation" is used by historians and theologians to refer to the western European movement, centering upon individuals such as Martin Luther, Huldrych Zwingli, and John Calvin, concerned with the moral, theological, and institutional reform of the Christian church in that region. Initially, up to about 1525, the Reformation may be regarded as revolving around Martin Luther and the University of Wittenberg, in modern-day north-eastern Germany. However, the movement also gained strength, independently at first, in the Swiss city of Zurich in the early 1520s. Through a complex series of developments, the Zurich Reformation gradually underwent a series of political and theological modifications, eventually coming to be associated primarily with the city of Geneva (now part of modern-day Switzerland, although then an independent city-state) and John Calvin.

The Reformation movement was complex and heterogeneous, and its agenda went for beyond the reform of the doctrine of the church. It addressed fundamental social, political, and economic issues, too complex to be discussed in any detail in this volume. The agenda of the Reformation varied from one country to another, with the theological issues which played major roles in one country (for example, Germany) often having relatively little impact elsewhere (for example, in England).

In response to the Reformation, the Catholic church moved to put its own house in order. Prevented from calling a council at an early date due to political instability in Europe resulting from tensions between France and Germany, the Pope of the day (Paul III) was eventually able to convene the Council of Trent (1545). This set itself the task of clarifying Catholic thought and practice and defending them against its evangelical opponents.

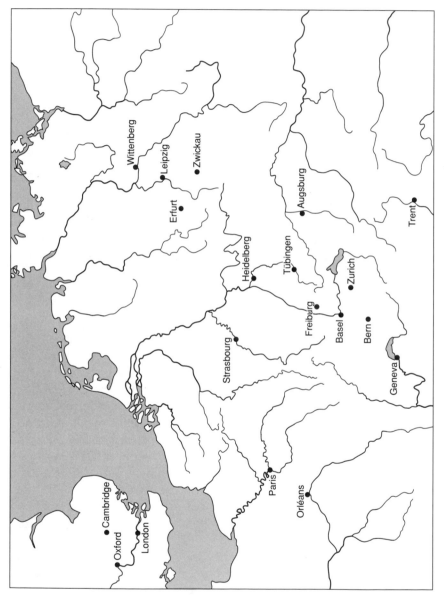

Map 3   Centers of theological and ecclesiastical activity at the time of the European Reformation

The Reformation itself was a western European phenomenon, concentrated especially in the central and northern parts of this region, although Calvinism penetrated as far east as Hungary. However, the emigration of large numbers of individuals to North America, which becomes increasingly significant from 1600 onward, led to post-Reformation Protestant and Catholic theologies being exported to that region. Harvard College is an example of an early center of theological education in New England. The Society of Jesus also undertook extensive missionary operations in the Far East, including India, China, and Japan. Christian theology gradually began to expand beyond its western European base and become a global phenomenon – a development which received final consolidation in the modern period, to which we shall turn shortly. Our attention now turns to a consideration of the terminology linked with the Reformation and post-Reformation periods.

A Clarification of Terms

The term "Reformation" is used in a number of senses, and it is helpful to distinguish them. Four elements may be involved in its definition, and each will be discussed briefly below: Lutheranism; the Reformed church, often referred to as "Calvinism"; the "radical Reformation," often still referred to as "Anabaptism"; and the "Counter-Reformation" or "Catholic Reformation." In its broadest sense, the term "Reformation" is used to refer to all four movements. The term is also used in a somewhat more restricted sense, meaning "the Protestant Reformation," excluding the Catholic Reformation. In this sense, it refers to the three Protestant movements noted above. In many scholarly works, however, the term "Reformation" is used to refer to what is sometimes known as the "magisterial Reformation," or the "mainstream Reformation" – in other words, that linked with the Lutheran and Reformed churches (including Anglicanism), and excluding the Anabaptists.

The unusual phrase "magisterial Reformation" needs a little explaining. The phrase draws attention to the manner in which the mainstream reformers related to secular authorities, such as princes, magistrates, or city councils. Whereas the radical reformers regarded such authorities as having no rights within the church, the mainstream reformers argued that the church was, at least to some extent, subject to the secular agencies of government. The magistrate had a right to authority within the church, just as the church could rely on the

authority of the magistrate to enforce discipline, suppress heresy, or
maintain order. The phrase "magisterial Reformation" is intended to
draw attention to this close relationship between the magistracy and
the church, which lay at the heart of the reforming program of writers
such as Martin Luther or Martin Bucer. All three senses of the word
"Reformation" will be encountered in the course of reading works
dealing with Christian theology. The term "magisterial Reformation"
is increasingly used to refer to the first two senses of the term (i.e.
covering Lutheranism and the Reformed church), taken together, and
the term "radical Reformation" to refer to the third (Anabaptism).

The term "Protestant" requires comment. It derives from the aftermath of the Diet of Speyer (February 1529), which voted to end the
toleration of Lutheranism in Germany. In April of the same year, six
German princes and fourteen cities protested against this oppressive
measure, defending freedom of conscience and the rights of religious
minorities. The term "Protestant" derives from this protest. It is therefore not strictly correct to apply the term "Protestant" to individuals
prior to April 1529, or to speak of events prior to that date as constituting "the Protestant Reformation." The term "evangelical" is often
used in the literature to refer to the reforming factions at Wittenberg
and elsewhere (e.g. in France and Switzerland) prior to this date.
Although the word "Protestant" is often used to refer to this earlier
period, this use is, strictly speaking, an anachronism.

The Lutheran Reformation

The Lutheran Reformation is particularly associated with the German
territories and the pervasive personal influence of one charismatic
individual – Martin Luther. Luther was particularly concerned with
the doctrine of justification, which formed the central point of his
religious thought. The Lutheran Reformation was initially an academic
movement, concerned primarily with reforming the teaching of theology at the University of Wittenberg. Wittenberg was an unimportant
university, and the reforms introduced by Luther and his colleagues
within the theology faculty attracted little attention. It was Luther's
personal activities – such as his posting of the famous Ninety-Five
Theses (31 October 1517) – which attracted considerable interest, and
brought the ideas in circulation at Wittenberg to the attention of a
wider audience.

The Ninety-Five Theses were a protest against the practice of selling
indulgences in order to raise money for the rebuilding of St Peter's
basilica in Rome. The theory underlying the sale of indulgences is
confused, but seems to have rested upon the idea of the gratitude of

the sinner for forgiveness of sins. Once sinners were assured that their sins had been forgiven by the church, acting on behalf of Christ, they would naturally wish to express that gratitude in some positive manner. Gradually, the giving of money to charity, including directly to church funds, came to be seen as the normal way of expressing appreciation for such forgiveness. It must be noted that this was not understood to mean that a sinner *purchased* forgiveness. The gift of money was a result of, not a condition for, forgiveness. But by Luther's time, misrepresentation and misunderstanding had set in. People seem to have believed that indulgences were a quick and convenient way of buying forgiveness of sins. Luther protested. Forgiveness was a matter of a changed relationship between a sinner and God, not a matter of financial speculation. The idea of forgiveness by grace had become corrupted into that of the purchase of God's favor.

Strictly speaking, the Lutheran Reformation only began in 1522, when Luther returned to Wittenberg from his enforced isolation in the Wartburg. Luther was condemned for "false doctrine" by the Diet of Worms in 1521. Fearing for his life, certain well-placed supporters removed him in secrecy to the castle known as the Wartburg, until the threat to his safety ceased. In his absence, Andreas Bodenstein von Karlstadt, one of Luther's academic colleagues at Wittenberg, began a program of reform at Wittenberg which seemed to degenerate into chaos. Convinced that he was needed if the Reformation was to survive Karlstadt's ineptitude, Luther emerged from his place of safety, and returned to Wittenberg.

At this point, Luther's program of academic reform changed into a program of reform of church and society. No longer was Luther's forum of activity the university world of ideas; he now found himself regarded as the leader of a religious, social, and political reforming movement which seemed to some contemporary observers to open the way to a new social and religious order in Europe. In fact, Luther's program of reform was much more conservative than that associated with his Reformed colleagues, such as Huldrych Zwingli. Furthermore, it met with considerably less success than some anticipated. The movement remained obstinately tied to the German territories, and – Scandinavia apart – never gained the foreign power bases which seemed to be like so many ripe apples, ready to fall into its lap. Luther's understanding of the role of the "godly prince" (which effectively ensured that the monarch had control of the church) does not seem to have had the attraction which might have been expected, particularly in the light of the generally republican sentiments of Reformed thinkers such as Calvin. The case of England is particularly illuminating: here, as in the Low Countries, the Protestant theology which gained the ascendancy was Reformed rather than Lutheran.

The Calvinist Reformation

The origins of the Calvinist Reformation, which brought the Reformed churches (such as the Presbyterians) into being, lie in developments within the Swiss Confederation. Whereas the Lutheran Reformation had its origins in an academic context, the Reformed church owed its origins to a series of attempts to reform the morals and worship of the church (but not necessarily its *doctrine*) according to a more biblical pattern. It must be emphasized that although Calvin gave this style of Reformation its definitive form, its origins are to be traced back to earlier reformers, such as Huldrych Zwingli and Heinrich Bullinger, based in the leading Swiss city of Zurich.

Although most of the early Reformed theologians, such as Zwingli, had an academic background, their reforming programs were not academic in nature. They were directed toward the church as they found it in Swiss cities such as Zurich, Berne, and Basel. Whereas Luther was convinced that the doctrine of justification was of central significance to his program of social and religious reform, the early Reformed thinkers had relatively little interest in doctrine, let alone one specific doctrine. Their reforming program was institutional, social, and ethical, in many ways similar to the demands for reform emanating from the humanist movement.

The consolidation of the Reformed church is generally thought to begin with the stabilization of the Zurich Reformation after Zwingli's death in battle (1531) under his successor, Heinrich Bullinger, and to end with the emergence of Geneva as its power base, and John Calvin as its leading spokesman, in the 1550s. The gradual shift in power within the Reformed church (initially from Zurich to Berne, and subsequently from Berne to Geneva) took place over the period 1520–60, eventually establishing the city of Geneva, its political system (republicanism), and its religious thinkers (initially Calvin, and after his death Theodore Beza) as predominant within the Reformed church. This development was consolidated through the establishment of the Genevan Academy (founded in 1559), at which Reformed pastors were trained.

The term "Calvinism" is often used to refer to the religious ideas of the Reformed church. Although still widespread in the literature relating to the Reformation, this practice is now generally discouraged. It is becoming increasingly clear that later sixteenth-century Reformed theology draws on sources other than the ideas of Calvin himself. To refer to later sixteenth- and seventeenth-century Reformed thought as "Calvinist" implies that it is essentially the thought of Calvin – and it is now generally agreed that Calvin's ideas were modified subtly by his successors. The term "Reformed" is now preferred, whether to refer to those churches (mainly in Switzerland, the Low Countries, and Germany) or religious thinkers (such as Theodore Beza, William Perkins, and John Owen) that based themselves upon Calvin's celebrated religious textbook, *The Institutes of the Christian Religion*, or church documents (such as the famous *Heidelberg Catechism*) based upon it.

Of the three constituents of the Protestant Reformation – Lutheran, Reformed or Calvinist, and Anabaptist – it is the Reformed wing which is of particular importance to the English-speaking world. Puritanism, which figures so prominently in seventeenth-century English history and is of such fundamental importance to the religious and political views of New England in the seventeenth century and beyond, is a specific form of Reformed Christianity. To understand the religious and political history of New England or the ideas of writers such as Jonathan Edwards, for example, it is necessary to come to grips with at least some of the theological insights and part of the religious outlook of Puritanism, which underlie their social and political attitudes.

The Radical Reformation (Anabaptism)

The term "Anabaptist" literally means "rebaptizer," and refers to what was perhaps the most distinctive aspect of Anabaptist practice: the insistence that only those who had made a personal, public profession of faith should be baptized. Anabaptism seems to have first arisen around Zurich, in the aftermath of Zwingli's reforms within the city in the early 1520s. It centered on a group of individuals (amongst whom we may note Conrad Grebel) who argued that Zwingli was not being faithful to his own reforming principles. He preached one thing, and practiced another. Although Zwingli professed faithfulness to the *sola scriptura*, "by scripture alone," principle, Grebel argued that he retained a number of practices – including infant baptism, the close link between church and magistracy, and the participation of Christians in warfare – which were not sanctioned or ordained by Scripture. In the hands of such thinkers as Grebel, the *sola scriptura* principle would be radicalized; reformed Christians would believe and practice only those things explicitly taught in Scripture. Zwingli was alarmed by this, seeing it as a destabilizing development which threatened to cut the Reformed church at Zurich off from its historical roots and its continuity with the Christian tradition of the past.

A number of common elements can be discerned within the various strands of the Anabaptist movement: a general distrust of external authority; the rejection of infant baptism in favor of the baptism of adult believers; the common ownership of property; and an emphasis

upon pacifism and non-resistance. To take up the third of these
points: In 1527, the governments of Zurich, Berne, and St Gallen
accused the Anabaptists of believing "that no true Christian can either
give or receive interest or income on a sum of capital; that all temporal
goods are free and common, and that all can have full property rights
to them." It is for this reason that "Anabaptism" is often referred to as
the "left wing of the Reformation" (Roland H. Bainton) or the "radical
Reformation" (George Hunston Williams). For Williams, the "radical
Reformation" was to be contrasted with the "magisterial Reformation,"
which he broadly identified with the Lutheran and Reformed movements. These terms are increasingly being accepted within Reformation scholarship, and you are likely to encounter them in your
reading of more recent studies of the movement.

The Catholic Reformation

This term is often used to refer to the revival within Roman Catholicism
in the period following the opening of the Council of Trent (1545). In
older scholarly works, the movement is often designated the "Counter-
Reformation": as the term suggests, the Roman Catholic church developed means of combating the Protestant Reformation, in order to
limit its influence. It is, however, becoming increasingly clear that the
Roman Catholic church countered the Reformation partly by reforming itself from within, in order to remove the grounds of Protestant
criticism. In this sense, the movement was a reformation of the Roman
Catholic church, as much as it was a reaction against the Protestant
Reformation.

The same concerns underlying the Protestant Reformation in northern Europe were channeled into the renewal of the Catholic church,
particularly in Spain and Italy. The Council of Trent, the foremost
component of the Catholic Reformation, clarified Catholic teaching on
a number of confusing matters, and introduced much-needed reforms
in relation to the conduct of the clergy, ecclesiastical discipline, religious education, and missionary activity. The movement for reform
within the church was greatly stimulated by the reformation of many
of the older religious orders, and the establishment of new orders
(such as the Jesuits). The more specifically theological aspects of the
Catholic Reformation will be considered in relation to its teachings on
Scripture and tradition, justification by faith, and the sacraments. As a
result of the Catholic Reformation, many of the abuses which originally
lay behind the demands for reform – whether these came from humanists or Protestants – were removed.

Key Theologians

The Reformation era is widely regarded as one of the most creative in the history of Christian theology. Three theologians are usually singled out as being of particular significance: Martin Luther, John Calvin, and Huldrych Zwingli. Of these, the first two are of especial importance. Although Zwingli is a major figure in his own right, he has been overshadowed by the creative talent and theological impact of Luther and Calvin.

Martin Luther (1483–1546)

Martin Luther was educated at the University of Erfurt, initially studying within the faculty of arts, before beginning the study of theology at the local Augustinian monastery. He gained an appointment as professor of biblical studies at the University of Wittenberg in 1512, and lectured on the Psalms (1513–15), Romans (1515–16), Galatians (1516–17), and Hebrews (1517–18). During this period, Luther's theology can be seen to have gone through a series of developments, especially in relation to the doctrine of justification. His close engagement with biblical texts during this period appears to have led him to become increasingly dissatisfied with the views of the *via moderna* on the subject.

Luther first came to public attention in 1517, through the publication of his Ninety-Five Theses on Indulgences. This was followed by the Leipzig Disputation (June–July 1519), in which Luther established a reputation as a radical critic of scholasticism. In 1520 he published three treatises which consolidated his growing reputation as a theological reformer. In the *Appeal to the Christian Nobility of the German Nation*, Luther argued passionately for the need for reform of the church. In both its doctrine and its practices, the church of the early sixteenth century had cast itself adrift from the New Testament. His pithy and witty German gave added popular appeal to some intensely serious theological ideas. Encouraged by the remarkable success of this work, Luther followed it up with *The Babylonian Captivity of the Christian Church*. In this powerful piece of writing, Luther argued that the gospel had become captive to the institutional church. The medieval church, he argued, had imprisoned the gospel in a complex system of priests and sacraments. The church had become the master of the gospel, where it should be its servant. This point was further developed in *The Liberty of a Christian*, in which Luther explored the implications of the doctrine of justification by faith for the Christian life.

Luther was perhaps the most creative of the reformers. Yet his theological impact does not rest upon any major work of theology. Most of Luther's writings were produced in response to some controversy. Only his two Catechisms can really be thought of as systematic presentations of the basic ideas of the Christian faith. Their largely pastoral role probably disqualifies them from being taken seriously as works of academic theology. Nevertheless, aspects of Luther's theology have had a deep impact upon western Christian thought. For example, his "theology of the cross," set out briefly in a document of 1518 (the *Heidelberg Disputation*) has had a considerable impact upon twentieth-century theology, as works such as Jürgen Moltmann's *Crucified God* indicate.

John Calvin (1509–64)

Calvin was born in Noyon, north-east of Paris, in 1509. Educated at the scholasticism-dominated University of Paris, he subsequently moved to the more humanist University of Orléans, at which he studied civil law. Although initially inclined to a career of scholarship, he underwent a conversion experience in his mid-twenties, which led to his becoming increasingly associated with reforming movements in Paris, and eventually being forced into exile in Basel.

The second generation of reformers were far more aware of the need for works of systematic theology than the first. Calvin, the major figure of the second period of the Reformation, saw the need for a work which would set out clearly the basic ideas of evangelical theology, justifying them on the basis of Scripture and defending them in the face of Catholic criticism. In 1536, he published a small work entitled *Institutes of the Christian Religion*, a mere six chapters in length. For the next quarter of a century, Calvin worked away at this, adding extra chapters and rearranging the material. By the time of its final edition (1559), the work had eighty chapters, and was divided into four books.

The first book deals with God the creator, and God's sovereignty over that creation. Book two concerns the human need for redemption, and the manner in which this redemption is achieved by Christ the mediator. The third book deals with the manner in which this redemption is appropriated by human beings, while the final book deals with the church and its relation to society. Although it is often suggested that predestination stands at the center of Calvin's system, this is not the case; the only principle which seems to govern Calvin's organization of his theological system is a concern to be faithful to

Scripture on the one hand, and to achieve maximum clarity of presentation on the other.

After winding up his affairs in Noyon early in 1536, Calvin decided to settle down to a life of private study in the great city of Strasbourg. Unfortunately, the direct route from Noyon to Strasbourg was impassable, due to the outbreak of war between Francis I of France and the Emperor Charles V. Calvin had to make an extended detour, passing through the city of Geneva which had recently gained its independence from the neighboring territory of Savoy. Geneva was then in a state of confusion, having just evicted its local bishop and begun a controversial program of reform under the Frenchmen Guillaume Farel and Pierre Viret. On hearing that Calvin was in the city, they demanded that he stay, and help the cause of the Reformation. They needed a good teacher. Calvin reluctantly agreed.

His attempts to provide the Genevan church with a solid basis of doctrine and discipline met with intense resistance. After a series of quarrels, matters reached a head on Easter Day 1538: Calvin was expelled from the city, and sought refuge in Strasbourg. Having arrived in Strasbourg two years later than he had anticipated, Calvin began to make up for lost time. In quick succession he produced a series of major theological works. Perhaps most importantly, he revised and expanded his *Institutes* (1539) and produced the first French translation of this work (1541). As pastor to the French-speaking congregation in the city, Calvin was able to gain experience of the practical problems facing Reformed pastors. Through his friendship with Martin Bucer, the Strasbourg reformer, Calvin was able to develop his thinking on the relation between the city and the church.

In Calvin's absence from Geneva, the religious and political situation had deteriorated. In September 1541 the city appealed to him to come back, and restore order and confidence there. The Calvin who returned to Geneva was a wiser and more experienced young man, far better equipped for the tasks awaiting him than he had been three years earlier. His experience at Strasbourg lent new realism to his theorizing about the nature of the church, which is reflected in his subsequent writings in the field. By the time of his death in 1564, Calvin had made Geneva the center of an international movement, which came to bear his name. Calvinism is still one of the most potent and significant intellectual movements in human history.

Huldrych Zwingli (1484–1531)

The Swiss reformer Huldrych Zwingli was educated at the universities of Vienna and Basel, before taking up parish duties in eastern

Switzerland. It is clear that he took a keen interest in the agenda of Christian humanism, especially the writings of Erasmus, and became committed to belief in the need to reform the church of his day. In 1519, he took up a pastoral position in the city of Zurich, where he used the pulpit of the Great Minster, the chief church within the city, to propagate a program of reform. Initially, this program was primarily concerned with the reformation of the morals of the church. However, it soon extended to include criticism of the existing theology of the church, especially its sacramental theology. The term "Zwinglian" is used especially to refer to the belief, associated with Zwingli, that Christ is not present at the eucharist, which is best seen as a memorial of Christ's death.

Zwingli was of major importance in relation to the early propagation of the Reformation, especially in eastern Switzerland. However, he never achieved the same impact as Luther or Calvin, lacking the creativity of the former and the systematic approach of the latter. The reader will encounter considerable variation in the spelling of Zwingli's forename, with "Ulrich" and "Huldreich" often being used in preference to "Huldrych."

Key Theological Developments

The Reformation was a complex movement, with a very broad agenda. The debate centered in part upon the sources of Christian theology; in part upon the doctrines which resulted from the application of those sources. We shall consider these matters individually.

The Sources of Theology

The mainstream Reformation was concerned not with establishing a new Christian tradition, but with the renewal and correction of an existing tradition. Arguing that Christian theology was ultimately grounded in Scripture, reformers such as Luther and Calvin argued for the need to return to Scripture as the primary and critical source of Christian theology. The slogan "by Scripture alone" (*sola scriptura*) became characteristic of the reformers, expressing their basic belief that Scripture was the sole necessary and sufficient source of Christian theology. However, as we shall see later (pp. 188–9), this did not mean that they denied the importance of tradition.

This new emphasis upon Scripture had a number of direct consequences, of which the following are of especial importance:

1 Beliefs which could not be demonstrated to be grounded in Scripture were either to be rejected, or to be declared as binding on no one. For example, the reformers had little time for the doctrine of the immaculate conception of Mary (that is, the belief that Mary, as the mother of Jesus, was conceived without any taint from sin). They regarded this as lacking in Scriptural basis, and thus discarded it.

2 A new emphasis came to be placed upon the public status of Scripture within the church. The expository sermon, the biblical commentary, and works of biblical theology (such as Calvin's *Institutes*) came to be characteristic of the Reformation.

The Doctrine of Grace

The first period of the Reformation is dominated by the personal agenda of Martin Luther. Convinced that the church had lapsed into an unwitting Pelagianism, Luther proclaimed the doctrine of justification by faith to whomever would listen to him. The question "How can I find a gracious God?" and the slogan "by faith alone" (*sola fide*) resonated throughout much of western Europe, and attracted him a hearing amongst a substantial section of the church. The issues involved in this doctrine are complex, and will be discussed in detail at the appropriate point later in this volume (see pp. 382–8).

The doctrine of justification by faith is especially associated with the Lutheran Reformation. Calvin, while continuing to honor this doctrine, initiated a trend which became of increasing importance in later Reformed theology: the discussion of grace in relation to the doctrine of predestination, rather than justification. For Reformed theologians, the ultimate statement of the "grace of God" was not to be seen in the fact that God justified sinners; rather, it was to be seen in God's election of humanity without reference to their foreseen merits or achievements. The doctrine of "unconditional election" (see p. 398) came to be seen as a concise summary of the unmerited nature of grace.

The Doctrine of the Sacraments

By the 1520s, the view had become well established within reforming circles that the sacraments were outward signs of the invisible grace of God. This forging of a link between the sacraments and the doctrine of justification (a development especially associated with Luther and his colleague at Wittenberg, Philip Melanchthon) led to a new interest in the theology of the sacraments. It was not long before this area of theology became the subject of considerable controversy, the reformers disagreeing with their Catholic opponents over the number and nature of the sacraments, and Luther and Zwingli arguing furiously over whether Christ was really present at communion services (see pp. 440–2).

The Doctrine of the Church

If the first generation of reformers were preoccupied with the question of grace, the second generation turned to address the question of the church. Having broken away from the mainstream Catholic church over the doctrine of grace, the reformers came under increasing pressure to develop a coherent theory of the church which would justify this break, and give a basis for the new evangelical churches springing up in the cities of western Europe. Where Luther is especially linked with the doctrine of grace, it is Martin Bucer and John Calvin who made the decisive contributions to the development of Protestant understandings of the church. Those understandings have since become increasingly significant in global Christianity, and will be considered in greater detail later in the present work (see pp. 410–17).

The Post-Reformation Movement: Confessionalism and Scholasticism

It seems to be a general rule of history that periods of enormous creativity are followed by eras of stagnation. The Reformation is no exception. Perhaps through a desire to preserve the insights of the Reformation, the post-Reformation period witnessed the development of a strongly scholastic approach to theology. The phenomenon of "confessionalism" set in, characterized by a concern for doctrinal correctness. A new emphasis was placed on "confessions" – that is, denominational statements of beliefs, such as the Lutheran "Augsburg Confession" of 1530. New tensions developed within Protestantism, especially between the followers of Luther and Calvin, as each group sought to justify its distinctive position. "Faith" increasingly came to refer to "a set of beliefs" rather than "a personal trust in God." A dead orthodoxy threatened to replace the dynamic faith of the reformers. The insights of the reformers were codified and perpetuated, through the development of a series of systematic presentations of Christian theology.

In the period after Calvin's death a new concern for method – that is, the systematic organization and coherent deduction of ideas – gained momentum. Reformed theologians found themselves having to defend their ideas against both Lutheran and Roman Catholic opponents. Aristotelianism, regarded with a certain degree of suspicion by Calvin, was now seized upon as an ally. It became increasingly important to demonstrate the internal consistency and coherence of Calvinism. As a result, many Calvinist writers turned to Aristotle, in the hope that his writings on method would offer hints as to how their theology might be placed upon a firmer rational foundation.

Four characteristics of the new approach to theology which resulted may be noted.

1 Human reason was assigned a major role in the exploration and defense of Christian theology.
2 Christian theology was presented as a logically coherent and rationally defensible system, derived from syllogistic deductions based upon known axioms. In other words, theology began from first principles, and proceeded to deduce its doctrines on their basis.
3 Theology was understood to be grounded upon Aristotelian philosophy, and particularly Aristotelian insights into the nature of method; later Reformed writers are better described as philosophical, rather than biblical, theologians.
4 Theology became oriented toward metaphysical and speculative questions, especially relating to the nature of God, God's will for humanity and creation, and above all the doctrine of predestination.

The starting point of theology thus came to be general principles, not a specific historical event. The contrast with Calvin will be clear. For Calvin, theology centered on and derived from the event of Jesus Christ, as witnessed to by Scripture. But for later Calvinism, general principles came to take the central place hitherto assigned to Christ.

A point of major importance here concerns the political situation in Europe, especially Germany, in the later sixteenth century. In the 1550s, Lutheranism and Roman Catholicism were well established in different regions of Germany. A religious stalemate had developed, in which further expansion into Roman Catholic regions by Lutheranism was no longer possible. Lutheran writers therefore concentrated upon defending Lutheranism at the academic level, by demonstrating its internal consistency and faithfulness to Scripture. They believed that by showing Lutheranism to be intellectually respectable, they might make it attractive to Roman Catholics, disillusioned with their own system of beliefs. But this was not to be the case. Roman Catholic writers responded with increasingly sophisticated works of systematic theology, drawing on the writings of Thomas Aquinas. The Society of Jesus (founded in 1534) rapidly established itself as a leading intellectual force within the Roman Catholic church. Its leading writers, such as Roberto Bellarmine and Francisco de Suarez, made major contributions to the intellectual defense of Roman Catholicism.

The situation in Germany became even more complicated during the 1560s and 1570s, as Calvinism began to make major inroads into previously Lutheran territory. Three major Christian denominations were now firmly established in the same area: Lutheranism, Calvinism, and Roman Catholicism. All three were under considerable pressure to identify themselves. Lutherans were obliged to explain how they differed from Calvinists on the one hand, and Roman Catholics on the other. Doctrine proved the most reliable way of identifying and explaining these differences: "We believe this, but they believe that." The period 1559–1622, characterized by its new emphasis upon doctrine, is generally referred to as the "period of orthodoxy." A new form of scholasticism began to develop within both Protestant and Roman Catholic theological circles, as both sought to demonstrate the rationality and sophistication of their systems.

Lutheranism and Calvinism were, in many respects, very similar. Thus both claimed to be evangelical, and rejected more or less the same central aspects of medieval Catholicism. But they needed to be distinguished. On most points of doctrine, Lutherans and Calvinists were in broad agreement. Yet there was one matter upon which they were radically divided: the doctrine of predestination. The emphasis placed upon the doctrine of predestination by Calvinists in the period 1559–1662 partly reflects the fact that this doctrine most sharply distinguished them from their Lutheran colleagues.

The importance of this point can easily be appreciated by comparing the German situation with that of England. The sixteenth-century English Reformation under Henry VIII (1509–47) bore little relation to its German equivalent. In Germany, there was a protracted struggle between Lutheran and Roman Catholic, as each attempted to gain influence in a disputed region. In England, Henry VIII simply declared that there would only be one national church within his realm. By royal command, there would only be one Christian body within England. The Reformed English church was under no pressure to define itself in relation to any other Christian body in the region. The manner in which the English Reformation initially proceeded demanded no doctrinal self-definition, in that the church in England was defined socially in precisely the same way before the Reformation as after, whatever political alterations may have been introduced. This is not to say that no theological debates took place in England at the time of the Reformation; it is to note that they were not seen as of decisive importance. They were not regarded as identity-giving.

The Lutheran church in Germany was obliged to define and defend its existence and boundaries by doctrine because it had broken away from the medieval Catholic church. That church continued to exist around Lutheran regions, forcing Lutheranism to carry on justifying its existence. The Henrician church in England, however, regarded itself as continuous with the medieval church. The English church was sufficiently well defined as a social unit to require no further definition at the doctrinal level.

The situation in England remained much the same under Elizabeth I. The "Elizabethan Settlement" (1559) laid down that there would only be one Christian church in England: the Church of England, which retained the monopoly of the pre-Reformation church, while replacing it with a church which recognized royal, rather than papal, authority. Roman Catholicism, Lutheranism, and Calvinism – the three Christian churches fighting it out for dominance of the continent of Europe – would not be tolerated within England. There was thus no particular reason for the Church of England to bother much about doctrinal questions. Elizabeth ensured that it had no rivals within England. One of the purposes of doctrine is to divide – and there was nothing for the Church of England to divide itself from. England was insulated from the factors which made doctrine so significant a matter on the mainland of Europe in the Reformation and immediate post-Reformation periods.

The following two developments are of especial importance during this period.

1 *A new concern for method* Reformers such as Luther and Calvin had relatively little interest in questions of method. For them, theology was primarily concerned with the exposition of Scripture. Indeed, Calvin's *Institutes* may be regarded as a work of "biblical theology," bringing together the basic ideas of Scripture into an orderly presentation. However, in the writings of Theodore Beza, Calvin's successor as director of the Genevan Academy (a training institute for Calvinist pastors throughout Europe), there is a new concern for questions of method, as noted above. The logical arrangement of material, and its grounding in first principles, comes to assume paramount importance. The impact of this development is perhaps most obvious in the way in which Beza handled the doctrine of predestination, to be noted later.

2 *The development of works of systematic theology* The rise of scholasticism within Lutheran, Calvinist, and Roman Catholic theological circles led to the appearance of vast works of systematic theology, comparable in many ways to Thomas Aquinas' *Summa Theologia*. These works aimed to present sophisticated and comprehensive accounts of Christian theology, demonstrating the strengths of their positions and the weaknesses of their opponents'.

The following writers should be noted as being of especial importance durng this period.

1 *Theodore Beza (1519–1605)*, a noted Calvinist writer, served as professor of theology at the Genevan Academy from 1559 to 1599. The three volumes of his *Tractationes theologicae* ("Theological Treatises," 1570–82) present a rationally coherent account of the main elements of Reformed theology, using Aristotelian logic. The result is a tightly argued and rationally defensible account of Calvin's theology, in which some of the unresolved tensions of that theology (chiefly relating to the doctrines of predestination and atonement) are clarified. Some writers have suggested that Beza's concern for logical clarity leads him to misrepresent Calvin at a number of critical points; others have argued that Beza merely streamlined Calvin's theology, tidying up some loose ends.

2 *Johann Gerhard (1582–1637)*, a Lutheran writer, was appointed professor of theology at Jena in 1616, where he remained for the rest of his teaching career. Gerhard recognized the need for a systematic presentation of Lutheran theology in the face of intense Calvinist opposition. The basic form of Lutheran works of systematic theology had been laid down in 1521, when Philip Melancthon published the first edition of his *Loci communes* ("Commonplaces"), in which subjects were treated topically, rather than systematically. Gerhard continued this tradition, but felt able to draw increasingly upon Aristotelian works of logic. His *Loci communes theologici* ("Theological Commonplaces," 1610–22) remained a classic of Lutheran theology for many years.

3 *Roberto Bellarmine (1542–1621)*, a Roman Catholic writer, entered the Society of Jesus in 1560, and subsequently became professor of controversial theology at Rome in 1576. He remained in this position until 1599, when he became a cardinal. His most significant work is generally regarded to be the *Disputationes de controversiis Christianae fidei* ("Disputations concerning the controversies of the Christian faith," 1586–93), in which he argued forcibly for the rationality of Catholic theology against its Protestant (both Lutheran and Calvinist) critics.

One influential element of the Reformed wing of the church demands further attention. This is the moment known as Puritanism, initially based in late sixteenth- and early seventeenth-century England, which drew extensively upon the theological heritage of Calvin and Beza, whilst demonstrating a considerable degree of pastoral concern and commitment. The term "Puritan" rapidly became abusive; the modern popular stereotype of the movement is still that of a bleak and dreary moralism. However, this stereotype is gradually being abandoned, as scholarship uncovers the religious dynamism and popular influence of the movement, especially in seventeenth-century North America. Leading English representatives of the movement include Richard Baxter (1615–91) and John Owen (1616–83). Their writings show a sharp interest in the relation between faith and experience, anticipating some attitudes later associated with Pietism, and especially in the pastoral aspects of Christian living. Baxter's *Reformed Pastor* (1656) remains a classic of its kind.

Pietism

As orthodoxy became increasingly influential within mainstream Protestantism, so its defects became clear. At its best, orthodoxy was concerned with the rational defense of Christian truth claims, and a concern for doctrinal correctness. Yet, too often, this came across as an academic preoccupation with logical niceties, rather than a concern for relating theology to the issues of everyday life. The term "Pietism" derives from the Latin word *pietas* (best translated as "piety" or "godliness"), and was initially a derogatory term used by the movement's opponents to describe its emphasis upon the importance of Christian doctrine for the everyday Christian life.

The Pietist movement is usually regarded as having been inaugurated with the publication of Philip Jakob Spener's *Pia desideria* ("Pious Wishes," 1675). In this work, Spener lamented the state of the German Lutheran church in the aftermath of the Thirty Years' War (1616–48), and set out proposals for the revitalization of the church of his day. Chief among these was a new emphasis upon personal Bible study. These proposals were treated with derision by academic theologians; nevertheless, they were to prove influential in German church circles, reflecting a growing disillusionment and impatience with the sterility of orthodoxy in the face of the shocking social conditions endured during the war. For Pietism, a reformation of doctrine must always be accompanied by a reformation of life.

Pietism developed in a number of different directions, especially in England and Germany. Among the representatives of the movement, two in particular should be noted.

1 *Nikolaus Ludwig Graf von Zinzendorf (1700–60)* founded the Pietist community generally known as the "Herrnhuter," named after the German village of Herrnhut. Alienated from what he regarded as the arid rationalism and barren orthodoxy of his time, he stressed the importance of a "religion of the heart," based on an intimate and personal relationship between Christ and the believer. A new emphasis was placed upon the role of "feeling" (as opposed to reason or doctrinal orthodoxy) within the Christian life, which may be regarded as laying the foundations of Romanticism in later German religious thought. Zinzendorf's emphasis upon a personally appropriated faith finds expression in the slogan "a living faith," which he opposed to the dead credal assent of Protestant orthodoxy. These ideas would be developed in one direction by F. D. E. Schleiermacher, and in another by John Wesley, who may be regarded as introducing Pietism to England.

2 *John Wesley (1703–91)* founded the Methodist movement within the Church of England, which subsequently gave birth to Methodism as a denomination in its own right. Convinced that he "lacked the faith whereby alone we are saved," Wesley paid a visit to Herrnhut in 1738, and was deeply impressed by what he found. The Pietist emphasis upon the need for a "living faith" and the role of experience in the Christian life led to his conversion experience at a meeting in Aldersgate Street in May 1738, in which he felt his heart to be "strangely warmed." Wesley's emphasis upon the experiential side of Christian faith, which contrasted sharply with the dullness of contemporary English Deism, led to a major religious revival in England.

Despite their differences, the various branches of Pietism succeeded in making Christian faith relevant to the experiential world of ordinary believers. The movement may be regarded as a reaction against a one-sided emphasis upon doctrinal orthodoxy, in favor of a faith which relates to the deepest aspects of human nature.

Key Names, Words, and Phrases

*Anabaptism
*Calvinist
Catholic Reformation
confessionalism
Deism
evangelical
Lutheran
Methodism
orthodoxy
Pietism
Protestant
Reformed

Those terms marked with an asterisk are discussed in more detail elsewhere in this work.

Questions for Chapter 3

1 What does the term "Reformation" mean?

2 Which reformer is especially associated with the doctrine of justification by faith alone?

3 How important was humanism to the origins and development of the Reformation?

4 Why did the reformers come to place such emphasis upon revising existing doctrines of the church?

5 What factors led to the development of (a) confessionalism and (b) Pietism?

4

The Modern Period, *c.*1700–the Present

From 1700 onward, Christian theology moved away from a western European context to become a global phenomenon. A number of stages may be discerned in this development. First, the colonization of North America by western Europeans, especially from Scandinavia, Germany, and England, led to the various schools of Protestant theology – Lutheran, Reformed, and Anabaptist – becoming firmly settled in a North American context. Jonathan Edwards (1703–58), closely linked with the religious revival generally known as the Great Awakening (*c.*1726–45), is unquestionably the most significant theologian to have operated in such a context. Later waves of immigration, especially from Ireland and Italy, led to Roman Catholic theology becoming of increasing significance.

The establishment of seminaries by various denominations (such as Princeton Theological Seminary by the Presbyterians) consolidated the importance of the United States of America as a leading center of Christian theological teaching and research. However, it was not until the middle of the twentieth century that America came to assume global significance in theological discussions; until that point, German and British theology tended to dominate, partly on account of the continuing immigration of European theologians into the United States. Such theologians, who had trained in European contexts, tended to maintain a European emphasis in their teaching and orientation.

Elsewhere, expansion continued. The enormous impact of Christian missions in Australasia, India, the Far East, and sub-Saharan Africa led to Christian theological seminaries, high schools, and universities becoming established in these regions, and gradually divesting themselves of their western European roots. The development of "local theologies" has become an issue of increasing importance in such regions, particularly as the perceived "Eurocentrism" of much Christian theologizing has been subjected to considerable critical comment on the part of native writers.

This is especially the case in Latin America, where there appears to be a growing reaction against the Roman Catholicism exported to the region with the *conquistadores*. The rise of liberation theology (see pp. 105–7), with its characteristic emphasis upon the importance of praxis, the prioritization of the situation of the poor, and the orientation of theology toward political liberation, has proved incapable of staunching a severe loss of individuals from the Roman Catholic church. The chief beneficiaries of this trend appear to be evangelicals and charismatics (see p. 110) in the region.

One of the most prominent features of western theology during the modern period has been the intellectual hegemony of German theology. The German-speaking lands of Europe, above all Germany and northern Switzerland, have long been the source of a rich and fertile theological tradition. Two leading figures of the Reformation, Martin Luther and Huldrych Zwingli, are witnesses to the importance of this tradition to the development of modern western theology. Since the Enlightenment, the prominence of the German-language tradition has become even more firmly established; a list of the leading theologians of the modern western tradition – including Karl Barth, Rudolf Bultmann, Jürgen Moltmann, Wolfhart Pannenberg, and Paul Tillich – has an unquestionably Germanic ring to it.

In recent years, however, this situation has changed. A new generation of German-language theologians of truly global significance has not emerged to succeed writers such as Bultmann, Moltmann, and Pannenberg. Instead, there has been a steady increase in the significance of English-language theology, especially that originating from the United States of America. With the increasing role played by English as the *lingua franca* of the world (the parallel with Latin in the Middle Ages being of significance), it seems likely that this development will be consolidated, at least in the opening years of the new millenium.

The idea of "modernity," like just about every other term used in this work, is difficult to define. What is characteristic of the "modern" period? When did it begin? And has it now ended? In one sense, "modern" could be understood to mean "most recent," in which case it makes no sense to speak of the "end of modernity." However, for many historians, "modernity" refers to a quite definite outlook, typical of much of western thought since the early eighteenth century, which is characterized by a confidence in humanity's ability to think for itself. Perhaps the classic expression of this attitude is to be found in the Enlightenment, with its emphasis upon the competence of unaided human reason to make sense of the world – including those aspects of that world traditionally reserved for theologians.

The modern period is of enormous importance to the theology of the nineteenth and twentieth centuries. It establishes the context within which many recent developments and debates are set, and gave rise to many movements which are a continuing presence within today's church and academy. For this reason, the present chapter devotes substantially more space to the analysis of movements of importance within the period under consideration than has been allocated in earlier chapters. We begin by considering the movement which has dominated the intellectual agenda of the period – the Enlightenment.

The Enlightenment

The English term "Enlightenment" passed into general circulation only in the closing decades of the nineteenth century. The German term *die Aufklärung* (which literally means "the clearing up") and the French term *les lumières* ("the lights") date from the eighteenth century, but do not convey much information about the nature of the movement in question. "Enlightenment" is a loose term, defying precise definition, embracing a cluster of ideas and attitudes characteristic of the period 1720–80, such as the free and constructive use of reason in an attempt to demolish old myths which were seen to have bound individuals and societies to the oppression of the past. If there is any common element underlying the movement, it perhaps lies more in *how* those who were sympathetic to its outlook thought than in *what* they thought.

The term "Age of Reason," often used as a synonym for the Enlightenment, is misleading. It implies that reason had been hitherto ignored or marginalized. Yet, as we saw earlier, the Middle Ages was just as much an "Age of Reason" as the Enlightenment; the crucial difference lay in the manner in which reason was used, and the limits which were understood to be imposed upon it. Nor was the eighteenth century consistently rational in every aspect. In fact, the Enlightenment included a remarkable variety of anti-rational movements, such as Mesmerism and Masonic rituals. Nevertheless, an emphasis upon the ability of human reason to penetrate the mysteries of the world is rightly regarded as a defining characteristic of the Enlightenment.

The term "rationalism" should also be used with caution when referring to the Enlightenment. In the first place, it should be noted that the term is often used in an uncritical and inaccurate way, designating the general atmosphere of optimism, grounded in a belief in scientific and social progress, which pervades much of the writing of the period. This use of the term is confusing, and should be avoided. Rationalism, in its proper sense, is perhaps best defined as the doctrine that the external world can be known by reason, and reason alone. This doctrine, which is characteristic of earlier writers such as Descartes, Leibniz, Spinoza, and Wolff, was subjected to intense criticism during the later eighteenth century, as the influence of John Locke's empiricist epistemology became widespread. Kant, often portrayed as an exponent of the sufficiency of pure reason, was in reality acutely aware of its limitations. The theory of knowledge developed in the *Critique of Pure Reason* (1781) may be regarded as an attempt to synthesize the insights of pure rationalism (which relies upon reason alone) and pure empiricism (which appeals to experience alone). This work may be regarded as bringing the early period of rationalism to a close. Despite according a particularly significant role to reason in his thought (as seen in *Religion within the Limits of Reason Alone*), Kant showed a keen appreciation of the implications of the empiricist emphasis upon sense experience. Nevertheless, rationalist attitudes persisted well into the nineteenth century, and constitute an important element of the general Enlightenment critique of Christianity.

The Enlightenment ushered in a period of considerable uncertainty for Christianity in western Europe and north America. The trauma of the Reformation and the resulting Wars of Religion had barely subsided on the continent of Europe before a new and more radical challenge to Christianity arose. If the sixteenth-century Reformation challenged the church to rethink its external forms and the manner in which it expressed its beliefs, the Enlightenment saw the intellectual credentials of Christianity itself (rather than any one of its specific forms) facing a major threat on a number of fronts. The origins of this challenge may be traced back to the seventeenth century, with the rise of Cartesianism on the continent of Europe, and the increasing influence of Deism in England. The growing emphasis upon the need to uncover the rational roots of religion had considerable negative implications for Christianity, as subsequent events were to prove.

The Enlightenment and Protestantism

It was Protestant theology, rather than Roman Catholic or Eastern Orthodox, which was especially open to influence from the new currents of thought which arose from the Enlightenment and its aftermath. Four main factors have been noted which may explain this observation, at least in part.

1 *The relative weakness of Protestant ecclesiastical institutions* The absence of an authoritarian centralized structure, such as the papacy, meant that national or regional Protestant churches were able to respond to local circumstances, intellectual and political, with a far greater freedom than Roman Catholic churches. Similarly, individual Protestant thinkers experienced a degree of academic freedom denied until quite recently to their Roman Catholic colleagues. The spirit of creative freedom which characterized Protestantism from its outset thus expressed itself in theological creativity and originality quite impossible for others.

2 *The nature of Protestantism itself* While the "essence of Protestantism" remains disputed, there is agreement that a spirit of protest is part of the birthright of the movement. The Protestant predisposition to challenge religious authority, and the commitment to the principle *ecclesia reformata, ecclesia semper reformanda* ("the reformed church must always be the church which is reforming itself"), encouraged a spirit of critical inquiry concerning Christian dogma. This attitude resonated with the ideals of the Enlightenment, leading to an alignment of many Protestant writers with the movement, and a willingness to absorb its methods and outlooks.

3 *The relation of Protestantism and the universities* From its inception, Protestantism recognized the importance of higher education in the training of its ministers. The foundation of the Genevan Academy and Harvard College are obvious illustrations of this point. During the late sixteenth and early seventeenth centuries, the Lutheran and Reformed churches in Germany established university faculties of theology as a means of ensuring a constant supply of well-educated clergy. During the eighteenth century, political protest was stifled in Germany; the only means by which radicalism could express itself was intellectual.

The German universities thus became centers of revolt against the Old Regime. As a result, German university theologians (who were almost all Protestant) aligned themselves with the Enlightenment, where the more conservative church leadership tended to side with the Old Regime. Radicalism was thus able to express itself theologically, at the level of ideas. Although apparently unable to achieve any significant social, political, or ecclesiastical change, radicalism was able to mount a significant challenge to the ideas which undergirded the churches. Protestant theology was thus significantly affected by the methods of the Enlightenment, whereas Roman Catholic theology was not.

4 *The varying local impact of the Enlightenment* It must be stressed that the Enlightenment was not a chronologically uniform movement.

Although well established in western central Europe by the eighteenth century, the Enlightenment cannot really be said to have taken hold in Russia or the countries of southern Europe (such as Spain, Italy, or Greece) until the late nineteenth or early twentieth century. These countries were the strongholds of Roman Catholicism or Eastern Orthodoxy. In consequence, theologians of their churches did not feel under pressure to respond to the intellectual forces which were of such major significance in regions historically associated with Protestantism.

The Enlightenment Critique of Christian Theology: A General Overview

The Enlightenment criticism of traditional Christianity was based upon the principle of the omnicompetence of human reason. A number of stages in the development of this belief may be discerned. First, it was argued that the beliefs of Christianity were rational, and thus capable of standing up to critical examination. This type of approach may be found in John Locke's *Reasonableness of Christianity* (1695), and within the early Wolffian school in Germany. Christianity was a reasonable supplement to natural religion. The notion of divine revelation was thus maintained.

Second, it was argued that the basic ideas of Christianity, being rational, could be derived from reason itself. There was no need to invoke the idea of divine revelation. According to this idea, as it was developed by John Toland in *Christianity not Mysterious* (1696) and by William Tindal in *Christianity as Old as Creation* (1730), Christianity was essentially the re-publication of the religion of nature. It did not transcend natural religion, but was merely an example of it. All so-called "revealed religion" was actually nothing other than the recon-firmation of what can be known through rational reflection on nature. "Revelation" was simply a rational reaffirmation of moral truths already available to enlightened reason.

Third, the ability of reason to judge revelation was affirmed. As critical reason was omnicompetent, it was argued that it was supremely qualified to judge Christian beliefs and practices, with a view to eliminating any irrational or superstitious elements. This view, as-sociated with Hermann Samuel Reimarus in Germany and the *philosophes* in France, placed reason firmly above revelation, and may be seen as symbolized in the enthronement of the Goddess of Reason in Notre Dame de Paris in 1793.

The Enlightenment was primarily a European and American phenomenon, and thus took place in cultures in which the most numerically significant form of religion was Christianity. This historical observation is of importance: The Enlightenment critique of religion in general was often particularized as a criticism of Christianity in general. It was Christian doctrines which were subjected to a critical assessment of unprecedented vigor. It was Christian sacred writings – rather than those of Islam or Hinduism – which were subjected to an unprecedented critical scrutiny, both literary and historical, with the Bible being treated "as if it were any other book" (Benjamin Jowett). It was the life of Jesus of Nazareth which was subjected to critical reconstruction, rather than that of Mohammed or the Buddha.

The Enlightenment attitude to religion was subject to a considerable degree of regional variation, reflecting a number of local factors peculiar to different situations. One of the most important such factors is Pietism, perhaps best known in its English and American form of Methodism. As noted earlier, this movement placed considerable emphasis upon the experiential aspects of religion – see, for example, John Wesley's notion of "experimental religion" (note that Wesley uses the word "experimental" to mean "experiential"). This concern for religious experience served to make Christianity relevant and accessible to the experiential situation of the masses, contrasting sharply with the intellectualism of, for example, Lutheran orthodoxy, which was perceived to be an irrelevance. Pietism forged a strong link between Christian faith and experience, thus making Christianity a matter of the heart, as well as of the mind.

As noted earlier, Pietism was well established in Germany by the end of the seventeenth century, whereas the movement developed in England only during the eighteenth century, and in France not at all. The Enlightenment thus preceded the rise of Pietism in England, with the result that the great evangelical revivals of the eighteenth century significantly blunted the influence of rationalism upon religion. In Germany, however, the Enlightenment followed after the rise of Pietism, and thus developed in a situation which had been significantly shaped by religious faith, even if it would pose a serious challenge to the received forms and ideas of that faith. (Interestingly, English Deism began to become influential in Germany at roughly the same time as German Pietism began to exert influence in England.) The most significant intellectual forces in the German Enlightenment were thus directed toward the reshaping (rather than the rejection or demolition) of the Christian faith.

In France, however, Christianity was widely perceived as both oppressive and irrelevant, with the result that the writers of the French Enlightenment – often referred to simply as *les philosophes* – were able to advocate the total rejection of Christianity as an archaic and discredited belief system. In his *Treaty on Tolerance*, Denis Diderot argued that English Deism had compromised itself, permitting religion to survive where it ought to have been eradicated totally.

The Enlightenment Critique of Christian Theology: Specific Issues

Having outlined the general principles of the Enlightenment challenge to traditional Christian thought, it is now appropriate to explore how these impacted on specific matters of doctrine. The rational religion of the Enlightenment found itself in conflict with six major areas of traditional Christian theology.

1 The possibility of miracles

Much traditional Christian apologetics concerning the identity and significance of Jesus Christ was based upon the "miraculous evidences" of the New Testament, culminating in the resurrection. The new emphasis upon the mechanical regularity and orderliness of the universe, perhaps the most significant intellectual legacy of Newtonianism, raised doubts about the New Testament accounts of miraculous happenings. Hume's *Essay on Miracles* (1748) was widely regarded as demonstrating the evidential impossibility of miracles. Hume emphasized that there were no contemporary analogues of New Testament miracles, such as the resurrection, thus forcing the New Testament reader to rely totally upon human testimony to such miracles. For Hume, it was axiomatic that no human testimony was adequate to establish the occurrence of a miracle, in the absence of a present-day analogue. Reimarus and G. E. Lessing denied that human testimony to a past event (such as the resurrection) was sufficient to make it credible if it appeared to be contradicted by present-day direct experience, no matter how well documented the original event may have been.

Similarly, Diderot declared that if the entire population of Paris were to assure him that a dead man had just been raised from the dead, he would not believe a word of it. This growing skepticism concerning the "miraculous evidences" of the New Testament forced traditional Christianity to defend the doctrine of the divinity of Christ on grounds other than miracles – which, at the time, it proved singularly incapable of doing. Of course, it must be noted that other religions claiming miraculous evidences were subjected to equally great skeptical criticism by the Enlightenment: Christianity happened to be singled out for particular comment on account of its religious domination of the cultural milieu in which the Enlightenment developed.

2 The notion of revelation

The concept of revelation was of central importance to traditional Christian theology. While many Christian theologians (such as Thomas Aquinas and John Calvin) recognized the possibility of a natural knowledge of God, they insisted that this required supplementation by supernatural divine revelation, such as that witnessed to in Scripture. The Enlightenment witnessed the development of an increasingly critical attitude to the very idea of supernatural revelation. In part, this new critical attitude was also due to the Enlightenment depreciation of history.

For Lessing, there was an "ugly great ditch" between history and reason (see pp. 313–16). Revelation took place in history – but of what value were the contingent truths of history in comparison with the necessary truths of reason? The *philosophes* in particular asserted that history could at best confirm the truths of reason, but was incapable of establishing those truths in the first place. Truths about God were timeless, open to investigation by human reason but not capable of being disclosed in "events" such as the history of Jesus of Nazareth.

3 The doctrine of original sin

The idea that human nature is in some sense flawed or corrupted, expressed in the orthodox doctrine of original sin, was vigorously opposed by the Enlightenment. Voltaire and Jean-Jacques Rousseau criticized the doctrine as encouraging pessimism with regard to human abilities, thus impeding human social and political development and encouraging *laissez-faire* attitudes. German Enlightenment thinkers tended to criticize the doctrine on account of its historical origins in the thought of Augustine of Hippo, dating from the fourth and fifth centuries, which they regarded as debarring it from permanent validity and relevance.

The rejection of original sin was of considerable importance, as the Christian doctrine of redemption rested upon the assumption that humanity required to be liberated from bondage to original sin. For the Enlightenment, it was the idea of original sin itself which was oppressive, and from which humanity required liberation. This intellectual liberation was provided by the Enlightenment critique of the doctrine.

4 The problem of evil

The Enlightenment witnessed a fundamental change in attitude toward the existence of evil in the world. For the medieval period, the existence of evil was not regarded as posing a threat to the coherence of Christianity. The contradiction implicit in the existence both of a benevolent divine omnipotence and of evil was not regarded as an obstacle to belief, but as simply as an academic theological problem. The Enlightenment saw this situation change radically: The existence of evil metamorphosed into a challenge to the credibility and coherence of Christian faith itself. Voltaire's novel *Candide* was one of many works to highlight the difficulties caused for the Christian worldview by the existence of natural evil (such as the famous Lisbon earthquake). The term "theodicy," coined by Leibniz, derives from this period, reflecting a growing recognition that the existence of evil was assuming a new significance within the Enlightenment critique of religion.

5   The status and interpretation of Scripture

Within orthodox Christianity, whether Protestant or Roman Catholic, the Bible was still widely regarded as a divinely inspired source of doctrine and morals, to be differentiated from other types of literature. The Enlightenment saw this assumption called into question, with the rise of the critical approach to Scripture. Developing ideas already current within Deism, the theologians of the German Enlightenment developed the thesis that the Bible was the work of many hands, at times demonstrating internal contradiction, and that it was open to precisely the same method of textual analysis and interpretation as any other piece of literature. These ideas may be seen in developed forms in works by J. A. Ernesti (1761) and J. J. Semler (1771). The effect of these developments was to weaken still further the concept of "supernatural revelation," and call into question the permanent significance of these foundational documents of the Christian faith.

6   The identity and significance of Jesus Christ

A final area in which the Enlightenment made a significant challenge to orthodox Christian belief concerns the person of Jesus of Nazareth. Two particularly important developments may be noted: the origins of the "quest of the historical Jesus" (see pp. 316–27), and the rise of the "moral theory of the atonement" (pp. 355–60).

Both Deism and the German Enlightenment developed the thesis that there was a serious discrepancy between the real Jesus of history and the New Testament interpretation of his significance. Underlying the New Testament portrait of the supernatural redeemer of humanity lurked a simple human figure, a glorified teacher of common sense. While a supernatural redeemer was unacceptable to Enlightenment rationalism, the idea of an enlightened moral teacher was not.

This idea, developed with particular rigor by Reimarus, suggested that it was possible to go behind the New Testament accounts of Jesus and uncover a simpler, more human Jesus, who would be acceptable to the new spirit of the age. And so the quest for the real and more credible "Jesus of history" began. Although this pursuit would ultimately end in failure, the later Enlightenment regarded the quest as holding the key to the credibility of Jesus within the context of a rational natural religion. Jesus' moral authority resided in the quality of his teaching and religious personality, rather than in the unacceptable orthodox suggestion that he was God incarnate.

The second area in which the ideas of orthodoxy concerning Jesus were challenged concerned the significance of his death. For orthodoxy, Jesus' death on the cross was interpreted from the standpoint of the resurrection (which the Enlightenment was not prepared to accept as an historical event) as a way in which God was able to forgive the sins of humanity. During the Enlightenment this "theory of the atonement" was subjected to increasing criticism, as involving arbitrary and unacceptable hypotheses such as that of original sin.

Jesus' death on the cross was reinterpreted in terms of a supreme moral example of self-giving and dedication, intended to inspire similar dedication and self-giving on the part of his followers. Where orthodox Christianity tended to treat Jesus' death (and resurrection) as possessing greater inherent importance than his religious teaching, the Enlightenment marginalized his death and denied his resurrection, in order to emphasize the quality of his moral teaching.

Theological Movements since the Enlightenment

It will be clear from the above that the Enlightenment had a major impact upon Christian theology, raising a series of critical questions concerning its sources, methods, and doctrines. However, despite its continuing influence over the modern period, the Enlightenment is generally regarded as having reached the zenith of its impact around the time of the French Revolution. A series of developments since then have moved Christian theology away from the agenda of the movement, even if its influence can still be discerned at points. In what follows, we shall consider major developments within Christian theology since the time of the Enlightenment.

In the course of discussing these movements, the contributions of several major theologians will be considered. In particular, the following should be noted: F. D. E. Schleiermacher (Romanticism); Karl Barth (neo-orthodoxy); Paul Tillich (liberal Protestantism). However, the modern period includes a galaxy of stars, and we do not propose to single out any individual writers for special discussion.

Romanticism

In the closing decade of the eighteenth century, increasing misgivings came to be expressed concerning the arid quality of rationalism. Reason, once seen as a liberator, came increasingly to be regarded as spiritually enslaving. These anxieties were not expressed so much within university faculties of philosophy, as within literary and artistic circles, particularly in the Prussian capital, Berlin, where the brothers Friedrich and August William Schlegel became particularly influential.

"Romanticism" is notoriously difficult to define. The movement is perhaps best seen as a reaction against certain of the central themes of the Enlightenment, most notably the claim that reality can be known to the human reason. This reduction of reality to a series of rationalized simplicities seemed, to the Romantics, to be a culpable and crude misrepresentation. Where the Enlightenment appealed to the human reason, Romanticism made an appeal to the human imagination, which was capable of recognizing the profound sense of mystery which arises from realizing that the human mind cannot comprehend even the finite world, let alone the infinity beyond this. This ethos is expressed well by the English poet William Wordsworth, who spoke of the human imagination in terms of transcending the limitations of human reason, and reaching beyond its bounds to sample the infinite through the finite. Imagination, he wrote,

> Is but another name for absolute power
> And clearest insight, amplitude of mind,
> And Reason in her most exalted mood.

Romanticism thus found itself equally unhappy with both traditional Christian doctrines and the rationalist moral platitudes of the Enlightenment: both failed to do justice to the complexity of the world, in an attempt to reduce the "mystery of the universe" – to use a phrase found in the writings of August William Schlegel – to neat formulae.

A marked limitation of the competence of reason may be discerned in such sentiments. Reason threatens to limit the human mind to what may be deduced; the imagination is able to liberate the human spirit from this self-imposed bondage, and allow it to discover new depths of reality – a vague and tantalizing "something," which can be discerned in the world of everyday actualities. The infinite is somehow present in the finite, and may be known through feeling and the imagination. As John Keats put it, "I am certain of nothing except the holiness of the heart's affections, and the truth of the imagination."

The reaction against the aridity of reason was thus complemented by an emphasis upon the epistemological significance of human feelings and emotions. Under the influence of Novalis (Friedrich von Hardenberg), German Romanticism came to develop two axioms concerning *das Gefühl* (This German term is perhaps best translated as "feeling" or "sentiment," though neither conveys the full range of meanings associated with the original. For this reason, it is often left untranslated; readers disliking the use of foreign-language terms can, however, replace it with "feeling.") First, "feeling" has to do with the individual subjective thinker, who becomes aware of his or her subjectivity and inward individuality. Rationalism may have made its appeal to individual reason; Romanticism retained the emphasis upon the individual, but supplanted a concern with reason by a new interest in the imagination and personal feeling. The Enlightenment looked inward to human reason; Romanticism looked inward to human feelings, seeing in these "the way to all mysteries" (Novalis).

Second, "feeling" is oriented toward the infinite and eternal, and provides the key to these higher realms. It is for this reason, Novalis declares, that the Enlightenment proscribed the imagination and feeling as "heretical," in that they offered access to the "magical idealism" of the infinite; by its wooden appeal to reason alone, the Enlightenment attempted to suppress knowledge of these higher worlds through an appeal to the aridities of philosophy. Human subjectivity and inwardness were now seen as a mirror of the infinite. A new emphasis came to be placed upon music as a "revelation of a higher order than any morality or philosophy" (Bettina von Arnim).

The development of Romanticism had considerable implications for Christianity in Europe. Those aspects of Christianity (especially Roman Catholicism) which rationalism found distasteful came to captivate the imaginations of the Romantics. Rationalism was seen to be experientially and emotionally deficient, incapable of meeting real human needs that were traditionally addressed and satisfied by Christian faith. As F. R. de Chateaubriant remarked of the situation in France in the first decade of the nineteenth century, "there was a need for faith, a desire for religious consolation, which came from the very lack of that consolation for so long." Similar sentiments can be instanced from the German context in the closing years of the eighteenth century.

That rationalism had failed to undermine religion is clear from developments in England, Germany, and North America. The new strength evident in German Pietism and English evangelicalism in the eighteenth century is evidence of the failure of rationalism to provide a cogent alternative to the prevailing human sense of personal need and meaning. Philosophy came to be seen as sterile, academic in the worst sense of the word, in that it was detached from both the outer realities of life and the inner life of the human consciousness.

It is against this background of growing disillusionment with rationalism, and a new appreciation of human "feeling," that the contribution of Friedrich Daniel Ernst Schleiermacher (1768–1834) is to be seen. Schleiermacher capitalized on this interest in feeling. He argued that religion in general, and Christianity in particular, was a matter of feeling or "self-consciousness." His major work of systematic theology, *The Christian Faith* (1821; revised 1834), is an attempt to show how Christian theology is related to a feeling of "absolute dependence." The structure of *The Christian Faith* is complex, centering on the dialectic between sin and grace. The work is organized in three parts. The first deals with the consciousness of God, concentrating upon such matters as creation. The second part handles the consciousness of sin, and its implications, such as an awareness of the possibility of redemption. The final part considers the consciousness of grace, and deals with such matters as the person and work of Christ. In this way, Schleiermacher is able to argue that "everything is related to the redemption accomplished by Jesus of Nazareth."

Schleiermacher's contribution to the development of Christian theology is considerable, and will be examined in depth at the appropriate points in this volume. However, our attention now turns to a movement which, although not strictly theological – indeed, it could be termed *a*theological – has had a major impact upon modern western theology. The movement in question is Marxism.

Marxism

Marxism, probably one of the most significant worldviews to emerge during the modern period, has had a major impact upon Christian theology during the last century, and is likely to continue to be an important dialogue partner in the years to come. Marxism may be regarded as the body of ideas associated with the German writer Karl Marx (1818–83). Until recently, however, the term also referred to a state ideology, characteristic of a number of states in eastern Europe and elsewhere, which regarded Christianity and other religions as reactionary, and adopted repressive measures to eliminate them.

The notion of materialism is fundamental to Marxism. This is not some metaphysical or philosophical doctrine which affirms that the world consists only of matter. Rather, it is an assertion that a correct understanding of human beings must begin with material production.

The way in which human beings respond to their material needs determines everything else. Ideas, including religious ideas, are responses to material reality. They are the superstructure which is erected upon a socio-economic substructure. In other words, ideas and belief systems are a response to a quite definite set of social and economic conditions. If these are radically altered (for example, by a revolution), the belief systems which they generated and sustained will pass away with them.

This first idea flows naturally into the second: the alienation of humanity. A number of factors bring about alienation within the material process, of which the two most significant are the division of labor and the existence of private property. The former causes the alienation of the worker from his product, whereas the second brings about a situation in which the interest of the individual no longer coincides with that of society as a whole. As productive forces are owned by a small minority of the population, it follows that societies are divided along class lines, with political and economic power being concentrated in the hands of the ruling class.

If this analysis is correct, Marx believed that the third conclusion naturally followed: Capitalism – the economic order just described – was inherently unstable, due to the tensions arising from productive forces. As a result of these internal contradictions, it would break down. Some versions of Marxism present this breakdown as happening without any need for assistance. Others present it as the result of a social revolution, led by the working class. The closing words of the *Communist Manifesto* (1848) seem to suggest the latter: "Workers have nothing to lose but their chains. They have a world to gain. Workers of the world, unite!"

So how do these ideas relate to Christian theology? In his 1844 political and economic manuscripts, Marx develops the idea that religion in general (he does not distinguish the individual religions) is a direct response to social and economic conditions. "The religious world is but the reflex of the real world." There is an obvious and important allusion here to Feuerbach's critique of religion, which we shall consider in a later section. Thus Marx argues that "religion is just the imaginary sun which seems to man to revolve around him, until he realizes that he himself is the center of his own revolution." In other words, God is simply a projection of human concerns. Human beings "look for a superhuman being in the fantasy reality of heaven, and find nothing their but their own reflection."

But why should religion exist at all? If Marx is right, why should people continue to believe such in a crude illusion? Marx's answer centers on the notion of alienation. "Humans make religion; religion does not make humans. Religion is the self-consciousness and self-esteem of people who either have not found themselves or who have already lost themselves again." Religion is the product of social and economic alienation. It arises from that alienation, and at the same time encourages that alienation by a form of spiritual intoxication which renders the masses incapable of recognizing their situation, and doing something about it. Religion is a comfort, which enables people to tolerate their economic alienation. If there were no such alienation, there would be no need for religion.

Materialism affirms that events in the material world bring about corresponding changes in the intellectual world. Religion is thus the result of a certain set of social and economic conditions. Change those conditions, so that economic alienation is eliminated, and religion will cease to exist. It will no longer serve any useful function. Unjust social conditions produce religion, and are in turn supported by religion. "The struggle against religion is therefore indirectly a struggle against *the world* of which religion is the spiritual fragrance."

Marx thus argues that religion will continue to exist, as long as it meets a need in the life of alienated people. "The religious reflex of the real world can . . . only then vanish when the practical relations of everyday life offer to man none but perfectly intelligible and reasonable relations with regard to his fellow men and to nature." In other words, a shake-up in the real world is needed to get rid of religion. Marx thus argues that when a non-alienating economic and social environment is brought about through communism, the needs which gave rise to religion will vanish. And with the elimination of those material needs, spiritual hunger will also vanish.

In practice, Marxism had virtually no influence until the period of World War I. This can be put down partly to some disagreements within the movement, and partly due to the lack of any real opportunities for political expansion. The internal problems are especially interesting. The suggestion that the working class could liberate itself from its oppression, and bring about a political revolution, soon proved to be illusory. It rapidly became clear that Marxists, far from being drawn from the ranks of the politically conscious working class, were actually depressingly middle-class (like Marx himself). Aware of this problem, Lenin developed the idea of a "vanguard party." The workers were so politically naïve that they needed to be led by professional revolutionaries, who alone could provide the overall vision and practical guidance that would be needed in bringing about and sustaining a world revolution.

The Russian Revolution gave Marxism the break it needed. However, although Marxism established itself in a modified form (Marxism-Leninism) within the Soviet Union, it proved unsuccessful elsewhere. Its successes in eastern Europe after World War II can be put down mainly to military strength and political destabilization. Its successes in Africa were largely due to the seductive appeal of Lenin's carefully devised concept of "imperialism," which allowed alienated elements in certain African and Asian countries to put their backwardness down to ruthless and systematic exploitation by the external agency of western capitalism, rather than any inherent deficiences.

The economic failure and political stagnation which resulted when such countries experimented with Marxism in the 1970s and 1980s soon led to disillusionment with this new philosophy. In Europe, Marxism found itself locked into a spiral of decline. Its chief advocates increasingly became abstract theoreticians, detached from working-class roots, with virtually no political experience. The idea of a socialist revolution gradually lost its appeal and its credibility. In the United States and Canada, Marxism had little, if any, social appeal in the first place, although its influence upon the academic world was more noticeable. The Soviet invasion of Czechoslovakia in 1968 resulted in a noticeable cooling in enthusiasm for Marxism within western intellectual circles.

However, Marx's ideas have found their way, suitably modified, into modern Christian theology. Latin American liberation theology can be shown to have drawn appreciatively on Marxist insights, even if the movement cannot really be described as "Marxist." We shall consider liberation theology in a later section (see pp. 105–7).

Liberal Protestantism

Liberal Protestantism is unquestionably one of the most important movements to have arisen within modern Christian thought. Its origins are complex. However, it is helpful to think of it as having arisen in response to the theological program set out by F. D. E. Schleiermacher, especially in relation to his emphasis upon human "feeling" and the need to relate Christian faith to the human situation. Classic liberal Protestantism had its origins in the Germany of the mid-nineteenth century, amidst a growing realization that Christian faith and theology alike required reconstruction in the light of modern knowledge. In England, the increasingly positive reception given to Charles Darwin's theory of natural selection (popularly known as the "Darwinian theory of evolution") created a climate in which some elements of traditional Christian theology (such as the doctrine of the seven days of creation) seemed to be increasingly untenable. From its outset, liberalism was committed to bridging the gap between Christian faith and modern knowledge.

Liberalism's program required a significant degree of flexibility in

relation to traditional Christian theology. Its leading writers argued
that reconstruction of belief was essential if Christianity were to remain a serious intellectual option in the modern world. For this reason,
they demanded a degree of freedom in relation to the doctrinal inheritance of Christianity on the one hand, and traditional methods
of biblical interpretation on the other. Where traditional ways of interpreting Scripture, or traditional beliefs, seemed to be compromised
by developments in human knowledge, it was imperative that they
should be discarded or reinterpreted to bring them into line with what
was now known about the world.

The theological implications of this shift in direction were considerable. A number of Christian beliefs came to be regarded as seriously
out of line with modern cultural norms; these suffered one of two
fates:

1 They were *abandoned*, as resting upon outdated or mistaken
  presuppositions. The doctrine of original sin is a case in point;
  this was put down to a misreading of the New Testament in
  the light of the writings of St Augustine, whose judgment on
  these matters had become clouded by his overinvolvement
  with a fatalist sect (the Manichees).

2 They were *reinterpreted*, in a manner more conducive to the
  spirit of the age. A number of central doctrines relating to
  the person of Jesus Christ may be included in this category,
  including his divinity (which was reinterpreted as an affirmation of Jesus exemplifying qualities which humanity as a
  whole could hope to emulate).

Alongside this process of doctrinal reinterpretation (which continued
in the "history of dogma" movement – see pp. 293–4) may be seen
a new concern to ground Christian faith in the world of humanity –
above all, in human experience and modern culture. Sensing potential
difficulties in grounding Christian faith in an exclusive appeal to
Scripture or the person of Jesus Christ, liberalism sought to anchor
that faith in common human experience, and interpret it in ways that
made sense within the modern worldview.

Liberalism was inspired by the vision of a humanity which was
ascending upward into new realms of progress and prosperity. The
doctrine of evolution gave new vitality to this belief, which was
nurtured by strong evidence of cultural stability in western Europe in
the late nineteenth century. Religion came increasingly to be seen
as relating to the spiritual needs of modern humanity, and giving
ethical guidance to society. The strongly ethical dimension of liberal

Protestantism is especially evident in the writings of Albrecht Benjamin Ritschl.

For Ritschl, the idea of the "kingdom of God" was of central importance. Ritschl tended to think of this as a static realm of ethical values, which would undergird the development of German society at this point in its history. History, it was argued, was in the process of being divinely guided toward perfection. Civilization is seen as part of this process of evolution. In the course of human history, a number of individuals appear who are recognized as being the bearers of special divine insights. One such individual was Jesus. By following his example and sharing in his inner life, other human beings are able to develop. The movement showed enormous and unbounded optimism in human ability and potential. Religion and culture were, it was argued, virtually identical. Later critics of the movement dubbed it "culture Protestantism" (*Kulturprotestantismus*), on account of their belief that it was too heavily dependent upon accepted cultural norms.

Many critics – such as Karl Barth in Europe and Reinhold Niebuhr in North America – regarded liberal Protestantism as based upon a hopelessly optimistic view of human nature. They believed that this optimism had been destroyed by the events of World War I, and that liberalism would henceforth lack cultural credibility. This has proved to be a considerable misjudgment. At its best, liberalism may be regarded as a movement committed to the restatement of Christian faith in forms which are acceptable within contemporary culture. Liberalism has continued to see itself as a mediator between two unacceptable alternatives: the mere restatement of traditional Christian faith (usually described as "traditionalism" or "fundamentalism" by its liberal critics), and the total rejection of Christianity. Liberal writers have been passionately committed to the search for a middle road between these two stark alternatives.

Perhaps the most developed and influential presentation of liberal Protestantism is to be found in the writings of Paul Tillich (1886–1965), who rose to fame in the United States in the late 1950s and early 1960s, toward the end of his career, and who is widely regarded as the most influential American theologian since Jonathan Edwards. Tillich's program can be summarized in the term "correlation." By the "method of correlation," Tillich understands the task of modern theology to be to establish a conversation between human culture and Christian faith. Tillich reacted with alarm to the theological program set out by Karl Barth, seeing this as a misguided attempt to drive a wedge between theology and culture. For Tillich, existential questions – or "ultimate questions," as he often terms them – are thrown up and revealed by human culture. Modern philosophy, writing, and the creative arts point to questions which concern humans. Theology then formulates answers to these questions, and by doing so it correlates the gospel to modern culture. The gospel must speak to culture, and it can do so only if the actual questions raised by that culture are heard. For David Tracy of the University of Chicago, the image of a dialogue between the gospel and culture is controlling: That dialogue involves the mutual correction and enrichment of both gospel and culture. There is thus a close relation between theology and apologetics, in that the task of theology is understood to be that of interpreting the Christian response to the human needs disclosed by cultural analysis.

The term "liberal" is thus probably best interpreted as applying to "a theologian in the tradition of Schleiermacher and Tillich, concerned with the reconstruction of belief in response to contemporary culture," in which form it describes many noted modern writers. However, it must be noted that the term "liberal" is widely regarded as imprecise and confusing. The British theologian John Macquarrie notes this point with characteristic clarity:

> What is meant by "liberal" theology? If it means only that the theologian to whom the adjective is applied has an openness to other points of view, then liberal theologians are found in all schools of thought. But if "liberal" becomes itself a party label, then it usually turns out to be extremely illiberal.

In fact, one of the more curious paradoxes of recent Christian theology is that some of the most dogmatic of its representatives actually lay claim to be liberals! Liberalism, in the traditional and honorable sense of the word, carries with it an inalienable respect for and openness to the views of others; as such, it ought to be a fundamental element of every branch of Christian theology (including neo-orthodoxy and evangelicalism, to be discussed shortly). However, the term has now come to have a developed meaning, often carrying with it overtones of suspicion, hostility, or impatience toward traditional Christian formulations and doctrines. This can be seen clearly in the popular use of the term, which often includes ideas such as the denial of the resurrection or of the uniqueness of Christ.

Liberalism has been criticized on a number of points, of which the following are typical.

1 It tends to place considerable weight upon the notion of a universal human religious experience. Yet this is a vague and ill-defined notion, incapable of being examined and assessed publicly. There are also excellent reasons for suggesting that "experience" is shaped by interpretation to a far greater extent than liberalism allows.

2   Liberalism is seen by its critics as placing too great an empha-
    sis upon transient cultural developments, with the result that
    it often appears to be uncritically driven by a secular agenda.
3   It has been suggested that liberalism is too ready to surrender
    distinctive Christian doctrines in an effort to become accept-
    able to contemporary culture.

Liberalism probably reached its zenith in North America during the
late 1970s and early 1980s. Although continuing to maintain a distinguished presence in seminaries and schools of religion, it is now
widely regarded as a waning force both in modern theology and in
church life in general. The weaknesses of liberalism have been seized
upon by critics within the post-liberal school, to be considered shortly.
Much the same criticism can also be directed against a movement
known loosely as "modernism," to which we may now turn.

Modernism

The term "modernist" was first used to refer to a school of Roman
Catholic theologians operating toward the end of the nineteenth century, which adopted a critical and skeptical attitude to traditional
Christian doctrines, especially those relating to Christology and soteriology. The movement fostered a positive attitude toward radical
biblical criticism, and stressed the ethical, rather than the more theological; dimensions of faith. In many ways, modernism may be seen
as an attempt by writers within the Roman Catholic church to come to
terms with the outlook of the Enlightenment which it had, until that
point, largely ignored.

"Modernism" is, however, a loose term, and should not be understood to imply the existence of a distinctive school of thought, committed to certain common methods or indebted to common teachers.
It is certainly true that most modernist writers were concerned to
integrate Christian thought with the spirit of the Enlightenment,
especially the new understandings of history and the natural sciences
which were then gaining the ascendancy. Equally, some drew inspiration from writers such as Maurice Blondel (1861–1949), who
argued that the supernatural was intrinsic to human existence, or
Henri Bergson (1859–1941), who stressed the importance of intuition
over intellect. Yet there is not sufficient commonality amongst the
French, English, and American modernists, nor between Roman
Catholic and Protestant modernism, to allow the term to be understood as designating a rigorous and well-defined school.

Amongst Roman Catholic modernist writers, particular attention should be paid to Alfred Loisy (1857–1940) and George Tyrrell (1861–1909). During the 1890s, Loisy established himself as a critic of traditional views of the biblical accounts of creation, and argued that a real development of doctrine could be discerned within Scripture. His most significant publication, *L'évangile et l'église* ("The gospel and the church"), appeared in 1902. This important work was a direct response to the views of Adolf von Harnack, published two years earlier as *What is Christianity?*, on the origins and nature of Christianity. Loisy rejected Harnack's suggestion that there was a radical discontinuity between Jesus and the church; however, he made significant concessions to Harnack's liberal Protestant account of Christian origins, including an acceptance of the role and validity of biblical criticism in interpreting the gospels. As a result, the work was placed upon the list of prohibited books by the Roman Catholic authorities in 1903.

The British Jesuit writer George Tyrrell followed Loisy in his radical criticism of traditional Catholic dogma. In common with Loisy, he criticized Harnack's account of Christian origins in *Christianity at the Crossroads* (1909), dismissing Harnack's historical reconstruction of Jesus as "the reflection of a Liberal Protestant face, seen at the bottom of a deep well." The book also included a defense of Loisy's work, arguing that the official Roman Catholic "hostility to the book and its author has created a general impression that it is a defence of Liberal Protestant against Roman Catholic positions, and that 'Modernism' is simply a protestantizing and rationalizing movement."

In part, this perception may be due to the growing influence of modernist attitudes within the mainstream Protestant denominations. In England, the Churchmen's Union was founded in 1898 for the advancement of liberal religious thought; in 1928, it altered its name to the Modern Churchmen's Union. Amongst those especially associated with this group may be noted Hastings Rashdall (1858–1924), whose *Idea of Atonement in Christian Theology* (1919) illustrates the general tenor of English modernism. Drawing somewhat uncritically upon the earlier writings of liberal Protestant thinkers such as Ritschl, Rashdall argued that the theory of the atonement associated with the medieval writer Peter Abelard was more acceptable to modern thought forms than traditional theories which made an appeal to the notion of a substitutionary sacrifice. This strongly moral or exemplarist theory of the atonement, which interpreted Christ's death virtually exclusively as a demonstration of the love of God, made a considerable impact upon English, and especially Anglican, thought in the 1920s and 1930s. Nevertheless, the events of World War I, and the subsequent rise of fascism in Europe in the 1930s, undermined the credibility of the movement. It was not until the 1960s that a renewed modernism or radicalism became a significant feature of English Christianity.

The rise of modernism in the United States follows a similar pattern. The growth of liberal Protestantism in the late nineteenth and early twentieth centuries was widely perceived as a direct challenge to more conservative evangelical standpoints. Newman Smyth's *Passing Protestantism and Coming Catholicism* (1908) argued that Roman Catholic modernism could serve as a mentor to American Protestantism in several ways, not least in its critique of dogma and its historical understanding of the development of doctrine. The situation became increasingly polarized through the rise of fundamentalism in response to modernist attitudes.

World War I ushered in a period of self-questioning within American modernism which was intensified through the radical social realism of writers such as H. R. Niebuhr. By the mid-1930s, modernism appeared to have lost its way. In an influential article in *The Christian Century* of December 4, 1935, Harry Emerson Fosdick declared the need "to go beyond modernism." In his *Realistic Theology* (1934), Walter Marshall Horton spoke of the rout of liberal forces in American theology. However, the movement gained new confidence in the post-war period, and arguably reached its zenith during the period of the Vietnam War.

However, we must now turn back to the opening of the twentieth century, to consider an earlier reaction against liberalism, which is especially associated with the name of Karl Barth: neo-orthodoxy.

Neo-Orthodoxy

World War I witnessed a disillusionment with, although not a final rejection of, the liberal theology which had come to be associated with Schleiermacher and his followers. A number of writers argued that Schleiermacher had, in effect, reduced Christianity to little more than religious experience, thus making it a human-centered rather than a God-centered affair. The war, it was argued, destroyed the credibility of such an approach. Liberal theology seemed to be about human values – and how could these be taken seriously, if they led to global conflicts on such a massive scale? By stressing the "otherness" of God, writers such as Karl Barth (1886–1968) believed that they could escape from the doomed human-centered theology of liberalism.

These ideas were given systematic exposition by Barth in the *Church Dogmatics* (1936–69), probably the most significant theological achievement of the twentieth century. Barth did not live to finish this enterprise, so that his exposition of the doctrine of redemption is incomplete. The primary theme which resonates throughout the *Dogmatics* is the need to take seriously the self-revelation of God in Christ through Scripture. Although this might seem to be little more than a reiteration of themes already firmly associated with Calvin or Luther, Barth brought a degree of creativity to his task which firmly established him as a major thinker in his own right.

The work is divided into five volumes, each of which is further subdivided. Volume I deals with the Word of God – for Barth, the source and starting point of Christian faith and Christian theology alike. Volume II deals with the doctrine of God, and volume III with the doctrine of the creation. Volume IV deals with the doctrine of reconciliation (or, perhaps one might say, atonement; the German term *Versöhnung* can mean both), and the incomplete volume V with the doctrine of redemption.

Apart from the predictable (and relatively non-informative) "Barthianism," two terms have been used to describe the approach associated with Barth. The term "dialectical theology" has been used, taking up the idea, found especially in Barth's 1919 commentary on Romans, of a "dialectic between time and eternity," or a "dialectic between God and humanity." The term draws attention to Barth's characteristic insistence that there is a contradiction or dialectic, rather than a continuity, between God and humanity. The second term is "neo-orthodoxy," which draws attention to the affinity between Barth and the writings of the period of Reformed orthodoxy, especially during the seventeenth century. In many ways, Barth can be regarded as entering into dialogue with several leading Reformed writers of this period.

Perhaps the most distinctive feature of Barth's approach is his "theology of the Word of God." According to Barth, theology is a discipline which seeks to keep the proclamation of the Christian church faithful to its foundation in Jesus Christ, as he has been revealed to us in Scripture. Theology is not a response to the human situation or to human questions; it is a response to the Word of God, which demands a response on account of its intrinsic nature.

Neo-orthodoxy became a significant presence in North American theology during the 1930s, especially through the writings of Reinhold Niebuhr and others, which criticized the optimistic assumptions of much liberal Protestant social thinking of the time.

Neo-orthodoxy has been criticized at a number of points. The following are of especial importance:

1   Its emphasis upon the transcendence and "otherness" of God leads to God being viewed as distant and potentially

irrelevant. It has often been suggested that this leads to extreme skepticism.

2 There is a certain circularity to the claim of neo-orthodoxy to be based only upon divine revelation, in that this cannot be checked out by anything other than an appeal to that same revelation. In other words, there are no recognized external reference points by which neo-orthodoxy's truth claims can be verified. This has led many of its critics to suggest that it is a form of *fideism* – that is to say, a belief system which is impervious to any criticism from outside.

3 Neo-orthodoxy has no helpful response to those who are attracted to other religions, which it is obliged to dismiss as distortions and perversions. Other theological approaches are able to account for the existence of such religions, and place them in relation to the Christian faith.

Feminism

Feminism has come to be a significant component of modern western culture. At its heart, feminism is a global movement working toward the emancipation of women. The older term for the movement – "women's liberation" – expressed the fact that it is at heart a liberation movement directing its efforts toward achieving equality for women in modern society, especially through the removal of obstacles – including beliefs, values, and attitudes – which hinder that process. Of late, the movement has become increasingly heterogeneous, partly on account of a willingness to recognize a diversity of approaches on the part of women within different cultures and ethnic groupings. Thus the religious writings of black women in North America are increasingly coming to be referred to as "black womanist theology."

Feminism has come into conflict with Christianity (as it has with most religions) on account of the perception that religions treat women as second-rate human beings, in terms of both the roles which those religions allocate to women, and the manner in which they are understood to image God. The writings of Simone de Beauvoir – such as *The Second Sex* (1945) – developed such ideas at length. A number of post-Christian feminists, including Mary Daly in her *Beyond God the Father* (1973) and Daphne Hampson in *Theology and Feminism* (1990), argue that Christianity, with its male symbols for God, its male savior figure, and its long history of male leaders and thinkers, is biased against women, and incapable of redemption. Women, they urge, should leave its oppressive environment. Others, such as Carol Christ in *Laughter of Aphrodite* (1987) and Naomi Ruth Goldenberg in *Changing of the Gods* (1979), argue that women may find religious emancipation by recovering the ancient goddess religions (or inventing new ones), and abandoning traditional Christianity altogether.

Yet the feminist evaluation of Christianity is far from as mono-lithically hostile toward Christianity as these writers might suggest. Feminist writers have stressed how women have been active in the shaping and development of the Christian tradition, from the New Testament onward, and have exercised significant leadership roles throughout Christian history. Indeed, responsible feminist writers have shown the need to reappraise the Christian past, giving honor and recognition to an army of faithful women, whose practice, de-fense, and proclamation of their faith had hitherto passed unnoticed by much of the Christian church and its (mainly male) historians.

The most significant contribution of feminism to Christian thought may be argued to lie in its challenge to traditional theological formu-lations. These, it is argued, are often patriarchal (that is, they reflect a belief in domination by males) and sexist (that is, they are biased against women). The following areas of theology are especially signifi-cant in this respect.

1 *The maleness of God* (see pp. 205–7) The persistent use of male pronouns for God within the Christian tradition is a target of criticism by many feminist writers. It is argued that the use of female pronouns is at least as logical as the use of their male counterparts, and might go some way toward correcting an excessive emphasis upon male role models for God. In her *Sexism and God-Talk* (1983), Rosemary Radford Ruether suggests that the term "God/ess" is a politically correct desig-nation for God, although the verbal clumsiness of the term is unlikely to enhance its appeal.

Sallie McFague's *Metaphorical Theology* (1982) argues for the need to recover the idea of the metaphorical aspects of male models of God, such as "father": *analogies* tend to stress the similarities between God and human beings; *metaphors* affirm that, amidst these similarities, there are significant dissimilarities between God and humans (for example, in the realm of gender).

2 *The nature of sin* Many feminist writers have suggested that no-tions of sin as pride, ambition, or excessive self-esteem are fundamen-tally male in orientation. This, it is argued, does not correspond to the experience of women, who tend to experience sin as *lack* of pride, *lack* of ambition, and *lack* of self-esteem. Of particular importance in this context is the feminist appeal to the notion of non-competitive rela-tionships, which avoids the patterns of low self-esteem and passivity which have been characteristic traditional female responses to male-dominated society. This point is made with particular force by Judith Plaskow in *Sex, Sin and Grace* (1980), a penetrating critique of Reinhold Niebuhr's theology from a feminist perspective.

3   *The person of Christ* (see pp. 270–308)   A number of feminist writers, most notably Rosemary Radford Ruether in *Sexism and God-Talk*, have suggested that Christology is the ultimate ground of much sexism within Christianity. In her *Consider Jesus: Waves of Renewal in Christology* (1990), Elizabeth Johnson has explored the manner in which the maleness of Jesus has been the subject of theological abuse, and suggests appropriate correctives. Two areas of especial importance may be noted.

First, the maleness of Christ has sometimes been used as the theological foundation for the belief that only the male human may adequately image God, or that only males provide appropriate role models or analogies for God. Second, the maleness of Christ has sometimes been used as the foundation for a network of beliefs concerning norms within humanity. It has been argued, on the basis of the maleness of Christ, that the norm of humanity is the male, with the female being somehow a second-rate, or less than ideal, human being. Thomas Aquinas, who describes women as misbegotten males (apparently on the basis of an obsolete Aristotelian biology), illustrates this trend, which has important implications for issues of leadership within the church.

In responding to these points, feminist writers have argued that the maleness of Christ is a contingent aspect of his identity, on the same level as his being Jewish. It is a contingent element of his historical reality, not an essential aspect of his identity. Thus it cannot be allowed to become the basis of the domination of females by males, any more than it legitimates the domination of Gentiles by Jews, or plumbers by carpenters.

The relevance of the feminist critique of traditional theology will be noted at appropriate points during the course of this volume.

Postmodernism

Postmodernism is generally taken to be something of a cultural sensibility without absolutes, fixed certainties, or foundations, which takes delight in pluralism and divergence, and which aims to think through the radical "situatedness" of all human thought. Postmodernism is a vague and ill-defined notion, which perhaps could be described as the general intellectual outlook arising after the collapse of modernism.

Although a number of writers still maintain that modernism is alive and active, this attitude is becoming increasingly rare.

Further, it should be noted that modernism itself is a vague idea. The very idea of postmodernism might be argued to "presuppose that our age is unified enough that we can speak of its ending" (David Kolb); nevertheless, much of western culture disagrees. The trauma of Auschwitz is a powerful and shocking indictment of the "pretense of new creation, the hatred of tradition, the idolatry of self" (Kolb) characteristic of modernism. It is modernism, especially with its compulsive desire to break totally with the past, which gave rise to the Nazi holocaust and the Stalinist purges. There has been a general collapse of confidence in the Enlightenment trust in the power of reason to provide foundations for a universally valid knowledge of the world, including God. Reason fails to deliver a morality suited to the real world in which we live. And with this collapse in confidence in universal and necessary criteria of truth, relativism and pluralism have flourished.

To give a full definition of postmodernism is virtually impossible; nevertheless, it is possible to identify its leading general features, in so far as it is likely to be encountered by the student of Christian theology, especially on North American college and university campuses. This is the precommitment to relativism or pluralism in relation to questions of truth. To use the language which has become characteristic of the movement, one could say that postmodernism represents a situation in which the signifier (or signifying) has replaced the signified as the focus of orientation and value.

In terms of the structural linguistics developed initially by Ferdinand de Saussure, and subsequently by Roman Jakobson and others, the recognition of the *arbitrariness* of the linguistic sign and its interdependence with other signs marks the end of the possibility of fixed, absolute meanings. Thus writers such as Jacques Derrida, Michel Foucault, and Jean Baudrillard argued that language was whimsical and capricious, and did not reflect any overarching, absolute linguistic laws. It was arbitrary, incapable of disclosing meaning. Baudrillard argued that modern society was trapped in an endless network of artificial sign systems, which *meant* nothing, and merely perpetuated the belief systems of those who created them.

One aspect of postmodernism which illustrates this trend particularly well, while also indicating its obsession with texts and language, is *deconstruction* – the critical method which virtually declares that the identity and intentions of the author of a text are irrelevant to the interpretation of the text, prior to insisting that, in any case, no meaning can be found in it. All interpretations are equally valid, or equally meaningless (depending upon your point of view). As Paul de Man, one of the leading American proponents of this approach, declared, the very idea of "meaning" smacked of fascism. It implied that someone had authority to define how a work of literature *ought* to be understood, and denied others the opportunity to exercise freedom of interpretation, thus stifling their creativity. This approach, which blossomed in the cultural situation of post-Vietnam America, was given intellectual respectability by academics such as de Man, Geoffrey Hartman, Harold Bloom, and J. Hillis Miller.

Theologically, the two following developments should be noted as being of especial importance. Although it is not clear what their long-term influence may be, they are likely to remain significant until the end of this century.

1 *Biblical interpretation* Traditional academic biblical interpretation had been dominated by the historico-critical method. This approach, which developed during the nineteenth century, stressed the import-ance of the application of critical historical methods, such as establish-ing the *Sitz im Leben*, or "situation in life," of gospel passages. It was challenged in the 1970s and 1980s through the rise of structuralism and post-structuralism.

A number of leading literary critics of the 1980s (such as Harold Bloom and Frank Kermode) ventured into the field of biblical in-terpretation, and challenged such ideas as "institutionally legitimized" or "scholarly respectable" interpretations of the Bible. The notion that there is *a* meaning to a biblical text – whether laid down by a church authority or by the academic community – is regarded with intense suspicion within postmodernism.

Amongst specific influences upon biblical interpretation, the follow-ing are of especial interest. Michel Foucault's analysis of the power relationship between the interpreter and the community raised a cluster of important questions concerning the potentially repressive function of "authorized" biblical interpreters. The works of Jacques Derrida raised the question of how a range of conflicting readings of Scripture could be created by the differential interpretation of biblical texts. Jean-François Lyotard suggested that what he styled *les grands récits*, the great biblical narratives, did little more than perpetuate secular ideologies based loosely on those narratives. This raised the question of how the Bible can be interpreted in such a way as to challenge, rather than endorse, the assumptions of western capitalism (although the writings of Latin American liberation theologians – see below – suggest that this problem is considerably less serious than Lyotard's rhetoric allows).

2 *Systematic theology* Postmodernism is, by its very nature, hostile to the notion of "systematization," or any claims to have discerned "meaning." Mark Taylor's study *Erring* is an excellent illustration of the impact of postmodernism on systematic theology. The image of "erring" – rather than more traditional approaches to theological system-building – leads Taylor to develop an anti-systematic theology which offers polyvalent approaches to questions of truth or meaning. Taylor's study represents an exploration of the consequences of Nietzsche's declaration of the "death of God." On the basis of this, Taylor argues for the elimination of such concepts as self, truth, and meaning. Language does not refer to anything, and truth does not correspond to anything.

Liberation theology

The term "liberation theology" could, in theory, be applied to any theology which is addressed to or deals with oppressive situations. In this sense, feminist theology could be regarded as a form of liberation theology, as the older term "women's liberation" suggests. Equally, Black theology is unquestionably concerned with the issue of liberation. However, in practice, the term is used to refer to a quite distinct form of theology, which has its origins in the Latin American situation in the 1960s and 1970s. In 1968, the Roman Catholic bishops of Latin America gathered for a congress at Medellín, Colombia. This meeting – often known as CELAM II – sent shock waves throughout the region by acknowledging that the church had often sided with oppressive governments in the region, and declaring that in future it would be on the side of the poor.

This pastoral and political stance was soon complemented by a solid theological foundation. In his *Theology of Liberation* (1971), the Peruvian theologian Gustavo Gutiérrez introduced the characteristic themes that would become definitive of the movement, and which we shall explore presently. Other writers of note include the Brazilian Leonardo Boff, the Urugayan Juan Luis Segundo, and the Argentinian José Miguel Bonino. This last is unusual in one respect, in that he is a Protestant (more precisely, a Methodist) voice in a conversation dominated by Roman Catholic writers.

The basic themes of Latin American liberation theology may be summarized as follows.

1 Liberation theology is oriented toward the poor and oppressed. "The poor are the authentic theological source for understanding Christian truth and practice" (Sobrino). In the Latin American situation, the church is on the side of the poor: "God is clearly and unequivocally on the side of the poor" (Bonino). The fact that God is on the side of the poor leads to a further insight: the poor occupy a position of especial importance in the interpretation of the Christian faith. All Christian theology and mission must begin with the "view from below," with the sufferings and distress of the poor.

2   Liberation theology involves critical reflection on practice. As Gutiérrez puts it, theology is a "critical reflection on Christian praxis in the light of the word of God." Theology is not, and should not be, detached from social involvement or political action. Whereas classical western theology regarded action as the result of reflection, liberation theology inverts the order: Action comes first, followed by critical reflection. "Theology has to stop explaining the world, and start transforming it" (Bonino). True knowledge of God can never be disinterested or detached, but comes in and through commitment to the cause of the poor. There is a fundamental rejection of the Enlightenment view that commitment is a barrier to knowledge.

At this point, the indebtedness of liberation theology to Marxist theory becomes evident. Many western observers have criticized the movement for this reason, seeing it as an unholy alliance between Christianity and Marxism. Liberation theologians have vigorously defended their use of Marx, on two major grounds. First, Marxism is seen as a "tool of social analysis" (Gutiérrez), which allows insights to be gained concerning the present nature of Latin American society, and the means by which the appalling situation of the poor may be remedied. Second, it provides a political program by which the present unjust social system may be dismantled, and a more equitable society created. In practice, liberation theology is intensely critical of capitalism and affirmative of socialism. Liberation theologians have noted Thomas Aquinas' use of Aristotle in his theological method, and argued that they are merely doing the same thing – using a secular philosopher to give substance to fundamentally Christian beliefs. For, it must be stressed, liberation theology declares that God's preference for and commitment to the poor is a fundamental aspect of the gospel, not some bolt-on option arising from the Latin American situation or based purely in Marxist political theory.

It will be clear that liberation theology is of major significance to recent theological debate. Two key theological issues may be considered as an illustration of its impact.

1   *Biblical hermeneutics*   Scripture is read as a narrative of liberation. Particular emphasis is laid upon the liberation of Israel from bondage in Egypt, the prophet's denunciation of oppression, and Jesus' proclamation of the gospel to the poor and outcast. Scripture is read, not from a standpoint of wishing to understand the gospel, but out

of a concern to apply its liberating insights to the Latin American situation. Western academic theology has tended to regard this approach with some impatience, believing that it has no place for the considered insights of biblical scholarship concerning the interpretation of such passages.

2 *The nature of salvation* (see pp. 360–4) Liberation theology has tended to equate salvation with liberation, and stressed the social, political, and economic aspects of salvation. The movement has laid particular emphasis upon the notion of "structural sin," noting that it is society, rather than individuals, that is corrupted and requires redemption. To its critics, liberation theology has reduced salvation to a purely worldly affair, and neglected its transcendent and eternal dimensions.

Black Theology

"Black theology" is the movement, especially significant in the United States during the 1960s and 1970s, which concerned itself with ensuring that the realities of Black experience were represented at the theological level. The first major evidence of the move toward theological emancipation within the American Black community dates from 1964, with the publication of Joseph Washington's *Black Religion*, a powerful affirmation of the distinctiveness of Black religion within the North American context. Washington emphasized the need for integration and assimilation of Black theological insights within mainstream Protestantism; however, this approach was largely swept to one side with the appearance of Albert Cleage's *Black Messiah*. Cleage, pastor of the Shrine of the Black Madonna in Detroit, urged Black people to liberate themselves from white theological oppression. Arguing that Scripture was written by black Jews, Cleage claimed that the gospel of a Black Messiah had been perverted by Paul in his attempt to make it acceptable to Europeans. Despite the considerable overstatements within the work, *Black Messiah* came to be a rallying point for black Christians, determined to discover and assert their distinctive identity.

The movement made several decisive affirmations of its theological distinctiveness during 1969. The "Black Manifesto" issued at the Interreligious Foundation for Community Organization meeting in Detroit, Michigan, placed the issue of the black experience firmly on the theological agenda. The statement by the National Committee of Black Churchmen emphasized the theme of liberation as a central motif of Black theology:

> Black Theology is a theology of black liberation. It seeks to plumb
> the black condition in the light of God's revelation in Jesus Christ,
> so that the black community can see that the gospel is commen-
> surate with the achievement of black humanity. Black Theology is
> a theology of "blackness." It is the affirmation of black humanity
> that emancipates black people from white racism, thus providing
> authentic freedom for both white and black people.

Although there are evident affinities between this statement and the
aims and emphases of Latin American liberation theology, it must be
stressed that, at this stage, there was no formal interaction between
the two movements. Liberation theology arose primarily within the
Roman Catholic church in South America, whereas Black theology
tended to arise within Black Protestant communities in North America.

The origins of the movement can be traced to the rise in black
consciousness which was so distinctive a feature of American history
in the 1960s. Three main stages can be distinguished within the development of the movement:

1   *1966–70*   During this developmental phase, Black theology
    emerged as a significant aspect of the civil rights struggle in
    general, and as a reaction against the dominance of whites in
    both seminaries and churches. At this stage, Black theology
    was developed within the black-led churches, and was not
    particularly academic in its outlook. The issues of primary
    importance centered on the use of violence to achieve justice,
    and the nature of Christian love.
2   *1970–77*   In this period of consolidation, the movement
    appears to have moved away from the churches to the semin-
    aries, as the movement became increasingly accepted within
    theological circles. The focus of the movement shifted from
    issues of practical concern to more explicitly theological
    issues, such as the nature of liberation and the significance
    of suffering.
3   *1977 onwards*   A new awareness of the development of liber-
    ation movements in other parts of the world, especially in
    Latin America, became of importance within Black theology.
    Alongside this new sense of perspective came a new commit-
    ment to serving black-led churches, and the fostering of fel-
    lowship and collaboration amongst those churches.

The most significant writer within the movement is generally agreed
to be James H. Cone, whose *Black Theology of Liberation* (1970) appealed
to the central notion of a God who is concerned for the black struggle

for liberation. Noting the strong preference of Jesus for the oppressed, Cone argued that "God was Black" – that is, identified with the oppressed. However, Cone's use of Barthian categories was criticized: why, it was asked, should a Black theologian use the categories of a white theology in articulating the black experience? Why had he not made fuller use of black history and culture? In later works, Cone responded to such criticisms by making a more pervasive appeal to "the Black experience" as a central resource in Black theology. Nevertheless, Cone has continued to maintain a Barthian emphasis upon the centrality of Christ as the self-revelation of God (while identifying him as "the Black Messiah"), and the authority of Scripture in interpreting human experience in general.

Postliberalism

One of the most significant developments in theology since about 1980 has been a growing skepticism over the plausibility of a liberal world-view. A number of developments have accompanied this retreat from liberalism, perhaps the most important of which has been the repristi-nation of more conservative viewpoints. One such development has been postliberalism, which has become especially associated with Yale Divinity School. Its central foundations are narrative approaches to theology, such as those developed by Hans Frei, and the schools of social interpretation which stress the importance of culture and lan-guage in the generation and interpretation of experience and thought.

Building upon the work of philosophers such as Alasdair MacIntyre, postliberalism rejects both the traditional Enlightenment appeal to a "universal rationality" and the liberal assumption of an immediate religious experience common to all humanity. Arguing that all thought and experience is historically and socially mediated, postliberalism bases its theological program upon a return to religious traditions, whose values are inwardly appropriated. Postliberalism is thus *anti-foundational* (in that it rejects the notion of a universal foundation of knowledge), *communitarian* (in that it appeals to the values, experi-ences, and language of a community, rather than prioritizing the individual), and *historicist* (in that it insists upon the importance of traditions and their associated historical communities in the shaping of experience and thought).

The most significant statement of the postliberal agenda remains George Lindbeck's *Nature of Doctrine* (1984). Rejecting "cognitive-propositional" approaches to doctrine as premodern, and liberal "experiential-expressive" theories as failing to take account of both hu-man experiential diversity and the mediating role of culture in human thought and experience, Lindbeck develops a "cultural-linguistic" approach which embodies the leading features of postliberalism.

The "cultural-linguistic" approach denies that there is some universal unmediated human experience which exists apart from human language and culture. Rather, it stresses that the heart of religion lies in living within a specific historical religious tradition, and interiorizing its ideas and values. This tradition rests upon a historically mediated set of ideas, for which the narrative is an especially suitable means of transmission.

Postliberalism is of particular importance in relation to two areas of Christian theology.

1 *Systematic theology* Theology is understood to be primarily a descriptive discipline, concerned with the exploration of the normative foundations of the Christian tradition, which are mediated through the scriptural narrative of Jesus Christ. Truth can be, at least in part, equated with fidelity to the distinctive doctrinal traditions of the Christian faith. This has caused critics of postliberalism to accuse it of retreating from the public arena into some kind of Christian ghetto. If Christian theology, as postliberalism suggests, is intrasystemic (that is, concerned with the exploration of the internal relationships of the Christian tradition), its validity is to be judged with reference to its own internal standards, rather than some publicly agreed or universal criteria. Once more, this has prompted criticism from those who suggest that theology ought to have external criteria, subject to public scrutiny, by which its validity can be tested.

2 *Christian ethics* Stanley Hauerwas is one of a number of writers to explore postliberal approaches to ethics. Rejecting the Enlightenment idea of a universal set of moral ideals or values, Hauerwas argues that Christian ethics is concerned with the identification of the moral vision of a historical community (the church), and with bringing that vision to actualization in the lives of its members. Thus ethics is intrasystemic, in that it concerns the study of the internal moral values of a community. To be moral is to identify the moral vision of a specific historical community, to appropriate its moral values, and to practice them within that community.

Evangelicalism

The term "evangelical" dates from the sixteenth century, and was then used to refer to Catholic writers wishing to revert to more biblical beliefs and practices than those associated with the late medieval church. It was used especially in the 1520s, when the terms *évangelique*

(French) and *evangelisch* (German) came to feature prominently in polemical writings of the early Reformation. The term is now used widely to refer to a transdenominational trend in theology and spirituality, which lays particular emphasis upon the place of Scripture in the Christian life. Evangelicalism now centers upon a cluster of four assumptions:

1   The authority and sufficiency of Scripture.
2   The uniqueness of redemption through the death of Christ upon the cross.
3   The need for personal conversion.
4   The necessity, propriety, and urgency of evangelism.

All other matters have tended to be regarded as adiaphora, "matters of indifference," upon which a substantial degree of pluralism may be accepted.

Of particular importance is the question of ecclesiology, an issue which will be considered at a later stage in this work (pp. 421–2). Historically, evangelicalism has never been committed to any particular theory of the church, regarding the New Testament as being open to a number of interpretations in this respect, and treating denominational distinctives as of secondary importance to the gospel itself. This most emphatically does not mean that evangelicals lack commitment to the church as the body of Christ; rather, it means that evangelicals are not committed to any one theory of the church. A corporate conception of the Christian life is not understood to be specifically linked with any one denominational understanding of the nature of the church. In one sense, this is a "minimalist" ecclesiology; in another, it represents an admission that the New Testament itself does not stipulate with precision any single form of church government, which can be made binding upon all Christians. This has had several major consequences, which are of central importance to an informed understanding of the movement.

1   Evangelicalism is transdenominational. It is not confined to any one denomination, nor is it a denomination in its own right. There is no inconsistency involved in speaking of "Anglican evangelicals," "Presbyterian evangelicals," "Methodist evangelicals," or even "Roman Catholic evangelicals."
2   Evangelicalism is not a denomination in itself, possessed of a distinctive ecclesiology, but is a trend within the mainstream denominations.
3   Evangelicalism itself represents an ecumenical movement. There is a natural affinity amongst evangelicals, irrespective

of their denominational associations, which arises from a common commitment to a set of shared beliefs and outlooks. The characteristic evangelical refusal to allow any specific ecclesiology to be seen as normative, while honoring those which are clearly grounded in the New Testament and Christian tradition, means that the potentially divisive matters of church ordering and government are treated as of secondary importance.

An essential question which demands clarification at this point concerns the relation between fundamentalism and evangelicalism. Fundamentalism arose as a reaction within some of the American churches to the rise of a secular culture. It was from its outset, and has remained, a counter-cultural movement, using central doctrinal affirmations as a means of defining cultural boundaries. Certain central doctrines – most notably, the absolute literal authority of Scripture and the second coming of Christ before the end of time (a doctrine usually referred to as "the premillennial return of Christ") – were treated as barriers, intended as much to alienate secular culture as to give fundamentalists a sense of identity and purpose. A siege mentality became characteristic of the movement; fundamentalist counter-communities viewed themselves as walled cities, or (to evoke the pioneer spirit) circles of wagons, defending their distinctiveness against an unbelieving culture.

The emphasis upon the premillennial return of Christ is of especial significance. This view has a long history; it never attained any especial degree of significance prior to the nineteenth century. However, fundamentalism appears to have discerned in the idea an important weapon against the liberal Christian idea of a kingdom of God upon earth, to be achieved through social action. "Dispensationalism" (see pp. 472–3), especially of a premillennarian type, became an integral element of fundamentalism.

Yet disquiet became obvious within American fundamentalism during the late 1940s and early 1950s. Neo-evangelicalism (as it has subsequently come to be known) began to emerge, committed to redressing the unacceptable situation created by the rise of fundamentalism. Fundamentalism and evangelicalism can be distinguished at three general levels.

1 Biblically, fundamentalism is totally hostile to the notion of biblical criticism, in any form, and is committed to a literal interpretation of Scripture. Evangelicalism accepts the principle of biblical criticism (although insisting that it be applied

responsibly), and recognizes the diversity of literary forms within Scripture.

2 Theologically, fundamentalism is narrowly committed to a set of doctrines, some of which evangelicalism regards as at best peripheral (such as those specifically linked with dispensationalism), and at worst utterly irrelevant. There is an overlap of beliefs (such as the authority of Scripture), which can too easily mask profound differences in outlook and temperament.

3 Sociologically, fundamentalism is a reactionary counter-cultural movement, with tight criteria of membership, and is especially associated with a "blue-collar" constituency. Evangelicalism is a cultural movement with increasingly loose criteria of self-definition, which is more associated with a professional or "white-collar" constituency. The element of irrationalism often associated with fundamentalism is lacking in evangelicalism, which has produced significant writings in areas of the philosophy of religion and apologetics.

The break between fundamentalism and neo-evangelicalism in the late 1940s and early 1950s changed both the nature and the public perception of the latter. Billy Graham, perhaps the most publicly visible representative of this new evangelical style, became a well-known figure in English society, and a role model for a younger generation of evangelical ordinands. The public recognition in America of the new importance and public visibility of evangelicalism dates from the early 1970s. The crisis of confidence within American liberal Christianity in the 1960s was widely interpreted to signal the need for the emergence of a new and more publicly credible form of Christian belief. In 1976, America woke up to find itself living in the "Year of the Evangelical," with a born-again Christian (Jimmy Carter) as its President, and an unprecedented media interest in evangelicalism, linked with an increasing involvement on the part of evangelicalism in organized political action.

Yet, despite its massive strength in the churches, evangelicalism has yet to produce theologians of truly international standing. In part, this is due to the characteristic emphasis of the movement: At one level, evangelicalism may be regarded primarily as a Scripture-centered spirituality. For this reason, theology is regarded as a derivative matter, of secondary importance to direct engagement with the biblical text. At the time of writing, evangelicalism has yet to have the impact upon global theology that has been associated, in the past, with movements such as neo-orthodoxy or liberalism. It is highly likely, however, that this situation will alter radically within the next generation.

Key Names, Words, and Phrases

Black theology
dialectical theology
Enlightenment
evangelicalism
feminism
liberalism
liberation theology
modernism
neo-orthodoxy
postliberalism
postmodernism
Quest of the Historical Jesus
Romanticism

Questions for Chapter 4

1   What are the main features of the Enlightenment?

2   Which areas of Christian theology were especially af-
    fected by the ideas of the Enlightenment? Why?

3   Summarize some of the features of the following move-
    ments: liberal Protestantism; neo-orthodoxy; evangelical-
    ism; liberation theology.

4   With which theological movements would you associate
    the following individuals: Karl Barth; Leonardo Boff;
    James Cone; Stanley Hauerwas; Rosemary Radford
    Ruether; F. D. E. Schleiermacher?

5   The list of theologians which follows includes examples
    of the following schools of thought or groups of writers:
    the Cappadocian fathers; humanism; liberal Protestant-
    ism; medieval scholasticism; Reformed theology. Some
    categories include more than one theologian. Assign
    the following theologians to those groups: Anselm of
    Canterbury; Basil of Caesarea; John Calvin; Erasmus of
    Rotterdam; Gregory of Nazianzen; Thomas Aquinas;
    Paul Tillich; William of Ockham.

Part II

Sources and Methods

5

Getting Started: Preliminaries

This chapter will survey some general points which underlie the discipline of Christian theology. Before engaging with the ideas of Christian theology, it is essential to explore the manner in which those ideas are derived. On what are they based? And how do they arise? The present chapter and that which follows aim to consider such matters, before we move on to deal with the substance of Christian theology in the third part of this work.

A Working Definition of Theology

The word "theology" is easily broken down into two Greek words: *theos* (God) and *logos* (word). "Theology" is thus discourse about God, in much the same way as "biology" is discourse about life (Greek: *bios*). If there is only one God, and if that God happens to be the "God of the Christians" (to borrow a phrase from the second-century writer Tertullian), then the nature and scope of theology are relatively well defined: Theology is reflection upon the God whom Christians worship and adore.

Yet Christianity came into existence in a polytheistic world, where belief in the existence of many gods was commonplace. Part of the task of the earliest Christian writers appears to have been to distinguish the Christian god from other gods in the religious marketplace. At some point, it had to be asked which god Christians were talking about, and how this god related to the "God of Abraham, Isaac, and Jacob," who figures so prominently in the Old Testament. The doctrine of the Trinity appears to have been, in part, a response to the pressure to *identify* the god that Christian theologians were speaking about (see pp. 263–4).

As time passed, polytheism began to be regarded as outdated and rather primitive. The assumption that there is only one god, and that this god was identical to the Christian god, became so widespread that, by the early Middle Ages in Europe, it seemed self-evident. Thus Thomas Aquinas, in developing arguments for the existence of God, did not think it worth demonstrating that the god whose existence he had proved was the "god of the Christians": after all, what other god was there? To prove the existence of God was, by definition, to prove the existence of the *Christian* god.

Theology was thus understood as systematic analysis of the nature, purposes, and activity of God. At its heart lay the belief that it was an attempt, however inadequate, to speak about a divine being, distinct from humans. Although "theology" was initially understood to mean "the doctrine of God," the term developed a subtly new meaning in the twelfth and thirteenth centuries, as the University of Paris began to develop. A name had to be found for the systematic study of the Christian faith at university level. Under the influence of Parisian writers such as Peter Abelard and Gilbert de la Porrée, the Latin word *theologia* came to mean "the discipline of sacred learning," embracing the totality of Christian doctrine, not merely the doctrine of God.

A further development is more recent. Since the time of the Enlightenment, partly in response to the development of sociology and anthropology, attention has shifted away from anything that lies beyond human investigation, such as God, to the study of the human phenomenon of religion. "Religious studies" or "the study of religions" is concerned with investigating religious matters – for example, the beliefs or religious practices of Christianity and Buddhism.

With this development has come a shift in the meaning of theology. Not all religions profess faith in one god: for example, Theravada Buddhism and Advaitin Hinduism seem to be radically atheist at heart, while other forms of Hinduism are polytheist. So where theology was once thought of as discourse about God, it now becomes analysis of religious beliefs – even if these beliefs make reference to no god at all, or to a cluster of gods, as in the Hindu pantheon. Even Oxford theologian John Macquarrie's helpful definition of theology is slightly vulnerable at this point: "Theology may be defined as the study which, through participation in and reflection upon a religious faith, seeks to express the content of this faith in the clearest and most coherent language available." Atheist writers, particularly during the heyday of the "death of God" movement in the 1960s, coined the term "atheology" to refer to a system of belief which was based on atheist assumptions. Furthermore, the Greek word *theos* is masculine. As a result, the word "theology" seems to imply reference to a male god. This has caused offense to many feminist writers, some of whom have urged that the term "thealogy" (from the Greek word *thea*, "goddess") should be used instead.

Alternative terms certainly exist. One example may be noted here: the older English word "divinity," which designates both "God" and "a system of thought which attempts to take rational trouble to make sense of God." Nevertheless, "theology" seems to be here to stay, despite the problems which it raises. The phrase "Christian theology" is used throughout this volume in the gender-neutral sense of the systematic study of the fundamental ideas of the Christian faith. "Theology is the *science* of faith. It is the conscious and methodical explanation and explication of the divine revelation received and grasped in faith" (Karl Rahner).

The Architecture of Theology

Etienne Gilson once likened the great systems of scholastic theology to "cathedrals of the mind." It is a powerful image, which suggests permanence, solidity, organization, and structure – qualities which were highly prized by the writers of the period. Perhaps the image of a great medieval cathedral, evoking gasps of admiration from parties of camera-laden tourists, seems out of place today; the most that many university teachers of theology can expect these days, it seems, is a patient tolerance. But the idea of theology possessing a *structure* remains important. For theology is a complex discipline, bringing together a number of related fields in an uneasy alliance. Some of them are noted below.

Biblical Studies

The ultimate source of Christian theology is the Bible, which bears witness to the historical grounding of Christianity in both the history of Israel and the life, death, and resurrection of Jesus Christ. (Note that the word-pairs "Scripture" and "the Bible," and "scriptural" and "biblical," are synonymous for the purposes of theology.) As is often pointed out, Christianity is about belief in a person (Jesus Christ), rather than belief in a text (the Bible). Nevertheless, the two are closely interlocked. Historically, we know virtually nothing about Jesus Christ, except what we learn from the New Testament. In trying to wrestle with the identity and significance of Jesus Christ, Christian theology is thus obliged to wrestle with the text which transmits knowledge of him. This has the result that Christian theology is intimately linked with the science of biblical criticism and interpretation – in other words, with the attempt to appreciate the distinctive literary and historical nature of the biblical texts, and to make sense of them.

The importance of biblical studies to theology is easily demonstrated. The rise of humanist biblical scholarship in the early 1500s demonstrated a series of translation errors in existing Latin versions of the Bible. As a result, pressure grew for the revision of some existing Christian doctrines, which were grounded in biblical passages which were once held to support them, but which now turned out to say something rather different. The sixteenth-century Reformation may plausibly be argued to represent an attempt to bring theology back into line with Scripture, after a period in which it had departed considerably from it.

Systematic Theology

Systematic theology is thus dependent upon biblical scholarship, although the extent of that dependence is controversial. The reader must therefore expect to find reference to modern scholarly debates over the historical and theological role of the Bible in the present volume. To give an example, it is impossible to understand the development of modern Christologies without coming to terms with at least some of the developments in biblical scholarship over the last two centuries. Rudolf Bultmann's kerygmatic approach to theology can be argued to bring together contemporary New Testament scholarship, systematic theology, and philosophical theology (specifically, existentialism). This illustrates a vitally important point: Systematic theology does not operate in a watertight compartment, isolated from other intellectual developments. It responds to developments in other disciplines (especially New Testament scholarship and philosophy).

Historical Theology

Theology has a history. This insight is too easily overlooked, especially by those of a more philosophical inclination. Christian theology can be regarded as an attempt to make sense of the foundational resources of faith in the light of what each day and age regards as first-rate methods. This means that local circumstances have a major impact upon theological formulations. Christian theology regards itself as universal, in that it is concerned with the application of God's saving action to every period in history. Yet it is also characterized by its particularity as an experience of God's saving work in particular cultures, and is shaped by the insights and limitations of persons who were themselves seeking to live the gospel within a particular context. The *universality* of Christianity is thus complemented, rather than contradicted, by its particular application.

Historical theology is the branch of theology which aims to explore the historical situations within which ideas developed or were specifically formulated. It aims to lay bare the connection between context and theology. For example, it demonstrates that it was no accident that the doctrine of justification by faith first became of foundational significance in the late Renaissance. It shows how, for example, the concept of salvation found in Latin American liberation theology is closely linked with the socio-economic situation of the region. It illustrates how secular cultural trends – such as liberalism or conservatism – find their corresponding expression in theology.

It may seem to be little more than stating a self-evident fact to say that Christianity often unconsciously absorbs ideas and values from its cultural backdrop. Yet that observation is enormously important. It points to the fact that there is a *provisional* or *conditional* element to Christian theology, which is not necessitated by or implied in its foundational resources. In other words, certain ideas which have often been regarded as Christian ideas often turn out to be ideas imported from a secular context. A classic example is the notion of the *impassibility of God* – that is, the idea that God cannot suffer. This idea was well established in Greek philosophical circles. Early Christian theologians, anxious to gain respect and credibility in such circles, did not challenge this idea. As a result, it became deeply embedded in the Christian theological tradition.

The study of the history of Christianity provides a powerful corrective to static views of theology. It allows us to see:

1 That certain ideas came into being under very definite circumstances; and that, occasionally, mistakes are made.
2 That theological development is not irreversible; the mistakes of the past may be corrected.

The study of historical theology is thus subversive, as it indicates how easily theologians are led astray by the "self-images of the age" (Alasdair MacIntyre). Nor is this something that is restricted to the past! Too often, modern trends in theology are little more than knee-jerk reactions to short-term cultural trends. The study of history makes us alert both to the mistakes of the past, and to the alarming way in which they are repeated in the present. "History repeats itself. It has to. Nobody listens the first time round" (Woody Allen).

It is for such reasons that the present volume aims to provide its readers with the maximum amount of historical background to contemporary issues. All too often, theological issues are conducted as if the debate began yesterday. An understanding of how we got to be where we are is essential to an informed debate of such issues.

Pastoral Theology

It cannot be emphasized too strongly that Christianity does not occupy its present position as a global faith on account of university faculties of theology or departments of religion. There is a strongly pastoral dimension to Christianity, which is generally inadequately reflected in the academic discussion of theology. Indeed, many scholars have argued that Latin American liberation theology represents an overdue correction of the excessively academic bias of western theology, with a healthy adjustment in the direction of social applicability. Theology is here seen as offering models for transformative action, rather than purely theoretical reflection.

This academic bias is, however, a recent development. Puritanism is an excellent instance of a movement which placed theological integrity alongside pastoral applicability, believing that each was incomplete without the other. The writings of individuals such as Richard Baxter and Jonathan Edwards are saturated with the belief that theology finds its true expression in pastoral care and the nurture of souls. In more recent years, this concern to ensure that theology finds its expression in pastoral care has led to a resurgence of interest in *pastoral theology*. This development is reflected in the present volume, which is written on the basis of the assumption that many of its readers, like its writer, are concerned to bring the full critical resources of Christian theology to the sphere of pastoral ministry.

Philosophical Theology

Theology is an intellectual discipline in its own right, concerned with many of the questions that have intrigued humanity from the dawn of history. Is there a God? What is God like? Why are we here? Questions such as this are asked outside the Christian community, as well as within it. So how do these conversations relate to one another? How do Christian discussions of the nature of God relate to those within the western philosophical tradition? Is there a common ground? Philosophical theology is concerned with what might be called "finding the common ground" between Christian faith and other areas of intellectual activity. Thomas Aquinas' Five Ways (that is, five arguments for the existence of God) are often cited as an example of philosophical theology, in which non-religious arguments or considerations are seen to lead to religious conclusions.

In the course of this work, we shall explore some of the areas in which philosophical considerations have made a considerable impact upon Christian theology. Examples include the patristic analysis of the nature of God, which shows a marked influence from classical Greek philosophy; Thomas Aquinas' arguments for the existence of God, which are influenced by Aristotelian physics; the Christology of nineteenth-century writers such as D. F. Strauss, which draw upon a Hegelian understanding of the historical process; and the existential approach to Christology, developed by Rudolf Bultmann. In each case, a philosophical system is treated as a resource or dialogue partner in the development of a theology. Many theologians have worked on the basis of the assumption that a philosophy provides a secure foundation on which theology may build.

Nevertheless, it must be noted that there exists a trend within Christian theology which has been severely critical of attempts to use secular philosophies in matters of theology. Tertullian raised the question in the second century: "What has Athens to do with Jerusalem? Or the Academy with the church?" More recently, the same critical reaction may be seen in the writings of Karl Barth (see pp. 98–100), who argued that the use of philosophy in this way ultimately made God's self-revelation dependent upon a particular philosophy, and compromised the freedom of God.

The Question of Prolegomena

Anyone beginning the study of an unfamiliar subject faces the same problem: Where should you begin? There seem to be so many ways of approaching subjects such as philosophy, the natural sciences, and theology that some kind of confusion over this question is inevitable. In theology, the debate over where theology should start has become known as the "question of prolegomena." The Greek term *prolegomena* could be translated as "forewords" – in other words, things that need to be said before beginning the study of theology itself.

The question of what starting point should be adopted is of importance not merely to theology, but also to a number of related subjects. An obvious example is apologetics, the discipline which aims to make Christianity credible to those outside the faith. For example, the second-century Apologists (writers such as Justin Martyr, whose concern was to gain a serious hearing for Christianity amongst its educated opponents) took considerable trouble to find experiences and beliefs which Christians shared with their pagan counterparts. By beginning from this point, they believed that they could show how Christianity built upon and complemented these shared experiences and ideas.

Since the time of the Enlightenment, the question of prolegomena has become of especial importance. Before theology can explore the content of the Christian faith, it has to be shown how anyone can know anything about God in the first place. Talking about *how* we can know anything about God comes to be at least as important as discussing *what* we know about God. Increasing secularization in Europe and North America meant that theologians could no longer assume that their audiences would have any sympathy with the Christian faith. Accordingly, many theologians regarded it as vitally important to find some common starting point, which would allow those outside the faith to have access to its insights.

Amongst these approaches, which seek to anchor Christian theology in the basic experiences of human existence, the following are especially important.

F. D. E. Schleiermacher argued that a common feature of human experience was "the feeling of absolute dependence." Christian theology expressed and interpreted this basic human emotion as "a feeling of dependence *upon God*," and related it to the Christian doctrines of sin and redemption.

Paul Tillich developed a "method of correlation" (see pp. 94–5), based on his belief that human beings asked certain "ultimate questions" about their existence. "In using the method of correlation, systematic theology proceeds in the following way: It makes an analysis of the human situation out of which the existential questions arise, and it demonstrates that the symbols used in the Christian message are the answers to these questions."

Karl Rahner drew attention to the importance of the basic human urge to transcend the limitations of human nature. Human beings are aware of a sense of being made for more than they now are, or more than they can ever hope to achieve by their own abilities. The Christian revelation supplies this "more," to which human experience points.

Nevertheless, such approaches (especially as developed by Schleiermacher and his immediate followers) have provoked hostile reactions. The most significant of these is to be found in the neo-orthodox school (see pp. 98–100), which protested against what it believed to be a reduction of theology to human needs, or an imprisonment of theology within the confines of some philosophy of human existence.

Barth declared that Christian theology was not in any sense dependent upon human philosophy, but was autonomous and self-supporting. God was perfectly capable of revealing himself without any human assistance. The word "prolegomena" was not to be understood as "things which need to be said before theology is possible." Rather, it was to be understood as "the things that must be said first in theology" – in other words, the doctrine of the Word of God.

There has thus been little agreement within Christian theology on this point. There has been a temptation to assume that philosophy is somehow capable of establishing a secure foundation upon which theology can build – particular favorites being Kant, Hegel, and Whitehead. Inevitably, this means that the credibility of such theologies is linked with the intellectual fortunes of the philosophies to which they are hitched.

Questions of method have dominated modern theology, not least on account of the challenge of the Enlightenment to establish reliable foundations for knowledge. However, as Jeffrey Stout of Princeton University observed: "Preoccupation with method is like clearing your throat: it can go on for only so long before you lose your audience." There has thus been a reaction against the contemporary preoccupation with method, especially within postliberalism (see pp. 109–10). Writers such as Hans Frei, George Lindbeck, and Ronald Thiemann have argued that Christian faith is like a language: Either you speak it, or you don't. Christianity is viewed as one option in a pluralist context, with no need to appeal to universal criteria or principles of argument. To its opponents, this represents little more than a degeneration into fideism – that is, a system which is justified by its own internal standards, which need not be shared or approved by anyone else.

The Nature of Faith

Since the time of the Enlightenment, the word "faith" has come to mean something like "a lower form of knowledge." Faith is understood to mean "partial knowledge," characterized by a degree of uncertainty, and based upon either a lack of evidence, or evidence which is inadequate to convince fully. Kant argued that faith (*Glaube*) is basically a belief which is held on grounds that are subjectively adequate, but objectively inadequate. Faith is thus seen as a firm commitment to a belief which is not adequately justified on the basis of the evidence available.

Although this understanding of faith may be adequate for many purposes, it is seriously inadequate for the purposes of Christian theology. Faith, as understood within the Christian tradition, has both epistemological and soteriological aspects; that is, it concerns how things (especially things about God) may be known, and also how salvation may be grasped. For example, Luther's doctrine of justification by faith alone cannot be understood if faith is understood to mean "a belief which goes beyond the evidence available."

To explore this point further, we may consider these two aspects of faith in more detail. The cognitive or epistemological aspects of faith are best discussed with reference to the works of Thomas Aquinas, while the soteriological aspects of faith are best brought out in the early writings of Martin Luther.

Faith and Knowledge

Aquinas adopts a strongly intellectualist approach to faith, treating it as something which is mid-way between knowledge (*scientia*) and opinion. For Aquinas, *scientia* has the sense of "something which is self-evidently true," or "something which can be demonstrated to be derived from something which is self-evidently true." In the case of *scientia*, truth compels assent on the part of the human intellect either because it is self-evidently correct, or because it is supported by such powerfully persuasive logical arguments that no rational mind could fail to be convinced. In the case of faith, however, the evidence is not sufficient to compel the human intellect to accept it.

Faith accepts as true the articles of the Christian faith, as they are summarized, for example, in the creeds. The object of faith is propositions about God, or about the Christian faith in general. To "have faith" is to accept these articles of faith as true, even though they cannot be demonstrated to be so beyond doubt, on the basis of the evidence available.

Aquinas insists upon the rationality of the Christian faith. In other words, he stresses that the contents of the Christian faith can be shown to be consistent with human reason. His arguments for the existence of God (the "Five Ways") are basically an attempt to show that the Christian belief in God is consistent with rational reflection on the world of human experience. Nevertheless, Aquinas is also concerned to insist that Christian faith and theology are ultimately a response to something which lies beyond human reason – divine revelation. We shall consider this point further elsewhere (see pp. 182–3).

The commonsense understanding of faith, as a lower form of knowledge, thus seems to be well grounded in the writings of Thomas Aquinas. It has had a profound impact upon the philosophy of religion, as well as upon popular understandings of the nature of Christian faith. For example, the popular understanding of the first statement of the creed, "I believe in God," is little more than "I believe that there is a god." Yet with the sixteenth-century Reformation, there came a sustained attempt to rediscover aspects of the biblical understanding of the nature of faith, which had become obscured by the scholastic concern for right knowledge of God. We can explore this by considering Luther's emphasis upon the soteriological aspects of faith.

Faith and Salvation

The most significant contribution to the classic evangelical understanding of faith was unquestionably made by Martin Luther. Luther's doctrine of justification by faith alone made faith, rightly understood, the cornerstone of his spirituality and theology. Luther's fundamental point is that "the Fall" (Genesis 1–3) is first and foremost a fall from faith. Faith is the right relationship with God (cf. Genesis 15: 6). To have faith is to live as God intends us to live.

Luther's notion of faith has three components.

1 Faith has a personal, rather than a purely historical, reference.
2 Faith concerns trust in the promises of God.
3 Faith unites the believer to Christ.

We shall consider each of these points individually.

1 *Faith is not simply historical knowledge* Luther argues that a faith which is content to believe in the historical reliability of the gospels is not a saving faith. Sinners are perfectly capable of trusting in the historical details of the gospels; but these facts of themselves are not adequate for true Christian faith. Saving faith concerns believing and trusting that Christ was born for us personally, and has accomplished for us the work of salvation.

2 *Faith includes an element of trust* (fiducia) The notion of trust is prominent in the Reformation conception of faith, as a nautical analogy used by Luther indicates: "Everything depends upon faith. The person who does not have faith is like someone who has to cross the sea, but is so frightened that he does not trust the ship. And so he stays where he is, and is never saved, because he will not get on board and cross over." Faith is not merely believing that something is true; it is being prepared to act upon that belief, and relying upon it. To use Luther's analogy: Faith is not simply about believing that a ship exists – it is about stepping into it, and entrusting ourselves to it.

But what are we being asked to trust? Are we being asked simply to have faith in faith? The question could perhaps be phrased more accurately: Who are we being asked to trust? For Luther, the answer was unequivocal: Faith is about being prepared to put one's trust in the promises of God, and the integrity and faithfulness of the God who made those promises. Faith is only as strong as the one in whom we believe and trust. The efficacy of faith does not rest upon the intensity with which we believe, but in the reliability of the one in whom we believe. It is not the greatness of our faith, but the greatness of God, which counts. As Luther put it:

> Even if my faith is weak, I still have exactly the same treasure and the same Christ as others. There is no difference. . . . It is like two people, each of whom owns a hundred guldens. One may carry them around in a paper sack, the other in an iron chest. But despite these differences, they both own the same treasure. Thus the Christ whom you and I own is one and the same, irrespective of the strength or weakness of your faith or mine.

The content of faith matters at least as much as, and probably far more than, its intensity. It is pointless to trust passionately in someone who is not worthy of trust; even a modicum of faith in someone who is totally reliable is vastly to be preferred. Trust is not, however, an occasional attitude. For Luther, it is an undeviating trusting outlook upon life, a constant stance of conviction of the trustworthiness of the promises of God.

3 *Faith unites the believer to Christ*   Luther states this principle clearly in his 1520 work, *The Liberty of a Christian*.

> Faith unites the soul with Christ as a bride is united with her bridegroom. As Paul teaches us, Christ and the soul become one flesh by this mystery (Ephesians 5: 31–2). And if they are one flesh, and if the marriage is for real – indeed, it is the most perfect of all marriages, and human marriages are poor examples of this one true marriage – then it follows that everything that they have is held in common, whether good or evil. So the believer can boast of and glory in whatever Christ possesses, as though it were his or her own; and whatever the believer has, Christ claims as his own. Let us see how this works out, and see how it benefits us. Christ is full of grace, life, and salvation. The human soul is full of

sin, death, and damnation. Now let faith come between them. Sin, death, and damnation will be Christ's. And grace, life, and salvation will be the believer's.

Faith, then, is not assent to an abstract set of doctrines. Rather, it is a "wedding ring", pointing to mutual commitment and union between Christ and the believer. It is the response of the whole person of the believer to God, which leads in turn to the real and personal presence of Christ in the believer. Faith makes both Christ and his benefits – such as forgiveness, justification, and hope – available to the believer.

Aquinas and Luther Compared

On the basis of this brief discussion, it will be clear that Aquinas and Luther adopt very different understandings of faith. The main points of difference may be summarized as follows.

1 Aquinas tends to adopt a philosophical approach to faith, where Luther's approach is more explicitly religious.
2 Aquinas tends to regard faith as relating to propositions about God; Luther understands it to relate to the promises of God.
3 Aquinas relates faith to evidence; Luther relates it to the personal trustworthiness of God.
4 Aquinas's notion of faith is theological, in that it relates to God himself; Luther's is more Christological, for two reasons. First, because the object of faith is to unite the believer to Christ; second, because Christ is the historical manifestation or demonstration of the faithfulness of God to the divine promises.

Can God's Existence be Proved?

The relation of faith and reason is often discussed in terms of whether God's existence can be proved, and whether such proof would be adequate to bring a non-believer to faith. Although some writers have suggested that this is the case, the general consensus within Christian theology seems to be that, although reason does not bring individuals to faith in God, believers are nonetheless able to give rational reasons for their faith in God.

Thomas Aquinas' contribution to this discussion is of major importance. Although some philosophers suggest that Aquinas was out to prove the existence of God, this is clearly not the case. In front of me, I have a copy of one of the standard editions of Aquinas' *Summa Theologiae* (see p. 44). It is more than four thousand pages long. His discussion of "whether God exists" occupies just over two pages. The phrase "proofs of God's existence" is not found in Aquinas' own discussion. Later writers have imposed it upon his thought. Yet it is perfectly clear that Aquinas does not believe in God on account of any of the considerations he mentions so briefly; his primary reason for believing in the existence of God is God's self-revelation. Aquinas expects his readers to share his faith in God, not to have to prove it to them first. The Austrian philosopher Ludwig Wittgenstein made this point clearly in his *Culture and Value*:

> A proof of God's existence ought really to be something by means of which one could convince oneself that God exists. But I think that what *believers* who have furnished such proofs have wanted to do is to give their "belief" an intellectual analysis and foundation, although they themselves would never have come to believe as a result of such proofs.

The classic statement of such questions, to which all modern discussion makes reference, is to be found in the writings of Anselm of Canterbury and Thomas Aquinas. The former developed what has come to be known as "the ontological argument" for the existence of God. The latter developed the "Five Ways," arguing from the effects of nature to their cause in God its creator. We shall consider these two categories of arguments individually.

The Ontological Argument

The "ontological argment" is first set out in Anselm's *Proslogion*, a work which dates from 1079. (The term "ontological" refers to the branch of philosophy which deals with the notion of "being.") Anselm himself does not refer to his discussion as an "ontological" argument. When his contemporaries wished to refer to his approach, they dubbed it "Anselm's argument" (*ratio Anselmi*). In fact, there is really no ontological character to the argument, as Anselm presents it; and Anselm never presents his reflections as an "argument" for the existence of God. The *Proslogion* is a work of meditation, not of logical argument. In the course of this work, Anselm reflects on how self-evident the idea of God has become to him, and what the implications of this might be.

Anselm begins by offering a crucially important definition of God. God is "that than which nothing greater can be conceived." This definition, which seems self-evidently true to Anselm (given his Christian understanding of what God is like) has important implications. Anselm expresses his point in a rather contorted manner, which requires a little explanation:

> It is possible to conceive of a being which cannot be conceived not to exist. Now this is greater than one which can be conceived not to exist. So if that than which nothing greater can be conceived, can be conceived not to exist, it is not that than which nothing greater can be conceived. But this is an irreconcilable contradiction. So there really is a being than which nothing greater can be conceived to exist, that it cannot be conceived not to exist; and you are that being, O Lord our God. . . . For if a mind could conceive of a being better than you, the creature would rise above the creator, and this would be absurd.

This is not the easiest of arguments to follow, and it might be helpful if we simplify the argument, to bring out the central point at issue.

God is defined as "that than which nothing greater can be conceived." Now the *idea* of such a being is one thing; the *reality* is another. Thinking of a hundred dollar bill is quite different from having a hundred dollar bill in your hands – and much less satisfying, as well. Anselm's point is this: The *idea* of something is inferior to the *reality*. So the idea of God as "that than which nothing greater can be conceived" contains a contradiction – because the *reality* of God would be superior to this *idea*. In other words, if this definition of God is correct, and exists in the human mind, then the corresponding reality must also exist.

There is an obvious logical weakness in this "argument" (although it must be stressed that Anselm does not really regard it as an argument in the first place). It is brought out clearly by Anselm's critic Gaunilo, who made a response known as *A Reply on Behalf of the Fool* (the reference being to Psalm 14: 1, cited by Anselm, "The fool says in his heart that there is no God"). Imagine, he suggests, an island, so lovely that a more perfect island cannot be conceived. By the same argument, Gaunilo suggested, that island must exist, in that the *reality* of the island is necessarily more perfect than the mere *idea*. In much the same way, we might argue that the idea of a hundred dollar bill seems, according to Anselm, to imply that we have such a bill in our hands.

Anselm, however, is not so easily dismissed. Part of his argument is that it is an essential part of the definition that God is "that than which nothing greater can be conceived." God belongs in a totally different category to islands or hundred dollar bills. It is part of the nature of God to transcend everything else. Once the believer has come to understand what the word "God" means, then God really does exist for him or her. This is the intention of Anselm's meditation: to reflect on how the Christian understanding of the nature of God reinforces belief in God's reality. The "argument" does not really have force outside this context of faith, and Anselm never intended it to be used in this general philosophical manner.

Thomas Aquinas' Five Ways

Aquinas believed that it was entirely proper to identify pointers toward the existence of God, drawn from general human experience of the world. So what kind of pointers does Aquinas identify? The basic line of thought guiding Aquinas is that the world mirrors God, as its creator – an idea which is given more formal expression in his doctrine of the "analogy of being" (see pp. 135–6). Just as an artist might sign a painting to identify it as his or her handiwork, so God has stamped a divine "signature" upon the creation. What we observe in the world – for example, its signs of ordering – can be explained on the basis of the existence of God as its creator. God is both its first cause and its designer. God both brought the world into existence, and impressed the divine image and likeness upon it.

So where might we look in creation to find evidence for the existence of God? Aquinas argues that the ordering of the world is the most convincing evidence of God's existence and wisdom. This basic assumption underlies each of the "Five Ways," although it is of particular importance in the case of the argument often referred to as the "argument from design" or the "teleological argument." We shall consider each of these "ways" individually.

The first way begins from the observation that things in the world are in motion or change. The world is not static, but is dynamic. Examples of this are easy to list. Rain falls from the sky. Stones roll down valleys. The earth revolves around the sun (a fact, incidentally, unknown to Aquinas). But how did nature come to be in motion? Why isn't it static?

Aquinas argues that everything which moves is moved by something else. For every motion, there is a cause. Things don't just move – they are moved. Now, each cause of motion must itself have a cause. And *that* cause must have a cause as well. And so Aquinas argues that there is a whole series of causes of motion lying behind the world as we know it. Now unless there is an infinite number of these causes, Aquinas argues, there must be a single cause right at the origin of the series. From this original cause of motion, all other motion is ultimately derived. This is the origin of the great chain of causality which we see reflected in the way the world behaves. From the fact that things are in motion, Aquinas thus argues for the existence of a single original cause of all this motion – and this, he concludes, is none other than God.

The second way begins from the idea of causation. In other words, Aquinas notes the existence of causes and effects in the world. One event (the effect) is explained by the influence of another (the cause). The idea of motion, which we looked at briefly above, is a good example of this cause-and-effect sequence. Using a line of reasoning similar to that used above, Aquinas thus argues that all effects may be traced back to a single original cause – which is God.

The third way concerns the existence of contingent beings. In other words, the world contains beings (such as human beings) that are not there as a matter of necessity. Aquinas contrasts this type of being with a necessary being (one that is there as a matter of necessity). Whilst God is a necessary being, Aquinas argues that humans are contingent beings. The fact that we *are* here needs explanation. Why are we here? What happened to bring us into existence?

Aquinas argues that a being comes into existence because something which already exists brought it into being. In other words, our existence is caused by another being. We are the effects of a series of causation. Tracing this series back to its origin, Aquinas declares that this original cause of being can only be someone whose existence is necessary – in other words, God.

The fourth way begins from human values, such as truth, goodness, and nobility. Where do these values come from? What causes them? Aquinas argues that there must be something which is in itself true, good, and noble, and that this brings into being our ideas of truth, goodness, and nobility. The origin of these ideas, Aquinas suggests, is God, who is their original cause.

The fifth and final way is the "teleological argument" itself. Aquinas notes that the world shows obvious traces of intelligent design. Natural processes and objects seem to be adapted with certain definite objectives in mind. They seem to have a purpose. They seem to have been designed. But things don't design themselves: They are caused and designed by someone or something else. Arguing from this observation, Aquinas concludes that the source of this natural ordering must be conceded to be God.

It will be obvious that most of Aquinas' arguments are rather similar. Each depends on tracing a causal sequence back to its single origin, and identifying this with God. A number of criticisms of the

"Five Ways" were made by Aquinas' critics during the Middle Ages, such as Duns Scotus and William of Ockham. The following are especially important.

1　Why is the idea of an infinite regression of causes impossible? For example, the argument from motion only really works if it can be shown that the sequence of cause and effect stops somewhere. There has to be, according to Aquinas, a Prime Unmoved Mover. But he fails to demonstrate this point.

2　Why do these arguments lead to belief in only *one* God? The argument from motion, for example, could lead to belief in a number of Prime Unmoved Movers. There seems to be no reason for insisting that there can only be *one* such cause.

3　These arguments do not demonstrate that God continues to exist. Having caused things to happen, God might cease to exist. The continuing existence of events does not necessarily imply the continuing existence of their originator. Aquinas' arguments, Ockham suggests, might lead to a belief that God existed once upon a time – but not necessarily now. Ockham developed a somewhat complex argument, based on the idea of God continuing to sustain the universe, which attempts to get round this difficulty.

In the end, Aquinas' arguments only go some way toward suggesting that it is reasonable to believe in a creator of the world, or an intelligent being who is able to cause effects in the world. Nevertheless, a leap of faith is still required. It still remains to be shown that this creator or intelligent being *is* the God whom Christians. know, worship, and adore. Aquinas' arguments could lead to faith in the existence of a god rather like that favored by the Greek philosopher Aristotle – an Unmoved Mover, who is distant from and uninvolved in the affairs of the world.

The Nature of Theological Language

Theology is "talk about God." But how can God ever be described or discussed using human language? Wittgenstein made this point forcefully: If human words are incapable of describing the distinctive aroma of coffee, how can they cope with something as subtle as God?

Analogy

Perhaps the most basic idea which underlies the theological reply to such questions is usually referred to as "the principle of analogy." The fact that God created the world points to a fundamental "analogy of being" (*analogia entis*) between God and the world. There is a continuity between God and the world on account of the expression of the being of God in the being of the world. For this reason, it is legitimate to use entities within the created order as analogies for God. In doing this, theology does not reduce God to the level of a created object or being; it merely affirms that there is a likeness or correspondence between God and that being, which allows the latter to act as a signpost to God. A created entity can be *like* God, without being *identical to* God.

Consider the statement "God is our Father." Aquinas argues that this should be understood to mean that God is *like* a human father. In other words, God is analogous to a father. In some ways God is like a human father, and in others not. There are genuine points of similarity. God cares for us, as human fathers care for their children (note Matthew 7: 9–11). God is the ultimate source of our existence, just as our fathers brought us into being. God exercises authority over us, as do human fathers. Equally, there are genuine points of dissimilarity. God is not a human being, for example. Nor does the necessity of a human mother point to the need for a divine mother.

The point that Aquinas is trying to make is clear. Divine self-revelation makes use of images and ideas which tie in with our world of everyday existence – yet which do not reduce God to that everyday world. To say that "God is our father" is not to say that God is just yet another human father. Nor, as we shall later explore, does it mean that God is to be thought of as *male* (see pp. 205–7). Rather, it is to say that thinking about human fathers helps us think about God. They are analogies. Like all analogies, they break down at points. However, they are still extremely useful and vivid ways of thinking about God, which allow us to use the vocabulary and images of our own world to describe something which ultimately lies beyond it.

In saying that "God is love," we are referring to our own capacity to love, in order to try and imagine this love in all its full perfection in God. We are not reducing the "love of God" to the level of human love. Rather, it is being suggested that human loves provides a pointer toward the love of God, which, to some limited extent, it is capable of mirroring.

But, as we all know from experience, analogies break down. There comes a point when they cannot be pressed further. How do we know when they break down? To illustrate this problem, we may consider an example from another area of theology, before moving on to consider its solution. The New Testament talks about Jesus giving his life as a "ransom" for sinners (Mark 10: 45; 1 Timothy 2: 6). What does this analogy mean? The everyday use of the word "ransom" suggests three ideas:

1 *Liberation*   A ransom is something which achieves freedom for a person who is held in captivity. When someone is kidnapped, and a ransom demanded, the payment of that ransom leads to liberation.
2 *Payment*   A ransom is a sum of money which is paid in order to achieve an individual's liberation.
3 *Someone to whom the ransom is paid*   A ransom is usually paid to an individual's captor, or an intermediary.

These three ideas thus seem to be implied by speaking of Jesus' death as a "ransom" for sinners. But are they *all* present in Scripture? There is no doubt whatsoever that the New Testament proclaims that we have been liberated from captivity through the death and resurrection of Jesus. We have been set free from captivity to sin and the fear of death (Romans 8: 21; Hebrews 2: 15). It is also clear that the New Testament understands the death of Jesus as the price which had to be paid to achieve our liberation (1 Corinthians 6: 20; 7: 23). Our liberation is a costly and a precious matter. In these two respects, the scriptural use of "redemption" corresponds to the everyday use of the word. But what of the third aspect?

There is not a hint in the New Testament that Jesus' death was the price paid to someone (such as the devil) to achieve our liberation. Some of the writers of the first four centuries, however, assumed that they could press this analogy to its limits, and declared that God had delivered us from the power of the devil by offering Jesus as the price of our liberation (see pp. 345–8). This idea surfaces repeatedly in patristic discussions of the meaning of the death of Christ. Yet it needs to be asked whether it rests upon pressing an analogy beyond its acceptable limits.

So how do we know whether an analogy has been pressed too far? How can the limits of such analogs be tested? Such questions have been debated throughout Christian history. An important twentieth-century discussion of this point may be found in British philosopher of religion Ian T. Ramsey's *Christian Discourse: Some Logical Explorations* (1965), which puts forward the idea that models or analogies are not freestanding, but interact with and qualify each other.

Ramsey argues that Scripture does not give us one single analogy (or "model") for God or for salvation, but uses a range of analogies. Each of these analogies or models illuminates certain aspects of our understanding of God, or the nature of salvation. However, these analogies also interact with each other. They modify each other. They help us understand the limits of other analogies. No analogy or parable is exhaustive in itself; taken together, however, the range of analogies and parables builds up to give a comprehensive and consistent understanding of God and salvation.

An example of how images interact may make this point clearer. Take the analogies of king, father, and shepherd. Each of these three analogies conveys the idea of authority, suggesting that this is of fundamental importance to our understanding of God. Kings, however, often behave in arbitrary ways, and not always in the best interests of their subjects. The analogy of God as a king might thus be misunderstood to suggest that God is some sort of tyrant. However, the tender compassion of a father toward his children commended by Scripture (Psalms 103: 13–18), and the total dedication of a good shepherd to the welfare of his flock (John 10: 11), show that this is not the intended meaning. Authority is to be exercised tenderly and wisely.

Aquinas' doctrine of analogy, then, is of fundamental importance to the way we think about God. It illuminates the manner in which God reveals himself to us through scriptural images and analogies, allowing us to understand how God can be *above* our world, and yet simultaneously be revealed *in and through* that world. God is not an object or a person in space and time; nevertheless, such persons and objects can help us deepen our appreciation of God's character and nature. God, who is infinite, may be revealed in and through human words and finite images.

Metaphor

The precise nature of the differences between analogies and metaphors remains disputed. Aristotle defined a metaphor as involving "the transferred use of a term that properly belongs to something else." So broad is this definition that it embraces just about every figure of speech, including analogy. In modern use, the word "metaphor" would be taken to mean something rather different, with the following being a useful definition. A metaphor is a way of speaking about one thing in terms which are suggestive of another. It is, to use Nelson Goodman's famous phrase, "a matter of teaching an old word new tricks." This definition clearly includes analogy; so what is the difference between them?

Once more, it is necessary to note that there is no general agreement on this matter. Perhaps a working solution to the problem could be stated as follows: Analogies seem to be *appropriate*, where metaphors involve a sense of surprise or initial incredulity. For example, consider the two statements which follow:

1 God is wise.
2 God is a lion.

In the first case, it is being affirmed that there is an analogical connection between the nature of God and the human notion of "wisdom." It is being suggested that, at both the linguistic and the ontological level, there is a direct parallel between human and divine notions of wisdom. Human wisdom serves as a analogy of divine wisdom. The comparison does not cause us any surprise.

In the second case, the comparison can cause a slight degree of consternation. It does not seem to be appropriate to compare God to a lion. However many similarities there may be between God and a lion, there are obviously many differences. For some modern writers, a metaphor mingles similarity and dissimilarity, stressing that there are both parallels and divergences between the two objects being compared.

With these points in mind, we may explore three features of metaphors which have attracted theological attention in recent decades.

1 Metaphors imply both *similarity* and *dissimilarity* between the two things being compared. It is perhaps for this reason that some recent writings – particularly those of Sallie McFague – have stressed the metaphorical, rather than the analogical, nature of theological language. As McFague puts it,

> A metaphor is seeing one thing *as* something else, pretending "this" is "that" because we do not know how to think or talk about "this", so we use "that" as a way of saying something about it. Thinking metaphorically means spotting a thread of similarity between two dissimilar objects, events, or whatever, and using the better-known as a way of speaking about the lesser-known.

To speak of "God as father" should be seen as a metaphor, rather than an analogy, implying significant differences between God and a father, rather than (as in the case of a analogy) a direct line of similarities.

2 Metaphors cannot be reduced to definitive statements. Perhaps the most attractive feature of metaphors for Christian theology is their *open-ended character.* Although some literary critics have suggested that metaphors can be reduced to a set of equivalent literal expressions, others have insisted that no limits can be set to the extent of the comparison. Thus the metaphor "God as father" cannot be reduced to a set of precise statements about God, valid for every place and every time. It is meant to be suggestive, allowing future readers and interpreters to find new meanings within it. A metaphor is not simply an elegant description or memorable phrasing of something that we already know. It is an invitation to discover further levels of meaning, which others may have overlooked or forgotten.

3 Metaphors often have strongly emotional overtones. Theological metaphors are able to express the emotional dimensions of Christian faith in a way which makes them appropriate to worship. For example, the metaphor of "God as light" has enormously powerful overtones, including those of illumination, purity, and glorification. Ian G. Barbour summarizes this aspect of metaphorical language as follows:

> Where poetic metaphors are used only momentarily, in one context, for the sake of an immediate expression or insight, *religious symbols* become part of the language of a religious community in its scripture and liturgy and in its continuing life and thought. Religious symbols are expressive of human emotions and feelings, and are powerful in calling forth response and commitment.

Accommodation

A third approach declines to speculate on the precise nature of theological language, and instead focuses on the general principles which seem to underlie the nature of theological language. The basic ideas of the approach we propose to consider derive from classical Greek rhetorical theory, taken up with enthusiasm by writers such as Origen. Origen suggests that God faced much the same problems in addressing sinful humanity as those experienced by a human father in trying to communicate to small children. "God condescends and comes down to us, accommodating to our weakness, like a schoolmaster talking a 'little language' to his children, or like a father caring for his own children and adopting their ways." When you are talking to small children, you have to appreciate that they have limited intellectual resources at their disposal. If you treat them as adults, and use words and ideas that are beyond their understanding and experience, you will fail to communicate with them. You have to adapt yourself to their capacities.

This approach was taken up in the sixteenth century by John Calvin, who developed the theory usually referred to by the term "accommodation." The word "accommodation" here means "adjusting or adapting to meet the needs of the situation and the human ability to comprehend it." In revelation, Calvin argues, God accommodates to the capacities of the human mind and heart. God paints a self-portrait which we are capable of understanding. The analogy which lies behind Calvin's thinking at this point is that of a human orator. Good speakers know the limitations of their audience, and adjust the way they speak accordingly. The gulf between the speaker and the hearer must be bridged if communication is to take place. God has to come down to our level in the process of revelation. Just as a human mother stoops down to reach her child, so God stoops down to come to our level.

An example of this accommodation is provided by the scriptural portraits of God. God is often, Calvin points out, represented as possessing a mouth, eyes, hands, and feet. That might seem to suggest that God is a human being. It might seem to imply that somehow the eternal and spiritual God has been reduced to a physical human being. (The point at issue is often referred to as "anthropomorphism" – in other words, God being portrayed in human form.) Calvin argues that God is obliged to configure the divine self-revelation in this pictorial manner on account of our weak intellects. Images of God which represent God as having a mouth or hands are divine "baby-talk," a way in which God comes down to our level and uses images which we can handle. More sophisticated ways of speaking about God are certainly proper – but we might not be able to understand them.

Calvin's concern was not to generalize concerning the nature of theological language – whether it is analogical or metaphorical, or any of the other figures of speech with which he was familiar. His basic concern was to stress that theological language cannot necessarily be taken at face value. Questions have to be asked concerning what is being said, and the way in which it is being said. A case study, of obvious scientific relevance, will make this point clear.

In the case of the biblical story of the creation (Genesis 1), Calvin argues that it is accommodated to the abilities and horizons of a relatively simple and unsophisticated people; it is not intended to be taken as a *literal* representation of reality. The author of Genesis, he declares, "was ordained to be a teacher of the unlearned and primitive, as well as the learned; and so could not achieve his goal without descending to such crude means of instruction." The phrase "six days of creation" does not designate six periods of twenty-four hours, but is simply an accommodation to human ways of thinking to designate an extended period of time. Similarly, the "water above the firmament" is simply an accommodated way of speaking about clouds.

The biblical accounts of creation were thus not to be taken literally.

They are "accommodated." The theologian has to decide on the nature and extent of that accommodation. It is this principle which underlies Calvin's response to a major controversy in which the status of theological language proved to be of decisive importance – the Copernican theory of the solar system. So important is this case study that it deserves to be considered in some detail, to illustrate the application of the ideas we have just been dealing with.

A Case Study: The Copernican Debate

One of the most significant confrontations between theology and the natural sciences took place during the sixteenth century, with the publication of Copernicus' heliocentric theory of the solar system. Up to that point, the generally accepted understanding was geocentric: The sun and every other heavenly body revolved around the earth. This theory seemed to be supported by the Bible, which referred, for example, to the motion of the sun.

In his *De revolutionibus orbium coelestium*, "On the revolutions of the heavenly bodies" (1543), Copernicus (1473–1543) argued that the earth revolved around the sun. With the publication of Copernicus' theory, a radical challenge was posed to the received view – and also to the accepted way of interpreting the Bible. As the scientific merits of Copernicus' theory became apparent, a new threat seemed to be posed to the authority and reliability of the Bible. How could Copernicus' heliocentric theory be reconciled with the Bible's apparently geocentric outlook?

There are excellent reasons for suggesting that Calvin's theological method may have been of decisive importance, both in gaining a sympathetic hearing for Copernicus' theory of the solar system, and in preserving the credibility of the Bible. At first sight, this might seem improbable. For the past hundred years, the attitude of reformers such as Calvin to Copernicus' heliocentric theory of the solar system has been the subject of ridicule. In his vigorously polemical *History of the Warfare of Science with Theology* (1896), Andrew Dickson White wrote:

> Calvin took the lead, in his *Commentary on Genesis*, by condemning all who asserted that the earth is not at the centre of the universe. He clinched the matter by the usual reference to the first verse of the ninety-third Psalm, and asked, "Who will venture to place the authority of Copernicus above that of the Holy Spirit?"

This assertion is repeated by writer after writer on the theme of "religion and science," including Bertrand Russell, in his *History of*

Western Philosophy. Yet nobody seems to have bothered to check their sources. For Calvin wrote no such words and expressed no such sentiments in any of his known writings. The reality is much more interesting.

In fact, Calvin may be regarded as making two major contributions to the appreciation and development of the natural sciences. First, he positively encouraged the scientific study of nature; second, he eliminated a major obstacle to the development of that study. His first contribution is specifically linked with his stress upon the orderliness of creation; both the physical world and the human body testify to the wisdom and character of God. Calvin thus commends the study of both astronomy and medicine. They are able to probe more deeply than theology into the natural world, and thus uncover further evidence of the orderliness of the creation and the wisdom of its creator.

Calvin thus gave a new religious motivation to the scientific investigation of nature, which came to be seen as a means of discerning the wise hand of God in creation. The *Belgic Confession* (1561), a Calvinist statement of faith which exercised particular influence in the Low Countries (an area which would become particularly noted for its botanists and physicists), declared that nature is "before our eyes as a most beautiful book in which all created things, whether great or small, are as letters showing the invisible things of God to us." God can thus be discerned through the detailed study of the creation.

These ideas were taken up with enthusiasm within the Royal Society, the most significant organization devoted to the advancement of scientific research and learning in England. Many of its early members were admirers of Calvin, familiar with his writings and their potential relevance to their fields of study. Thus Richard Bentley (1662–1742) delivered a series of lectures in 1692, based on Newton's *Principia Mathematica* (1687), in which the regularity of the universe, as established by Newton, is interpreted as evidence of design. There are unambiguous hints here of Calvin's reference to the universe as a "theater of the glory of God," in which humans are an appreciative audience. The detailed study of the creation leads to an increased awareness of the wisdom of its creator.

It is Calvin's second major contribution which is of especial interest to us here. Calvin is widely regarded as having eliminated a significant obstacle to the development of the natural sciences: biblical literalism, which remains influential within fundamentalist circles today. Calvin insisted that not all biblical statements concerning God or the world were to be taken literally, for they were accommodated to the abilities of their audiences. Scripture, in apparently speaking of the sun rotating around the earth, was simply accommodating itself to the worldview of its audience, not making scientific statements about the universe. Calvin's discussion of the relationship between scientific findings and the statements of the Bible is generally regarded as one of his most valuable contributions to Christian thought. The impact of these ideas upon scientific theorizing, especially during the seventeenth century, was considerable. For example, the seventeenth-century English writer Edward Wright defended Copernicus' heliocentric theory of the solar system against biblical literalists by arguing, in the first place, that Scripture was not concerned with physics, and in the second, that its manner of speaking was "accommodated to the understanding and way of speech of the common people, like nurses to little children." Both these arguments derive directly from Calvin, who may be argued to have made a fundamental contribution to the emergence of the natural sciences at these points.

Commitment and Neutrality in Theology

To what extent should theologians be "committed"? To put this question in an especially pointed way: Can Christian theology be taught by someone who is not a Christian? Is commitment to the Christian faith an essential qualification for anyone who wants to teach or study Christian theology?

This question has been debated at length within the Christian tradition. The debate is usually regarded as having got fully under way in the twelfth century, with the founding of the University of Paris. Public confrontations developed between thinkers who believed that theology was about a committed defense of the Christian faith (Bernard of Clairvaux), and those who insisted that theology was an academic discipline, demanding detachment on the part of its practitioners (Peter Abelard). Significantly, the former tended to be based in monasteries, and the latter in universities.

The debate is unresolved, in that each view has a number of significant arguments in its favor. The following are the main points put forward by each side.

First, let us consider two arguments for detachment and neutrality.

1   A total detachment on the part of a scholar is necessary in the quest for truth. If a scholar is already committed to a theory (such as the truth of Christianity), this will prejudice his or her evaluation of the material to be studied. With the Enlightenment came the idea that "commitment" and "truth" were mutually incompatible. The only person who is intellectually qualified to pass judgment on the Christian faith is someone who is neutral toward it.

2 Theology must be prepared to ask hard questions about its intellectual credibility, its methods, and its ideas. The critical environment of a modern university forces theologians to ask the hard questions which otherwise might not get asked. "If theology were now forced to disappear from the universities on the grounds maintained by many people (that it is essentially tied to authority and therefore unscientific), this would be a severe setback for the Christian understanding of truth" (Wolfhart Pannenberg). David Tracy's emphasis upon the need for Christianity to ground Christian truth claims in public, universal norms of intelligibility and justification also points firmly in this direction.

Having considered two of the arguments advocated for neutrality, we may now note three in support of commitment.

1 Latin American liberation theologians have been scathing of the notion of "academic detachment," regarding this as a severe hindrance to the cause of social justice and political transformation. If something is true, ought one not to be committed to it? Basing themselves partly on Marxist principles, and partly on some fairly traditional Christian ideas, liberation theologians have argued that there is no tension between truth and commitment: indeed, the former demands the latter.

2 Scholarship is in reality precommitted, whether it realizes this or not. For example, the sophisticated analysis of the nature of theories in physics or psychology offered by Roy A. Clouser in *The Myth of Religious Neutrality* suggests that precommitments exercise a major, if hidden, role in these areas. Far from being "neutral," such disciplines turn out to have hidden commitments. Might not the same be true of theology? In other words, even those who claim to be "detached" are, in reality, servants of hidden precommitments and presuppositions.

3 Christian theology arises in response to the faith of a community. It is, to use the celebrated phase of Anselm of Canterbury, *fides quaerens intellectum*, "faith seeking understanding" (see pp. 48–9). Faith implies commitment. To study Christian theology as a purely academic subject, from a disinterested standpoint, is to lose sight of the fact that Christianity is about proclamation, prayer, and worship. It is these activities which give rise to theology – and if a theologian does not proclaim the faith, pray to God, and worship the risen Christ, he or she cannot really be said to have understood what theology is all about.

Each of these arguments for and against neutrality has its strengths and weaknesses. For example, consider the suggestion that only someone outside the Christian faith can provide a reliable account of its ideas – i.e. that the person best qualified to write about Christian theology is someone who is not a Christian. This suggestion has its strengths. An outside observer is more likely to ask hard questions, to make critical judgments, and to notice the strangeness of things which those inside the Christian faith take as self-evident. Yet, because the outside observer does not share the inner dynamics of the Christian faith – such as its life of prayer or worship – he or she will not be able to understand the motivation for theological development. A critical perspective is achieved at the cost of a lack of understanding.

For reasons such as these, the debate about commitment in theology has found itself at something of a stalemate. In recent decades, however, a social development has taken place which is tending to lead to Christian theology being studied in seminaries, rather than universities – and hence in a committed context. With the rise of multiculturalism in Europe, North America, and Australia, there has been increasing disquiet within secular circles over the privileged status of Christian theology in the universities. Why should Christian – and not Jewish or Islamic – thought be given this special status?

The result of this development in the United States has been the birth of "faculties of religion" or "faculties of religious studies," which aim to study a variety of specific religions, or religion in general, rather than Christianity. As most individuals studying Christian theology do so with a view to ordination, the result of this has tended to be an exodus of students to the seminaries, where *Christian* theology is taught. Thus a significant number of major theologians – including major European Roman Catholic theologians such as Hans Urs von Balthasar and Yves Congar – have never held university appointments. Equally, many modern American evangelical theologians prefer to remain in seminary contexts, rather than work within the "religious studies" faculties of secular universities.

Orthodoxy and Heresy

The terms "orthodoxy" and "heresy" have now largely lost their original theological meanings. The rise of anti-authoritarian attitudes in modern times has led to "orthodoxy" (that is, literally, "right opinion") being seen as little more than "a dogma imposed upon people by coercive authority," with "heresy" often being viewed as the victim of suppression by intolerant church or state authorities. As we shall see, Walter Bauer (1877–1960) advanced the thesis that forms of Christianity which later generations regarded as "heretical" were actually earlier and more influential than "orthodox" views; the Roman church deliberately suppressed these ideas, declaring them to be heretical, and enforced its own less popular ideas as "orthodoxy." Recent scholarship has cast considerable doubt on this thesis, although it remains popular in more liberal circles today.

It should be noted that heresy has often been associated with marginalized social groupings: for example, the Donatists (a group of heretics in late fourth-century North Africa; see pp. 407–9) drew their support mainly from the indigenous Berber people of the region, whereas their Catholic opponents were mainly Roman settlers. While the Christian church has frequently fallen to the temptation of suppressing its opponents, inside and outside its ranks, the notion of "heresy" is and remains of genuine theological importance, and needs to be examined more closely. In what follows, we shall consider both historical and theological aspects of the ideas of heresy and orthodoxy.

Historical Aspects

The ideas of "orthodoxy" and "heresy" are especially associated with the early church. So how did they develop? Are we to think of heresy as a degeneration from orthodoxy? In his study *Orthodoxy and Heresy in Earliest Christianity* (1934), Walter Bauer argued that the basic unity within the early Christian churches did not seem to be located at the level of doctrines, but at the level of relationship with the same Lord. Christian unity lay in the worship of the same Lord, rather than in the formal statement of doctrine (which is how "orthodoxy" tends to be defined).

Bauer went on to argue that a variety of views which were tolerated in the early church gradually began to be regarded with suspicion by the later church. An orthodox consensus began to emerge, in which opinions that had once been tolerated were discarded as inadequate. But how was this distinction between heresy and orthodoxy drawn? Bauer argued that "orthodoxy" was the result of the growing power of Rome, which increasingly came to impose its own views upon others, and using the term "heresy" to refer to views it rejected. Bauer's argument is that, to him, the difference between orthodoxy and heresy often seems arbitrary. Bauer's hostility to the idea of doctrinal norms reflects his conviction that these were a late development within Christianity.

A more nuanced approach to the same question is taken by the Oxford patristic scholar Henry Chadwick. In his essay "The Circle and the Ellipse" (1959), Chadwick contrasted a patristic view of orthodoxy, which regarded only Rome as normative, and the rival view, which recognized that all Christian communities were linked by the foundational events which took place at Jerusalem and continued to be of defining importance in the process of the forging of doctrinal orthodoxy. Where Bauer focused on the single center of Rome, Chadwick suggested that the image of an ellipse, with its two foci at Rome and Jerusalem, was more appropriate. Historically, Chadwick's account appears to be much the more plausible.

Theological Aspects

The debate over the historical origins of the notions of heresy and orthodoxy might suggest that the ideas are of purely antiquarian interest. In fact, there is a continuing theological significance associated with the ideas. Heresy is important theologically. This point is perhaps best seen from one of the most important discussions of heresy, found in F. D. E. Schleiermacher's *Christian Faith* (1821–2). Schleiermacher argued that heresy was that which preserved the *appearance* of Christianity, yet contradicted its *essence*:

> If the distinctive essence of Christianity consists in the fact that in it all religious emotions are related to the redemption wrought by Jesus Christ, there will be two ways in which heresy can arise. That is to say: This fundamental formula will be retained in general . . . but *either* human nature will be so defined that a redemption in the strict case cannot be accomplished, *or* the Redeemer will be defined in such a way that he cannot accomplish redemption.

Schleiermacher's discussion of heresy is of such interest that we shall consider it in detail, partly because it illuminates the distinction between heresy and unbelief, and partly because it shows the continuing need for the notion of "heresy" in theology, even if the word itself has become discredited through overuse.

If, as Schleiermacher suggests, the distinctive essence of Christianity consists in the fact that God has redeemed us through Jesus Christ, and through no one else and in no other way, it must follow that the Christian understanding of God, Jesus Christ, and human nature should be consistent with this understanding of redemption. Thus the Christian understanding of God must be such that God can effect the redemption of humanity through Christ; the Christian understanding of Christ must be such that God may effect our redemption through him; the Christian understanding of humanity must be such that redemption is both possible and genuine. In other words, it is essential that the Christian understanding of God, Christ, humanity is *consistent with* the principle of redemption through Christ alone.

According to Schleiermacher, the rejection or denial of the principle that God has redeemed us through Jesus Christ is nothing less than the rejection of Christianity itself. In other words, to deny that God has redeemed us through Jesus Christ is to deny the most fundamental truth claim which the Christian faith dares to make. The distinction between what is *Christian* and what is not lies in whether this principle is accepted: The distinction between what is *orthodox* and what is *heretical*, however, lies in how this principle, once conceded and accepted, is understood. In other words, heresy is not a form of unbelief; it is something that arises within the context of faith itself. For Schleiermacher, heresy is fundamentally *an inadequate or inauthentic form of Christian faith*.

Heresy arises through accepting the basic principle, but interpreting its terms in such a way that internal inconsistency results. In other words, the principle is granted, but it is inadequately understood. The principle may be accepted, and yet

1   be interpreted in such a way that Christ cannot effect the redemption of humanity; *or*
2   be interpreted in such a way that humanity – the object of justification – cannot be justified, properly speaking.

Let us examine each of these possibilities.

Who is the redeemer? The answer given to this question must be able to account for the uniqueness of his office and for his ability to mediate between God and humanity. There must therefore be an essential similarity between Christ and ourselves, if he is able to mediate between us and God, and yet at the same time there must be something fundamentally different about him. Not every human being is a redeemer. Heresy can arise simply by failing to uphold these two points simultaneously, so that the affirmation of one amounts to the denial of the other.

If the superiority of Jesus Christ over us is emphasized, without maintaining his essential similarity to us, his ability to reconcile us to God is lost, in that he no longer has a point of contact with those whom he is supposed to redeem. On the other hand, if his similarity to us is emphasized, without acknowledging that in at least one respect he is fundamentally different, then the redeemer himself requires redemption. If the redeemer is treated as being similar in every respect to us, he must be acknowledged to share our need for redemption. Therefore either all of us are actually redeemers, to a greater or lesser extent, or else the redeemer cannot redeem.

It will be obvious that the doctrine of redemption through Christ requires that the redeemer should share our common humanity, except our need for redemption. According to Schleiermacher, orthodox Christianity has upheld this crucial insight by insisting that Jesus Christ is at one and the same time both God and a human being. It would be much simpler to suggest that Jesus was just God, or just human; but to uphold the possibility and actuality of our redemption, it is necessary to insist that both are true.

From the above discussion, it will be obvious that two heresies may arise through upholding the principle of redemption through Christ, but interpreting the person of Christ in such a way that this redemption becomes impossible. On the one hand, Jesus Christ loses his point of contact with those he is meant to redeem – thus giving rise to the heresy generally known as *Docetism*. On the other, he loses his essential dissimilarity from those whom he came to redeem, and comes to be treated simply as a particularly enlightened human being – thus giving rise to the heresy which Schleiermacher styles *Ebionitism*.

In a similar manner, Schleiermacher explores the question: Who are the redeemed? The answer to this question must be capable of explaining why redemption is necessary from outside humanity itself – in other words, why we cannot redeem ourselves. The object of redemption must both require redemption in the first place, and be capable of accepting that redemption when it is offered. These two aspects of the question must be maintained at one and the same time, just like the humanity and divinity of Christ.

If the human need for redemption is granted, yet our impotence to redeem ourselves is denied, the conclusion follows that we could be the agents of our own redemption. Reconciliation could then be effected by at least some individuals, if not by all, to varying degrees – which immediately contradicts the principle of redemption through Jesus Christ alone. And if our ability to accept redemption, once it is offered to us, is denied, that redemption again becomes an impossibility. Broadly speaking, these two positions correspond to the Pelagian and the Manichaean heresies.

The four heresies described above may, according to Schleiermacher, be regarded as the four natural heresies of the Christian faith, each of which arises through an inadequate interpretation of the doctrine of justification by faith. It is no accident that these were by far the most important heresies to be debated in the early church.

In this chapter, we have explored a number of issues which are preparatory to engaging with the study of theology. The aim has been, in effect, to clear the ground a little, before we move on to deal with specific issues of substance relating to theology. Much the same remarks must apply to the next chapter, which aims to explore the sources upon which theology must draw.

Questions for Chapter 5

1 Is it necessary to prove God's existence?

2 How would you distinguish between an analogy and a metaphor?

3 How convincing do you find Anselm's "ontological argument" for the existence of God?

4 What theological issues were at stake in the Copernican debate?

5 Do you have to be a Christian to be a Christian theologian?

6

The Sources of Theology

Christian theology, like most disciplines, draws upon a number of sources. There has been considerable discussion within the Christian tradition concerning the identity of these sources, and their relative importance for theological analysis. The present chapter aims to explore the identity of these sources, and provide an assessment of their potential for constructive theology.

Broadly speaking, four main sources have been acknowledged within the Christian tradition:

1 Scripture;
2 reason;
3 tradition;
4 experience.

Each of these sources has a distinct contribution to make within the discipline of theology, and will be considered in detail at the appropriate point in our discussion. We begin, however, by considering an idea which is of fundamental importance to Christian theology – that of revelation.

The Idea of Revelation

A central theme of Christian theology down the ages has been that human attempts to discern fully the nature and purposes of God are ultimately unsuccessful. Although a natural knowledge of God is generally held to be possible (the early writings of Karl Barth being a notable exception to this consensus), this is limited both in scope and in depth. The idea of *revelation* expresses the pervasive belief of Christian theology, to the effect that we need to be "told what God is like" (Eberhard Jüngel).

The 1960s saw a major upheaval in Christian theology, with many traditional ideas being challenged and redefined. One such challenge was to the notion of revelation. Two issues emerged, each of which seemed to call into doubt the traditional Christian understanding of revelation. In the first place, F. G. Downing suggested that the modern interest in revelation was due not to the biblical material itself, but to the prominence of epistemological issues in modern philosophy. The prominence of questions concerning "right knowledge" in, for example, the philosophy of science had been improperly transferred to theology. The Bible, it was argued, was concerned with salvation, not knowledge. The dominant question in the New Testament was "What must I *do* to be saved?" not "What must I *know*?" In response to this, it was pointed out that the biblical conception of salvation is often expressed in terms of "knowledge," and that human salvation was understood to rest upon the knowledge of the possibility of salvation in Christ, and the proper response which was necessary for salvation to take place. "Knowledge of God," understood biblically, does not mean simply "information about God," but a life-giving and salvation-bringing self-disclosure of God in Christ.

In the second place, biblical scholars such as James Barr argued that the issue of revelation appeared to be of marginal importance to both the Old and the New Testaments. They suggested that revelational language was neither fundamental to, nor uniform within, the biblical writings. However, it soon became clear that their analyses rested upon the uncritical acceptance of systematically developed ideas of "revelation," rather than a careful consideration of the revelational vocabulary of Scripture itself. It is certainly true that medieval or modern notions of revelation are not found explicitly stated in either the Old or the New Testament. However, this by no means indicates that revelational language is absent from, or marginalized within, Scripture.

It is certainly correct to say that the New Testament does not regard "revelation" as meaning "disclosure of a hitherto unknown God." In its everyday use, the term "revelation" might be taken to imply "making something known in all its fulness," or "the total disclosure of what had hitherto been obscure or unclear." Yet to speak of a "revelation of God" in a theological context is not to imply that the self-revelation of God is *total*. As Gerald O'Collins puts it:

Revelation can occur between persons without there being an utterly complete disclosure of personalities. Take the following statement: "He revealed to me his wishes in the matter." No full, continuing personal communion is asserted. But something has been disclosed and that too in a context which affords some insight into the other's personality. To see something of his personality is not equivalent to seeing nothing at all. May we not use "reveal" in some such qualified sense of God, and speak of a genuine experience of God which communicates something, and yet falls short of being full disclosure?

O'Collins here expresses a general consensus within Christian theology. For example, many writers within the Greek Orthodox tradition stress that the revelation of God does not abolish the mystery of God. John Henry Newman's doctrine of "reserve" emphasizes the same point. There is always more to God than what we can come to know. Again, Luther suggests that God's self-revelation is only partial – yet that partial revelation is reliable and adequate. He develops the idea of a "hidden revelation of God" – one of the most important aspects of his "theology of the cross" – to make this point.

There is a consensus within Christian theology to the effect that nature (or creation) bears a witness to God its creator. This natural knowledge of God is to be supplemented by revelation, which gives access to information which is not otherwise available. Yet the idea of revelation implies more than imparting knowledge of God; it carries with it the idea of the *self-disclosure* of God. In speaking about other persons, we might draw a distinction between "knowing about someone" and "knowing someone." The former implies cerebral knowledge, or an accumulation of data about an individual (such as her height, weight, and so on). The latter implies a personal relationship.

In its developed sense, "revelation" does not mean merely the transmission of a body of knowledge, but the personal self-disclosure of God within history. God has taken the initiative through a process of self-disclosure, which reaches its climax and fulfillment in the history of Jesus of Nazareth. This point has been stressed in the twentieth century by writers influenced by various types of personalist philosophies – such as Friedrich Gogarten, Dietrich Bonhoeffer, and Emanuel Hirsch. Emil Brunner, who also belongs to this group of thinkers, emphasized the importance of the doctrine of the incarnation to revelation: In Christ may be seen the personal self-disclosure of God. Believers are "God's dialogue partners in history." Revelation takes a personal form. We shall explore this question further in dealing with the idea of a personal God (pp. 207–13).

Models of Revelation

Revelation, in common with most theological notions, is a complex concept. In an attempt to unravel and cast light on its various components, theologians have used various models of revelation. In what follows, we shall consider four such models. It must be stressed that these are not mutually exclusive. The affirmation of one does not imply the negation of any one or all four of the remainder. Correctly understood, they represent different emphases within the Christian understandings of revelation.

Revelation as Doctrine

This approach has been characteristic of conservative evangelical and Catholic neo-scholastic schools, and, in modified or supplemented forms, continues to exercise considerable influence within the Christian tradition. Whereas evangelicals have stressed the role of Scripture in the mediation of revelation, Catholic neo-scholastics have generally given considerably more weight to the role of tradition, and especially the teaching office of the church (the *magisterium*). The term "the deposit of revelation" or "the deposit of truth," meaning the accumulated insights of the church over the years, is often employed in such contexts. According to this approach, revelation is to be thought of primarily (although not exclusively) in propositional forms.

This approach has been severely criticized, most notably by post-liberal theologian George Lindbeck in his *Nature of Doctrine* (see pp. 109–10). Lindbeck designates this view of revelation as "propositionalist" or "cognitive." It views revelation as "informative propositions or truth claims about objective realities." Lindbeck argues that this approach is to be rejected as intellectualist and literalist, and resting on the mistaken assumption that it is possible to state the objective truth about God definitively, exhaustively, and timelessly in propositional form.

Lindbeck's criticism of "cognitive" theories of revelation or doctrine has considerable force when directed against neo-scholastic understandings of revelation. For example, the view of the neo-scholastic writer Hermann Dieckmann, to the effect that supernatural revelation transmits conceptual knowledge by means of propositions, is clearly open to serious criticism along the lines suggested by Lindbeck. Nevertheless, not all cognitive theories of doctrine are vulnerable in this respect. It is necessary to make a clear distinction between the view that an exhaustive and unambiguous account of God is transmitted through revelation conceptually by propositions, on the one hand, and the view that there is a genuinely cognitive element to doctrinal statements, on the other. For example, most theologians of the medieval period actually understood revelation as a dynamic concept, a "perception of divine truth, tending toward this truth." For such theologians, revelation provides *reliable* yet *incomplete* descriptions of reality.

Nor need a propositional approach to revelation exclude other approaches. Perhaps the greatest weakness within Christian theology is a reluctance to recognize that models are complementary, rather than mutually exclusive. To assert that revelation involves information about God is not to deny that it can also involve the mediation of the presence of God, or the transformation of human experience.

Revelation as Presence

This model of revelation is especially associated with writers of the dialectical school of theology (see pp. 98–100) influenced by the dialogical personalism of Martin Buber (see pp. 210–13). Perhaps the most important statement of the approach may be found in Emil Brunner's *Truth as Encounter*, which sets out the idea of revelation as a personal communication of God – that is to say, a communication or impartation of the personal presence of God within the believer. "The Lordship and love of God can be communicated in no other way than by God's self-giving."

Brunner's point is that God does not merely convey information in the process of revelation. Revelation concerns the conveying of God's personal presence, rather than mere information concerning God. Brunner, basing himself upon Martin Buber's analysis of "I–Thou" and "I–It" relationships, insists that there is a strongly relational element to revelation. God is experienced as a "Thou" rather than an "It." Revelation is teleological, a process directed toward a goal – and that goal is the establishment of a mutual relationship between the revealing God and responding humanity.

Brunner's concept of "truth as encounter" thus conveys the two elements of a correct understanding of revelation: It is *historical* and it is *personal*. By the former, Brunner wishes us to understand that truth is not something permanent within the eternal world of ideas which is disclosed or communicated to us in revelation; rather, it is something which *happens* in space and time. Truth comes into being, as the act of God in time and space. By the latter, Brunner intends to emphasize that the content of this *act* of God is none other than the *person* of God, rather than a complex of ideas or doctrines concerning God. The revelation of God is God's self-impartation to humanity. For Brunner, divine revelation is necessarily Christocentric: He counters the false objectivism of orthodoxy's doctrine of propositional revelation with Luther's dictum to the effect that the Scriptures are "the manger in which Christ is laid."

On the basis of this approach, Brunner develops a critique of any notion of revelation which represents itself as words or propositions about God. These objectify God, in the sense of reducing God to the status of an *object*, rather than a *person*. "No speech, no word, is adequate to the mystery of God as a Person." Revelation cannot be understood as the impartation of data about God: "It is never the mere communication of knowledge, but a life-giving and life-renewing fellowship." Revelation is thus understood primarily as the communication or establishment of a personal relationship.

Of course, related ideas can be instanced from earlier periods in church history. The recognition that revelation involves a personal presence is stated with particular clarity in John Henry Newman's hymn "Praise to the Holiest":

> And that a higher gift than grace
> Should flesh and blood refine;
> God's presence and God's very self
> And essence all-divine.

Revelation as Experience

A third influential model centers upon human experience. God is understood to be revealed or made known through the experience of the individual. We shall consider this approach in more detail later in this chapter, in exploring the value and function of religious experience as a source of theology. One of the greatest weaknesses of the model is the criticisms directed against it by Ludwig Feuerbach (1804–72), who argued that such "experience" was little more than "experience of the self." We shall consider the experiential approach in considerably more detail shortly (pp. 192–200).

Revelation as History

A quite distinct approach, especially associated with the German theologian Wolfhart Pannenberg, centers on the theme "revelation as history" (see pp. 332–6). According to Pannenberg, Christian theology is based upon an analysis of universal and publicly accessible history, rather than the inward subjectivity of personal human existence or a special interpretation of that history. History itself is (or has the capacity to become) revelation. For Pannenberg, revelation is essentially a public and universal historical event which is recognized and *interpreted* as an "act of God." Pannenberg's "Dogmatic Theses on the Doctrine of Revelation" set out this position in seven theses, of which the first five are of especial interest in relation to this model of revelation:

1 The self-revelation of God in Scripture did not take place directly, after the fashion of a theophany, but indirectly, in the acts of God in history. (A "theophany" is an appearance of God in a temporary form, not necessarily material, which is to be contrasted with the incarnation, in which God is understood to have been revealed permanently in the person of Christ.)
2 Revelation is not completely apprehended at the beginning, but only at the end of revelatory history.
3 In contrast to special divine manifestations, the revelation of God in history is publicly and universally accessible, and open to anyone who has eyes to see it.
4 The universal revelation of God is not fully realized in the history of Israel; it was first realized in the destiny of Jesus of Nazareth, in so far as the end of history is anticipated in that destiny.
5 The Christ-event cannot be regarded as revealing God in isolation; it is set in the context of the history of God's dealings with Israel.

On this basis, Pannenberg is able to argue for the resurrection of Christ as a central act of divine revelation in history, a point to which we shall return later in our analysis of the resurrection.

Pannenberg's approach to revelation has aroused excitement and criticism in about equal measure. The idea of establishing the gospel on the basis of universal history seemed a daring and creative gesture, allowing theology to reclaim the intellectual high ground that many had thought had long been forfeited to Marxism. In particular, it seemed to bypass the trap laid by Ludwig Feuerbach (see pp. 199–200), who had argued that Schleiermacher's approach to revelation, beginning from human experience, was little more than a theology constructed through the objectification of human feelings. Pannenberg, by his appeal to history, is able to avoid the line of thought which leads to Feuerbach's impasse by insisting that theology arises out of history, not out of human feelings of redemption or the presence of God.

Natural Theology: Its Scope and Limits

The doctrine of creation gives theological foundation to the notion of a natural knowledge of God. If God created the world, it is to be expected that his creation should bear the mark of the divine handiwork. Just as an artist's distinctive style might be evident in her sculpturing, or a painter might sign his name on his work, so the presence of God, it is argued, can be discerned within the creation. But what part of creation? Three answers may be picked out from the considerable variety offered by Christian theology down the centuries.

1 *Human reason* Augustine of Hippo addresses this question at some length in *De Trinitate* ("On the Trinity"). His line of argument can be summed up as follows. If God is indeed to be discerned within his creation, we ought to expect to find him at the height of that creation. Now the height of God's creation, Augustine argues (basing himself on Genesis 1 and 2), is human nature. And, on the basis of the neo-Platonic presuppositions which he inherited from his cultural milieu, Augustine further argued that the height of human nature is the human capacity to reason. Therefore, he concluded, one should expect to find traces of God (or, more accurately, "vestiges of the Trinity") in human processes of reasoning. On the basis of this belief, Augustine develops what have come to be known as "psychological analogies of the Trinity."

2 *The ordering of the world* We have already seen how Thomas Aquinas' arguments for the existence of God base themselves on the perception that there is an ordering within nature, which requires to be explained. Equally, the fact that the human mind can discern and investigate this ordering of nature is of considerable significance. There seems to be something about human nature which prompts it to ask questions about the world. And there seems to be something about the world which allows answers to those questions to be given. The noted theoretical physicist and Christian apologist John Polkinghorne comments on this point as follows, in his *Science and Creation*:

> We are so familiar with the fact that we can understand the world that most of the time we take it for granted. It is what makes science possible. Yet it could have been otherwise. The universe might have been a disorderly chaos rather than an orderly cosmos. Or it might have had a rationality which was inaccessible to us. . . . There is a congruence between our minds and the universe, between the rationality experienced within and the rationality observed without.

There is a deep-seated congruence between the rationality present in our minds, and the rationality – the *orderedness* – which we observe as present in the world. Thus the abstract structures of pure mathematics – a free creation of the human mind – provide important clues to understanding the world. All of this, Polkinghorne argues, is a form of natural theology, preparing the way for the full knowledge of the Christian revelation.

3   *The beauty of the world*   A number of theologians have developed natural theologies, based on the sense of beauty which arises from contemplating the world. Hans Urs von Balthasar is an example of a twentieth-century writer who stresses the theological importance of beauty. But perhaps the most powerful exploration of this theme is made by the celebrated American theologian, Jonathan Edwards. In his *Personal Narrative*, Edwards wrote thus of his "sheer beholding of God's beauty":

> As I was walking there and looking up into the sky and clouds, there came into my mind so sweet a sense of the glorious *majesty* and *grace* of God, that I know not how to express. I seemed to see them both in a sweet conjunction . . . it was a sweet and gentle, and holy majesty; and also a majestic meekness.

This sense of aesthetic ecstasy pervades Edwards's autobiographical writings, especially his *Miscellanies*. The perception of beauty that we experience "when we are delighted with flowery meadows and gentle breezes" is, for Edwards, an intimation of the holiness of God, which Scripture clarifies and confirms, placing it upon a reliable theological foundation.

These, then, are merely some of the ways in which Christian theologians have attempted to describe the manner in which God can be known, however fleetingly, through nature. But what of the relation between a general and a more special knowledge of God? How are we to understand their relation? One model will be considered in detail: Calvin's distinction between "knowledge of God the creator" and "knowledge of God the redeemer." In part, this model has been selected on account of the widespread misconception that Calvin denies a natural knowledge of God, on account of the corruption of the human mind. But it is also representative of the general account offered by theologians of the relation of natural and revealed knowledge of God.

Knowledge of God the Creator – Knowledge of God the Redeemer

The first book of Calvin's *Institutes* opens with discussion of this fundamental problem of Christian theology: How do we know anything about God? Calvin affirms that a general knowledge of God may be discerned throughout the creation – in humanity, in the natural order, and in the historical process itself. Two main grounds of such knowledge are identified: one subjective, the other objective. The first ground is a "sense of divinity" (*sensus divinitatis*) or a "seed of religion" (*semen religionis*), implanted within every human being by God. God has endowed human beings with some inbuilt sense or presentiment of the divine existence. It is as if something about God has been engraved in the heart of every human being. Calvin identifies three consequences of this inbuilt awareness of divinity: the universality of religion (which, if uninformed by the Christian revelation, degenerates into idolatry), a troubled conscience, and a servile fear of God. All of these, Calvin suggests, may serve as points of contact for the Christian proclamation. The second such ground lies in experience of and reflection upon the ordering of the world. The fact that God is creator, together with an appreciation of the divine wisdom and justice, may be gained from an inspection of the created order, culminating in humanity itself.

It is important to stress that Calvin makes no suggestion whatsoever that this knowledge of God from the created order is peculiar to, or restricted to, Christian believers. Calvin is arguing that *anyone*, by intelligent and rational reflection upon the created order, should be able to arrive at the idea of God. The created order is a "theater" or a "mirror" for the displaying of the divine presence, nature, and attributes. Although invisible and incomprehensible, God wills to be known under the form of created and visible things, by donning the garment of creation.

Calvin thus commends the natural sciences (such as astronomy), on account of their ability to illustrate further the wonderful ordering of creation, and the divine wisdom which this indicates (see pp. 141–2). Significantly, however, Calvin makes no appeal to specifically *Christian* sources of revelation. His argument is based upon empirical observation and ratiocination. If Calvin introduces scriptural quotations, it is to consolidate a general natural knowledge of God, rather than to establish that knowledge in the first place. There is, he stresses, a way of discerning God which is common to those inside and outside the Christian community.

Having thus laid the foundations for a general knowledge of God,

Calvin stresses its shortcomings; his dialogue partner here is the classical Roman writer Cicero, whose *On the Nature of the Gods* is perhaps one of the most influential classical expositions of a natural knowledge of God. Calvin argues that the epistemic distance between God and humanity, already of enormous magnitude, is increased still further on account of human sin. Our natural knowledge of God is imperfect and confused, even to the point of contradiction on occasion. A natural knowledge of God serves to deprive humanity of any excuse for ignoring the divine will; nevertheless, it is inadequate as the basis of a fully fledged portrayal of the nature, character, and purposes of God.

Having stressed this point, Calvin then introduces the notion of revelation; Scripture reiterates what may be known of God through nature, while simultaneously clarifying this general revelation and enhancing it. "The knowledge of God, which is clearly shown in the ordering of the world and in all creatures, is still more clearly and familiarly explained in the Word." It is only through Scripture that the believer has access to knowledge of the redeeming actions of God in history, culminating in the life, death, and resurrection of Jesus Christ. For Calvin, revelation is focused upon the person of Jesus Christ; our knowledge of God is mediated through him. God may thus be fully known only through Jesus Christ, who may in turn be known only through Scripture; the created order, however, provides important points of contact for and partial resonances of this revelation.

The basic idea here, then, is that a knowledge of God the creator may be had both through nature and through revelation, with the latter clarifying, confirming, and extending what may be known through the former. Knowledge of God the redeemer – which for Calvin is a distinctively *Christian* knowledge of God – may only be had by the Christian revelation, in Christ and through Scripture.

If this positive approach to a natural knowledge of God represents the majority report within the Christian tradition, it is important to acknowledge that there have been other views. Perhaps the most negative attitude to have been adopted in recent Christian theology is that of Karl Barth, whose 1934 controversy with Emil Brunner over this issue has become something of a *cause célèbre*.

The Barth–Brunner Debate

In 1934, the Swiss theologian Emil Brunner published a work entitled *Nature and Grace*. In this work, he argued that "the task of our theological generation is to find a way back to a legitimate natural theology." Brunner located this approach in the doctrine of creation, specifically the idea that human beings are created in the *imago Dei*, the "image of God." Human nature is constituted in such a way that there is an analogy with the being of God. Despite the sinfulness of human nature, the ability to discern God in nature remains. Sinful human beings remain able to recognize God in nature and the events of history, and to be aware of their guilt before God. There is thus a "point of contact" (*Anknüpfungspunkt*) for divine revelation within human nature.

In effect, Brunner is arguing that human nature is constituted in such a way that there is a ready-made point of contact for divine revelation. Revelation addresses a human nature which already has some idea of what that revelation is about. For example, take the gospel demand to "repent of sin." Brunner argues that this makes little sense, unless human beings already have some idea of what "sin" is. The gospel demand to repent is thus addressed to an audience which already has at least something of an idea of what "sin" and "repentance" might mean. Revelation brings with it a fuller understanding of what sin means – but in doing so, it builds upon an existing human awareness of sin.

Barth reacted with anger to this suggestion. His published reply to Brunner – which brought their long-standing friendship to an abrupt end – has one of the shortest titles in the history of religious publishing: *Nein!* Barth was determined to say "no!" to Brunner's positive evaluation of natural theology. It seemed to imply that God needed help to become known, or that human beings somehow cooperated with God in the act of revelation. "The Holy Spirit . . . needs no point of contact other than that which that same Spirit establishes," was his angry retort. For Barth, there was no "point of contact" inherent within human nature. Any such "point of contact" was itself the result of divine revelation. It is something that is evoked by the Word of God, rather than something which is a permanent feature of human nature.

Underlying this exchange is another matter, which is too easily overlooked. The Barth–Brunner debate took place in 1934, the year in which Hitler gained power in Germany. Underlying Brunner's appeal to nature is an idea, which can be traced back to Luther, known as "the orders of creation." According to Luther, God providentially established certain "orders" within creation, in order to prevent it collapsing into chaos. Those orders included the family, the church, and the state. (The close alliance between church and state in German Lutheran thought reflects this idea.) Nineteenth-century German liberal Protestantism had absorbed this idea, and developed a theology which allowed German culture, including a positive assessment of the state, to become of major importance theologically. Part of Barth's concern is that Brunner, perhaps unwittingly, has laid a theological foundation for allowing the state to become a model for God. And who wanted to model God on Adolf Hitler?

Scripture

The terms "Bible" and "Scripture," along with the derived adjectives "biblical" and "scriptural," are virtually interchangeable. Both designate a body of texts which are recognized as authoritative for Christian thinking (although the nature and extent of that authority is a matter of debate). It must be stressed that the Bible is not merely the object of formal academic study within Christianity; it is also read and expounded within the context of public worship, and is the subject of meditation and devotion on the part of individual Christians.

The adjective *canonical* is often used to refer to Scripture. This term, deriving from the Greek word *kanon* (meaning "rule" or "yardstick"), is used to indicate that limits have been set, by the consensus of the Christian community, to the texts which may be regarded as "scriptural," and hence as authoritative for Christian theology. A long-standing debate between Roman Catholic and Protestant theologians concerns the status of a further group of texts which are often referred to as "apocryphal" or "deutero-canonical."

A comparison of the contents of the Old Testament in the Hebrew Bible on the one hand, and the Greek and Latin versions (such as the Septuagint or Vulgate) on the other, shows that the latter contain a number of works not found in the former. Following the lead of Jerome, the sixteenth-century reformers argued that the only Old Testament writings which could be regarded as belonging to the canon of Scripture were those originally included in the Hebrew Bible.

A distinction was thus drawn between the "Old Testament" and the "Apocrypha": The former consisted of works found in the Hebrew Bible, while the latter consisted of works found in the Greek and Latin Bibles but *not* in the Hebrew Bible. While some reformers allowed that the apocryphal works were edifying reading, there was general agreement that these works could not be used as the basis of Christian theology. In 1546, the Council of Trent defined the "Old Testament" as "those Old Testament works contained in the Greek and Latin Bibles," thus eliminating any distinction between "Old Testament" and "Apocrypha."

In practice, this distinction is not as significant as might at first seem to be the case. An examination of the sixteenth-century debates over the matter suggest that the only theological issue of any real

Box 1   Abbreviations of the books of the Bible

Old Testament

Genesis	Ge	Zephaniah	Zep
Exodus	Ex	Haggai	Hag
Leviticus	Lev	Zechariah	Zec
Numbers	Nu	Malachi	Mal
Deuteronomy	Dt		
Joshua	Jos	*New Testament*	
Judges	Jdg		
Ruth	Ru	Matthew	Mt
1 Samuel	1 Sa	Mark	Mk
2 Samuel	2 Sa	Luke	Lk
1 Kings	1 Ki	John	Jn
2 Kings	2 Ki	Acts	Ac
1 Chronicles	1 Ch	Romans	Ro
2 Chronicles	2 Ch	1 Corinthians	1 Co
Ezra	Ezr	2 Corinthians	2 Co
Nehemiah	Ne	Galatians	Gal
Esther	Est	Ephesians	Eph
Job	Job	Philippians	Php
Psalms	Ps	Colossians	Col
Proverbs	Pr	1 Thessalonians	1 Th
Ecclesiastes	Ecc	2 Thessalonians	2 Th
Song of Songs	SS	1 Timothy	1 Ti
Isaiah	Isa	2 Timothy	2 Ti
Jeremiah	Jer	Titus	Tit
Lamentations	La	Philemon	Phm
Ezekiel	Eze	Hebrews	Heb
Daniel	Da	James	Jas
Hosea	Hos	1 Peter	1 Pe
Joel	Joel	2 Peter	2 Pe
Amos	Am	1 John	1 Jn
Obadiah	Ob	2 John	2 Jn
Jonah	Jnh	3 John	3 Jn
Micah	Mic	Jude	Jude
Nahum	Na	Revelation	Rev
Habakkuk	Hab		

importance which was linked to this question was whether it was proper to pray for the dead. The (apocryphal) Books of the Maccabees encourage this practice, which Protestant theologians were not inclined to accept.

The issue which remains of real theological significance today concerns the canon of Scripture. Does the fact that the church drew up the canon imply that the church has authority over Scripture? Or did the church merely recognize and give formal assent to an authority which the canonical Scriptures already possessed? The former position is particularly attractive to Catholic, and the latter to Protestant scholars. In practice, there has been increased recognition of late that the community of faith and Scripture, the people and the book, coexist with one another, and that attempts to draw sharp lines of distinction between them are somewhat arbitrary. The canon of Scripture may be regarded as emerging organically from a community of faith already committed to using and respecting it.

Box 2   Referring to books of the Bible

The standard method of referring to the Bible involves *three* elements. First, the *book* in question is identified (note that the term "book" is invariably used, even when the "book" in question is actually a letter). This is followed by the *chapter* of the book, followed by the *verse(s)* within that chapter.

The book may be identified in a full or abbreviated form. The chapter may be given in roman or arabic numerals. The chapter and verse numbers are usually separated by a colon or period. However, occasionally the verse numbers are printed in superscript.

The following are all commonly encountered ways of referring to one of the most familiar sayings from St Paul, which has become widely known as "the grace."

2 Corinthians 13.14   II Corinthians xiii, 14
2 Cor. 13[14]   2 Co 13:14

Note the following points:
1 It is not necessary to distinguish between the Old and New Testaments in referring to biblical works.
2 It is not necessary to identify the author of a biblical book when referring to it.

Box 3   Common terms used in relation to the Bible

Pentateuch	The first five books of the Old Testament (Genesis, Exodus, Leviticus, Numbers, and Deuteronomy)
Five books of the Law	The first five books of the Old Testament (Genesis, Exodus, Leviticus, Numbers, and Deuteronomy)
Major prophets	The first four prophetic writings of the Old Testament (Isaiah, Jeremiah, Ezekiel, and Daniel)
Minor prophets	The twelve remaining prophetic writings of the Old Testament (Hosea, Joel, Amos, Obadiah, Jonah, Micah, Nahum, Habakkuk, Zephaniah, Haggai, Zechariah, and Malachi)
Synoptic gospels	The first three gospels (Matthew, Mark, and Luke)
Pastoral epistles (or letters)	A way of referring collectively to 1 Timothy, 2 Timothy, and Titus, which takes note of their particular concern for pastoral matters and church order
Catholic epistles (or letters)	Those New Testament letters which are not explicitly addressed to individuals (James, 1 Peter, 2 Peter, 1 John, 2 John, 3 John, Jude). In older works, sometimes referred to as "epistles general"

Old and New Testaments

The Christian terms "Old Testament" and "New Testament" are strongly theological in nature. These Christian terms rest upon the belief that the contents of the Old Testament belong to a period of God's dealings with the world which has in some way been superseded or relativized by the coming of Christ in the New Testament. Roughly the same collection of texts is referred to by Jewish writers as "the law, prophets, and writings," and by Christian writers as "the Old Testament." There is thus no particular reason why someone who is not a Christian should feel obliged to refer to this collection of books as the "Old Testament," apart from custom of use.

The Christian theological framework which leads to this distinction is that of "covenants" or "dispensations." The basic Christian belief that the coming of Christ inaugurates something *new* expresses itself in a distinctive attitude toward the Old Testament, which could basically be summarized thus: Religious *principles and ideas* (such as the notion of a sovereign God who is active in human history) are appropriated; religious *practices* (such as dietary laws and sacrificial routines) are not.

How, then, are the Old and New Testaments related to one another, according to Christian theology? One option was to treat the Old Testament as the writings of a religion which had nothing to do with Christianity. This approach is especially associated with the second-century writer Marcion, who was excommunicated in the year 144. According to Marcion, Christianity was a religion of love, which had no place whatsoever for law. The Old Testament relates to a different God from the New; the Old Testament God, who merely created the world, was obsessed with the idea of law. The New Testament God, however, redeemed the world, and was concerned with love. According to Marcion, the purpose of Christ was to depose the Old Testament God (who bears a considerable resemblance to the Gnostic "demiurge," a semi-divine figure responsible for fashioning the world), and usher in the worship of the true God of grace.

There are faint echoes of this idea in the writings of Luther. Although Luther insists that both Old and New Testaments relate to the actions of the same God, he nevertheless insists upon the total opposition of law and grace. Judaism, according to Luther, was totally preoccupied with the idea of justification by works, believing that it was possible to merit favor in the sight of God by one's achievements. The gospel, in contrast, emphasized that justification was completely gratuitous, resting only on the grace of God. Although grace could be detected in the Old Testament (e.g. Isaiah 40–55), and law in the New (e.g. the Sermon on the Mount, Matthew 5–7), Luther often seemed to suggest that the Old Testament was primarily a religion of law, contrasted with the New Testament emphasis on grace.

The majority position within Christian theology has on the one hand emphasized the *continuity* between the two testaments, while on the other noting the *distinction* between them. Calvin provides a lucid and typical discussion of their relation, to which we may turn.

Calvin argues that there exists a fundamental similarity and continuity between Old and New Testaments on the basis of three considerations. First, Calvin stresses the immutability of the divine will. God cannot do one thing in the Old Testament, and follow it by doing something totally different in the New. There must be a fundamental continuity of action and intention between the two. Second, both celebrate and proclaim the grace of God manifested in Jesus Christ. The Old Testament may only be able to witness to Jesus Christ "from a distance and darkly"; nevertheless, its witness to the coming of Christ is real. In the third place, both testaments possess the "same signs and sacraments," bearing witness to the same grace of God.

Calvin thus argues that the two testaments are identical. In terms of their substance and content, there is no radical discontinuity between them. The Old Testament happens to occupy a different chronological position in the divine plan of salvation from the New; its content (rightly understood), however, is the same. Calvin proceeds to identify five points of difference between Old and New Testaments, relating to form, rather than substance.

1 The New Testament possesses greater clarity than the Old, particularly in relation to invisible things. The Old Testament tends to be pervaded by a certain preoccupation with things visible and tangible, which might obscure the invisible goals, hopes, and values which lay behind them. Calvin illustrates this point with reference to the land of Canaan: The Old Testament tends to treat this earthly possession as an end in itself, whereas the New Testament regards it as a reflection of the future inheritance reserved for believers in heaven.

2 The Old and New Testaments adopt significantly different approaches to imagery. The Old Testament employs a mode of representation of reality which, Calvin suggests, leads to an indirect encounter with the truth, through various figures of speech and visual images; the New Testament, however, allows an immediate experience of truth. The Old Testament presents "only the image of truth, . . . the shadow instead of the substance," giving a "foretaste of that wisdom which would one day be clearly revealed"; the New Testament presents the truth directly in all its fulness.

3 A third difference between the two testaments centers on the distinction between law and gospel, or the letter and the spirit. The Old Testament lacks the empowering activity of the Holy Spirit, whereas the New is able to deliver this power. The law can thus command, forbid, and promise, but lacks the necessary resources to effect any fundamental change within human nature which renders such commands necessary in the first place. The gospel is able to "change or correct the perversity which naturally exists in all humans." It is interesting to note that the radical antithesis between law and gospel, so characteristic of Luther (and Marcion before him), is quite lacking. Law and gospel are continuous with each other, and do not stand in diametrical opposition.

4 Developing this previous distinction, Calvin argues that a fourth distinction can be discerned in the differing emotions evoked by the law and the gospel. The Old Testament evokes fear and trembling, and holds the conscience in bondage, whereas the New produces a response of freedom and joy.

5   The Old Testament revelation was confined to the Jewish nation; the New Testament revelation is universal in its scope. Calvin restricts the sphere of the old covenant to Israel; with the coming of Jesus Christ, this partition was broken down, as the distinction between Jew and Greek, between those who were circumcised and those who were not, was abolished. The calling of the Gentiles thus distinguishes the New from the Old Testament.

Throughout this discussion of the distinction between the Old and New Testaments, and the superiority of the latter over the former, Calvin is careful to allow that certain individuals within the old covenant – for example, the patriarchs – were able to discern hints of the new covenant. At no point do the divine purposes or nature alter; they are merely made clearer, in accordance with the limitations imposed upon human understanding. Thus, to give but one example, it was not as if God had originally determined to restrict grace to the Jewish nation alone, and then decided to make it available to everyone else as well; rather, the evolutionary thrust of the divine plan was only made clear with the coming of Jesus Christ. Calvin summarizes this general principle with the assertion that "where the entire law is concerned, the gospel differs from it only in clarity of presentation." Christ is shown forth and the grace of the Holy Spirit is offered in both Old and New Testaments – but more clearly and more fully in the latter.

The Word of God

The phrases "the Word of God" and "the Word of the Lord" are at least as deeply rooted in Christian worship as they are in Christian theology. "Word" implies action and communication. Just as a person's character and will are expressed through the words he or she uses, so Scripture (especially the Old Testament) understands God to address the people, who are thus made aware of God's intentions and will for them.

The term "Word of God" is complex and highly nuanced, bringing together a cluster of ideas. Three broad, and clearly related, senses of the term may be discerned, both within the Christian tradition and within Scripture itself.

1   The phrase is used to refer to Jesus Christ as the Word of God made flesh (John 1: 14). This is the most highly developed use of the term in the New Testament. In speaking of Christ

as the "Word of God incarnate," Christian theology has attempted to express the idea that the will, purposes, and nature of God are made known in history through the person of Jesus Christ. It is the deeds, character, and theological identity of Jesus Christ, and not merely the words that he uttered, which make known the nature and purpose of God.

2 The term is also used to refer to "the gospel of Christ," or "the message or proclamation about Jesus." In this sense, the term refers to what God achieved and made known through the life, death, and resurrection of Christ.

3 The term is used in a general sense to refer to the whole Bible, which can be regarded as setting the scene for the advent of Christ, telling the story of his coming, and exploring the implications of his life, death, and resurrection for believers.

Considerations of this kind lie behind Karl Barth's use of the phrase "Word of God." Barth's doctrine of "the threefold form of the Word of God" distinguishes a threefold movement, from the Word of God in Christ, to the witness to this Word in Scripture, and finally to the proclamation of this Word in the preaching of the community of faith. There is thus a direct and organic connection between the preaching of the church and the person of Jesus Christ.

Narrative Theology

The literary form which dominates Scripture is that of a narrative. What implications does this observation have for relating Scripture to theology? The recently developed concept of "narrative theology" has much to say on this theme.

Narrative theology is based on the observation that the Bible tells stories about God, just as much as it makes doctrinal or theological statements. For example, the Old Testament could be said to be dominated by the telling and retelling of the story of how God led Israel out of Egypt into the promised land, and all that this implies for the people of God. There are stories of battles, love affairs, betrayals, healings, the building of temples, and disastrous sieges.

In a similar way, the New Testament is also dominated by a story of God's redeeming action in history, this time centering on the life, death, and resurrection of Jesus Christ. What does this story mean for Christians? How does it affect the way in which they think and act? It is helpful to think of Paul's letters, for example, as systematic attempts to spell out the relevance of the story of Jesus Christ for Christians.

It is insights like these which lie behind the emergence of one of the most important theological movements to develop in the last few decades – *narrative theology*. It has developed largely in North America, with many observers detecting especially close links with Yale Divinity School and writers based there such as Hans Frei, George Lindbeck, and Ronald Thiemann. Although the term "narrative theologian" has failed to gain general acceptance, narrative theology has come to have a major impact on much English-language theology since the early 1970s. The basic feature of narrative theology is the particular attention it pays to narratives, or stories, in relation to Christian theology. As we shall see, this has proved to be of considerable interest and importance in giving a new sense of direction to theology, and especially in reforging the often neglected link between systematic theology and the study of Scripture.

The origins of this movement are complex. One of its most important sources was a writer who was neither theologian nor biblical scholar, but a specialist in secular literature. In his highly acclaimed study *Mimesis: The Representation of Reality in Western Literature* (1946), Erich Auerbach compared scenes from classical literature, such as Homer's *Odyssey*, with a series of biblical passages, drawn from both Old and New Testaments. Time and time again, Auerbach argued, the biblical narrative had a far greater depth of history, time, and consciousness. There was a depth of realism to their accounts that was lacking in other works of the period. Auerbach thus pointed to the narrative quality of Scripture as distinctive, setting the scene for its theological exploitation. This was not long in coming.

Perhaps the more specifically theological roots of narrative theology can be traced back to Karl Barth, who gave new dignity and meaning to Scripture as "the story of God." Others suggest that a major impetus was given to the movement, especially in North America, by H. Richard Niebuhr's *The Meaning of Revelation* (1941). Niebuhr's constant emphasis upon the revelation of God in history led him to note that narratives were an especially appropriate way of expressing that revelation. God chose to become revealed in history and historical forms (such as in the exodus from Egypt and the history of Jesus Christ). The literary form most appropriate to represent that revelation was thus a narrative – a story. (The word "story," it must be stressed, does not imply a "work of fiction.") Both the Old and the New Testaments bear witness to this point, with their constant use of narratives to express God's involvement and revelation in human history.

However, since the Enlightenment of the eighteenth century, with its emphasis upon generally available rational truths (see pp. 185–7), these insights were widely neglected. One of the most important contributions to their recovery was made by Yale theologian Hans

Frei, in his justly celebrated work *The Eclipse of Biblical Narrative*. Frei pointed out how the Enlightenment's drive to reduce theology to general rational concepts led to a disregard for the narrative quality of the biblical writings. Theology, according to the Enlightenment, was about general principles which could be established by reason. There was no need to make an appeal to history, except in a supportive role. A related approach came to be associated with Rudolf Bultmann (1884–1976), who embarked on a program of "demythologization" (see pp. 470–2). At the heart of this program was the idea that it was possible to extract the timeless significance of Jesus, which Bultmann located in the proclamation about Jesus, from the scriptural narratives concerning him. Demythologization, whatever else it may have been, was basically an attempt to get to the real meaning of the scriptural narrative about Jesus, so that the narratives could be set to one side. Once the timeless significance of Jesus had been established, the original narratives concerning him would serve no further useful purpose.

It is perhaps no accident that the death of Bultmann in 1968 may be seen as marking a new interest in the narrative quality of Scripture. The radical criticism of Christianity during the 1960s, which perhaps found its most famous expression in the "death of God" movement (see pp. 220–2), had spent itself. The time seemed right to begin the reconstruction of faith. Amongst those writers who believed that narrative theology held the key to that reconstruction, we may note the following: Hans Frei, James Gustafson, Stanley Hauerwas, George Lindbeck, and Ronald Thiemann, often loosely grouped together as "postliberal" thinkers (see pp. 109–10). It must, however, be stressed that narrative theology is by no means a well-defined movement: It is difficult (and probably not especially worthwhile) to place specific theologians firmly in this category.

What, then, are the advantages and drawbacks of such an approach? Why has it gained such a following in academic theology? The following points are important in understanding the appeal of this new approach, especially amongst writers concerned to reclaim the centrality of Scripture in modern theology.

1 Narrative is the main literary type found in Scripture. Indeed, some recent writers have even suggested that it is the *only* literary form in Scripture – an obvious, though perhaps understandable, exaggeration. It can occur in various forms: The Old Testament histories, the gospel accounts of the history of Jesus, and the parables which Jesus himself told – all are examples of narratives. To approach theology from a narrative point of view is, potentially, to be much more faithful to Scripture itself than to take a more theoretical approach. Other significant Christian documents – for example, the creeds – all maintain an emphasis on narrative, especially when affirming faith in Jesus Christ. To affirm faith in Jesus is to affirm faith in the narrative of his birth, crucifixion, death, resurrection, and ascension – a continuous story, centering upon Jesus Christ, and casting light on his identity and his significance.

2 The approach avoids the dulling sense of *abstraction* which is often claimed to be a feature of much academic theological writing. The abstract, generalizing approach of theology is set to one side. Instead, narrative theology invites us to reflect upon a story – a vivid, memorable account of something that actually happened (such as the story of Jesus), or that may be treated as if it really happened (such as the parables of Jesus). There is an appeal to the imagination (a point especially stressed by writers such as C. S. Lewis), a sense of realism, of personal involvement, which is often conspicuously absent from theology.

3 Narrative theology affirms that God meets us in history, and speaks to us as one who has been involved in history. The doctrine of the incarnation affirms that the story of Jesus Christ is also the story of God. Narrative theology declares that God really became involved in our world of space and time, that God really entered into history, that God really came to meet us where we are. Often, systematic theology creates the impression that God has presented us with a set of ideas, as if revelation were some kind of data bank (see pp. 154–5). Narrative theology enables us to recover the central insight that God became involved in our history. God's story intersects with our story. We can understand our story by relating it to the story of God, as we read it in Scripture.

This aspect of narrative theology has had a considerable impact, most strikingly in the field of ethics. Stanley Hauerwas is perhaps the most distinguished of a group of ethical writers who have argued that the gospel narratives set out a pattern of behavior which is appropriate for Christian believers. The story of Jesus Christ, for example, is seen as establishing a pattern which is characteristic of the story of Christian believers. Ethics, approached from a narrative standpoint, becomes thoroughly grounded in real life. The gospel is not primarily about a set of ethical principles; it is about the effect of an encounter with God upon the lives of individuals and the histories of nations. By relating such stories, the biblical writers are able to declare: "This is the result of being transformed by the grace of God. That is an appropriate model for Christian behavior."

4 Recognition of the narrative character of Scripture allows us to appreciate how Scripture effectively conveys the tension between the limited knowledge on the part of the human characters in the story, and the omniscience of God. In his *Art of Biblical Narrative* (1985),

Robert Alter makes this point as follows: "The biblical tale might usefully be regarded as a narrative experiment in the possibilities of moral, spiritual and historical knowledge, undertaken through a process of studied contrasts between the variously limited knowledge of the human characters and the divine omniscience quietly but firmly represented by the narrator." Perhaps Job illustrates this point with especial clarity in the Old Testament. The narrative structure of Scripture allows the reader to see the story from God's point of view, and appreciate the interplay between the human ignorance or misunderstanding of the situation and its reality, seen from God's point of view.

Thus far, we have been considering the advantages of narrative theology. But the movement has raised difficulties. For example, is the Christian narrative the *only* authoritative story? Or are there other narratives which may claim to be authoritative? What has been said thus far might suggest that narrative theology is especially attractive to conservative theologians. Yet many liberal theologians find narrative theology attractive, because it does not claim to be exclusive or universal; other stories (such as those of Hinduism) could conceivably be regarded as having equal validity (see pp. 448–50). Indeed, the question of the authority of narratives is often evaded within many modern theological circles, especially those sympathetic to liberalism or postmodernism (see pp. 92–6; 102–5).

Perhaps a more important difficulty, however, centers upon the *truth* of the narrative. Narrative theology focuses its attention upon the literary structure of Scripture. It thus tends to ignore more historical factors. In concentrating upon the literary structure of narratives, the simple historical question: Is this true? Did it really happen? tends to be ignored. How can we tell the difference between fiction and history? Both possess narrative structures – yet they have a very different historical and theological status. This point is given added weight through the recent rise of postmodernism, which argues that it is impossible to decide whether a given interpretation of a text is true or false. An appeal to the "narrative" of Scripture is inadequate to answer this crucial question.

Methods of Interpretation of Scripture

Every text demands to be interpreted; Scripture is no exception. There is a sense in which the history of Christian theology can be regarded as the history of biblical interpretation. In what follows, we shall explore some of the approaches to biblical interpretation likely to be of interest to students of theology. It will, however, be clear that the vastness of the subject makes it impossible to do more than give a representative selection of approaches to the matter.

We open our discussion by dealing with the patristic period. The *Alexandrian* school of biblical interpretation drew on the methods devised by the Jewish writer Philo of Alexandria (*c*.30 BC–*c*.45 AD) and earlier Jewish traditions, which allowed the literal interpretation of Scripture to be supplemented by an appeal to allegory. But what is an allegory? The Greek philosopher Heracleitus had defined it as "saying one thing, and meaning something other than what is said." Philo argued that it was necessary to look beneath the surface meaning of Scripture to discern a deeper meaning which lay beneath the surface of the text. These ideas were taken up by a group of theologians based in Alexandria, of which the most important are generally agreed to be Clement, Origen, and Didymus the Blind. (Indeed, Jerome playfully referred to the last-mentioned as "Didymus the Sighted," on account of the spiritual insights which resulted from his application of the allegorical method of biblical interpretation.)

The scope of the allegorical method can be seen from Origen's interpretation of key Old Testament images. Joshua's conquest of the promised land, interpreted allegorically, referred to Christ's conquest of sin upon the cross, just as the sacrificial legislation in Leviticus pointed ahead to the spiritual sacrifices of Christians. It might at first sight seem that this represents a degeneration into *eisegesis*, in which the interpreter simply reads any meaning he or she likes into the text of Scripture. However, as the writings of Didymus (which were rediscovered in an ammunition dump in Egypt during World War II) make clear, this need not be the case. It seems that a consensus developed about the images and texts of the Old Testament which were to be interpreted allegorically. For example, Jerusalem regularly came to be seen as an allegory of the church.

In contrast, the *Antiochene* school placed an emphasis upon the interpretation of Scripture in the light of its historical context. This school, especially associated with writers such as Diodore of Tarsus, John Chrysostom, and Theodore of Mopsuestia, gave an emphasis to the historical location of Old Testament prophecies, which is quite absent from the writings of Origen and other representatives of the Alexandrian tradition. Thus Theodore, in dealing with Old Testament prophecy, stresses that the prophetic message was relevant to those to whom it was directly addressed, as well as having a developed meaning for a Christian readership. Every prophetic oracle is to be interpreted as having a single consistent historical or literal meaning. In consequence, Theodore tended to interpret relatively few Old Testament passages as referring directly to Christ, whereas the

Alexandrian school regarded Christ as the hidden content of many Old Testament passages, both prophetic and historical.

In the western church a slightly different approach can be seen to develop. In many of his writings, Ambrose of Milan developed a threefold understanding of the senses of Scripture: In addition to the *natural* sense, the interpreter may discern a *moral* sense and a *rational* or *theological* sense. Augustine chose to follow this approach, and instead argued for a twofold sense – a *literal–fleshly–historical* approach and an *allegorical–mystical–spiritual* sense, although he allowed that some passages could possess both senses. "The sayings of the prophets are found to have a threefold meaning, in that some have in mind the earthly Jerusalem, others the heavenly city, and others refer to both." To understand the Old Testament at a purely historical level is unacceptable; the key to its understanding lies in its correct interpretation. Amongst the major lines of "spiritual" interpretation, the following should be noted: Adam represents Christ; Eve represents the church; Noah's ark represents the cross; the door of Noah's ark represents Christ's pierced side; the city of Jerusalem represents the heavenly Jerusalem.

> These hidden meanings of inspired Scripture we can track down to the best of our ability, with varying degrees of success. Yet we all hold firmly to the principle that all these historical events and their narrative always have some foreshadowing of things to come, and that they are always to be interpreted with reference to Christ and his church.

By the use of such lines of analysis, Augustine is able to stress the unity of the Old and New Testaments. They bear witness to the same faith, even if their modes of expression may be different (an idea developed by John Calvin). Augustine expresses this idea in a text which has become of major importance to biblical interpretation, especially as it bears on the relation between Old and New Testaments: "The New Testament is hidden in the Old; the Old is made accessible by the New" (*In Vetere Novum latet et in Novo Vetus patet*).

This distinction between the *literal* or *historical* sense of Scripture on the one hand, and a deeper *spiritual* or *allegorical* meaning on the other, came to be generally accepted within the church during the early Middle Ages. The standard method of biblical interpretation used during the Middle Ages is usually known as the *Quadriga*, or the "fourfold sense of Scripture." The origins of this method lie specifically in the distinction between the literal and spiritual senses. Scripture possesses four different senses. In addition to the literal sense, three non-literal senses could be distinguished: the allegorical, defining what Christians are to believe; the tropological or moral, defining what Christians are to do; and the anagogical, defining what Christians were to hope for. The four senses of Scripture were thus the following:

1   The *literal* sense of Scripture, in which the text could be taken at face value.
2   The *allegorical* sense, which interpreted certain passages of Scripture to produce statements of doctrine. Those passages tended either to be obscure, or to have a literal meaning which was unacceptable, for theological reasons, to their readers.
3   The *tropological* or *moral* sense, which interpreted such passages to produce ethical guidance for Christian conduct.
4   The *anagogical* sense, which interpreted passages to indicate the grounds of Christian hope, pointing toward the future fulfillment of the divine promises in the New Jerusalem.

A potential weakness was avoided by insisting that nothing should be believed on the basis of a non-literal sense of Scripture, unless it could first be established on the basis of the literal sense. This insistence on the priority of the literal sense of Scripture may be seen as an implied criticism of the allegorical approach adopted by Origen, which virtually allowed interpreters of Scripture to read into any passage whatever "spiritual" interpretations they liked. As Luther states this principle in 1515: "In the Scriptures no allegory, tropology, or anagogy is valid, unless that same truth is explicitly stated literally somewhere else. Otherwise, Scripture would become a laughing matter."

Luther is fully aware of the distinctions noted above, and has no hesitation in using them to the full in his biblical exposition. In his analysis of the Psalter, he distinguishes eight senses of the Old Testament. This amazing precision (which may strike some readers as typical of scholasticism) results from combining the four senses of Scripture with the insight that each of these senses can be interpreted *historically* or *prophetically*. Luther argues that a distinction had to be made between what he terms "the killing letter" (*litera occidens*) – in other words, a crudely literal or historical reading of the Old Testament – and "the life-giving spirit" (*spiritus vivificans*) – in other words, a reading of the Old Testament which is sensitive to its spiritual nuances and prophetic overtones. As a worked example, we may consider Luther's analysis of an Old Testament image using this eight-fold scheme of interpretation.

The image in question is Mount Zion, which can be interpreted either in a woodenly historical and literal sense as a reference to ancient Israel, or as a prophetic reference to the New Testament church. Luther explores the possibilities as follows:

1   Historically, according to "the killing letter":
    (a)   literally: the land of Canaan;
    (b)   allegorically: the synagogue, or a prominent person within it;
    (c)   tropologically: the righteousness of the Pharisees and the Law;
    (d)   anagogically: a future glory on earth.
2   Prophetically, according to "the life-giving spirit":
    (a)   literally: the people of Zion;
    (b)   allegorically: the church, or a prominent person within it;
    (c)   tropologically: the righteousness of faith;
    (d)   anagogically: the eternal glory of the heavens.

The *Quadriga* was a major component of academic study of the Bible within scholastic theological faculties of universities. But it was not the only option available to biblical interpreters in the first two decades of the sixteenth century. Indeed, Luther may be argued to be the only reformer to make significant use of this scholastic approach to biblical interpretation. By far the most influential approach to the subject within reforming and humanist circles in the early Reformation period was that associated with Erasmus of Rotterdam, to which we may now turn.

Erasmus' *Handbook of the Christian Soldier* (see p. 46) made much of the distinction between the "letter" and the "spirit" – that is, between the words of Scripture and their real meaning. Especially in the Old Testament, the words of the text are like a shell, containing – but not identical with – the kernel of the meaning. The surface meaning of the text often conceals a deeper hidden meaning, which it is the task of the enlightened and responsible exegete to uncover. Biblical interpretation, according to Erasmus, is concerned with establishing the underlying sense, not the letter, of Scripture. There are strong affinities here with the Alexandrian school, noted earlier.

Zwingli's basic concern echoes that of Erasmus. The interpreter of the Bible is required to establish the "natural sense of Scripture" – which is not necessarily identical with the literal sense of Scripture. Zwingli's humanist background allows him to distinguish various figures of speech, especially alloiosis, catachresis, and synecdoche. An example will make this point clear. Take the statement of Christ at the Last Supper, in which, when breaking the bread, he spoke the words "this is my body" (Matthew 26: 26). The literal sense of these words would be "this piece of bread is my body," but the natural sense is "this piece of bread signifies my body" (see p. 441).

Zwingli's search for the deeper meaning of Scripture (to be contrasted with the superficial meaning) is well illustrated by the story of
Abraham and Isaac (Genesis 22). The historical details of the story are
too easily assumed to be its real meaning. In fact, Zwingli argues, the
real meaning of that story can only be understood when it is seen as
a prophetic anticipation of the story of Christ, in which Abraham
represents God and Isaac is a figure (or, more technically, "type") of
Christ.

With the advent of the modern period, the science of biblical interpretation has become considerably more complex, reflecting the
increased acceptance within academic circles of new rational methods
of interpretation, grounded in the assumptions of the Enlightenment.
It is impossible to survey these developments adequately in the
scope of this work. However, it will be helpful to note some broad
tendencies in biblical interpretation during the last two and a half
centuries. Under the influence of the Enlightenment, four main
approaches can be seen in academic biblical interpretation.

1 The *rational* approach, found in the writings of H. S. Reimarus.
This regards both Old and New Testaments as resting on a series
of supernatural fictions. By a process of radical logical criticism, he
argued that the supernatural elements of the Bible could not be taken
seriously. It was therefore necessary to interpret Scripture along
rational lines, as stating (although in a somewhat muddled manner)
the universal truths of the religion of reason. With the general collapse
in confidence in both the universality and the theological competence
of reason in more recent times, the attractions of this approach have
dwindled drastically.

2 The historical approach, which treats Scripture as an account of
Christian origins. F. C. Baur, probably the most distinguished early
representative of this tradition, argued that it was no longer per-
missible to explain the origins of the Christian faith in terms of "the
only-begotten Son of God descending from the eternal throne of the
Godhead to earth, and becoming a human person in the womb of
the virgin." Instead, Baur argued that it was possible to account for
the origins of Christianity in rational and non-supernatural terms.
Believing that Hegelianism held the key to explaining how Christianity
came into being, Baur made a direct appeal to its philosophy of
history as an alternative explanation to the traditional accounts of the
origins of Christian faith, and interpreted the New Testament in its
light. With the waning of Hegelianism, Baur's impact also diminished.

3 The *sociological* approach. By the 1890s, many liberal Christians
had lost interest in matters of Christian doctrine or theology, and
begun to explore the wider category of "religion" in general – a trend
which undergirds the development of faculties of "religious studies"

in many western universities. Yet religion is a social phenomenon; concerned with far more than "ideas" as such, it comes under the category of "social history." The way was thus opened for a socio-logical approach to biblical interpretation, which treated Christianity as a specific example of a general phenomenon – religion. An example of this approach is provided by Sir James's Frazer's *Golden Bough* (1890–1915), which applied comparative ethnology (the study of peoples and their traditions) to the Bible on an unprecedented scale.

4 The *literary* approach, which is concerned to do justice to the distinctive literary categories of Scripture. One such approach which has had major impact of late is *narrative theology*, which has been discussed at length earlier in this chapter (see pp. 170–4).

Theories of the Inspiration of Scripture

The notion that the special status of Scripture within Christian the-ology rests upon its divine origins, however vaguely this may be stated, can be discerned both in the New Testament itself, and in subsequent reflection on it. An important element in any discussion of the manner in which Scripture is inspired, and the significance which is to be attached to this, is 2 Timothy 3: 16–17, which speaks of Scripture as "God-breathed" (*theopneustos*). This idea was common in early Christian thought, and was not regarded as controversial. The Greek-speaking Jewish philosopher Philo of Alexandria (*c*.30 BC–*c*.AD 45) regarded Scripture as fully inspired, and argued that God used the authors of scriptural books as passive instruments for communicating the divine will.

The issue began to surface as potentially controversial at the time of the Reformation, especially through the writings of John Calvin. Calvin was concerned to defend the authority of Scripture against two groups of people. On the one hand were those on the more Catholic wing of the church, who argued that the authority of Scripture rested in its being recognized as authoritative by the Church. On the other were the more radical evangelical writers, such as the Anabaptists, who argued that every individual had the right to ignore Scripture altogether in favor of some direct personal divine revelation. Calvin declared that the Spirit worked through Scripture (not bypassing it, as the radicals held), and that the Spirit lent direct authority to Scripture by inspiring it, thus doing away with the need for any external support to its authority (such as that of the church).

This point is important, in that it indicates that the reformers did not see the issue of inspiration as linked with the absolute historical reliability or factual inerrancy of the biblical texts. Calvin's doctrine of accommodation implied that God revealed himself in forms tailored to the abilities of the communities which were to receive this revelation; thus in the case of Genesis 1, Calvin suggests that a whole series of ideas – such as the "days of creation" – are simply accommodated ways of speaking, a kind of divine "baby-talk." The development of ideas of "biblical infallibility" or "inerrancy" within Protestantism can be traced to the United States in the middle of the nineteenth century.

With the coming of the Enlightenment, the idea of the Bible having special status was called into question, largely on account of the pre-suppositions of the rationalism of the period, and increased interest in the critical study of Scripture. A number of approaches to the issue of inspiration which developed around this period are of interest.

1 J. G. Herder, strongly influenced by the outlook of Romanticism, argued that the idea of inspiration was to be interpreted in an artistic or aesthetic sense. In his *Spirit of Hebrew Poetry* (1782–3), Herder suggested that the most appropriate model for biblical inspiration was provided by works of art. Just as one might speak of a great novel, poem, or painting as "inspired," so the same idea can be applied to Scripture. Inspiration is thus seen as a human achievement, rather than a gift of God.

2 The Old Princeton School, represented by Charles Hodge (1797–1878) and Benjamin B. Warfield (1851–1921), developed strongly supernatural theories of inspiration, in conscious opposition to the naturalist approach favored by Herder. "Inspiration is that extra-ordinary, supernatural influence . . . exerted by the Holy Ghost on the writers of our Sacred Books, by which their words were rendered also the words of God, and, therefore, perfectly infallible." Although Warfield is careful to stress that the humanity and individuality of biblical writers are not abolished by inspiration, he nonetheless insists that their humanity "was so dominated that their words became at the same time the words of God, and thus, in every case and all alike, absolutely infallible."

3 Others held that inspiration was also to be regarded as God's guidance of the *reader* of Scripture, which enabled that reader to recognize the word of God in the biblical text. As we have just seen, Warfield located the inspiration of Scripture in the biblical text itself, thus implying that Scripture was *objectively*, in itself, the word of God for all who read it. Others argued for a *subjective* understanding of inspiration, by which the reader's perception of Scripture – rather than Scripture itself – was to be regarded as "inspired." Augustus H. Strong (1836–1921) stressed that the authority of Scripture could not be located simply in the words of Scripture, as if these could have authoritative status apart from their reception by individual believers, or the community of faith. Inspiration thus had to be recognized to have objective and subjective aspects.

Having considered some questions relating to Scripture as a source of Christian theology, we may now turn to a consideration of the role of reason.

Reason

The second major resource to be considered is human reason. Although the importance of reason for Christian theology has always been recognized, it assumed an especial importance at the time of the Enlightenment (see pp. 78–86). We open our discussion by considering the changing emphasis which has come to be placed upon reason within the Christian tradition.

Reason and Revelation: Three Models

In that human beings are rational, it is to be expected that reason should have a major role to play in theology. There has, however, been considerable debate within Christian theology concerning what that role might be. Three broad categories of positions can be discerned.

1 *Theology is a rational discipline.* This position, associated with writers such as Thomas Aquinas, works on the assumption that the Christian faith is fundamentally rational, and can thus be both supported and explored by reason. Aquinas' Five Ways, considered earlier, illustrate his belief that reason is capable of lending support to the ideas of faith.

But Aquinas, and the Christian tradition which he represented, did not believe that Christianity was limited to what could be ascertained by reason. Faith goes beyond reason, having access to truths and insights of revelation, which reason could not hope to fathom or discover unaided. Reason has the role of building upon what is known by revelation, exploring what its implications might be. In this sense, theology is a *scientia* – a rational discipline, using rational methods to build upon and extend what is known by revelation.

The noted historian of medieval Christian thought, Etienne Gilson, made a delightful comparison between the great theological systems of the Middle Ages and the cathedrals which sprang up throughout Christian Europe at this time: The former were, he remarked, "cathedrals of the mind." Christianity is like a cathedral which rests upon the bedrock of human reason, but whose superstructure rises beyond the realms accessible to pure reason. It rests upon rational foundations; but the building erected on that foundation went far beyond what reason could uncover.

2 *Theology is the re-publication of the insights of reason.* By the middle of the seventeenth century, especially in England and Germany, a new attitude began to develop. Christianity, it was argued, was reasonable. But where Thomas Aquinas understood this to mean that faith rested securely upon rational foundations, the new school of thought had different ideas. If faith is rational, they argued, it must be capable of being deduced in its entirety by reason. Every aspect of faith, every item of Christian belief, must be shown to derive from human reason.

An excellent example of this approach is to be found in the writings of Lord Herbert of Cherbury, especially *De veritatis religionis*, "On the truth of religion," which argued for a rational Christianity based upon the innate sense of God and human moral obligation. This had two major consequences. First, Christianity was in effect *reduced* to those ideas which could be proved by reason. If Christianity was rational, then any parts of its system which could not be proved by reason could not be counted as "rational." They would have to be discarded. And second, reason was understood to take priority over revelation. Reason comes first, revelation comes second.

Reason thus came to be regarded as being capable of establishing what is right without needing any assistance from revelation; Christianity has to follow, being accepted where it endorses what reason has to say, and being disregarded where it went its own way. So why bother with the idea of revelation, when reason could tell us all we could possibly wish to know about God, the world, and ourselves? This absolutely settled conviction in the total competence of human reason underlies the rationalist depreciation of the Christian doctrine of revelation in Jesus Christ and through Scripture.

3 *Theology is redundant; reason reigns supreme.* Finally, this potentially rationalist position was pushed to its logical outcome. As a matter of fact, it was argued, Christianity does include a series of major beliefs which are inconsistent with reason. Reason has the right to judge religion, in that it stands above it. This approach is usually termed "Enlightenment rationalism," and is of such importance that it will be considered in more detail. We begin by looking at an English movement which laid the foundations of this form of rationalism in religion – Deism.

Deism

The term "deism" (from the Latin *deus*, "god") is often used in a general sense to refer to that view of God which maintains God's creatorship, but denies a continuing divine involvement with, or special presence within, that creation. It is often contrasted with "theism" (from the Greek *theos*, "god"),which allows for continuing divine involvement within the world.

In its more specific sense, Deism is used to refer to the views of a group of English thinkers during the "Age of Reason," in the late seventeenth and early eighteenth centuries. In his *Principal Deistic Writers* (1757), Leland grouped together a number of writers – including Lord Herbert of Cherbury, Thomas Hobbes, and David Hume – under the broad term "deist." Close examination of their religious views shows that they have relatively little in common, apart from a general skepticism of specifically Christian ideas.

John Locke's *Essay Concerning Human Understanding* (1690) developed an idea of God which became characteristic of much later Deism. Indeed, Locke's *Essay* can be said to lay much of the intellectual foundations of Deism. Locke argued that "reason leads us to the knowledge of this certain and evident truth, that there is an *eternal, most powerful and most knowing Being*." The attributes of this being are those which human reason recognizes as appropriate for God. Having considered which moral and rational qualities are suited to the deity, Locke argues that "we enlarge every one of these with our idea of infinity, and so, putting them together, make our complex *idea of God*." In other words, the idea of God is made up of human rational and moral qualities, projected to infinity.

Matthew Tindal's *Christianity as Old as Creation* (1730) argued that Christianity was nothing other than the "republication of the religion of nature." God is understood as the extension of accepted human ideas of justice, rationality, and wisdom. This universal religion is available at all times and in every place, whereas traditional Christianity rested upon the idea of a divine revelation which was not accessible to those who lived before Christ. Tindal's views were propagated before the modern discipline of the sociology of knowledge created skepticism of the idea of "universal reason," and are an excellent model of the rationalism characteristic of the movement, and which later became influential within the Enlightenment.

The ideas of English Deism percolated through to the continent of Europe (especially to Germany) through translations, and through the writings of individuals familiar with and sympathetic to them, such as Voltaire's *Philosophical Letters*. Enlightenment rationalism, to which we now turn, is often considered to be the final flowering of the bud of English Deism.

Enlightenment Rationalism

The basic presupposition of Enlightenment rationalism is that human reason is perfectly capable of telling us everything we need to know about the world, ourselves, and God (if there is one). One of the most graphic portrayals of this enormous confidence in reason is the frontispiece to the eighteenth-century rationalist philosopher Christian Wolff's ambitiously titled book *Reasonable Thoughts about God, the World, the Human Soul, and just about everything else* (1720). The engraving in question portrays a world enveloped in shadows and gloom, representing the old ideas of superstition, tradition, and faith. But on part of the engraving, the sun has broken through, lighting up hills and valleys, and bringing smiles to the faces of what we must assume to have been a hitherto rather gloomy group of peasants. The message is clear: Reason enlightens, dispelling the fog and darkness of Christian faith, and ushering in the glorious light of human rationality. Divine revelation is an irrelevance, if it exists at all. The consequences of this approach were noted in more detail earlier, as we surveyed the general impact of the Enlightenment upon Christian theology.

At this point, we need to stress the difference between "reason" and "rationalism," which may appear identical to some readers. *Reason* is the basic human faculty of thinking, based on argument and evidence. It is theologically neutral, and poses no threat to faith – unless it is regarded as the only source of knowledge about God. It then becomes *rationalism*, which is an exclusive reliance upon human reason alone, and a refusal to allow any weight to be given to divine revelation.

Enlightenment rationalism may be said to rest upon the belief that unaided human reason can deliver everything that humanity needs to know. There is no need to listen to other voices, having first consulted reason. By definition, the Christian cannot have anything to say that is at one and the same time distinctive and right. If it is distinctive, it departs from the path of reason – and thus must be untrue. To be different is, quite simply, to be wrong.

An excellent example of this rationalist critique of Christianity can be seen in relation to the doctrine of Christ (how could Jesus be both God and man at one and the same time?) and the doctrine of the Trinity (how can one God be three persons simultaneously,

within lapsing into crude logical contradiction?). One of the early
American presidents, Thomas Jefferson, who was deeply influenced
by eighteenth-century French rationalism, poured reasoned scorn
upon the doctrine of the Trinity:

> When we shall have done away with the incomprehensible jargon
> of the Trinitarian arithmetic, that three are one and one is three;
> when we shall have knocked down the artificial scaffolding, reared
> to mask from view the very simple structure of Jesus; when, in
> short, we shall have unlearned everything which has been taught
> since his day, and got back to the pure and simple doctrines he
> inculcated, we shall then be truly and worthily his disciples.

Jesus was really a very simple rational teacher, who taught a very
simple and reasonable gospel about a very simple and rational idea of
God. And at every point, Christianity chose to make things more
complicated than they need be.

A direct consequence of this was the movement in New Testament
studies known as the "quest of the historical Jesus" (see pp. 316–27).
This quest, which dates from the late eighteenth century, was based
upon the belief that the New Testament got Jesus entirely wrong. The
real Jesus – the "Jesus of history" – was a simple Galilean teacher,
who taught entirely sensible ideas based upon reason. The New
Testament quite erroneously presented him as the risen savior of
sinful humanity.

Reason was thus held to be able to judge Christ. In his celebrated
work *Religion within the Limits of Reason Alone*, Immanuel Kant argued
powerfully for the priority of reason and conscience over the authority
of Jesus Christ. Where Jesus endorses what reason has to say, he is to
be respected; where he goes against or goes beyond reason, he is to be
rejected. Iris Murdoch writes of this type of approach in *The Sovereignty
of the Good*:

> How recognizable, how familiar to us, is the man so beautifully
> portrayed in the *Grundlegung*, who confronted even with Christ
> turns away to consider the judgement of his own conscience and
> to hear the voice of his own reason. Stripped of the exiguous
> metaphysical background which Kant was prepared to allow him,
> this man is still with us, free, independent, lonely, powerful,
> rational, responsible, brave, the hero of so many novels and books
> of moral philosophy.

Enlightenment rationalism, then, upheld the sovereignty of reason,
arguing that human reason was capable of establishing all that it was
necessary to know about religion without recourse to the idea of

"revelation." Furthermore, reason possessed an ability to judge the truths of religions, such as Christianity, and eliminate vast tracts of its ideas as "irrational." Influential though such ideas were in the late eighteenth and nineteenth centuries, they are now regarded with suspicion. The following section explores why.

Criticisms of Enlightenment Rationalism

A series of developments, of which we may here note a few, have destroyed the credibility of the Enlightenment approach. This approach could be said to rest upon the idea of the "immediately given," whether in reason or in experience. Knowledge rests upon a foundation, whether this is self-evident truths, immediately recognized as such by the human mind, or immediate experience, deriving directly from contact with the outside world. But these foundations do not seem to exist.

We may begin by exploring reason itself. Surely human reason is capable of basing itself upon self-evident first principles, and, by following these through logically, deducing a complete system? Just about everyone who favors this approach makes some sort of appeal to Euclid's five principles of geometry. On the basis of his five principles, he was able to construct his entire geometrical system. Philosophers, such as Spinoza, were deeply attracted to this: maybe they could use the same method in philosophy. On a set of certain assumptions, a great secure edifice of philosophy and ethics could be erected. But the dream turned sour. The discovery of non-Euclidian geometry during the nineteenth century destroyed the appeal of this analogy. It turned out that there were other ways of doing geometry, each just as internally consistent as Euclid's. But which is right? The question cannot be answered. They are all different, each with its own especial merits and problems.

Much the same observation is now made concerning rationalism itself. Where once it was argued that there was one single rational principle, it is now conceded that there are – and always have been – many different "rationalities." Enlightenment thinkers appear to have been shielded from this disconcerting fact by the limitations of their historical scholarship, which remained firmly wedded to the classical western tradition. But this illusion has now been shattered. At the end of his brilliant analysis of rational approaches to reason, Alasdair MacIntyre concludes:

> Both the thinkers of the Enlightenment and their successors proved unable to agree as to precisely what those principles were

which would be found undeniable by all rational persons. One
kind of answer was given by the authors of the *Encyclopédie*, a
second by Rousseau, a third by Bentham, a fourth by Kant, a fifth
by the Scottish philosophers of common sense and their French
and American disciples. Nor has subsequent history diminished
the extent of such disagreement. Consequently, the legacy of
the Enlightenment has been the provision of an ideal of rational
justification which it has proved impossible to attain.

Reason promises much, yet fails to deliver its much-vaunted benefits.
It is for such reasons that Hans-Georg Gadamer wrote scathingly of
the "Robinson Crusoe dream of the historical Enlightenment, as
artificial as Crusoe himself." The notion of "universal rationality" is
today viewed by many as little more than a fiction. Postmodernism
has argued that there exist a variety of "rationalities," each of which
has to be respected in its own right; there is no privileged vantage
point, no universal concept of "reason," which can pass judgment
upon them.

Having considered Scripture and reason as theological resources,
we may now turn to consider the idea of tradition.

Tradition

The word "tradition" implies not merely something that is handed
down, but an active process of reflection by which theological or
spiritual insights are valued, assessed, and transmitted from one
generation to another. Three broad approaches to tradition may be
detected within Christian theology.

A Single-Source Theory of Tradition

In response to various controversies within the early church, especially
the threat from Gnosticism, a "traditional" method of understanding certain passages of Scripture began to develop. Second-century
patristic theologians such as Irenaeus of Lyons began to develop the
idea of an authorized way of interpreting certain texts of Scripture,
which he argued went back to the time of the Apostles themselves.
Scripture could not be allowed to be interpreted in any arbitrary
or random way: it had to be interpreted within the context of the
historical continuity of the Christian church. The parameters of its
interpretation were historically fixed and "given." "Tradition" here

means simply "a traditional way of interpreting Scripture within the community of faith." This is a *single-source* theory of theology: Theology is based upon Scripture, and "tradition" refers to a "traditional way of interpreting Scripture."

The mainstream Reformation adopted this approach, insisting that traditional interpretations of Scripture – such as the doctrine of the Trinity or the practice of infant baptism – could be retained, provided they could be shown to be consistent with Scripture. On the basis of this observation, it will be clear that it is incorrect to suggest that the magisterial reformers elevated private judgment above the corporate judgment of the church, or that they descended into some form of individualism. This is, however, unquestionably true of the radical Reformation (see below).

This approach remains the "majority report" within modern Christian thought. Nevertheless, two significant alternative positions should be noted.

A Dual-Source Theory of Tradition

In the fourteenth and fifteenth centuries a somewhat different understanding of tradition from that noted above developed. "Tradition" was understood to be a separate and distinct source of revelation, *in addition to Scripture*. Scripture, it was argued, was silent on a number of points – but God had providentially arranged for a second source of revelation to supplement this deficiency: A stream of unwritten tradition, going back to the Apostles themselves. This tradition was passed down from one generation to another within the church. This is a *dual-source* theory of theology: Theology is based upon two quite distinct sources, Scripture and unwritten tradition.

A belief which is not to be found in Scripture may thus, on the basis of this dual-source theory, be justified by an appeal to an unwritten tradition. This position was defended strongly at the Council of Trent, which was charged with stating and defending the Roman Catholic position against the threat posed by the Reformation. Trent ruled that Scripture could not be regarded as the only source of revelation; tradition was a vital supplement, which Protestants irresponsibly denied. "All saving truths and rules of conduct . . . are contained in the written books and in the unwritten traditions, received from the mouth of Christ himself or from the apostles themselves." Interestingly, however, the Second Vatican Council (1962–5) seems to move away from this approach, in favor of the "traditional interpretation of Scripture" approach, noted above.

These two approaches just discussed affirm the value of tradition.

A third approach, which in effect rejected tradition, came to be influential within the radical wing of the Reformation, often known as "Anabaptism," and subsequently was developed by writers sympathetic to the Enlightenment.

The Total Rejection of Tradition

For radical theologians of the sixteenth century, such as Thomas Müntzer and Caspar Schwenkfeld, every individual had the right to interpret Scripture as he or she pleased, subject to the guidance of the Holy Spirit. For the radical Sebastian Franck, the Bible "is a book sealed with seven seals which none can open unless he has the key of David, which is the illumination of the Spirit." The way was thus opened for individualism, with the private judgment of the individual raised above the corporate judgment of the church. Thus the radicals rejected the practice of infant baptism (to which the magisterial Reformation remained committed) as non-scriptural. (There is no explicit reference to the practice in the New Testament.) Similarly, doctrines such as the Trinity and the divinity of Christ were rejected as resting upon inadequate scriptural foundations. The radicals had no place whatsoever for tradition. As Sebastian Franck wrote in 1530: "Foolish Ambrose, Augustine, Jerome, Gregory – of whom not one even knew the Lord, so help me God, nor was sent by God to teach. Rather, they were all apostles of Antichrist."

This approach was developed further during the Enlightenment, which was anxious to liberate itself from the shackles of tradition. Political emancipation from the oppression of the past (a key theme of the French Revolution) meant a total abandoning of the political, social, and religious ideas of the past. One of the reasons why Enlightenment thinkers placed such a high value upon human reason was that it relieved them of the need to appeal to tradition for ideas; any ideas worth knowing about were accessible to reason alone.

A respect for tradition was thus seen as capitulation to the authority of the past, a self-imposed bondage to outdated social, political, and religious structures. "Modern thought was born in a crisis of authority, took shape in flight from authority, and aspired from the start to autonomy from all traditional influence whatsoever" (Jeffrey Stout). Or, as Michael Polanyi puts it:

> We were warned that a host of unproven beliefs were instilled in us from earliest childhood. That religious dogma, the authority of the ancients, the teaching of the schools, the maxims of the nursery, all were united to a body of tradition which we tended to

accept merely because these beliefs had been previously held by others, who wanted us to embrace them in our turn.

The Enlightenment thus represented a radical rejection of tradition. Reason required no supplementation by voices from the past.

Theology and Worship: The Importance of Liturgical Tradition

One of the most important elements of the Christian tradition is fixed forms of worship, usually known as "liturgy." In recent years there has been a rediscovery of the fact that Christian theologians pray and worship, and that this devotional context shapes their theological reflections. This point has been appreciated since the first centuries of the Christian church. The tag *lex orandi, lex credendi*, which could be translated roughly as "the way you pray determines what you believe," expresses the fact that theology and worship interact with each other. What Christians believe affects the manner in which they pray and worship; the manner in which Christians pray and worship affects what they believe.

Two controversies within the early church, centering on Gnosticism and Arianism, illustrate the importance of this point particularly well. On the basis of their radical dualism between the "physical" and the "spiritual," the Gnostics argued that matter was inherently evil. In refuting this position, Irenaeus pointed to the fact that bread, wine, and water were used in the Christian sacraments. How could they be evil, if they were given so prominent a position in Christian worship?

Arius argued that Christ was supreme amongst God's creatures. His opponents, such as Athanasius, retorted that this Christology was totally inconsistent with the way in which Christians worshipped. Athanasius stressed the theological importance of the practice of praying to Christ and worshipping him. If Arius was right, Christians were guilty of idolatry, through worshipping a creature, rather than God. Where Arius believed that theology should criticize liturgy, Athanasius believed that worship patterns and practices had to be taken into account by theologians.

In recent times, there has been renewed interest in the relation between liturgy and theology. In his *Doxology*, the Methodist writer Geoffrey Wainwright drew attention to the way in which theological motifs were incorporated into Christian worship from the earliest of times. The liturgy of the church includes intellectual elements, and is not purely emotive in character. As a result, the close relationship between theology and liturgy, noted above, is entirely natural, in that worship and theological reflection are linked together organically.

In his *On Liturgical Theology* (1984), the Roman Catholic theologian Aidan Kavanagh argued that worship was the primary source and stimulus of Christian theology. Kavanagh drew a sharp distinction between *primary theology* (worship) and *secondary theology* (theological reflection). This suggests that worship has the upper hand over theology. But what happens if liturgical development becomes irresponsible? Does theology have a role in *limiting* or *criticizing* liturgy? This question of the relative authority of the *lex orandi* and *lex credendi* remains to be further explored, and is likely to be the subject of lively debate for some time to come.

Religious Experience

"Experience" is an imprecise term. The origins of the word are relatively well understood: It derives from the Latin term *experientia*, which could be interpreted as "that which arises out of travelling through life" (*ex-perientia*). In this broad sense, it means "an accumulated body of knowledge, arising through first-hand encounter with life." When one speaks of "an experienced teacher" or "an experienced doctor," the implication is that the teacher or doctor has learned her craft through first-hand application.

Yet the term has developed an acquired meaning, which particularly concerns us here. It has come to refer to the inner life of individuals, in which those individuals become aware of their own subjective feelings and emotions. It relates to the inward and subjective world of experience, as opposed to the outward world of everyday life. A series of writings, including William James's celebrated study *The Varieties of Religious Experience* (1902), have stressed the importance of the subjective aspects of religion in general, and Christianity in particular. Christianity is not simply about ideas (as our discussion of Scripture, reason, and tradition might suggest); it is about the interpretation and transformation of the inner life of the individual. This concern with human experience is particularly associated with the movement generally known as *existentialism*, which we may consider briefly, before moving on.

Existentialism: A Philosophy of Human Experience

In what way do human beings differ from other forms of life? Humans have always been aware of some basic distinction between themselves on the one hand, and all other forms of life on the other. But what *is* this difference? And what does it *mean* to exist? Perhaps the most important thing which distinguishes human beings from other forms of life is the fact that they are aware of their own existence, and ask questions about it.

The rise of existentialist philosophy is ultimately a response to this crucial insight. We not only exist: We *understand*, we *are aware* that we exist, and we are aware that our existence will one day be terminated by death. The sheer fact of our existence is important to us, and we find it difficult, probably impossible, to adopt a totally detached attitude to it. Existentialism is basically a protest against the view that human beings are "things," and a demand that we take the personal existence of the individual with full seriousness.

The term "existentialism" can bear two meanings. At its most basic level, it means an *attitude* toward human life which places special emphasis upon the immediate, real-life experience of individuals. It is concerned with the way in which individuals encounter others, and gain an understanding of their finitude. In a more developed sense, the term refers to a *movement*, which probably reached its zenith in the period 1938–68, the origins of which lie primarily in the writings of the Danish philosopher Søren Kierkegaard (1813–55). Kierkegaard stressed the importance of individual decision and an awareness of the limits of human existence. In terms of the history of modern theology, the most important contribution to the development of existentialism was made by Martin Heidegger (1888–1976), particularly in his *Being and Time* (1927). This work provided Rudolf Bultmann with the basic ideas and vocabulary he required to develop a Christian existentialist account of human existence, and the manner in which this is illuminated and transformed by the gospel.

Heidegger's work is dominated by the theme of "Being" (*Dasein*). Especially in his *Commentary on John's Gospel*, Bultmann argued that Heidegger's existentialist vocabulary expressed the basic ideas of the New Testament in secular terms. Of fundamental importance is Heidegger's distinction between "inauthentic existence" and "authentic existence," which Bultmann creatively reinterprets in the light of the New Testament.

According to Bultmann, the New Testament recognizes two types of human existence. First, there is unbelieving, unredeemed existence, which is an inauthentic form of existence. Here, individuals refuse to recognize themselves for what they really are: creatures who are dependent upon God for their well-being and salvation. Such individuals seek to justify themselves by trying to secure existence through moral actions or material prosperity. This attempt at self-sufficiency on the part of humanity is designated by both the Old and New Testaments as "sin."

Against this inauthentic mode of human existence, the New Testament sets the mode of believing, redeemed existence, in which we abandon all security created by ourselves, and trust in God. We recognize the illusion of our self-sufficiency, and trust instead in the sufficiency of God. Instead of denying that we are God's creatures, we recognize and exult in this fact, and base our existence upon it. Instead of clinging to transitory things for security, we learn to abandon faith in this transitory world in order that we may place our trust in God himself. Instead of trying to justify ourselves, we learn to recognize that God offers us our justification as a free gift. Instead of denying the reality of our human finitude and the inevitability of death, we recognize that these have been faced and conquered through the death and resurrection of Jesus Christ, whose victory becomes our victory through faith.

The rise of existentialism is a reflection of the importance attached to the inner world of human experience in the modern period. Nevertheless, it must be appreciated that this concern with human experience is not something new; it can arguably be discerned in both Old and New Testaments, and it permeates the writings of Augustine of Hippo. Martin Luther declared that "experience makes a theologian," and argued that it was impossible to be a proper theologian without an experience of the searing and terrifying judgment of God upon human sin. As we noted earlier, the literary movement known as Romanticism (see pp. 87–9) gave considerable importance to the role of "feeling," and opened the way for a new interest in this aspect of Christian life.

Experience and Theology: Two Models

Two main approaches to the question of the relation of experience to theology may be discerned within Christian theology:

1 Experience provides a foundational resource for Christian theology.
2 Christian theology provides an interpretive framework within which human experience may be interpreted.

The second has been the dominant theme, and will be considered in more detail.

Experience as a foundational resource

The idea that human religious experience can act as a foundational resource for Christian theology has obvious attractions. It suggests that Christian theology is concerned with human experience – something which is common to all humanity, rather than the exclusive preserve of a small group. To those who are embarrassed by the "scandal of particularity" the approach has many merits. It suggests that all the world religions are basically human responses to the same religious experience – often referred to as "a core experience of the transcendent." Theology is thus the Christian attempt to reflect upon this common human experience, in the knowledge that the same experience underlies the other world religions. We shall return to this point later in dealing with the question of the relation of Christianity to the other religions.

This approach also has considerable attractions for Christian apologetics, as the writings of Paul Tillich and David Tracy make clear. If humans share a common experience, whether they choose to regard it as "religious" or not, Christian theology can address that experience. The problem of agreeing upon a common starting point is thus avoided; the starting point is already provided, in human experience. Apologetics can demonstrate that the Christian gospel makes sense of common human experience. This approach is probably seen at its best in Paul Tillich's volume of sermons *The Courage to Be*, which attracted considerable attention after its publication in 1952. It seemed to many observers that Tillich had succeeded in correlating the Christian proclamation with common human experience.

But there are difficulties here. The most obvious is that there is actually very little empirical evidence for a "common core experience" throughout human history and culture. The idea is easily postulated, and virtually impossible to verify. This criticism has found its most mature and sophisticated expression in the "Experiential-Expressive Theory of Doctrine," to use a term employed by the distinguished Yale theologian George Lindbeck. In his volume *The Nature of Doctrine* (1984), Lindbeck provides an important analysis of the nature of Christian doctrine (pp. 109–10).

Lindbeck suggests that theories of doctrine may be divided into three general types. The *cognitive-propositionalist* theory lays stress upon the cognitive aspects of religion, emphasizing the manner in which doctrines function as truth claims or informative propositions (see pp. 154–5). The *experiential-expressive* theory interprets doctrines as non-cognitive symbols of inner human feelings or attitudes. A third possibility, which Lindbeck himself favors, is the *cultural-linguistic* approach to religion. Lindbeck associates this model with a "rule" or "regulative" theory of doctrine. It is Lindbeck's criticism of the second of these approaches which is of particular interest to us at this point.

The "experiential-expressive" approach, according to Lindbeck, sees religions, including Christianity, as public, culturally conditioned

manifestations and affirmations of pre-linguistic forms of consciousness, attitudes, and feelings. In other words, there is some common
universal "religious experience," which Christian theology (as well as
other religions) attempts to express in words. The experience comes
first; the theology comes in later. As Lindbeck argues, the attraction of
this approach to doctrine is grounded in a number of features of late
twentieth-century western thought. For example, the contemporary
preoccupation with inter-religious dialogue is considerably assisted by
the suggestion that the various religions are diverse expressions of a
common core experience, such as an "isolable core of encounter" or
an "unmediated awareness of the transcendent."

The principal objection to this theory, thus stated, is its resistance
to verification. As Lindbeck points out, "religious experience" is a
hopelessly vague idea. "It is difficult or impossible to specify its
distinctive features, and yet unless this is done, the assertion of
commonality becomes logically and empirically vacuous." The assertion that "the various religions are diverse symbolizations of one and
the same core experience of the Ultimate" is ultimately an unverifiable
hypothesis, not least on account of the difficulty of locating and
describing the "core experience" concerned. As Lindbeck rightly
points out, this would appear to suggest that there is "at least the
logical possibility that a Buddhist and a Christian might have basically
the same faith, although expressed very differently." The theory can
only be credible if it is possible to isolate a common core experience
from religious language and behavior, and demonstrate that the latter
two are articulations of or responses to the former.

For such reasons, the second approach to the understanding of the
relation between experience and theology has regained a hearing.

Experience as something which requires to be interpreted

According to this approach, Christian theology provides a framework
within which the ambiguities of experience may be interpreted.
Theology aims to interpret experience. It is like a net which we can
cast over experience, in order to capture its meaning. Experience is
seen as something which is to be interpreted, rather than something
which is itself capable of interpreting.

The classic example of this approach is usually thought to be Martin
Luther's "theology of the cross," which is of continuing significance
as a critique of the role of experience in theology. Luther's position is
that experience is of vital importance to theology; without experience,
theology is impoverished and deficient, an empty shell waiting to
be filled. Yet experience cannot by itself be regarded as a reliable theological resource; it must be interpreted and corrected by theology.

Luther suggests that we attempt to imagine what it was like for the disciples of Jesus on the first Good Friday. They had given up everything to follow Jesus. Their whole reason for living centered on him. He seemed to have the answers to all their questions. Then, in front of their eyes, he was taken from them and publicly executed. God was experienced as being absent. There was no way in which anyone experienced God as being present on that occasion. Even Jesus himself seems to have had a momentary sense of the absence of God – "My God, my God, why have you forsaken me?" (Matthew 27: 46).

This way of thinking, according to Luther, demonstrates how unreliable experience and feelings can be as guides to the presence of God. Those around the cross did not experience the presence of God – so they concluded that God was absent from the scene. The resurrection overturns that judgment: God was present in a hidden manner, which experience mistook for absence. Theology interprets our feelings, even to the point of contradicting them when they are misleading. It stresses the faithfulness of God and the reality of the resurrection hope – even where experience seems to suggest otherwise. Theology thus gives us a framework for making sense of the contradictions of experience. God may be experienced as absent from the world – yet theology insists that this experience is provisional and flawed, and cannot be taken at face value.

Yet theology also allows experience to be interpreted in a more positive manner. The dialectic between the Christian doctrines of creation and sin can be deployed to provide an interpretation of a common human experience – an awareness of dissatisfaction, or a curious sense of longing for something undefined. To illustrate the relation between theology and experience, we may consider Augustine's analysis of the implications for experience of the Christian doctrine of creation.

According to Augustine, it is a consequence of the Christian doctrine of creation that we are made in the image of God. There is thus an inbuilt capacity within human nature to relate to God. Yet, on account of the fallenness of human nature, this potential is frustrated. There is now a natural tendency to try to make other things fulfill this need. Created things thus come to be substituted for God. And they do not satisfy. Human beings are thus left with a feeling of longing – longing for something undefinable.

This phenomenon has been recognized since the dawn of human civilization. In his dialogue *Gorgias*, Plato compares human beings to leaky jars. Somehow, human beings are always unfulfilled. Perhaps the greatest statement of this feeling, and its most famous theological interpretation, may be found in the famous words of Augustine:

"You have made us for yourself, and our hearts are restless until they rest in you."

Throughout Augustine's reflections, especially in his autobiographical *Confessions*, the same theme recurs. Humanity is destined to remain incomplete in its present existence. Its hopes and deepest longings will remain nothing but hopes and longings. The themes of creation and redemption are brought together by Augustine, to provide an interpretation of the human experience of "longing." Because humanity is created in the image of God, it desires to relate to God, even if it cannot recognize that desire for what it is. Yet on account of human sin, humanity cannot satisfy that desire unaided. And so a real sense of frustration, of dissatisfaction, develops. And that dissatisfaction – though not its theological interpretation – is part of common human experience. Augustine expresses this feeling when he states that he "is groaning with inexpressible groanings on my wanderer's path, and remembering Jerusalem with my heart lifted up toward it – Jerusalem my home land, Jerusalem my mother."

Augustine finds one of his finest recent apologetic interpreters in the writings of the twentieth-century Oxford literary critic and theologian C. S. Lewis. Perhaps one of the most original aspects of Lewis's writing is his persistent and powerful appeal to the religious imagination, in developing Augustine's maxim *desiderium sinus cordis* ("longing makes the heart deep"). Like Augustine, Lewis was aware of certain deep human emotions which pointed to a dimension of our existence beyond time and space. There is, Lewis suggested, a deep and intense feeling of longing within human beings, which no earthly object or experience can satisfy. Lewis terms this sense "joy," and argues that it points to God as its source and goal (hence the title of his celebrated autobiography, *Surprised by Joy*). Joy, according to Lewis, is "an unsatisfied desire which is itself more desirable than any other satisfaction . . . anyone who has experienced it will want it again."

Lewis addressed this question further in a sermon entitled "The Weight of Glory," preached at the University of Oxford on June 8, 1941. Lewis spoke of "a desire which no natural happiness will satisfy," "a desire, still wandering and uncertain of its object and still largely unable to see that object in the direction where it really lies." There is something self-defeating about human desire, in that what is desired, when achieved, seems to leave the desire unsatisfied. Lewis illustrates this from the age-old quest for beauty, using recognizably Augustinian imagery:

> The books or the music in which we thought the beauty was located will betray us if we trust to them; it was not *in* them, it only came *through* them, and what came through them was

longing. These things – the beauty, the memory of our own past –
are good images of what we really desire; but if they are mistaken
for the thing itself they turn into dumb idols, breaking the hearts
of their worshippers. For they are not the thing itself; they are
only the scent of a flower we have not found, the echo of a tune
we have not heard, news from a country we have not visited.

The basic point being emphasized is thoroughly Augustinian: the
creation creates a sense of longing for its creator, which it cannot
satisfy by itself. In this way, an essentially Augustinian framework
is applied to common human experience, to provide a plausible
theological interpretation.

Feuerbach's Critique of Experience-Based Theologies

As noted above, many theologians regarded experience-based theologies as providing an escape from the impasse of Enlightenment
rationalism, or from difficulties relating to the alleged particularity of
Christian revelation. F. D. E. Schleiermacher is an excellent instance of
a theologian concerned to use human experience as a starting point
for Christian theology. In particular, Schleiermacher drew attention to
the importance for theology of "a feeling of absolute dependence." By
exploring the nature and origins of this feeling, it was possible to
trace it back to its origins with God. This approach has enormous
attractions. However, as Ludwig Feuerbach demonstrated, it is also
enormously problematical.

In the foreword to the first edition of his highly influential *Essence of
Christianity* (1841), Ludwig Feuerbach states that the "purpose of this
work is to show that the supernatural mysteries of religion are based
upon quite simple natural truths." The leading idea of the work
is deceptively simple: Human beings have created the gods, who
embody their own idealized conception of their aspirations, needs,
and fears. Human "feeling" has nothing to do with God; it is
of purely human origin, misunderstood by an overactive human
imagination. "If feeling is the essential instrumentality or organ of
religion, then God's nature is nothing other than an expression of the
nature of feeling . . . The divine essence, which is comprehended
by feeling, is actually nothing other than the essence of feeling,
enraptured and delighted with itself – nothing but self-intoxicated,
self-contented feeling."

For Schleiermacher, the nature of the religious self-consciousness
was such that the existence of the redeemer could be inferred from it;
for Feuerbach, this species of self-consciousness was nothing more

and nothing less than human beings' awareness of themselves. It is experience of oneself, not of God. "God-consciousness" is merely human self-awareness, not a distinct category of human experience.

Feuerbach's analysis continues to be influential in western liberal Christianity. The existence of God is held to be grounded in human experience. But, as Feuerbach emphasizes, human experience might be nothing other than experience of *ourselves*, rather than of God. We might simply be projecting our own experiences, and calling the result "God," where we ought to realize that they are simply experiences of our own very human natures. Feuerbach's approach represents a devastating critique of humanity-centered ideas of Christianity.

It may be noted that Feuerbach's critique of religion loses much of its force when dealing with non-theistic religions, or theologies (such as that of Karl Barth) which claim to deal with a divine encounter with humanity from outside. However, when it is applied to a theistic construction or interpretation of human emotional or psychological states, it is in its element. Has anyone really spoken about God or Christ? Or have we simply projected our longings and fears on to an imaginary transcendent plane, or on to a distant historical figure about whom we know so little?

The growing conviction that Christology must be objectively grounded in the history of Jesus of Nazareth (especially prominent, for example, in the writings of Wolfhart Pannenberg) is due at least in part to Feuerbach's critique of religion. The very idea of "God" was, according to Feuerbach, an illusion which we could in principle avoid, and, with sufficient progress in self-knowledge, could discard altogether. It is, of course, a small – and perhaps an inevitable – step from this assumption to the Marxist view that religious feeling is itself the product of an alienated social existence.

This chapter has provided a brief exploration of the resources available to Christian theology, and some of the debates concerning their potential and their limitations. In the chapters which follow, we shall explore the results of their application, as we enter into the field of Christian theology in the proper sense of the term. All that has been said thus far is by way of introduction; we may now begin to explore the themes for which the ground has been prepared.

Questions for Chapter 6

1 Why is the idea of revelation so important to Christian theology?

2 What issues were at stake in the controversy between Emil Brunner and Karl Barth over natural theology?

3 Why has "narrative theology" become so popular recently?

4 Give some examples of the way in which Christian worship affects Christian theology.

5 What does it mean to "experience" God?

Part III

Christian Theology

7

The Doctrine of God

In preceding chapters, we have been considering the historical development of Christian theology, as well as some issues of sources and methods. Issues relating to history and method will be a recurring feature of the remainder of this work. However, this remaining part of the volume is primarily devoted to questions of theological substance. The most appropriate way of beginning such a discussion is by considering the Christian doctrine of God. The present chapter will explore some general issues relating to the doctrine of God, concentrating upon a series of questions of particular relevance to the modern period – questions raised by the rise of feminism, a new concern for the suffering of the world, and increased anxiety concerning the environment. The chapter which follows will deal with the distinctively Christian doctrine of the Trinity, perhaps one of the most difficult aspects of Christian theology for the student to come to terms with.

We begin our discussion of the Christian doctrine of God by turning to deal with a question of gender. Is God male? Indeed, can one speak of God as having "gender" in the first place?

Is God Male?

Both Old and New Testaments use male language about God. The Greek word *theos* is unquestionably masculine, and most of the analogies used for God throughout Scripture – such as father, king, and shepherd – are male. Does this mean that God *is* male?

Earlier, we noted the analogical nature of theological language (pp. 135–6), by which persons or social roles, largely drawn from the rural world of the ancient Near East, were seen to be suitable models for the divine activity or personality. One such analogy is that of a father. Yet the statement that "a father in ancient Israelite society is a suitable model for God" is not equivalent to saying that "God is male," or that "God is confined to the cultural parameters of ancient Israel." Mary Hayter, reflecting on such issues in her work *New Eve in Christ* (1983), writes:

> It would appear that certain "motherly prerogatives" in ancient Hebrew society – such as carrying and comforting small children – became metaphors for Yahweh's activity *vis-à-vis* his children Israel. Likewise, various "fatherly prerogatives" – such as disciplining a son – became vehicles for divine imagery. Different cultures and ages have different ideas about which roles are proper to the mother and which to the father.

To speak of God as father is to say that the role of the father in ancient Israel allows us insights into the nature of God. It is not to say that God *is* a male human being. Neither male nor female sexuality is to be attributed to God. For sexuality is an attribute of the created order, which cannot be assumed to correspond directly to any such polarity within the creator God.

Indeed, the Old Testament avoids attributing sexual functions to God, on account of the strongly pagan overtones of such associations. The Canaanite fertility cults emphasized the sexual functions of both gods and goddesses; the Old Testament refuses to endorse the idea that the gender or the sexuality of God is a significant matter. As Mary Hayter puts it:

> Today a growing number of feminists teach that the God/ess combines male and female characteristics. They, like those who assume that God is exclusively male, should remember that *any* attribution of sexuality to God is a reversion to paganism.

There is no need to revert to pagan ideas of gods and goddesses to recover the idea that God is neither masculine nor feminine; those ideas are already potentially present, if neglected, in Christian theology. Wolfhart Pannenberg develops this point further in his *Systematic Theology* (1990):

> The aspect of fatherly care in particular is taken over in what the Old Testament has to say about God's fatherly care for Israel. The sexual definition of the father's role plays no part . . . To bring sexual differentiation into the understanding of God would mean

polytheism; it was thus ruled out for the God of Israel . . . The fact
that God's care for Israel can also be expressed in terms of a
mother's love shows clearly enough how little there is any sense
of sexual distinction in the understanding of God as Father.

In an attempt to bring out the fact that God is not male, a number
of recent writers have explored the idea of God as "mother" (which
brings out the female aspects of God), or as "friend" (which brings
out the more gender-neutral aspects of God). An excellent example of
this is provided by Sallie McFague, in her *Models of God*. Recognizing
that speaking of "God as father" does not mean that God is male, she
writes:

> God as mother does not mean that God is mother (or father). We
> imagine God as both mother and father, but we realize how
> inadequate these and any other metaphors are to express the
> creative love of God . . . Nevertheless, we speak of this love in
> language that is familiar and dear to us, the language of mothers
> and fathers who give us life, from whose bodies we come, and
> upon whose care we depend.

Interestingly, the new interest in the question of the "maleness" of
God has led to a careful reading of the spiritual literature of earlier
periods in Christian history, and a rediscovery of the extent to which
female imagery has been used to describe God in the past. Julian of
Norwich is by no means the only Christian writer of the Middle
Ages to describe God as "mother" – and by doing so, to bring out
thoroughly orthodox aspects of the nature of God.

A Personal God

Down the ages, theologians and ordinary Christian believers alike
have had no hesitation in speaking about God in personal terms. For
example, Christianity has ascribed to God a whole series of attributes
– such as love and purpose – which seemed to have strongly personal
associations. Many writers have pointed out that the Christian practice
of prayer seems to be modeled on the relationship between a child
and a parent. Prayer expresses a gracious relationship which "is
simply trust in a person whose whole dealing with us proves him
worthy of trust" (John Oman).

One of Paul's leading soteriological images, "reconciliation," is
clearly modeled on human personal relationships. It implies that the
transformation through faith of the relationship between God and

sinful human beings is like the reconciliation of two persons – perhaps an alienated husband and wife.

There are thus powerful reasons for suggesting that the idea of a "personal God" is integral to the Christian outlook. But such a suggestion raises a number of difficulties, which require careful consideration. The following problems are particularly important.

1   It might be taken to imply that God is a human being. To speak of God as "a person" is to reduce God to our level. Paul Tillich points to "difficulties of location" in speaking of God in personal terms. To refer to God as a person is to imply that God, in common with human beings, is located at some definite place. Given the modern understanding of the universe, this assumption seems very out of place.

2   The doctrine of the Trinity speaks of God as "three persons." To speak of God as "a person" thus amounts to a denial of the Trinity. Historically, this objection is well justified. In the sixteenth century, those writers who spoke of God as "*a* person" were generally denying that God was *three* persons. Thus, in his *Philosophical Commentaries*, Bishop Berkeley made a note not to speak of God as "a person" for this very reason.

These difficulties can, however, be mitigated. In response to the first, it may be pointed out that talking of God as "a person" is analogical. To say that God is like a person is to affirm the divine ability and willingness to relate to others. This does not imply that God is human, or located at a specific point in the universe. All analogies break down at some point. These aspects of the analogy are not intended to be taken up.

In response to the Trinitarian difficulty, it will be noticed that the word "person" has changed its meaning significantly over the centuries. The word "person" does not have the same meaning in the two sentences which follow:

1   God is three persons.
2   God is a person.

We shall explore this point further in dealing with the doctrine of the Trinity itself (see pp. 247–69). Our attention now turns to further exploration of the term "person."

Defining "Person"

In everyday English, the word person has come to mean little more than "an individual human being." This makes it somewhat problematic to speak of a "personal God." However, as might be expected, there are hidden depths to the idea of personhood, which are too easily overlooked. The English word "person" derives from the Latin *persona*, which originally had the sense of a "mask."

The development of the meaning of *persona* is a fascinating subject in its own right. There may be an etymological connection between this Latin word and the Etruscan word for the goddess Persephone. (Etruscan was the language of a region of ancient Italy, near Rome.) Masks were worn by those participating in her festivals, which tended, by all reports, to degenerate into orgies. By the time of Cicero, the word had acquired a range of meanings. Although the sense of "mask" still predominated, important overtones had developed. Masks were used much in Roman theaters, being worn by actors to indicate the parts they were playing in dramas. *Persona* thus came to mean both "a theatrical mask" and "a theatrical character" or "a role in a play."

The early development of this idea in Christian theology is due to Tertullian. For Tertullian, a person is a being who speaks and acts. (The theatrical origins of the word can be seen clearly.) The final development of this definition is due to Boethius. Writing at the beginning of the sixth century, he offered the following definition: *persona est naturae rationabilis individua substantia*, "a person is the individual substance of a rational nature."

For early Christian writers, the word "person" is an expression of the individuality of a human being, as seen in his or her words and actions. Above all, there is an emphasis upon the idea of social relationships. A person is someone who plays a role in a social drama, who relates to others. A person has a part to play within a network of social relationships. "Individuality" does not imply social relationships, whereas "personality" relates to the part played by an individual in a web of relationships, by which that person is perceived to be distinctive by others. The basic idea expressed by the idea of "a personal God" is thus a God with whom we can stand in a relationship which is analogous to that which we could have with another human person.

It is helpful to consider what overtones the phrase "an impersonal God" would convey. The phrase suggests a God who is distant or aloof, who deals with humanity (if God deals with us at all) in general terms which take no account of human individuality. The idea of a personal relationship, such as love, suggests a reciprocal character to God's dealings with us. This idea is incorporated into the notion of a personal God, but not into impersonal conceptions of the nature of God. There are strongly negative overtones to the idea of "impersonal," which have passed into Christian thinking about the nature of God.

This point can be more fully appreciated by considering the impersonal concepts of God associated with Aristotle and Spinoza. As C. C. J. Webb points out:

> Aristotle does not and could not speak of a love of God for us in any sense. God, according to the principles of Aristotle's theology, can know and love nothing less than himself . . . He is utterly transcendent, and beyond the reach of personal communion. It is very instructive to study the modifications which Aristotle's faithful follower, St Thomas Aquinas, has to introduce into his master's notion of God, in order to make room for the providence of God for man, and the communion of man with God which his religious faith and religious experience demanded.

Spinoza experienced the same difficulty. He allowed that we, as human beings, should love God; yet he could not allow that this love is in any way reciprocated by God. It is a one-way street. Spinoza did not permit the two-way relationship implied by a personal God who loves, and is loved by, individual human beings.

So how can we begin to explore the idea of what it means to be a "person" in more detail? In a moment, we shall consider a significant twentieth-century contribution to this discussion, in the form of dialogical personalism. But we should first return to the question of why Christians speak of God both as "a person" and as "three persons."

When Christians now speak of God as a person, they are referring to the fact that it is possible to enter into a personal relationship with God. Human personal relationships are declared to be appropriate analogies or models for our relationship with God. Paul's use of the image of reconciliation is important here, as it implies an analogy between the reconciliation of two estranged people, and of sinful human beings to God.

To speak of God as three persons is to recognize the complexity of this relationship with God, and the manner in which it is established. It is to appreciate the complexity of the divine activity which lies behind God's ability to relate to us as persons. It is to understand that a network of relationships exists within the Godhead itself, and that this network undergirds our relationship with God. These points will be explored further in our discussion of the Trinity itself. Our attention now turns to a modern philosophical analysis of the idea of a "person" which is of considerable interest to Christian theology.

Dialogical Personalism

In his major work *I and Thou* (1927), the Jewish writer Martin Buber drew a fundamental distinction between two categories of relations:

I–*Thou* relations, which are "personal," and I–*It* relations, which are impersonal. (The use of the archaic word "thou" may irritate some readers; unfortunately, it has to be used, as there is no other way in English to indicate that the "you" is singular, not plural. The English word "you" can be used to address an individual or a group of people. Also, Buber's work was originally published in German, with the title *Ich und Du*; the German pronoun "du" suggests familiarity – another idea that is not necessarily conveyed by the English word "you.") We shall explore these basic distinctions further, before considering their theological importance.

1   *I–It relations*. Buber uses this category to refer to the relation between subjects and objects – for example, between a human being and a pencil. The human being is active, whereas the pencil is passive. This distinction is often referred to in more philosophical language as a *subject–object relation*, in which an active subject (in this case, the human being) relates to an inactive object (in this case, the pencil). According to Buber, the subject acts as an *I*, and the object as an *It*. The relation between the human being and pencil could thus be described as an *I–It* relation.

2   *I–Thou relations*. With this category, we come to the heart of Buber's philosophy. An I–Thou relation exists between two active subjects– between two *persons*. It is something which is *mutual* and *reciprocal*. "The I of the primary word I–Thou makes its appearance as a person, and becomes conscious of itself." In other words, Buber is suggesting that human personal relationships exemplify the essential features of an I–Thou relation. It is the relationship itself, that intangible and invisible bond which links two persons, which is the heart of Buber's idea of an I–Thou relation.

I–It knowledge is indirect, mediated through an object, and has a specific content. In contrast, I–Thou knowledge is direct, immediate, and lacks a specific content. An "It" is known by measurable parameters – its height, weight, color, and so on. We can give a good physical description of it. But a "Thou" is known directly. The English language allows us to make a vital distinction between "knowing *about* something" and "*knowing* someone." Roughly the same distinction lies behind Buber's categories of "I–It" and "I–Thou" relations. We know about an "It" – but we know, *and are known by*, a "Thou." To "know about" something is to be able to express the content of that knowledge. Yet strictly speaking, there is no content to "knowing someone." The "knowledge" in question cannot really be expressed.

For Buber, an "I–Thou" relation is thus *mutual, reciprocal, symmetrical*, and *content-less*. Both partners retain their own subjectivity in the encounter, in which they become aware of the other person as a subject, rather than an object. Whereas an I–It relation can be thought of as the active subject pursuing and investigating the passive object, an I–Thou relation involves the encounter of two mutually active subjects. It is the relationship – something which has no real content, but which really exists nonetheless – which is the real focus of personal interaction. It is, to use Buber's terms, "not a specific *content*, but a *Presence*, a Presence as power."

What, then, are the theological consequences of this approach? How does Buber's philosophy help us to understand and explore the idea of God as a person? A number of key ideas emerge, all of which have important and helpful theological applications. Furthermore, Buber anticipated some of these himself. In the final sections of *I and Thou*, he explores the implications of his approach to thinking and speaking about God – or, to use his preferred term, "the Absolute Thou."

1   Buber's approach affirms that God cannot be reduced to a concept, or to some neat conceptual formulation. According to Buber, only "Its" can be treated in this way. For Buber, God is the "Thou who can, by its nature, never become an It. That is, God is a being who escapes all attempts at objectification and transcends all description." Theology must learn to acknowledge and wrestle with the presence of God, realizing that this presence cannot be reduced to a neat package of contents.

2   The approach allows valuable insights into the idea of revelation (see pp. 155–6). For Christian theology, God's revelation is not simply a making known of facts about God, but a self-revelation of God. Revelation of ideas about God is to be supplemented by revelation of God as a person, a presence as much as a content. We could make sense of this by saying that revelation includes knowledge of God as an "It" and as a "Thou." We come to know things about God; yet we also come to know God. Similarly, "knowledge of God" includes knowledge of God as both It and Thou. "Knowing God" is not simply a collection of data about God, but a personal relationship.

3   Buber's "dialogical personalism" also avoids the idea of God as an object, perhaps the weakest and most heavily criticized aspect of some nineteenth-century liberal theology. The characteristic nineteenth-century phrase "man's quest for God" summed up the basic premise of this approach: God is an "It," a passive object, waiting to be discovered by (male) theologians, who are viewed as active subjects. Writers within the dialectical school, especially Emil Brunner in his *Truth as Encounter*, argued that God had to be viewed as a Thou, an active subject. As such, God could take the initiative away from

humans, through self-revelation and a willingness to be known in a historical and personal form – namely, Jesus Christ. Theology would thus become the human response to God's self-disclosure, rather than the human quest for God.

This emphasis upon a "personal God" raises a number of questions, one of which concerns the extent to which human experiences can be said to be shared by God. If God is personal, one can speak of God "loving" people. But how far can this be taken? Can, for example, one speak of God "suffering"?

Can God Suffer?

Christian theology throws up many fascinating questions. Some of them are interesting in themselves. Others are interesting because they open up wider issues. A question which belongs to both of these categories is this: Can God be said to suffer? If God can be said to suffer, a point of contact is immediately established between God and the pain of the human world. God cannot then be thought of as being immune from the suffering of the creation. The implications of this for reflecting upon the problem of evil and suffering would be considerable.

But the question is also of interest in another respect. It invites us to consider why so many writers have an inbuilt aversion to thinking and speaking about "a suffering God." To explore this point, we may consider the historical background to early Christian theology. Although Christianity had its origins in Palestine, it rapidly expanded into other areas of the eastern Mediterranean world, such as modern-day Turkey and Egypt, establishing strongholds in cities such as Antioch and Alexandria. In the course of doing so, it came into contact with Hellenistic culture, and Greek ways of thinking.

One of the major questions that arise from this observation is the following. Did Christian theologians, operating in a Hellenistic environment, inadvertently incorporate some Greek ideas into their thought? In other words, did a basically Palestinian gospel become distorted by being refracted through a Hellenistic prism? Particular attention was focused on the introduction of metaphysical terms into theology. Some scholars regarded this as the imposition of a static Greek way of thinking upon a dynamic semitic worldview. The result, they argued, was a distortion of the gospel.

Since the time of the Enlightenment, this question has been taken with considerable seriousness. A movement of major importance in this respect is known as the "history of dogma" movement (a working translation of the somewhat formidable German term *Dogmengeschichte*). Writers such as Adolf von Harnack (1851–1930) studied the historical development of Christian doctrine with a view to establishing whether this kind of deformation could be identified and eliminated. In his substantial *History of Dogma* (1886–9), which takes up seven volumes in English translation, Harnack argued that metaphysics should never have been allowed to find its way into Christian theology. For Harnack, the classic example of a doctrine which rested on metaphysical, rather than evangelical, foundations was the incarnation.

Many writers who felt that Harnack was wrong to single out the doctrine of the incarnation for criticism in this way nevertheless believed that classical Greek ideas had found their way into Christian theology. The search for these unwelcome intruders continued. It is now generally agreed that the idea of a God who lies beyond suffering may represent exactly the sort of thing that Harnack was worried about. In what follows, we shall explore the classic pagan idea of the *apatheia* or "impassibility" of God – the view according to which God lies beyond all human emotions and pain.

The Classic View: The Impassibility of God

The notion of perfection dominates the classical understanding of God, as it is expressed in the Platonic dialogues, such as *The Republic*. To be perfect is to be unchanging and self-sufficient. It is therefore impossible for such a perfect being to be affected or changed by anything outside itself. Furthermore, perfection was understood in very static terms. If God is perfect, change in any direction is an impossibility. If God changes, it is either a move *away from* perfection (in which case God is no longer perfect), or *toward* perfection (in which case, God was not perfect in the past). Aristotle, echoing such ideas, declared that "change would be change for the worse," and thus excluded his divine being from change and suffering.

This understanding passed into Christian theology at an early stage. Philo, a Hellenistic Jew whose writings were much admired by early Christian writers, wrote a treatise entitled *Quod Deus immutabilis sit* ("That God is unchangeable"), which vigorously defended the impassibility of God. Biblical passages which seemed to speak of God suffering were, he argued, to be treated as metaphors, and not to be allowed their full literal weight. To allow that God changes was to deny the divine perfection. "What greater impiety could there be than to suppose that the Unchangeable changes?" asked Philo. It seemed to be an unanswerable question.

For Philo, God could not be allowed to suffer, or undergo anything which could be spoken of as "passion." Anselm of Canterbury, influenced by this idea, argued that God was compassionate in terms of our experience, but not in terms of the divine being itself. The language of love and compassion is treated as purely figurative when used in relation to God. We may *experience* God as compassionate; this does not mean that God *is* compassionate. Anselm meditates along these lines in his *Proslogion*:

> You are compassionate in terms of our experience, but not in terms of your being. . . . For when you see us in our wretchedness, we experience the effect of compassion, but you do not experience that feeling. So you are compassionate, in that you save the wretched and spare those who sin against you; and yet you are not compassionate, in that you are affected by no sympathy for wretchedness.

Thomas Aquinas develops this approach, especially when reflecting on the love of God for sinners. Love implies vulnerability and, potentially, that God could be affected by our sorrows, or moved by our misery. Thomas Aquinas dismissed this possibility: "Mercy is especially to be attributed to God, provided that it is considered as an effect, not as a feeling of suffering. . . . It does not belong to God to sorrow over the misery of others."

An obvious difficulty arises here. Jesus Christ suffered and died on the cross. Traditional Christian theology declared that Jesus Christ was God incarnate. It therefore seems to follow that God suffered in Christ. (The issue in question is the "communication of attributes," to be discussed at pp. 291–3). Not so, declared most of the patristic writers, deeply influenced by the pagan idea of the impassibility of God. Christ suffered in his human nature, not his divine nature. God thus did not experience human suffering, and remained unaffected by this aspect of the world.

A Suffering God

We have seen how the idea of an impassible God achieved considerable influence during the patristic and medieval periods. Yet there were protests against these developments. Perhaps the most celebrated of these is Martin Luther's "theology of the cross," which emerged during the period 1518–19. In the *Heidelberg Disputation*

(1518), Luther contrasted two rival ways of thinking about God. A *theologia gloriae* ("theology of glory") perceives God's glory, power, and wisdom in creation. A *theologia crucis* ("theology of the cross") discerns God hidden in the suffering and humiliation of the cross of Christ. Luther deliberately uses the phrase *Deus crucifixus*, "a crucified God", as he speaks of the manner in which God shares in the sufferings of the crucified Christ.

In the late twentieth century, it has become "the new orthodoxy" to speak of a suffering God. Jürgen Moltmann's *The Crucified God* (1974) is widely regarded as the most significant and influential work to have expounded this idea, and has been the subject of intense discussion. What pressures led to the rediscovery of the idea of a suffering God? Three can be identified, all focusing on the period immediately after World War I. These three factors, taken together, gave rise to widespread skepticism concerning traditional ideas about the impassibility of God.

1 *The rise of protest atheism* The sheer horror of World War I made a deep impact upon western theological reflection. The suffering of the period led to a widespread perception that liberal Protestantism was fatally compromised by its optimistic views of human nature. It is no accident that dialectical theology arose in the aftermath of this trauma. Another significant response was the movement known as "protest atheism," which raised a serious moral protest against belief in God. How could anyone believe in a God who was above such suffering and pain in the world?

Traces of such ideas can be found in Fyodor Dostoyevsky's nineteenth-century novel *The Brothers Karamazov*. The ideas were developed more fully in the twentieth century, often using Dostoyevsky's character Ivan Karamazov as a model. Karamazov's rebellion against God (or, perhaps more accurately, against the *idea* of God) has its origins in his refusal to accept that the suffering of an innocent child could ever be justified. Albert Camus developed such ideas in *L'homme révolté* ("The Rebel"), which expressed Karamazov's protest in terms of a "metaphysical rebellion." Writers such as Jürgen Moltmann saw in this protest against an invulnerable God "the only serious atheism." This intensely moral form of atheism demanded a credible theological response – a theology of a suffering God.

2 *The rediscovery of Luther* In 1883 – the celebration of the 400th anniversary of Luther's birth – the Weimar edition of Luther's works was launched. The resulting availability of Luther's works (many of which were hitherto unpublished) led to a resurgence in Luther scholarship, especially in German theological circles. Scholars such as

Karl Holl opened the way for a new interest in the reformer during the 1920s. The result was a perceptible quickening in interest in many of Luther's ideas, especially the "theology of the cross." Luther's ideas about the "God who is hidden in suffering" became available at almost exactly the moment when they were needed.

3 *The growing impact of the "history of dogma" movement* Although this movement reached its climax in the closing days of the nineteenth century, it took some while for the implications of its program to percolate into Christian theology as a whole. By the time World War I had ended, there was a general awareness that numerous Greek ideas (such as the impassibility of God) had found their way into Christian theology. Sustained attention was given to eliminating these ideas. Protest atheism created a climate in which it was apologetically necessary to speak of a suffering God. The "history of dogma" movement declared that Christian thinking had taken a wrong turn in the patristic period, and that this could be successfully reversed. Christian declarations that God was above suffering, or invulnerable, were now realized to be inauthentic. It was time to recover the authentically Christian idea of the suffering of God in Christ.

Three additional considerations may also be noted. First, the rise of process thought gave new impetus to speaking of God as "a fellow-sufferer who understands" (A. N. Whitehead). Yet many who welcomed this insight were hesitant over the theological framework which engendered it. Process thought's emphasis upon the primacy of creativity seemed inconsistent with much traditional Christian thinking concerning the transcendence of God. An acceptable alternative was to ground the notion of God as a fellow-sufferer in the self-limitation of God, especially in the cross of Christ.

Second, fresh studies of the Old Testament – such as Abraham Heschel's *God of the Prophets* (1930) and T. F. Fretheim's *Suffering of God* (1984) – drew attention to the manner in which the Old Testament often portrayed God as sharing in the *pathos* of Israel. God is hurt and moved by the suffering of God's people. If classical theism could not accommodate that insight, it was argued, then so much the worse for it.

Third, the notion of "love" itself has been the subject of considerable discussion in the present century. Theologians rooted in the classical tradition – such as Anselm and Aquinas – defined love in terms of expressions and demonstrations of care and good will toward others. It is thus perfectly possible to speak of God "loving impassibly" – that is, loving someone without being emotionally affected by that person's situation. Yet the new interest in the has raised questions over this notion of love. Can one really speak of "love," unless there is some mutual sharing of suffering and feelings? Surely "love" implies the lover's intense awareness of the suffering of the beloved, and thus some form of sharing in its distress? Such considerations have undermined the intuitive plausibility (yet not, interestingly, the intellectual credibility) of an impassible God.

Amongst major contributions to the discussion of the theological implications of a "suffering God," two should be singled out as being of special importance.

1 In *The Crucified God* (1974), Jürgen Moltmann argued that the cross is both the foundation and the criterion of true Christian theology. The passion of Christ, and especially his cry of Godforsakenness – "My God! My God! Why have you forsaken me?" (Mark 15: 34) – stands at the center of Christian thinking. The cross must be seen as an event between the Father and the Son, in which the Father suffers the death of his Son in order to redeem sinful humanity.

Moltmann argues that a God who cannot suffer is a *deficient*, not a perfect, God. Stressing that God cannot be *forced* to change or undergo suffering, Moltmann declares that God willed to undergo suffering. The suffering of God is the direct consequence of the divine *decision* to suffer, and the divine *willingness* to suffer:

> A God who cannot suffer is poorer than any human. For a God who is incapable of suffering is a being who cannot be involved. Suffering and injustice do not affect him. And because he is so completely insensitive, he cannot be affected or shaken by anything. He cannot weep, for he has no tears. But the one who cannot suffer cannot love either. So he is also a loveless being.

Moltmann here brings together a number of the considerations we noted earlier, including the idea that love involves the lover participating in the sufferings of the beloved.

2 In *A Theology of the Pain of God* (1946), the Japanese writer Kazoh Kitamori argued that true love was rooted in pain. "God is the wounded Lord, having pain in himself." God is able to give meaning and dignity to human suffering on account of the fact that he also is in pain, and suffers. Like Moltmann, Kitamori draws heavily upon Luther's theology of the cross.

The idea of a suffering God might at first sight seem to be heretical in the eyes of Christian orthodoxy. The patristic period identified two unacceptable views relating to the suffering of God – *patripassianism* and *theopaschitism*. The former was regarded as a heresy, and the latter as a potentially misleading doctrine. They merit brief discussion before proceeding further.

Patripassianism arose during the third century, and was associated with writers such as Noetus, Praxeas, and Sabellius. It centered on the belief that the Father suffered as the Son. In other words, the suffering of Christ on the cross is to be regarded as the suffering of the Father. According to these writers, the only distinction within the Godhead was a succession of modes or operations. In other words, Father, Son, and Spirit were just different modes of being, or expressions, of the same basic divine entity. This form of modalism, often known as Sabellianism, will be explored further in relation to the doctrine of the Trinity.

Theopaschitism arose during the sixth century, and was linked with writers such as John Maxentius. The basic slogan associated with the movement was "one of the Trinity was crucified." The formula can be interpreted in a perfectly orthodox sense (it reappears as Martin Luther's celebrated formula "the crucified God"), and was defended as such by Leontius of Byzantium. However, it was regarded as potentially misleading and confusing by more cautious writers, including Pope Hormisdas (died 523), and the formula gradually fell into disuse.

The doctrine of a suffering God rehabilitates theopaschitism, and interprets the relation of the suffering of God and of Christ in such a way that it avoids the patripassian difficulty. For example, Kitamori distinguishes the ways in which Father and Son suffer. "God the Father who hid himself in the death of God the Son is God in pain. Therefore the pain of God is neither merely the pain of God the Son, nor merely the pain of God the Father, but the pain of two persons who are essentially one." Perhaps the most sophisticated statement of this doctrine is to be found in Jürgen Moltmann's *Crucified God*, which develops the following position.

The Father and the Son suffer – but they experience that suffering in different manners. The Son suffers the pain and death of the cross; the Father gives up and suffers the loss of the Son. Although both Father and Son are involved in the cross, their involvement is not *identical* (the patripassian position), but *distinct*. "In the passion of the Son, the Father himself suffers the pains of abandonment. In the death of the Son, death comes upon God himself, and the Father suffers the death of his Son in his love for forsaken man."

Moltmann's confident assertion that "death comes upon God" naturally leads us to consider whether God can be thought of as having died.

The Death of God?

If God can suffer, can God also die? Or is God now dead? These questions demand consideration as part of any discussion of the suffering of God in Christ. Hymns, as much as theology textbooks, bear witness to the beliefs of Christianity. A number of significant hymns of the Christian church make reference to the death of God, exulting in the paradox that the immortal God should die on the cross. Perhaps the most celebrated example is Charles Wesley's eighteenth-century hymn "And can it be?," which includes the following lines:

> Amazing love! how can it be
> That thou, my God, shouldst die for me?

These lines express the idea of the immortal God being given up to death as an expression of love and commitment. This thought is also expressed elsewhere in that same hymn, as here:

> 'Tis mystery all! th'immortal dies!
> Who can explore his strange design?

But how, one wonders, can one speak of God "dying"?

For a few weeks in 1965, theology hit the national headlines in the United States. *Time* magazine ran an edition declaring that God was dead. Slogans such as "God is dead" and "the death of God" became of national interest. In its issue of February 16, 1966, the *Christian Century* provided a satirical application form for its readers to join the "God-Is-Dead-Club." New terms began to appear in the learned journals: "theothanasia," "theothanatology," and "theothanatopsis" became buzz words, before happily lapsing into fully merited obscurity.

Two quite distinct lines of interpretation may be discerned lying behind the slogan "the death of God."

1 The belief, especially linked with the nineteenth-century German philosopher Nietzsche, that human civilization has reached the stage at which it may dispense with the notion of God. The crisis of faith in the west, especially western Europe, which developed during the nineteenth century, finally matured. The historian of modern thought Carl Becker describes this development in the following words:

> It was as if a rumour, started no one knew when, had at last become too insistent to be longer disregarded: the rumour that God, having departed secretly in the night, was about to cross the

frontiers of the known world and leave mankind in the lurch. What we have to realize is that in those years God was on trial.

The same sentiment is expressed in T. S. Eliot's poem "The Rock":

> But it seems that something has happened that has never happened before: though we know not just when, or why, or how, or where.
> Men have left GOD not for other gods, they say, but for no god; and this has never happened before.

Nietzsche's declaration (*The Happy Science*, 1882), that "God is dead! God remains dead! And we have killed him!" thus expresses the general cultural atmosphere which finds no place for God. This secular outlook is well explored in Gabriel Vahanian's *Death of God: The Culture of our Post-Christian Era* (1961). William Hamilton expressed this feeling as follows:

> We are not talking about the absence of the experience of God, but about the experience of the absence of God . . . The death of God must be affirmed; the confidence with which we thought we could speak of God is gone . . . There remains a sense of not having, of not believing, of having lost, not just the idols or the gods of religion but God himself. And this is an experience that is not peculiar to a neurotic few, nor is it private or inward. Death of God is a public event in our history.

Although subsequent predictions of the total secularization of western society remain conspicuously unfulfilled, the "death of God" motif seems to capture the atmosphere of an important moment in western cultural history.

This development had important implications for those Christian theologians who took their lead from cultural developments. In his *Secular Meaning of the Gospel* (1963), Paul van Buren, arguing that the word "God" had ceased to have any meaning, sought to ascertain how the gospel might be stated in purely atheological terms. Belief in a transcendent God was replaced by commitment to a "Jesus-ethic," centered on respect for the lifestyle of Jesus. Thomas J. J. Altizer's *Gospel of Christian Atheism* (1966) refocused the question by suggesting that, while it was no longer acceptable to talk about Jesus being God, one could still talk about God being Jesus – thus giving a moral authority to Jesus' words and deeds, even if belief in a God was no longer to be retained.

2 The totally distinct belief that Jesus Christ has such a high profile of identification with God that one can speak of God "dying"

in Christ. Just as God suffers in Christ, so one can speak of God experiencing death or "perishability" (Eberhard Jüngel) in the same manner. This approach is considerably less interesting culturally, although it is probably much more significant theologically. Partly in reaction to developments in the United States, especially the widespread circulation given to the slogan "God is dead," Eberhard Jüngel wrote a paper entitled "The Death of the Living God" (1968), in which he argued that, through the death of Christ, God becomes involved in *Vergänglichkeit* – a German word which is often translated as "perishability," but is perhaps better rendered as "transience" or "transitoriness." Jüngel, who developed these ideas at greater length in *God as the Mystery of the World* (1983), thus sees the theme of "the death of God" as an important affirmation of God's self-identification with the transitory world of suffering.

Developing related ideas in his *Crucified God*, Jürgen Moltmann speaks (a little cryptically, one feels) of "death in God." God identifies with all who suffer and die, and thus shares in human suffering and death. These aspects of human history are thereby taken up into the history of God. "To recognize God in the cross of Christ . . . means to recognize the cross, inextricable suffering, death and hopeless rejection in God." Moltmann makes this point using a poignant episode from a famous passage in Elie Wiesel's novel *Night*, describing an execution at Auschwitz. As a crowd watched three people die by hanging, someone asked "Where is God?" Moltmann uses this episode to make the point that, through the cross of Christ, God tastes and is affected by death. God knows what death is like.

The Omnipotence of God

The Nicene creed opens with the confident words "I believe in God, the Father almighty . . ." Belief in an "almighty" or omnipotent God is thus an essential element of traditional Christian faith. But what does it mean to speak of God being "omnipotent"? The common-sense approach to the matter defines omnipotence like this: If God is omnipotent, then God can do anything. Of course, God cannot make a square circle, or a round triangle; this is a logical self-contradiction. But the idea of divine omnipotence seems to imply that God must be able to do anything which does not involve obvious contradiction.

A more subtle problem is raised by the following question: Can God create a stone which is too heavy to lift? If God cannot create such a stone, the idea of total divine omnipotence would seem to be denied. Yet if God could create such a stone, then there is something else which God *cannot* do – namely, lift that stone. And so, again, God turns out not to be omnipotent.

Such logical explorations are unquestionably valuable, in that they cast light on the difficulties of speaking about God. One of the most important rules of Christian theology is to ask closely concerning the meaning of words. Words with one meaning in a secular context often have more developed, subtle or nuanced meanings in a theological setting. "Omnipotence" is an excellent example, as we shall see.

Defining Omnipotence

We may explore the definition of omnipotence by considering some arguments developed by C. S. Lewis in his celebrated book *The Problem of Pain*. Lewis begins by stating the problem as follows:

> "If God were good, he would wish to make his creatures perfectly happy, and if God were almighty he would be able to do what he wished. But the creatures are not happy. Therefore God lacks either the goodness, or power, or both." This is the problem of pain, in its simplest form.

But what does it mean to say that God is omnipotent? Lewis argues that it does *not* mean that God can do anything. Once God has opted to do certain things, or to behave in a certain manner, then other possibilities are excluded.

> If you choose to say "God can give a creature free will and at the same time withhold free will from it", you have not succeeded in saying *anything* about God: meaningless combinations of words do not suddenly acquire a meaning because we prefix to them the two other words: "God can". It remains true that all *things* are possible with God: the intrinsic impossibilities are not things but non-entities.

God, then cannot do anything that is *logically* impossible. But Lewis takes the case further: God cannot do anything that is inconsistent with the divine nature. It is not merely logic, he argues, but the very nature of God, which prevents God from doing certain things.

The point at issue here was made firmly by Anselm of Canterbury in his *Proslogion*, as he meditated upon the nature of God.

> How can you be omnipotent, if you cannot do all things? But how can you do all things, if you cannot be corrupted, or tell lies, or

make the true into the false? . . . Or is the ability to do these things
not power but powerlessness?

In other words, certain possibilities are the result of the absence,
rather than the presence, of power. For example, consider the question: Can God sin? Christian theology has tended to dismiss this
question as nonsensical. Aquinas's reponse is characteristic:

> To sin is to fall short of full activity. Therefore to be able to sin
> is to be able to fail in something, which is not consistent with
> omnipotence. It is because God is omnipotent that he cannot sin.

There is, however, another issue at stake, which was explored by
writers such as William of Ockham in an appeal to "the two powers of
God." We shall explore this in the section which follows.

The Two Powers of God

How can God act absolutely reliably, without being subject to some
external agency which compels God to act in this way? This question
was debated with some heat at Paris in the thirteenth century, in
response to a form of determinism linked with the writer Averroes.
For Averroes, the reliability of God ultimately rested upon external
pressures. God was compelled to act in certain ways – and thus acted
reliably. This approach was, however, regarded with intense suspicion
by most theologians, who saw it as a crude denial of the freedom of
God. But how could God be said to act reliably, unless it was through
external compulsion?

The answer given by writers such as Duns Scotus and William of
Ockham can be stated as follows: The reliability of God is ultimately
grounded in the divine nature itself. God does not act reliably because
someone or something makes God act in this way, but because of a
deliberate and free divine *decision* to act like this.

In his discussion of the opening line of the Apostles' creed – "I
believe in God the Father almighty" – Ockham asks precisely what is
meant by the word "almighty" (*omnipotens*). It cannot, he argues,
mean that God is *presently* able to do everything; rather, it means that
God was *once* free to act in this way. God has now established an
order of things which reflects a loving and righteous divine will – and
that order, once established, will remain until the end of time.

Ockham uses two terms to refer to these different options. The
"absolute power of God" (*potentia absoluta*) refers to the options which
existed before God had committed himself to any course of action or

world ordering. The "ordained power of God" (*potentia ordinata*) refers to the way things now are, which reflects the order established by God their creator. These do not represent two different sets of options now open to God. They represent two different moments in the great history of salvation. And our concern is with the ordained power of God, the way in which God orders the creation at present.

The distinction is important, yet difficult. In view of this, we shall explore it in a little more detail. Ockham is inviting us to consider two very different situations in which we might speak of the "omnipotence of God." The first is this: God is confronted with a whole array of possibilities – such as creating the world, or not creating the world. God can choose to actualize any of these possibilities. This is the *absolute* power of God.

But then God chooses some options, and brings them into being. We are now in the realm of the ordained power of God – a realm in which God's power is restricted, by virtue of God's own decision. Ockham's point is this: By choosing to actualize some options, God has to choose not to actualize others. Choosing to do something means choosing to reject something else. Once God has chosen to create the world, the option of *not* creating the world is set to one side. This means that there are certain things which God could do *once* which can *no longer* be done. Although God could have decided not to create the world, God has now deliberately rejected that possibility. And that rejection means that this possibility is no longer open.

This leads to what seems, at first sight, to be a paradoxical situation. On account of the divine omnipotence, God is not now able to do everything. By exercising the divine power, God has limited options. For Ockham, God *cannot* now do everything. God has deliberately limited the possibilities. God chose to limit the options which are now open. Is that a contradiction? No. If God is really capable of doing anything, then God must be able to become committed to a course of action – and stay committed to it. This notion of divine self-limitation, explored by Ockham, is important in modern theology, and merits further exploration.

The Notion of Divine Self-Limitation

The idea of God's self-limitation began to be explored with new interest in the nineteenth century, specifically within a Christological context. The favored framework for the discussion of the idea of divine self-limitation was usually that suggested by Philippians 2: 6–7, which speak of Christ "emptying himself." The term "kenoticism" (from the Greek *kenosis*, "an emptying") came to be widely used to refer to this approach.

Writers in the German tradition such as Gottfried Thomasius (1802–75), F. H. R. von Frank (1827–94), and W. F. Gess (1819–91) argued that God chose a course of self-limitation in becoming incarnate in Christ. Thomasius adopted the position that God (or, more accurately, the divine Logos) set aside (or became emptied of) the divine *metaphysical* attributes (such as omnipotence, omniscience, and omnipresence) in Christ, while retaining the *moral* attributes (such as the divine love, righteousness, and holiness). Gess, however, insisted that God set aside all the attributes of divinity in the incarnation, thus making it virtually impossible to speak of Christ being "divine" in any sense of the term.

In England, the idea of kenoticism was later in developing, and took a somewhat different form. Convinced that traditional Christologies did not do justice to the humanity of Christ (tending to portray him in terms which approached Docetism), writers such as Charles Gore (1853–1932) and P. T. Forsyth (1848–1921) argued that those attributes of divinity which tended to be seen as obliterating Christ's humanity had been set to one side. Thus Gore's *Incarnation of the Son of God* (1891) developed the idea that Christ's full earthly humanity involved a voluntary self-emptying of his divine knowledge, with a resulting human ignorance. There was thus no difficulty raised by the observation that the gospel records seemed to suggest that Jesus was possessed of a limited knowledge at points.

Perhaps the most dramatic statement of this notion of divine self-limitation can be found in Dietrich Bonhoeffer's *Letters and Papers from Prison*:

> God lets himself be pushed out of the world on to the cross. He is weak and powerless in the world, and that is precisely the way, the only way, in which he is with us and helps us . . . The Bible directs us to God's powerlessness and suffering; only the suffering God can help.

In an age which has become increasingly suspicious of the idea of "power," it is perhaps refreshing to be reminded that talk about "God almighty" does not necessarily imply that God is a tyrant, but that God chooses to stand alongside people in their powerlessness – a major theme in interpretations of the cross of Christ, to which we shall return shortly.

God in Process Thought

The origins of process thought are generally agreed to lie in the writings of the American philosopher Alfred North Whitehead (1861–1947), especially his *Process and Reality* (1929). Reacting against the rather static view of the world associated with traditional metaphysics (expressed in ideas such as "substance" and "essence"), Whitehead conceived of reality as a process. The world, as an organic whole, is something dynamic, not static; something which *happens*. Reality is made up of building blocks of "actual entities" or "actual occasions," and is thus characterized by becoming, change, and event.

All these "entities" or "occasions" (to use Whitehead's original terms) possess a degree of freedom to develop, and be influenced by their surroundings. It is perhaps at this point that the influence of biological evolutionary theories can be discerned: like the later writer Pierre Teilhard de Chardin, Whitehead is concerned to allow for development within creation, subject to some overall direction and guidance. This process of development is thus set against a permanent background of order, which is seen as an organizing principle essential to growth. Whitehead argues that God may be identified with this background of order within the process. Whitehead treats God as an "entity," but distinguishes God from other entities on the grounds of imperishability. Other entities exist for a finite period; God exists permanently. Each entity thus receives influence (Whitehead uses the term "prehend" to describe this act of appropriating experience) from two main sources: previous entities and God.

Causation is thus not a matter of an entity being coerced to act in a given manner: It is a matter of *influence* and *persuasion*. Entities influence each other in a "dipolar" manner – mentally and physically. Precisely the same is true of God, as of other entities. God can only act in a persuasive manner, within the limits of the process itself. God "keeps the rules" of the process. Just as God influences other entities, so God is also influenced by them. God, to use Whitehead's famous phrase, is "a fellow-sufferer who understands." God is thus affected and influenced by the world.

Process thought thus redefines God's omnipotence in terms of persuasion or influence within the overall world-process. This is an important development, as it explains the attraction of this way of understanding God's relation to the world in relation to the problem of evil. The traditional free-will defense of God in the face of evil is persuasive (although the extent of that persuasion is contested) in the case of moral evil – in other words, evil resulting from human decisions and actions. But what of natural evil? What of earthquakes, famines, and other natural disasters?

Process thought argues that God cannot force nature to obey the divine will or purpose for it. God can only attempt to influence the process from within, by persuasion and attraction. Each entity enjoys a degree of freedom and creativity, which God cannot override. Where the traditional free-will defense of moral evil argues that human beings are free to disobey or ignore God, process theology argues that individual components of the world are likewise free to ignore divine attempts to influence or persuade them. They are not bound to respond to God. God is thus absolved of responsibility for both moral and natural evil.

While this understanding of the persuasive nature of God's activity has obvious merits, critics of process thought have suggested that too high a price is paid. The traditional idea of the transcendence of God appears to have been abandoned, or radically reinterpreted in terms of the primacy and permanency of God as an entity within the process. In other words, the divine transcendence is understood to mean little more than that God outlives and surpasses other entities.

Whitehead's basic ideas have been developed by a number of writers, most notably Charles Hartshorne (1897–), Schubert Ogden (1928–), and John B. Cobb (1925–). Hartshorne modified Whitehead's notion of God in a number of directions, perhaps most significantly by suggesting that the God of process thought should be thought of more as a person than as an entity. This allows him to meet one of the more significant criticisms of process thought: that it compromises the idea of divine perfection. How can a perfect God change? Is not change tantamount to an admission of imperfection? Hartshorne redefines perfection in terms of a *receptivity to change which does not compromise God's superiority*. In other words, God's ability to be influenced by other entities does not mean that God is reduced to their level. God surpasses other entities, although affected by them.

For many commentators, the real strength of process theology lies in its insights into the origin and nature of suffering within the world. Those strengths are best appreciated through an analysis of the various alternatives on offer within the Christian tradition concerning suffering – an area of theology which has come to be known as "theodicy," to which we now turn.

Theodicies: The Problem of Evil

A major problem which concerns the doctrine of God centers on the existence of evil in the world. How can the presence of evil or suffering be reconciled with the Christian affirmation of the goodness of the God who created the world? In what follows, we shall explore some of the options available within the Christian tradition.

Irenaeus

Irenaeus represents a major element within Greek patristic thought, which regards human nature as a potentiality. Humans are created with certain capacities for growth toward maturity. That capacity for Godward growth requires contact with and experience of good and evil, if truly informed decisions are to be made. This tradition tends to view the world as a "vale of soul-making" (to use a term taken from the English poet John Keats), in which encounter with evil is seen as a necessary prerequisite for spiritual growth and development.

This view is not developed fully in the writings of Irenaeus. In the modern period, it has found an able exponent in John Hick, who is widely regarded as the most influential and persuasive exponent of such an approach. In his *Evil and the God of Love*, Hick emphasizes that human beings are created incomplete. In order for them to become what God intends them to be, they must participate in the world. God did not create human beings as automatons, but as individuals who are capable of responding freely to God. Unless a real choice is available between good and evil, the biblical injunctions to "choose good" are meaningless. Good and evil are thus necessary presences within the world, in order that informed and meaningful human development may take place.

The argument is obviously attractive, not least on account of its emphasis upon human freedom. It also resonates with the experience of many Christians, who have found that God's grace and love are experienced most profoundly in situations of distress or suffering. However, criticism has been directed against one aspect of this approach in particular. The objection is often raised that it appears to lend dignity to evil, by allocating it a positive role within the purposes of God. If suffering is seen simply as a means of advancing the spiritual development of humanity, what are we to make of those events – such as Hiroshima or Auschwitz – which destroy those who encounter them? This approach, to its critics, seems merely to encourage acquiesence in the presence of evil in the world, without giving any moral direction or stimulus to resist and overcome it.

Augustine

The distinctive approach adopted by Augustine has had a major impact upon the western theological tradition. By the fourth century, the problems raised by the existence of evil and suffering had begun to become something of a theological embarrassment. Gnosticism – including its variant form, Manichaeism, with which Augustine became fascinated as a young man – had no difficulty in accounting for the existence of evil. It arose on account of the fundamentally evil nature of matter. The entire purpose of salvation was to redeem humanity from the evil material world, and transfer it to a spiritual realm which was uncontaminated by matter.

A central aspect of many Gnostic systems was the idea of a demiurge – that is, a demigod who was responsible for forging the world, in its present form, out of pre-existent matter. The sorry state of the world was put down to the inadequacies of this demigod. The redeemer god was thus regarded as being quite distinct from the creator demigod.

Augustine, however, could not accept this approach. For him, creation and redemption were the work of the one and the same God. It was therefore impossible to ascribe the existence of evil to creation, for this merely transferred blame to God. For Augustine, God created the world good, meaning that it was free from the contamination of evil. So where does evil come from? Augustine's fundamental insight is that evil is a direct consequence of the misuse of human freedom. God created humanity with the freedom to choose good or evil. Sadly, humanity chose evil; as a result, the world is contaminated by evil.

This, however, did not really resolve the problem, as Augustine himself appreciated. How could humans choose evil, if there was no evil to choose? Evil had to be an option within the world, if it were to be accessible to human choice. Augustine therefore located the origin of evil in satanic temptation, by which Satan lured Adam and Eve away from obedience to their creator. In this way, he argued, God could not be regarded as being responsible for evil.

Still the problem was not resolved. For where did Satan come from, if God created the world good? Augustine traces the origin of evil back by another step. Satan is a fallen angel, who was originally created good, like all the other angels. However, this particular angel was tempted to become like God, and assume supreme authority. As a result, he rebelled against God, and thus spread that rebellion to the world. But how, Augustine's critics asked, could a good angel turn out to be so bad? How are we to account for the original fall of that angel? And there, Augustine appears to have been reduced to silence.

Karl Barth

Thoroughly dissatisfied with existing approaches to evil, Karl Barth called for a complete rethinking of the entire issue. Barth, who was particularly concerned with the Reformed approach to the issue of providence, believed that a central theological flaw had developed in relation to the notion of the omnipotence of God. He argued that the Reformed doctrine of providence had become virtually indistinguishable from that of Stoicism. (In passing, we may note that many scholars of the Reformation make precisely this point in relation to Zwingli's doctrine of providence, which appears to be based upon the Stoic writer Seneca to a far greater extent than upon the New Testament!) For Barth, the notion of the omnipotence of God must always be understood in the light of God's self-revelation in Christ.

On the basis of this principle, Barth argued that there was a need for a "radical rethinking of the whole issue." He suggested that the Reformed doctrine of omnipotence rested largely upon logical deduction from a set of premises about God's power and goodness. Barth, whose theological program is distinguished by its "Christological concentration," argued for a more Christological approach. Barth thus rejected *a priori* notions of omnipotence, in favor of a belief in the triumph of God's grace over unbelief, evil, and suffering. A confidence in the ultimate triumph of the grace of God enables believers to maintain their morale and hope in the face of a world which is seemingly dominated by evil. Barth himself had Nazi Germany in mind as he developed this notion; his ideas have proved useful elsewhere, and may be argued to be reflected in the theodicies which have been characteristic of liberation theology in more recent years.

Nevertheless, one aspect of Barth's theodicy has caused considerable discussion. Barth describes evil as *das Nichtige* – a mysterious power of "nothingness," which has its grounds in what God did *not* will in the act of creation. "Nothingness" is that which contradicts the will of God. It is not "nothing," but that which threatens to *reduce* to nothing, and thus poses a threat to the purposes of God in the world. For Barth, the ultimate triumph of grace ensures that "nothingness" need not be feared. However, his critics have found the idea of "nothingness" problematic, and have charged him with lapsing into arbitary metaphysical speculation at a point at which fidelity to the biblical narrative is of central importance.

Recent Contributions

The question of suffering remains high on the agenda of modern theology, and has been given a new sense of urgency and importance through the impact of the horrors of World War II, and the continued struggle of oppressed people against those who oppress them. A number of approaches may be noted, each of which can be set against a different backdrop.

1   Liberation theology develops a distinctive approach to suffering, based upon its emphasis upon the poor and the oppressed (see pp. 105–7). The suffering of the poor is not viewed as passive acquiescence in suffering; rather, it is seen as participation in the struggle of God against suffering in the world – a struggle which involves direct confrontation with suffering itself. This idea, in various forms, can be discerned in the writings of Latin American liberation theologians. However, it is generally thought to find its most powerful expression in the writings of Black theology, especially those of James Cone. The sequence of the cross and resurrection is interpreted in terms of a present struggle against evil, conducted in the knowledge of God's final victory over all suffering and that which causes it. Similar themes can be noted in the writings of Martin Luther King, especially his "Death of Evil upon the Seashore."

2   Process theology locates the origins of suffering and evil within the world in a radical limitation upon the power of God (pp. 227–8). God has set aside the ability to coerce, retaining only the ability to persuade. Persuasion is seen as a means of exercising power in such a manner that the rights and freedoms of others are respected. God is obliged to persuade every aspect of the process to act in the best possible manner. There is, however, no guarantee that God's benevolent persuasion will lead to a favorable outcome. The process is under no obligation to obey God.

   God intends good for the creation, and acts in its best interests. However, the option of coercing everything to do the divine will cannot be exercised. As a result, God is unable to prevent certain things happening. Wars, famines, and holocausts are not things which God desires; they are, however, not things which God can prevent, on account of the radical limitations placed upon the divine power. God is thus not responsible for evil; nor can it be said, in any way, that God *desires* or *tacitly accepts* its existence. The metaphysical limits placed upon God are such as to prevent any interference in the natural order of things.

3   A third strand in recent thinking on suffering has drawn upon Old Testament themes. Jewish writers such as Elie Wiesel, retaining at least the vestiges of a belief in the fundamental goodness of God, point to the numerous passages in the Old Testament which *protest*

against the presence of evil and suffering in the world. This approach has been picked up by a number of Christian writers, including John Roth, who has named the approach "protest theodicy." The protest in question is seen as part of the faithful and trusting response of a faithful people to their God, in the face of uncertainties and anxieties concerning God's presence and purposes in the world.

God as Creator

The doctrine of God as creator has its foundations firmly laid in the Old Testament (e.g. Genesis 1, 2). In the history of theology, the doctrine of God the creator has often been linked with the authority of the Old Testament. The continuing importance of the Old Testament for Christianity is often held to be grounded in the fact that the God of which it speaks is the same God to be revealed in the New Testament. The creator god and the redeemer god are one and the same. In the case of Gnosticism, a vigorous attack was mounted on both the authority of the Old Testament and the idea that God was creator of the world.

For Gnosticism, in most of its significant forms, a sharp distinction was to be drawn between the God who redeemed humanity from the world, and a somewhat inferior deity (often termed "the demiurge") who created that world in the first place. The Old Testament was regarded by the Gnostics as dealing with this lesser deity, whereas the New Testament was concerned with the redeemer God. As such, belief in God as creator and in the authority of the Old Testament came to be interlinked at an early stage. Of the early writers to deal with this theme, Irenaeus of Lyons is of particular importance.

A distinct debate centered on the question of whether creation was to be regarded as *ex nihilo* – that is to say, out of nothing. In one of his dialogues (*Timaeus*), Plato developed the idea that the world was made out of pre-existent matter, which was fashioned into the present form of the world. This idea was taken up by most Gnostic writers, who, followed here by individual Christian theologians such as Theophilus and Justin Martyr, professed a belief in pre-existent matter, which was shaped into the world in the act of creation. In other words, creation was not *ex nihilo*; rather, it was to be seen as an act of construction, on the basis of material which was already to hand, as one might construct an igloo out of snow, or a house from stone. The existence of evil in the world was thus to be explained on the basis of the intractability of this pre-existent matter. God's options in creating the world were limited by the poor quality of the material available. The presence of evil or defects within the world is thus to be ascribed not to God, but to deficiencies in the material from which the world was constructed.

However, the conflict with Gnosticism forced reconsideration of this issue. In part, the idea of creation from pre-existent matter was discredited by its Gnostic associations; in part, it was called into question by an increasingly sophisticated reading of the Old Testament creation narratives. Writers such as Theophilus of Antioch insisted upon the doctrine of creation *ex nihilo*, which may be regarded as gaining the ascendancy from the end of the second century onward. From that point, it became the received doctrine within the church.

Implications of the doctrine of creation

The doctrine of God as creator has several major implications, of which several may be noted here.

1 A distinction must be drawn between God and the creation. A major theme of Christian theology from the earliest of times has been to resist the temptation to merge the creator and the creation. The theme is clearly stated in Paul's letter to the Romans, the opening chapter of which criticizes the tendency to reduce God to the level of the world. According to Paul, there is a natural human tendency, as a result of sin, to serve "created things rather than the creator" (Romans 1: 25). A central task of a Christian theology of creation is to distinguish God from the creation, while at the same time to affirm that it is *God's* creation.

This process may be seen at work in the writings of Augustine; it is of considerable importance in the writings of reformers such as Calvin, who were concerned to forge a world-affirming spirituality in response to the general monastic tendency to renounce the world, evident in writings such as Thomas à Kempis' *Imitation of Christ*, with its characteristic emphasis upon the "contempt of the world." There is a dialectic in Calvin's thought between the world, as the creation of God himself, and the world as the fallen creation. In that it is God's creation, it is to be honored, respected, and affirmed; in that it is a fallen creation, it is to be criticized with the object of redeeming it. These two insights could be described as the twin foci of the ellipse of Calvin's world-affirming spirituality. A similar pattern can be discerned in Calvin's doctrine of human nature, where – despite his stress upon the sinful nature of fallen humanity – he never loses sight of the fact that it remains God's creation. Though stained by sin, it remains the creation and possession of God, and is to be valued for that reason. The doctrine of creation thus leads to a critical world-affirming spirituality, in which the world is affirmed, without falling into the snare of treating it as if it were God.

2 Creation implies God's authority over the world. A characteristic biblical emphasis is that the creator has authority over the creation. Humans are thus regarded as part of that creation, with special functions within it. The doctrine of creation leads to the idea of *human stewardship of the creation*, which is to be contrasted with a secular notion of *human ownership of the world*. The creation is not ours; we hold it in trust for God. We are meant to be the stewards of God's creation, and are responsible for the manner in which we exercise that stewardship. This insight is of major importance in relation to ecological and environmental concerns, in that it provides a theoretical foundation for the exercise of human responsibility toward the planet.

3 The doctrine of God as creator implies the goodness of creation. Throughout the first biblical account of creation, we encounter the affirmation "And God saw that it was good" (Genesis 1: 10, 18, 21, 25, 31). (The only thing that is "not good" is that Adam is alone. Humanity is created as a social being, and is meant to exist in relation with others.) There is no place in Christian theology for the Gnostic or dualist idea of the world as an inherently evil place. As we shall explore elsewhere, even though the world is fallen through sin, it remains God's good creation, and capable of being redeemed.

This is not to say that the creation is presently perfect. An essential component of the Christian doctrine of sin is the recognition that the world has departed from the trajectory upon which God placed it in the work of creation. It has become deflected from its intended course. It has fallen from the glory in which it was created. The world as we see it is not the world as it was intended to be. The existence of human sin, evil, and death are themselves tokens of the extent of the departure of the created order from its intended pattern. For this reason, most Christian reflections on redemption include the idea of some kind of restoration of creation to its original integrity, in order that God's intentions for his creation might find fulfillment. Affirming the goodness of creation also avoids the suggestion, unacceptable to most theologians, that God is responsible for evil. The constant biblical emphasis upon the goodness of creation is a reminder that the destructive force of sin is not present in the world by God's design or permission.

4 Creation implies that human beings are created in the image of God. This insight, central to any Christian doctrine of human nature, will be discussed at greater length later (pp. 369–71); it is, however, of major importance as an aspect of the doctrine of creation itself. "You made us for yourself, and our hearts are restless until they find their rest in you" (Augustine of Hippo). With these words, the importance of the doctrine of creation for a right understanding of human experience (pp. 192–200), nature, and destiny is established.

Models of God as Creator

The manner in which God acts as creator has been the subject of intense discussion within the Christian tradition. A number of models of, or ways of picturing, the manner in which God is to be thought of as creating the world have been developed, each of which casts some degree of light upon the matter. As is inevitable with analogies, there are limits upon the manner in which they may be used responsibly; part of the challenge of theology is to test those limits.

1 *Emanation* The image that dominates this approach, especially associated with the theologians of the early church, is that of light or heat radiating from the sun, or from a human source such as a fire. This image of creation (hinted at in the Nicene creed's phrase "light from light") suggests that the creation of the world can be regarded as an overflowing of the creative energy of God. Just as light derives from the sun and reflects its nature, so the created order derives from God, and expresses the divine nature. There is, on the basis of this model, a *natural* or *organic* connection between God and the creation.

However, the model has weaknesses, of which two may be noted. First, the image of a sun radiating light, or a fire radiating heat, implies an involuntary emanation, rather than a conscious decision to create. The Christian tradition has consistently emphasized that the act of creation rests upon a prior decision on the part of God to create, which this model cannot adequately express. This naturally leads on to the second weakness, which relates to the impersonal nature of the model in question. The idea of a personal God, expressing a personality both in the very act of creation and in the subsequent creation itself, is difficult to convey by this image.

2 *Construction* Many biblical passages portray God as a master builder, deliberately constructing the world (for example, Psalm 127: 1). The imagery is powerful, conveying the ideas of purpose, planning, and a deliberate intention to create. The image is important, in that it draws attention to both the creator and the creation. In addition to bringing out the skill of the creator, it also allows the beauty and ordering of the resulting creation to be appreciated, both for what it is in itself, and for its testimony to the creativity and care of its creator.

However, the image has an obvious deficiency, which relates to a point made earlier concerning Plato's dialogue *Timaeus*. This portrays creation as involving pre-existent matter. Here, creation is understood as giving shape and form to something which is already there – an idea which, we have seen, is in serious tension with the doctrine of creation *ex nihilo*. The image of God as a builder would seem to imply the assembly of the world from material which is already to hand, which is clearly deficient.

3 *Artistic expression*   Many Christian writers, from various periods in the history of the church, speak of creation as the "handiwork of God," comparing it to a work of art which is both beautiful in itself, as well as expressing the personality of its creator. This model of creation as the "artistic expression" of God as creator is particularly well expressed in the writings of Jonathan Edwards. In his *Personal Narrative*, Edwards speaks of his experience of the beauty of God the creator during a stroll. "As I was walking there and looking up into the sky and clouds, there came into my mind so sweet a sense of the glorious majesty and grace of God that I know not how to express."

The image is profoundly helpful, in that it supplements a deficiency of both the two models noted above – namely, their impersonal character. The image of God as artist conveys the idea of personal expression in the creation of something beautiful. Once more, the potential weaknesses need to be noted: For example, the model could easily lead to the idea of creation from pre-existent matter, as in the case of a sculptor with a statue carved from an already existing block of stone. However, it offers us at least the possibility of thinking about creation from nothing, as with the author who writes a novel, or the composer who creates a melody and harmony. It also encourages us to seek for the self-expression of God in the creation, and gives added theological credibility to a natural theology.

God's Presence within the World

In what sense can God be said to be present and active within the world? A number of models have been developed to articulate the richness of the Christian understanding of this matter, and are probably best regarded as complementary rather than competitive.

1 *The monarchical model*   According to this approach, God governs the world as sovereign Lord. All events are totally subordinate to

God's guidance and control. We have already seen that the idea of "omnipotence" needs careful qualification if it can be applied to God; nevertheless, this particular model perhaps brings out most clearly the idea of the power of God, both in creation and in redemption. God's power is understood to be demonstrated both in the bringing of the world into being, and also in the raising of Christ from the dead. The model is open to a number of criticisms, most obviously the charge that it encourages belief in a God of power, running the risk of overlooking or repressing the more tender images of God as mother or shepherd.

2 *The Deist model* Deism traditionally defended the idea that God created the world, and endowed it with the ability to develop and function without the need for his continuing presence or interference. This viewpoint, which became especially influential in the eighteenth century, regarded the world as a watch, and God as the watchmaker. God endowed the world with a design, such that it could subsequently function on its own. The model has considerable strengths, not least in its affirmation of the ordering and intelligent design of the created order (a point which was especially appreciated in the age of Newtonian physics). However, its minimization of the idea of a continuing divine presence within the world, and especially the absence of any idea of creation being dependent upon God's continuing sustenance, make it deficient in the eyes of many writers.

3 *The neo-Thomist model* Drawing on the insights of Thomas Aquinas concerning causality (which find expression in his "Five Ways"), his later followers developed the idea of a complex network of primary and secondary causes. This approach avoids the "absentee God" difficulty of Deism by insisting upon the continuing presence and activity of God within creation. However, this action is seen as subtle, resting upon the idea of God as *primary cause* and natural agencies as *secondary causes*. God, according to this view, both creates these secondary causes in the first place, and then subsequently works through them.

Each secondary cause – such as a human being, or a natural force – has a particular characteristic or inclination, reflecting its distinctive identity and place within creation. God works through these secondary causes, as a joiner works through his saw or a musician through her violin. Although God can work without the need for secondary causes (as in the case of miracles), the normal pattern of divine activity is through secondary causes. Hence a woman who loves her son could be said to express the love of God, in that God is the primary cause of that love. Nevertheless, the reality and distinctiveness of that secondary cause are maintained; even though God is implicated in that love, it remains the woman's love for her son.

This approach respects the integrity and reality of natural causes, and insists that we see the primary causality of God behind an apparently natural causality. However, this view – like many others – is confronted with difficulties over the problem of evil. The suggestion that evil may be explained by a good primary cause (God) having to work through inadequate secondary causes (humans or natural processes) has an obvious attraction; one cannot expect a good violinist to play well on a faulty violin. Yet the secondary causes through which God now works were themselves created by that same God. The problem has thus been deferred by one stage, rather than resolved.

4 *Process thought*   As we noted in our earlier extended discussion of this approach (pp. 227–8), it avoids many of the difficulties associated with the models just considered. The idea of "sympathetic influence" avoids the notion of God as power, and absolves God from responsibility for the evil or failures of the world. God, according to this view, may attempt to influence events within the process. God is viewed as a creative participant in the cosmos. However, the notion of God *controlling* events is quite unacceptable to this model, and impossible within its defining parameters. Evil is thus not to be ascribed to God. Nevertheless, the model seems to evacuate God of most of the traditional notions of divinity, causing many to be skeptical concerning its theological credentials. Is this really *God* that is being described? This common complaint reflects a fundamental difficulty with this model for many theologians.

5 *Existentialism*   The importance of existentialism as a philosophy of human existence was explored earlier (pp. 192–4). This approach seems to avoid many of the tricky questions concerning the nature of God's presence in the world. As noted earlier, existentialism focuses upon human existence. The "presence of God" is thus radically restricted to a divine impact or impression upon the subjective world of individual experience. Bultmann's account of the function of the *kerygma* suggests that God confronts individuals through the Christian proclamation, and subsequently achieves a presence within their lives through a transformed personal existence. There are obvious affinities here with the neo-Thomist approach just noted, with the *kerygma* functioning as a secondary cause.

While avoiding many of the difficulties traditionally associated with the idea of God's presence in the world, this approach seems to radically curtail God's presence to the subjective existence of the individual. God acts only in personal existence; it is not meaningful to speak of God acting in the world. Thus one cannot speak of God acting in the resurrection (as with the monarchical model); for Bultmann, the resurrection was an event in the personal experience of the disciples, not in the external world as such. Once more, this seems to lose sight of a considerable element of the Christian understanding of God!

6 *Dialogical personalism* This model, which draws upon the philosophy of Martin Buber (pp. 210–13) is related to the existentialist approach, noted above. Here, the presence of God is linked with the idea of an immediate relationship. God is experienced as present within the context of a relationship. "The Thou confronts me. But I enter into a direct relationship to it" (Martin Buber). The presence of God is thus localized or focused on the notion of an encounter with something undefinable, which is recognized as being a "Thou." The strengths and weaknesses of this approach are similar to those of the existentialist model just discussed.

The Holy Spirit

The doctrine of the Holy Spirit deserves a full chapter in its own right. The Holy Spirit has long been the cinderella of the Trinity. The other two sisters may have gone to the theological ball; the Holy Spirit got left behind every time. But not now. The rise of the charismatic movement within virtually every mainstream church has ensured that the Holy Spirit figures prominently on the theological agenda. A new experience of the reality and power of the Spirit has had a major impact upon the theological discussion of the person and work of the Holy Spirit.

Models of the Holy Spirit

"God is spirit" (John 4: 24). But what does this tell us about God? The English language uses at least three words – "wind," "breath," and "spirit" – to translate a single Hebrew term, *ruach*. This important Hebrew word has a depth of meaning which it is virtually impossible to reproduce in English. *Ruach*, traditionally translated simply as "spirit," is associated with a range of meanings, each of which casts some light on the complex associations of the Christian notion of the Holy Spirit.

1 *Spirit as wind*   The Old Testament writers are careful not to identify God with the wind, and thus reduce God to the level of a natural force. Nevertheless, a parallel is drawn between the power of the wind, and that of God. To speak of God as spirit is to call to mind the surging energy of the "Lord of Hosts," and remind Israel of the power and dynamism of the God who had called Israel out of Egypt. This image of the spirit as redemptive power is perhaps stated in its most significant form in the account of the exodus from Egypt, in which a powerful wind divides the Red Sea (Exodus 14: 21). Here, the idea of *ruach* conveys both the power and the redemptive purpose of God.

The image of the wind also allowed the pluriformity of human experience of God to be accounted for, and visualized in a genuinely helpful manner. The Old Testament writers were conscious of experiencing the presence and activity of God in two quite distinct manners. Sometimes God was experienced as a judge, one who condemned Israel for its waywardness; yet at other times, God is experienced as one who refreshes the chosen people, like water in a dry land. The image of the wind conveyed both these ideas in a powerful manner.

It must be remembered that Israel bordered the Mediterranean Sea on the west, and the great deserts on the east. When the wind blew from the east, it was experienced as a mist of fine sand which scorched vegetation and parched the land. Travellers' accounts of these winds speak of their remarkable force and power. Even the light of the sun is obliterated by the sand-storm thrown up by the wind. This wind was seen by the biblical writers as a model for the way in which God demonstrated the finitude and transitoriness of the creation. "The grass withers and the flowers fall, when the breath of the Lord blows on them" (Isaiah 40: 7). Just as the scorching east wind, like the Arabian sirocco, destroyed plants and grass, so God was understood to destroy human pride (see Psalm 103: 15–18; Jeremiah 4: 11). Just as a plant springs up, fresh and green, only to be withered before the blast of the hot desert wind, so human empires rise only to fall before the face of God.

At the time when the prophet Isaiah was writing, Israel was held captive in Babylon. To many, it seemed that the great Babylonian empire was a permanent historical feature, which nothing could change. Yet the transitoriness of human achievements when the "breath of the Lord" blows upon them is asserted by the prophet, as he proclaims the pending destruction of that empire. God alone is permanent, and all else is in a state of flux and change. "The grass withers and the flowers fall, but the word of our God stands for ever" (Isaiah 40: 8).

The western winds, however, were totally different. In the winter, the west and south-west winds brought rain to the dry land as they blew in from the sea. In the summer, the western winds did not bring rain, but coolness. The intensity of the desert heat was mitigated through these gentle cooling breezes. And just as this wind brought refreshment, by moistening the dry ground in winter and cooling the heat of the day in summer, so God was understood to refresh human spiritual needs. In a series of powerful images, God is compared by the Old Testament writers to the rain brought by the western wind (Hosea 6: 3), refreshing the land.

2 *Spirit as breath* The idea of spirit is associated with life. When God created Adam, God breathed into him the breath of life, as a result of which he became a living being (Genesis 2: 7). The basic difference between a living and a dead human being is that the former breathes, and the latter does not. This led to the idea that life was dependent upon breath. God is the one who breathes the breath of life into empty shells, and brings them to life. God brought Adam to life by breathing into him. The famous vision of the valley of the dry bones (Ezekiel 37: 1–14) also illustrates this point: Can these dry bones live? The bones only come to life when breath enters into them (Ezekiel 37: 9–10). The model of God as spirit thus conveys the fundamental insight that God is the one who gives life, even the one who is able to bring the dead back to life.

It is thus important to note that *ruach* is often linked with God's work of creation (e.g. Genesis 1: 2; Job 26: 12–13; 33: 4, Psalm 104: 27–31), even if the precise role of the Spirit is left unspecified. There is clearly an association between "Spirit" and the giving of life through creation.

3 *Spirit as charism* The technical term "charism" refers to the "filling of an individual with the spirit of God," by which the person in question is enabled to perform tasks which would otherwise be impossible. The gift of wisdom is often portrayed as a consequence of the endowment of the Spirit (Genesis 41: 38–9; Exodus 28: 3, 35: 31; Deuteronomy 34: 9). At times, the Old Testament attributes gifts of leadership or military prowess to the influence of the Spirit (Judges 14: 6, 19; 15: 14, 15). However, the most pervasive aspect of this feature of the Spirit relates to the question of prophecy.

The Old Testament does not offer much in the way of clarification concerning the manner in which the prophets were inspired, guided, or motivated by the Holy Spirit. In the pre-exilic era, prophecy is often associated with ecstatic experiences of God, linked with wild behavior (1 Samuel 10: 6, 19: 24). Nevertheless, the activity of prophecy gradually became associated with the *message* rather than the *behavior* of the prophet. The prophet's credentials rest upon an endowment with the Spirit (Isaiah 61: 1; Ezekiel 2: 1–2; Micah 3: 8; Zechariah 7: 12), which authenticates the prophet's message – a message which is usually described as "the word [*dabhar*] of the Lord."

The Debate over the Divinity of the Holy Spirit

The early church found itself puzzled by the Spirit, and unable to make much in the way of theological sense of this area of doctrine. In part, this reflects the fact that theological debate was centered elsewhere. The Greek patristic writers had, in their view, more important things to do than worry about the Spirit, when vital political and Christological debates were raging all around them. However, a debate eventually developed over the status of the Holy Spirit. The theological development of the early church was generally a response to public debates; once a serious debate got under way, doctrinal clarification was the inevitable outcome.

The debate in question centered upon the *pneumatomachoi* or "opponents of the Spirit." These writers argued that neither the person nor the works of the Spirit were to be regarded as having the status or nature of a divine person. In response to this, writers such as Athanasius and Basil of Caesarea made an appeal to the formula which had by then become universally accepted for baptism. Since the time of the New Testament (see Matthew 28: 18–20), Christians were baptized in the name of "the Father, Son, and Holy Spirit." Athanasius argued that this had momentous implications for an understanding of the status of the person of the Holy Spirit. In his *Letter to Serapion*, Athanasius declared that the baptismal formula clearly pointed to the Spirit sharing the same divinity as the Father and the Son. This argument eventually prevailed.

However, patristic writers were hesitant to speak openly of the Spirit as "God," in that this practice was not sanctioned by Scripture – a point discussed at some length by Basil of Caesarea in his treatise on the Holy Spirit (374–5). This caution can be seen in the final statement of the doctrine of the Holy Spirit formulated by a Council meeting at Constantinople in 381. The Spirit was here described, not as God, but as "the Lord and giver of life, who proceeds from the Father, and is worshipped and glorified with the Father and Son." The language is unequivocal; the Spirit is to be treated as having the same dignity and rank as the Father and Son, even if the term "God" is not to be used explicitly. The precise relation of the Spirit to Father and Son would subsequently become an item of debate in its own right, as the *filioque* controversy indicates (see pp. 266–9).

The admission of the full divinity of the Spirit thus took place at a relatively late stage in the development of patristic theology. In terms of the logical advance of doctrines, the following historical sequence can be discerned.

> Stage 1: the recognition of the full divinity of Jesus Christ.
> Stage 2: the recognition of the full divinity of the Spirit.
> Stage 3: the definitive formulation of the doctrine of the Trinity, embedding and clarifying these central insights, and determining their mutual relationship.

This sequential development is acknowledged by Gregory of Nazianzen, who pointed to a gradual progress in clarification and understanding of the mystery of God's revelation in the course of time. It was, he argued, impossible to deal with the question of the divinity of the Spirit until the issue of the divinity of Christ had been settled.

> The Old Testament preached the Father openly and the Son more obscurely. On the other hand, the New Testament revealed the Son, and hinted at the divinity of the Holy Spirit. Now the Spirit dwells in us, and is revealed more clearly to us. It was not proper to preach the Son openly, while the divinity of the Father had not yet been admitted. Nor was it proper to accept the Holy Spirit before the divinity of the Son had been acknowledged . . . Instead, by gradual advances and . . . partial ascents, we should move forward and increase in clarity, so that the light of the Trinity should shine.

Augustine: The Spirit as Bond of Love

One of the most significant contributions to the development of the theology of the Holy Spirit (an area of theology occasionally referred to as *pneumatology*) is due to Augustine. Augustine had become a Christian partly through the influence of Marius Victorinus, who had himself converted to Christianity from a pagan background. Victorinus had a distinct approach to the role of the Spirit, as can be seen from a hymn which he had penned:

> Help us, Holy Spirit, the bond [*copula*] of Father and Son,
> When you rest, you are the Father; when you proceed, the Son;
> In binding all in one, you are the Holy Spirit.

Although the theology of these lines seems modalist (to anticipate a Trinitarian heresy we shall explore later: see pp. 256–7), an idea of considerable importance is nevertheless expressed: that the Spirit is the "bond of Father and Son" (*patris et filii copula*).

It is this idea which Augustine would take up and develop with considerable skill in his *On the Trinity*. Augustine insisted upon the distinctiveness of the Spirit; nevertheless, despite this distinctive identity, the Spirit is what is common to the Father and Son. The Father is only the Father of the Son, and the Son only the Son of the Father; the Spirit, however, is the Spirit of both Father and Son.

> According to Holy Scripture, the Holy Spirit is neither only the Spirit of the Father, nor only the Spirit of the Son, but is the Spirit of both. For this reason, the Spirit is able to teach us that love which is common both to the Father and to the Son and through which they love each other.

This idea of the Spirit as "bond of love" has important implications for Augustine's doctrine of the Trinity, and his doctrine of the church. We shall explore the former in the following chapter; the latter merits discussion at this earlier stage.

Augustine regards the Spirit as the bond of unity between Father and Son on the one hand, and between God and believers on the other. The Spirit is a gift, given by God, which unites believers both to God and to other believers. The Holy Spirit forges bonds of unity between believers, upon which the unity of the church ultimately depends. The church is the "temple of the Holy Spirit," within which the Holy Spirit dwells. The same Spirit which binds together the Father and Son in the unity of the Godhead also binds together believers in the unity of the church.

Having discussed the doctrine of God in general, our attention now turns to the more complex area of the doctrine of the Trinity, which seeks to give expression to a sequence of distinctively Christian insights concerning God.

Questions for Chapter 7

1 "God reveals himself as Lord" (Karl Barth). What difficulties does this statment raise by its use of masculine language in relation to God?

2 Many Christians talk about having a "personal relationship" with God. What might they mean by this?

3 "God can do anything." How would you respond to this definition of divine omnipotence?

4 Why do so many Christians believe that God suffers? What difference does it make?

5 Summarize and assess the main ways of thinking of God as the creator of the world.

8

The Doctrine of the Trinity

The doctrine of the Trinity has traditionally been placed toward the beginning of works of Christian theology, not least on account of the influence of the creeds of Christendom upon such works. The creeds open with a declaration of faith in God; it therefore seemed natural to most theologians to follow this pattern, placing any discussion about the doctrine of God at the opening of their works. Thus Thomas Aquinas, perhaps the finest representative of this classical tradition of doing theology, considered it only natural to begin his *Summa Theologiae* with a discussion of God in general, and the Trinity in particular. However, it must be stressed that this pattern is not the only one which could be adopted. To illustrate this point, we shall consider the location of the discussion of the doctrine of God in Schleiermacher's *Christian Faith*.

As we noted earlier, Schleiermacher's approach to theology is to begin with the common human experience of a "feeling of absolute dependence," which is then interpreted in a Christian sense as "a feeling of absolute dependence *upon God*." As a result of a long process of inference from this feeling of dependence, Schleiermacher finally reaches the doctrine of the Trinity. This doctrine is placed right at the end of the work, as an appendix. For some, this demonstrates that Schleiermacher regarded the Trinity as an appendix to his theology; for others, it suggested that it was the last word that the theologian can utter concerning God.

The doctrine of the Trinity is unquestionably one of the most perplexing aspects of Christian theology, and requires careful discussion. In what follows, we shall attempt to present the considerations which led to the evolution of the doctrine as clearly as possible. We may begin by considering its biblical foundations.

The Biblical Foundations of the Trinity

The casual reader of Scripture will discern a mere two verses in the entire Bible which seem, at first glance, to be capable of a Trinitarian interpretation: Matthew 28: 19 and 2 Corinthians 13: 14. Both these verses have become deeply rooted in the Christian consciousness, the former on account of its baptismal associations, and the latter through the common use of the formula in Christian prayer and devotion. Yet these two verses, taken together or in isolation, can hardly be thought of as constituting a doctrine of the Trinity.

Happily, the ultimate grounds of the doctrine are not to be sought exclusively in these two verses. Rather, the foundations of the doctrine of the Trinity are to be found in the pervasive pattern of divine activity to which the New Testament bears witness. The Father is revealed in Christ through the Spirit. There is the closest of connections between the Father, Son, and Spirit in the New Testament writings. Time after time, New Testament passages link together these three elements as part of a greater whole. The totality of God's saving presence and power can only, it would seem, be expressed by involving all three elements (for example, see 1 Corinthians 12: 4–6; 2 Corinthians 1: 21–2; Galatians 4: 6; Ephesians 2: 20–2; 2 Thessalonians 2: 13–14; Titus 3: 4–6; 1 Peter 1: 2).

The same Trinitarian structure can be seen in the Old Testament. Three major "personifications" of God can be discerned within its pages, which naturally lead on to the Christian doctrine of the Trinity. These are:

1 *Wisdom* This personification of God is especially evident in the Wisdom literature, such as Proverbs, Job, and Ecclesiastes. The attribute of divine wisdom is here treated as if it were a person (hence the idea of "personification"), with an existence apart from, yet dependent upon, God. Wisdom (who is always treated as female, incidentally) is portrayed as active in creation, fashioning the world in her imprint (see Proverbs 1: 20–3; 9: 1–6; Job 28; Ecclesiastes 24).

2 *The Word of God* Here, the idea of God's speech or discourse is treated as an entity with an existence independent of God, yet originating with God. The Word of God is portrayed as going forth into the world to confront men and women with the will and purpose of God, bringing guidance, judgment, and salvation (see Psalm 119: 89; Psalm 147: 15–20; Isaiah 55: 10–11).

3 *The Spirit of God* The Old Testament uses the phrase "the

spirit of God" to refer to God's presence and power within the creation. The spirit is portrayed as being present in the expected Messiah (Isaiah 42: 1–3), and as being the agent of a new creation which will arise when the old order has finally passed away (Ezekiel 36: 26, 37: 1–14).

These three "hypostatizations" of God (to use a Greek word in place of the English "personification") do not amount to a doctrine of the Trinity in the strict sense of the term. Rather, they point to a pattern of divine activity and presence in and through creation, in which God is both immanent and transcendent. A purely unitarian conception of God proved inadequate to contain this dynamic understanding of God. And it is this pattern of divine activity which is expressed in the doctrine of the Trinity.

The doctrine of the Trinity can be regarded as the outcome of a process of sustained and critical reflection on the pattern of divine activity revealed in Scripture, and continued in Christian experience. This is not to say that Scripture contains a doctrine of the Trinity; rather, Scripture bears witness to a God who demands to be understood in a Trinitarian manner. We shall explore the evolution of the doctrine and its distinctive vocabulary in what follows.

The Historical Development of the Doctrine: The Terms

The vocabulary associated with the doctrine of the Trinity is unquestionably one of the biggest difficulties to students. The phrase "three persons, one substance" is not exactly illuminating, to say the least. However, understanding how the terms came to emerge is perhaps the most effective way of appreciating their meaning and importance.

The theologian who may be argued to be responsible for the development of the distinctive Trinitarian terminology is Tertullian. According to one analysis, Tertullian was responsible for coining 509 new nouns, 284 new adjectives, and 161 new verbs in the Latin language. Happily, not all seem to have caught on. It is thus hardly surprising that a shower of new words resulted when he turned his attention to the doctrine of the Trinity. Three of these are of particular importance.

1 *Trinitas* Tertullian invented the word "Trinity" (Latin: *Trinitas*), which has become so characteristic a feature of Christian theology since

his time. Although other possibilities had been explored, Tertullian's influence was such that this term became normative within the western church.

2 *Persona* Tertullian introduced this Latin term to translate the Greek word *hypostasis*, which had begun to gain acceptance in the Greek-speaking church. Scholars have debated at length over what Tertullian meant by this Latin term, which is invariably translated into English as "person" (on which see pp. 208–13). The following explanation commands a wide degree of assent, and casts some light on the complexities of the Trinity.

The term *persona* literally means "a mask," such as that worn by an actor in a Roman drama. At this time, actors wore masks to allow the audiences to understand which of the different characters in the drama they were playing. The term *persona* thus came to have a developed meaning, along the lines of "the role that someone is playing." It is quite possible that Tertullian wanted his readers to understand the idea of "one substance, three persons" to mean that the one God played three distinct yet related roles in the great drama of human redemption. Behind the plurality of roles lay a single actor. The complexity of the process of creation and redemption did not imply that there were many gods; simply that there was one God, who acted in a multiplicity of manners within the "economy of salvation" (a term which will be expained in more detail in the following section).

3 *Substantia* Tertullian introduced this term to express the idea of a fundamental unity within the Godhead, despite the inherent complexity of the revelation of God within history. "Substance" is what the three persons of the Trinity have in common. It must not be thought of as something which exists independently of the three persons; rather, it expresses their common foundational unity, despite their outward appearance of diversity.

The Historical Development of the Doctrine: The Ideas

The development of the doctrine of the Trinity is best seen as organically related to the evolution of Christology (see pp. 279–81; 294–306). It became increasingly clear that there was a consensus to the effect that Jesus was "of the same substance" (*homoousios*) as God, rather than just "of similar substance" (*homoiousios*). But if Jesus was God, in any meaningful sense of the word, what did this imply about God? If Jesus was God, were there now two Gods? Or was a radical reconsideration of the nature of God appropriate? Historically, it is possible to argue that the doctrine of the Trinity is closely linked with the development of the doctrine of the divinity of Christ. The more emphatic the church became that Christ was God, the more it came under pressure to clarify how Christ related to God.

The starting point for Christian reflections on the Trinity is, as we have seen, the New Testament witness to the presence and activity of God in Christ and through the Spirit. For Irenaeus, the whole process of salvation, from its beginning to its end, bore witness to the action of Father, Son, and Holy Spirit. Irenaeus made use of a term which featured prominently in future discussion of the Trinity: "the economy of salvation." That word "economy" needs clarification. The Greek word *oikonomia* basically means "the way in which one's affairs are ordered" (the relation to the modern sense of the word will thus be clear). For Irenaeus, the "economy of salvation" meant "the way in which God has ordered the salvation of humanity in history."

At the time, Irenaeus was under considerable pressure from Gnostic critics, who argued that the creator God was quite distinct from (and inferior to) the redeemer God (see pp. 15–16). In the form favored by Marcion, this idea took the following form: The Old Testament God is a creator God, and totally different from the redeemer God of the New Testament. As a result, the Old Testament should be shunned by Christians, who should concentrate their attention upon the New Testament. Irenaeus vigorously rejected this idea. He insisted that the entire process of salvation, from the first moment of creation to the last moment of history, was the work of the one and the same God. There was a single economy of salvation, in which the one God – who was both creator and redeemer – was at work to redeem his creation.

In his *Demonstration of the Preaching of the Apostles*, Irenaeus insisted upon the distinct yet related roles of Father, Son, and Spirit within the economy of salvation. He affirmed his faith in:

> God the Father uncreated, who is uncontained, invisible, one God, creator of the universe . . . and the Word of God, the Son of God, our Lord Jesus Christ, who . . . in the fulness of time, to gather all things to himself, became a human among humans, to . . . destroy death, bring life, and achieve fellowship between God and humanity . . . And the Holy Spirit . . . was poured out in a new way on our humanity to make us new throughout the world in the sight of God.

This passage brings out clearly the idea of an economic Trinity – that is to say, an understanding of the nature of the Godhead in which each person is responsible for an aspect of the economy of salvation. Far from being a rather pointless piece of theological speculation, the doctrine of the Trinity is grounded directly in the complex human experience of redemption in Christ, and is concerned with the explanation of this experience.

Tertullian gave the theology of the Trinity its distinctive vocabulary (see above); he also shaped its distinctive form. God is one; nevertheless, God cannot be regarded as something or someone totally isolated from the created order. The economy of salvation demonstrates that God is active in creation. This activity is complex; on analysis, this divine action reveals both a *unity* and a *distinctiveness*. Tertullian argues that *substance* is what unites the three aspects of the economy of salvation; *person* is what distinguishes them. The three persons of the Trinity are distinct, yet not divided (*distincti non divisi*), different yet not separate or independent of each other (*discreti non separati*). The complexity of the human experience of redemption is thus the result of the three persons of the Godhead acting in distinct yet coordinated manners in human history, without any loss of the total unity of the Godhead.

By the second half of the fourth century, the debate concerning the relation of the Father and the Son gave every indication of having been settled. The recognition that Father and Son were "of one being" settled the Arian controversy, and established a consensus within the church over the divinity of the Son. But further theological construction was necessary. What was the relation of the Spirit to the Father? And to the Son? There was a growing consensus that the Spirit could not be omitted from the Godhead. The Cappadocian fathers, especially Basil of Caesarea, defended the divinity of the Spirit in such persuasive terms that the foundation was laid for the final element of Trinitarian theology to be put in its place. The divinity and co-equality of Father, Son, and Spirit had been agreed; it now remained to develop Trinitarian models to allow this understanding of the Godhead to be visualized.

In general, eastern theology tended to emphasize the distinct individuality of the three persons or *hypostases*, and to safeguard their unity by stressing the fact that both the Son and the Spirit derived from the Father. The relation between the persons or *hypostases* is ontological, grounded in what those persons are. Thus the relation of the Son to the Father is defined in terms of "being begotten" and "sonship." As we shall see, Augustine moves away from this approach, preferring to treat the persons in relational terms. We shall return to these points shortly, in discussing the *filioque* controversy (see pp. 266–9).

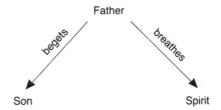

Figure 1   *The eastern approach to the Trinity*

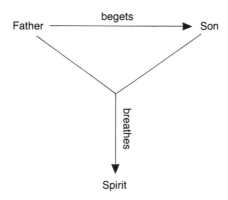

Figure 2   *The western approach to the Trinity*

The western approach, however, was more marked by its tendency to begin from the unity of God, especially in the work of revelation and redemption, and to interpret the relation of the three persons in terms of their mutual fellowship. It is this position which is characteristic of Augustine, and which we shall explore later (see pp. 257–60).

The eastern approach might seem to suggest that the Trinity consists of three independent agents, doing quite different things. This possibility was excluded by two later developments, which are usually referred to by the terms "mutual interpenetration" (*perichoresis*) and "appropriation." Although these ideas find their full development at a later stage in the development of the doctrine, they are unquestionably hinted at by both Irenaeus and Tertullian, and find more substantial expression in the writings of Gregory of Nyssa. We may usefully consider both these ideas at this stage.

Perichoresis

This Greek term, which is often found in either its Latin (*circumincessio*) or English ("mutual interpenetration") forms, came into general use in the sixth century. It refers to the manner in which the three persons of the Trinity relate to one another. The concept of *perichoresis* allows the individuality of the persons to be maintained, while insisting that each person shares in the life of the other two. An image often used to express this idea is that of "a community of being," in which each person, while maintaining its distinctive identity, penetrates the others and is penetrated by them.

This notion has important implications for Christian political thought, as Leonardo Boff (see p. 105) and other theologians concerned with political theology have made clear. The mutual relationships amongst three co-equal persons within the Godhead have been argued to provide a model both for human relationships within communities and for Christian political and social theorizing. Our attention now turns to a related idea of importance in this connection.

Appropriation

This second idea is related to *perichoresis*, and follows on from it. The modalist heresy (see p. 256) argued that God could be considered as existing in different "modes of being" at different points in the economy of salvation, so that, at one point, God existed as Father and created the world; at another, God existed as Son and redeemed it. The doctrine of appropriation insists that the works of the Trinity are a unity; every person of the Trinity is involved in every outward action of the Godhead. Thus Father, Son, and Spirit are all involved in the work of creation, which is not to be viewed as the work of the Father alone. For example, Augustine of Hippo pointed out that the Genesis creation account speaks of God, the Word, and the Spirit (Genesis 1: 1–3), thus indicating that all three persons of the Trinity were present and active at this decisive moment in salvation history.

Yet it is *appropriate* to think of creation as the work of the Father. Despite the fact that all three persons of the Trinity are implicated in creation, it is properly seen as the distinctive action of the Father. Similarly, the entire Trinity is involved in the work of redemption (although, as we shall see later, a number of theories of salvation, or *soteriologies*, ignore this Trinitarian dimension of the cross, and are impoverished as a result). It is, however, *appropriate* to speak of redemption as being the distinctive work of the Son.

Taken together, the doctrines of *perichoresis* and appropriation allow us to think of the Godhead as a "community of being," in which all is shared, united, and mutually exchanged. Father, Son, and Spirit are not three isolated and diverging compartments of a Godhead, like three subsidiary components of an international corporation.

Rather, they are differentiations within the Godhead, which become evident within the economy of salvation and the human experience of redemption and grace. The doctrine of the Trinity affirms that, beneath the surface of the complexities of the history of salvation and our experience of God lies one God, and one God only.

One of the most sophisticated statements of this points was made by Karl Rahner, in his treatise *The Trinity* (1970). Rahner's discussion of the doctrine of the Trinity is one of the most interesting aspects of his thought. Sadly, however, it is also one of the most difficult aspects of the thought of a writer not noted for his clarity of expression. (The story is told of the American theologian who expressed his delight to a German colleague over the way in which Rahner's German writings were becoming available in English. "It's just great the way Rahner's being translated into English." His colleague laughed bitterly, and replied: "We're still waiting for someone to translate him into German.")

One of the central features of Rahner's discussion concerns the relation of the "economic" and "essential" (or "immanent") Trinities. These do not constitute two different Godheads; rather, they are two different manners of approaching the same Godhead. The "essential" or "immanent" Trinity can be regarded as an attempt to formulate the Godhead outside the limiting conditions of time and space; the "economic Trinity" is the manner in which the Trinity is made known within the "economy of salvation," that is to say, in the historical process itself. Rahner lays down the following axiom: "The economic Trinity is the immanent Trinity, and vice versa." In other words,

1 The God who is known in the economy of salvation corresponds to the way in which God actually is. They are the same God. God's self-communication takes on a threefold form because God is *in se* threefold. God's self-revelation corresponds to God's essential nature.
2 Human experience of God's action in the economy of salvation is also experience of God's inner history and immanent life. There is only one network of divine relationships; that network exists in two distinct forms, one eternal, and the other historical. One is above history; the other is shaped and conditioned by the limiting factors of history.

It will be clear that this approach (which summarized a broad consensus within Christian theology) ties up some loose ends left by the notion of "appropriation," and allows a rigorous correlation between God's self-disclosure in history, and God's eternal being.

Two Trinitarian Heresies

In an earlier section, we introduced the idea of heresy, maing the point that the term is best understood as *an inadequate version of Christianity*. In an area of theology as complex as that of the doctrine of the Trinity, it is hardly surprising that a variety of ways of approaching the subject should have developed. Nor should it be cause for surprise that some of them turned out, on closer inspection, to be seriously inadequate. The two heresies which follow are the most important for the student of theology.

Modalism

The term "modalism" was introduced by the German historian of dogma, Adolf von Harnack, to describe the common element of a group of Trinitarian heresies, associated with Noetus and Praxeas in the late second century, and Sabellinus in the third. Each of these writers was concerned to safeguard the unity of the Godhead, fearing a lapse into some form of tritheism as a result of the doctrine of the Trinity. (As will become clear, this fear was amply justified.) This vigorous defense of the absolute unity of God (often referred to as "monarchianism," from the Greek words meaning "single principle of authority") led these writers to insist that the self-revelation of the one and only God took place in different ways at different times. The divinity of Christ and the Holy Spirit is to be explained in terms of three different ways or modes of divine self-revelation (hence the term "modalism"). The following Trinitarian sequence is thus proposed.

1 The one God is revealed in the manner of creator and lawgiver. This aspect of God is referred to as "the Father."
2 The same God is then revealed in the manner of savior, in the person of Jesus Christ. This aspect of God is referred to as "the Son."
3 The same God is then revealed in the manner of the one who sanctifies and gives eternal life. This aspect of God is referred to as "the Spirit."

There is thus no difference, save that of appearance and chronological location, between the three entities in question. There are three terms for the same God. This led directly to the doctrine of patripassianism, as noted earlier (p. 219): The Father suffers as the Son, in that there is no fundamental or essential difference between the Father and the Son.

Tritheism

If modalism represented one simple solution to the dilemma posed by the Trinity, tritheism offered an equally neat way out. Tritheism invites us to imagine the Trinity as consisting of three equal, independent, and autonomous beings, each of whom is divine. Many students will regard this as an absurd idea. However, the same idea can be stated in more subtle forms, as can be seen from the understated form of tritheism which is often regarded as undergirding the understanding of the Trinity found in the writings of the Cappadocian fathers – Basil of Caesarea, Gregory of Nazianzen and Gregory of Nyssa – writing in the late fourth century.

The analogy which these writers use to describe the Trinity has the virtue of simplicity. We are asked to imagine three human beings. Each of them is distinct; yet they share a common humanity. So it is with the Trinity: There are three distinct persons, yet with a common divine nature. When all is said and done, this analogy leads directly to an understated tritheism. Yet the treatise in which Gregory of Nyssa develops this analogy is entitled *That There Are Not Three Gods*! In fact, Gregory develops his analogy with a degree of sophistication which blunts the *prima facie* charge of tritheism; however, even the most studious reader of the work is often left with the lingering impression of three distinct independent entities within the Trinity.

The Trinity: Four Models

As we have noted, the Trinity is a remarkably difficult area of Christian theology. In what follows, we shall survey four approaches, classic and modern, to this doctrine. Each of these approaches casts light on aspects of the concept, and allows insights to be gained concerning its foundations and implications. Perhaps the most important of these classic expositions is that of Augustine, whereas in the modern period, that of Karl Barth is of outstanding importance.

Augustine

Augustine takes up many elements of the emerging consensus on the Trinity. This can be seen in his vigorous rejection of any form of subordinationism (that is, treating the Son and Spirit as inferior to the Father within the Godhead). Augustine insists that the action of the entire Trinity is to be discerned behind the actions of each of its persons. Thus humanity is not merely created in the image of God; it is created in the image of the Trinity. An important distinction is drawn between the eternal Godhead of the Son and the Spirit, and their place in the economy of salvation. Although the Son and Spirit may appear to be posterior to the Father, this judgment only applies to their role within the process of salvation. Although the Son and Spirit may appear to be subordinate to the Father in history, in eternity all are co-equal. This is an important anticipation of the later distinction between the *essential Trinity*, grounded in God's eternal nature, and the *economic Trinity*, grounded in God's self-revelation within history.

Perhaps the most distinctive element of Augustine's approach to the Trinity concerns his understanding of the person and place of the Holy Spirit; we shall consider specific aspects of this in a later section, as part of our discussion of the *filioque* controversy (see pp. 266–9). However, Augustine's conception of the Spirit as the love which unites the Father and Son demands attention at this early stage.

Having identified the Son with "wisdom" (*sapientia*), Augustine proceeds to identify the Spirit with "love" (*caritas*). He concedes that he has no explicit biblical grounds for this identification; nevertheless, he regards it as a reasonable inference from the biblical material. The Spirit "makes us dwell in God, and God in us." This explicit identification of the Spirit as the basis of union between God and believers is important, as it points to Augustine's idea of the Spirit as the giver of community. The Spirit is the divine gift which binds us to God. There is, Augustine argues, therefore a corresponding relation within the Trinity itself. God already exists in the kind of relation to which he wishes to bring us. And just as the Spirit is the bond of union between God and the believer, so the Spirit exercises a comparable role within the Trinity, binding the persons together. "The Holy Spirit . . . makes us dwell in God, and God in us. But that is the effect of love. So the Holy Spirit is God who is love."

This argument is supplemented by a general analysis of the importance of love (*caritas*) within the Christian life. Augustine, basing himself loosely on 1 Corinthians 13: 13 ("These three remain: faith, hope and love. But the greatest of these is love"), argues along the following lines:

1   God's greatest gift is love;
2   God's greatest gift is the Holy Spirit;
3   therefore the Holy Spirit is love.

Both these lines of argument are brought together in the following passage:

> Love is of God, and its effect in us is that we dwell in God, and he in us. This we know, because he has given us his Spirit. Now the Spirit is God who is love. If among God's gifts there is none greater than love, and if there is no greater gift than the Holy Spirit, we naturally conclude that the one who is said to be both God and of God is love.

This style of analysis has been criticized for its obvious weaknesses, not least in leading to a curiously depersonalized notion of the Spirit. The Spirit appears as a sort of glue, binding Father and Son together, and binding both to believers. The idea of "being bound to God" is a central feature of Augustine's spirituality, and it is perhaps inevitable that this concern will appear prominently in his discussion of the Trinity.

One of the most distinctive features of Augustine's approach to the Trinity is his development of "psychological analogies." The reasoning which lies behind the appeal to the human mind in this respect can be summarized as follows. It is not unreasonable to expect that, in creating the world, God has left a characteristic imprint upon that creation. But where is that imprint (*vestigium*) to be found? It is reasonable to expect that God would plant this distinctive imprint upon the height of his creation. Now the Genesis creation accounts allow us to conclude that humanity is the height of God's creation. Therefore, Augustine argues, we should look to humanity in our search for the image of God.

However, Augustine then takes a step which many observers feel to have been unfortunate. On the basis of his neo-Platonic worldview, Augustine argues that the human mind is to be regarded as the apex of humanity. It is therefore to the individual human mind that the theologian should turn, in looking for "traces of the Trinity" (*vestigia Trinitatis*) in creation. The radical individualism of this approach, coupled with its obvious intellectualism, means that he chooses to find the Trinity in the inner mental world of individuals, rather than – for example – in personal relationships (an approach favored by medieval writers, such as Richard of St Victor). Furthermore, a first reading of *On the Trinity* suggests that Augustine seems to regard the inner workings of the human mind as telling us as much about God as the economy of salvation. Although Augustine stresses the limited value of such analogies, he himself appears to make more use of them than this critical appraisal would warrant.

Augustine discerns a triadic structure to human thought, and argues that this structure of thought is grounded in the being of God. He himself argues that the most important such triad is that of mind, knowledge, and love (*mens*, *notitia*, and *amor*), although the related triad of memory, understanding, and will (*memoria*, *intelligentia*, and *voluntas*) is also given considerable prominence. The human mind is an image – inadequate, to be sure, but still an image – of God himself. So just as there are three such faculties in the human mind, which are not ultimately totally separate and independent entities, so there can be three "persons" in God.

There are some obvious weaknesses here, possibly even some fatal weaknesses. As has often been pointed out, the human mind cannot be reduced to three entities in quite this neat and simplistic manner. In the end, however, it must be pointed out that Augustine's appeal to such "psychological analogies" is actually illustrative, rather than constitutive. They are intended to be visual aids (although visual aids that are grounded in the doctrine of creation) to insights that may be obtained from Scripture and reflection on the economy of salvation. Augustine's doctrine of the Trinity is not ultimately grounded in his analysis of the human mind, but in his reading of Scripture, especially of the Fourth Gospel.

Augustine's presentation of the Trinity exercised a major influence over later generations, especially during the Middle Ages. Thomas Aquinas' *Treatise on the Trinity* largely represents an elegant restatement of Augustine's ideas, rather than a subtle modification and correction of their deficiencies. Similarly, in the *Institutes* Calvin is content to offer an interpretation of Scripture which is largely a direct repetition of Augustine's approach to the Trinity, indicating a settled consensus within the western tradition at this point. If Calvin distances himself from Augustine at any point, it is in relation to the "psychological analogies." "I doubt if analogies drawn from human things are much use here," he remarked drily, when considering the intra-Trinitarian distinctions.

The most significant restatements of the doctrine of the Trinity within the western tradition date from the twentieth century. We shall consider a variety of approaches, beginning with the most significant: that of Karl Barth.

Karl Barth

Barth sets the doctrine of the Trinity at the opening of his *Church Dogmatics*. This simple observation is important, for he totally inverts the position in which it was placed by his rival, Schleiermacher. For Schleiermacher, the Trinity is perhaps the last word which can be said about God; for Barth, it is the word which must be spoken before revelation is even a possibility. It is thus placed at the opening of the *Church Dogmatics*, because its subject matter makes that dogmatics possible in the first place. The doctrine of the Trinity undergirds and guarantees the actuality of divine revelation to sinful humanity. It is an "explanatory confirmation," as Barth puts it, of revelation. It is an exegesis of the fact of revelation.

"*God* reveals himself. He reveals himself *through himself*. He reveals *himself*." With these words (which I have found to be impossible to translate into inclusive language), Barth sets up the revelational framework which leads to the formulation of the doctrine of the Trinity. *Deus dixit!*; God has spoken in revelation – and it is the task of theology to inquire concerning what this revelation presupposes and implies. For Barth, theology is *Nach-Denken*, a process of "thinking afterwards" about what is contained in God's self-revelation. We have to "inquire carefully into the relation between our knowing of God, and God himself in his being and nature." With such statements, Barth sets up the context of the doctrine of the Trinity: Given that God's self-revelation has taken place, what must be true of God if this can have happened? What does the actuality of revelation have to tell us about the being of God? Barth's starting point for his discussion of the Trinity is not a doctrine or an idea, but the actuality of God's speaking and God's being heard. For how can God be heard, when sinful humanity is incapable of hearing the Word of God?

The above paragraph is simply a paraphrase of sections of the first half-volume of Barth's *Church Dogmatics*, entitled "The Doctrine of the Word of God," punctuated by occasional quotations. There is an enormous amount being said in this, and it requires unpacking. Two themes need to be carefully noted.

1 Sinful humanity is fundamentally incapable of hearing the Word of God.
2 Nevertheless, sinful humanity has heard the Word of God, in that this Word makes its sinfulness known to it.

The very fact that revelation takes place thus requires explanation. For Barth, this implies that humanity is passive in the process of reception; the process of revelation is, from its beginning to its end, subject to the sovereignty of God as Lord. For revelation to *be* revelation, God must be capable of effecting self-revelation to sinful humanity, despite their sinfulness.

Once this paradox has been appreciated, the general structure of Barth's doctrine of the Trinity can be followed. In revelation, Barth argues, God must be as shown in the divine self-revelation. There must be a direct correspondence between the revealer and the revelation. If "God reveals himself as Lord" (a characteristically Barthian assertion), then God must be Lord "antecedently in himself." Revelation is the reiteration in time of what God actually is in eternity. There is thus a direct correspondence between:

1   the revealing God;
2   the self-revelation of God.

To put this in the language of Trinitarian theology, the Father is revealed in the Son.

So what about the Spirit? Here we come to what is perhaps the most difficult aspect of Barth's doctrine of the Trinity: the idea of "revealedness" (*Offenbarsein*). To explore this, we will have to use an illustration, not used by Barth himself. Imagine two individuals, walking outside Jerusalem on a spring day around the year AD 30. They see three men being crucified, and pause to watch. The first points to the central figure, and says "There is a common criminal being executed." The second, pointing to the same man, replies, "There is the Son of God dying for me." To say that Jesus *is* the self-revelation of God will not do in itself; there must be some means by which Jesus is *recognized* as the self-revelation of God. And it is this recognition of revelation as revelation that constitutes the idea of *Offenbarsein*.

How is this insight achieved? Barth is quite clear: Sinful humanity is not capable of reaching this insight unaided. Barth is not prepared to allow humanity any positive role in the interpretation of revelation, believing that this was to subject divine revelation to human theories of knowledge. (As we have seen, he has been heavily criticized for this, even by those, such as Emil Brunner, who might otherwise be sympathetic to his aims.) The interpretation of revelation as revelation must itself be the work of God – more accurately, the work of the Spirit. Humanity does not become capable of hearing the word of the Lord (*capax verbi domini*), and then hear the word; hearing and capacity to hear are given in the one act by the Spirit.

All this might seem to suggest that Barth is really some kind of modalist, treating the different moments of revelation as different "modes of being" of the same God. It must be conceded immediately that there are those who charge him with precisely this deficiency. Nevertheless, more considered reflection perhaps moves us away from this judgment, although other criticisms can certainly be made. For example, the Spirit fares rather badly in Barth's exposition, which in this respect can be argued to mirror weaknesses in the western tradition as a whole. However, whatever its weaknesses may be,

Barth's discussion of the Trinity is generally regarded as having rein-stated the importance of the doctrine after a period of sustained neglect within dogmatic theology.

Robert Jenson

Writing from a Lutheran perspective, but deeply versed in the Re-formed tradition, the contemporary American theologian Robert Jenson has provided a fresh and creative restatement of the traditional doctrine of the Trinity. In many ways, it is appropriate to regard Jenson as providing a development of Barth's position, with its characteristic emphasis upon the need to remain faithful to God's self-revelation. *The Triune Identity: God According to the Gospel* (1982) provides a funda-mental reference point for discussion of the doctrine in a period which has seen fresh interest develop in this hitherto neglected matter.

Jenson argues that "Father, Son, and Holy Spirit" is the proper name for the God whom Christians know in and through Jesus Christ. It is imperative, he argues, that God should have a proper name. "Trinitarian discourse is Christianity's effort to identify the God who has claimed us. The doctrine of the Trinity comprises both a proper name, 'Father, Son and Holy Spirit'. . . and an elaborate development and analysis of corresponding identifying descriptions." Jenson points out that ancient Israel was set in a polytheistic context, in which the term "god" conveyed relatively little information. It was necessary to *name* the god in question. A similar situation was confronted by the writers of the New Testament, who were obliged to identify the god at the heart of their faith, and distinguish this god from the many other gods worshipped and acknowledged in the region, especially in Asia Minor.

The doctrine of the Trinity thus *identifies* and *names* the Christian God – but identifies and names this God in a manner consistent with the biblical witness. It is not a name which we have chosen; it is a name which has been chosen for us, and which we are authorized to use. In this way, Jensen defends the priority of God's self-revelation against human constructions of concepts of divinity.

"The gospel identifies its God thus: God is the one who raised Israel's Jesus from the dead. The whole task of theology can be described as the unpacking of this sentence in various ways. One of these produces the church's trinitarian language and thought." We noted in an earlier section the manner in which the early church tended to accidentally confuse distinctively Christian ideas about God with those deriving from the Hellenistic context into which it ex-panded. The doctrine of the Trinity, Jenson affirms, is and was a necessary defense mechanism against such developments. It allows the church to discover the distinctiveness of its creed, and avoid becoming absorbed by rival conceptions of God.

However, the church could not ignore its intellectual context. If, on the one hand, its task was to defend the Christian notion of God against rival conceptions of divinity, another of its tasks was to provide "a metaphysical analysis of the gospel's triune identification of God." In other words, it was obliged to use the philosophical categories of its day to explain precisely what Christians believed about their God, and how this distinguished them from alternatives. Paradoxically, the attempt to distinguish Christianity from Hellenism led to the introduction of Hellenistic categories into Trinitarian discourse.

The doctrine of the Trinity thus centers on the recognition that God is named by Scripture, and within the witness of the church. Within the Hebraic tradition, God is identified by historical events. Jenson notes how many Old Testament texts identify God with reference to divine acts in history – such as the liberation of Israel from its captivity in Egypt. The same pattern is evident in the New Testament: God is recognized to be identified with reference to historical events, supremely the resurrection of Jesus Christ. God comes to be identified in relation to Jesus Christ. Who is God? Which god are we talking about? The God who raised Christ from the dead. As Jenson puts it, "the emergence of a semantic pattern in which the uses of 'God' and 'Jesus Christ' are mutually determining" is of fundamental importance within the New Testament.

Jenson thus recovers a personal conception of God from metaphysical speculation. "Father, Son, and Holy Spirit" is a *proper name*, which we are asked to use in naming and addressing God. "Linguistic means of identification – proper names, identifying descriptions, or both – are a necessity of religion. Prayers, like other requests and praises, must be addressed." The Trinity is thus an instrument of theological precision, which forces us to be precise about the God under discussion.

John Macquarrie

John Macquarrie, an Anglo-American writer with roots in a Scottish Presbyterian tradition, approaches the doctrine of the Trinity from an existentialist perspective (see pp. 192–4). His approach illuminates both the strengths and weaknesses of the existentialist approach to theology. Broadly speaking, these may be stated as follows:

- The strength of the approach is that it gives a powerful additional dimension to Christian theology, by indicating the ways in which this theology may be correlated with the structures of human existence.

• The weakness of the approach is that, although capable of *existential enhancement* of existing Christian doctrines, it is less valuable in *establishing* those doctrines in the first place.

In what follows, we shall explore these points by considering Macquarrie's existentialist approach to the doctrine, as found in his *Principles of Christian Theology* (1966).

Macquarrie argues that the doctrine of the Trinity "safeguards a dynamic as opposed to a static understanding of God." But how can a dynamic God simultaneously be stable? Macquarrie's reflections on this tension lead him to conclude that "if God had not revealed himself as triune, we should have been compelled to think of him in some such way." He explores the dynamic conception of God within the Christian tradition in the following manner.

1   The Father is to be understood as *primordial Being*. By this, we are meant to understand "the ultimate act or energy of letting-be, the condition that there should be anything whatsoever, the source not only of whatever is but of all possibilities of being."

2   The Son is to be conceived as *expressive Being*. "Primordial Being" needs to express itself in the world of beings, which it does by "flowing out through expressive Being." In adopting this approach, Macquarrie picks up the idea of the Son being the Word or Logos, the agent of the Father in the creation of the world. He explicitly relates this form of Being to Jesus Christ: "Christians believe that the Father's Being finds expression above all in the finite being of Jesus."

3   The Holy Spirit is to be understood as *unitive Being*, in that it "is the function of the Spirit to maintain, strengthen and, where need be, restore the unity of Being with the beings." The task of the Spirit is to promote new and higher levels of unity between God and the world (between "Being" and "beings," to use Macquarrie's terms); it leads the beings back up into a new and richer unity with Being which let them be in the first place.

It will be clear that Macquarrie's approach is genuinely helpful, in that it links the doctrine of the Trinity with the existential situation of humanity. Yet its weakness also becomes evident, in that there appears to be a certain artificiality involved in the assignment of existential functions to the persons of the Trinity. One wonders what would have happened if the Trinity had happened to have four members; perhaps Macquarrie would have devised a fourth category of Being to deal with this situation? But this is a weakness of existential approaches in general, rather than this specific approach in particular.

The *filioque* Controversy

One of the most significant events in the early history of the church was agreement throughout the Roman Empire, both east and west, on the Nicene creed. This document was intended to bring doctrinal stability to the church in a period of considerable importance in its history. Part of that agreed text referred to the Holy Spirit "proceeding from the Father." By the ninth century, however, the western church routinely altered this phrase, speaking of the Holy Spirit "proceeding from the Father and the Son." The Latin term *filioque*, "and from the Son," has since come to refer to this addition, now normative within the western church, and the theology which it expresses. This idea of a "double procession" of the Holy Spirit was a source of intense irritation to Greek writers: Not only did it raise serious theological difficulties for them, it also involved tampering with the supposedly inviolable text of the creeds. Many scholars see this bad feeling as contributing to the split between the eastern and western churches, which took place around 1054 (see p. 27).

The *filioque* debate is of importance, both as a theological issue in itself, and also as a matter of some importance in the contemporary relations between the eastern and western churches. We therefore propose to explore the issues in some detail. The basic issue at stake is whether the Spirit may be said to proceed *from the Father alone*, or *from the Father and the Son*. The former position is associated with the eastern church, and is given its most weighty exposition in the writings of the Cappadocian fathers; the latter is associated with the western church, and is developed in Augustine's treatise *On the Trinity*.

The Greek patristic writers insisted that there was only one source of being within the Trinity. The Father alone was the sole and supreme cause of all things, including the Son and the Spirit within the Trinity. The Son and the Spirit derive from the Father, but in different manners. In searching for suitable terms to express this relationship, theologians eventually fixed on two quite distinct images: the Son is *begotten* of the Father, while the Spirit *proceeds* from the Father. These two terms are intended to express the idea that both Son and Spirit derive from the Father, but in different ways. The vocabulary is clumsy, reflecting the fact that the Greek words involved (*gennesis* and *ekporeusis*) are difficult to translate into modern English.

To assist in understanding this complex process, the Greek fathers used two images. The Father pronounces his word; at the same time as he utters this word, he breathes out in order to make this word capable of being heard and received. The imagery used here, which is strongly grounded in the biblical tradition, is that of the Son as the

Word of God, and the Spirit as the breath of God. An obvious question arises here: Why should the Cappadocian fathers, and other Greek writers, spend so much time and effort on distinguishing Son and Spirit in this way? The answer is important. A failure to distinguish the ways in which Son and Spirit derive from the one and the same Father would lead to God having two sons, which would have raised insurmountable problems.

Within this context, it is unthinkable that the Holy Spirit should proceed from the Father and the Son. Why? Because it would totally compromise the principle of the Father as the sole origin and source of all divinity. It would amount to affirming that there were *two* sources of divinity within the one Godhead, with all the internal contradictions and tensions that this would generate. If the Son were to share in the exclusive ability of the Father to be the source of all divinity, this ability would no longer be exclusive. For this reason, the Greek church regarded the western idea of a "double procession" of the Spirit with something approaching stark disbelief.

The Greek tradition, however, was not entirely unanimous on this point. Cyril of Alexandria had no hesitation in speaking of the Spirit as "belonging to the Son," and related ideas were not slow to develop within the western church. Early western Christian writers were deliberately vague about the precise role of the Spirit within the Godhead. In his treatise *On the Trinity*, Hilary of Poitiers contented himself with a declaration that he would "say nothing about [God's] Holy Spirit except that he is [God's] Spirit." This vagueness led some of his readers to suspect that he was really a binitarian, believing in the full divinity only of Father and Son. However, in other passages from the same treatise, it becomes clear that Hilary regards the New Testament as pointing to the Spirit proceeding from both Father and Son, rather than from the Father alone.

This understatement of the procession of the Spirit from Father and Son was developed and given its classic statement by Augustine. Possibly building upon the position hinted at by Hilary, Augustine argued that the Spirit had to be thought of as proceeding from the Son. One of his main proof texts was John 20: 22, in which the risen Christ is reported as having breathed upon his disciples, and said: "Receive the Holy Spirit." Augustine explains this as follows in *On the Trinity*:

> Nor can we say that the Holy Spirit does not also proceed from the Son. After all, the Spirit is said to be the Spirit of both the Father and the Son. . . . [John 20: 22 is then cited] . . . The Holy Spirit proceeds not only from the Father, but also from the Son.

In making this statement, Augustine thought that he was summarizing a general consensus within both the eastern and western churches. Unfortunately, his knowledge of Greek does not appear to have been good enough to allow him to appreciate that the Greek-speaking Cappadocian writers adopted a rather different position. Nevertheless, there are points at which Augustine is obviously concerned to defend the distinctive role of the Father within the Godhead:

> God the Father alone is the one from whom the Word is born, and from whom the Spirit principally proceeds. Now I have added the word "principally," because we find that the Holy Spirit also proceeds from the Son. Nevertheless, the Father gave the Spirit to the Son. It was not as if the Son already existed and possessed the Spirit. Whatever the Father gave to the only-begotten Word, he gave by begetting him. Therefore he begot him in such a way that the common gift should be the Spirit of both.

So what did Augustine think he was doing, in understanding the role of the Spirit in this way? The answer lies in his distinctive understanding of the Spirit as the "bond of love" between Father and Son. Augustine developed the idea of relation within the Godhead, arguing that the persons of the Trinity are defined by their relations to one another. The Spirit is thus to be seen as the relation of love and fellowship between the Father and Son, a relation which Augustine believed to be foundational to the Fourth Gospel's presentation of the unity of will and purpose of Father and Son.

We can summarize the root differences between the two approaches as follows.

1   The *Greek* intention was to safeguard the unique position of the Father as the sole source of divinity. In that both the Son and Spirit derive from him, although in different but equally valid manners, their divinity is in turn safeguarded. To the Greeks, the Latin approach seemed to introduce two separate sources of divinity into the Godhead, and to weaken the vital distinction between Son and Spirit. The Son and Spirit are understood to have distinct, yet complementary roles; whereas the western tradition sees the Spirit as the *Spirit of Christ*. Indeed, a number of modern writers from this tradition, such as the Russian writer Vladimir Lossky, have criticized the western approach. In his essay "The Procession of the Holy Spirit," Lossky argues that the western approach inevitably depersonalizes the Spirit, leads to a misplaced emphasis upon the person and work of Christ, and reduces the Godhead to an impersonal principle.

2   The *Latin* intention was to ensure that the Son and Spirit were adequately distinguished from one another, yet shown to be mutually related to one another. The strongly relational approach to the idea of "person" adopted made it inevitable that the Spirit would be treated in this way. Sensitive to the Greek position, later Latin writers stressed that they did not regard their approach as presupposing two sources of divinity in the Godhead. The Council of Lyons stated that "the Holy Spirit proceeds from the Father and the Son, *yet not as from two origins but as from one origin.*" However, the doctrine remains a source of contention, which is unlikely to be removed in the foreseeable future.

Having now considered the Christian doctrine of God, we may turn to the second of major theme of Christian theology – the identity and significance of Jesus Christ. We have already noted how the Christian doctrine of the Trinity emerges from Christological considerations. It is now appropriate to explore the development of Christology as a subject in its own right.

Questions for Chapter 8

1   Many theologians prefer to speak of "Creator, Redeemer, and Sustainer," rather than the traditional "Father, Son, and Holy Spirit." What is gained by this approach? And what difficulties does it raise?

2   How could you reconcile these two statements: "God is a person"; "God is three persons"?

3   Is the Trinity a doctrine about God, or about Jesus Christ?

4   Summarize the doctrine of the Trinity found in the writings of either Augustine of Hippo or Karl Barth.

5   Does it matter whether the Spirit proceeds from the Father alone, or from both the Father and the Son?

9

The Doctrine of the
Person of Christ

The area of Christian theology traditionally known as "Christology" deals with the person of Jesus Christ. The present chapter deals with the understandings of the person of Christ which have been of importance within the Christian tradition. As will become clear, the issues to be discussed in this chapter can be described as "classic," in the sense that they dominated the Christological agenda of the Christian tradition before the rise of the Enlightenment. The Enlightenment raised a new series of questions, opening up a network of debates without any real parallel in the period before 1700. These issues will be discussed at length in the chapter which follows. Our concern in the present chapter is the documentation of classic approaches to Christology.

The Relation between Christology and Soteriology

Older works of Christian theology often draw a sharp distinction between "the person of Christ" or "Christology" on the one hand, and "the work of Christ" or "soteriology" on the other. This distinction is maintained in this present work, for purely educational reasons, in that a full discussion of both areas could not be contained within the limits of a single chapter. However, the distinction is increasingly regarded as being unhelpful, save for presentational reasons. Theologically, the close connection between the two areas is now generally recognized. Amongst the considerations which led to this development, the following are of especial importance.

1 *The Kantian distinction between the* Ding-an-sich *("thing in itself")
and its perception*   Kant's argument is that we cannot know things
directly, but only in so far as we can perceive them or apprehend their
impact. Although the ultimate philosophical justification of this assertion lies beyond the scope of this volume, its theological implications
are clear: The identity of Jesus is known through his impact upon
us. In other words, the person of Christ becomes known through
his work. There is thus an organic link between Christology and
soteriology. This is the approach adopted by Albrecht Ritschl in his
Christian Doctrine of Justification and Reconciliation (1874). Ritschl argued
that it was improper to separate Christology and soteriology, in that
we perceive "the nature and attributes, that is the determination of
being, only in the effect of a thing upon us, and we think of the
nature and extent of its effect upon us as its essence."

2 *The growing realization of the affinities between* functional *and* ontological *Christologies* – that is, between Christologies which make affirmations about the function or work of Christ, and those which
make affirmations concerning his identity or being. Athanasius is one
of the earliest Christian writers to make this connection explicit. Only
God can save, he asserts. Yet Christ is savior. What does this statement concerning the *function* of Christ tell us about his *identity*? If
Jesus Christ is capable of functioning as savior, who must he be?
Christology and soteriology are thus seen as two sides of the same
coin, rather than two independent areas of thought. "A separation between Christology and soteriology is not possible, because in general
the soteriological interest, the interest in salvation, in the *beneficia
Christi*, is what causes us to ask about the figure of Jesus" (Wolfhart
Pannenberg).

The importance of this point can be seen by comparing a Nestorian-
style Christology (which stresses the humanity of Christ, especially in
relation to his moral example: see p. 292) with a Pelagian soteriology
(which stresses the total freedom of the human will: see pp. 371–7).
For Pelagius, humanity had the ability to do right; it merely needed
to be told what to do. The moral example of Christ provided this
example. This exemplarist view of Christ is thus linked with a view of
human nature which minimizes the extent of human sin, and the
strange and tragic history of humanity in general. As the English
theologian Charles Gore pointed out incisively a century ago, in an
often-quoted passage:

> Inadequate conceptions of Christ's person go hand in hand with in-
> adequate conceptions of what human nature wants. The Nestorian
> conception of Christ . . . qualifies Christ for being an example of
> what man can do, and into what wonderful union with God he

can be assumed if he is holy enough; but Christ remains one man among many, shut in within the limits of a single human personality, and influencing man only from outside. He can be a Redeemer of man if man can be saved from outside by bright example, but not otherwise. The Nestorian Christ is logically associated with the Pelagian man . . . The Nestorian Christ is the fitting Saviour of the Pelagian man.

Although Gore perhaps overstates his point, an important point of connection between Christology and soteriology is identified. An exemplarist soteriology, with its associated understanding of the nature and role of the moral example of Jesus Christ, is ultimately the correlative of a Pelagian view of the situation and abilities of humanity. The ontological gap between Christ and ourselves is contracted, in order to minimize the discontinuity between his moral personality and ours. Christ is the supreme human example, who evinces an authentically human lifestyle which we are alleged to be capable of imitating. Our view of who Jesus is ultimately reflects our understanding of the situation of fallen humanity.

Despite this consensus, there is continuing disagreement over the emphasis to be given to soteriological considerations in Christology. For example, as will become clear later, the approach adopted by Rudolf Bultmann appears to reduce Christology to the mere fact "that" an historical figure existed, to whom the *kerygma* (that is, the proclamation of Christ) can be traced and attached (see p. 324). The primary function of the *kerygma* is to transmit the soteriological content of the Christ-event. A related approach, found in the writings of A. E. Biedermann and Paul Tillich, draws a distinction between the "Christ principle" and the historical person of Jesus. This has led some writers, most notably Wolfhart Pannenberg, to express anxiety that a Christology might simply be constructed out of soteriological considerations (and thus be vulnerable to the criticisms of Ludwig Feuerbach), rather than being grounded in the history of Jesus himself (see p. 199).

The Place of Jesus Christ in Christian Theology

The person of Jesus Christ is of central importance to Christian theology. Whereas "theology" could be defined as "talk about God" in general, "Christian theology" accords a central role to Jesus Christ. The nature of that role is complex, and is best understood by considering its various components. The first such component is historical, whereas the three others are more explicitly theological in character.

Jesus Christ is the Historical Point of Departure for Christianity

This observation is relatively uncontroversial. However, its interpretation is complex. Consider, for example, the question of whether Jesus of Nazareth introduced anything *new* into the world. For the writers of the Enlightenment, Jesus of Nazareth did little more than re-publish a religion of nature, which was promptly corrupted by his followers, including Paul. There was nothing new about his words and deeds. The insights of Jesus, where they were valid, could all be obtained through the use of an omnicompetent human reason. Rationalism thus argued that Jesus had nothing that was both *right* and *new* to say; where he was right, he merely agreed with what sound human reason always knew to be the case; if he said anything that was new (that is, hitherto unknown to reason), this would, by definition, be irrational and hence of no value.

A very different approach is associated with German liberal Protestantism (see pp. 93–4), especially as this is developed in the writings of Albrecht Benjamin Ritschl. Ritschl argues that Jesus of Nazareth brought something *new* to the human situation, something which reason had hitherto neglected. "Jesus was conscious of a *new and hitherto unknown relation to God.*" Where rationalists believed in a universal rational religion, of which individual world religions were at best shadows, Ritschl argued that this was little more than a dream of reason, an abstraction without any historical embodiment. Christianity possesses certain definite theological and cultural characteristics as a historical religion, partly due to Jesus of Nazareth.

Important though this historical consideration might be, Christian theology has generally located the significance of Jesus Christ in three specifically *theological* areas, which we shall consider in what follows. Nevertheless, it must be stressed that this historical dimension to the significance of Jesus Christ is of continuing importance. Christianity is not a set of self-contained and freestanding ideas; it represents a sustained response to the questions raised by the life, death, and resurrection of Jesus Christ. Christianity is an historical religion, which came into being in response to a specific set of events, which center upon Jesus Christ, and to which Christian theology is obliged to return in the course of its speculation and reflection.

This point is of importance in understanding the continuing importance of Scripture within the Christian tradition. Christology and scriptural authority are inextricably linked, in that it is Scripture which brings us to a knowledge of Jesus Christ. The New Testament is the only document we possess which the Christian church has recognized as authentically embodying and recollecting its understanding of Jesus, and the impact he had upon people's lives and thought. The reports we have concerning Jesus from extracanonical sources are of questionable reliability, and strictly limited value. The authority of Scripture thus rests partly upon historical considerations. However, those historical considerations are to be supplemented with theological reflections – for example, that it is through Jesus Christ that the distinctively Christian knowledge of God comes about, and this knowledge of Jesus is given only in Scripture. We shall now move on to consider such explicitly theological considerations.

Jesus Christ Reveals God

A central element of Christian theology centers upon the idea of a *revelatory presence of God* in Christ (see pp. 281; 302–4). Jesus Christ is regarded as making God known in a particular and specific manner, distinctive to Christianity. Perhaps the most radical statement of this conviction may be found in Karl Barth's *Church Dogmatics*:

> When Holy Scripture speaks of God, it concentrates our attention and thoughts upon one single point and what is to be known at that point . . . And if we look closer, and ask: who and what is at this point upon which our attention and thoughts are concentrated, which we are to recognise as God, . . . then from its beginning to its end, the Bible directs us to the name of Jesus Christ.

This conviction has been central to mainstream Christianity down the ages. Thus the writer of 2 Clement, probably to be dated from the middle of the second century, opens his letter with the affirmation that "we must think of Jesus Christ as of God." The noted Anglican writer Arthur Michael Ramsey states precisely the same theological principle as Barth, even if his style is more restrained: "The importance of the confession 'Jesus is Lord' is not only that Jesus is divine but that God is Christlike."

This "Christological concentration" has been the subject of considerable debate amongst those concerned for dialogue between Christianity and other religions, and we shall return to consider its implications at a later stage in this work. Our concern at this stage is simply to note that, as a matter of historical fact, Christian theology has recognized that it is impossible to speak of "God" within the parameters of the Christian tradition without relating such statements to the person and work of Jesus Christ.

Jesus Christ is the Bearer of Salvation

A central theme of mainstream Christian thought is that salvation, in the Christian sense of the term, is manifested in and through, and constituted on the basis of, the life, death, and resurrection of Jesus Christ (see pp. 337–40). It must be noted that the term "salvation" is complex. To assert that "Jesus Christ makes salvation possible" is not to deny that other modes of salvation are accessible by other means; it is simply to insist that, within the Christian tradition, the distinctively Christian understanding of what salvation is can only be realized on the basis of Jesus Christ.

Once more, this central core of Christian belief has been the subject of some concern on the part of revisionists, alarmed at its potential implications for dialogue between Christianity and other religions, and we shall return to explore it at the appropriate point in this work.

Jesus Christ Defines the Shape of the Redeemed Life

A central issue in Christian spirituality and ethics concerns the nature of Christian existence, in relation to both its spiritual and its ethical dimensions. The New Testament itself is strongly *Christomorphic* in its view of the redeemed life – that is to say, it affirms that Jesus Christ not only makes that life possible; he also determines its shape. The New Testament imagery of "being conformed to Christ" expresses this notion well. The issues involved are of some importance, especially in relation to the question of the manner in which Jesus Christ can be an ethical or spiritual example for believers.

New Testament Christological Affirmations

The New Testament is the primary source for Christology. However, the New Testament's reflections on the significance of Christ are to be set in an Old Testament context. For example, the very term "Christ" – so easily treated as a surname – is actually a *title*, with a range of meanings which can only be fully appreciated in the light of the Old Testament expectation concerning the coming of God's messiah (Greek: *Christos*). In this section, we shall explore the main lines of Christological affirmations to be found in the New Testament.

Messiah

The Greek word *Christos* translates the Hebrew term *mashiah*, most familiar in its anglicized form of "Messiah," with the root meaning of "one who has been anointed." Although ancient Israel anointed both prophets and priests, the term is primarily reserved for the anointing of a king. Within the context of ancient Israel's strongly theocentric worldview, the king was regarded as someone who was appointed by God. Anointing – that is, the rubbing or covering of someone with olive oil – was thus a public sign of having been chosen by God for the task of kingship.

The term became linked to a set of expectations concerning the future of Israel, which focused on the anticipated coming of a new king who, like David, would rule over a renewed people of God. There is evidence that such expectations reached new heights during the period of Roman occupation, with nationalist feelings becoming closely linked to messianic expectations. The discovery of the Dead Sea Scrolls has cast much light on such expectations at this time. To designate any first-century Palestinian as "the anointed one" would be to make a powerful and deeply evocative affirmation of the importance of such a person.

The New Testament evidence for the use of this title for Jesus is complex, and its interpretation is open to dispute. However, it seems that a good case can be made for suggesting that the following four statements are plausible:

1   Jesus was regarded by some of those who were attracted to him as a potential political liberator, who would rally his people to throw off the Roman domination.
2   Jesus himself never permitted his followers to describe him as "Messiah" – something which has subsequently come to be known as the "messianic secret" (William Wrede).
3   If Jesus regarded himself as the Messiah, it was not in the politicized form that was associated with Zealot or other strongly nationalist circles.
4   The contemporary expectation was that of a victorious Messiah. The fact that Jesus suffered was seriously at odds with this expectation. If Jesus was a Messiah, he was not the kind of Messiah that people were expecting.

What, then, is the significance of the term for an understanding of the significance of Jesus? In terms of establishing Jesus' relation to Israel, the term is enormously important. It suggests that Jesus is to be regarded as the fulfillment of classic Jewish expectations, and lays the foundations for an understanding of the continuities between Judaism and Christianity. This issue may have been important in first-century Palestine, and continues to be of importance in connection with Jewish – Christian relations today. However, the issue became increasingly irrelevant to Christian writers, who were primarily concerned with accurately placing Jesus on the map of humanity and divinity. The term "Messiah" refers to a human leader, and thus serves to stress the humanity of Jesus. The early church soon found itself focusing on other New Testament Christological titles, as it sought to clarify the relation of Jesus's humanity and divinity. One of the most important terms to be discussed was "Son of God," to which we now turn.

Son of God

The Old Testament used the term "Son of God" in a broad sense, perhaps best translated as "belonging to God." It was applied across a wide spectrum of categories, including the people of Israel in general (Exodus 4: 22), and especially the Davidic king and his successors who were to rule over that people (2 Samuel 7: 14). In this minimalist sense, the term could be applied equally to Jesus and to Christians. Jesus himself does not appear to have explicitly used the term of himself. It is found used in this way elsewhere in the New Testament, especially by Paul and in the letter to the Hebrews. Paul, for example, stated that Jesus had "been declared Son of God" on account of the resurrection (Romans 1: 4).

Paul uses the term "Son of God" in relation to both Jesus and believers. However, a distinction is drawn between the sonship of believers, which arises through adoption, and that of Jesus, which originates from his being "God's own son" (Romans 8: 31). In the Fourth Gospel and the Johannine letters, the term "son" (*huios*) is reserved for Jesus, while the more general term "children" (*tekna*) is applied to believers. The basic notion appears to be that believers are enabled, through faith, to enter into the same kind of relationship as that which Jesus enjoys with the Father; nevertheless, the relationship between Jesus and the Father is either prior to, or foundational for, that between believers and God.

These observations raise an important issue, which must be noted here. Some readers will find references to "Son of God" problematical, on account of the use of exclusive language. The simple solution is to replace the masculine "son" with the inclusive term "child." Although this substitution is understandable, it blurs a series of crucial distinctions in the New Testament. For Paul, all believers – whether male or female – are "sons of God" by adoption. The point being made is that all believers enjoy inheritance rights – rights which, under the cultural conditions of the period, were enjoyed only by male children. In view of this major cultural problem, the present work will use the traditional exclusive language forms "Son of God" and "Son of Man" to deal with New Testament Christological titles, in much the same way as the traditional terms "Father" and "Son" are retained in the earlier analysis of the Trinity (see pp. 247–69).

Son of Man

For many Christians, the term "Son of Man" stands as a natural counterpart to "Son of God." It is an affirmation of the humanity of Christ, just as the latter term is an complementary affirmation of his divinity. However, it is not quite as simple as this. The term "Son of Man" (Hebrew *ben-adam* or Aramaic *bar nasha*) is used in three main contexts in the Old Testament:

1 as a form of address to the prophet Ezekiel;
2 to refer to a future eschatological figure (Daniel 7: 13–14), whose coming signals the end of history and the coming of divine judgment;
3 to emphasize the contrast between the lowliness and frailty of human nature and the elevated status or permanence of God and the angels (Numbers 23: 19; Psalm 8: 14).

The third such meaning relates naturally to the humanity of Jesus, and may underlie at least some of its references in the synoptic gospels. It is, however, the second use of the term which has attracted most scholarly attention.

Rudolf Bultmann argued that Daniel 7: 13–14 pointed to the expectation of the coming of a "Son of Man" at the end of history, and argued that Jesus shared this expectation. References by Jesus to "the Son of Man coming in clouds with great power and glory" (Mark 13: 26) are thus, according to Bultmann, to be understood to refer to a figure *other than* Jesus. Bultmann suggested that the early church subsequently merged "Jesus" and "Son of Man," understanding them to be the one and the same. The early church thus invented the application of the term to Jesus.

This view has not, however, commanded universal assent. Other scholars have argued that the term "Son of Man" carries a range of associations, including suffering, vindication, and judgment, thus making it natural to apply it to Jesus. George Caird is one New

Testament scholar to develop such an approach, arguing that Jesus used the term "to indicate his essential unity with mankind, and above all with the weak and humble, and also his special function as predestined representative of the new Israel and bearer of God's judgement and kingdom."

Lord

The acknowledgement that "Jesus Christ is Lord" (Romans 10: 9) appears to have become one of the earliest Christian confessions of faith, serving to distinguish those who believed in Jesus from those who did not. The term "Lord" (Greek *kyrios* and Aramaic *mar*) appears to have had powerful theological associations, partly on account of its use to translate the Tetragrammaton – the four Hebrew characters used to represent the sacred name of God in the Hebrew version of the Old Testament, often represented in English as YHWH or "Yahweh." It was regarded as improper within Judaism to pronounce the name of God; an alternative word (*adonai*) was therefore used. In the Septuagint Greek translation of the Old Testament, the term *kyrios* is used to translated the name of God.

The Greek word *kyrios* thus came to be regarded as reserved for God. The important Jewish historian Josephus records an important incident in which Jews refused to take part in the emperor-cult which was a central part of the civil religion of the Roman Empire. They refused to address the emperor as "lord" (*kyrios*), clearly on account of their belief that this term was appropriate to God alone. The use of the term to refer to Jesus in the New Testament thus draws on this rich tradition of association, implying a high degree of identity between Jesus and God. This trend is illustrated by a number of passages within the New Testament, which take Old Testament passages referring to God, and apply them to Christ. Perhaps the most significant such occurrence is to be found at Philippians 2: 10–11, a passage which is clearly pre-Pauline. Here, a very early Christian writer, whose identity will probably remain forever unknown, takes the great Old Testament declaration (Isaiah 45: 23) that every knee will bow to the Lord God, and transfers it to the Lord Jesus Christ.

God

The New Testament was written against a background of the strict monotheism of Israel. The idea that anyone could be described as "God" would have been blasphemous within this context. Nevertheless, New Testament scholar Raymond Brown has argued that there are three clear instances of Jesus being called "God" in the New Testament, with the momentous implications that this involves. These are:

1 the opening section of the Fourth Gospel, which includes the affirmation "the Word was God" (John 1: 1).
2 the confession of Thomas, in which he addresses the risen Christ as "my Lord and my God" (John 20: 28).
3 the opening of the letter to the Hebrews, in which a psalm is addressed to Jesus as God (Hebrews 1: 8).

Given the strong reluctance of New Testament writers to speak of Jesus as "God," because of their background in the strict monotheism of Israel, these three affirmations – to which other possible cases may easily be added – are of considerable significance.

To these verses may be added a series of important New Testament passages which speak of the significance of Jesus in *functional* terms – that is to say, in terms which identify him as performing certain functions or tasks associated with God. Several of these prove to be of considerable significance.

1 *Jesus is the savior of humanity*   The Old Testament affirmed that there was only one savior of humanity – God. In the full knowledge that it was God alone who was Savior, that it was God alone who could save, the first Christians nevertheless affirmed that Jesus was Savior, that Jesus could save. A fish came to be a symbol of faith to the early Christians, as the five Greek letters spelling out "fish" in Greek (I-CH-TH-U-S) came to represent the slogan "Jesus Christ, Son of God, Savior." For the New Testament, Jesus saves his people from their sins (Matthew 1: 21); in his name alone is there salvation (Acts 4: 12); he is the "captain of salvation" (Hebrews 2: 10); he is the "Savior, who is Christ the Lord" (Luke 2: 11). And in these affirmations, and countless others, Jesus is understood to function as God, doing something which, properly speaking, only God can do.

2 *Jesus is worshipped*   Within the Jewish context in which the first Christians operated, it was God and God alone who was to be worshipped. Paul warned the Christians at Rome that there was a constant danger that humans would worship creatures, when they ought to be worshipping their creator (Romans 1: 23). Yet the early Christian church worshipped Christ as God – a practice which is clearly reflected even in the New Testament. Thus 1 Corinthians 1: 2 speaks of Christians as those who "call upon the name of our Lord Jesus Christ," using language which reflects the Old Testament formulas for worshipping or adoring God (such as Genesis 4: 26, 13: 4; Psalm 105: 1; Jeremiah 10: 25; Joel 2: 32). Jesus is clearly understood to function as God, in that he is an object of worship.

3 *Jesus reveals God* "Anyone who has seen me, has seen the Father" (John 14: 9). These remarkable words, so characteristic of the Fourth Gospel, emphasize the belief that the Father speaks and acts in the Son – in other words, that God is revealed in and by Jesus. To have seen Jesus is to have seen the Father – in other words, Jesus is understood, once more, to function as God.

The Patristic Debate over the Person of Christ

The patristic period saw considerable attention being paid to the doctrine of the person of Christ. The debate was conducted primarily within the eastern church; interestingly, Augustine of Hippo never wrote anything of consequence on Christology. The period proved to be definitive, laying down guidelines for the discussion of the person of Christ which remained normative until the dawn of the Enlightenment debates on the relation of faith and history, to be considered in the next chapter.

The task confronting the patristic writers was basically the development of a unified Christological scheme, which would bring together and integrate the various Christological hints and statements, images and models, found within the New Testament – some of which have been considered briefly above. That task proved complex. In view of its enormous importance for Christian theology, we shall consider its main stages of development in what follows.

Early Contributions: From Justin Martyr to Origen

The first period of the development of Christology centered on the question of the divinity of Christ. That Jesus Christ was human appeared to be something of a truism to most early patristic writers. What required explanation – indeed, what appeared *exciting* – about Christ concerned the manner in which he differed from, rather than approximated to, other human beings.

Two early viewpoints were quickly rejected as heretical. *Ebionitism*, a primarily Jewish sect which flourished in the early centuries of the Christian era, regarded Jesus as an ordinary human being, the human son of Mary and Joseph. This reduced Christology was regarded as totally inadequate by its opponents, and soon passed into oblivion.

More significant was the diametrically opposed view, which came to be known as *Docetism*, from the Greek verb *dokeo*, "to seem or appear." This approach – which is probably best regarded as a tendency within theology rather than a definite theological position – argued that Christ was totally divine, and that his humanity was merely an appearance. The sufferings of Christ are thus treated as apparent rather than real. Docetism held a particular attraction for the Gnostic writers of the second century, during which period it reached its zenith. By this time, however, other viewpoints were in the process of emerging, which would eventually eclipse this tendency. Justin Martyr represents one such viewpoint.

Justin Martyr, amongst the most important of the second-century Apologists, was especially concerned to demonstrate that the Christian faith brought to fruition the insights of both classical Greek philosophy and Judaism. Adolf von Harnack summarized the manner in which Justin achieved this objective: he argued that "Christ is the Logos and Nomos." Of particular interest is the Logos-Christology which Justin develops, in which he exploits the apologetic potential of the idea of the Logos, current in both Stoicism and the Middle Platonism of the period.

The Logos (a Greek term which usually translated as "word" – e.g. as it occurs at John 1: 14) is to be thought of as the ultimate source of all human knowledge. The one and the same Logos is known by both Christian believers and pagan philosophers; the latter, however, have only partial access to it, whereas Christians have full access to it, on account of its manifestation in Christ. Justin allows that pre-Christian secular philosophers, such as Heraclitus or Socrates, thus had partial access to the truth, on account of the manner in which the Logos is present in the world.

An idea of especial importance in this context is that of the *logos spermatikos*, which appears to derive from Middle Platonism. The divine Logos sowed seeds throughout human history; it is therefore to be expected that this "seed-bearing Logos" will be known, even if only in part, by non-Christians. Justin is therefore able to argue that Christianity builds upon and fulfills the hints and anticipations of God's revelation which are to be had through pagan philosophy. The Logos was known temporarily through the theophanies (that is, appearances or manifestations of God) in the Old Testament; Christ brings the Logos to its fullest revelation. Justin states this point clearly in his *Second Apology*:

> Our religion is clearly more sublime than any human teaching in
> this respect: the Christ who has appeared for us human beings
> represents the Logos principle in all its fulness . . . For everything

that the philosophers and lawgivers declared or discovered that is true was brought about by investigation and perception, in accordance with that portion of the Logos to which they had access. But because they did not know the whole of the Logos, who is Christ, they often contradicted each other.

The world of Greek philosophy is thus set firmly in the context of Christianity: it is a prelude to the coming of Christ, who brings to fulfillment what it had hitherto known only in part.

It is in the writings of Origen that the Logos-Christology appears to find its fullest development. It must be made clear that Origen's Christology is complex, and that its interpretation at points is highly problematical. What follows is a simplification of his approach. In the incarnation, the human soul of Christ is united with the Logos. On account of the closeness of this union, Christ's human soul comes to share in the properties of the Logos. Origen illustrates this idea with an often quoted analogy:

> If a lump of iron is constantly kept in a fire, it will absorb its heat through all its pores and veins. If the fire is continuous, and the iron is not removed, it becomes totally converted to the other . . . In the same way, the soul which has been constantly placed in the Logos and Wisdom and God, is God in all that it does, feels, and understands.

Nevertheless, Origen insists that, although both the Logos and Father are co-eternal, the Logos is subordinate to the Father.

We noted above that Justin Martyr argued that the Logos was accessible to all, even if only in a fragmentary manner, but that its full disclosure only came in Christ. Related ideas can be found in other writers to adopt the Logos-Christology, including Origen. Origen adopts an illuminationist approach to revelation, in which God's act of revelation is compared to being enlightened by the "rays of God," which are caused by "the light which is the divine Logos." For Origen, both truth and salvation are to be had outside the Christian faith.

The Arian Controversy

The Arian controversy remains a landmark in the development of classical Christology, and therefore demands more extensive discussion than was afforded to earlier themes of the patristic period. Certain aspects of the history of the controversy remain obscure, and are likely to remain so, despite the best efforts of historians to clarify them. What concerns us here are the theological aspects of the debate, which are comparatively well understood. However, it must be stressed that we know Arius' views mainly in the form in which they have been mediated to us *by his opponents*, which raises questions about the potential bias of their presentation. What follows is an attempt to present Arius' distinctive Christological ideas as fairly as possible, on the basis of the few reliable sources now available to us.

Arius emphasizes the self-subsistence of God. God is the one and only source of all created things; nothing exists which does not ultimately derive from God. This view of God, which many commentators have suggested is due more to Hellenistic philosophy than to Christian theology, clearly raises the question of the relation of the Father to the Son. In his *Against the Arians*, Arius' critic Athanasius represents him as making the following statements on this point.

> God was not always a father. There was a time when God was all alone, and was not yet a father; only later did he become a father. The Son did not always exist. Everything created is out of nothing . . . so the Logos of God came into existence out of nothing. There was a time when he was not. Before he was brought into being, he did not exist. He also had a beginning to his created existence.

These statements are of considerable importance, and bring us to the heart of Arianism. The following points are of especial significance.

The Father is regarded as existing before the Son. "There was a time when he was not." This decisive affirmation places Father and Son on different levels, and is consistent with Arius' rigorous insistence that the Son is a creature. Only the Father is "unbegotten"; the Son, like all other creatures, derives from this one source of being. However, Arius is careful to emphasize that the Son is not like every other creature. There is a distinction of rank between the Son and other creatures, including human beings. Arius has some difficulty in identifying the precise nature of this distinction. The Son, he argued, is "a perfect creature, yet not as one among other creatures; a begotten being, yet not as one among other begotten beings." The implication seems to be that the Son outranks other creatures, while sharing their essentially created and begotten nature.

An important aspect of Arius' distinction between Father and Son concerns the unknowability of God. Arius emphasizes the utter transcendence and inaccessibility of God. God cannot be known by any other creature. Yet, as we noted above, the Son is to be regarded as a creature, however elevated above all other creatures. Arius presses home his logic, arguing that the Son cannot know the Father. "The one who has a beginning is in no position to comprehend or lay hold

of the one who has no beginning." This important affirmation rests
upon the radical distinction between Father and Son. Such is the gulf
fixed between them, that the latter cannot know the former unaided.
In common with all other creatures, the Son is dependent upon the
grace of God if he (the Son) is to perform whatever function has been
ascribed to him. It is considerations such as these which have led
Arius' critics to argue that, at the levels of revelation and salvation,
the Son is in precisely the same position as other creatures.

But what about the many biblical passages which seem to suggest
that the Son is far more than a mere creature? Arius' opponents were
easily able to bring forward a series of biblical passages, pointing to
the fundamental unity between Father and Son. On the basis of the
controversial literature of the period, it is clear that the Fourth Gospel
was of major importance to this debate, with John 3: 35, 10: 30, 12: 27,
14: 10, 17: 3, and 17: 11 being discussed frequently. Arius' response to
such texts is significant: The language of "sonship" is variegated
in character, and metaphorical in nature. To refer to the "Son" is
an honorific, rather than a theologically precise, way of speaking.
Although Jesus Christ is referred to as "Son" in Scripture, this metaphorical way of speaking is subject to the controlling principle of a God
who is totally different in essence from all created beings – including
the Son. Arius's position can be summarized in the following manner.

1   The Son is a creature, who, like all other creatures, derives
    from the will of God.
2   The term "Son" is thus a metaphor, an honorific term intended
    to underscore the rank of the Son among other creatures. It
    does not imply that Father and Son share the same being or
    status.
3   The status of the Son is itself a consequence not of the *nature
    of the Son*, but of the *will of the Father*.

Athanasius had little time for Arius' subtle distinctions. If the Son is
a creature, then the Son is a creature like any other creature, including
human beings. After all, what other kind of creaturehood is there? For
Athanasius, the affirmation of the creaturehood of the Son had two
decisive consequences, each of which had uniformly negative implications for Arianism.

First, Athanasius makes the point that it is only God who can save.
God, and God alone, can break the power of sin, and bring us to
eternal life. An essential feature of being a creature is that one requires
to be redeemed. No creature can save another creature. Only the
creator can redeem the creation. Having emphasized that it is God
alone who can save, Athanasius then makes the logical move which

the Arians found difficult to counter. The New Testament and the
Christian liturgical tradition alike regard Jesus Christ as Savior. Yet, as
Athanasius emphasized, only God can save. So how are we to make
sense of this?

The only possible solution, Athanasius argues, is to accept that
Jesus is God incarnate. The logic of his argument at times goes
something like this:

1 No creature can redeem another creature.
2 According to Arius, Jesus Christ is a creature.
3 Therefore, according to Arius, Jesus Christ cannot redeem
   humanity.

At times, a slightly different style of argument can be discerned,
resting upon the statements of Scripture and the Christian liturgical
tradition.

1 Only God can save.
2 Jesus Christ saves.
3 Therefore Jesus Christ is God.

Salvation, for Athanasius, involves divine intervention. Athanasius
thus draws out the meaning of John 1: 14 by arguing that the "Word
became flesh": in other words, God entered into our human situation,
in order to change it.

The second point that Athanasius makes is that Christians worship
and pray to Jesus Christ. This represents an excellent case study of the
importance of Christian practices of worship and prayer for Christian
theology. By the fourth century, prayer to and adoration of Christ
were standard features of the way in which public worship took place.
Athanasius argues that if Jesus Christ were a creature, then Christians
were guilty of worshipping a creature instead of God – in other
words, they had lapsed into idolatry. Christians, Athanasius stresses,
are totally forbidden to worship anyone or anything except God alone.
Athanasius thus argued that Arius seemed to be guilty of making
nonsense of the way in which Christians prayed and worshipped.
Athanasius argued that Christians were right to worship and adore
Jesus Christ, because by doing so, they were recognizing him for what
he was – God incarnate.

The Arian controversy had to be settled somehow, if peace was to
be established within the church. Debate came to center upon two
terms as possible descriptions of the relation of the Father to the
Son. The term *homoiousios*, "of like substance" or "of like being," was
seen by many as representing a judicious compromise, allowing the

proximity between Father and Son to be asserted without requiring any further speculation on the precise nature of their relation. However, the rival term *homoousios*, "of the same substance" or "of the same being," eventually gained the upper hand. Though differing by only one letter from the alternative term, it embodied a very different understanding of the relationship between Father and Son. The fury of the debate prompted Gibbon to comment in his *Decline and Fall of the Roman Empire* that never had there been so much energy spent over a single vowel. The Nicene creed – or, more accurately, the Niceno-Constantinopolitan creed – of 381 declared that Christ was "of the same substance" with the Father. This affirmation has since come to be widely regarded as a benchmark of Christological orthodoxy within all the mainstream Christian churches, whether Protestant, Catholic, or Orthodox.

In turning to deal with Athanasius' response to Arius, we have begun to touch upon some of the features of the Alexandrian school of Christology. It is therefore appropriate now to explore these in more detail, and compare them with the views of the rival school of Antioch.

The Alexandrian School

The outlook of the Alexandrian school, to which Athanasius is to be assigned, is strongly soteriological in character. Jesus Christ is the redeemer of humanity, where "redemption" means "being taken up into the life of God" or "being made divine," a notion traditionally expressed in terms of *deification*. Christology gives expression to what this soteriological insight implies. We could summarize the trajectory of Alexandrian Christology along the following lines: If human nature is to be deified, it must be united with the divine nature. God must become united with human nature in such a manner that the latter is enabled to share in the life of God. This, the Alexandrians argued, was precisely what had happened in and through the incarnation of the Son of God in Jesus Christ. The Second Person of the Trinity assumed human nature, and by doing so, ensured its divinization. God became human, in order that humanity might become divine.

Alexandrian writers thus placed considerable emphasis upon the idea of the Logos assuming human nature. The term "assuming" is important; a distinction is drawn between the Logos "dwelling within humanity" (as in the case of the Old Testament prophets), and the Logos taking human nature upon itself (as in the incarnation of the Son of God). Particular emphasis came to be placed upon John 1: 14 ("the Word became flesh"), which came to embody the fundamental insights of the school, and the liturgical celebration of Christmas. To celebrate the birth of Christ was to celebrate the coming of the Logos to the world, and its taking human nature upon itself in order to redeem it.

This clearly raised the question of the relation of the divinity and humanity of Christ. Cyril of Jerusalem is one of many writers within the school to emphasize the reality of their union in the incarnation. The Logos existed "without flesh" before its union with human nature; after that union, there is only one nature, in that the Logos united human nature to itself. This emphasis upon the one nature of Christ distinguishes the Alexandrian from the Antiochene school, which was more receptive to the idea of two natures within Christ. Cyril states this point as follows:

> We do not affirm that the nature of the Logos underwent a change and became flesh, or that it was transformed into a whole or perfect human consisting of flesh and body; rather, we say that the Logos . . . personally united itself to a human nature with a living soul, became a human being, and was called the Son of Man, but not of mere will or favor.

This raised the question of what kind of human nature had been assumed. Apollinarius of Laodicea had anxieties about the increasingly widespread belief that the Logos assumed human nature in its entirety. It seemed to him that this implied that the Logos was contaminated by the weaknesses of human nature. How could the Son of God be allowed to be tainted by purely human directive principles? The sinlessness of Christ would be compromised, in Apollinarius' view, if he were to possess a purely human mind; was not the human mind the source of sin and rebellion against God? Only if the human mind were to be replaced by a purely divine motivating and directing force could the sinlessness of Christ be maintained. For this reason, Apollinarius argued that, in Christ, a purely human mind and soul were replaced by a divine mind and soul. "The divine energy fulfills the role of the animating soul and of the human mind" in Christ. The human nature of Christ is thus incomplete.

This idea appalled many of Apollinarius' colleagues. The Apollinarian view of Christ may have had its attractions for some; others, however, were shocked by its soteriological implications. It was pointed out above (p. 287) that soteriological considerations are of central importance to the Alexandrian approach. How could human nature be redeemed, it was asked, if only part of human nature had been assumed by the Logos? Perhaps the most famous statement of this position was made by Gregory of Nazianzen, who stressed the redemptive importance of the assumption of human nature in its totality at the incarnation:

> The unassumed is the unhealed; however, that which is united to his Godhead is saved. If only half of Adam fell, then Christ assumes and saves only that half of his nature. But if his nature fell in its totality, then it must all be united to the nature of him who was begotten, and thus be saved in its totality. Let them not begrudge us our salvation in its totality, or clothe the savior with nothing more than bones and nerves and something which looks like humanity.

The Antiochene School

The school of Christology which arose in Asia Minor (modern-day Turkey) differed considerably from its Egyptian rival at Alexandria. One of the most significant points of difference relates to the context in which Christological speculation was set. The Alexandrian writers were motivated primarily by soteriological considerations. Concerned that deficient understandings of the person of Christ were linked with inadequate conceptions of salvation, they used ideas derived from secular Greek philosophy to ensure a picture of Christ which was consistent with the full redemption of humanity. As we have seen, the idea of the Logos was of particular importance, especially when linked with the notion of incarnation.

The Antiochene writers differed here. Their concerns were moral, rather than purely soteriological, and they drew much less significantly on the ideas of Greek philosophy. The basic trajectory of much Antiochene thinking on the identity of Christ can be traced along the following lines. On account of their disobedience, human beings exist in a state of corruption, from which they are unable to extricate themselves. If redemption is to take place, it must be on the basis of a new obedience on the part of humanity. In that humanity is unable to break free from the bonds of sin, God is obliged to intervene. This leads to the coming of the redeemer as one who unites humanity and divinity, and thus to the re-establishment of an obedient people of God.

The two natures of Christ are vigorously defended. Christ is at one and the same time both God and a human being. Against the Alexandrian criticism that this was to deny the unity of Christ, the Antiochenes responded that they upheld that unity, whilst simultaneously recognizing that the one redeemer possessed both a perfect human and a perfect divine nature. There is a "perfect conjunction" between the human and divine natures in Christ. The complete unity of Christ is thus not inconsistent with his possessing two natures, divine and human. Theodore of Mopsuestia stressed this, in asserting that the glory of Jesus Christ "comes from God the Logos, who assumed him and united him to himself. . . . And because of this exact conjunction which this human being has with God the Son, the whole creation honors and worships him."

The Alexandrians remained suspicious; this seemed to amount to a doctrine of "two sons" – that is, that Jesus Christ was not a single person, but two, one human and one divine. Yet this option is explicitly excluded by the leading writers of the school, such as Nestorius. Christ is, according to Nestorius, "the common name of the two natures":

> Christ is indivisible in that he is Christ, but he is twofold in that he is both God and a human being. He is one in his sonship, but is twofold in that which takes and that which is taken. . . . For we do not acknowledge two Christs or two sons or "only-begottens" or Lords; not one son and another son, not a first "only-begotten" and a new "only-begotten," not a first and second Christ, but one and the same.

So how did the Antiochene theologians envisage the mode of union of divine and human natures in Christ? We have already seen the "assumption" model which had gained the ascendancy at Alexandria, by which the Logos assumed human flesh. What model was employed at Antioch? The answer could be summarized as follows:

> Alexandria: Logos assumes a general human nature.
> Antioch: Logos assumes a specific human being.

Theodore of Mopsuestia often implied that the Logos did not assume "human nature" in general, but a specific human being. Theodore appears to suggest that, instead of assuming a general or abstract human nature, the Logos assumed a specific concrete human individual. This seems to be the case in his work *On the Incarnation*: "In coming to indwell, the Logos united the assumed [human being] as a whole to itself, and made him to share with it in all the dignity in which the one who indwells, being the Son of God by nature, possesses."

So how are the human and divine natures related? Antiochene writers were convinced that the Alexandrian position led to the "mingling" or "confusion" of the divine and human natures of Christ. To avoid this error, they devised a manner of conceptualizing the relationship between the two natures which maintained their distinct identities. This "union according to good pleasure" involves the human and divine natures of Christ being understood to be rather like watertight compartments within Christ. They never interact, or mingle with one another. They remain distinct, being held together by the good pleasure of God. The "hypostatic union" – that is, the union of the divine and human natures in Christ – rests in the will of God.

This might seem to suggest that Theodore of Mopsuestia regarded the union of the divine and human natures as being a purely moral union, like that of a husband and wife. It also leads to a suspicion that the Logos merely puts on human nature, as one would put on a coat: The action involved is temporary and reversible, and involves no fundamental change to anyone involved. However, the Antiochene writers do not seem to have intended these conclusions to be drawn. Perhaps the most reliable way of approaching their position is to suggest that their desire to avoid confusing the divine and human natures within Christ led them to stress their distinctiveness – yet in so doing, to inadvertently weaken their link in the hypostatic union.

The "Communication of Attributes"

An issue of major concern to many patristic writers centered on the question of the "communication of attributes," a notion often discussed in terms of the Latin phrase *communicatio idiomatum*. The issue involved can be explored as follows. By the end of the fourth century, the following propositions had gained widespread acceptance within the church:

1 Jesus is fully human.
2 Jesus is fully divine.

If both these statements are simultaneously true, it was argued, then what was true of the humanity of Jesus must also be true of his divinity – and vice versa. An example might be the following:

Jesus Christ is God.
Mary gave birth to Jesus.
Therefore Mary is the Mother of God.

This kind of argument became increasingly commonplace within the late fourth-century church; indeed, it often served as a means of testing the orthodoxy of a theologian. A failure to agree that Mary was the "mother of God" became seen as tantamount to a refusal to accept the divinity of Christ.

But how far can this principle be pressed? For example, consider the following line of argument:

> Jesus suffered on the cross.
> Jesus is God.
> Therefore God suffered on the cross.

The first two statements are orthodox, and commanded widespread assent within the church. But the conclusion drawn from them was widely regarded as unacceptable, as we noted in our earlier discussion of the idea of "a suffering God" (pp. 218–19). It was axiomatic to most patristic writers that God could not suffer. The patristic period witnessed much agonizing over the limits that could be set to this approach. Thus, Gregory of Nazianzen insisted that God must be considered to suffer; otherwise the reality of the incarnation of the Son of God was called into question. However, it was the Nestorian controversy which highlighted the importance of the issues.

By the time of Nestorius, the title *theotokos* (literally, "bearer of God") had become widely accepted within both popular piety and academic theology. Nestorius was, however, alarmed at its implications. It seemed to deny the humanity of Christ. Why not call Mary *anthropotokos* ("bearer of humanity") or even *Christotokos* ("bearer of the Christ")? His suggestions were met with outrage and indignation, on account of the enormous theological investment which had come to be associated with the term *theotokos*. Nevertheless, Nestorius may be regarded as making an entirely legitimate point.

In more recent theology, the most interesting radical application of the "communication of attributes" is generally thought to be that of Martin Luther. Luther had no hesitation in arguing along the following lines:

> Jesus Christ was crucified.
> Jesus Christ is God.
> Therefore God was crucified.

As we noted earlier, the phrase "the crucified God" is one of Luther's most famous bequests to modern theology. Or, again:

> Jesus Christ suffered and died.
> Jesus Christ is God.
> Therefore God suffered and died.

Luther's distinctive "theology of the cross" may be regarded as a radical application of the "communication of attributes."

However, he also employs the argument in a different direction. One of the most classic cases is the following:

God is the creator of the world.
Jesus Christ is God.
Therefore Jesus Christ is creator of the world.

Luther can therefore happily picture the first Christmas, with Jesus Christ lying in the manger, and declare that the child in the manger is the one who created heaven and earth. This radical approach has found its way into many of the Christian church's best-loved Christmas carols, often as a means of emphasizing the self-humiliation of God in the incarnation, or the veiled majesty and glory of the Christ-child. The following lines from "See Amid the Winter's Snow" are typical:

> Low within a manger lies
> He who built the starry skies
> He who throned in height sublime
> Reigns above the cherubim.

Adolf von Harnack on the Evolution of Patristic Christology

On the basis of his historical studies of the development of Christian doctrine, Harnack argued forcefully that the transition of the gospel from its original Palestinian milieu, dominated by Hebraic modes of thought and rationality, to a Hellenistic milieu, characterized by radically different modes of thinking, represented a decisive turning point in the history of Christian thought. The notion of dogma, Harnack argues, owes nothing to the teaching of Jesus Christ, or to primitive Christianity in its original Palestinian context. Rather, it is due to the specific historical location, characterized by Hellenistic modes of thought and patterns of discourse, within which the dogmatic statements of the early church were formulated.

For Harnack, the gospel is nothing other than Jesus Christ himself. "Jesus does not belong to the gospel as one of its elements, but was the personal realization and power of the gospel, and we still perceive him as such." Jesus himself *is* Christianity. In making this assertion, however, Harnack implies no *doctrine* of Jesus; the basis of the assertion is partly historical (based on an analysis of the genesis of Christianity), and partly a consequence of Harnack's personalist religious assumptions (Jesus' significance resides primarily in the impact he has upon individuals). Nevertheless, the transmission of the gospel within a

Hellenistic milieu, with its distinct patterns of rationality and modes of discourse, led to the attempt to conceptualize and give metaphysical substance to the significance of Jesus.

In the first edition of his *History of Dogma*, Harnack illustrates this trend with reference to Gnosticism, the Apologists, and particularly the Logos-Christology of Origen. To a certain extent, the development of doctrine may be likened, in Harnack's view, to a chronic degenerative illness. In the specific case of Christology, Harnack detects in the shift from soteriology (an analysis of the personal impact of Jesus) to speculative metaphysics a classical instance of the Greek tendency to retreat into the abstract.

Harnack makes three historical observations in support of this thesis.

1   A Christology (that is, a doctrine of the *person* of Christ) is not part of the proclamation of Jesus of Nazareth. Jesus' own message is not a Christology; it includes no self-referring affirmations. It is this point which underlies Harnack's famous – and often totally misunderstood – statement that "the gospel, as Jesus proclaimed it, has to do with the Father only and not the Son."

2   In the history of Christian thought, a concern with Christology was both chronologically and conceptually posterior to a concern with soteriology.

3   The concern with Christology arose within a Hellenistic culture, which echoed a characteristic Greek concern for abstract speculation.

Harnack's observations prompted a new interest in the study of the patristic period, which led to growing criticism of his position. Perhaps the most significant such criticism concerns his oversimplification of the nature of "Hellenism." Nevertheless, Harnack's critique of the patristic period is of importance; we have already seen how the patristic notion of an "impassible God" appears to rest on the uncritical absorption of secular ideas into Christianity. Harnack may not be correct in his suggestion that patristic Christology, and above all the idea of incarnation, is erroneous; nevertheless, he warns us of the dangers of regarding the patristic writers as having an authoritative status in matters of doctrine. They are as open to criticism as any others in the long history of Christian thought.

Models of Divine Presence in Christ

One of the perennial tasks of Christian theology has been the clarification of the relationship between human and divine elements in the person of Jesus Christ. The Council of Chalcedon (451) may be regarded as laying down a controlling principle for classical Christology, which has been accepted as definitive within much Christian theology. The principle in question could be summarized like this: Provided that it is recognized that Jesus Christ is both truly divine and truly human, the precise manner in which this is articulated or explored is not of fundamental importance. Oxford patristic scholar Maurice Wiles summarized Chalcedon's aims as follows:

> On the one hand was the conviction that a saviour must be fully divine; on the other was the conviction that what is not assumed is not healed. Or, to put the matter in other words, the source of salvation must be God; the locus of salvation must be humanity. It is quite clear that these two principles often pulled in opposite directions. The Council of Chalcedon was the church's attempt to resolve, or perhaps rather to agree to live with, that tension. Indeed, to accept both principles as strongly as did the early church is already to accept the Chalcedonian faith.

In part, Chalcedon's decision to insist upon the two natures of Christ, whilst accepting a plurality of interpretations regarding their relation, reflects the political situation of the period. At a time in which there was considerable disagreement within the church over the most reliable way of stating the "two natures of Christ," the Council was obliged to adopt a realistic approach, and give its weight to whatever consensus it could find. That consensus concerned the recognition that Christ was both divine and human, but *not* how the divine and human natures related to each other.

An important minority viewpoint must, however, be noted. Chalcedon did not succeed in establishing a consensus throughout the entire Christian world. A dissenting position became established during the sixth century, and is now generally known as *monophysitism* – literally, the view that there is "only one nature" (Greek: *monos*, "only one," and *physis*, "nature") in Christ. The nature in question is understood to be divine, rather than human. The intricacies of this viewpoint lie beyond the scope of this volume; the reader should note that it remains normative within most Christian churches of the eastern Mediterranean world, including the Coptic, Armenian, Syrian, and Abyssinian churches. (The rival Chalcedonian position, which recognized two natures in Christ, one human and the other divine, is occasionally referred to as *dyophysitism*, from the Greek terms for "two natures.")

As Christian theology has expanded into a variety of different cultural contexts, and adopted various philosophical systems as vehicles for theological exploration, it is no cause for surprise that a variety of ways of exploring the relation between the human and divine natures of Christ can be found within the Christian tradition. In what follows, we shall explore some of these approaches.

The Example of a Godly Life

The Enlightenment raised a series of challenges to Christology, which will be explored further in the following chapter. One such challenge was to the notion of Jesus Christ differing in kind from other human beings. If Jesus Christ differed from other human beings, it was in relation to the extent to which he possessed certain qualities – qualities which were, in principle, capable of being imitated or acquired by everyone else. The particular significance of Christ resides in his being an *example* of a godly life – that is, a life which resonates with the divine will for humanity.

This view can be shown to be one aspect of the Antiochene Christology, which was especially concerned to bring out the moral aspects of Christ's character. For a number of Antiochene writers, Christ's divinity serves to give authority and weight to his human moral example. It is also an important aspect of the Christology of the medieval writer Peter Abelard, who was concerned to stress the subjective impact of Christ upon believers. However, these writers all retained the classical conception of the "two natures" of Christ. With the Enlightenment, the affirmation of the divinity of Christ became increasingly problematic. Two main approaches came to be developed.

The Enlightenment itself witnessed the development of a *degree Christology*, which located the significance of Jesus Christ in his human moral example. In his life, Christ was an outstanding moral educator, whose teachings were authoritative, not on account of his identity, but on account of their resonance with the moral values of the Enlightenment itself. In his death, he provided an example of self-giving love which the Enlightenment regarded as foundational to its morality. If Jesus Christ can be spoken of as "divine," it is in the sense of embodying or exemplifying the lifestyle which ought to typify the person who stands in a correct moral relationship to God, to other human beings, and to the world in general.

Liberal Protestantism came to focus upon the inner life of Jesus Christ, or his "religious personality," as being of decisive importance. In Jesus Christ, the appropriate inner or spiritual relationship of the believer to God may be discerned. It is the "inner life of Jesus" which is regarded as being of decisive importance to faith. The "religious personality of Jesus" is seen as something that is compelling, capable of being assimilated by believers, and hitherto without parallel in the religious and cultural history of humanity. An excellent representative of this approach may be found in Wilhelm Herrmann, who understands Jesus to have made *known* and made *available* something that is new, and that this is thence made known in the inner life of the Christian.

It is the "impression of Jesus" which the believer gains from the gospels which is of decisive importance. This gives rise to a personal certainty of faith, which is grounded in an inner experience. "There arises in our hearts the certainty that God himself is turning toward us in this experience." Perhaps the most significant statement of such views is found in the 1892 essay, "The Historical Christ as the Ground of our Faith." In this essay, which is basically a study of the manner in which the historical figure of Jesus can function as the basis of faith, Herrmann drew a sharp distinction between the "historical fact of the person of Jesus" and the "fact of the personal life of Jesus," understanding by the latter the psychological impact of the figure of Jesus upon the reader of the gospels.

A Symbolic Presence

A related approach treats the traditional Christological formulas as *symbols of a presence of God* in Christ, which is not to be understood as a *substantial* presence. This *symbolic* presence points to the possibility of the same presence being available and accessible to others. Perhaps the most important representative of this position is Paul Tillich, for whom Jesus of Nazareth symbolizes a universal human possibility, which can be achieved without specific reference to Jesus.

For Tillich, the event upon which Christianity is based has two aspects: The fact which is called "Jesus of Nazareth," and the reception of this fact by those who claimed him as the Christ. The factual or objective-historical Jesus is not the foundation of faith, apart from his reception as the Christ. Tillich has no interest in the historical figure of Jesus of Nazareth: All that he is prepared to affirm about him (in so far as it relates to the foundation of faith) is that it was a "personal life," analogous to the biblical picture, who might well have had a name other than "Jesus." "Whatever his name, the New Being was and is active in this man."

The symbol "Christ" or "Messiah" means "the one who brings the new state of things, the New Being." The significance of Jesus lies in his being the historical manifestation of the New Being. "It is the Christ who brings the New Being, who saves men from the old being, that is from existential estrangement and its destructive consequences." In one personal life, that of Jesus of Nazareth, "essential manhood" has appeared under the conditions of existence without being conquered by them. We are, in effect, presented with a philosophy of existence which attaches itself to the existence of Jesus of Nazareth in the most tenuous of manners, and which would not be significantly disadvantaged if the specific historical individual Jesus of Nazareth did not exist.

Jesus may thus be said to be a symbol which illuminates the mystery of being, although other sources of illumination are available. Tillich here regards Jesus of Nazareth as a symbol of a particular moral or religious principle. Tillich emphasizes that God himself cannot appear under the conditions of existence, in that he is the ground of being. The "New Being" must therefore come from God, but cannot *be* God. Jesus was a human being who achieved a union with God open to every other human being. Tillich thus represents a degree Christology, which treats Jesus as a symbol of our perception of God.

This approach has particular attractions for those committed to inter-faith dialogue, such as Paul Knitter and John Hick. On the basis of this approach, Jesus Christ can treated as one symbol among many others of a universal human possibility – namely, relating to the transcendent, or achieving salvation. Jesus is one symbol of humanity's relationship to the transcendent; others are to be found elsewhere among the world's religions.

Christ as Mediator

A major strand of Christological reflection concentrates upon the notion of mediation between God and humanity. The New Testament refers to Christ as a mediator at several points (Hebrews 9: 15; 1 Timothy 2: 5), thus lending weight to the notion that the presence of God in Christ is intended to mediate between a transcendent God and fallen humanity. This idea of "presence as mediation" takes two quite distinct, yet ultimately complementary, forms: The mediation of revelation on the one hand, and of salvation on the other.

The Logos-Christology of Justin Martyr and others is an excellent instance of the notion of the mediation of revelation through Christ. Here, the Logos is understood to be a mediating principle which bridges the gap between a transcendent God and God's creation. Although present in a transient manner in the Old Testament prophets, the Logos becomes incarnate in Christ, thus providing a fixed point of mediation between God and humanity. A related approach is found in Emil Brunner's *The Mediator* (1927), and in a more developed form in his 1938 work *Truth as Encounter*. In the latter, Brunner argued that faith was primarily a personal encounter with the God who meets us personally in Jesus Christ. Brunner was convinced that the early church had misunderstood revelation as the divine impartation of doctrinal truth about God, rather than the self-revelation of God. For Brunner, "truth" is itself a personal concept. Revelation cannot be conceived propositionally or intellectually, but must be understood as an act of God, and supremely the act of Jesus Christ.

God *is revealed* personally and historically in Jesus Christ (pp. 155–6). The concept of "truth as encounter" thus conveys the two elements of a correct understanding of revelation: It is *historical* and it is *personal*. By the former, Brunner wishes us to understand that truth is not something permanent within the eternal world of ideas which is disclosed or communicated to us, but something which *happens* in space and time. Truth comes into being as the act of God in time and space. By the latter point, Brunner intends to emphasize that the content of this act of God is none other than *God*, rather than a complex of ideas or doctrines concerning God. The revelation of God is God's self-impartation to us. In revelation, God communicates *God*, not *ideas* about God – and this communication is concentrated and focused in the person of Jesus Christ, as appropriated by the Holy Spirit. Although Brunner's rejection of any cognitive dimension to revelation seems overstated, a significant point is being made, with important Christological implications.

The more strongly soteriological approach to this issue is best seen in Calvin's *Institutes*, in which the person of Christ is interpreted in terms of the mediation of salvation from God to humanity. Christ is in effect seen as a unique channel or focus, through which God's re-deeming work is directed toward and made available to humanity. Humanity, as originally created by God, was good in every respect. On account of the Fall, natural human gifts and faculties have been radically impaired. As a consequence, both the human reason and human will are contaminated by sin. Unbelief is thus seen as an act of will as much as of reason; it is not simply a failure to discern the hand of God within the created order, but a deliberate decision *not* to discern it and *not* to obey God.

Calvin develops the consequences of this at two distinct, although related, levels. At the epistemic level, humans lack the necessary rational and volitional resources to discern God fully within the created order. There are obvious parallels here with the Logos-Christology of Justin Martyr. At the soteriological level, humans lack what is required in order to be saved; they do not *want* to be saved (on account of the debilitation of the mind and will through sin), and they are *incapable* of saving themselves (in that salvation presupposes obedience to God, now impossible on account of sin). True knowledge of God and salvation must both therefore come from outside the human situation.

In such a manner, Calvin lays the foundations for his doctrine of the mediatorship of Jesus Christ.

Calvin's analysis of the knowledge of God and of human sin lays the foundation for his Christology. Jesus Christ is the mediator between God and humanity. In order to act as such a mediator, Jesus Christ must be both divine and human. In that it was impossible for us to ascend to God, on account of our sin, God chose to descend to us instead. Unless Jesus Christ was a himself a human being, other human beings could not benefit from his presence or activity. "The Son of God became the Son of Man, and received what is ours in such a way that he transferred to us what is his, making that which is his by nature to become ours through grace."

In order for Christ to redeem us from sin, it was necessary, Calvin argued, for the primordial human disobedience toward God to be outweighed by an act of human obedience. Through his obedience to God *as a human being*, Christ presented an offering to God which compensated for sin, discharging any debt and paying any penalty which may be due on its account. Through his suffering, he satisfied the debt of sin; through his defeat of death, he broke the power of death over the human race. Calvin does not allow that Christ's humanity participates in every feature of his divinity. Later writers termed this aspect of Calvin's thought the *extra Calvinisticum*. According to Calvin, God became incarnate, and yet may still be said to have remained in heaven. God, in all God's totality, cannot be said to be concentrated into the single historical existence of Jesus Christ.

Calvin's stress upon the mediatorial presence of God in Christ leads him to posit a close connection between the person and the work of Christ. Drawing on a tradition going back to Eusebius of Caesarea, Calvin argues that Christ's work may be summarized under three offices or ministries (the *munus triplex Christi*) – prophet, priest, and king. The basic argument is that Jesus Christ brings together in his person the three great mediatorial offices of the Old Testament. In his *prophetic* office, Christ is the herald and witness of God's grace. He is a teacher endowed with divine wisdom and authority. In his *kingly* office, Christ has inaugurated a kingship which is heavenly, not earthly; spiritual, not physical. This kingship is exercised over believers through the action of the Holy Spirit. Finally, through his *priestly* office, Christ is able to reinstate us within the divine favor, through offering his death as a satisfaction for our sin. In all these respects, Christ brings to fulfillment the mediatorial ministries of the Old Covenant, allowing them to be seen in a new and clearer light as they find their fulfillment in his mediatorship.

Presence of the Spirit

An important way of understanding the presence of God in Christ is by viewing Jesus as the bearer of the Holy Spirit. The roots of this idea lie in the Old Testament, and especially in the notion of charismatic leaders or prophets, endowed and anointed with the gift of the Holy Spirit. Indeed, the term "Messiah," as noted above, has close links with the idea of "being anointed with the Holy Spirit." There are excellent reasons for supposing that such an approach to Christology may have become influential in early Palestinian Christianity.

On the basis of what we know of the messianic expectations of first-century Palestine, it may be argued that there was a strong belief in the imminent coming of a bringer of eschatological salvation, who would be a bearer of the Spirit of the Lord (Joel 2: 28–32 is of especial importance). Even in his earthly ministry, Jesus appears to have been identified as the one upon whom the Spirit of God rested. The anointing of Jesus with the Spirit at the time of his baptism is of particular importance in this respect. An early approach to this question became known as *adoptionism*; this view, especially associated with Ebionitism, regarded Jesus as an ordinary human being, yet endowed with special divine charismatic gifts subsequent to his baptism.

The understanding of Jesus as the bearer of the Spirit has proved attractive to many who have difficulty with the classical approaches to Christology. An excellent example is provided by the British patristic scholar G. W. H. Lampe, in his 1976 Bampton Lectures at Oxford University, entitled *God as Spirit*. Lampe argued that the particular significance of Jesus of Nazareth resided in his being the bearer of the Spirit of God, and thus an example of a spirit-filled Christian existence, showing "the indwelling presence of God as Spirit in the freely responding spirit of man as this is concretely exhibited in Christ and reproduced in some measure in Christ's followers."

Perhaps a more significant development of this approach may be found in the writings of the German theologian Walter Kasper, especially in his *Jesus the Christ*. Here, Kasper argues for a pneumatologically oriented Christology, which does justice to the fact that the New Testament often portrays Christ in terms of the central Old Testament concept of the "Spirit of the Lord." For Kasper, the uniqueness of Jesus within the synoptic gospels resides in his spirit-filled existence. Jesus' real identity can only be accounted for in terms of an unprecedented relationship to the Spirit. This Spirit, according to Kasper, is the life-giving power of the creator, who inaugurates the eschatological age of healing and hope.

In Jesus, Kasper sees the Spirit of the Lord at work, effecting a new and unprecedented relationship between God and humanity, a development confirmed and consolidated by the resurrection. In terms of this Spirit-Christology, Kasper regards Jesus as the focal point at which the universal saving intention of God becomes a unique historical person. In this way, the Spirit opens up the possibility of others entering into the inner life of God. The same Spirit who permeated the life of Jesus is now made available to others, in order that they might share in the same inner life of God.

An anxiety about this approach has been raised by Wolfhart Pannenberg. In *Jesus – God and Man*, Pannenberg argues that any Christology which begins from the notion of the presence of the Spirit in Jesus will inevitably lapse into some form of adoptionism. The presence of the Spirit in Jesus is neither a necessary nor a sufficient ground for maintaining the divinity of Christ. God would be present in Jesus "only as the power of the Spirit which fills him." Jesus could, according to Pannenberg, be viewed simply as a prophetic or charismatic figure – in other words, as a human being who had been "adopted" by God, and endowed with the gift of the Spirit. As we have seen, for Pannenberg it is the resurrection of Jesus, rather than the presence of the Spirit in his ministry, which is of decisive importance in this respect.

Nevertheless, Kasper is perhaps less vulnerable to Pannenberg's critique than at first might seem to be the case. Pannenberg's anxiety is that an approach such as Kasper's might lead to a Christology which places Jesus on a par with an Old Testament prophet or charismatic religious leader. However, Kasper insists that the resurrection of Jesus is of decisive importance. Both Pannenberg and Kasper regard the resurrection as having a retroactive character. Pannenberg locates this in terms of the validation and justification of the religious claims of Jesus during his ministry. Kasper, on the other hand, sees the resurrection as linked with the work of the Spirit, and justifies this with reference to pivotal New Testament texts (especially Romans 8: 11 and 1 Peter 3: 18). The Christian understanding of the role of the Spirit is grounded in the role of the Spirit at the resurrection, which excludes an adoptionist Christology.

Revelational Presence

As we noted earlier, the idea of "revelation" is complex, embracing the idea of a final disclosure or "unveiling" of God at the end of time, as well as the more general and restricted idea of "making God known" (see pp. 151–63). Both these ideas have been of significance in more recent theology, as the notion of a Christologically determined concept of God gained influence in twentieth-century German the-

ology. Jürgen Moltmann's *Crucified God* is an excellent example of a
work which seeks to build up an understanding of the nature of God,
on the basis of the assumption that God is disclosed through the cross
of Christ. In what follows, we shall explore the distinct, though
related, approaches to "revelational presence" associated with Karl
Barth and Wolfhart Pannenberg.

Karl Barth's *Church Dogmatics* may be regarded as probably the most
extensive and complex exposition of the idea of the "revelational
presence of God in Christ." Barth frequently emphasizes that all
theology necessarily possesses an implicit Christological perspective
and foundation, which it is the task of theology to make explicit. Barth
rejects any deductive Christology based upon a "Christ-principle" in
favor of one based upon "Jesus Christ himself as witnessed to in Holy
Scripture."

Every theological proposition in the *Church Dogmatics* may be regarded as Christological, in the sense that it has its point of departure in Jesus Christ. It is this feature of Barth's later thought which
has led to its being described as "Christological concentration" or
"Christomonism." Hans Urs von Balthasar illustrates this "Christological concentration" by comparing it to an hour-glass, in which the
sand pours from the upper to the lower section through a constriction.
Similarly, the divine revelation proceeds from God to the world, from
above to below, only through the central event of the revelation of
Christ, apart from which there is no link between God and humanity.

It must be made clear that Barth is not suggesting that the doctrine
of either the person or the work of Christ (or both, if they are deemed
inseparable) should stand at the center of a Christian dogmatics, nor
that a Christological idea or principle should constitute the systematic
speculative midpoint of a deductive system. Rather, Barth is arguing
that the act of God which is Jesus Christ underlies theology in its totality. A "Church dogmatics" must be "Christologically determined," in
that the very possibility and reality of theology is determined by the
actuality of the act of divine revelation, by the speaking of the Word of
God, by the revelational presence of God in Jesus Christ.

A more eschatological approach is associated with Wolfhart
Pannenberg, especially in the 1968 work *Jesus – God and Man*. For
Pannenberg, the resurrection of Christ must be interpreted within the
context of the apocalyptic worldview. Within this context, Pannenberg
argues, the resurrection of Jesus must be seen as the anticipation of
the general resurrection of the dead at the end of time. It thus brings
forward into history both that resurrection and other aspects of the
apocalyptic expectation of the end-time – including the full and final
revelation of God. The resurrection of Jesus is thus organically linked
with the self-revelation of God in Christ:

Only at the end of all events can God be revealed in his divinity, that is, as the one who works all things, who has power over everything. Only because in Jesus' resurrection the end of all things, which for us has not yet happened, has already occurred can it be said of Jesus that the ultimate already is present in him, and so also that God himself, his glory, has made its appearance in Jesus in a way that cannot be surpassed. Only because the end of the world is already present in Jesus' resurrection is God himself revealed in him.

The resurrection thus establishes Jesus' identity with God, and allows this identity with God to be read back into his pre-Easter ministry, in terms of a "revelational presence."

Pannenberg is careful to stress that the "revelation" he has in mind is not simply the "disclosure of facts or statements about God." He insists upon the notion of *self-revelation* – a personal revelation which cannot be detached from the person of God. We can only speak of Christ revealing God if there is a revelational presence of God in Christ:

> The concept of God's self-revelation contains the idea that the revealer and what is revealed are identical. God is both the subject and content of this self-revelation. To speak of a self-revelation of God in Christ means that the Christ-event, that *Jesus*, belongs to the essence of God. If this is not the case, then the human event of the life of Jesus would veil the God who is active in that life, and thus exclude the full revelation of God. Self-revelation in the proper sense of the word only takes place where the medium through which God is made known is something that is not alien to God. . . . The concept of self-revelation demands the identity of God with the event that reveals God.

Substantial Presence

The doctrine of the incarnation, especially as developed within the Alexandrian school, affirms the presence of the divine nature or substance within Christ. The divine nature assumes human nature in the incarnation. Patristic writers affirmed the reality of the union of divine and human substances in the incarnation through designating Mary *theotokos* – that is, "bearer of God." The notion of a substantial presence of God within Christ was of vital importance to the Christian church in its controversy with Gnosticism. A central Gnostic notion was that matter was evil and sinful, so that redemption was a purely spiritual affair. Irenaeus links the idea of a substantial presence of God in

Christ with the symbolic affirmation of this in the bread and wine of the eucharist.

> If the flesh is not saved, then the Lord did not redeem us with his blood, the cup of the eucharist is not a sharing in his blood, and the bread which we break is not a sharing in his body. For the blood cannot exist apart from veins and flesh and the rest of the human substance which the divine Logos truly became, in order to redeem us.

This Christological approach is closely linked with the image of salvation as *deification*. Symeon the New Theologian (949–1022) stated this with particular clarity, as he reflected on the union of the human soul with God:

> Your nature is your essence, and your essence your nature; thus, uniting with your body, I participate in your nature, and I truly take as mine a part of your essence, uniting with your divinity . . . You have made me, a mortal by my nature, a god, god by adoption, god by your grace, by the power of your Spirit, uniting miraculously, God that you are, the two extremes.

We shall return to this concept later, in the course of our discussion of the nature of salvation (see pp. 360–1).

The idea of a substantial presence of God in Christ became of particular importance within Byzantine theology, and formed one of the theological foundations of the practice of portraying God in images – or, to use the more technical term, *icons*. There had always been resistance to this practice within the eastern church, on account of its emphasis upon the ineffability and transcendence of God. The *apophatic* tradition in theology sought to preserve the mystery of God by stressing the divine unknowability. The veneration of icons appeared to be totally inconsistent with this, and seemed to many to be dangerously close to paganism. In any case, did not the Old Testament forbid the worship of images?

Germanus, patriarch of Constantinople, argued vigorously for the use of icons in public worship and private devotion on the basis of the following incarnational argument. "I represent God, the invisible one, not as invisible, but in so far as God has become visible for us by participation in flesh and blood." A similar approach was taken by John of Damascus, who argued that, in worshipping icons, he was not worshipping any created object as such, but the creator God who had chosen to redeem humanity through the material order:

> In former times, God, who has not body or form, could not be represented in any manner. But today, I can represent what is visible

of God, since God has appeared in human flesh and lived among
us. I do not venerate matter, but I venerate the creator of matter,
who became matter for my sake, who assumed life in human
flesh, and who, through matter, accomplished my salvation.

This position was regarded as untenable by the iconoclastic party (so
called because they wanted to break up icons). To portray God in an
image was to imply that God could be described or defined – and that
was to imply an unthinkable limitation on the part of God. Aspects
of this debate can still be discerned within the Greek and Russian
Orthodox churches, where the veneration of icons remains an integral
element of spirituality.

Kenotic Approaches to Christology

During the early seventeenth century, a controversy developed between Lutheran theologians based at the universities of Giessen and
Tübingen. The question at issue can be stated as follows. The gospels
make no reference to Christ making use of all his divine attributes
(such as omniscience) during his period on earth. How is this to
be explained? Two options seemed to present themselves to these
Lutheran writers as appropriately orthodox solutions: Either Christ
used his divine powers in secret, or he abstained from using them
altogether. The first option, which came to be known as *krypsis*, was
vigorously defended by Tübingen; the second, which came to be
known as *kenosis*, was defended with equal vigor by Giessen.

Yet it must be noted that both parties were in agreement that Christ
possessed the central attributes of divinity – such as omnipotence and
omnipresence – during the period of the incarnation. The debate was
over the question of their use: Were they used in secret, or not at all?
A much more radical approach came to be developed during the nineteenth century, which saw a developing appreciation of the humanity
of Jesus, especially his religious personality. Thus A. E. Biedermann
stated that "the religious principle of Christianity is to be more precisely defined as the religious personality of Jesus, that is, that relation
between God and humanity which, in the religious self-consciousness
of Jesus, has entered into the history of humanity as a new religious
fact with the power to inspire faith."

The roots of this idea can be argued to lie in German Pietism,
especially in the form this takes in the writings of Nikolaus von
Zinzendorf (1700–60), whose "religion of the heart" laid particular
emphasis upon an intimate personal relationship between the believer
and Christ. It was developed and redirected by F. D. E. Schleiermacher,

who regarded himself as a "Herrnhuter" (that is, a follower of Zinzendorf) "of a higher order." Schleiermacher's understanding of the manner in which Christ is able to assimilate believers into his fellowship has strong parallels with Zinzendorf's analysis of the role of religious feelings in the spiritual life, and their grounding in the believer's fellowship with Christ.

Nevertheless, the importance attached to the human personality of Jesus left a number of theological loose ends. What about the divinity of Christ? Where did this come into things? Was not the emphasis upon Christ's humanity equivalent to a neglect of his divinity? Such questions and suspicions were voiced within more orthodox circles during the 1840s and early 1850s. However, during the later 1850s an approach to Christology was mapped out which seemed to have considerable potential in this respect. At one and the same time, it defended the divinity of Christ, yet justified an emphasis upon his humanity. The approach in question is known as "kenoticism," and is especially associated with the German Lutheran writer Gottfried Thomasius.

In his *Person and Work of Christ* (1852–61) Thomasius argues that the incarnation involves *kenosis*, the deliberate setting aside of all divine attributes, so that, in the state of humiliation, Christ has voluntarily abandoned all priviliges of divinity. It is therefore entirely proper to stress his humanity, especially the importance of his suffering as a human being. Thomasius' approach to Christology was much more radical than that of the early kenoticists. The incarnation involves Christ's *abandoning* of the attributes of divinity. They are set to one side during the entire period from the birth of Christ to his resurrection. Basing himself on Philippians 2: 6–8, Thomasius argued that in the incarnation, the second person of the Trinity reduced himself totally to the level of humanity. A theological and spiritual emphasis upon the humanity of Christ was thus entirely justified.

This approach to Christology was criticized by Isaak August Dorner (1809–84), on the grounds that it introduced change into God himself. The doctrine of the immutability of God was thus, he argued, compromised by Thomasius' approach. Interestingly, this insight contains much truth, and can be seen as an anticipation of the twentieth-century debate over the question of the "suffering of God," noted earlier. The approach was also taken up with some enthusiasm in England. In his 1889 Bampton Lectures at Oxford University, Charles Gore argued that Christ had emptied himself of the divine attributes, especially omniscience, in the incarnation. This prompted leading traditionalist Darwell Stone to charge that Gore's view "contradicted the practically unanimous teaching of the fathers, and is inconsistent with the immutability of the divine nature." Once more, such comments point to the close connection between Christology and theology, and indicate the importance of Christological considerations for the development of the doctrine of "a suffering God."

In the present chapter, we have surveyed some classical themes of Christology. The issues involved will probably continue to be subjects for perennial debate within Christian theology, and it is essential that the student becomes familiar with at least some of the questions discussed here. However, these issues were largely overshadowed during the period of the Enlightenment, as questions of a more historical nature came to the fore – questions which will be considered in the following chapter.

Questions for Chapter 9

1   Can Christian theology do without Jesus Christ?

2   Explore the use of one of the major New Testament titles for Jesus. What are the implications of speaking of Jesus in this way?

3   Summarize the main points of difference between the Alexandrian and Antiochene approaches to Christology.

4   What theological insights are linked with the belief that Jesus Christ is "God incarnate"?

5   What is meant by speaking of Jesus as "the mediator"?

Faith and History: A New Christological Agenda

The modern period has seen a series of developments of fundamental importance to Christology, which have no real parallel in previous Christian history. In view of the importance of these developments, they are considered here in some detail. The previous chapter explored the development of classical Christology, which continues to be a major aspect of theological reflection within the church. However, the rise of the Enlightenment worldview led to the credibility of classical Christology being challenged on a number of fronts. The present chapter documents these developments, and assesses their impact upon Christology.

The Enlightenment and Christology

In chapter 4 we explored the basic features of Enlightenment rationalism, noting especially its emphasis upon the ability of human reason to uncover the ordering of the world and the place and purpose of human beings within it. It will thus be clear that the rational religion of the Enlightenment found itself in conflict with a number of major areas of traditional Christian theology with a direct bearing upon Christology. We shall first outline these general areas of interest, before exploring some of them in greater detail in later sections.

The Enlightenment emphasis upon the competence of reason raised questions concerning the necessity of divine revelation. If reason was capable of discovering the nature and purposes of God, what continuing role was there for a historical revelation of God in the person of Jesus Christ? Reason seemed to make revelation – and thus any idea of a "revelational presence" in Christ – superfluous. The significance of Jesus Christ was thus stated in terms of his moral teaching and example. Far from being a supernatural redeemer of humanity, it was argued, Christ was actually the "moral educator of humanity," offering the world a religious teaching which was consistent (although to what extent was a matter of debate) with the highest ideals of human reason. In his life, Jesus was an educator; in his death, he was an example of self-giving love for humanity.

The Enlightenment also insisted that history was homogeneous. This had two major consequences. In the first place, it led to a contraction of the ontological gap between Christ and other human beings. Christ was to be regarded as a human being like other human beings. If he differed from others, it was in the extent to which he possessed certain qualities. The difference between Christ and others was one of *degree*, rather than *kind*. In the second place, it led to growing historical skepticism concerning the resurrection. If history was continuous and homogeneous, the absence of resurrections in present-day human experience must, it was argued, cast serious doubt upon the New Testament reports of the resurrection. The Enlightenment thus tended to treat the resurrection as a non-event, at best a simple misunderstanding of a spiritual experience, and at worst a deliberate cover-up to hide the shameful end of Jesus' ministry on the cross. We shall explore this point further below.

In view of its emphasis upon the resurrection, the New Testament must therefore be regarded as having misrepresented the significance of Christ. Whereas Jesus of Nazareth was actually little more than a thoroughly human itinerant rabbi, the New Testament writers presented him as a savior and risen Lord. These beliefs were, it was argued, often little more than fanciful additions to or misunderstandings of the history of Jesus. By appropriate use of the latest historical methods, some writers of the Enlightenment period believed that it was possible to reconstruct Jesus "as he actually was." The origins of the "quest of the historical Jesus" (as opposed to the "mythical Christ of faith") lie in this period, based on such considerations.

Two specific aspects of the Enlightenment critique of classical Christology are of such importance that they require to be noted in more detail.

The Critique of Miracles

Much traditional Christian apologetics concerning the identity and significance of Jesus Christ was based upon the "miraculous evidences" of the New Testament, culminating in the resurrection. The new emphasis upon the mechanical regularity and orderliness of the universe, perhaps the most significant intellectual legacy of Newtonianism, raised doubts concerning the New Testament accounts of miraculous happenings. Hume's *Essay on Miracles* (1748) was widely regarded as demonstrating the evidential impossibility of miracles. Hume emphasized that there were no contemporary analogs of New Testament miracles, such as the resurrection, thus forcing the New Testament reader to rely totally upon human testimony to such miracles. For Hume, it was a matter of principle that no human testimony was adequate to establish the occurrence of a miracle, in the absence of a present-day analog.

In the 1760s and 1700s, H. S. Reimarus and G. E. Lessing denied that human testimony to a past event (such as the resurrection) was sufficient to make it credible if it appeared to be contradicted by present-day direct experience, no matter how well documented the original event may have been. Similarly, the leading French rationalist Denis Diderot declared that if the entire population of Paris were to assure him that a dead man had just been raised from the dead, he would not believe a word of it. This growing skepticism concerning the "miraculous evidences" of the New Testament forced traditional Christianity to defend the doctrine of the divinity of Christ on grounds other than miracles – which, at the time, it proved singularly incapable of doing. Of course, it must be noted that other religions claiming miraculous evidences were subjected to equally great skeptical criticism by the Enlightenment: Christianity happened to be singled out for particular comment on account of its religious domination of the cultural milieu in which the Enlightenment developed.

The Development of Doctrinal Criticism

The Enlightenment witnessed the origin of the discipline of doctrinal criticism, in which the received teachings of the Christian church were subjected to a penetrating analysis concerning their historical origins and foundations. The origins of the "history of dogma" (to use the traditional English rendering of the German term *Dogmengeschichte*) date from the period of the Enlightenment; the consolidation of the discipline dates from later, more specifically from the period of liberal Protestantism, especially during the second half of the nineteenth century. The discipline is generally regarded as having been initiated in the eighteenth century by Johann Friedrich Wilhelm Jerusalem, who argued that dogmas such as the doctrine of the two natures and the Trinity were not to be found in the New Testament. If anything, these arose through confusion of the Platonic *logos*-concept with that found in the Fourth Gospel, and the mistaken apprehension that Jesus personified, rather than exemplified, this *logos*. The history of dogma was thus a history of mistakes – mistakes, however, which were in principle reversible, were it not for the immovable hostility of the institutional churches to any such reconstruction.

In terms of Christology, this movement reached its peak of influence under Adolf von Harnack, who argued that a series of Christological developments were due to the influence of Greek ideas during the patristic period. The doctrine of the incarnation was not part of the gospel at all; it was a Hellenistic addition to an essentially simple Palestinian gospel (see pp. 293–4).

One of the most significant works dating from this period argued that a series of assumptions, each of central importance to the Anselmian doctrine of penal substitution, had become incorporated into Christian theology by what were little more than historical accidents. In his *System der reinen Philosophie* (1778), G. S. Steinbart argued that historical investigation disclosed the intrusion of three "arbitrary assumptions" into Christian reflection on salvation:

1 the Augustinian doctrine of original sin;
2 the concept of satisfaction;
3 the doctrine of the imputation of the righteousness of Christ.

For such reasons, Steinbart felt able to declare the substructure of orthodox Protestant thinking on the person and work of Christ to be little more than a relic of a bygone era.

It will thus be clear that the dawn of the Enlightenment represented a major new challenge to traditional Christology, obliging it to engage with questions which hitherto had not featured prominently, if at all, on its agenda. The Enlightenment set the parameters for future Christian discussion, not just of the *nature* but also of the *plausibility* of its theological heritage. Although the credibility of the Enlightenment worldview, especially its emphasis upon the total adequacy of human reason, has been severely challenged through the recognition of the non-universal character of human rationality and the social mediation of traditions of discourse and reasoning, the Enlightenment continues to remain a fundamental reference point for modern Christian thought.

It is now appropriate to begin to explore the Christologies of the Enlightenment in more detail.

The Problem of Faith and History

The problems which confront the Christian appeal to the history of Jesus of Nazareth as the climax of God's self-revelation in history can be summarized under three broad headings. How can we be sure about what really happened in Palestine at the time of Jesus? And, assuming that we can rest assured concerning the reliability of that knowledge, how can a series of events in history give us access to universal truth? And surely the vast difference between modern western culture and that of first-century Palestine makes it impossible to do anything with the history of Jesus? We could state these points more formally in as a set of three difficulties, as follows.

1 A *chronological* difficulty, on account of the distance of the past from the present. How can we be certain of what happened nearly two thousand years ago?
2 A *metaphysical* difficulty, posed by the nature of history itself. How can the history of Jesus of Nazareth give access to truth? At first sight, accidental historical truths seem to be rather different from universal and necessary rational truths.
3 An *existential* problem, which arises from the cultural distance between first-century Palestine and modern western society. How can modern human existence relate to a religious message of the distant past?

It will be clear that these three elements are not absolutely distinct. There is a significant degree of interaction between them. However, together they build up to form the overall problem of "faith and history" which has been of such importance in relation to modern German Christology. We shall consider each of these elements in turn, basing our discussion on the writings of Gottfried Ephraim Lessing, a leading German rationalist writer and critic of traditional Christianity. Lessing's discussion of these three difficulties is widely regarded as having set the agenda for modern discussion of these questions. From 1780 onward, Christology was obliged to address and answer each of these difficulties. In what follows, we shall consider the difficulties, and indicate the responses.

The Chronological Difficulty

The gospel accounts of Jesus Christ place him firmly in the past. We are unable to verify those accounts, but are obliged to rely upon the eyewitness reports which underlie the gospels for our knowledge of Jesus. But, Lessing asked, how reliable are those accounts? Why should we trust reports from the past, when they cannot be verified in the present? As we shall see later, Lessing regards this difficulty to be felt with particular force in relation to the resurrection of Christ, which he regards as resting upon distinctly shaky historical foundations.

There is thus uncertainty about what happened in the past. However, Lessing argues that the problem goes deeper than this. Even if we could be certain about the past, a new difficulty would arise: What conceivable value has historical knowledge? How can an historical event give rise to ideas? We shall explore this difficulty in what follows.

The Metaphysical Difficulty

If one pole of the Enlightenment critique of traditional Christianity was a belief in the omnicompetence of reason, a second pole was a growing skepticism concerning the value of history as a source of knowledge. There was a growing belief that history – including historical figures or events – could not give access to the kind of knowledge that was necessary for a rational religious or philosophical system. How can the move from history (which is a collection of accidental and contingent truths) to reason (which is concerned with necessary and universal truths) take place? Lessing argued there was a gap between *historical* and *rational* truth which could not be bridged.

> If no historical truth can be demonstrated, then nothing can be demonstrated by means of historical truths. That is: Accidental truths of history can never become the proof of necessary truths of reason. . . . That, then, is the ugly great ditch which I cannot get across, however often and however earnestly I have tried to make the leap.

Lessing's phrase an "ugly great ditch" between faith and history has been seen as summing up the gulf fixed between historical and rational approaches to Christian theology.

"If on historical grounds I have no objection to the statement that this Christ himself rose from the dead, must I therefore accept that this risen Christ was the Son of God?" In answering this question in the negative, Lessing draws a distinction between two different classes of truth. If the chronological ditch concerned a dispute about historical facts – what actually happened in the past – the second ditch concerned the interpretation of those events. How can the transition from the "accidental truths of history" to the "necessary truths of reason" be made? Lessing argued that these are two radically different and totally incommensurable classes of truth.

Rational truth was regarded as possessing the qualities of necessity, eternity, and universality. It was the same at all times and all places. Human reason was capable of penetrating to this universal static realm of truth, which could act as the foundation of all human knowledge. This notion of truth can be found in a definitive form in the writings of Benedict Spinoza, who argued that human reason is capable of basing itself upon self-evident first principles, and, by following these through logically, deducing a complete moral system. Just about everyone who favors this approach makes some sort of appeal to Euclid's five principles of geometry. On the basis of his five principles, he was able to construct his entire geometrical system. Many of the more rationalist philosophers, such as Leibniz and Spinoza, were deeply attracted to this, believing that they could use the same method in philosophy. From a set of certain assumptions, a great secure edifice of philosophy and ethics could be erected. Of course, the dream later turned sour. The discovery of non-Euclidian geometry during the nineteenth century destroyed the appeal of this analogy. It turned out that there were other ways of doing geometry, each just as internally consistent as Euclid's (see pp. 186–7). But this development was not known to writers such as Spinoza or Lessing, who believed that reason was capable of erecting a self-sufficient and universally valid system on the basis of the necessary truths of reason.

Part of Lessing's case against orthodoxy here concerns the "scandal of particularity." Why should one specific historical event have such momentous significance? Why should the history of Jesus of Nazareth – even assuming that it could be known with a degree of certainty that Lessing personally believed to be impossible – be elevated to such epistemological heights? Lessing argued that the universal human faculty of reason, available at all times and in all places to all people, avoided this scandal. Rationalism thus possessed both a moral and an intellectual superiority to the particularist Christology associated with traditional Christianity.

Lessing's assumption about the existence of a universal rationality has, however, been subject to considerable criticism in modern times. The sociology of knowledge has demonstrated that, for example, "Enlightenment rationalism" is far from being universal, but is merely one of a number of intellectual options. The suggestion that historicity limits intellectual options raises a number of difficulties for Enlightenment rationalism. For our purposes, it is particularly important to stress that individuals (whether theologians, philosophers, or natural scientists) do not begin their quest for knowledge *de novo*, as if they were isolated from society and history. The Enlightenment emphasis upon knowledge gained through individual critical reflection, deriving from Descartes, has been the subject of considerable criticism in recent years on account of its uncritical rejection of the corporate foundations of knowledge.

The Existential Difficulty

Finally, Lessing poses a series of questions which are existential in their orientation. What, he asks, can the *relevance* of such an outdated and archaic message be for the modern world? The original Christian message is implausible for the modern reader. There is an insuperable credibility gap between a first-century and an eighteenth-century worldview. How can learned and culturally sensitive Europeans enter into the backward world of the New Testament and appropriate its outdated religious message?

It is difficult to analyse this aspect of Lessing's discussion of the problem of faith and history, simply because he himself appears to have some difficulty in conceptualizing the point at issue. Nevertheless, the point is important, and will be a recurring feature of our study of modern German Christology. Perhaps it could be said that it is only with the rise of existentially oriented Christologies in the twentieth century that Lessing's point has been fully addressed, and answered.

The Quest of the Historical Jesus

Both English Deism and the German Enlightenment developed the thesis that there was a serious discrepancy between the real Jesus of history and the New Testament interpretation of his significance. Underlying the New Testament portrait of the supernatural redeemer of humanity lurked a simple human figure, a glorified teacher of common sense. While the idea of a supernatural redeemer was unacceptable to Enlightenment rationalism, that of an enlightened moral teacher was not. This view, developed with particular rigor by Reimarus, suggested that it was possible to go behind the New Testament accounts of Jesus, and uncover a simpler, more human Jesus, who would be acceptable to the new spirit of the age. And so the quest for the real and more credible "Jesus of history" began. Although this quest would ultimately end in failure, the later Enlightenment regarded it as holding the key to the credibility of Jesus within the context of a rational natural religion. Jesus' moral authority resided in the quality of his teaching and religious personality, rather than in the unacceptable orthodox suggestion that he was God incarnate. And it is this suggestion which underlies the celebrated "quest of the historical Jesus."

The Original Quest of the Historical Jesus

The original "quest of the historical Jesus" was based upon the presupposition that there was a radical gulf between the historical figure of Jesus, and the interpretation which the Christian church had placed upon him. The "historical Jesus," who lies behind the New Testament, was a simple religious teacher; the "Christ of faith" was a misrepresentation of this simple figure by early church writers. By going back to the historical Jesus, a more credible version of Christianity would result, stripped of all unnecessary and inappropriate dogmatic additions (such as the idea of the resurrection or the divinity of Christ). Such ideas, although frequently expressed by English Deists of the seventeenth century, received their classic statements in Germany in the late eighteenth century, especially through the posthumously published writings of Hermann Samuel Reimarus (1694–1768).

Reimarus became increasingly convinced that both Judaism and Christianity rested upon fraudulent foundations, and conceived the idea of writing a major work which would bring this fact to public attention. The resulting work labored under the title of *An Apology for the Rational Worshipper of God*. The volume subjected the entire biblical canon to the standards of rationalist criticism. However, reluctant to cause any controversy, Reimarus did not publish the work. It remained in manuscript form until his death.

At some point, the manuscript fell into the hands of Lessing, who decided to publish a selection of extracts from the work. These "fragments of an unknown writer," published in 1774, caused a sensation. The volume contained five fragments, now generally known as the "Wolfenbüttel Fragments," and included a sustained attack on the historicity of the resurrection.

The final fragment, entitled "On the Aims of Jesus and His Disciples," concerned the nature of our knowledge of Jesus Christ, and raised the questions of whether the gospel accounts of Jesus had been tampered with by the early Christians. Reimarus argued that there was a radical difference between the beliefs and intentions of Jesus himself, and those of the apostolic church. Jesus' language and images of God were, according to Reimarus, those of a Jewish apocalyptic visionary, with a radically limited chronological and political reference and relevance. Jesus accepted the late Jewish expectation of a Messiah who would deliver his people from Roman occupation, and believed that God would assist him in this task. His cry of dereliction on the cross represented his final realization that he had been deluded and mistaken.

However, the disciples were not prepared to leave things like this. They invented the idea of a "spiritual redemption" in the place of Jesus' concrete political vision of an Israel liberated from foreign occupation. They invented the idea of the resurrection of Jesus, in order to cover up the embarrassment caused by his death. As a result, the disciples invented doctrines quite unknown to Jesus, such as his death being an atonement for human sin, adding such ideas to the biblical text to make it harmonize with their beliefs. As a result, the New Testament as we now have it is riddled with fraudulent interpolations. The real Jesus of history is concealed from us by the apostolic church, which has substituted a fictitious Christ of faith, the redeemer of humanity from sin.

In his masterly survey *The Quest of the Historical Jesus*, Albert Schweitzer summarizes the importance of Reimarus' radical suggestions as follows: According to Reimarus, if

> we desire to gain an historical understanding of Jesus' teaching, we must leave behind what we learned in the catechism regarding the metaphysical divine sonship, the Trinity, and similar dogmatic conceptions, and go out into a wholly Jewish world of thought. Only those who carry the teachings of the catechism back into the preaching of the Jewish Messiah will arrive at the idea that he was the founder of a new religion. To all unprejudiced persons it is manifest that "Jesus has not the slightest intention of doing away with the Jewish religion and putting another in its place."

Jesus was simply a Jewish political figure, who confidently expected to cause a decisive and victorious popular rising against Rome, and was shattered by his failure.

Although Reimarus found few, if any, followers at the time, he raised questions which would become of fundamental importance in subsequent years. In particular, his explicit distinction between the legitimate historical Jesus and the fictitious Christ of faith proved to be of enormous significance. The resulting "quest of the historical Jesus" arose as a direct result of the growing rationalist suspicion that the New Testament portrayal of Christ was a dogmatic invention. It was possible to reconstruct the real historical figure of Jesus, and disentangle him from the dogmatic ideas in which the apostles had clothed him.

The Quest for the Religious Personality of Jesus

A more subtle version of this approach is linked with the rise of liberal Protestantism in the nineteenth century (see pp. 92–6). The emergence of movements such as Romanticism led to rationalism increasingly being regarded as outmoded (see pp. 87–9). A new interest developed in "the human spirit" and in the more specifically religious aspects of human life. This led to a new interest in the religious personality of Jesus. Ideas such as the "divinity" of Christ were regarded as outmoded; the idea of a "religious personality" of Jesus, which could be imitated by anyone, seemed a much more acceptable way of restating Christological issues in the modern period. As a result, renewed attention was paid to the nature of the New Testament sources upon which the life of the historical Jesus could be constructed. It was widely believed that the new literary approach to the New Testament in general, and the synoptic gospels in particular, would permit scholars to establish a firmly drawn and lifelike portrait which would bring out clearly the personality of Jesus.

The assumption underlying this "life of Jesus" movement in the later nineteenth century was that the remarkable religious personality of Jesus, whose shape could be determined by conscientious historical inquiry, would provide a solid historical foundation for faith. The firm ground of historical truth upon which Christian faith depended was thus not supernatural or anti-rational (a perceived weakness of traditional Christology), but merely the religious personality of Jesus, a fact of history open to scientific investigation. The impression which he made upon his contemporaries could be reproduced in his followers of every age. The remarkable number of "lives of Jesus" produced in the later nineteenth century in England, America, and France, as well as in Germany itself, is an adequate testimony to the popular appeal of the ideas underlying the "life of Jesus" movement. Through it, the religious personality of the "far-off mystic of the Galilean hills" (to use Lord Morley's famous phrase) could be brought into the present, uncluttered by cultural irrelevancies, in order to form the basis of faith for the coming generation.

It was, of course, inevitable that the portrayals of the religious personality of Jesus were radically subjective, so that the rediscovered Jesus of history turned out to be merely the embodiment of an ideal figure by the progressive standards of the nineteenth century. The relativity of historical research was not immediately obvious to the nineteenth-century "life of Jesus" movement, whose adherents regarded themselves as practitioners of the objective historical method, rather than as a historically conditioned phenomenon in themselves. Earlier writers had labored under misunderstandings; they had access to the most sophisticated historical methods and resources, which allowed them access to the authentic history of Jesus. They certainly saw him as he had never been seen before; sadly, they believed that they saw him as he actually was.

The Critique of the Quest, 1890–1910

The illusion could not last. The most sustained challenge to the "life of Jesus" movement developed on a number of fronts during the final decade of the nineteenth century. Three main criticisms of the "religious personality" Christology of liberal Protestantism emerged in the two decades before World War I; we shall consider them individually.

1 The *apocalyptic critique*, primarily associated with Johannes Weiss (1863–1914) and Albert Schweitzer (1875–1965), maintained that the strongly eschatological bias of Jesus' proclamation of the kingdom of God called the essentially Kantian liberal interpretation of the concept into question. In 1892, Johannes Weiss published *Jesus' Proclamation of the Kingdom of God*. In this book, he argued that the idea of the "kingdom of God" was understood by the liberal Protestants to mean the exercise of the moral life in society, or a supreme ethical ideal. In other words, it was conceived primarily as something subjective, inward, or spiritual, rather than in spatio-temporal terms. For Weiss himself, Ritschl's concept of the kingdom of God was essentially continuous with that of the Enlightenment. It was a static moral concept without eschatological overtones. The rediscovery of the eschatology of the preaching of Jesus called into question not merely this understanding of the kingdom of God, but also the liberal portrait of Christ in general. The kingdom of God was thus not to be seen as a settled and static realm of liberal moral values, but as a devastating apocalyptic moment which overturned human values (see pp. 466–8).

For Schweitzer, however, the whole character of Jesus' ministry was conditioned and determined by his apocalyptic outlook. It is this idea which has become familiar to the English-speaking world as "thoroughgoing eschatology." Where Weiss regarded a substantial part (but not all) of the teaching of Jesus as being conditioned by his radical eschatological expectations, Schweitzer argued for the need to recognize that every aspect of the teaching and attitudes of Jesus was determined by his eschatological outlook. Where Weiss believed that only part of Jesus' preaching was affected by this outlook, Schweitzer argued that the entire content of Jesus' message was consistently and thoroughly conditioned by apocalyptic ideas – ideas which were quite alien to the settled outlook of late nineteenth-century western Europe.

The result of this consistent eschatological interpretation of the person and message of Jesus of Nazareth was a portrait of Christ as a remote and strange figure, an apocalyptic and wholly unworldly person, whose hopes and expectations finally came to nothing. Far from being an incidental and dispensable "husk" which could be discarded in order to reach the true "kernel" of Jesus' teaching concerning the universal fatherhood of God, eschatology was an essential and dominant characteristic of his outlook. Jesus thus appears to us as a strange figure from an alien first-century Jewish apocalyptic milieu, so that, in Schweitzer's famous words, "he comes to us as one unknown."

2   The *skeptical critique*, associated particularly with William Wrede (1859–1906), called into question the historical status of our knowledge of Jesus in the first place. History and theology were closely intermingled in the synoptic narratives, and could not be disentangled. According to Wrede, Mark was painting a theological picture in the guise of history, imposing his theology upon the material which he had at his disposal. The Second Gospel was not objectively historical, but was actually a creative theological reinterpretation of history. It was thus impossible to go behind Mark's narrative and reconstruct the history of Jesus, in that – if Wrede is right – this narrative is itself a theological construction, beyond which one cannot go. The "quest of the historical Jesus" thus comes to an end, in that it proves impossible to establish a historical foundation for the "real" Jesus of history. Wrede identified the following three radical and fatal errors underlying the Christologies of liberal Protestantism.

First, although the liberal theologians appealed to later modifications of an earlier tradition when faced with unpalatable features of the synoptic accounts of Jesus (such as miracles, or obvious contradictions between sources), they failed to apply this principle consistently. In other words, they failed to realize that the later belief of the community had exercised a normative influence over the evangelist at every stage of his work.

Second, the motives of the evangelists were not taken into account. The liberal theologians tended simply to exclude those portions of the narratives they found unacceptable, and content themselves with what remained. By doing so, they failed to take seriously the fact that the evangelist himself had a positive statement to make, and substituted for this something quite distinct. The first priority should be to approach the gospel narratives on their own terms, and to establish what the evangelist wished to convey to his readers.

Third, the psychological approach to the gospel narratives tends to confuse what is conceivable with what actually took place, being based upon an inadequate foundation. In effect, liberal theologians tended to find in the gospels precisely what they were seeking, on the basis of a "sort of psychological guesswork" which appeared to value emotive descriptions more than strict accuracy and certainty of knowledge.

3 The *dogmatic critique*, expressed by Martin Kähler (1835–1912), challenged the theological significance of the reconstruction of the historical Jesus. The "historical Jesus" was an irrelevance to faith, which was based upon the "Christ of faith." Kähler rightly saw that the dispassionate and provisional Jesus of the academic historian cannot become the object of faith. Yet how can Jesus Christ be the authentic basis and content of Christian faith, when historical science can never establish certain knowledge concerning the historical Jesus? How can faith be based upon an historical event without being vulnerable to the charge of historical relativism? It was precisely these questions which Kähler addressed in his *The So-Called Historical Jesus and the Historic Biblical Christ* (1892).

Kähler states his two objectives in this work as follows: first, to criticize and reject the errors of the "life of Jesus" movement; and second, to establish the validity of an alternative approach. For Kähler:

> The historical Jesus of modern writers conceals the living Christ from us. The Jesus of the "life of Jesus" movement is merely a modern example of a brain-child of the human imagination, no better that the notorious dogmatic Christ of Byzantine Christology. They are both equally far removed from the real Christ. In this respect, historicism is just as arbitrary, just as humanly arrogant, just as speculative and "faithlessly gnostic," as that dogmatism which was itself considered modern in its own day.

Kähler concedes immediately that the "life of Jesus" movement was completely correct in so far as it contrasted the biblical witness to Christ with an abstract dogmatism. He nevertheless insists upon its futility, a view summarized in his well-known statement to the effect that the entire life of Jesus movement is a blind alley. His reasons for making this assertion are complex.

The most fundamental reason is that Christ must be regarded as a "supra-historical" rather than a "historical" figure, so that the critical historical method cannot be applied in his case. The critical historical method could not deal with the supra-historical (and hence supra-human) characteristics of Jesus, and hence was obliged to ignore or deny them. In effect, the critical historical method could only lead to an Arian or Ebionite Christology, on account of its latent dogmatic presuppositions. This point, made frequently throughout the essay, is developed with particular force in relation to the psychological interpretation of the personality of Jesus, and the related question concerning the use of the principle of analogy in the critical historical method.

Kähler notes that the psychological interpretation of the personality of Jesus is dependent upon the (unrecognized) presupposition that the distinction between ourselves and Jesus is one of degree (*Grade*) rather than kind (*Art*), which Kähler suggests must be criticized on dogmatic grounds. More significantly, Kähler challenged the principle of analogy in the interpretation of the New Testament portrayal of Christ in general, which inevitably led to Jesus being treated as analogous to modern human beings, and hence to a reduced or degree Christology. If it is assumed from the outset that Jesus is an ordinary human being, who differs from other humans only in degree and not in nature, then this assumption will be read back into the biblical texts, and dictate the resulting conclusion – that Jesus of Nazareth is a human being who differs from us only in degree.

Second, Kähler argued that "we do not possess any sources for a life of Jesus which an historian could accept as reliable and adequate." This is not to say that the sources are unreliable and inadequate for the purposes of *faith*. Kähler is rather concerned to emphasize that the gospels are not the accounts of disinterested, impartial observers, but rather accounts of the faith of believers, which cannot be isolated, either in form or content, from that faith: The gospel accounts "are not the reports of alert impartial observers, but are throughout the testimonies and confessions of believers in Christ." In that "it is only through these accounts that we are able to come into contact with him," it will be clear that the "biblical portrait of Christ" is of decisive importance for faith.

What is important for Kähler is not who Christ was, but what he presently does for believers. The "Jesus of history" lacks the soteriological significance of the "Christ of faith." The thorny problems of Christology may therefore be left behind in order to develop soteriology, "the knowledge of faith concerning the person of the savior." In effect, Kähler argues that the "life of Jesus" movement has done little more than create a fictitious and pseudo-scientific Christ, devoid of existential significance. For Kähler, "the real Christ is the preached Christ." Christian faith is not based upon this historical Jesus, but upon the existentially significant and faith-evoking figure of the Christ of faith.

Considerations such as these gradually came to dominate the theological scene, and may be regarded as reaching their climax in the writings of Rudolf Bultmann, to which we may now turn.

The Retreat from History: Rudolf Bultmann

Bultmann regarded the entire enterprise of the historical reconstruction of Jesus as a blind alley. History was not of fundamental importance to Christology; it was merely necessary that Jesus existed, and that the Christian proclamation (which Bultmann terms the *kerygma*) is somehow grounded in his person. Bultmann thus famously reduced the entire historical aspect of Christology to a single word – "that." It is necessary only to believe "that" Jesus Christ lies behind the gospel proclamation (or *kerygma*).

For Bultmann, the cross and the resurrection are indeed historical phenomena (in that they took place within human history) – but they must be discerned by faith as divine acts. The cross and the resurrection are linked in the *kerygma* as the divine act of judgment and the divine act of salvation. It is this divine act which is of continuing significance, and not the historical phenomenon which acted as its bearer. The *kerygma* is thus concerned not with matters of historical fact, but with conveying the necessity of a decision on the part of its hearers, and thus transferring the eschatological moment from the past to the here and now of the proclamation itself:

> This means that Jesus Christ encounters us in the *kerygma* and nowhere else, just as he confronted Paul himself and forced him to a decision. The *kerygma* does not proclaim universal truths or a timeless idea – whether it is an idea of God or of the redeemer – but an historical fact... Therefore the *kerygma* is neither a vehicle for timeless ideas nor the mediator of historical information: What is of decisive importance is that the *kerygma* is Christ's "that," his "here and now," a "here and now" which becomes present in the address itself.

One cannot therefore go behind the *kerygma*, using it as a "source" in order to reconstruct an "historical Jesus" with his "messianic consciousness," his "inner life," or his "heroism." That would merely be "Christ according to the flesh," who no longer exists. It is not the historical Jesus, but Jesus Christ, the one who is preached, who is the Lord.

This radical move away from history alarmed many. How could anyone rest assured that Christology was properly grounded in the person and work of Jesus Christ? How could anyone begin to check out Christology, if the history of Jesus was an irrelevance? It seemed to an increasing number of writers, within the fields of both New Testament and dogmatic studies, that Bultmann had merely cut a Gordian knot, without resolving the serious historical issues at stake.

For Bultmann, all that could be, and could be required to be, known about the historical Jesus was the fact that (*das Dass*) he existed. For the New Testament scholar Gerhard Ebeling, the person of the historical (*historisch*) Jesus is the fundamental basis (*das Grunddatum*) of Christology, and if it could be shown that Christology was a misinterpretation of the significance of the historical Jesus, Christology would be brought to an end. In this, Ebeling may be seen as expressing the concerns which underlie the "new quest of the historical Jesus," to be discussed in the following section.

Ebeling pointed to a fundamental deficiency in Bultmann's Christology: Its total lack of openness to investigation (perhaps "verification" is too strong a term) in the light of historical scholarship. Might not Christology rest upon a mistake? How can we rest assured that there is a justifiable transition from the preaching *of* Jesus to the preaching *about* Jesus? Ebeling develops criticisms which parallel those of Ernst Käsemann, but with a theological, rather than a purely historical, focus.

The New Quest of the Historical Jesus

A "new quest of the historical Jesus" is generally regarded as having been inaugurated with Ernst Käsemann's lecture of October 1953 on the problem of the historical Jesus. The full importance of this lecture only emerges if it is viewed in the light of the presuppositions and methods of the Bultmannian school up to this point. Käsemann conceded that the synoptic gospels are primarily theological documents, and that their theological statements are often expressed in the form of the historical. In this, he endorsed and recapitulated key axioms of the Bultmann school, here based upon insights of Kähler and Wrede.

Nevertheless, Käsemann immediately went on to qualify these assertions in a significant manner. Despite their obviously theological concerns, the evangelists nevertheless believed that they had access to historical information concerning Jesus of Nazareth, and that this historical information was expressed and embodied in the text of the synoptic gospels. The gospels include both the *kerygma* and historical narrative.

Building on this insight, Käsemann points to the need to explore the continuity between the preaching *of* Jesus and the preaching *about* Jesus. There is an obvious discontinuity between the earthly Jesus and the exalted and proclaimed Christ; yet a thread of continuity links them, in that the proclaimed Christ is already present, in some sense, in the historical Jesus. It must be stressed that Käsemann is not suggesting that a new inquiry should be undertaken concerning the historical Jesus in order to provide historical legitimation for the *kerygma*; still less is he suggesting that the discontinuity between the historical Jesus and the proclaimed Christ necessitates the deconstruction of the latter in terms of the former. Rather, Käsemann is pointing to the *theological* assertion of the identity of the earthly Jesus and the exalted Christ being *historically grounded* in the actions and preaching of Jesus of Nazareth. The theological affirmation is, Käsemann argues, dependent upon the historical demonstration that the *kerygma* concerning Jesus is already contained in a nutshell or embryonic form in the ministry of Jesus. In that the *kerygma* contains historical elements, it is entirely proper and necessary to inquire concerning the relation of the Jesus of history and the Christ of faith.

It will be clear that the "new quest of the historical Jesus" is qualitatively different from the discredited quest of the nineteenth century. Käsemann's argument rests upon the recognition that the discontinuity between the Jesus of history and the Christ of faith does not imply that they are unrelated entities, with the latter having no grounding or foundation in the former. Rather, the *kerygma* may be discerned in the actions and preaching of Jesus of Nazareth, so that there is a continuity between the preaching of Jesus and the preaching about Jesus. Where the older quest had assumed that the discontinuity between the historical Jesus and the Christ of faith implied that the latter was potentially a fiction, who required to be reconstructed in the light of objective historical investigation, Käsemann stressed that such reconstruction is neither necessary nor possible.

The growing realization of the importance of this point led to intensive interest developing in the question of the historical foundations of the *kerygma*. Four positions of interest may be noted.

1 Joachim Jeremias, perhaps representing an extreme element in this debate, seemed to suggest that the basis of the Christian faith lies in what Jesus actually said and did, in so far as this can be established by theological scholarship. The first part of his *New Testament Theology* was thus devoted in its totality to the "proclamation of Jesus" as a central element of New Testament theology.

2 Käsemann himself identified the continuity between the historical Jesus and the kerygmatic Christ in their common declaration of the dawning of the eschatological kingdom of God. Both in the preaching of Jesus and in the early Christian *kerygma*, the theme of the coming of the kingdom is of major importance.

3 As we saw above, Gerhard Ebeling located the continuity in the notion of the "faith of Jesus," which he understood to be analogous to the "faith of Abraham" (described in Romans 4) – a prototypical faith, historically exemplified and embodied in Jesus of Nazareth, and proclaimed to be a contemporary possibility for believers.

4 Günter Bornkamm laid particular emphasis upon the note of authority evident in the ministry of Jesus. In Jesus, the actuality of God confronts humanity, and calls it to a radical decision. Whereas Bultmann located the essence of Jesus' preaching in the future coming of the kingdom of God, Bornkamm shifted the emphasis from the future to the present confrontation of individuals with God through the person of Jesus. This theme of "confrontation with God" is evident in both the ministry of Jesus and the proclamation about Jesus, providing a major theological and historical link between the earthly Jesus and the proclaimed Christ.

The "new quest of the historical Jesus" was thus concerned to stress the continuity between the historical Jesus and the Christ of faith. Whereas the "old quest" had the aim of discrediting the New Testament portrayal of Christ, the "new quest" ended up consolidating it, by stressing the continuities between the preaching of Jesus himself, and the church's preaching about Jesus.

Since then, there have been other developments in the field. In the 1970s and 1980s particular attention has been directed toward exploring the relation between Jesus and his environment in first-century Judaism. This development, which is especially associated with English and American writers such as Geza Vermes and E. P. Sanders, has renewed interest in the Jewish background to Jesus, and further emphasized the importance of history in relation to Christology. The Bultmannian approach – which devalues the significance of history in Christology – is widely regarded as discredited, at least for the moment. However, theological fashions change, and it would be a foolish person who concluded that the present interest in history will remain a permanent feature of the theological landscape!

The Resurrection of Christ: Event and Meaning

The question of the relation of faith and history often comes to focus on the question of the resurrection of Christ. This question – more specifically, whether Christ was indeed raised from the dead, and, if so, what that event might mean – brings together the central components of the Enlightenment critique of traditional Christianity. In what follows, we shall outline the main positions to have developed during the modern period, and assess their significance.

The Enlightenment: The Resurrection as Non-Event

The characteristic Enlightenment emphasis on the omnicompetence of reason and the importance of contemporary analogs to past events led to the development of an intensely skeptical attitude toward the resurrection in the eighteenth century. Lessing provides an excellent example of this attitude. He confesses that he does not have personal first-hand experience of the resurrection of Jesus Christ; so why, he asks, should he be asked to believe in something which he has not seen? The problem of chronological distance, according to Lessing, is made all the more acute on account of his doubts (which he evidently assumes others will share) concerning the reliability of the eyewitness reports. Our faith eventually rests upon the authority of others, rather than the authority of our own experience and rational reflection upon it.

> But since the truth of these miracles has completely ceased to be demonstrable by miracles happening now, since they are no more than reports of miracles . . . I deny that they can and should bind me to the very least faith in the other teachings of Jesus.

In other words, as men and women are not raised from the dead now, why should we believe that such a thing happened in the past? At issue here is a central theme of the Enlightenment: human autonomy. Reality is rational, and human beings have the necessary epistemological capacities to uncover this rational ordering of the world. Truth is not something which demands to be accepted on the basis of an external authority; it is to be recognized and accepted by the autonomous thinking person, on the basis of the perception of congruence between what that individual knows to be true, and the alleged "truth" which presents itself for verification. Truth is something which is discerned, not something which is imposed. For Lessing, being obligated to accept the testimony of others is tantamount to a compromising of human intellectual autonomy. There are no contemporary analogs for the resurrection. Resurrection is not an aspect of modern-day experience. So why trust the New Testament reports? For Lessing, the resurrection is little more than a misunderstood non-event.

David Friedrich Strauss: The Resurrection as Myth

In his *Life of Jesus* (1835), Strauss provided a radical new approach to the question of the resurrection of Christ. Strauss himself noted that the resurrection of Christ is of central importance to Christian faith:

> The root of faith in Jesus was the conviction of his resurrection. He who had been put to death, however great during his life, could not, it was thought, be the Messiah: his miraculous restoration to life proved so much the more strongly that he *was* the Messiah. Freed by his resurrection from the kingdom of shades, and at the same time elevated above the sphere of earthly humanity, he was now translated to the heavenly regions, and had taken his place at the right hand of God.

Strauss noted that this understanding of what he termed "the Christology of the orthodox system" had come under considerable attack since the Enlightenment, not least on account of its presupposition that miracles (such as a resurrection) are impossible.

On the basis of this *a priori* assumption, which corresponds neatly to the Enlightenment worldview, Strauss declared his intention to explain "the origin of faith in the resurrection of Jesus without any corresponding miraculous fact." In other words, Strauss was concerned to explain how Christians came to believe in the resurrection, when there was no objective historical basis for this belief. Having excluded the resurrection as a "miraculous objective occurrence," Strauss located the origin of the belief at the purely subjective level. Belief in the resurrection is not to be explained as a response to "a life objectively restored," but is "a subjective conception in the mind." Faith in the resurrection of Jesus is the outcome of an exaggerated "recollection of the personality of Jesus himself," by which a memory has been projected into the idea of a living presence. A dead Jesus is thus transfigured into an imaginary risen Christ – a *mythical* risen Christ, to use the appropriate term.

Strauss's distinctive contribution to the debate was to introduce the category of "myth" – a reflection of the gospel writers' social conditioning and cultural outlook. To suggest that their writings were partly "mythical" was thus not so much a challenge to their integrity, but simply an acknowledgment of the premodern outlook of the period in which they were written. The gospel writers must be regarded as sharing the mythical worldview of their cultural situation. Strauss distances himself from Reimarus' suggestion that the evangelists distorted their accounts of Jesus of Nazareth, whether unconsciously or deliberately. He argues that mythical language is the natural mode of expression of a primitive group culture which had yet to rise to the level of abstract conceptualization.

For Reimarus, the gospel writers were confused or liars – more likely the latter. Strauss moved the discussion away from this judgment by his introduction of the category of "myth." The resurrection was to be viewed not as a deliberate fabrication, but as an interpretation of events (especially the memory and "subjective vision" of Jesus) in terms which made sense in first-century Palestine culture, dominated by a mythical worldview. Belief in the resurrection as an objective event must be regarded as becoming impossible with the passing of that worldview.

Strauss's *Life of Jesus*, along with other rationalizing works of the same period, such as Ernest Renan's work of the same name (1863), attracted enormous attention. The resurrection, traditionally seen as the basis of Christian faith, was now viewed as its product. Christianity was seen as relating to the memory of a dead Jesus, rather than the celebration of a risen Christ. However, the debate was far from over. In what follows, we shall consider later developments in this intriguing chapter of modern theology. Perhaps Strauss's most acute reinterpreter in the twentieth century has been Rudolf Bultmann, to whose distinctive views on the resurrection we may now turn.

Rudolf Bultmann: The Resurrection as an Event in the Experience of the Disciples

Bultmann shared Strauss's basic conviction that, in this scientific age, it is impossible to believe in miracles. As a result, belief in an objective resurrection of Jesus is no longer possible; however, it may well prove to be possible to make sense of it in another manner. History, Bultmann argued, is "a closed continuum of effects in which individual events are connected by the succession of cause and effect." The resurrection, in common with other miracles, would thus disrupt the closed system of nature. Similar points had been made by other thinkers sympathetic to the Enlightenment.

Belief in an objective resurrection of Jesus, although perfectly legitimate and intelligible in the first century, cannot be taken seriously today. "It is impossible to use electric light and radio equipment and, when ill, to claim the assistance of modern medical and clinical discoveries, and at the same time believe in the New Testament world of spirits and miracles." The human understanding of the world and of human existence has changed radically since the first century, with the result that modern humanity finds the mythological worldview of the New Testament unintelligible and unacceptable. A worldview is given to someone with the age in which they live, and they are in no position to alter it. The modern scientific and existential worldview means that that of the New Testament is now discarded and unintelligible.

For this reason, the resurrection is to be regarded as "a mythical event, pure and simple." The resurrection is something which happened in the subjective experience of the disciples, not something which took place in the public arena of history. For Bultmann, Jesus has indeed been raised – he has been raised up into the *kerygma*. The preaching of Jesus himself has been transformed into the Christian proclamation of Christ. Jesus has become an element of Christian preaching; he has been raised up and taken up into the proclamation of the gospel:

> All speculation concerning the modes of being of the risen Jesus, all the narratives of the empty tomb and all the Easter legends, whatever elements of historical facts they may contain, and as true as they may be in their symbolic form, are of no consequence. To believe in the Christ present in the *kerygma* is the meaning of the Easter faith.

Consistent with his anti-historical approach in general, Bultmann directs attention away from the historical Jesus toward the proclamation of Christ. "Faith in the church as the bearer of the *kerygma* is the Easter faith which consists in the belief that Jesus Christ is present in the *kerygma*."

Karl Barth: The Resurrection as an Historical Event beyond Critical Inquiry

Barth wrote a small work entitled *The Resurrection of the Dead* in 1924. However, his mature views on the relation of the resurrection to history date from considerably later, and have clearly been influenced by Bultmann. Barth's essay "Rudolf Bultmann – An Attempt to Understand Him" (1952) set out his misgivings concerning Bultmann's approach. This was followed up by a sustained engagement with the issues at stake in volume 4, part 1, of *Church Dogmatics* (1953). In what follows, we shall attempt to set out Barth's position, and compare it with that of Bultmann.

In his early writings, Barth argued that the empty tomb was of minimal importance in relation to the resurrection. However, he became increasingly alarmed at Bultmann's existential approach to the resurrection, which seemed to imply that it had no objective historical foundation. For this reason, Barth came to place considerable emphasis upon the gospel accounts of the empty tomb. The empty tomb is "an indispensable sign" which "obviates all possible misunderstanding." It demonstrates that the resurrection of Christ was not a purely inward, interior, or subjective event, but something which left a mark upon history.

This would seem to suggest that Barth regarded the resurrection as being open to historical investigation, to clarify its nature and confirm its place in the public history of the world, rather than in the private interior experience of the first believers. Yet this is not so. He consistently refuses to allow the gospel narratives to be subjected to critical historical scrutiny. It is not entirely clear why. The following factor appears to have weighed heavily in his thinking at this point.

Barth emphasizes that Paul and the other Apostles are not calling for the "acceptance of a well-attested historical report," but for "a decision of faith." Historical investigation cannot legitimate or provide security for such faith; nor can faith become dependent upon the provisional results of historical inquiry. In any case, faith is a response to the risen Christ, not to the empty tomb. Barth was quite clear that the empty tomb, taken by itself, was of little value in laying the foundation for faith in the risen Christ. The absence of Christ from his tomb does not necessarily imply his resurrection: "He might, in fact, have been stolen, he might have only appeared to be dead."

As a result, Barth is left in what initially seems to be a highly vulnerable position. Concerned to defend the resurrection as an act in public history against Bultmann's subjectivist approach, he is not prepared to allow that history to be critically studied. In part, this rests upon his passionate belief that historical scholarship cannot lay the basis for faith; in part, it reflects his assumption that the resurrection of Christ is part of a much larger network of ideas and events, which cannot be disclosed or verified by historical inquiry. However much one may sympathize with Barth's theological concerns at this point, it is difficult to avoid the conclusion that he lacks credibility. It is perhaps for this reason that the approach of Wolfhart Pannenberg has been the subject of considerable attention.

Wolfhart Pannenberg: The Resurrection as an Historical Event Open to Critical Inquiry

The most distinctive feature of Pannenberg's theological program, as it emerged during the 1960s, is the appeal to universal history. Such views are developed and justified in the 1961 volume *Revelation as History*, edited by Pannenberg, in which these ideas are explored at some length. Pannenberg's essay "Dogmatic Theses on the Doctrine of Revelation" opens with a powerful appeal to universal history:

> History is the most comprehensive horizon of Christian theology.
> All theological questions and answers have meaning only within

the framework of the history which God has with humanity, and through humanity with the whole creation, directed towards a future which is hidden to the world, but which has already been revealed in Jesus Christ.

These crucially important opening sentences sum up the distinctive features of Pannenberg's theological program at this stage in his career. They immediately distinguish him from the ahistorical theology of Bultmann and his school on the one hand, and the suprahistorical approach of Martin Kähler on the other. Christian theology is based upon an analysis of universal and publicly accessible history. For Pannenberg, revelation is essentially a public and universal historical event which is recognized and *interpreted* as an "act of God." To his critics, this seemed to reduce faith to insight, and deny any role to the Holy Spirit in the event of revelation.

Pannenberg's argument takes the following form. History, in all its totality, can only be understood when it is viewed from its end-point. This point alone provides the perspective from which the historical process can be seen completely, and thus be properly understood. However, where Marx argued that the social sciences, by predicting the goal of history to be the hegemony of socialism, provided the key to the interpretation of history, Pannenberg declared that this was provided only in Jesus Christ. The end of history is disclosed proleptically in the history of Jesus Christ. In other words, the end of history, which has yet to take place, has been disclosed in advance of the event in the person and work of Christ.

This idea of a "proleptic disclosure of the end of history" is grounded in the apocalyptic worldview which, Pannenberg argues, provides the key to understanding the New Testament interpretation of the significance and function of Jesus. Whereas Bultmann chose to demythologize the apocalyptic elements of the New Testament, Pannenberg treats them as a hermeneutical grid or framework by which the life, death, and resurrection of Christ may be interpreted.

Perhaps the most distinctive, and certainly the most commented upon, aspect of this work is Pannenberg's insistence that the resurrection of Jesus is an objective historical event, witnessed by all who had access to the evidence. Whereas Bultmann treated the resurrection as an event within the experiential world of the disciples, Pannenberg declared that it belonged to the world of universal public history.

This immediately raised the question of the historicity of the resurrection. As noted earlier, a group of Enlightenment writers had argued that our only knowledge of the alleged resurrection of Jesus was contained in the New Testament. In that there were no contemporary analogs for such a resurrection, the credibility of those reports had to be seriously questioned. In a similar vein, Ernst Troeltsch had argued for the homogeneity of history: In that the resurrection of Jesus appeared to radically disrupt that homogeneity, it was to be regarded as of dubious historicity. Pannenberg initially responded to these difficulties in an essay on "Redemptive Event and History," and subsequently in *Jesus – God and Man*. His basic argument against this position can be set out as follows.

Troeltsch, in Pannenberg's view, has a pedantically narrow view of history, which rules out certain events in advance, on the basis of a set of provisional judgments which have improperly come to have the status of absolute laws. Troeltsch's unwarranted "constriction of historico-critical inquiry" was "biased" and "anthropocentric." It presupposed that the human viewpoint is the only acceptable and normative standpoint within history. Analogies, Pannenberg stresses, are always analogies *viewed from the standpoint of the human observer*; that standpoint is radically restricted in its scope, and cannot be allowed to function as the absolutely certain basis of critical inquiry. Pannenberg is too good a historian to suggest that the principle of analogy should be abandoned; it is, after all, a proven and useful tool of historical research. Yet, Pannenberg insists, that is all that it is: It is a working tool, and cannot be allowed to define a fixed view of reality.

If the historian sets out to investigate the New Testament already precommitted to the belief "dead people do not rise again," that conclusion will merely be read back into the New Testament material. The judgment "Jesus did not rise from the dead" will be the presupposition, not the conclusion, of such an investigation. Pannenberg's discussion of this question represents an impassioned and impressive plea for a neutral approach to the resurrection. The historical evidence pointing to the resurrection of Jesus must be investigated without the prior dogmatic presupposition that such a resurrection could not have happened.

Having argued for the historicity of the resurrection, Pannenberg turns to deal with its interpretation within the context of the apocalyptic framework of meaning. The end of history has proleptically taken place in the resurrection of Jesus from the dead. This maxim dominates Pannenberg's interpretation of the event. The resurrection of Jesus anticipates the general resurrection at the end of time, and brings forward into history both that resurrection and the full and final revelation of God. The resurrection of Jesus is thus organically linked with the self-revelation of God in Christ; it establishes Jesus' identity with God, and allows this identity with God to be read back into his pre-Easter ministry. It thus functions as the foundation of a series of central Christological affirmations, including the divinity of Christ (however this is expressed) and the incarnation.

Resurrection and the Christian Hope

The resurrection of Jesus Christ assumes a number of functions within Christian theology. As we have seen, one foundational role of the resurrection relates to the Christological affirmation of the divinity of Christ. Even in the New Testament, the exalted status of Jesus of Nazareth – however this is conceptualized – is seen as being linked to his resurrection. The Australian writer Peter Carnley, surveying New Testament scholarship on this issue, comments that:

> Most contemporary New Testament scholars have been anxious to affirm that the resurrection is not just a loosely connected appendage to a set of beliefs that might be formulated concerning Jesus' nature and identity as the Christ of God. The datum for faith in Christ is not just the historical life of Jesus from his birth to his crucifixion. Even if some inkling of his divine significance was arrived at during his lifetime, it was shattered by his premature and devastating death. Genuine Christian faith is a post-Easter phenomenon, and the presentation of his life and death in the gospels is made in the retrospective light of it. Indeed, it was the resurrection faith which initiated the various attempts of the early church to express its understanding of the uniqueness of Christ's person.

However, it must be appreciated that the resurrection of Jesus serves an additional function within Christian theology. It establishes and undergirds the Christian hope. This has both *soteriological* and *eschatological* implications. At the soteriological level, it enables the death of Christ upon the cross to be interpreted in terms of God's victory over death and a coalition of allied forces and powers (pp. 345–9). At the eschatological level, it gives both foundation and substance to the Christian hope of eternal life (p. 466). We shall explore these elements later in the present volume; our concern at this stage is merely to alert the reader to the multifaceted theological significance of the resurrection of Christ.

Our primary concern in the present chapter has been to address the issue of faith and history raised by the Enlightenment. It will be clear that the Enlightenment and post-Enlightenment Christological debate has been of major interest, raising a cluster of issues which seem set to continue to be the subject of debate for some time to come. The general collapse of confidence in the Enlightenment worldview has led to a related retreat from its Christological agenda, and a return to a significant part of the concerns of classical Christology. Much the same may be said of the doctrine of the work of Christ, to which we may now turn.

Questions for Chapter 10

1 What did Lessing mean when he spoke of an "ugly great ditch" between faith and history?

2 Suppose, for the sake of argument, that the New Testament gets Jesus wrong. How could we correct it?

3 In what ways does the "quest of the historical Jesus" reflect the agenda of the Enlightenment?

4 Assess the contribution of either Martin Kähler or Albert Schweitzer to the failure of the "quest of the historical Jesus."

5 If the bones of Jesus Christ were to be discovered in Palestine, what would remain of Christianity?

11

The Doctrine of Salvation in Christ

The two previous chapters have considered a network of issues concerning the identity of Jesus Christ. As noted in the course of that discussion, a central consideration in determining the identity of Jesus Christ relates to his function. There is an organic relationship between the two central questions:

> Who is Jesus Christ?
> What did Jesus Christ achieve?

The identity and function of Jesus Christ can, as we noted earlier, be thought of as two sides of the same coin. The close connection between *functional* and *ontological* Christologies (pp. 270–1) should be noted in this respect.

Christian Approaches to Salvation

"Salvation" is a complex notion. It does not necessarily have any specifically *Christian* reference. The term can be used in a thoroughly secular manner. For example, it was common for Soviet writers, especially during the late 1920s, to speak of Lenin as the "savior" of the Soviet peoples. Military coups in African states during the 1980s frequently resulted in the setting up of "councils of salvation," concerned to restore political and economic stability. Salvation can be a purely secular notion, concerned with political emancipation or the general human quest for liberation.

Even at the religious level, salvation is not a specifically Christian idea. Many – but not, it must be stressed, all – of the world's religions have concepts of salvation. They differ enormously, in relation to both their understanding of how that salvation is achieved, and the shape or form which it is understood to take. One of the most difficult tasks facing those in the past who, in the tradition of the Enlightenment, wished to argue that "all religions were basically the same" has been to show that there is an underlying unity amongst the religions, despite all their obvious differences in relation to these two questions. It is generally thought that this quest has failed, on account of the astonishing variety of the phenomena in question.

Christianity is, therefore, not in any sense distinctive or unique in attaching importance to the idea of salvation. The distinctiveness of the Christian approach to salvation lies in two distinct areas: In the first place, salvation is understood to be grounded in the life, death, and resurrection of Jesus Christ; in the second, the specific shape of salvation, within the Christian tradition, is itself formed by Christ. These ideas are complex, and require further exploration before we can proceed.

Salvation is Linked with Jesus Christ

First, salvation – however that is subsequently defined – is understood to be linked with the life, death, and resurrection of Jesus Christ. That there is such a link is characteristic of Christian theology down the ages. A significant debate in more recent theological literature has concerned whether the cross can be said to be *constitutive* or *illustrative*. In his *Doctrine of Reconciliation* (1898), the noted German theologian Martin Kähler posed the following question concerning theories of the atonement: "Did Christ just make known some insights concerning an unchangeable situation – or did he establish a new situation?" With this question we come to a central aspect of soteriology. Does the cross of Christ illustrate the saving will of God, giving shape to a hitherto vague notion? Or does it make such a salvation possible in the first place? Is it illustrative or constitutive?

The former approach has been characteristic of much writing inspired by the Enlightenment, which treats the cross as a historical symbol of a timeless truth. John Macquarrie firmly defends this approach in his *Principles of Christian Theology* (1977):

> It is not that, at a given moment, God adds the activity of reconciliation to his previous activities, or that we can set a time when his reconciling activity began. Rather, it is the case that at a given time there was a new and decisive interpretation of an activity that

had always been going on, an activity that is equiprimordial with creation itself.

A similar approach is associated with Oxford theologian Maurice F. Wiles, who argues in his *Remaking of Christian Doctrine* (1974) that the Christ-event is "in some way a demonstration of what is true of God's eternal nature." Christ is here understood to reveal the saving will of God, not to establish that saving will in the first place. The coming of Christ is an expression and public demonstration of God's saving will.

Yet the debate is far from over. In his *Actuality of Atonement* (1988), the London-based theologian Colin Gunton suggests that non-constitutive approaches to the atonement run the risk of falling back into exemplarist and subjective doctrines of salvation. It is, he argues, necessary to say that Christ does not just reveal something of importance to us; he achieves something for us – something without which salvation would not be possible. Raising the question of whether "the real evil of the world is faced and healed *ontologically* in the life, death and resurrection of Jesus," Gunton argues that there must be a sense in which Christ is a "substitute" for us: He does for us something that we ourselves cannot do. To deny this is to revert to some form of purely subjective understanding of salvation.

Gunton's approach may be regarded as characteristic of much of the pre-Enlightenment Christian discussion of the foundations of salvation, which reflects the fundamental conviction that something new happened in Christ, which makes possible and available a new way of life. This approach continues to be definitive within modern evangelicalism, and has exercised a deep and continuing influence over the hymns and liturgies of the Christian church.

Salvation is Shaped by Jesus Christ

Alongside the characteristic Christian insistence that salvation is linked with Jesus Christ may be found a further Christological assertion: Salvation is shaped by Christ. In other words, Jesus Christ provides a model or paradigm for the redeemed life. While the Christian tradition has been thoroughly unsympathetic to the idea that the imitation of Christ in itself *is* or *gives rise to* the Christian life, there is widespread agreement that Christ in some sense gives shape or specification to that life.

The idea that the mere external imitation of Christ gives rise to the Christian life has generally been regarded as Pelagian. The main-stream Christian approach has tended to argue that the Christian life is made possible through Christ, while recognizing two quite distinct manners in which the resulting Christian life is "shaped" by him.

1 The Christian life takes the form of the believer's sustained attempt to imitate Christ. Having become a Christian, the believer now treats Christ as an example of the ideal relationship to God and other people, and attempts to mimic this relationship. This approach may perhaps be seen at its best in the works of some later medieval spiritual writers, especially within a monastic situation, such as the medieval writer Thomas à Kempis' famous *Imitation of Christ*. It places emphasis upon the human responsibility to bring one's life into line with the example set by Christ.

2 The Christian life is a process of "being conformed to Christ," in which the outward aspects of the believer's life are brought into line with the inward relationship to Christ, established through faith. This approach is characteristic of writers such as Luther and Calvin, and is based on the idea of God conforming the believer to the likeness of Christ through the process of renewal and regeneration brought about by the Holy Spirit.

The Eschatological Dimension of Salvation

A final issue which must be addressed at this early stage concerns the chronology of salvation. Is salvation to be understood as something which has happened to the believer? Or is it something currently happening? Or is there an eschatological dimension to it – in other words, is there something which has yet to happen? The only answer to such questions which can be given on the basis of the New Testament is that salvation includes past, present, and future reference. We may illustrate this by considering Paul's statements on justification and related themes.

In dealing with Paul, it is tempting to adopt a simplistic approach to the chronological question just noted. For example, one could attempt to force justification, sanctification, and salvation into a neat past–present–future framework, as follows:

1 justification: a past event, with present implications (sanctification);
2 sanctification: a present event, dependent upon a past event (justification), which has future implications (salvation);
3 salvation: a future event, already anticipated and partially experienced in the past event of justification and the present event of sanctification, and dependent upon them.

But this is clearly inadequate. Justification has future, as well as past, reference (Romans 2: 13, 8: 33; Galatians 5: 4–5), and appears to relate to both the beginning of the Christian life and its final consummation. Similarly, sanctification can also refer to a past event (1 Corinthians 6: 11) or a future event (1 Thessalonians 5: 23). And salvation is an exceptionally complex idea, embracing not simply a future event, but something which has happened in the past (Romans 8: 24; 1 Corinthians 15: 2) or which is taking place now (1 Corinthians 1: 18).

Justification language appears in Paul with reference to both the inauguration of the life of faith and also its final consummation. It is a complex and all-embracing notion, which anticipates the verdict of the final judgment (Romans 8: 30–4), declaring in advance the verdict of ultimate acquittal. The believer's present justified Christian existence is thus an anticipation of and advance participation in deliverance from the wrath to come, and an assurance in the present of the final eschatological verdict of acquittal (Romans 5: 9–10).

This very brief discussion indicates the complexity of the issues at stake. The Christian understanding of salvation presupposes that something *has* happened, that something *is now happening*, and that something further *will still happen* to believers.

The Foundations of Salvation: The Cross of Christ

The term "theory of the atonement" has become commonplace in English-language theology as a term for "a way of understanding the work of Christ." The term was used especially extensively in the nineteenth and early twentieth centuries. However, there is increasing evidence that this term is seen as cumbersome and unhelpful by many modern Christian writers, across the entire spectrum of theological viewpoints. In view of this trend, it has been avoided in the present work. The term "soteriology" (from the Greek *soteria*, "salvation") is increasingly used to refer to what were traditionally designated "theories of the atonement" or "the work of Christ." Soteriology embraces two broad areas of theology: the question of how salvation is possible and in particular how it relates to the history of Jesus Christ; and the question of how "salvation" itself is to be understood. These questions have been the subject of intense discussion through-out Christian history, especially during the modern period.

Discussions of the meaning of the cross and resurrection of Christ are best grouped around four central controlling themes or images. It must be stressed that these are not mutually exclusive, and that it is normal to find writers adopting approaches which incorporate elements drawn from more than one such category. Indeed, it can be argued that the views of most writers on this subject cannot be reduced to or confined within a single category, without doing serious violence to their ideas.

The Cross as a Sacrifice

The New Testament, drawing on Old Testament imagery and expectations, presents Christ's death upon the cross as a sacrifice. This approach, which is especially associated with the Letter to the Hebrews, presents Christ's sacrificial offering as an effective and perfect sacrifice, which was able to accomplish that which the sacrifices of the Old Testament were only able to intimate, rather than achieve. In particular, Paul's use of the Greek term *hilasterion* (Romans 3: 25) points to a sacrificial interpretation of Christ's death.

This idea is developed subsequently within the Christian tradition. For example, in taking over the imagery of sacrifice, Augustine states that Christ "was made a sacrifice for sin, offering himself as a whole burnt offering on the cross of his passion." In order for humanity to be restored to God, the mediator must sacrifice himself; without this sacrifice, such restoration is an impossibility. In his *Festal Letter VII*, Athanasius explored the idea of Christ's sacrifice in terms of the passover sacrifice of the lamb:

> He became incarnate for our sakes, so that he might offer himself to the Father in our place, and redeem us through his offering and sacrifice. . . . This is he who, in former times, was sacrificed as a lamb, having been foreshadowed in that lamb. But afterwards, he was slain for us. For Christ, our passover, is sacrificed.

Augustine brought new clarity to the discussion, through his crisp and highly influential definition of a sacrifice set out in *City of God*: "A true sacrifice is offered in every action which is designed to unite us to God in a holy fellowship." On the basis of this definition, Augustine has no difficulties in speaking of Christ's death as a sacrifice: "By his death, which is indeed the one and most true sacrifice offered for us, he purged, abolished, and extinguished whatever guilt there was by which the principalities and powers lawfully detained us to pay the penalty." In this sacrifice, Christ was both victim and priest; he offered himself up as a sacrifice: "He offered sacrifice for our sins. And where did he find that offering, the pure victim that he would offer? He offered himself, in that he could find no other."

The sacrificial offering of Christ on the cross came to be linked especially with one aspect of the "threefold office of Christ" (*munus triplex Christi*). According to this typology, which dates from the middle of the sixteenth century, the work of Christ could be summarized under three "offices": prophet (by which Christ declares the will of God); priest (by which he makes sacrifice for sin); and king (by which he rules with authority over his people). The general acceptance of this taxonomy within Protestantism in the late sixteenth and seventeenth centuries led to a sacrificial understanding of Christ's death becoming of central importance within Protestant soteriologies. Thus John Pearson's *Exposition of the Creed* (1659) insists upon the necessity of the sacrifice of Christ in redemption, and specifically links this with the priestly office of Christ.

> The redemption or salvation which the Messiah was to bring consisteth in the freeing of a sinner from the state of sin and eternal death into a state of righteousness and eternal life. Now a freedom from sin could not be wrought without a sacrifice propitiatory, and therefore there was a necessity of a priest.

Since the Enlightenment, however, there has been a subtle shift in the meaning of the term. A metaphorical extension of meaning has come to be given priority over the original. Whereas the term originally referred to the ritual offering of slaughtered animals as a specifically religious action, it increasingly came to mean heroic or costly action on the parts of individuals, especially the giving up of one's life, with no transcendent reference or expectation.

This trend may be seen developing in John Locke's *Reasonableness of Christianity* (1695). Locke argues that the only article of faith required of Christians is that of belief in Christ's Messiahship; the idea of a sacrifice for sin is studiously set to one side. "The faith required was to believe Jesus to be the Messiah, the anointed, who had been promised by God to the world . . . I do not remember that Christ anywhere assumes to himself the title of a priest, or mentions anything relating to his priesthood."

These arguments are developed further by the Deist writer Thomas Chubb (1679-1747), especially in his *True Gospel of Jesus Christ Vindicated* (1739). Arguing that the true religion of reason was that of conformity to the eternal rule of right, Chubb argues that the idea of Christ's death as a sacrifice arises from the apologetic concerns of the early Christian writers, which led them to harmonize this religion of reason with the cult of the Jews: "As the Jews had their temple, their altar, their high priest, their sacrifices and the like, so the apostles, in order to make Christianity bear a resemblance to Judaism, found out something or other in Christianity, which they by a figure of speech called by those names." Chubb, in common with the emerging Enlightenment tradition, dismissed this as spurious. "God's disposition to show mercy . . . arises wholly from his own innate goodness or mercifulness, and not from anything external to him, whether it be the sufferings and death of Jesus Christ or otherwise."

Even the noted English critic of Deism, Joseph Butler, in attempting to reinstate the notion of sacrifice in his *Analogy of Religion* (1736), found himself in difficulty, given the strongly rationalist spirit of the age. In upholding the sacrificial nature of Christ's death, he found himself obliged to concede more than he cared to:

> How and in what particular way [the death of Christ] had this efficacy, there are not wanting persons who have endeavoured to explain; but I do not find that Scripture has explained it. We seem to be very much in the dark concerning the manner in which the ancients understood atonements to be made, i.e. pardon to be obtained by sacrifice.

Horace Bushnell's *Vicarious Sacrifice* (1866) illustrates this same trend in the Anglo-American theology of the period, but in a more constructive manner. Through his suffering, Christ awakens our sense of guilt. His vicarious sacrifice demonstrates that God suffers on account of evil. In speaking of the "tender appeals of sacrifice," Bushnell might seem to align himself with purely exemplarist understandings of the death of Christ; however, Bushnell is adamant that there are objective elements to atonement. Christ's death affects God, and expresses God. There are strong anticipations of later theologies of the suffering of God, when Bushnell declares:

> Whatever we may say or hold or believe concerning the vicarious sacrifice of Christ, we are to affirm in the same manner of God. The whole Deity is in it, in it from eternity. . . . There is a cross in God before the wood is seen on the hill. . . . It is as if there were a cross unseen, standing on its undiscovered hill, far back in the ages.

The use of sacrificial imagery has become noticeably less widespread since 1945, especially in German-language theology. It is highly likely that this relates directly to the rhetorical debasement of the term in secular contexts, especially in situations of national emergency. The secular use of the imagery of sacrifice, often degenerating into little more than slogan-mongering, is widely regarded as having tainted and compromised both the word and the concept. The frequent use of such phrases as "he sacrificed his life for King and country" in Britain during World War I, and Adolf Hitler's extensive use of sacrificial imagery in justifying economic hardship and the loss of civil liberties as the price of German national revival in the late 1930s, served to render the term virtually unusable for many in Christian teaching and preaching, on account of its negative associations. Nevertheless, the idea continues to be of importance in modern Roman Catholic sacramental theology, which continues to regard the eucharist as a sacrifice, and finds in this notion a rich source of theological imagery.

The Cross as a Victory

The New Testament and early church laid considerable emphasis upon the victory gained by Christ over sin, death, and Satan through his cross and resurrection (see pp. 465–6). This theme of victory, often linked liturgically with the Easter celebrations, was of major importance within the western Christian theological tradition until the Enlightenment. The theme of "Christ the victor" (*Christus victor*) brought together a series of themes, centering on the idea of a decisive victory over forces of evil and oppression.

The image of Christ's death as a ransom came to be of central importance to Greek patristic writers, such as Irenaeus. We noted earlier, in discussing the theological role of analogies, that the New Testament speaks of Jesus giving his life as a "ransom" for sinners (Mark 10: 45; 1 Timothy 2: 6). The word "ransom" suggests three related ideas:

1 *Liberation* A ransom is something which achieves freedom for a person who is held in captivity.
2 *Payment* A ransom is a sum of money which is paid in order to achieve an individual's liberation.
3 *Someone to whom the ransom is paid* A ransom is usually paid to an individual's captor, or his agent.

These three ideas thus seem to be implied by speaking of Jesus' death as a "ransom" for sinners. At any rate, that was the conclusion of Origen, perhaps the most speculative of early patristic writers. If Christ's death was a ransom, Origen argued, it must have been paid to someone. But to whom? It could not have been paid to God, in that God was not holding sinners to ransom. Therefore it had to be paid to the devil.

Gregory the Great developed this idea still further. The devil had acquired rights over fallen humanity, which God was obliged to respect. The only means by which humanity could be released from this satanic domination and oppression was through the devil exceeding the limits of his authority, and thus being obliged to forfeit his rights. So how could this be achieved? Gregory suggests that it could come about if a sinless person were to enter the world, yet in the form of a normal sinful person. The devil would not notice until it was too late: In claiming authority over this sinless person, the devil would have overstepped the limits of his authority, and thus be obliged to abandon his rights.

Gregory suggests the image of a baited hook: Christ's humanity is the bait, and his divinity the hook. The devil, like a great sea-monster, snaps at the bait – and then discovers, too late, the hook. "The bait tempts in order that the hook may wound. Our Lord therefore, when coming for the redemption of humanity, made a kind of hook of himself for the death of the devil." Other writers explored other images for the same idea – that of trapping the devil. Christ's death was like a net for catching birds, or a trap for catching mice. It was this aspect of this approach to the meaning of the cross that caused the most disquiet subsequently. It seemed that God was guilty of deception.

The imagery of victory over the devil proved to have enormous popular appeal. The medieval idea of "the harrowing of hell" bears witness to its power. According to this, after dying upon the cross, Christ descended to hell, and broke down its gates in order that the imprisoned souls might go free. The idea rested (rather tenuously, it has to be said) upon 1 Peter 3: 18–22, which makes reference to Christ "preaching to the spirits in prison." The hymn "Ye Choirs of New Jerusalem," written by Fulbert of Chartres, expresses this theme in two of its verses, picking up the theme of Christ, as the "lion of Judah" (Revelation 5: 5), defeating Satan, the serpent (Genesis 3: 15):

> For Judah's lion bursts his chains
>   Crushing the serpent's head;
> And cries aloud through death's domain
>   To wake the imprisoned dead.
>
> Devouring depths of hell their prey
>   At his command restore;
> His ransomed hosts pursue their way
>   Where Jesus goes before.

A similar idea can be found in a fourteenth-century English mystery play, which describes the "harrowing of hell" in the following manner.

> And when Christ was dead, his spirit went in haste to hell. And soon he broke down the strong gates that were wrongfully barred against him. . . . He bound Satan fast with eternal bonds, and so

shall Satan ever remain bound until the day of doom. He took with him Adam and Eve and others that were dear to him . . . all these he led out of hell and set in paradise.

With the advent of the Enlightenment, however, the *Christus victor* approach began to fall out of theological favor, increasingly being regarded as outmoded and unsophisticated. However great the popular appeal of the "harrowing of hell" may have been to medieval peasants, it was regarded as utterly primitive by the more sophisticated standards of the Enlightenment. The following factors appear to have contributed to this development.

1   Rational criticism of belief in the resurrection of Christ (pp. 82; 85–6) raised doubts concerning whether one could even begin to speak of a "victory" over death.
2   The imagery traditionally linked with this approach to the cross – such as the existence of a personal devil in the form of Satan, and the domination of human existence by oppressive or satanic forces of sin and evil – was dismissed as premodern superstition.

The rehabilitation of this approach in the modern period is usually dated to 1931, with the appearance of Gustaf Aulén's *Christus victor*. This short book, which originally appeared in German as an article in *Zeitschrift für systematische Theologie* (1930), has exercised a major influence over English-language approaches to the subject. Aulén argued that the classic Christian conception of the work of Christ was summed up in the belief that the risen Christ had brought new possibilities of life to humanity through his victory over the powers of evil. In a brief and very compressed account of the history of theories of the atonement, Aulén argued that this highly dramatic "classic" theory had dominated Christianity until the Middle Ages, when more abstract legal theories began to gain ground. A new concern for the morality of atonement led to a focus on justice-centered theories of the atonement, with a gradual loss of interest in the more morally problematic *Christus victor* approach. The situation was radically reversed through Luther, who reintroduced the theme, perhaps as a reaction against the spiritual aridity of scholastic theories of the atonement. However, Aulén argued, the scholastic concerns of Protestant orthodoxy led to its being relegated once more to the background. Aulén declared that it was time to reverse this process, and rediscover the theory, which deserved a full and proper hearing in the modern period.

Historically, Aulén's case was soon found to be wanting. Its claims to be treated as the "classic" theory of the atonement had been overstated. The idea of Christ as the victor over death and Satan was indeed an important component of the general patristic understanding of the nature of salvation; however, it was just one image or approach amongst many others. Aulén had exaggerated its importance for patristic writers. His critics pointed out that, if any theory could justly lay claim to the title of "the classic theory of the atonement," it would be the notion of redemption through unity with Christ.

Nevertheless, Aulén's views were sympathetically received. In part, this reflects growing disenchantment with the Enlightenment world-view in general; more fundamentally, perhaps, it represents a growing realization of the reality of evil in the world, fostered by the horrors of World War I. The insights of Sigmund Freud, which drew attention to the manner in which adults could be spiritually imprisoned by their subconscious, raised serious doubts about the Enlightenment view of the total rationality of human nature, and lent new credibility to the idea that humans are held in bondage to unknown and hidden forces. Aulén's approach seemed to resonate with a growing realization of the darker side of human nature. It had become intellectually respectable to talk about "forces of evil."

Aulén's approach also offered a third possibility, which mediated between the two alternatives then on offer within mainstream liberal Protestantism – both of which were increasingly coming to be regarded as flawed. The classic legal theory was regarded as raising difficult theological questions, not least concerning the morality of atonement; the subjective approach, which regarded Christ's death as doing little more than arousing human religious sentiment, seemed to be seriously religiously inadequate. Aulén offered an approach to the meaning of the death of Christ which bypassed the difficulties of legal approaches, yet vigorously defended the objective nature of the atonement. Nevertheless, Aulén's *Christus victor* approach did raise some serious questions. It offered no rational justification for the manner in which the forces of evil are defeated through the cross of Christ. Why the cross? Why not in some other manner?

Since then, the image of victory has been developed in writings on the cross. Rudolf Bultmann extended his program of demythologization to the New Testament theme of victory, interpreting it as a victory over inauthentic existence and unbelief. Paul Tillich offered a reworking of Aulén's theory, in which the victory of Christ on the cross was interpreted as a victory over existential forces which threaten to deprive us of authentic existence. Bultmann and Tillich, in adopting such existentialist approaches, thus converted a theory of the atonement which was originally radically objective into a subjective victory within the human consciousness.

In his *Past Event and Present Salvation* (1989), Oxford theologian Paul Fiddes emphasized that the notion of "victory" retains a place of significance within Christian thinking about the cross. Christ's death does more than impart some new knowledge to us, or express old ideas in new manners. It makes possible a new mode of existence:

> The victory of Christ actually *creates* victory in us. . . . The act of Christ is one of those moments in human history that "opens up new possibilities of existence." Once a new possibility has been disclosed, other people can make it their own, repeating and reliving the experience.

The Cross and Forgiveness

A third approach centers on the idea of the death of Christ providing the basis by which God is enabled to forgive sin. The notion is traditionally associated with the eleventh-century writer Anselm of Canterbury, who developed an argument for the necessity of the incarnation on this basis. This model became incorporated into classical Protestant dogmatics during the period of orthodoxy, and finds its expression in many hymns of the eighteenth and nineteenth centuries. In part, Anselm's reason for developing this model appears to have been a deep-seated dissatisfaction with the *Christus victor* approach, which seemed to rest upon a series of highly questionable assumptions about the "rights of the devil" (*ius diaboli*), and an implicit suggestion that God acted with less than total honesty in redeeming humanity.

Anselm was unable to understand why the devil can be said to have "rights" of any kind over fallen humanity, let alone why God should be under any obligation to respect them. At best, the devil might be allowed to have a *de facto* power over humanity – a power which exists as a matter of fact, even if it is an illegitimate and unjustified power. Yet this cannot be thought of as a *de jure* authority – that is, an authority firmly grounded in some legal or moral principle. "I do not see what force this has," he comments, in dismissing the idea. Equally, Anselm is dismissive of any notion that God deceives the devil in the process of redemption. The entire trajectory of redemption is grounded in and reflects the righteousness of God.

Anselm's emphasis falls totally upon the righteousness of God. God redeems humanity in a manner that is totally consistent with the divine quality of righteousness. Anselm's *Cur Deus homo?* is a sustained engagement with the question of the possibility of human redemption, cast in the form of a dialogue. In the course of his

analysis, he demonstrates – although how successfully is a matter
of dispute – both the necessity of the incarnation and the saving
potential of the death and resurrection of Jesus Christ. The argument
is complex, and can be summarized as follows.

1   God created humanity in a state of original righteousness,
    with the objective of bringing humanity to a state of eternal
    blessedness.
2   That state of eternal blessedness is contingent upon human
    obedience to God. However, through sin, humanity is unable
    to achieve this necessary obedience, which appears to frus-
    trate God's purpose in creating humanity in the first place.
3   In that it is impossible for God's purposes to be frustrated,
    there must be some means by which the situation can be
    remedied. However, the situation can only be remedied if a
    satisfaction is made for sin. In other words, something has to
    be done, by which the offense caused by human sin can be
    purged.
4   There is no way in which humanity can provide this necessary
    satisfaction. It lacks the resources which are needed. On the
    other hand, God possesses the resources needed to provide
    the required satisfaction.
5   A "God–man" would possess both the *ability* (as God) and
    the *obligation* (as a human being) to pay the required satisfac-
    tion. Therefore the incarnation takes place, in order that the
    required satisfaction may be made, and humanity redeemed.

A number of points require comment. First, sin is conceived of as
an offense against God. The weight of that offense appears to be
proportional to the status of the offended party. For many scholars,
this suggests that Anselm has been deeply influenced by the feudal
assumptions of his time, perhaps regarding God as the equivalent of
the "lord of the manor."

Second, there has been considerable debate over the origins of the
idea of a "satisfaction." It is possible that the idea may derive from the
Germanic laws of the period, which stipulated that an offense had to
be purged through an appropriate payment. However, most scholars
believe that Anselm was appealing directly to the existing penitential
system of the church. A sinner, seeking penance, was required
to confess every sin. In pronouncing forgiveness, the priest would
require that the penitent should do something (such as go on a
pilgrimage or undertake some charitable work) as a "satisfaction" –
that is, a means of publicly demonstrating gratitude for forgive-

ness. It is possible that Anselm derived the idea from this source.

However, despite the obvious difficulties which attend Anselm's approach, an important advance had been made. Anselm's insistence that God is totally and utterly obliged to act according to the principles of justice throughout the redemption of humanity marks a decisive break with the dubious morality of the *Christus victor* view. In taking up Anselm's approach, later writers were able to place it on a more secure foundation by grounding it in the general principles of law. The sixteenth century was particularly appreciative of the importance of human law, and saw it as an appropriate model for God's forgiveness of human sin. Three main models came to be used at this time to understand the manner in which the forgiveness of human sins is related to the death of Christ.

1 *Representation* Christ is here understood to be the covenant representative of humanity. Through faith, believers come to stand within the covenant between God and humanity. All that Christ has achieved through the cross is available on account of the covenant. Just as God entered into a covenant with his people Israel, so he has entered into a covenant with his church. Christ, by his obedience upon the cross, represents his covenant people, winning benefits for them as their representative. By coming to faith, individuals come to stand within the covenant, and thus share in all its benefits, won by Christ through his cross and resurrection – including the full and free forgiveness of our sins.

2 *Participation* Through faith, believers participate in the risen Christ. They are "in Christ," to use Paul's famous phrase. They are caught up in him, and share in his risen life. As a result of this, they share in all the benefits won by Christ, through his obedience upon the cross. One of those benefits is the forgiveness of sins, in which they share through faith. New Testament scholar E. P. Sanders states the importance of "participation in Christ" for Paul in the following words:

> The prime significance which the death of Christ has for Paul is not that it provides atonement for past transgressions (although he holds the common Christian view that it does so), but that, by *sharing* in Christ's death, one dies to the *power* of sin or to the old aeon, with the result that one belongs to God. . . . The transfer takes place by *participation* in Christ's death.

Participating in Christ thus entails the forgiveness of sins, and sharing in his righteousness. This idea is central to both Luther's and Calvin's soteriology, as Luther's image of the marriage between Christ and the believer makes clear.

3 *Substitution* Christ is here understood to be a substitute, the one who goes to the cross in our place. Sinners ought to have been crucified, on account of their sins. Christ is crucified in their place. God allows Christ to stand in our place, taking our guilt upon himself, so that his righteousness – won by obedience upon the cross – might become ours.

With the onset of the Enlightenment, this approach to the atonement was subjected to a radical critique. The following major points of criticism were directed against it.

1 It appeared to rest upon a notion of original guilt, which Enlightenment writers found unacceptable. Each human being was responsible for his or her own moral guilt; the very notion of an inherited guilt, as it was expressed in the traditional doctrine of original sin, was to be rejected.

2 The Enlightenment insisted upon the rationality, and perhaps above all the morality, of every aspect of Christian doctrine. This theory of the atonement appeared to be morally suspect, especially in its notions of transferred guilt or merit. The central idea of "vicarious satisfaction" was also regarded with acute suspicion: In what sense was it moral for one human being to bear the penalties due for another?

These criticisms were given added weight through the development of the discipline of the "history of dogma" (see pp. 213–14). The representatives of this movement, from G. S. Steinbart through to Adolf von Harnack, argued that a series of assumptions, each of central importance to the Anselmian doctrine of penal substitution, had become incorporated into Christian theology by what were little more than historical accidents. For example, in his *System of Pure Philosophy* (1778), Steinbart argued that historical investigation disclosed the intrusion of three "arbitrary assumptions" into Christian reflection on salvation:

1   the Augustinian doctrine of original sin;
2   the concept of satisfaction;
3   the doctrine of the imputation of the righteousness of Christ.

For such reasons, Steinbart felt able to declare the substructure of orthodox Protestant thinking on the atonement to be a relic of a bygone era.

More recently, the idea of guilt – a central aspect of legal approaches to soteriology – has been the subject of much discussion, especially in the light of Freud's views on the origin of guilt in childhood experiences. For some twentieth-century writers, "guilt" is simply a psychosocial projection, whose origins lie not in the holiness of God but in the muddleheadedness of human nature. These psychosocial structures are then, it is argued, projected on to some imaginary screen of "external" reality, and treated as if they were objectively true. While this represents a considerable overstatement of the case, it has the advantage of clarity, and allows us to gain an appreciation of the considerable pressure that this approach to the atonement is currently facing.

Nevertheless, this view of the cross continues to find significant supporters. The collapse of the evolutionary moral optimism of liberal Protestantism in the wake of World War I (see pp. 98–100) did much to raise again the question of human guilt, and the need for redemption from outside the human situation. Two significant contributions to this discussion may be regarded as precipitated directly by the credibility crisis faced by liberal Protestantism at this time.

P. T. Forsyth's *Justification of God* (1916), written in England during World War I, represents an impassioned plea to allow the notion of the "justice of God" to be rediscovered. Forsyth is less concerned than Anselm for the legal and juridical aspects of the cross; his interest centers on the manner in which the cross is inextricably linked with "the whole moral fabric and movement of the universe." The doctrine of the atonement is inseparable from "the rightness of things." God acts to restore this "rightness of things," in that he makes available through the cross a means of moral regeneration – something which the war demonstrated that humanity needed, yet was unable to provide itself.

> The cross is not a theological theme, nor a forensic device, but the crisis of the moral universe on a scale far greater than earthly war. It is the theodicy of the whole God dealing with the whole soul of the whole world in holy love, righteous judgement and redeeming grace.

Through the cross, God aims to restore the rightness of the world through rightful means – a central theme of Anselm's doctrine of atonement, creatively restated.

More significant is the extended discussion of the theme of "atonement" or "reconciliation" (the German term *Versöhnung* can bear both meanings) to be found in Karl Barth's *Church Dogmatics*. The central

section (volume 4, part 1, section 59, 2) addressing the issue is entitled
– significantly – "The Judge Judged in Our Place." The title derives
from the *Heidelberg Catechism*, which speaks of Christ as the judge who
"has represented me before the judgment of God, and has taken away
all condemnation from me." The section in question can be regarded
as an extended commentary on this classic text of the Reformed
tradition, dealing with the manner in which the judgment of God in
the first place is made known and enacted, and in the second, is taken
upon God himself (a central Anselmian theme, even if Anselm failed
to integrate it within a Trinitarian context).

The entire section is steeped in the language and imagery of guilt,
judgment, and forgiveness. In the cross, we can see God exercising
his rightful judgment of sinful humanity (Barth uses the compound
term *Sündermensch* – "person of sin" – to emphasize that "sin" is not
a detachable aspect of human nature). The cross exposes human
delusions of self-sufficiency and autonomy of judgment, which Barth
sees encapsulated in the story of Genesis 3: "Human beings want to be
their own judges."

Yet alteration of the situation demands that its inherent wrongness
be acknowledged. For Barth, the cross of Christ represents the locus
in which the righteous judge makes known his judgment of sinful
humanity, and simultaneously takes that judgment upon himself.

> What took place is that the Son of God fulfilled the righteous
> judgement on us human beings by himself taking our place as a
> human being, and in our place undergoing the judgement under
> which we had passed . . . Because God willed to execute his judge-
> ment on us in his Son, it all took place in his person, as *his*
> accusation and condemnation and destruction. He judged, and
> it was the judge who was judged, who allowed himself to be
> judged. . . . Why did God become a human being? So that God as
> a human being might do and accomplish and achieve and com-
> plete all this for us wrongdoers, in order that in this way there
> might be brought about by him our reconciliation with him, and
> our conversion to him.

The strongly substitutionary character of this will be evident. God
exercises his righteous judgment by exposing our sin, by taking it
upon himself, and thus by neutralizing its power.

The cross thus both speaks "for us" and "against us." Unless the
cross is allowed to reveal the full extent of our sin, it cannot take that
sin from us:

> The "for us" of his death on the cross included and encloses this
> terrible "against us." Without this terrible "against us," it would

not be the divine and holy and redemptive and effectively helpful "for us," in which the conversion of humanity and the world to God has become an event.

The Cross as a Moral Example

A central aspect of the New Testament understanding of the meaning of the cross relates to the demonstration of the love of God for humanity. Augustine of Hippo was but one of many patristic writers to stress that one of the motivations underlying the mission of Christ was the "demonstration of the love of God toward us." Perhaps the most important medieval statement of this emphasis can be found in the writings of Peter Abelard. It must be stressed that Abelard does not, as some of his interpreters suggest, *reduce* the meaning of the cross to a demonstration of the love of God. This is one amongst many components of Abelard's soteriology, which includes traditional ideas concerning Christ's death as a sacrifice for human sin. It is Abelard's emphasis upon the subjective impact of the cross that is distinctive.

For Abelard, "the purpose and cause of the incarnation was that Christ might illuminate the world by his wisdom, and excite it to love of himself." In this, Abelard restates the Augustinian idea of Christ's incarnation as a public demonstration of the extent of the love of God, with the intent of evoking a response of love from humanity. "The Son of God took our nature, and in it took upon himself to teach us by both word and example even to the point of death, thus binding us to himself through love." This insight is pressed home with considerable force, as the subjective impact of the love of God in Christ is explored further:

> Everyone is made more righteous, that is more loving toward God, after the passion of Christ than before, because people are incited to love . . . And so our redemption is that great love for us shown in the passion of Christ, which not only sets us free from the bondage of sin, but also gains for us the true liberty of the children of God, so that we should fulfill all things not so much through fear as through love.

Abelard fails to provide an adequate theological foundation to allow us to understand precisely why Christ's death is to be understood as a demonstration of the love of God. Nevertheless, his approach to the meaning of the death of Christ brought home the powerful subjective impact of that death, which had been totally ignored by contemporary writers, such as Anselm of Canterbury.

With the rise of the Enlightenment worldview, increasingly critical approaches were adopted to theories of the atonement which incorporated transcendent elements – such as the idea of a sacrifice which had some impact upon God, or Christ dying in order to pay some penalty or satisfaction which was due for sin. The increasingly skeptical attitude to the resurrection associated with the Enlightenment tended to discourage theologians from incorporating this element into their theologies of atonement with anything even approaching the enthusiasm of earlier generations. As a result, the emphasis of theologians sympathetic to the Enlightenment came to focus upon the cross itself.

However, many Enlightenment theologians also had difficulties with the "two natures" doctrine. The form of Christology which perhaps expresses the spirit of the Enlightenment most faithfully is a degree Christology – that is to say, a Christology which recognizes a difference of degree, but not of nature, between Christ and other human beings. Jesus Christ was recognized as embodying certain qualities which were present, actually or potentially, in all other human beings, the difference lying in the superior extent to which he embodied them.

When such considerations are applied to theories of atonement, a consistent pattern begins to emerge. This can be studied from the writings of G. S. Steinbart, I. G. Töllner, G. F. Seiler, and K. G. Bretschneider. Its basic features can be summarized as follows.

1   The cross has no transcendent reference or value; its value relates directly to its impact upon humanity. Thus the cross represents a "sacrifice" only in that it represents Christ giving up his life.
2   The person who died upon the cross was a human being, and the impact of that death is upon human beings. That impact takes the form of inspiration and encouragement to model ourselves upon the moral example set us in Jesus himself.
3   The most important aspect of the cross is that it demonstrates the love of God toward us.

This approach became enormously influential in rationalist circles throughout nineteenth-century Europe. The mystery and apparent irrationalism of the cross had been neutralized; what remained was a powerful and dramatic plea for the moral improvement of humanity, modeled on the lifestyle and attitudes of Jesus Christ. The model of a martyr, rather than a savior, describes the attitude increasingly adopted toward Jesus within such circles.

The most significant challenge to this rationalist approach to the cross was expressed by F. D. E. Schleiermacher, who insisted upon the *religious* – as opposed to purely moral – value of the death of Christ. Christ did not die to make or endorse a moral system; he came in order that the supremacy of the consciousness of God could be established in humanity. Schleiermacher argues that redemption consists in the stimulation and elevation of the natural human God-consciousness through the "entrance of the living influence of Christ." He attributes to Christ "an absolutely powerful God-consciousness." This, he argues, possesses an assimilative power of such intensity that it is able to bring about the redemption of humanity.

Schleiermacher seems to have in mind something like the model of a charismatic political leader, who is able to communicate his vision with such clarity and power that it is both understood by his audience, and also captivates them in such a way that they are transformed by it, and come to be caught up in it. Yet it remains his idea; he has assumed others into it, without compromising his personal unique-ness, in that it is and remains *his* vision:

> Let us now suppose that some person for the first time combines a naturally cohesive group into a civil community (legend tells of such cases in plenty); what happens is that the idea of the state first comes to consciousness in him, and takes possession of his personality as its immediate dwelling-place. Then he assumes the rest into the living fellowship of the idea. He does so by making them clearly conscious of the unsatisfactoriness of their present condition by effective speech. The power remains with the founder of forming in them the idea which is the innermost principle of his own life, and of assuming them into the fellowship of that life.

Yet this is not exemplarism, in the strict sense of the word. Two central German terms – *Urbildlichkeit* and *Vorbildlichkeit* – are employed by Schleiermacher in exploring this question, both of which are dif-ficult to adequately translate into English.

1 *Urbildlichkeit* may be rendered as "the quality of being an ideal." For Schleiermacher, Jesus of Nazareth is the ideal of human God-consciousness, and the ultimate in human piety (*Frömmigkeit*). Taken on its own, this notion might seen to come close to the rationalist notion of Jesus as a human moral example. Scheliermacher is able to evade this, in two ways. First, he stresses that Jesus of Nazareth is not simply a moral example, someone who illustrates permanent moral truths. He is the one ideal example of a perfect human consciousness of God – a *religious*, rather than a purely moral or rational idea. Second, Christ possesses the ability to communicate this God-consciousness to others, as noted above – a quality which Schleiermacher discusses in terms of *Vorbildlichkeit*.

2 *Vorbildlichkeit* may be translated as "the quality of being able to evoke his ideal in others." Jesus of Nazareth is not simply the instantiation of an ideal, but one who possesses an ability to evoke or arouse this quality in others.

On the basis of this approach, Schleiermacher criticizes existing manners of conceiving the person of Christ. For Enlightenment writers, Jesus of Nazareth was merely a religious teacher of humanity, or perhaps the exemplar of a religious or moral principle. As noted earlier, this does not mean that Jesus established such principles or teachings; their authority lies in their being recognized to be consonant with rational ideas and values. The authority of Jesus is thus derivative and secondary, while that of reason is immediate and primary. Schleiermacher designates this as an "empirical" understanding of the work of Christ, which "attributes a redemptive activity on the part of Christ, but one which is held to consist only in bringing about an increasing perfection in us, and which cannot take place other than by teaching and example." Nevertheless, Schleiermacher was – and is – often represented as teaching a view of the atonement as *Lebenserhöhung*, a kind of moral elevation of life. His distinctive ideas ultimately proved to be capable of being assimilated to purely exemplarist understandings, rather than posing a coherent challenge to them.

The most significant statement of an exemplarist approach in England is to be found in the 1915 Bampton Lectures of the noted modernist Hastings Rashdall (see pp. 96–7). In these lectures, Rashdall launched a vigorous attack on traditional approaches to the atonement. The only interpretation of the cross which was adequate for the needs of the modern age was that already associated with the medieval writer Peter Abelard:

> The church's early creed, "There is none other name given among men by which we may be saved" may be translated so as to be something of this kind: "There is none other ideal given among men by which we may be saved, except the moral ideal which Christ taught us by his words, and illustrated by his life and death of love."

Although Abelard did not actually hold precisely the opinions which Rashdall attributed to him, Rashdall's argument is independent of this fact. In an age which had discovered both Darwinianism and biblical criticism, there was no longer any place for any understanding of Christ's death which was based upon an objective notion of sin or divine punishment. Other later English writers who adopted similar or related approaches include G. W. H. Lampe and John Hick. In his essay "The Atonement: Law and Love," contributed to the liberal Catholic volume *Soundings*, Lampe launched a fierce attack on legal approaches to his subject, before commending an exemplarist approach based on "the paradox and miracle of love."

The position of John Hick is of especial interest, in that it relates to the place of the work of Christ in inter-faith dialogue. The religious pluralist agenda has certain important theological consequences. Traditional Christian theology does not lend itself particularly well to the homogenizing agenda of religious pluralists (see pp. 462–3). The suggestion that all religions are more or less talking about vaguely the same thing finds itself in difficulty in relation to certain essentially Christian ideas – most notably, the doctrines of the incarnation, atonement, and the Trinity. The suggestion that something unique is made possible or available through the death of Christ is held to belittle non-Christian religions.

In response to this pressure, a number of major Christological and theological developments may be noted. Doctrines such as the incarnation, which imply a high profile of identification between Jesus Christ and God, are discarded, in favor of various degree Christologies, which are more amenable to the reductionist program of liberalism. This has important implications for soteriology, as will become clear. A sharp distinction is drawn between the *historical person* of Jesus Christ, and the *principles* which he is alleged to represent. Paul Knitter is but one of a small galaxy of pluralist writers concerned to drive a wedge between the "Jesus-event" (which is unique to Christianity) and the "Christ-principle" (accessible to all religious traditions, and expressed in their own distinctive, but equally valid, ways). Viewed in this pluralist light, the cross of Christ is thus understood to make known something which is accessible in other manners, and which is a universal religious possibility. Thus Hick argues that the Christ-event is only "one of the points at which God has been and still is creatively at work within human life"; his distinctiveness relates solely to his being a "visible story," and not an "additional truth."

The chief difficulty associated with purely exemplarist approaches to the cross concerns their understanding of human sin. The Enlightenment tended to regard the idea of "sin" as a hangover from a period of superstition, which the modern age could dispense with. If "sin" had any real meaning, it was that of "ignorance concerning the true nature of things." Christ's death was thus treated as the correlative of this notion of sin – the conveying of information concerning God to a confused or ignorant humanity.

However, this idea of sin seemed rather weak and inadequate in the light of the atrocities of World War II, such as Auschwitz. The Enlightenment belief in the fundamental goodness of human nature received a severe setback through such events. A growing anxiety about the plausibility of the Enlightenment view of sin has brought in its wake a growing disenchantment with the Enlightenment notion of "redemption through knowledge" – including exemplarist approaches to the meaning of the death of Christ.

The Nature of Salvation in Christ

As noted earlier, the idea of "salvation" is exceptionally complex. One of the tasks of theology is to provide a critical analysis of the constituent elements of this idea. However, even this project is considerably more complex than it might seem. Different aspects of the Christian understanding of salvation have proved to have especial attraction for different periods of church history, or specific situations, reflecting the manner in which one aspect of this understanding interlocks with the specifics of the situation it addresses.

Recent studies of the theory of Christian mission have laid considerable emphasis upon the importance of *contextualization* and the notion of the *receptor-orientation* of the Christian proclamation. In other words, the Christian gospel is recognized to address specific situations, and to *contextualize* the notion of salvation in those situations. To those who are oppressed, whether spiritually or politically, the gospel message is that of liberation. To those who are burdened by the weight of personal guilt, the "good news" is that of forgiveness and pardon.

The gospel is thus related to the specific situation of its audience – in other words, it is *receptor-oriented*. If any of the following models of salvation were to be regarded as totally constitutive of the Christian understanding of salvation, a severely truncated and reduced gospel would result. In what follows, we shall explore a selection of components of this understanding, and indicate the situations in which they have particular appeal and relevance. However, it must be appreciated that others – such as salvation as moral perfection or deliverance from the transience of this world – could easily be instanced.

Deification

"God became human, in order that humans might become God." This theological refrain may be discerned as underlying much of the soteriological reflection of the eastern Christian tradition, both during the patristic period and in the modern Greek and Russian Orthodox theological traditions. As the citation suggests, there is an especially strong link between the doctrine of the incarnation and this understanding of salvation. For Athanasius, salvation consists in the human participation in the being of God. The divine Logos is imparted to humanity through the incarnation. On the basis of the assumption of a universal human nature, Athanasius concluded that the Logos did not merely assume the specific human existence of Jesus Christ, but that of human nature in general. As a consequence, all human beings are able to share in the deification which results from the incarnation. Human nature was created with the object of sharing in the being of God; through the descent of the Logos, this capacity is finally realized.

A distinction must be drawn between the idea of deification as "becoming God" (*theosis*) and as "becoming like God" (*homoiosis theoi*). The first, associated with the Alexandrian school, conceives of deification as a union with the substance of God; the second, associated with the Antiochene school, interprets the believer's relationship with God more in terms of a participation in that which is divine, often conceived in terms of ethical perfection. The distinction between these approaches is subtle, and reflects significantly different Christologies.

Righteousness in the Sight of God

"How do I find a gracious God?" Martin Luther's question has resonated down the centuries for those who shared his heartfelt conviction that sinners could not hope to find acceptance in the sight of a righteous God. For Luther, the question of salvation came to be linked with the issue of how guilt-ridden humans could ever possess a righteousness which would enable them to stand in God's presence. This concern is by no means outdated, as can be seen from C. S. Lewis's words in *Mere Christianity*: "In my most clearsighted moments not only do I not think myself a nice man, but I know that I am a very nasty one. I can look at some of the things I have done with horror and loathing." Such concerns naturally led to the use of legal or forensic categories in relation to the question of justification. For Luther, the gospel offered a justifying righteousness to believers – a righteousness which would shield them from condemnation, and permit them to enter into the presence of God (see pp. 381–3).

Such insights were developed within later Protestant orthodoxy, and achieved a wide circulation in popular Protestant devotional writings and hymns. In a period in which the threat of divine punishment was taken with considerable seriousness (witness Jonathan

Edwards' passionate sermons on this theme), the idea of deliverance from condemnation on account of sin was regarded as of central importance to the gospel. One of the hymns to express this concern for righteousness in the sight of God with particular force is Charles Wesley's "And Can it Be?," the last verse of which includes the following lines:

> No condemnation now I dread;
> Jesus, and all in him, is mine!
> Alive in him, my living head,
> And clothed in righteousness divine.

Authentic Human Existence

The rise of existentialism brought with it a new concern for authentic human existence (pp. 192–4). Existentialism, protesting against the dehumanizing tendency to treat humans as objects devoid of any subjective existence, demanded that attention be paid to the inner lives of individuals. Martin Heidegger's distinction between "authentic existence" and "inauthentic existence" represented an important statement of the bipolar structure of human existence. Two options were open. Rudolf Bultmann, developing such an approach, argued that the New Testament spoke of two possible modes of human existence: An authentic or redeemed existence, characterized by faith in God, and an inauthentic existence, characterized by being fettered to the transient material order. For Bultmann, Christ made possible and available, through the *kerygma*, authentic existence.

Bultmann does not entirely reduce salvation to the notion of "authentic existence," as if Christianity related solely to the experiential world of individuals. However, the emphasis which he placed upon this notion tended to create the impression that this was the sum total of the "salvation" offered through the gospel. A related approach was developed by Paul Tillich, using a slightly different set of terms. Within the context of Tillich's system, "salvation" does indeed seem to be reduced to little more than a general human philosophy of existence, offering insights to those who are aware of tensions within their personal existence. This outlook has been criticized by many concerned with the transcendent elements of salvation, as well as those wishing to draw attention to the political and social aspects of the Christian gospel, such as liberation theology.

Political Liberation

Latin American liberation theology places considerable emphasis upon the idea of salvation as liberation (see pp. 105–7). The title of Leonardo Boff's *Jesus Christ Liberator* makes this point forcefully. Salvation is here contextualized in the political world of Latin America, including its radical and pervasive poverty, and the struggle for social and political justice. God is seen to side with the exploited peoples of the world, as in the deliverance of Israel from captivity and oppression under Pharaoh. Similarly, Jesus appears to have expressed and exercised a preferential option for the poor in his teaching and ministry. Jesus Christ brings liberation, through both his teaching and his lifestyle.

Liberation theology has been criticized for viewing both the figure of Jesus and the concept of salvation in the light of a predetermined interpretive grid derived from the Latin American context. However, all Christologies and soteriologies are vulnerable to this charge. For example, the writers of the Enlightenment interpreted both the person and the work of Jesus Christ in terms of a predetermined framework, derived in part from the middle-class European context in which most of them existed, and partly from the severely rationalist outlook characteristic of the movement. Equally, it can be argued that the Greek patristic writers tended to view Christ through a Hellenistic prism, which had significant consequences for their Christologies and soteriologies. However, the criticism just noted has validity, if the understanding of either the person or the work of Christ is *reduced* to a purely political or social conception of liberation.

Spiritual Freedom

The *Christus victor* approach to the death and resurrection of Christ lays considerable emphasis upon the notion of Christ's victory over forces which enslave humanity – such as satanic oppression, evil spirits, fear of death, or the power of sin. The early patristic writers had little difficulty in regarding these forces as real oppressive and hostile presences in the everyday world. In consequence, the proclamation of liberty from their oppression through the cross and resurrection of Christ came to be of central importance, as can be seen from the Easter homilies of writers such as John Chrystostom. Similar ideas can be shown to be prominent in the popular devotional and spiritual writings of the Middle Ages. Martin Luther continued this tradition, placing considerable emphasis upon the objective power of Satan in the world, and the liberation resulting from the gospel.

With the rise of the Enlightenment worldview, belief in objective evil spirits or a personal devil became increasingly problematic. Writers sympathetic to the Enlightenment generally dismissed such beliefs as outmoded superstitions which had no place in the modern world. If the idea of "salvation as victory" was to remain current, it would have to be reinterpreted. Such a process can be seen taking place in the writings of Paul Tillich, where salvation is understood in terms of a victory over *subjective* forces which enslave humanity and trap it in inauthentic modes of existence. What the patristic writers treated as objective forces were thus treated as subjective or existential.

The Scope of Salvation in Christ

The Christian tradition has witnessed intense debate over the extent of the salvation which is made available and possible through Christ. Two central assumptions, both of which are deeply grounded in the New Testament, may be discerned as exercising a controlling influence over this discussion:

1   The affirmation of the universal saving will of God.
2   The affirmation that salvation is possible only in and through Christ.

The various approaches to the scope of salvation rest upon different manners of resolving the dialectic between these assumptions.

An important parallel should be noted here between the discussion of the scope of salvation and the relation of Christianity to other religions, to be discussed at greater length in chapter 15.

Universalism: All will be Saved

The view that all people will be saved, irrespective of whether they have heard or responded to the Christian proclamation of redemption in Christ, has exerted a powerful influence within the Christian tradition. It represents a powerful affirmation of the universal saving will of God, and its ultimate actualization in the universal redemption of all people. Its most significant early exponent was Origen, who defended the idea at length in his *De principis* ("First principles"). Origen was deeply suspicious of any form of dualism – that is, any belief system which acknowledged the existence of two supreme powers, one good and one evil. This belief was characteristic of many forms of Gnosticism, and was very influential in the eastern Mediterranean world in the late second century.

Arguing that dualism was fatally flawed, Origen pointed out that this had important implications for the Christian doctrine of salvation. To reject dualism is to reject the idea that God and Satan rule over their respective kingdoms for eternity. In the end, God will overcome evil, and restore creation to its original form. In its original form, creation was subject to the will of God. It therefore follows, on the basis of this "restorationist" soteriology, that the final redeemed version of creation cannot include anything along the lines of "a hell" or "a kingdom of Satan." All "will be restored to their condition of happiness . . . in order that the human race . . . may be restored to that unity promised by the Lord Jesus Christ."

Related ideas have been developed in the twentieth century, most notably by Karl Barth. We shall explore his approach elsewhere in the context of his doctrine of predestination, to allow the relation of his doctrines of salvation and grace to be appreciated more fully (pp. 400–2). A different approach may be found in the writings of John A. T. Robinson, a radical English theologian active in the 1960s, especially in his *In the End God* (1968). In this book, Robinson considers the nature of the love of God. "May we not imagine a love so strong that ultimately no one will be able to restrain himself from free and grateful surrender?" This notion of omnipotent love functions as the central idea of Robinson's universalism. In the end, love will conquer all, making the existence of hell an impossibility. "In a universe of love there can be no heaven which tolerates a chamber of horrors."

Only Believers will be Saved

The position to be discussed in this section is one of the most influential positions in relation to the scope of salvation. Its most vigorous defender in the early church was Augustine, who consciously distanced himself from the universalism associated with Origen by stressing the need for faith as a precondition for salvation. In doing so, Augustine cited a large number of New Testament passages which emphasize the conditionality of salvation or eternal life upon faith. A classic example of such a text is John 6: 51, in which Christ refers to himself as a bread which, if eaten, will bring eternal life. "I am the living bread that came down from heaven. If anyone eats of this bread, they will live for ever. This bread is my flesh, which I will give for the life of the world."

This position was maintained by most writers of the Middle Ages.

Thomas Aquinas argued that an act of faith was a necessary condition of salvation. This view is echoed in many popular devotional writings of the period, including the highly sophisticated *Divine Comedy* of Dante Aligheri. In canto 19 of *Paradise* (the third and final part of the trilogy), Dante deals with the question of what happens to those who die without having heard or responded in faith to the Christian proclamation. The answer given is subtle, and appears to rest upon the affirmation of the need of faith in Christ:

> To this high empery
> none ever rose but through belief in Christ
> either before or after his agony.

One of the most vigorous defenders of this position at the time of the Reformation was John Calvin, who dismissed the views of his fellow reformer Huldrych Zwingli to the effect that pious pagans could attain salvation. "All the more vile is the stupidity of those people who open heaven to all the impious and unbelieving, without the grace of him whom Scripture teaches to be the only door by which we enter into salvation."

So what do such writers make of the biblical assertions that God wishes all to be saved, and all to come to a knowledge of the truth? Augustine and Calvin argue that such texts are to be interpreted sociologically: God wishes *all kinds of people* – but not *all people* – to be saved. Redemption embraces all nationalities, cultures, languages, geographical regions, and walks of life. This is the soteriological equivalent of the doctrine of the catholicity of the church, to be considered later.

However, a number of modified versions of this approach should be noted. For example, is it necessary to have a fully *Christian* faith in God in order to be saved? This question is of major importance in relation to an understanding of mission and evangelism, and also of the relation of Christianity to other religions. In his sermon "On Faith," John Wesley argued for the need for faith in God in order to be saved – but affirmed that this faith need not be explicitly Christian in character. The requirement for salvation is "such a divine conviction of God, and the things of God, as, even in its infant state, enables every one that possesses it to fear God and work righteousness. And whosoever, in every nation, believes thus far, the Apostle declares is accepted." What, then, is the advantage of a specifically Christian belief, as opposed to this more general theistic belief? According to Wesley, two differences may be noted. First, such people have yet to attain the full benefits of the redeemed life. They are "servants of

God" but not "sons of God." Second, they do not have full assurance of salvation, which is only possible on the basis of Christ.

A similar position is associated with the twentieth-century literary critic and apologist C. S. Lewis. In his *Mere Christianity*, Lewis argues that those who commit themselves to the pursuit of goodness and truth will be saved, even if they have no formal knowledge of Christ. Although Lewis has philosophers in mind, he extends his approach to include other religions. "There are people in other religions who are being led by God's secret influence to concentrate on those parts of their religion which are in agreement with Christianity, and who thus belong to Christ without knowing it." There are clear parallels here with the writings of the Jesuit theologian Karl Rahner, to be discussed later (pp. 461–2).

Particular Redemption: Only the Elect will be Saved

A final approach which should be noted is variously termed "limited atonement" or "particular redemption." This has Reformed associations, and is particularly influential in such circles in the United States. The basis of the doctrine lies in the Reformed doctrine of predestination, to be discussed in the next chapter. However, its historical origins can be discerned in the ninth century, in the writings of Godescalc of Orbais (also known as Gottschalk). Godescalc argued along the following lines. Let us suppose that Christ died for all people. But not all people will be saved. Therefore it follows that Christ died to no effect for those who are not saved. This raises the gravest of questions concerning the efficacy of his death. But if Christ died only for those who are to be saved, he will have succeeded in his mission in every case. Therefore Christ died only for those who are to be saved.

Related lines of argument can be discerned in the later sixteenth century, and especially during the seventeenth century. The doctrine which emerged at this time, especially within Puritan circles, can be summarized as follows: Christ died only for the elect. Although his death is sufficient to achieve the redemption of all people, it is effective only for the elect. As a result, Christ's work was not in vain. All those for whom he died are saved. Although this approach has a logical coherence to it, its critics tend to regard it as compromising the New Testament's affirmation of the universality of God's love and redemption.

The present chapter has explored central aspects of the Christian doctrine of salvation, demonstrating both the richness and the variety of Christian thinking on the subject. It is clear that there is a close connection between the doctrine of salvation and that of grace, especially in relation to predestination. For this reason, we shall now move on to consider these, and related, matters in more detail.

Questions for Chapter 11

1   How are Christian understandings of the person of Christ related to understandings of the work of Christ?

2   Assess the importance of one of the following approaches to the meaning of the cross: a victory over sin and death; forgiveness of sin; a demonstration of the love of God toward humanity.

3   From what are we saved?

4   Is a human response to salvation necessary?

5   How are the cross and resurrection related in Christian understandings of salvation?

12

The Doctrines of Human Nature, Sin, and Grace

The previous chapter considered the foundations of the Christian doctrine of salvation, paying particular attention to the basis and nature of salvation. A series of issues relating to salvation remain to be addressed: What must human beings do in order to share in the salvation which is made known and made available through Christ's death upon the cross? The issues which this question raises are traditionally discussed under the general heading of "the doctrine of grace," which embraces an understanding of human nature and sin, as well as the role of God in salvation. There is the closest of connections within the Christian tradition between the doctrine of salvation on the one had, and that of grace on the other. We have already explored some aspects of these doctrines in earlier discussions; it is now time to explore them at greater length individually.

The Place of Humanity within Creation

The Christian tradition, basing itself largely upon the accounts of creation found in the book of Genesis, has insisted that humanity is the height of God's creation, set over and above the animal kingdom. The theological justification of this rests largely upon the doctrine of creation in the image of God, to which we now turn.

A text of central importance to a Christian understanding of human nature is Genesis 1: 27, which speaks of humanity being made in God's image – an idea which is often expressed with reference to the Latin slogan *imago Dei*. What does this affirmation mean? Especially during the patristic period, the idea was interpreted in terms of human reason. The "image of God" is the human rational faculty, which here mirrors the wisdom of God. Augustine argues that it is this faculty which distinguishes humanity from the animal kingdom: "We ought therefore to cultivate in ourselves the faculty through which we are superior to the beasts, and to reshape it in some way. . . . So let us therefore use our intelligence . . . to judge our behavior." It should be emphasized that Augustine does not use this theological premise to justify the human exploitation of animals, as has sometimes been suggested. Augustine's point is that the central distinctive element of human nature is its God-given ability to relate to God. Although human reason has been corrupted by the fall, it may be renewed by grace: "For after original sin, humanity is renewed in the knowledge of God according to the image of its creator."

The fact that humanity is created in the image of God is widely regarded as establishing the original uprightness and dignity of human nature. Thus Greek patristic writers emphasize the state of blessedness enjoyed by Adam and Eve in the garden of Eden. Athanasius taught that God created human beings in the image of God, thus endowing humanity with a capacity which was granted to no other creature – that of being able to relate to and partake in the life of God. This fellowship with the Logos is seen at its most perfect in Eden, when Adam enjoyed a perfect relation with God. However, things went wrong. Athanasius stresses that Adam and Eve could only enjoy a perfect relationship with God as long as they were not distracted by the material world. For the Cappadocians, the fact that Adam was created in the image of God meant that he was free from all the normal weaknesses and disabilities which subsequently afflicted human nature – such as death.

Cyril of Jerusalem emphasized that there was no need for Adam or Eve to fall from this state of grace. The fall took place as a result of their decision to turn away from God to the material world. As a result, the image of God in human nature has been defaced and disfigured. In that all of humanity traces its origins to Adam and Eve, he argued, it follows that all humanity shares in this defacement of the image of God.

However, the Greek patristic writers did not express this fall in terms of a doctrine of original sin, such as that which would later be associated with Augustine. Most Greek writers insisted that sin arises from an abuse of the human free will. Gregory of Nazianzen and Gregory of Nyssa both taught that infants are born without sin, an idea which stands in contrast with Augustine's doctrine of the universal sinfulness of fallen humanity. Chrysostom, commenting on Paul's assertion that the many were made sinners through the disobedience of Adam (Romans 5: 19), interprets the passage to mean

that all are made *liable* to punishment and death. The idea of transmitted *guilt*, a central feature of Augustine's later doctrine of original
sin, is totally absent from the Greek patristic tradition.

Nevertheless, aspects of Augustine's notion of original sin can be
discerned in the writings of the period. The Oxford patristic scholar J.
N. D. Kelly identifies three areas in which a notion of "original sin"
can be discerned in the Greek patristic tradition.

1 All humanity is understood to be involved, in some manner,
   in the disobedience of Adam. A strong sense of the mystical
   unity of all humanity with Adam can be discerned within the
   writings of this period. All of humanity is somehow wounded
   by Adam's disobedience.
2 The fall of Adam is understood to affect the human moral
   nature. All human moral weaknesses, including lust and
   greed, can be put down to Adam's sin.
3 Adam's sin is often represented as being transmitted, in some
   undefined manner, to his posterity. Gregory of Nyssa speaks
   of a predisposition to sin within human nature, which can be
   put down, at least in part, to the sin of Adam.

It is, however, during the Pelagian debate, to which we will now turn,
that the issues of this chapter were first debated at length during the
patristic period.

The Pelagian Controversy

The Pelagian controversy, which erupted in the early fifth century,
brought a cluster of questions concerning human nature, sin, and
grace into sharp focus. Up to this point, there had been relatively little
controversy within the church over human nature. The Pelagian controversy changed that, and ensured that the issues associated with
human nature were placed firmly on the agenda of the western church.

The controversy centered upon two individuals: Augustine of Hippo
and Pelagius. The controversy is complex, at both the historical and
the theological level, and, given its impact upon western Christian
theology, needs to be discussed at some length. We shall summarize
the main points of the controversy under four heads:

1 the understanding of the "freedom of the will";
2 the understanding of sin;

3   the understanding of grace;
4   the understanding of the grounds of justification.

The "Freedom of the Will"

For Augustine, the total sovereignty of God and genuine human responsibility and freedom must be upheld at one and the same time, if justice is to be done to the richness and complexity of the biblical statements on the matter. To simplify the matter, by denying either the sovereignty of God or human freedom, is to seriously compromise the Christian understanding of the way in which God justifies man. In Augustine's own lifetime, he was obliged to deal with two heresies which simplified and compromised the gospel in this way. Manichaeism was a form of fatalism (to which Augustine himself was initially attracted) which upheld the total sovereignty of God but denied human freedom, while Pelagianism upheld the total freedom of the human will while denying the sovereignty of God. Before developing these points, it is necessary to make some observations concerning the term "free will."

The term "free will" (translating the Latin term *liberum arbitrium*) is not biblical, but derives from Stoicism. It was introduced into western Christianity by the second-century theologian Tertullian. (We noted earlier Tertullian's gift for coining new theological terms: see p. 249). Augustine retained the term, but attempted to restore a more Pauline meaning to it by emphasizing the limitations placed upon the human free will by sin. Augustine's basic ideas can be summarized as follows. First, natural human freedom is affirmed: We do not do things out of any necessity, but as a matter of freedom. Second, human free will has been weakened and incapacitated – but not eliminated or destroyed – through sin. In order for that free will to be restored and healed, it requires the operation of divine grace. Free will really does exist; it is, however, distorted by sin.

In order to explain this point, Augustine deploys a significant analogy. Consider a pair of scales, with two balance pans. One balance pan represents good, and the other evil. If the pans are properly balanced, the arguments in favor of doing good or doing evil could be weighed, and a proper conclusion drawn. The parallel with the human free will is obvious: We weigh up the arguments in favor of doing good and evil, and act accordingly. But what, asks Augustine, if the balance pans are loaded? What happens if someone puts several heavy weights in the balance pan on the side of evil? The scales will still work, but they are seriously biased toward making an evil decision. Augustine argues that this is exactly what has happened to humanity through sin. The human free will is biased toward evil. It really exists, and really can make decisions – just as the loaded scales still work. But instead of giving a balanced judgment, a serious bias exists toward evil. Using this and related analogies Augustine argues that the human free will really exists in sinners, but that it is compromised by sin.

For Pelagius and his followers (such as Julian of Eclanum), however, humanity possessed total freedom of the will, and was totally responsible for its own sins. Human nature was essentially free and well created, and was not compromised or incapacitated by some mysterious weakness. According to Pelagius, any imperfection in man would reflect negatively upon the goodness of God. For God to intervene in any direct way to influence human decisions was equivalent to compromising human integrity. Going back to the analogy of the scales, the Pelagians argued that the human free will was like a pair of balance pans in perfect equilibrium, and not subject to any bias whatsoever. There was no need for divine grace in the sense understood by Augustine (although Pelagius did have a quite distinct concept of grace, as we shall see later).

In 413, Pelagius wrote a lengthy letter to Demetrias, who had recently decided to turn her back on wealth in order to become a nun. In this letter, Pelagius spelled out with remorseless logic the consequences of his views on human free will. God has made humanity, and knows precisely what it is capable of doing. Hence all the commands given to us are capable of being obeyed, and are meant to be obeyed. It is no excuse to argue that human frailty prevents these commands from being fulfilled. God has made human nature, and only demands of it what it can endure. Pelagius thus makes the uncompromising assertion that "since perfection is possible for humanity, it is obligatory." The moral rigor of this position, and its unrealistic view of human nature, served only to strengthen Augustine's hand as he developed the rival understanding of a tender and kindly God attempting to heal and restore wounded human nature.

The Nature of Sin

For Augustine, humanity is universally affected by sin as a consequence of the fall. The human mind has become darkened and weakened by sin. Sin makes it impossible for the sinner to think clearly, and especially to understand higher spiritual truths and ideas. Similarly, as we have seen, the human will has been weakened (but not eliminated) by sin. For Augustine, the simple fact that we are sinners means that we are in the position of being seriously ill, and

unable to diagnose our own illness adequately, let alone cure it. It is
through the grace of God alone that our illness is diagnosed (sin), and
a cure made available (grace).

The essential point which Augustine makes is that we have no
control over our sinfulness. It is something which contaminates our
lives from birth, and dominates our lives thereafter. It is a state over
which we have no decisive control. We could say that Augustine
understands humanity to be born with a sinful disposition as part of
human nature, with an inherent bias toward acts of sinning. In other
words, sin causes sins: The state of sinfulness causes individual acts of
sin. Augustine develops this point with reference to three important
analogies: original sin as a "disease," as a "power," and as "guilt."

1 The first analogy treats sin as a hereditary disease, which is
passed down from one generation to another. As we saw above, this
disease weakens humanity, and cannot be cured by human agency.
Christ is thus the divine physician, by whose "wounds we are healed"
(Isaiah 53: 5), and salvation is understood in essentially sanative or
medical terms. We are healed by the grace of God, so that our minds
may recognize God and our wills may respond to the divine offer of
grace.
2 The second analogy treats sin as a power which holds us captive, and from whose grip we are unable to break free by ourselves.
The human free will is captivated by the power of sin, and may only
be liberated by grace. Christ is thus seen as the liberator, the source of
the grace which breaks the power of sin.
3 The third analogy treats sin as an essentially judicial or forensic
concept – guilt – which is passed down from one generation to another. In a society which placed a high value on law, such as the
later Roman Empire, in which Augustine lived and worked, this was
regarded as a particularly helpful way of understanding sin. Christ
thus comes to bring forgiveness and pardon.

For Pelagius, however, sin is to be understood in a very different
light. The idea of a human disposition toward sin has no place in
Pelagius' thought. For Pelagius, the human power of self-improvement
could not be thought of as being compromised. It was always possible
for humans to discharge their obligations toward God and their neighbors. Failure to do so could not be excused on any grounds. Sin
was to be understood as an act committed willfully against God.
Pelagianism thus seems to be a rigid form of moral authoritarianism –
an insistence that humanity is under obligation to be sinless, and an
absolute rejection of any excuse for failure. Humanity is born sinless,
and sins only through deliberate actions. Pelagius insisted that many

Old Testament figures actually remained sinless. Only those who were morally upright could be allowed to enter the church – whereas Augustine, with his concept of fallen human nature, was happy to regard the church as a hospital where fallen humanity could recover and grow gradually in holiness through grace (see pp. 409–10).

The Nature of Grace

One of Augustine's favorite biblical texts is John 15: 5, "apart from me you can do nothing." In Augustine's view, we are totally dependent upon God for our salvation, from the beginning to the end of our lives. Augustine draws a careful distinction between the natural human faculties – given to humanity as its natural endowment – and additional and special gifts of grace. God does not leave us where we are naturally, incapacitated by sin and unable to redeem ourselves, but gives us grace in order that we may be healed, forgiven, and restored. Augustine's view of human nature is that it is frail, weak, and lost, and needs divine assistance and care if it is to be restored and renewed. Grace, according to Augustine, is God's generous and quite unmerited attention to humanity, by which this process of healing may begin. Human nature requires transformation through the grace of God, so generously given.

Pelagius used the term "grace" in a very different way. First, grace is to be understood as the natural human faculties. For Pelagius, these are not corrupted or incapacitated or compromised in any way. They have been given to humanity by God, and they are meant to be used. When Pelagius asserted that humanity could, through grace, choose to be sinless, what he meant was that the natural human faculties of reason and will should enable humanity to choose to avoid sin. As Augustine was quick to point out, this is not what the New Testament understands by the term.

Second, Pelagius understood grace to be external enlightenment provided for humanity by God. Pelagius gave several examples of such enlightenment – for example, the Ten Commandments, and the moral example of Jesus Christ. Grace informs us what our moral duties are (otherwise, we would not know what they were); it does not, however, assist us to perform them. We are enabled to avoid sin through the teaching and example of Christ. Augustine argued that this was "to locate the grace of God in the law and in teaching." The New Testament, according to Augustine, envisaged grace as divine assistance to humanity, rather than just moral guidance. For Pelagius, grace was something external and passive, something outside us. Augustine understood grace as the real and redeeming presence of

God in Christ within us, transforming us; something that was internal and active.

For Pelagius, then, God created humanity, and provided information concerning what is right and what is wrong – and then ceased to take any interest in humanity, apart from the final day of judgment. On that day, individuals will be judged according to whether they have fulfilled all their moral obligations in their totality. Failure to have done so will lead to eternal punishment. Pelagius' exhortations to moral perfection are characterized by their emphasis upon the dreadful fate of those who fail in this matter. For Augustine, however, humanity was created good by God, and then fell away from him – and God, in an act of grace, came to rescue fallen humanity from its predicament. God assists us by healing us, enlightening us, strengthening us, and continually working within us in order to restore us. For Pelagius, humanity merely needed to be shown what to do, and could then be left to achieve it unaided; for Augustine, humanity needed to be shown what to do, and then gently aided at every point, if this objective was even to be approached, let alone fulfilled.

The Basis of Salvation

For Augustine, humanity is justified as an act of grace: Even human good works are the result of God working within fallen human nature. Everything leading up to salvation is the free and unmerited gift of God, given out of love for sinners. Through the death and resurrection of Jesus Christ, God is enabled to deal with fallen humanity in this remarkable and generous manner, giving us that which we do not deserve (salvation), and withholding from us that which we do deserve (condemnation).

Augustine's exposition of the parable of the laborers in the vineyard (Matthew 20: 1–10) is of considerable importance in this respect. As we shall see, Pelagius argued that God rewarded each individual strictly on the basis of merit. Augustine, however, pointed out that this parable indicates that the basis of the reward given to the individual is the promise made to that individual. Augustine emphasized that the laborers did not work for equal periods in the vineyard, yet the same wage (a denarius) was given to each. The owner of the vineyard had promised to pay each individual a denarius, providing he worked from the time when he was called to sundown – even though this meant that some worked all day, and others only for an hour.

Augustine thus drew the important conclusion that the basis of our justification is the divine promise of grace made to us. God is faithful to that promise, and thus justifies sinners. Just as the laborers who began work in the vineyard so late in the day had no claim to a full day's wages, except through the generous promise of the owner, so sinners have no claim to justification and eternal life, except through the gracious promises of God, received through faith.

For Pelagius, however, humanity is justified on the basis of its merits: Human good works are the result of the exercise of the totally autonomous human free will, in fulfillment of an obligation laid down by God. A failure to meet this obligation opens the individual to the threat of eternal punishment. Jesus Christ is involved in salvation only to the extent that he reveals, by his actions and teaching, exactly what God requires of the individual. If Pelagius can speak of "salvation in Christ," it is only in the sense of "salvation through imitating the example of Christ."

It will thus be clear that Pelagianism and Augustinianism represent two radically different outlooks, with sharply divergent under-standings of the manner in which God and humanity relate to one another. Augustinianism would eventually gain the upper hand within the western theological tradition; nevertheless, Pelagianism continued to exercise influence over many Christian writers down the ages, not least those who felt that an emphasis upon the doctrine of grace could too easily lead to a devaluation of human freedom and moral responsibility.

The Concepts of Grace and Merit

The repercussions of the Pelagian controversy were considerable. It forced discussion of a number of issues upon the church, especially during the medieval period, in which Augustine's legacy was sub-jected to a process of evaluation and development. Two notions were debated at especial length – grace and merit. The modern discussion of the meaning of both terms may be said to have been initiated by Augustine, in the course of the Pelagian controversy.

At its heart, the term "grace" (*gratia*) has a connection with the idea of "a gift." This idea is taken up by Augustine, who stresses that salvation is a gift from God, rather than a reward. This immediately suggests a tension between the ideas of "grace" and "merit," the former referring to a gift and the latter to a reward. In fact, the question is considerably more complex than this, and merits – if the pun may be excused – careful discussion. In what follows, we shall consider the medieval debate over the meaning of the terms, to illustrate some of the issues at stake, and also as background material to the Reformation debates on the issues.

Grace

Augustine explored the nature of grace using several images, as noted earlier (pp. 373–6). Two may be noted once more in the present context. First, grace is understood as a liberating force, which sets human nature free from its self-incurred bondage to sin. Augustine used the term "the captive free will" (*liberum arbitrium captivatum*) to describe the free will which is so heavily influenced by sin, and argued that grace is able to liberate the human free will from this bias, to give the "liberated free will" (*liberum arbitrium liberatum*). To go back to the scales analogy, grace removes the weights loading the scales toward evil, and allows us to recognize the full weight of the case for choosing God. Thus Augustine was able to argue that grace, far from abolishing or compromising the human free will, actually establishes it.

Second, grace is understood as the healer of human nature. One of Augustine's favorite analogies for the church is that of a hospital, full of sick people. Christians are those who recognize that they are ill, and seek the assistance of a physician, in order that they may be healed. Thus Augustine appeals to the parable of the good Samaritan (Luke 10: 30–4), in suggesting that human nature is like the man who was left for dead by the roadside, until he was rescued and healed by the Samaritan (representing Christ as redeemer, according to Augustine). On the basis of illustrations such as these, Augustine argues that the human free will is unhealthy, and needs healing.

In exploring the functions of grace, Augustine developed three main notions, which have had a major impact upon western theology. The three categories are as follows.

1 *Prevenient grace* The Latin term *preveniens* literally means "going ahead"; in speaking of "prevenient grace," Augustine is defending his characteristic position, that God's grace is active in human lives before conversion. Grace "goes ahead" of humanity, preparing the human will for conversion. Augustine stresses that grace does not become operational in a person's life only after conversion; the process leading up to that conversion is one of preparation, in which the prevenient grace of God is operative.

2 *Operative grace* Augustine stresses that God effects the conversion of sinners without any assistance on their part. Conversion is a purely divine process, in which God operates upon the sinner. The term "operative grace" is used to refer to the manner in which prevenient grace does not rely upon human cooperation for its effects, in contrast with cooperative grace.

3 *Cooperative grace* Having achieved the conversion of the sinner,

God now collaborates with the renewed human will in achieving regeneration and growth in holiness. Having liberated the human will from its bondage to sin, God is now able to cooperate with that liberated will. Augustine uses the term "cooperative grace" to refer to the manner in which grace operates within human nature after conversion.

The theologians of the early Middle Ages were generally content to regard "grace" as a shorthand term for the graciousness or liberality of God. However, increasing pressure for systematization led to the development of an increasingly precise and meticulous vocabulary of grace. The most important statement of the medieval understanding of the nature and purpose of grace is that of Thomas Aquinas. Although Aquinas treats Augustine's analysis of grace with considerable respect, it is clear that he has considerable misgivings concerning its viability. A fundamental distinction is drawn between two different types of grace, as follows.

1 *Actual grace* (often referred to by the Latin slogan *gratia gratis data*, or "grace which is freely given"). Aquinas understands this to mean a series of divine actions or influences upon human nature.

2 *Habitual grace* (often referred to by the Latin slogan *gratia gratis faciens*, or "grace which makes pleasing"). Aquinas understands this to mean a created habit of grace, within the human soul. This notion is difficult, and requires further explanation.

Aquinas argues that there is an enormous gulf between humanity and God. God cannot establish a direct presence within human nature. Instead, an intermediate stage is established, in which the human soul is made ready for the habitation of God. This permanent alteration to the human soul is termed "a habit of grace," where the term "habit" means "something which is permanent." Habitual grace is thus a substance, "something supernatural in the soul." This change in human nature is regarded by Aquinas as the basis of human justification. Something has happened to human nature, which allows it to be acceptable to God. Whereas the reformers would locate the basis of justification in God's gracious favor, by which sinners are accepted in the sight of God, Aquinas argues for the need for an intermediary in the process of being accepted by God – the habit of grace, or "habitual grace."

The idea of "habitual grace" became the subject of considerable criticism in the later Middle Ages. William of Ockham, armed with his "razor," set out to eliminate unnecessary hypotheses from every area of theology. It seemed to him that a habit of grace was totally unnecessary. God was perfectly capable of accepting a sinner directly, without the need for any intermediate stage or intermediate entity. The principle "God can do directly what could otherwise be done through intermediate causes" led Ockham to question the need for habitual grace. So persuasive was his argument that, by the end of the fifteenth century, the notion was widely regarded as discredited. Grace increasingly came to be understood as "the gracious favor of God" – that is, as a divine attitude, rather than as a substance.

Merit

The Pelagian controversy drew attention to the question of whether salvation was a reward for good behavior, or a free gift of God (see pp. 371–7). The debate indicated the importance of clarifying what the term "merit" actually meant. Once more, it was the medieval period which saw clarification of the term. By the time of Thomas Aquinas, the following points had been generally agreed.

1   There is no way in which human beings can claim salvation as a "reward," on the basis of strict justice. Salvation is an act of God's grace, in which sinners are enabled to gain something which would otherwise lie completely beyond them. Left to their own devices, humanity would be unable to achieve their own salvation. The view that humans could earn their salvation through their own achievements was rejected as Pelagianism.

2   Sinners cannot earn salvation, in that there is nothing which they can achieve or perform which obliges God to reward them with faith or justification. The beginning of the Christian life is a matter of grace alone. However, although the grace of God *operates* on sinners to achieve their conversion, it subsequently *cooperates* with them to bring about their growth in holiness. And this cooperation leads to merit, by which God rewards the moral actions of believers.

3   A distinction is drawn between two kinds of merit: *congruous* and *condign* merit. Condign merit is a merit which is justified on the basis of the moral actions of the individual in question; congruous merit is based upon the liberality of God.

Despite this general consensus, a debate developed during the later Middle Ages over the ultimate ground of merit, with two rival positions being distinguishable. The debate illustrates the growing influence of voluntarism in the later Middle Ages. The older position, which can be described as *intellectualist*, is represented by writers such as Thomas Aquinas. Aquinas argued for a direct proportional representation between the moral and the meritorious value of an action on the part of a believer. The divine intellect recognizes the inherent value of an action, and rewards it accordingly.

In contrast, the *voluntarist* approach, represented by William of Ockham, placed the emphasis upon the divine will. God determines the meritorious value of an action, by an act of divine will. For Ockham, the intellectualist approach compromised the freedom of God, in that God was placed under an obligation to reward a moral action with a meritorious response. In defending the divine freedom, Ockham argued that God had to be free to reward a human action in any way that seemed fit. There was thus no direct link between the moral and the meritorious value of a human action. To his critics, Ockham seemed to have snapped the connection between human and divine notions of justice and fairness – an issue to which we shall return when we consider the issue of predestination, which brings the role of the will of God into full focus.

Our attention now turns to the great controversy which engulfed the church at the time of the Reformation, centering upon the doctrine of justification by faith.

The Doctrine of Justification by Faith

At the heart of the Christian faith lies the idea that human beings, finite and frail though they be, can enter into a relationship with the living God. As we have seen, this idea is articulated in a number of metaphors or images, such as "salvation" and "redemption," initially in the writings of the New Testament (especially the Pauline letters) and subsequently in Christian theological reflection, based upon these texts. By the late Middle Ages, one image had come to be seen as especially significant: justification.

The term "justification" and the verb "to justify" came to signify "entering into a right relationship with God," or perhaps "being made righteous in the sight of God." The doctrine of justification came to be seen as dealing with the question of what an individual had to do in order to be saved. As contemporary sources indicate, this question came to be asked with increasing frequency as the sixteenth century dawned. The rise of humanism brought with it a new emphasis upon individual consciousness, and a new awareness of human individuality. In the wake of this dawn of the individual consciousness came a new interest in the doctrine of justification – the question of how human beings, *as individuals*, could enter into a relationship with

God. How could a sinner hope to do this? This question lay at the heart of the theological concerns of Martin Luther, and came to dominate the early phase of the Reformation. In view of the importance of the doctrine to this period, we shall consider it in some detail, beginning with Luther's discussion of the doctrine.

Martin Luther's Theological Breakthrough

In 1545, the year before he died, Luther contributed a preface to the first volume of the complete edition of his Latin writings, in which he described how he came to break with the church of his day. The preface was clearly written with the aim of introducing Luther to a readership which may not know how Luther came to hold the radical reforming views linked with his name. In this "autobiographical fragment" (as it is usually known), Luther aimed to provide those readers with background information about the development of his vocation as a reformer. After dealing with some historical preliminaries, taking his narrative up to the year 1519, he turned to describe his personal difficulties with the problem of the "righteousness of God":

> I had certainly wanted to understand Paul in his letter to the Romans. But what prevented me from doing so was not so much cold feet as that one phrase in the first chapter: "the righteousness of God is revealed in it" (Romans 1: 17). For I hated that phrase, "the righteousness of God," which I had been taught to understand as the righteousness by which God is righteous, and punishes unrighteous sinners. Although I lived a blameless life as a monk, I felt that I was a sinner with an uneasy conscience before God. I also could not believe that I had pleased him with my works. Far from loving that righteous God who punished sinners, I actually hated him . . . I was in desperation to know what Paul meant in this passage. At last, as I meditated day and night on the relation of the words "the righteousness of God is revealed in it, as it is written, the righteous person shall live by faith," I began to understand that "righteousness of God" as that by which the righteous person lives by the gift of God (faith); and this sentence, "the righteousness of God is revealed," to refer to a passive righteousness, by which the merciful God justifies us by faith, as it is written, "the righteous person lives by faith." This immediately made me feel as though I had been born again, and as though I had entered through open gates into paradise itself. From that moment, I saw the whole face of Scripture in a new light . . . And now, where I had once hated the phrase, "the righteousness of God," I began to love and extol it as the sweetest of phrases, so that this passage in Paul became the very gate of paradise to me.

What is Luther talking about in this famous passage, which vibrates with the excitement of discovery? It is obvious that his understanding of the phrase "the righteousness of God" has changed radically. But what is the nature of this change?

The basic change is fundamental. Originally Luther regarded the precondition for justification as a human work, something which the sinner had to perform, before he or she could be justified. Increasingly convinced, through his reading of Augustine, that this was an impossibility, Luther could only interpret the "righteousness of God" as a *punishing* righteousness. But in this passage, he narrates how he discovered a "new" meaning of the phrase – a righteousness which God *gives* to the sinner. In other words, God himself meets the precondition, graciously giving sinners what they require if they are to be justified. An analogy (not used by Luther) may help bring out the difference between these two approaches.

Let us suppose that you are in prison, and are offered your freedom on condition that you pay a heavy fine. The promise is real – so long as you can meet the precondition, the promise will be fulfilled. As we noted earlier, Pelagius works on the presupposition, initially shared by Luther, that you have the necessary money stacked away somewhere. As your freedom is worth far more, you are being offered a bargain. So you pay the fine. This presents no difficulties, so long as you have the necessary resources. Luther increasingly came to share the view of Augustine – that sinful humanity just doesn't have the resources needed to meet this precondition. To go back to our analogy, Augustine and Luther work on the assumption that, as you don't have the money, the promise of freedom has little relevance to your situation. For both Augustine and Luther, therefore, the good news of the gospel is that you have been *given* the necessary money with which to buy your freedom. In other words, the precondition has been met for you by someone else.

Luther's insight, which he describes in this autobiographical passage, is that the God of the Christian gospel is not a harsh judge who rewards individuals according to their merits, but a merciful and gracious God who bestows righteousness upon sinners as a gift. The general consensus amongst Luther scholars is that his theology of justification underwent a decisive alteration at some point in 1515.

Luther on Justifying Faith

Central to Luther's insights was the doctrine of "justification by faith alone." The idea of "justification" is already familiar. But what about the phrase "by faith alone"? What is the nature of justifying faith?

"The reason why some people do not understand why faith alone justifies is that they do not know what faith is." In writing these words, Luther draws our attention to the need to inquire more closely concerning that deceptively simple word "faith." Three points relating to Luther's idea of faith may be singled out as having special importance to his doctrine of justification. Each of these points was taken up and developed by later writers, such as Calvin, indicating that Luther made a fundamental contribution to the development of Reformation thought at this point. These three points are:

1 Faith has a personal, rather than a purely historical, reference.
2 Faith concerns trust in the promises of God.
3 Faith unites the believer to Christ.

We shall consider each of these points individually.

1 First, faith is not simply historical knowledge. Luther argues that a faith which is content to believe in the historical reliability of the gospels is not a faith which justifies. Sinners are perfectly capable of trusting in the historical details of the gospels; but these facts of themselves are not adequate for true Christian faith. Saving faith involves believing and trusting that Christ was born *pro nobis*, born for us personally, and has accomplished for us the work of salvation.

2 Second, faith is to be understood as "trust" (*fiducia*). The notion of trust is prominent in the Reformation conception of faith, as a nautical analogy used by Luther indicates. "Everything depends upon faith. The person who does not have faith is like someone who has to cross the sea, but is so frightened that he does not trust the ship. And so he stays where he is, and is never saved, because he will not get on board and cross over." Faith is not merely believing that something is true; it is being prepared to act upon that belief, and relying upon it. To use Luther's analogy: Faith is not simply about believing that a ship exists – it is about stepping into it, and entrusting ourselves to it.

3 In the third place, faith unites the believer with Christ. Luther stated this principle clearly in his 1520 work, *The Liberty of a Christian*, cited earlier in this connection (p. 128). Faith is not assent to an abstract set of doctrines, but is a union between Christ and the believer. It is the response of the whole person of the believer to God, which leads in turn to the real and personal presence of Christ in the believer. "To know Christ is to know his benefits," wrote Philip Melanchthon, Luther's colleague at Wittenberg. Faith makes both Christ and his benefits – such as forgiveness, justification, and hope – available to the believer.

The doctrine of "justification by faith" thus does not mean that the sinner is justified because he or she believes, on account of that faith. This would be to treat faith as a human action or work. Luther insists that God provides everything necessary for justification, so that all that the sinner needs to do is to receive it. God is active, and humans are passive, in justification. The phrase "justification *by* grace *through* faith" brings out the meaning of the doctrine more clearly: The justification of the sinner is based upon the grace of God, and is received through faith. The doctrine of justification by faith alone is an affirmation that God does everything necessary for salvation. Even faith itself is a gift of God, rather than a human action. God himself meets the precondition for justification. Thus, as we saw, the "righteousness of God" is not a righteousness which judges whether or not we have met the precondition for justification, but the righteousness which is given to us so that we may meet that precondition.

The Notion of Forensic Justification

One of the central insights of Luther's doctrine of justification by faith alone is that the individual sinner is incapable of self-justification. It is God who takes the initiative in justification, providing all the resources necessary to justify that sinner. One of those resources is the "righteousness of God." In other words, the righteousness on the basis of which the sinner is justified is not his own righteousness, but a righteousness which is given to him by God. Augustine had made this point earlier: Luther, however, gives it a subtle new twist, which leads to the development of the concept of "forensic justification."

The point at issue is difficult to explain, and centers on the question of the location of justifying righteousness. Both Augustine and Luther are agreed that God graciously gives sinful humans a righteousness which justifies them. But where is that righteousness located? Augustine argued that it was to be found within believers; Luther insisted that it remained outside believers. For Augustine, the righteousness in question is internal; for Luther, it is external.

For Augustine, God bestows justifying righteousness upon the sinner, in such a way that it becomes part of his or her person. As a result, this righteousness, although originating from *outside* the sinner, becomes part of his or her person. For Luther, the righteousness in question remains outside the sinner: It is an "alien righteousness" (*iustitia aliena*). God treats, or "reckons," this righteousness *as if* it were part of the sinner's person. In his Romans lectures of 1515–16, Luther developed the idea of the "alien righteousness of Christ," imputed – not imparted – to us by faith, as the grounds of justification. His comments on Romans 4: 7 are especially important:

> The saints are always sinners in their own sight, and therefore always justified outwardly. But the hypocrites are always righteous in their own sight, and thus always sinners outwardly. I use the term "inwardly" to show how we are in ourselves, in our own sight, in our own estimation; and the term "outwardly" to indicate how we are before God and in his reckoning. Therefore we are righteous outwardly when we are righteous solely by the imputation of God and not of ourselves or of our own works.

Believers are righteous on account of the alien righteousness of Christ, which is imputed to them – that is, treated as if it were theirs through faith. Earlier, we noted that an essential element of Luther's concept of faith is that it unites the believer to Christ. Justifying faith thus allows the believer to link up with the righteousness of Christ, and be justified on its basis. Christians are thus "righteous by the imputation of a merciful God."

Through faith, the believer is clothed with the righteousness of Christ, in much the same way, Luther suggests, as Ezekiel 16: 8 speaks of God covering our nakedness with his garment. For Luther, faith is the right (or righteous) relationship to God. Sin and righteousness thus co-exist; we remain sinners inwardly, but are righteous extrinsically, in the sight of God. By confessing our sins in faith, we stand in a right and righteous relationship with God. From our own perspective we are sinners; but in the perspective of God, we are righteous.

Luther does not necessarily imply that this co-existence of sin and righteousness is a permanent condition. The Christian life is not static, as if – to use a very loose way of speaking – the relative amounts of sin and righteousness remained constant throughout. Luther is perfectly aware that the Christian life is dynamic, in that the believer grows in righteousness. Rather, his point is that the existence of sin does not negate our status as Christians. God shields our sin through his righteousness. This righteousness is like a protective covering, under which we may battle with our sin. This approach accounts for the persistence of sin in believers, while at the same time accounting for the gradual transformation of the believer and the future elimination of that sin. But it is not necessary to be perfectly righteous to be a Christian. Sin does not point to unbelief, or a failure on the part of God; rather, it points to the continued need to entrust one's person to the gentle care of God. Luther thus declares, in a famous phrase, that a believer is "at one and the same time righteous and a sinner" (*simul iustus et peccator*); righteous in hope, but a sinner in fact; righteous in the sight and through the promise of God, yet a sinner in reality.

These ideas were subsequently developed by Luther's follower Philip Melanchthon to give the doctrine now generally known as "forensic justification." Where Augustine taught that the sinner is *made righteous* in justification, Melanchthon taught that he is *counted as righteous* or *pronounced to be righteous*. For Augustine, "justifying righteousness" is *imparted*; for Melanchthon, it is *imputed*. Melanchthon drew a sharp distinction between the event of being *declared* righteous and the process of being *made* righteous, designating the former "justification" and the latter "sanctification" or "regeneration." For Augustine, both were simply different aspects of the same thing. According to Melanchthon, God pronounces the divine judgment – that the sinner is righteous – in the heavenly court (*in foro divino*). This legal approach to justification gives rise to the term "forensic justification," from the Latin word *forum* ("marketplace" or "courtyard") – the place traditionally associated with the dispensing of justice in classical Rome.

The importance of this development lies in the fact that it marks a complete break with the teaching of the church up to that point. From the time of Augustine onward, justification had always been understood to refer to both the event of being declared righteous and the process of being made righteous. Melanchthon's concept of forensic justification diverged radically from this. As it was taken up by virtually all the major reformers subsequently, it came to represent a standard difference between the Protestant and Roman Catholic churches from that point onward. In addition to their differences on how the sinner was justified, there was now an additional disagreement on what the word "justification" designated in the first place. As we shall see, the Council of Trent, the Roman Catholic church's definitive response to the Protestant challenge, reaffirmed the views of Augustine on the nature of justification, and censured the views of Melanchthon as woefully inadequate.

Calvin on Justification

The model of justification which would eventually gain the ascendancy in the later Reformation was formulated by Calvin in the 1540s and 1550s. The basic elements of his approach can be summarized as follows. Faith unites the believer to Christ in a "mystic union." (Here, Calvin reclaims Luther's emphasis upon the real and personal presence of Christ within believers, established through faith.) This union with Christ has a twofold effect, which Calvin refers to as "a double grace." First, the believer's union with Christ leads directly to his or her *justification*. Through Christ, the believer is declared to be righteous in the sight of God. Second, on account of the believer's union with Christ – and *not* on account of his or her justification – the believer begins the process of being made like Christ through regeneration. Calvin asserts that both justification and regeneration are the results of the believer's union with Christ through faith.

The Council of Trent on Justification

By 1540, Luther had become something of a household name throughout Europe. His writings were being read and digested, with various degrees of enthusiasm, even in the highest ecclesiastical circles in Italy. Something had to be done, if the Catholic church was to re-establish its credibility in relation to this matter. The Council of Trent, summoned in 1545, began the long process of formulating a comprehensive response to Luther. High on its agenda was the doctrine of justification.

The sixth session of the Council of Trent was brought to its close on January 13, 1547. The Tridentine Decree on Justification sets out the Roman Catholic teaching on justification with a considerable degree of clarity. Trent's critique of Luther's doctrine of justification can be broken down into four main sections:

1 The nature of justification.
2 The nature of justifying righteousness.
3 The nature of justifying faith.
4 The assurance of salvation.

We shall consider each of these four matters individually.

1 *The nature of justification*   In his earlier phase, around the years 1515–19, Luther tended to understand justification as a process of becoming, in which the sinner was gradually conformed to the likeness of Jesus Christ through a process of internal renewal (see pp. 385–6). In his later writings, however, dating from the mid-1530s and beyond, perhaps under the influence of Melanchthon's more forensic approach to justification (see p. 387), Luther tended to treat justification as a matter of being declared to be righteous, rather than a process of becoming righteous. Increasingly, he came to see justification as an event, which was complemented by the distinct process of regeneration and interior renewal through the action of the Holy Spirit.

Justification alters the outer status of the sinner in the sight of God (*coram Deo*), while regeneration alters the sinner's inner nature.

Trent strongly opposed this view, and vigorously defended the idea, originally associated with Augustine, that justification is the process of regeneration and renewal within human nature, which brings about a change in both the outer status and the inner nature of the sinner. The fourth chapter of the Decree provides the following precise definition of justification:

> The justification of the sinner may be briefly defined as a translation from that state in which a human being is born a child of the first Adam, to the state of grace and of the adoption of the sons of God through the second Adam, Jesus Christ our Savior. According to the gospel, this translation cannot come about except through the cleansing of regeneration, or a desire for this, as it is written, "Unless someone is born again of water and the Holy Spirit, he or she cannot enter into the Kingdom of God" (John 3: 5).

Justification thus includes the idea of regeneration. This brief statement is amplified in the seventh chapter, which stresses that justification "is not only a remission of sins but also the sanctification and renewal of the inner person through the voluntary reception of the grace and gifts by which an unrighteous person becomes a righteous person." This point was given further emphasis through canon 11, which condemned anyone who taught that justification takes place "either by the sole imputation of the righteousness of Christ or by the sole remission of sins, to the exclusion of grace and charity . . . or that the grace by which we are justified is only the good will of God."

In brief, then, Trent maintained the medieval tradition, stretching back to Augustine, which saw justification as comprising both an event and a process – the event of being declared to be righteous through the work of Christ, and the process of being made righteous through the internal work of the Holy Spirit. Reformers such as Melanchthon and Calvin distinguished these two matters, treating the word "justification" as referring only to the process of being declared to be righteous; the accompanying process of internal renewal, which they termed "sanctification" or "regeneration," they regarded as theologically distinct.

Serious confusion thus resulted: Roman Catholics and Protestants used the same word "justification" to mean very different things. Trent used the term "justification" to mean what, to Protestants, was *both* justification *and* sanctification.

2 *The nature of justifying righteousness*   Luther placed emphasis upon the fact that sinners possessed no righteousness in themselves. They had nothing within them which could ever be regarded as the basis of God's gracious decision to justify them. Luther's doctrine of the "alien righteousness of Christ" (*iustitia Christi aliena*) made it clear that the righteousness which justified sinners was outside them. It was imputed, not imparted; external, not internal.

Early critics of the Reformation argued, following Augustine, that sinners were justified on the basis of an internal righteousness, graciously infused or implanted within their persons by God. This righteousness was itself given as an act of grace; it was not something merited. But, they argued, there had to be something within individuals which could allow God to justify them. Luther dismissed this idea. God can justify individuals directly, rather than through an intermediate gift of righteousness.

Trent strongly defended the Augustinian idea of justification on the basis of an internal righteousness. The seventh chapter makes this point perfectly clear:

> The single formal cause [of justification] is the righteousness of God – not the righteousness by which he himself is righteous, but the righteousness by which he makes us righteous, so that, when we are endowed with it, we are "renewed in the spirit of our mind" (Ephesians 4: 23), and are not only counted as righteous, but are called, and are in reality, righteous. . . . Nobody can be righteous except God communicates the merits of the passion of our Lord Jesus Christ to him or her, and this takes place in the justification of the sinner.

The phrase "single formal cause" needs explanation. A "formal" cause is the *direct*, or most immediate, cause of something. Trent is thus stating that the direct cause of justification is the righteousness which God graciously imparts to us – as opposed to more distant causes of justification, such as the "efficient cause" (God), or the "meritorious cause" (Jesus Christ).

But the use of the word "single" should also be noted. One proposal for reaching agreement between Roman Catholic and Protestant, which gained especial prominence at the Colloquy of Ratisbon in 1541, was that *two* causes of justification should be recognized – an external righteousness (the Protestant position) and an internal righteousness (the Roman Catholic position). This compromise seemed to hold some potential. Trent, however, had no time for it. The use of the word "single" was deliberate, intended to eliminate the idea that there could be more than one such cause. The *only* direct cause of justification was the interior gift of righteousness.

3 *The nature of justifying faith*   Luther's doctrine of justification by faith alone came in for severe criticism. Canon 12 condemns a central aspect of Luther's notion of justifying faith, when it rejects the idea that "justifying faith is nothing other than confidence in the mercy of God, which remits sin for the sake of Christ." In part, this rejection of Luther's doctrine of justification reflects the ambiguity, noted above (p. 389), concerning the meaning of the term "justification." Trent was alarmed that anyone should believe that they could be justified – in the Tridentine sense of the term – by faith, without any need for obedience or spiritual renewal. Trent, interpreting "justification" to mean *both* the beginning of the Christian life *and* its continuation and growth, believed that Luther was suggesting that simply trusting in God (without any requirement that the sinner be changed and renewed by God) was the basis of the entire Christian life.

In fact, Luther meant nothing of the sort. He was affirming that the Christian life was begun through faith, and faith alone; good works followed justification, and did not cause that justification in the first place. Trent itself was perfectly prepared to concede that the Christian life was begun through faith, thus coming very close indeed to Luther's position. As chapter 8 of the Decree on Justification declares, "we are said to be justified by faith, because faith is the beginning of human salvation, the foundation and root of all justification, without which is it impossible to please God." This is perhaps a classic case of a theological misunderstanding, resting upon the disputed meaning of a major theological term.

4 *The assurance of salvation*   For Luther, as for the reformers in general, one could rest assured of one's salvation. Salvation was grounded upon the faithfulness of God to his promises of mercy; to fail to have confidence in salvation was, in effect, to doubt the reliability and trustworthiness of God. Yet this must not be seen as a supreme confidence in God, untroubled by doubt. Faith is not the same as certainty; although the theological foundation of Christian faith may be secure, the human perception of and commitment to this foundation may waver.

The Council of Trent regarded the reformers' doctrine of assurance with considerable skepticism. Chapter 9 of the Decree on Justification, entitled "Against the Vain Confidence of Heretics," criticized the "ungodly confidence" of the reformers. While no one should doubt God's goodness and generosity, the reformers erred seriously when they taught that "nobody is absolved from sins and justified, unless they believe with certainty that they are absolved and justified, and that absolution and justification are effected by this faith alone." Trent insisted that "nobody can know with a certainty of faith which is not subject to error, whether they have obtained the grace of God."

Trent's point seems to be that the reformers were seen to be making human confidence or boldness the grounds of justification, so that justification rested upon a fallible human conviction, rather than upon the grace of God. The reformers, however, saw themselves as stressing that justification rested upon the promises of God; a failure to believe boldly in such promises was tantamount to calling the reliability of God into question.

In the present section, we have considered the importance of the doctrine of justification to the sixteenth-century Reformation, when this doctrine came to the fore as an issue of controversy. It remains an issue of controversy, although in a different context. Our attention now turns to some developments relating to the doctrine of justification in recent New Testament scholarship.

Justification in Recent New Testament Scholarship

In recent years, a considerable debate on the relation of Paul's views on justification to those of first-century Judaism has developed, centering upon the writings of E. P. Sanders. His first major work to address this theme was *Paul and Palestinian Judaism* (1977), followed several years later by the more important *Paul, the Law and the Jewish People* (1983). Sanders' work represents a demand for a complete reappraisal of our understanding of Paul's relation to Judaism. Sanders noted that Paul has too often been read through Lutheran eyes.

According to the Lutheran interpretation of Paul (which, in marked contrast to the Reformed standpoint, linked with Bullinger and Calvin, stresses the divergence between the law and the gospel), Paul criticized a totally misguided attempt on the part of Jewish legalists to find favor and acceptance in the sight of God by earning righteousness through performing works of the law. This view, Sanders argued, colored the analysis of such Lutheran writers as Ernst Käsemann and Rudolf Bultmann. These scholars, perhaps unwittingly, read Paul through Lutheran spectacles, and thus failed to realize that Paul had to be read against his proper historical context in first-century Judaism.

According to Sanders, Palestinian Judaism at the time of Paul could be characterized as a form of "covenantal nomism." The Law is to be regarded as an expression of the covenant between God and Israel, and is intended to spell out as clearly and precisely as possible what forms of human conduct are appropriate within the context of this covenant. Righteousness is thus defined as behavior or attitudes consistent with being the historical covenant people of God. "Works of the law" are thus not understood (as Luther suggested) as the means by which Jews believed they could gain access to the covenant; for they already stood within it. Rather, these works are an expression of the fact that the Jews already belonged to the covenant people of God, and were living out their obligations to that covenant.

Sanders rejected the opinion that "the righteousness which comes from the law" is "a meritorious achievement which allows one to demand reward from God and is thus a denial of grace." "Works of the law" were understood as the basis not of entry to the covenant, but of maintaining that covenant. As Sanders puts it, "works are the condition of remaining 'in,' but they do not earn salvation." If Sanders is right, the basic features of Luther's interpretation of Paul are incorrect, and require radical revision.

What, then, is Paul's understanding of the difference between Judaism and Christianity, according to Sanders? Having argued that Jews never believed in salvation by works or unaided human effort, what does Sanders see as providing the distinctive advantage of Christianity over Judaism?

Having argued that it is not correct to see Judaism as a religion of merit and Christianity as a religion of grace, Sanders argues as follows. Judaism sees the Jewish people's hope of salvation as resting upon "their status as God's covenant people who possess the law," whereas Christians believe in "a better righteousness based solely upon believing participation in Christ." Paul, like Judaism, was concerned with the issue of entering into and remaining within the covenant. The basic difference is Paul's declaration that the Jews have no national charter of privilege; membership of the covenant is open to all who have faith in Christ, and who thus stand in continuity with Abraham (Romans 4).

Sanders' analysis is important, not least in that it forces us to ask hard questions about Paul's relation to his Jewish background, and the relation between the idea of participating in Christ and justification. (Interestingly, both Martin Luther and John Calvin made the notion of participating in Christ of central importance to their doctrines of justification, Calvin to the point of making justification the consequence of such participation). But is he right? The debate over this matter continues, and is likely to go on for some time. But the following points seem to be sufficiently well established to note at this juncture.

First, Sanders is rather vague about why Paul is convinced of the superiority of Christianity over Judaism. Judaism is presented as being wrong, simply because it is not Christianity. They are different dispensations of the same covenant. But Paul seems to regard Christianity as far more than some kind of dispensational shift within Judaism. R.

H. Gundry is one of a number of scholars to stress that salvation history does not account for all that Paul says, much less for the passion with which he says it.

Second, Sanders suggests that both Paul and Judaism regard works as the principle of continuing in salvation through the covenant. Yet Paul appears to regard good works as evidential, rather than instrumental. In other words, they are demonstration of the fact that the believer stands within the covenant, rather than instrumental in maintaining him within that covenant. One enters within the sphere of the covenant through faith. There is a radical new element here, which does not fit in as easily with existing Jewish ideas as Sanders seems to imply. Sanders may well be right in suggesting that good works are both a *condition for* and a *sign of* remaining within the covenant. Paul, however, sees faith as the necessary and sufficient condition for and sign of being in the covenant, with works (at best) a sign of remaining within its bounds.

Third, Sanders tends to regard Paul's doctrine of justification in a slightly negative light, as posing a challenge to the notion of a national ethnic election. In other words, Paul's doctrine of justification is a subtle challenge to the notion that Israel has special religious rights on account of its national identity. However, N. T. Wright has argued that Paul's doctrine of justification should be viewed positively, as an attempt to redefine who comes within the ambit of the promises made by God to Abraham. Such approaches treat justification as Paul's redefinition of how the inheritance of Abraham genuinely embraces the Gentiles apart from the law.

The Doctrine of Predestination

In discussing the nature of grace earlier in this chapter, we noted the close relationship between "grace" and "graciousness." God is under no obligation to bestow grace upon anyone, as if it were a commodity which functioned as a reward for meritorious actions. Grace is a gift, as Augustine never tired of emphasizing. Yet this emphasis upon the gift-character of grace, as will become clear, leads directly to the doctrine of predestination, often regarded as one of the most enigmatic and puzzling aspects of Christian theology. To explore how this connection developed, we shall consider some aspects of the theology of Augustine, before moving on to deal with the definitive exposition of a doctrine of predestination in the Reformed theological tradition.

Augustine of Hippo

Grace is a gift, not a reward. This insight is fundamental to Augustine (see pp. 375–6). If grace were a reward, humans could purchase their salvation through good works. They could earn their redemption. Yet this, according to Augustine, was totally contrary to the New Testament proclamation of the doctrine of grace. Affirming the gift-character of grace was a bulwark against inadequate theories of salvation. We have already spent much time dealing with Augustine's understanding of grace, and need not develop this point further here.

Augustine's insight has much to commend it. However, on further inspection, it proved to have its darker side. As the Pelagian controversy became increasingly hardened and bitter, the more negative implications of Augustine's doctrine of grace became clearer. In what follows, we shall explore those implications.

If grace is a gift, God must be free to offer it, or not to offer it, on the basis of any external consideration. If it is offered on the basis of any such consideration, it is no longer a gift – it is a reward for a specific action or attitude. Grace, according to Augustine, only remains gracious if it is nothing more and nothing less than a gift, reflecting the liberality of the one who gives. But the gift is not given to all. It is particular. Grace is only given to some. Augustine's defense of "the graciousness of God," which rests on his belief that God must be free to give or withhold grace, thus entails the recognition of the *particularity*, rather than the *universality*, of grace.

If this insight is linked with Augustine's doctrine of sin, its full implications become clear. All of humanity is contaminated by sin, and unable to break free from its grasp. Only grace can set humanity free. Yet grace is not bestowed universally; it is only granted to some individuals. As a result, only some will be saved – those to whom grace is given.

Augustine emphasized that this did not mean that some were predestined to damnation. It meant that God had selected some from the mass of fallen humanity. The chosen few were indeed predestined for salvation. The remainder were not, according to Augustine, actively condemned to damnation; they were merely not elected to salvation. Augustine tends (although he is not entirely consistent in this respect) to treat predestination as something which is *active* and *positive* – a deliberate decision to redeem on God's part. However, as his critics pointed out, this decision to redeem some was also a decision *not* to redeem others.

This question surfaced with new force during the great predestinarian controversy of the ninth century, in which the Benedictine monk Godescalc of Orbais (c.804–c.869, also known as Gottschalk) developed a doctrine of double predestination similar to that later to be associated with Calvin and his followers. Pursuing with relentless logic the implications of his assertion that God has predestined some to eternal damnation, Godescalc pointed out that it was thus quite improper to speak of Christ dying for such individuals; if he had, he would have died in vain, for their fate would be unaffected.

Hesitant over the implications of this assertion, Godescalc proposed that Christ died *only for the elect*. The scope of his redeeming work was restricted, limited only to those who were predestined to benefit from his death. Most ninth-century writers reacted to this assertion with disbelief. It was, however, to resurface in later Calvinism.

John Calvin

Calvin is often regarded as making the doctrine of predestination the center of his theological system. A close reading of his *Institutes* does not, however, bear out this often-repeated judgment. Calvin adopts a distinctly low-key approach to the doctrine, devoting a mere four chapters to its exposition (book III, chapters 21–4). Predestination is defined as "the eternal decree of God, by which he determined what he wished to make of every man. For he does not create everyone in the same condition, but ordains eternal life for some and eternal damnation for others." In writing of predestination at one point, Calvin appears to speak of it as a "horrible decree": "The decree, I admit, is *horribile*." However, the Latin term *horribile* is better translated as "awesome"; Calvin's own French translation of the passage (1560) reads: "I confess that this decree must frighten us" (*doit nous épouvanter*).

The very location of Calvin's discussion of predestination in the 1559 edition of the *Institutes* is significant in itself. It follows his exposition of the doctrine of grace. It is only after the great themes of this doctrine – such as justification by faith – have been expounded that Calvin turns to consider the mysterious and perplexing subject of predestination. Logically, predestination ought to precede such an analysis; predestination, after all, establishes the grounds of an individual's election, and hence his or her subsequent justification and sanctification. Yet Calvin declines to be subservient to the canons of such logic. Why?

Calvin's analysis of predestination begins from observable facts. Some believe the gospel. Some do not. The primary function of the doctrine of predestination is to explain why some individuals respond to the gospel, and others do not. It is an attempt to explain the variety of human responses to grace. Calvin's predestinarianism is to be regarded as reflection upon the data of human experience, interpreted in the light of Scripture, rather than something which is deduced on the basis of preconceived ideas concerning divine omnipotence. Belief in predestination is not an article of faith in its own right, but is the final outcome of scripturally informed reflection on the effects of grace upon individuals in the light of the enigmas of experience.

This is, it must be stressed, no theological innovation. Calvin is not introducing a hitherto unknown notion into the sphere of Christian theology. Many theologians of the late medieval period, especially writers of the "modern Augustinian school" (see p. 35) such as Gregory of Rimini and Hugolino of Orvieto, taught a doctrine of absolute double predestination – that God allocates some to eternal life, others to eternal condemnation, without any reference to their merits or demerits. Their fate rested totally upon the will of God, rather than their individualities. Indeed, it is possible that Calvin has actively appropriated this aspect of late medieval Augustinianism, which certainly bears an uncanny resemblance to his own teaching.

Far from being a central premise of Calvin's thought, predestination is an ancillary doctrine, concerned with explaining a puzzling aspect of the consequences of the proclamation of the gospel of grace. Yet as Calvin's followers sought to develop and recast his thinking in the light of new intellectual developments, it was perhaps inevitable (if this lapse into a potentially predestinarian mode of speaking may be excused) that alterations to his structuring of Christian theology might occur. In the section which follows, we shall explore the understandings of predestination which gained influence within Calvinism after Calvin's death.

Reformed Orthodoxy

It is not correct to speak of Calvin developing a "system" in the strict sense of the term. Calvin's religious ideas, as presented in the 1559 *Institutes*, are *systematically arranged*, on the basis of pedagogical considerations; they are not, however, *systematically derived* on the basis of a leading speculative principle. Calvin regarded biblical exposition and systematic theology as virtually identical, and refused to make the distinction between them which became commonplace after his death. However, as noted earlier, a new interest in the area of method developed after Calvin's death. The question of the proper starting point for theology became increasingly debated (see pp. 68–72).

It is this concern for establishing a logical starting point for theology which allows us to understand the new importance which came to be attached to the doctrine of predestination within Reformed orthodoxy.

Calvin focused upon the specific historical event of Jesus Christ and then moved out to explore its implications (that is, to deploy the appropriate technical language, Calvin's approach is analytic and inductive). In contrast, Theodore Beza – a later follower of Calvin (see p. 71) – begins from general principles and proceeds to deduce their consequences for Christian theology (that is, his approach is deductive and synthetic).

So what general principles does Beza use as a logical starting point for his theological systematization? The answer is that he bases his system on the divine decrees of election – that is, the divine decision to elect certain people to salvation, and others to damnation. All the remainder of theology is concerned with the exploration of the consequences of these decisions. The doctrine of predestination thus assumes the status of a controlling principle.

One major consequence of this development may be noted: the doctrine of "limited atonement" or "particular redemption." (The term "atonement" is often used to refer to "the benefits resulting from the death of Christ.") Consider the following question. For whom did Christ die? The traditional answer to this question took the following form: Christ died for everyone; yet although his death has the potential to redeem all, it is only effective for those who choose to allow it to have this effect. This doctrine was regarded with intense distaste by Arminanism, to which we shall presently turn.

Before doing so, the idea of "Five Point Calvinism" needs to be introduced. This term refers to the five central principles of Reformed soteriology (that is, the understanding of redemption associated with Calvinist writers), as they were laid down definitively by the Synod of Dort (1618–19). The "Five Points" are often referred to using the mnemonic TULIP:

T   total depravity of sinful human nature;
U   unconditional election, in that humans are not predestined on the basis of any foreseen merit, quality, or achievement;
L   limited atonement, in that Christ died only for the elect;
I   irresistible grace, by which the elect are infallibly called and redeemed;
P   perseverance of the saints, in that those who are truly predestined by God cannot in any way defect from that calling.

An important controversy emerged within Calvinist circles concerning the logical ordering of the "decrees of election." Two classic positions may be discerned within this notoriously pedantic debate, which has often become a symbol of theological obscurantism.

1   The *infralapsarian* position, associated with Francis Turrettini (1623–87), stated that election presupposes the fall of humanity. The decrees of election are thus oriented toward all of humanity as a "mass of sin" (*massa perditionis*). In other words, God's decision to predestine some to election and others to damnation is in response to the event of the fall. The object of the decision is fallen human beings.
2   The alternative *supralapsarian* position, associated with Beza, regards election as prior to the fall. Here, the object of the divine decree of predestination is seen as humanity prior to the fall. The fall is thus seen as a means of carrying out the decree of election.

A third position may also be noted, associated especially with Moses Amyraut (1596–1664) and the Calvinist Academy at Saumur, France. This position, often referred to as *hypothetical universalism*, has had relatively little impact within Calvinism.

Arminianism

Arminianism takes its name from Jakob Arminius (1560–1609), who reacted against the Reformed doctrine of particular redemption. For him, Christ had died for all, not merely for the elect. Such views were taken up within Dutch Reformed circles in the aftermath of the Synod of Dort, leading to the publication of the *Remonstrance* of 1610. This statement affirmed the universal character and scope of Christ's work:

> God, by an eternal and unchangeable decree in Christ before the existence of the world, determined to elect from the fallen and sinful human race to everlasting life all those who, through God's grace, believe in Jesus Christ and persevere in faith and obedience. . . . Christ the Savior of the world died for all and every human being, so that he obtained, through his death on the cross, reconciliation and pardon for all, in such a way, however, that only the faithful actually enjoy the same.

The idea of predestination is thus maintained: However, its frame of reference is radically altered. Whereas the Synod of Dort understood predestination to be an individual matter, the Arminians understood it corporately: God has predestined that a specific group of people will be saved – namely, those who believe in Jesus Christ. By believing, individuals fulfilled the predestined condition of salvation.

Arminianism soon achieved a major presence within eighteenth-century evangelicalism. Despite the more Calvinist views of George

Whitefield, Arminian ideas were forcefully stated within Methodism by Charles Wesley (1707–88). For example, his hymn "Would Jesus have a Sinner Die?" states the doctrine of the universal redemption of humanity with considerable force:

> O let thy love my heart constrain,
> Thy love for *every* sinner free,
> That *every* fallen soul of man,
> May taste the grace that found out me;
> That all mankind with me may prove
> Thy sovereign, everlasting love.

The position also achieved considerable prominence in North America during the eighteenth century: Jonathan Edwards' writings make frequent reference to the inconsistencies and shortcomings of his Arminian opponents.

Karl Barth

One of the most interesting features of Karl Barth's theology is the manner in which it interacts with the theology of the period of Reformed orthodoxy. It is in part the seriousness with which Barth takes the writings of this period that has given rise to the term "neo-orthodoxy" to refer to Barth's general approach (pp. 98–100). Barth's treatment of the Reformed doctrine of predestination is especially interesting, in that it demonstrates the manner in which he can take traditional terms, and give them a radically new meaning within the context of his theology.

Barth's discussion of predestination (*Church Dogmatics*, volume 2, part 2) is based upon two central affirmations:

1 Jesus Christ is the electing God;
2 Jesus Christ is the elected human being.

This strongly Christological orientation of predestination is maintained throughout his analysis of the doctrine. "In its simplest and most comprehensive form, the doctrine of predestination consists of the assertion that the divine predestination is the election of Jesus Christ. But the concept of election has a double reference – to the elector and the elected." So exactly what has God predestined? Barth's answer to this has several components, of which the following are especially important.

1 "God has chosen to be the friend and partner of humanity." God has elected, in a free and sovereign decision, to enter into fellowship with humanity. Barth thus affirms God's commitment to humanity, despite its sin and fallenness.

2 God chose to demonstrate that commitment in giving Christ for the redemption of humanity. "According to the Bible, this was what took place in the incarnation of the Son of God, in his death and passion, and in his resurrection from the dead." The very act of the redemption of humanity is the expression of God's self-election as redeemer of fallen humanity.

3 God elected to bear totally the pain and cost of redemption. God chose to accept the cross of Golgotha as a royal throne. God chose to accept the lot of fallen humanity, especially in suffering and death. God chose the path of self-humiliation and self-abasement, in order to redeem humanity.

4 God elected to take from us the negative aspects of his judgment. God rejects Christ in order that we might not be rejected. The negative side of predestination, which ought, Barth suggests, properly to have fallen upon sinful humanity, is instead directed toward Christ, the electing God and elected human being. God willed to bear the "rejection and condemnation and death" which are the inevitable consequences of sin. Thus "rejection cannot again become the portion or affair of humanity." Christ bore what sinful humanity ought to have borne, in order that they need never bear it again.

> In so far as predestination contains a No, it is not a No spoken against humanity. In so far as it involves exclusion and rejection, it is not the exclusion and rejection of humanity. In so far as it is directed to perdition and death, it is not directed to the perdition and death of humanity.

Barth thus eliminates any notion of a "predestination to condemnation" on the part of humanity. The only one who is predestined to condemnation is Jesus Christ who, "from all eternity willed to suffer for us."

The consequences of this approach are clear. Despite all appearances to the contrary, humanity cannot be condemned. In the end, grace will triumph, even over unbelief. Barth's doctrine of predestination eliminates the possibility of the rejection of humanity. In that Christ has borne the penalty and pain of rejection by God, this can never again become the portion of humanity. Taken together with his characteristic emphasis upon the "triumph of grace," Barth's doctrine of predestination points to the universal restoration and salvation of humanity – a position which has occasioned a degree of criticism from others who would otherwise be sympathetic to his general position. Emil Brunner is an example of such a critic:

> What does this statement, "that Jesus is the only really rejected person," mean for the situation of humanity? Evidently this: That there is no possibility of condemnation. . . . The decision has already been made in Jesus Christ – for all of humanity. Whether they know it or not, believe it or not, is not so important. They are like people who seem to be perishing in a stormy sea. But in reality they are not in a sea in which one can drown, but in shallow waters, in which it is impossible to drown. Only they do not know it.

Predestination and Economics: The Weber Thesis

One of the most fascinating consequences of the Calvinist emphasis upon predestination is its impact upon the attitudes of those who held the belief. Of especial importance is the question of *assurance*: How may the believer know that he or she really is amongst the elect? Although Calvin stressed that works are not the grounds of *salvation*, he nevertheless allowed it to be understood that they are, in some vague way, the grounds of *assurance*. Works may be regarded as "the testimonies of God dwelling and ruling within us." Believers are not saved by works; rather, their salvation is demonstrated by works. "The grace of good works . . . demonstrates that the spirit of adoption has been given to us." This tendency to regard works as evidence of election may be seen as the first stage in the articulation of a work ethic with significant pastoral overtones: It is by worldly activism that the believer can assure his or her troubled conscience that he or she is amongst the elect.

Anxiety over this question of election was subsequently a pervasive feature of Calvinist spirituality, and was generally treated at some length by Calvinist preachers and spiritual writers. The basic answer given, however, remained substantially the same: The believer who performs good works has indeed been chosen. Theodore Beza makes the point as follows:

> For this cause St Peter admonishes us to make our vocation and election sure by good works. Not that they be the cause of our vocation and election. . . . But forasmuch as good works bring testimony to our conscience that Jesus Christ dwells within us, and consequently we cannot perish, being elected to salvation.

Again, we find the same point being made: Works testify to, but do not cause, salvation; they are the consequence, not the precondition, of salvation. By a process of *a posteriori* reasoning, the believer may infer his or her election from its consequences (good works). In addition to glorifying God and demonstrating the believer's thankfulness, such human moral action serves a vital psychological role for the anxious Christian conscience, by assuring the believer that he or she is indeed one of the elect.

This idea was often stated in terms of the "practical syllogism," an argument constructed along the following lines:

> All who are elected exhibit certain signs as a consequence of that election.
> But I exhibit those signs.
> Therefore I am amongst the elect.

This *syllogismus practicus* thus locates the grounds of certainty of election in the presence of "certain signs" in the life of the believer. There was thus a significant psychological pressure to demonstrate one's election to oneself and the world in general by exhibiting its signs – amongst which was the wholehearted commitment to serve and glorify God by laboring in the world. It is this pressure which, according to sociologist Max Weber, lies behind the emergence of capitalism within Calvinist societies.

The popular version of the Weber thesis declares that capitalism is a direct result of the Protestant Reformation. This is historically untenable, and, in any case, is not what Weber actually said. Weber stressed that he had

> no intention whatsoever of maintaining such a foolish and doctrinaire thesis as that the spirit of capitalism . . . could only have arisen as a result of certain effects of the Reformation. In itself, the fact that certain important forms of capitalistic business organizations are known to be considerably older than the Reformation is a sufficient refutation of such a claim.

Rather, Weber argued that a new "spirit of capitalism" emerged in the sixteenth century. It is not so much *capitalism* as *a specific form of* capitalism which needs to be explained.

Protestantism, Weber argued, generated the psychological preconditions essential to the development of modern capitalism. Indeed, Weber located the fundamental contribution of Calvinism as lying in its generation of psychological impulses on account of its belief systems. Weber laid especial stress upon the notion of "calling," which he linked with the Calvinist idea of predestination. Calvinists, assured of their personal salvation, were enabled to engage in worldly

activity without serious anxiety regarding their salvation as a consequence. The pressure to prove one's election led to the active pursuit
of worldly success – a success which, as history indicates, was generally not slow in coming.

It is not our concern here to provide a critique of the Weber thesis.
In some circles, it is regarded as utterly discredited; in others, it lives
on. Our concern is simply to note that Weber rightly discerned that
religious ideas could have a powerful economic and social impact
upon early modern Europe. The very fact that Weber suggested that
the religious thought of the Reformation was capable of providing the
stimulus needed for the development of modern capitalism itself is a
powerful testimony to the need to study theology if human history is
to be fully understood. It also indicates that apparently abstract ideas
– such as predestination – can prove to have a very concrete impact
upon history!

The present chapter has briefly surveyed a vast amount of material
relating to the Christian understandings of human nature, sin, and
grace. Only a fraction of the debates within the Christian tradition have
been explored. Nevertheless, central landmarks have been identified,
which remain of decisive importance to the continuing debates within
Christianity on such issues.

Questions for Chapter 12

1   Give a concise summary of the main issues at stake in
    the Pelagian controversy.

2   Why did Augustine believe in original sin?

3   You are explaining the idea of grace to a non-theologian
    with a limited attention span. What could you say about
    the idea, in 200 words or less?

4   Martin Luther is associated with the doctrine of
    "justification by faith alone." What did he mean by this?
    And what were the alternatives he rejected?

5   "If you aren't predestined, then go and get yourself
    predestined." How does this attitude relate to Weber's
    thesis concerning the origins of capitalism?

13

The Doctrine of the Church

The Christian doctrine of the church, usually referred to as *ecclesiology* (Greek: *ekklesia*, "church"), is of major importance to anyone proposing to engage in pastoral ministry of any kind. Ecclesiological questions break into ministry at point after point. What sort of body is the church? Ecclesiology is that area of theology which seeks to give theoretical justification to an institution which has undergone development and change down the centuries, set against an altering social and political context. To study Christian understandings of the church is to gain insights into the way in which institutions adapt in order to survive. The Reformation is a particularly important period, when a cluster of ecclesiologies developed, each responding to different needs, perceptions, and opportunities. The present chapter aims to explore some of the issues which arise from this remarkable history of development down the ages.

The Early Development of Ecclesiology

Ecclesiology was not a major issue in the early church. The eastern church showed no awareness of the potential importance of the issue. Most Greek patristic writers of the first five centuries contented themselves with describing the church using recognizably scriptural images, without choosing to probe further. Thus Isidore of Pelusium defined the church as "the assembly of saints joined together by correct faith and an excellent manner of life." The following elements can be discerned as having achieved a wide consensus at the time:

1   The church is a spiritual society, which replaces Israel as the
    people of God in the world.
2   All Christians are made one in Christ, despite their different
    origins and backgrounds.
3   The church is the repository of true Christian teaching.
4   The church gathers the faithful throughout the world together,
    in order to enable them to grow in faith and holiness.

In part, this lack of interest in the doctrine of the church reflected
the political situation of the time. The church was at best a barely
tolerated, and at worst a vigorously persecuted, organization within
the sphere of authority of a hostile pagan state – namely, the Roman
Empire. With the conversion of Constantine, the situation changed
radically. Increasingly, theologians began to draw parallels between
the empire and the church – whether negatively (as with Hippolytus
of Rome, who saw the empire as a satanic imitation of the church),
or positively (as with Eusebius, who saw the empire as a divinely
ordained institution, charged with the task of preparing the world for
the coming of the kingdom of Christ).

One practical issue led to increased reflection on an ecclesiological
issue. At an early stage, rivalry developed between the leaders of the
churches, especially those at Rome and Constantinople. A number of
centers were held in particular esteem during the first four centuries,
of which Alexandria, Antioch, Constantinople, Jerusalem, and Rome
were of notable importance. However, by the end of the fourth
century, it was becoming increasingly clear that Rome, as the center of
the Roman Empire, had acquired a position of especial prominence.
The term "pope," from the Latin *papa*, "father," was initially used of
any Christian bishop; gradually, the term came to be used more often
of the most important bishop in the church – the bishop of Rome.
From 1073, the title was reserved exclusively for the bishop of Rome.
The question therefore began to arise: What authority does the bishop
of Rome have outside his own diocese?

In practical terms, the answer was quite simple: a lot. The bishop of
Rome (we shall use the term "pope" from now on, despite the slight
anachronism this involves) was often called upon to arbitrate in church
disputes of various kinds, throughout the entire Mediterranean.
When Nestorius and Cyril of Jerusalem became embroiled in endless
Christological debates in the fifth century, and it became clear that no
resolution was in sight, they each hastened to Rome to gain papal
support.

But did this priority rest upon any theological foundation? The
eastern churches had no hesitation in declaring that it did not. Others,
however, were not so sure. The pope was the successor to St Peter,

who had been martyred at Rome. In view of the apparent "primacy of Peter" in the New Testament (Matthew 16: 18), did this not give the successors of Peter authority over others? It seemed to many, even within the eastern churches, that, in some inscrutable manner, the spiritual authority of Peter had been transmitted to his successors as bishops of Rome. Cyprian of Carthage is an example of a western writer who is a vigorous defender of the primacy of the Roman see throughout the Christian world. This question would become of renewed importance at a number of junctures in church history, of which the Reformation is a particularly obvious instance.

The Donatist Controversy

In the end, it was the western church which forced the pace of theological reflection on the nature and identity of the church. It seems to be a general rule of the development of Christian doctrine that development is occasioned by controversy. A stimulus seems to have been required to provoke sustained theological reflection. In the case of ecclesiology, that stimulus was provided by a controversy centering upon Roman North Africa, which has passed into history as "the Donatist controversy."

Under the Roman emperor Diocletian (284–313), the Christian church was subject to various degrees of persecution. The beginnings of the persecution date from 303; it finally ended with the conversion of Constantine, and the issuing of the Edict of Milan in 313. Under an edict of February 303, Christian books were ordered to be burned and churches demolished. Those Christian leaders who handed over their books to be burned came to be known as *traditores* – "those who handed over." The modern word "traitor" derives from the same root. Once such *traditor* was Felix of Aptunga, who later consecrated Caecilian as Bishop of Carthage in 311.

Many local Christians were outraged that such a person should have been allowed to be involved in this consecration, and declared that they could not accept the authority of Caecilian as a result. The hierarchy of the Catholic church was tainted as a result of this development. The church ought to be pure, and should not be permitted to include such people. By the time Augustine returned to Africa in 388, a breakaway faction had established itself as the leading Christian body in the region, with especially strong support from the local African population. Sociological issues clouded theological debate; the Donatists (so named after the breakaway African church leader Donatus: see p. 20) tended to draw their support from the indigenous population, whereas the Catholics drew theirs from Roman colonists.

The theological issues involved are of considerable importance, and relate directly to a serious tension within the theology of a leading figure of the African church in the third century – Cyprian of Carthage. In his *Unity of the Catholic Church* (251), Cyprian had defended two major related beliefs. First, schism is totally and absolutely unjustified. The unity of the church cannot be broken, on any pretext whatsoever. To step outside the bounds of the church is to forfeit any possibility of salvation. Second, it therefore follows that lapsed or schismatic bishops are deprived of all ability to administer the sacraments or act as a minister of the Christian church. By passing outside the sphere of the church, they have lost their spiritual gifts and authority. They should therefore not be permitted to ordain priests or bishops. Any whom they have ordained must be regarded as invalidly ordained; any whom they have baptized must be regarded as invalidly baptized.

But what happens if a bishop lapses under persecution, and subsequently repents? Cyprian's theory is profoundly ambiguous, and is open to two lines of interpretation.

1   By lapsing, the bishop has committed the sin of apostasy (literally, "falling away"). He has therefore placed himself outside the bounds of the church, and can no longer be regarded as administering the sacraments validly.
2   By his repentance, the bishop has been restored to grace, and is able to continue administering the sacraments validly.

The Donatists adopted the first such position, the Catholics (as their opponents came to be universally known) the second.

The Donatists believed that the entire sacramental system of the Catholic church had become corrupted. It was therefore necessary to replace *traditores* with people who had remained firm in their faith under persecution. It was also necessary to rebaptize and reordain all those who had been baptized and ordained by *traditores*. Inevitably, this resulted in the formation of a breakaway faction. By the time Augustine returned to Africa, the breakaway faction was larger than the church it had broken away from.

Yet Cyprian had totally forbidden schism of any kind. One of the greatest paradoxes of the Donatist schism is that it resulted from principles which were due to Cyprian – yet contradicted those very same principles. As a result, both Donatists and Catholics appealed to Cyprian as an authority – but to very different aspects of his teaching. The Donatists stressed the outrageous character of apostasy; the Catholics equally emphasized the impossibility of schism. A stalemate resulted. That is, until Augustine arrived, and became Bishop of Hippo in the region. Augustine was able to resolve the tensions within the legacy of Cyprian, and put forward an "Augustinian" view of the church, which has remained enormously influential ever since.

First, Augustine emphasizes the *sinfulness of Christians*. The church is not meant to be a society of saints, but a "mixed body" (*corpus permixtum*) of saints and sinners. Augustine finds this image in two biblical parables: the parable of the net which catches many fishes, and the parable of the wheat and the tares. It is this latter parable (Matthew 13: 24–31) which is of especial importance, and requires further discussion.

The parable tells of a farmer who sowed seed, and discovered that the resulting crop included both wheat and tares – grain and weeds. What could be done about it? To attempt to separate the wheat and the weeds while both were still growing would be to court disaster, probably involving damaging the wheat while trying to get rid of the weeds. But at the harvest, all the plants – wheat and tares – are cut down and sorted out without any danger of damaging the wheat. The separation of the good and the evil thus takes place at the end of time, not in history.

For Augustine, this parable refers to the church in the world. It must expect to find itself including both saints and sinners. To attempt a separation in this world is premature and improper. That separation will take place in God's own time, at the end of history. No human can make that judgment or separation in God's place. So in what sense is the church holy? For Augustine, the holiness in question is not that of its members, but of Christ. The church cannot be a congregation of saints in this world, in that its members are contaminated with original sin. However, the church is sanctified and made holy by Christ – a holiness which will be perfected and finally realized at the last judgment.

In addition to this theological analysis, Augustine makes the practical observation that the Donatists failed to live up to their own high standards of morality. The Donatists, Augustine suggests, were just as capable as Catholics of getting drunk or beating people up.

Second, Augustine argues that schism and *traditio* (the handing over of Christian books, or any form of lapse from faith) are indeed both sinful – but that, for Cyprian, schism is by far the more serious sin. The Donatists are thus guilty of serious misrepresentation of the teaching of the great North African martyr bishop.

On the basis of these considerations, Augustine argues that Donatism is fatally flawed. The church is, and is meant to be, a mixed body. Sin is an inevitable aspect of the life of the church in the present age, and is neither the occasion nor the justification for schism. Yet precisely the schism which Augustine feared and detested so much would eventually come about in the sixteenth century, with the formation of breakaway Protestant churches in western Europe as a result of the Reformation. It is to these major developments that we now turn.

The Reformation Controversies

The sixteenth century was a period of crucial importance for reflection on the nature and identity of the Christian church. The reformers were convinced that the church of their day and age had lost sight of the doctrine of grace, which Luther regarded as the center of the Christian gospel. Thus Luther declared that his doctrine of justification by faith alone was the *articulus stantis et cadentis ecclesiae*, "the article by which the church stands or falls." Convinced that the Catholic church had lost sight of this doctrine, he concluded (with some reluctance, it would seem) that it had lost its claim to be considered the authentic Christian church.

His Catholic opponents responded to this suggestion with derision: Luther was simply creating a breakaway faction which had no connection with the church. In other words, he was a schismatic – and had not Augustine himself condemned schism? Had not he placed enormous emphasis upon the unity of the church, which Luther now threatened to disrupt? Luther, it seemed, could only uphold Augustine's doctrine of grace by rejecting Augustine's doctrine of the church. It is in the context of this tension between two aspects of Augustine's thought, which proved to be incompatible in the sixteenth century, that the Reformation understandings of the nature of the church are to be seen.

Martin Luther

Luther's early views on the nature of the church reflect his emphasis on the Word of God: The Word of God goes forth conquering, and wherever it conquers and gains true obedience to God *is* the church.

> The sure mark by which the Christian congregation can be recognized is that the pure gospel is preached there. For just as the banner of an army is the sure sign by which one can know what kind of lord and army have taken to the field, so too the gospel is the sure sign by which one knows where Christ and his army are encamped . . . Likewise, where the gospel is absent and human teachings rule, there no Christians live but only pagans, no matter how numerous they are and how holy and upright their life may be.

An episcopally ordained ministry is therefore not necessary to safeguard the existence of the church, whereas the preaching of the gospel is essential to the identity of that church. "Where the word is, there is faith; and where faith is, there is the true church." The visible church is constituted by the preaching of the Word of God: No human assembly may claim to be the "church of God" unless it is founded on this gospel. It is more important to preach the same gospel as the Apostles than to be a member of an institution which is historically derived from them. A similar understanding of the church was shared by Philip Melanchthon, Luther's colleague at Wittenberg, who conceived of the church primarily in terms of its function of administering the means of grace.

But if the church was defined not in *institutional* terms, but by the preaching of the gospel, how could Luther distinguish his views from those of the radical reformers? Luther himself had conceded that "the church is holy even where the fanatics [Luther's term for the radicals] are dominant, so long as they do not deny the word and the sacraments." Luther asserted the need for an institutional church, declaring that the historical institution of the church is a divinely ordained means of grace. But in countering the radicals by asserting that the church was indeed visible and institutional, Luther found himself having difficulty in distinguishing his views from those of his Catholic opponents. He himself fully appreciated this problem:

> We on our part confess that there is much that is Christian and good under the papacy; indeed, everything that is Christian and is good is to be found there and has come to us from this source. For instance, we confess that in the papal church there are the true Holy Scriptures, true baptism, the true sacrament of the altar, the true keys to the forgiveness of sins, the true office of the ministry, the true catechism in the form of the Lord's Prayer, the Ten Commandments and the articles of the Creed.

Luther is thus obliged to assert that "the false church has only the appearance, although it also possesses the Christian offices." In other words, the medieval church may have *looked like* the real thing, but it was really something rather different.

It will thus be clear that there are certain difficulties and shortcomings associated with Luther's approach. In part, this may reflect the general belief within reforming circles during the 1520s that separation from the Catholic church was a temporary matter. What point was there in developing extensive theories of the church, to give legitimation to the breakaway evangelical factions, when reunion with a reformed Catholic church was only a matter of time? It was only in the 1540s, when such reunion was finally realized to be nothing more than a dream, that Protestant theologians began to give sustained attention to formulating distinctively Protestant doctrines of the church. John Calvin is perhaps the most significant such writer.

John Calvin

An event of major importance to the Reformation took place in 1541. The Colloquy of Regensburg (or Ratisbon) collapsed. This conference represented a last-ditch attempt to reach a compromise between Catholics and Protestants, which would allow the latter to rejoin the church from which they had temporarily withdrawn. It must be stressed that the reformers initially regarded themselves as having removed themselves from the Catholic church only temporarily. There was a full expectation of a return, once the situation had improved. The failure of Regensburg put paid to that hope.

A new situation now developed. Up to 1541, there had been no real need for Protestant writers to develop theories of the church. Luther's early ecclesiology is actually a holding measure, designed to justify a temporary withdrawal from the church. It lacks rigor and conviction, precisely because Luther believed that there was no need to develop a full-blown theory of the church. After all, a return to the Catholic church was just around the corner. The second generation of reformers, amongst whom Calvin stands out as supreme, were faced with the challenge of developing a coherent and systematic ecclesiology, on the basis of the realization that separation from the main body of the Catholic church would continue indefinitely.

For Calvin, the marks of the true church were:

1 that the Word of God should be preached, and
2 that the sacraments should be rightly administered.

Since the Roman Catholic church did not conform even to this minimalist definition of the church, the evangelicals were perfectly justified in leaving it. And as the evangelical churches conformed to this definition of a church, there was no justification for further division within them. This point is of particular importance, reflecting Calvin's political judgment that further fragmentation of the evangelical congregations would be disastrous to the cause of the Reformation.

Calvin further argued that there were specific scriptural directions regarding the right order of ministry in the visible church, so that a specific form of ecclesiastical order now became an item of doctrine. In other words, he included a specific form of ecclesiastical administration (and he here borrows the term *administratio* from the field of secular government) in "the gospel purely preached."

Calvin's minimalist definition of the church now took on a new significance. The true church is indeed to be found where the gospel is rightly preached, and the sacraments rightly administered – and understood to be included within this definition is a specific form of ecclesiastical institution and administration. Calvin referred to the "order by which the Lord willed his church to be governed," and developed a detailed theory of church government based upon his exegesis of the New Testament, drawing extensively upon the terminology of the imperial Roman administration. Contrary to what the radicals asserted, Calvin insisted that a specific form of church structure and administration is laid down by Scripture. Thus Calvin held that the ministerial government of the church is divinely ordained, as are the distinctions between "minister," "elder," "deacon," and "people."

Calvin drew an important distinction between the *visible* and the *invisible* church. At one level, the church is the community of Christian believers, a visible group. It is also, however, the fellowship of saints and the company of the elect – an *invisible* entity. In its invisible aspect, the church is the invisible assembly of the elect, known only to God; in its visible aspect, it is the community of believers on earth. The former consists only of the elect; the latter includes both good and evil, elect and reprobate. The former is an object of faith and hope, the latter of present experience. The distinction between them is eschatological: The invisible church is the church which will come into being at the end of time, as God ushers in the final judgment of humanity. Calvin stresses that all believers are obliged to honor and to remain committed to the visible church, despite its weaknesses, on account of the invisible church, the true body of Christ. Despite this, there is only one church, a single entity with Jesus Christ as its head.

The distinction between the visible and invisible churches has two important consequences. In the first place, it is to be expected that the visible church will include both the elect and the reprobate. Augustine of Hippo had made this point against the Donatists, using the parable of the tares (Matthew 13: 24–31) as his basis. It lies beyond human competence to discern their difference, correlating human qualities with divine favor (in any case, Calvin's doctrine of predestination precludes such grounds of election).

In the second place, however, it is necessary to ask which of the various visible churches corresponds to the invisible church. Calvin thus recognizes the need to articulate objective criteria by which the authenticity of a given church may be judged. Two such criteria are stipulated: "Wherever we see the Word of God preached purely and listened to, and the sacraments administered according to the institution of Christ, we cannot doubt that a church exists." It is thus not the quality of its members, but the presence of the authorized means of grace, which constitutes a true church. Interestingly, Calvin does not follow the example of Martin Bucer – the Strasbourg reformer from whom he learned so much – in making discipline a mark of the true church; although passionately concerned with the need for charitable discipline of church members, Calvin did not regard this as essential to the definition or evaluation of the credentials of a church.

Calvin is also of importance in relation to another aspect of the doctrine of the church. Having defined the nature of the church, Calvin proceeds to explore its importance. Why is there any need for a church – understood, that is, as an institution, rather than a building – in the first place? Just as God redeemed human beings within the historical process through the incarnation, so God sanctifies them within that same process by founding an institution dedicated to that goal. God uses certain definite earthly means to work out the salvation of the elect. The church is thus identified as a divinely founded body, within which God effects the sanctification of the elect. Calvin expresses this idea as follows:

> I shall begin then, with the church, into the bosom of which God is pleased to gather his children, not only so that they may be nourished by her assistance and ministry while they are infants and children, but also so that they may be guided by her motherly care until they mature and reach the goal of faith. "For what God has joined together, no one shall divide" (Mark 10: 9). For those to whom God is Father, the church shall also be their mother.

Calvin confirms this high doctrine of the church by citing the two great ecclesiological maxims of Cyprian of Carthage: "You cannot have God as your father unless you have the church for your mother," and "Outside the church there is no hope of remission of sins nor any salvation" (see pp. 407–8).

Calvin's doctrine of the church reminds us that it is seriously inadequate to portray the reformers as rampant radical individualists, with no place for corporate conceptions of the Christian life. The image of the "church as mother" (which Calvin gladly borrows from Cyprian of Carthage) underscores the corporate dimensions of Christian faith:

> Let us learn from this simple word "mother" how useful (indeed, how necessary) it is to know her. There is no other way to life, unless this mother conceives us in her womb, nourishes us at her breast, and keeps us under her care and guidance.

Powerful theological imagery nestles within this way of speaking, above all that of the word of God which conceives us within the womb of the church. But it is the practical aspects of this way of thinking about the church which command our attention at this point. The institution of the church is a necessary, helpful, God-given, and God-ordained means of spiritual growth and development. The contrast with the radical Reformation, to which we now turn, will be clear.

The Radical Reformation View of the Church

For the radicals, such as Sebastian Franck and Menno Simons, the apostolic church had been totally compromised through its close links with the state, dating back to the conversion of the Emperor Constantine. As an institution, the church was corrupted by human power struggles and ambition. Franck wrote thus:

> I believe that the outward Church of Christ, including all its gifts and sacraments, because of the breaking in and laying waste by antichrist right after the death of the Apostles, went up into heaven, and lies concealed in the Spirit and in truth. I am thus quite certain that for fourteen hundred years now there has existed no gathered Church nor any sacrament.

The true church was in heaven, and its institutional parodies were on earth.

The radical emphasis upon the need for the church to become separated from secular society is especially clear in its discussion of attitudes to authority. The radical Reformation conceived of the church as an "alternative society" within the mainstream of sixteenth-century European culture. Just as the pre-Constantinian church existed within the Roman Empire, yet refused to conform to its standards, so the radical Reformation envisaged itself existing parallel to, but not within, its sixteenth-century environment. For Menno Simons, the church was "an assembly of the righteous," at odds with the world, and not a "mixed body":

> In truth, those who merely boast of his name are not the true congregation of Christ. The true congregation of Christ is those who are truly converted, who are born from above of God, who are of a regenerate mind by the operation of the Holy Spirit through the hearing of the Word of God, and have become the children of God.

It will be clear that there are strong parallels with the Donatist view of the church as a holy and pure body (see pp. 407–8), isolated from the corrupting influences of the world, and prepared to maintain its purity and distinctiveness by whatever disciplinary means proved necessary.

This notion of the church as a faithful remnant in conflict with the world harmonized with the Anabaptist experience of persecution by the forces of Antichrist, personified in the magistrates. The radical Reformation was generally hostile to the use of coercion, and advocated a policy of non-resistance. Jakob Hutter gave this apolitical stance a theological justification through an appeal to the example of Christ: "As all can see, we have no physical weapons, such as spears or muskets. We wish to show, by our words and deeds, that we are true followers of Christ." Hans Denck appealed to the meekness of Christ, and his silence before his accusers, in declaring that "force is not an attribute of God."

The clearest statement of the general Anabaptist attitude toward secular authority may be found in the Schleitheim Confession (1527), the sixth and seventh articles of which explain and justify the policy of non-involvement in secular affairs and non-resistance to secular authorities. Coercion has its place "outside the perfection of Christ" (that is, outside the radical community); inside that community, physical force has no place.

> The sword is ordained of God outside the perfection of Christ . . . It is not appropriate for a Christian to serve as a magistrate, for the following reasons. The government magistracy is according to the flesh, but the Christian's is according to the Spirit. Their houses and dwelling places are in this world, but the Christian's is in heaven; their citizenship is of this world, but the Christian's is in heaven; the weapons of their war and conflict are physical, and against the flesh, whereas the Christian's weapons are spiritual, against the fortification of the devil. The worldlings are armed with steel and iron, but the Christian is armed with the armor of God, with truth, righteousness, peace, faith, salvation, and the word of God.

Anabaptism maintained discipline within its communities through "the ban" – a means by which church members could be excluded from Anabaptist congregations. This means of discipline was regarded as essential to the identity of a true church. Part of the Anabaptist case for radical separation from the mainstream churches (a practice which continues to this day among the Amish of Lancaster County, Pennsylvania) was the failure of those churches to maintain proper discipline within their ranks. The Schleitheim Confession grounded its doctrine of the ban on Christ's words, as they are recorded in Matthew 18: 15–20:

> The ban shall be used in the case of all those who have given them-selves to the Lord, to walk in his commandments, and with all those who are baptized into the one body of Christ and are called brothers or sisters, yet who lapse on occasion, and inadvertently fall into error and sin. Such people shall be admonished twice in secret, and on the third occasion, they shall be disciplined publicly, or banned according to the command of Christ (Matthew 18).

The "ban" was seen as being both deterrent and remedial in its effects, providing both an incentive for banned individuals to amend their way of life and a disincentive for others to imitate them in their sin. The Polish Racovian Catechism lists five reasons for maintaining rigorous discipline within Anabaptist communities, most of which reflect its policy of radical separation:

1   So that the fallen church member may be healed, and brought back into fellowship with the church.
2   To deter others from committing the same offense.
3   To eliminate scandal and disorder from the church.
4   To prevent the word of the Lord falling into disrepute outside the congregation.
5   To prevent the glory of the Lord being profaned.

Despite its pastoral intentions, the "ban" often came to be interpreted harshly, with congregation members often avoiding all social contact (known as "shunning") with both the banned individual and his or her family.

The Notes of the Church

A central theme of ecclesiology relates to the four "notes" or "marks" of the church – that is to say, the four defining characteristics of the Christian church, as stated in the creeds of Christendom. These creeds affirm belief in "one holy catholic and apostolic church." The four adjectives included in this phrase – "one," "holy," "catholic," and "apostolic" – have come to be known as the "notes" or "marks" of the church, and have been of importance to ecclesiological discussion since the fourth century. In what follows, we shall consider each briefly.

"One"

The unity of the church has been of central importance to Christian thinking on the subject. The World Council of Churches, one of the more important agencies in the modern period to be concerned with Christian unity, defines itself as "a fellowship of churches, which confess our Lord Jesus Christ as God and Savior." Yet that very definition concedes the existence of a plurality of churches – Anglican, Baptist, Lutheran, Methodist, Orthodox, Presbyterian, Roman Catholic, and so on. How can one speak of "one church," when there are so many churches? Or "the unity of the church," when it is so clearly disunited at the institutional level?

Two episodes in church history may be noted as being of especial importance in relation to this question. The first relates to North Africa in the third century, when division within the church became a potentially destructive issue. The Decian persecution (250–1) led to many Christians lapsing or abandoning their faith in the face of persecution. Division arose immediately over how these individuals should be treated: Did such a lapse mark the end of their faith, or could they be reconciled to the church by penance? Opinions differed sharply, and serious disagreement and tension resulted. (The Donatist controversy, discussed earlier, may be regarded as a development of this unresolved problem, in response to the later Diocletian persecution.)

In his *On the Unity of the Catholic Church* (251), written in direct response to the crisis arising from the Decian persecution, Cyprian of Carthage insisted upon the absolute unity of the church, comparing it to the "seamless robe of Christ," which could not be divided because it had been woven from the top throughout. Destroy its unity, and its identity was simultaneously devastated.

> Whoever is separated from the church is joined with an adultress, and separated from the promises of the church. None who leaves the church of Christ can attain the rewards of Christ. None can have God for a father unless they have the church as their mother. If any had been able to escape outside Noah's Ark, there might be a way of escape for those who are outside the church.

There is only one church, and outside its bounds salvation is impossible. *Extra ecclesiasm nulla salus* – "outside the church there is no salvation." Cyprian was subsequently martyred, which led to his distinctive ideas on unity achieving a hallowed status within the region – and forcing Augustine to give them a comparable emphasis within his own writings.

The sixteenth-century Reformation also witnessed controversy over this issue. How, it was asked, could the reformers justify forming breakaway churches, and thus compromising the unity of the church? (It must be remembered that the Reformation took place in a western European context, where the only significant ecclesiastical body was the hitherto more or less undivided Roman Catholic church.) As noted earlier, the reformers' response was to argue that the medieval church had become corrupted to the point at which it could no longer be regarded as a church, in the strict sense of the word. The scene was thus set for an explosive increase in denominations.

Once the principle of breaking away from a parent ecclesiastical body for doctrinal reasons was established, little could be done to check it. Thus the Church of England broke away from the medieval Catholic church in the sixteenth century; in the eighteenth century, Methodism broke away from the church of England; in the nineteenth century, Methodism subdivided into Welseyan and Calvinist churches, divided over the issue of predestination. From the sixteenth century onward, it became clear that the idea of "one church" could no longer be understood sociologically or institutionally.

Faced with this apparent contradiction between a theoretical belief in "one church" and the brute reality of a plurality of churches, some Christian writers have developed approaches to allow the latter to be understood within the framework of the former. Four approaches may be noted, each with distinctive strengths and weaknesses.

1 An imperialist approach, which declares that there is only one empirical church which deserves to be treated as the true church, with all others being fraudulent, or at best approximations to the real thing. This position was characteristic of Roman Catholicism prior to the Second Vatican Council (1962–5), which took the momentous step of recognizing other churches as separated Christian brothers and sisters.

2 A Platonic approach, which draws a fundamental distinction between the empirical church (that is, the church as a visible historical reality) and the ideal church. This has found relatively little support in mainstream Christian theology, although some scholars have argued that this idea may be detected in the Reformation distinction between the "visible" and "invisible" churches. However, as we noted above, this distinction is better interpreted along eschatological lines.

3 An eschatological approach, which suggests that the present disunity of the church will be abolished on the last day. The present situation is temporary, and will be resolved at the time of eschatological fulfillment. This understanding lies behind Calvin's distinction between the "visible" and "invisible" churches (pp. 413–14).

4 A biological approach, which likens the historical evolution of the church to the development of the branches of a tree. This image, developed by the eighteenth-century German Pietist writer Nicolas von Zinzendof, and taken up with enthusiasm by Anglican writers of the following century, allows the different empirical churches – e.g. the Roman Catholic, Orthodox, and Anglican churches – to be seen as possessing an organic unity, despite their differences.

However, in recent years, many theologians concerned with ecumenism (deriving from the Greek word *oecumene*, "the whole world," and now generally understood to mean "the movement concerned with the fostering of Christian unity") argued that the true basis of the "unity of the church' required to be recovered, after centuries of distortion. The maxim *ubi Chrisus, ibi ecclesia* ("where Christ is, there is also the church"), which derives from Ignatius of Antioch (see p. 424 for the original quotation) pointed to the unity of the church lying in Christ, rather than in any historical or cultural factor. Throughout the New Testament, they argued, the diversity of local churches is not regarded as compromising the unity of the church. The church already possesses a unity through its common calling from God, which expresses itself in different communities in different cultures and situations. "Unity" must not be understood *sociologically* or *organizationally*, but *theologically*. Hans Küng stresses this point in his magisterial study *The Church*:

> The unity of the church is a spiritual entity. . . . It is one and the same God who gathers the scattered from all places and all ages and makes them into one people of God. It is one and the same Christ who through his word and Spirit unites all together in the same bond of fellowship of the same body of Christ. . . . The Church *is* one, and therefore *should be* one.

The point that Küng makes is that the unity of the church is grounded in the saving work of God in Christ. This is in no way inconsistent with that one church adapting itself to local cultural conditions, leading to the formation of local churches. As Küng puts it:

> The unity of the church presupposes a multiplicity of churches; the various churches do not need to deny their origins or their specific situations; their language, their history, their customs and traditions, their way of life and thought, their personal structure will differ fundamentally, and no one has the right to take this from them. The same thing is not suitable for everyone, at every time, and in every place.

An illustration of this may be provided from Anglicanism, a family of churches which owes its historical origins to the English Reformation. The Thirty-Nine Articles (1571), which established the identity of the movement at that time, do not commit Anglicanism to anything other than an affirmation of the main points of the Catholic faith, allowing a considerable degree of freedom in relation to areas of potential division (evident in the nuanced discussion of the highly contentious issue of predestination at Article XVII). If Anglicanism possesses "essentials," they are "essentials" that are common to the whole church of God, of which Anglicanism is part. Anglicanism's distinctive features may be argued to lie in its application of the gospel to a specific historical situation – England, and subsequently the British colonies. The American Anglican theologian Louis Weil states this point as follows:

> The gospel in Anglicanism is, then, one facet in a vast mosaic. In its essentials, it corresponds to the gospel as it has been proclaimed and believed all over the world. Yet it is also characterized by its particularity as an experience of God's saving work in particular cultures, and is shaped by the insights and limitations of persons who were themselves seeking to live the gospel within a particular context.

This represents an affirmation of the fundamental unity of the Christian church, while noting the need for adaptation to local circumstances.

The rapid growth of evangelicalism in the modern church is of considerable importance in relation to the doctrine of the church. Evangelicalism is a world-wide transdenominational movement, which is able to co-exist within every major denomination in the western church, including the Roman Catholic church. Evangelicalism is not inextricably locked into any specific denominational constituency. An evangelical commitment to a corporate conception of the Christian life does not entail the explicit definition of a theology of the church (see pp. 110–13). Precisely because evangelicalism has no defining or limiting ecclesiology, it can accommodate itself to virtually any form of church order.

This is well illustrated by the history of the movement. Evangelical attitudes are now known to have been deeply embedded within the Italian church during the 1520s and 1530s, with prominent Italian church leaders (including several cardinals) meeting regularly in a number of cities to study Scripture and the writings of the Protestant reformers. No tension was seen between an evangelical spirituality and a Catholic ecclesiology; it was only when the situation was radically politicized in the 1540s through the intrusion of imperial politics into theological debate that evangelicalism came to be seen as a destabilizing influence within the Italian church.

Similar developments are now known to be taking place within the Roman Catholic church in the United States, as an increasing number of members find evangelicalism conducive to their spiritual needs, yet do not feel (and are not made to feel) that their espousal of an evangelical spirituality entails abandoning their loyalty to Catholic church structures. The unity of the church is here grounded, not in any specific ecclesiastical organizational system, but in a common commitment to the *evangel* – the good news of Jesus Christ.

"Holy"

Earlier, we noted that the idea of the unity of the church appeared to be fatally compromised by rampant denominationalism. The theoretical unity of the church appeared to be contradicted by the empirical reality, in which the church appeared as divided and fragmented. Precisely the same tension between theory and experience arises through the assertion that the church is "holy," when both the past history and present experience of that institution point to sinfulness on the part of both the church and its members.

How is the theoretical holiness of the church to be reconciled with the sinfulness of Christian believers? The most significant attempt to bring experience into line with theory can be seen in sectarian movements such as Donatism and Anabaptism. Both these movements laid considerable emphasis upon the empirical holiness of church members, leading to the exclusion from the church of members who were deemed to have lapsed from these public standards of sanctity. This rigorist approach seemed to contradict substantial parts of the New Testament, which affirmed the fallibility and forgivability – if the neologism may be excused – of believers. Others have asserted that a distinction may be made between the holiness of the church, and the sinfulness of its members. This raises the theoretical difficulty of whether a church can exist without members, and seems to suggest a disembodied church without any real connection with human beings.

A different approach draws upon an eschatological perspective. The church is at present as sinful as its members; nevertheless, it will finally be purified on the last day. "Whenever I have described the church as being without spot or wrinkle, I have not intended to imply that it was like this already, but that it should prepare itself to be like this, at the time when it too will appear in glory" (Augustine). "That the church will be . . . without spot or wrinkle . . . will only be true in our eternal home, not on the way there. We would deceive ourselves if we were to say that we have no sin, as 1 John 1: 8 reminds us" (Thomas Aquinas).

Probably the most helpful approach to this mark of the church is to explore the meaning of the term "holy" in greater detail. In ordinary English, the term has acquired associations of "morality," "sanctity," or "purity," which often seem to bear little relation to the behavior of fallen human beings. The Hebrew term *kadad*, which underlies the New Testament concept of "holiness," has the sense of "being cut off," or "being separated." There are strong overtones of *dedication*: To be "holy" is to be set apart for and dedicated to the service of God. A fundamental element – indeed, perhaps *the* fundamental element – of the Old Testament idea of holiness is that of "something or someone whom God has set apart." The New Testament restricts the idea almost entirely to personal holiness. It refers the idea to individuals, declining to pick up the idea of "holy places" or "holy things." People are "holy" in that they are dedicated to God, and distinguished from the world on account of their calling by God. A number of theologians have suggested a correlation between the idea of "the church" (the Greek word for which can bear the meaning of "those who are called out"), and "holy" (that is, those who have been separated from the world, on account of their having been called by God).

To speak of the "holiness of the church" is thus primarily to speak of the holiness of the one who called that church and its members. The church has been separated from the world, in order to bear witness to the grace and salvation of God. In this sense, there are obvious connections between the church being "holy" and the church being "apostolic." The term "holy" is theological, not moral, in its connotations, affirming the calling of the church and its members, and the hope that the church will one day share in the life and glory of God.

"Catholic"

In modern English, the term "catholic" is often confused, especially in non-religious circles, with "Roman Catholic." Although this confusion is understandable, the distinction must be maintained. It is not only Roman Catholics who are catholic, just as it is by no means only Eastern Orthodox writers who are orthodox in their theology. Indeed, many Protestant churches, embarrassed by the use of the term "catholic" in the creeds, have replaced it with "universal," arguing that this brings greater intelligibility to belief in "one holy universal and apostolic church."

The term "catholic" derives from the Greek phrase *kath' holou* ("referring to the whole"). The Greek words subsequently found their way into the Latin word *catholicus*, which came to have the meaning "universal or general." This sense of the word is retained in the English phrase "catholic taste," meaning a "wide-ranging taste" rather than a "taste for things that are Roman Catholic." Older versions of the English Bible often refer to some of the New Testament letters (such as those of James and John) as "catholic epistles," meaning that they are directed to all Christians (rather than those of Paul, which are directed to the needs and situations of individual identified churches, such as those at Rome or Corinth).

At no point does the New Testament use the term "catholic" to refer to the church as a whole. The New Testament uses the term *ekklesia* to refer to local churches or worshipping communities, which it nevertheless understands to represent or embody something which transcends that local body. While an individual church is not the church in its totality, it nevertheless shares in that totality. It is this notion of "totality" which is subsequently encapsulated in the term "catholic." The term is introduced in later centuries, in an attempt to bring together central New Testament insights and attach them to a single term. The first known use of the phrase "the catholic church" occurs in the writings of Ignatius of Antioch, who was martyred at Rome around 110: "Where Jesus Christ is, there is the catholic church." Other writings of the second century use the term to refer to the existence of a universal church alongside local congregations.

The meaning of the term changed fundamentally with the conversion of Constantine. By the end of the fourth century, the term *ecclesia catholica* ("the catholic church") had come to mean "the imperial church" – that is, the only legal religion within the Roman Empire. Any other form of belief, including Christian beliefs which diverged from the mainstream, was declared to be illegal.

Further expansion of the church in this period contributed to a developing understanding of the term "catholic." By the beginning of the fifth century, Christianity was firmly established throughout the entire Mediterranean world. In response to this development, the term "catholic" came to be interpreted as "embracing the entire world."

In terms of its early development, the term "catholic" as applied to the church thus went through three stages of meaning:

1 A universal and all-embracing church, which underlies and undergirds individual local churches. In this sense, the term is descriptive and non-polemical, pointing to the fact that a local church was the representative of the universal church. There is an obvious correlation here between the notions of "unity" and "catholicity."
2 A church which is orthodox in its theology. The term now

takes on a strongly prescriptive and polemical tone. "Catholicism" is now contrasted with "schism" and "heresy," by which individuals place themselves outside the boundaries of a doctrinally orthodox church.

3   A church which extends throughout the world. In the first phase of the Christian church, this interpretation of the term would have been implausible, given the localized character of Christianity. However, the strongly missionary character of Christianity (linked, as we shall see, with the idea of "apostolicity") led to the expansion of the church throughout the civilized world of the Mediterranean. The term thus came to possess a geographical reference, originally absent.

As noted earlier, a fundamental re-examination of the notion of "catholicity" took place at the time of the Reformation. It seemed to many that the catholicity and unity of the church were destroyed simultaneously with the fragmentation of the western European church in the sixteenth century. Protestant writers argued that the essence of catholicity lay, not in church institutions, but in matters of doctrine. The fifth-century writer Vincent of Lérins had defined catholicity in terms of "that which is believed everywhere, at all times, and by all people." The reformers argued that they remained catholic, despite having broken away from the medieval church, in that they retained the central and universally recognized elements of Christian doctrine. Historical or institutional continuity was secondary to doctrinal fidelity. For this reason, the mainstream Protestant churches insisted they were simultaneously *catholic* and *reformed* – that is, maintaining continuity with the apostolic church at the level of teaching, having eliminated spurious non-biblical practices and beliefs.

The notion of "catholicity" which has come to the fore in recent years, especially in ecumenical discussions subsequent to the Second Vatican Council, is the oldest sense of the term – namely, that of totality. Local churches and particular denominations are to be seen as the manifestations, representations, or embodiments of the one universal church. As Hans Küng states this position:

> The catholicity of the church therefore consists in a notion of entirety, based on identity, and resulting in universality. From this it is clear that unity and catholicity go together; if the church is one, it must be universal; if it is universal, it must be one. Unity and catholicity are two interwoven dimensions of one and the same church.

"Apostolic"

The term "apostolic," like "catholic," is not used to refer to the church in the New Testament. Unlike "catholic," it is restricted to Christian use, and is therefore not subject to the kinds of confusion with secular ideas noted in the case of other marks of the church. The fundamental sense of the term is "originating with the Apostles" or "having a direct link with the Apostles." It is a reminder that the church is founded on the apostolic witness and testimony.

The term "Apostle" requires explanation. Its use in the New Testament suggests that it bears two related meanings:

1 one who has been commissioned by Christ, and charged with the task of preaching the good news of the kingdom;
2 one who was a witness to the risen Christ, or to whom Christ revealed himself as risen.

In declaring the church to be "apostolic," the creeds thus appear to emphasize the historical roots of the gospel, the continuity between the church and Christ through the Apostles whom he appointed, and the continuing evangelistic and missionary tasks of the church.

Having considered aspects of the Christian understanding of the church, we may now turn to a discussion of a related area of theology – the sacraments.

Questions for Chapter 13

1 Give a concise summary of the issues at stake in the Donatist controversy.

2 Augustine of Hippo wrote of the Christian church being like a hospital. Why?

3 The doctrine of the church is often described as "the Achilles' heel of the Reformation." Why?

4 "How can anyone speak of one church, when there are thousands of Christian denominations?" Summarize and assess the answers that could be given to this objection.

5 "How can the church be holy, when it is full of sinners?" What answers could be given to this question?

14

The Doctrine of the Sacraments

Our attention now turns to a set of issues centering on the sacraments. As with the doctrine of the church, the issues at stake are of considerable relevance to any who are studying theology with a view to entering pastoral ministry. However, they are also of interest to any studying theology for more academic reasons.

As will soon become clear, the term "sacrament" is notoriously difficult to define, given the controversy within the Christian churches upon the nature and number of the sacraments. In general terms, a sacrament may be thought of as an external rite or sign, which in some way conveys grace to believers. The most sustained debates within the church on the identity and function of the sacraments took place during the sixteenth century. For this reason, the discussion of sacramental theology will include extensive reference to the debates of this era. However, the Donatist controversy (see pp. 407–10) also resulted in several issues of importance being debated. The most convenient way of handling the material under consideration is to deal with the issues raised by the Donatist controversy and the Reformation.

The chief debates within Christian history which relate to the sacraments concern the following issues:

1 What is a sacrament?
2 How many sacraments are there?
3 What is the correct name for the sacrament which Christians have variously termed "the mass," "holy communion," "the eucharist," "the Lord's supper," and "the breaking of the bread"?
4 In what sense is Christ present at the eucharist?

The third question is unanswerable! In the present work, the term "eucharist" has been used as a convenient compromise, which has the advantage of possessing an adjectival form ("eucharistic"). Readers of the work who find this term unacceptable must regard themselves as completely at liberty to substitute alternatives, wherever these are appropriate. No attempt is being made to prescribe this term as correct or normative. In practice, it may be noted that the term "mass" tends to have Roman Catholic, and "Lord's supper" Protestant, connotations.

The Definition of a Sacrament

In the previous chapter, we noted that the first centuries were characterized by a relative lack of interest in the doctrine of the church. Much the same can be said in relation to the sacraments. During the second century, some discussions of a general sacramental nature can be found in such writings as the *Didache*, and the works of Irenaeus. It is only in the writings of Augustine that the issues, including that of the definition of a sacrament, begin to be fully addressed.

Augustine is generally regarded as having laid down the general principles relating to the definition of sacraments. These principles are as follows:

1   A sacrament is a *sign*. "Signs, when applied to divine things, are called sacraments."
2   The sign must bear some relation to the thing which is signified. "If sacraments did not bear some resemblance to the things of which they are the sacraments, they would not be sacraments at all."

These definitions are still imprecise and inadequate. For example, does it follow that every "sign of a sacred thing" is to be regarded as a sacrament? In practice, Augustine understood by "sacraments" a number of things that are no longer regarded as sacramental in character – for example, the creed and the Lord's prayer. As time passed, it became increasingly clear that the definition of a sacrament simply as "a sign of a sacred thing" was inadequate. It was during the earlier Middle Ages – the period of sacramental development *par excellence* – that further clarification took place.

In the first half of the twelfth century, the Paris theologian Hugh of St Victor revised the definition, as follows:

> Not every sign of a sacred thing can properly be called a sacra-
> ment. After all, the letters in sacred writings, or statues and pic-
> tures, are all "signs of sacred things," but cannot be called sacra-
> ments for that reason. . . . Anyone wanting a fuller and better
> definition of a sacrament can define it as follows: "A sacrament
> is a physical or material element set before the external senses,
> representing by likeness, signifying by its institution, and con-
> taining by sanctification, some invisible and spiritual grace."

There are thus four essential components to the definition of a
sacrament:

1   A "physical or material" element – such as the water of
    baptism, the bread and wine of the eucharist, or the oil of ex-
    treme unction. ("Extreme unction" is the practice of anointing
    those who are terminally ill with consecrated olive oil.)
2   A "likeness" to the thing which is signified, so that it can rep-
    resent the thing signified. Thus the eucharistic wine can be
    argued to have a "likeness" to the blood of Christ, allowing it
    to represent that blood in a sacramental context.
3   Authorization to signify the thing in question. In other words,
    there must be a good reason for believing that the sign in
    question is *authorized* to represent the spiritual reality to which
    it points. An example – indeed, the primary example – of the
    "authorization" in question is institution at the hands of Jesus
    Christ himself.
4   An efficacity, by which the sacrament is capable of conferring
    the benefits which it signifies to those who partake in it.

This fourth point is of especial importance. In medieval theology, a
careful distinction was drawn between the "sacraments of the Old
Covenant" (such as circumcision) and the "sacraments of the New
Covenant." The essential distinction between them is that the sacraments of the Old Covenant merely signified spiritual realities, whereas
the sacraments of the New Covenant actualized what they signified.
The thirteenth-century Franciscan writer Bonaventure made this point
as follows, using a medicinal analogy.

> In the Old Law, there were ointments of a kind, but they were
> figurative and did not heal. The disease was lethal, but the
> anointings were superficial. . . . Genuinely healing ointments must
> bring both spiritual anointing and a life-giving power; it was only
> Christ our Lord who did this, since . . . through his death, the
> sacraments have the power to bring to life.

However, Hugh of St Victor's definition of a sacrament remained unsatisfactory. According to Hugh, the following items were "sacraments": the incarnation, the church, and death. Something was still missing. By this time, there was general agreement that there were seven sacraments – baptism, confirmation, the eucharist, penance, marriage, ordination, and extreme unction. But by Hugh's definition, penance could not be a sacrament. It contained no material element. Theory and practice were thus seriously out of line.

The final touches were put to the definition by Peter Lombard, who – by omitting one vital aspect of Hugh's definition – was able to bring theory into line with practice. Peter's achievement was to omit reference to any "physical or material element" in his definition, which takes the following form: "A sacrament is precisely defined as a sign of the grace of God, and a form of invisible grace, which is such that it bears its likeness and exists as its cause." This definition fits each of the seven sacraments noted above, and excludes such things as the creed and the incarnation. As the definition was included in Peter's *Four Books of the Sentences*, it passed into general use in later medieval theology, and remained virtually unchallenged until the time of the Reformation.

In his reforming treatise of 1520, *The Babylonian Captivity of the Church*, Luther launched a major attack on the Catholic understanding of the sacraments. Taking advantage of the latest humanist philological scholarship, he asserted that the Vulgate use of the term *sacramentum* was largely unjustified on the basis of the Greek text (see p. 53). Where the Roman Catholic church recognized seven sacraments, Luther initially recognized three (baptism, eucharist, penance), and shortly afterwards two (baptism and eucharist). The transition between these two views can be seen in the *Babylonian Captivity* itself, and we may pause to examine this change and understand its basis.

The work opens with a powerful statement of principle, which sets to one side the medieval consensus regarding the sacraments:

> I deny that there are seven sacraments, and for the present maintain that there are only three: baptism, penance, and the bread. All three have been subjected to a miserable captivity by the Roman authorities, and the church has been robbed of all her freedom.

By the end of the work, however, Luther has come to place considerable emphasis upon the importance of a visible physical sign. Luther signaled this significant change in his views with the following statement:

> Yet it has seemed right to restrict the name of sacrament to those promises of God which have signs attached to them. The remainder, not being connected to signs, are merely promises. Hence, strictly speaking, there are only two sacraments in the church of God – baptism and the bread. For only in these two do we find the divinely instituted sign and the promise of the forgiveness of sins.

Penance thus ceased to have sacramental status, according to Luther, because the two essential characteristics of a sacrament were

1   the Word of God;
2   an outward sacramental sign (such as water in baptism, and bread and wine in the eucharist).

The only true sacraments of the New Testament church were thus baptism and eucharist; penance, having no external sign, could no longer be regarded as a sacrament.

Like Luther, the Swiss reformer Zwingli had grave misgivings about the word "sacrament" itself. He argued that the term has the basic sense of "oath," and initially treated the sacraments of baptism and eucharist (the remaining five sacraments of the Catholic system being rejected) as signs of God's faithfulness to the church and the divine gracious promise of forgiveness. Thus in 1523, he wrote that the word "sacrament" could be used to refer to those things which "God has instituted, commanded, and ordained with the Word, which is as firm and sure as if God had sworn an oath to this effect." However, Zwingli later came to see the sacraments as signifying the allegiance of believers to the church, rather than of God to believers, a point we shall consider at pp. 437–8.

The Council of Trent, reacting to the Protestant approaches to the sacraments, responded by defending the position outlined by Peter Lombard.

> If anyone says that the sacraments of the new law were not all instituted by our Lord Jesus Christ, or that there are more or less than seven, namely, baptism, confirmation, eucharist, penance, extreme unction, ordination, and marriage, or that any one of these seven is not truly and intrinsically a sacrament, let them be condemned.

This basic position has remained characteristic of Roman Catholic theology since the sixteenth century.

The Donatist Controversy: Sacramental Efficacy

In the previous chapter, we noted the issues which lay behind the Donatist controversy (pp. 407–10). A central issue, of direct relevance to the material to be considered in the present chapter, concerns the personal worthiness or holiness of the minister who administers the sacraments. The Donatists refused to recognize that a *traditor* – that is to say, a Christian minister whose personal credentials had been compromised or tainted through collaboration with the Roman authorities during the Diocletian persecution – could administer the sacraments. Accordingly, they argued that baptisms, ordinations, and eucharists administered by such ministers were invalid.

This attitude rested in part upon the authority of Cyprian of Carthage. Cyprian had argued that no true sacraments exist outside the church. Heretical baptism was thus not valid, as heretics did not accept the faith of the church, and were thus outside its bounds. Logically unassailable though Cyprian's views may have been, they failed to allow for the situation which arose during the Donatist controversy – that is, ministers who are of orthodox faith, but whose personal conduct is held to be unworthy of their calling. Were doctrinally orthodox yet morally inferior ministers entitled to administer the sacraments? And were such sacraments invalid?

Pressing Cyprian's views beyond their apparent intended limits, the Donatists argued that ecclesiastical actions could be regarded as invalid on account of subjective imperfections on the part of the person administering them. The Donatists thus held that those who were baptized or ordained by Catholic priests or bishops who had not joined the Donatist movement required to be rebaptized and reordained at the hands of Donatist ministers. The sacraments derive their validity from the personal qualities of the person who administers them.

Responding to this approach, Augustine argued that Donatism laid excessive emphasis upon the qualities of the human agent, and gave insufficient weight to the grace of Jesus Christ. It is, he argued, impossible for fallen human beings to make distinctions concerning who is pure and impure, worthy or unworthy. This view, which is totally consistent with his understanding of the church as a "mixed body" of saints and sinners, holds that the efficacy of a sacrament rests, not upon the merits of the individual administering it, but upon the merits of the one who instituted them in the first place – Jesus Christ. The validity of sacraments is independent of the merits of those who administer them.

Having said this, Augustine qualifies it in an important context. A distinction must be drawn, he argues, between "baptism" and "the right to baptize." Although baptism is valid, even when administered by those who are heretics or schismatics, this does not mean that the right to baptize is indiscriminately distributed amongst all peoples. The right to confer baptism exists only within the church, and supremely in those ministers whom it has chosen and authorized to administer the sacraments. The authority to administer the sacraments of Christ was committed by him to the Apostles, and through them and their successors the bishops to the ministers of the Catholic church.

The theological issue at stake has come to be represented by two Latin slogans, each reflecting a different understanding of the grounds of the efficacy of the sacraments.

1 Sacraments are efficacious *ex opere operantis* – literally, "on account of the work of the one who works." Here, the efficacity of the sacrament is understood to be dependent upon the personal qualities of the minister.
2 Sacraments are efficacious *ex opere operato* – literally, "on account of the work which is worked." Here, the efficacity of the sacrament is understood to be dependent upon the grace of Christ, which the sacraments represent and convey.

The Donatist position is consistent with an *ex opere operantis*, and Augustine's with an *ex opere operato*, understanding of sacramental causality. The latter view became normative within the western church, and was maintained by the mainstream reformers during the sixteenth century.

The Function of the Sacraments

In the course of the development of Christian theology, a number of understandings of the role of the sacraments have developed. In what follows, we shall consider the four most significant views of the function of the sacraments. It must be stressed that these are not mutually incompatible. The view that sacraments convey grace is not, for example, inconsistent with the related view that sacraments reassure believers of the promises of God. The debate has tended to center on which of the functions are essential to a right understanding of the sacraments.

Sacraments Convey Grace

We noted earlier the insistence on the part of medieval writers that sacraments *convey* the grace which they signify. Traces of this view may be found in the second century; Ignatius of Antioch declared that the eucharist was "the medicine of immortality and the antidote that we should not die, but live for ever in Jesus Christ." The idea is clearly that the eucharist does not merely *signify* eternal life, but is somehow instrumental in *effecting* it. The idea is developed subsequently by many writers, especially Ambrose of Milan. Writing in the fourth century, Ambrose argued that in baptism, the Holy Spirit "coming upon the font or upon those who are to be baptized, effects the reality of regeneration."

An important distinction, due to Augustine, relates to this point. Augustine distinguishes the sacrament from the "force [*virtus*] of the sacrament." The former is merely a sign, whereas the latter produces the effect to which the sign points. It is clear that a major function of the sacraments, in the thought of Augustine and his medieval successors, is that of the efficacious bestowal of grace.

Medieval writers sympathetic to Duns Scotus argued that it was not strictly proper to speak of the sacraments *causing* grace. The fourteenth-century writer Peter of Aquila put this point as follows:

> When Peter Lombard states that the sacraments effect what they signify, this must not be understood to mean that the sacraments themselves cause grace, in the strict sense of the word. Rather, God effects grace at the presence of the sacraments.

The sacraments are thus seen as causes in the sense of a *causa sine qua non* – that is, an indispensable precondition – rather than as causes in the stricter sense of the word.

Such views were rejected by the reformers, who found themselves embarrassed by Augustine's insistence upon the efficacious nature of the sacraments, especially baptism. Peter Martyr Vermigli is an example of a sixteenth-century Protestant writer who is critical of Augustine at this point:

> Augustine grievously erred in this doctrine, in ascribing too much to baptism. He does not acknowledge that it is merely an outward symbol of regeneration, but holds that, by the very act of being baptized, we are regenerated and adopted, and enter into the family of Christ.

The efficacious nature of the sacraments was reaffirmed by the Council of Trent, which criticized the Protestant tendency (seen above in Vermigli) to treat sacraments as signs, but not causes, of grace.

> If anyone says that the sacraments of the new law do not contain the grace that they signify, or that they do not confer that grace upon those who do not place obstacles in its path (as though they were only outward signs of grace or righteousness, received through faith, and certain marks of Christian profession by which believers are, at the human level, distinguished from non-believers), let them be condemned.

Trent prefers to speak of the sacraments "conferring" grace (rather than "causing" grace), thus allowing the Scotist position, noted above, to be maintained.

Sacraments Strengthen Faith

This understanding of the role of the sacraments became of especial importance during the sixteenth-century Reformation, partly on account of the importance placed upon the idea of trust (*fiducia*) as a defining characteristic of justifying faith. For the first generation of reformers, the sacraments were God's response to human weakness. Knowing our difficulty in receiving and responding to divine promises, the Word of God has been supplemented with visible and tangible signs of the gracious favor. The sacraments represent the promises of God, mediated through objects of the everyday world. In his *Propositions on the Mass* (1521), Melanchthon stressed that sacraments were primarily a gracious divine accommodation to human weakness. In a series of sixty-five propositions, Melanchthon put forward what he regarded as a reliable and responsible approach to the place of the sacraments in Christian spirituality. "Signs are the means by which we may be both reminded and reassured of the word of faith."

In an ideal world, Melanchthon suggests, human beings would be prepared to trust God on the basis of the Word alone. However, one of the weaknesses of fallen human nature is its need for signs (Melanchthon appeals to the Old Testament story of Gideon as he makes this point). For Melanchthon, sacraments are signs: "What some call sacraments, we call signs – or, if you prefer, sacramental signs." These sacramental signs enhance our trust in God. "In order to mitigate this distrust in the human heart, God has added signs to the word." Sacraments are thus signs of the grace of God, added to the promises of grace in order to reassure and strengthen the faith of fallen human beings.

Luther made a similar point, defining sacraments as "promises with signs attached to them" or "divinely instituted signs and the promise of forgiveness of sins." Interestingly, Luther uses the term "pledge" to emphasize the security-giving character of the eucharist. The bread and the wine reassure us of the reality of the divine promise of forgiveness, making it easier for us to accept it, and, having accepted it, to hold it firmly.

> In order that we might be certain of this promise of Christ, and truly rely on it without any doubt, God has given us the most precious and costly seal and pledge – Christ's true body and blood, given under the bread and wine. These are the very same as those with which he obtained for us the gift and the promise of this precious and gracious treasure, surrendering his life in order that we might receive and accept the promised grace.

This approach is also commended by the Second Vatican Council, which emphasized the dynamic role which sacraments assume in the advancement of maturity in the life of faith:

> Sacraments not only presuppose faith, but by words and objects they also nourish, strengthen, and express it. That is why they are called "sacraments of faith." They do indeed impart grace, but in addition, the very act of celebrating them disposes the faithful most effectively to receive this grace in a fruitful manner, to worship God rightly, and to practice charity.

Sacraments Enhance Unity and Commitment within the Church

The unity of the church was a source of major concern during the patristic period, especially as division arose in response to the Decian and Diocletian persecutions. Cyprian of Carthage, as we saw earlier (p. 408), laid considerable emphasis upon the unity of the church, and urged its members to work toward greater harmony within and commitment to the church. This point is developed by Augustine, with especial reference to the sacraments. For a society to have any degree of cohesion, there must be some act in which all can share, which both demonstrated and enhanced that unity. "In no religion, whether true or false, can people be held together in association, unless they are gathered together with some common share in some visible signs or sacraments." Although this point was understood by medieval writers, it found its most forceful expression at the time of the Reformation, especially in the writings of Huldrych Zwingli.

Luther asserted that a central function of the sacraments was to reassure believers that they are truly members of the body of Christ, and heirs of the kingdom of God. He developed this point at some length in his 1519 treatise *The Blessed Sacrament of the Holy and True Body of Christ*, stressing the psychological assurance that it makes available to believers:

> To receive this sacrament in bread and wine, then, is nothing else than to receive a sure sign of this fellowship and union with Christ and all the saints. It is as if citizens were given a sign, a document, or some other token, to assure them that they are indeed citizens of the city, and members of that particular community. . . . In this sacrament, therefore, we are given a sure sign from God that we are united with Christ and the saints, and have all things in common with them, and that Christ's suffering and life are our own.

This emphasis upon the sacraments as tokens of belonging to the Christian community is, as will become clear presently, perhaps more characteristic of Zwingli than of Luther; nevertheless, it is a significant element of Luther's thought at this point.

For Zwingli, the purpose of the sacraments is primarily to demonstrate that an individual belongs to the community of faith. Baptism represents the public declaration that a child is a member of the household of God. Zwingli pointed out that in the Old Testament infant males were circumcised within days of their birth as a sign of their membership of the people of Israel. Circumcision was the rite laid down by the Old Testament covenant to demonstrate that the circumcised child belonged to the covenant community. The child had been born into a community, to which it now belonged – and circumcision was a sign of belonging to this community.

It had been a long-standing tradition within Christian theology to see baptism as the Christian equivalent of circumcision. Developing this idea, Zwingli argued that baptism is the New Testament equivalent of the Old Testament rite of circumcision. It is gentler than circumcision, in that it involves no pain or shedding of blood, and more inclusive, in that it embraces both male and female infants. Further, Zwingli stressed that baptism was the sign of belonging to a community – the church. The fact that the child was not conscious of this belonging was irrelevant: It *was* a member of the Christian community, and baptism was the public demonstration of this membership. The contrast with Luther on this point will be obvious.

In a similar way, attendance at the eucharist represents a continuing public declaration of loyalty to the church. Zwingli develops this meaning of the eucharist with a military analogy drawn from his experience as an army chaplain for the Swiss Confederacy:

> If a man sews on a white cross, he proclaims that he wishes to be a confederate. And if he makes the pilgrimage to Nähenfels and gives God praise and thanksgiving for the victory vouchsafed to our forefathers, he testifies that he is a confederate indeed. Similarly, whoever receives the mark of baptism is the one who is resolved to hear what God says to him, to learn the divine precepts, and to live his life in accordance with them. And whoever in the congregation gives thanks to God in the remembrance or supper testifies to the fact that he rejoices in the death of Christ from the depths of his heart, and thanks him for it.

The reference is to the victory of the Swiss over the Austrians in 1388 near Nähenfels, in the canton of Glarus. This victory is usually regarded as marking the beginning of the Swiss (or Helvetic) Confederation, and it was commemorated by a pilgrimage to the site of the battle on the first Thursday in April.

Zwingli makes two points. First, the Swiss soldier wears a white cross (now incorporated into the Swiss national flag, of course) as a *Pflichtszeichen*, demonstrating publicly his allegiance to the Confederacy. Similarly, the Christian demonstrates his allegiance to the church publicly, initially by baptism, and subsequently by participating in the eucharist. Baptism is the "visible entry and sealing into Christ." Second, the historical event which brought the Confederacy into being is commemorated as a token of allegiance to that same Confederacy. Similarly, the Christian commemorates the historical event which brought the Christian church into being (the death of Jesus Christ) as a token of his commitment to that church. The eucharist is thus a memorial of the historical event leading to the establishment of the Christian church, and a public demonstration of the believer's allegiance to that church and its members. This is related to Zwingli's memorialist approach to the eucharist, which we shall explore further later (p. 442).

Sacraments Reassure Us of God's Promises Toward Us

Once more, this function is especially associated with the reformers, who laid particular emphasis upon faith as the human correlative to the promises of God. The reformers were deeply aware of the weakness of fallen human nature, and knew that it required considerable reassurance concerning God's love and commitment. Luther regarded the death of Christ as a token of both the trustworthiness and the enormous price of the grace of God. Luther developed this point by using the idea of a "testament," understood in the sense of a "last will and testament." This point is taken to its full extent in his 1520 work, *The Babylonian Captivity of the Christian Church*.

> A testament is a promise made by someone who is about to die, in which a bequest is defined and heirs appointed. A testament thus involves, in the first place, the death of the testator, and in the second, the promise of an inheritance and the naming of heirs. . . . We see these things clearly in the words of Christ. Christ testifies concerning his death when he says, "This is my body, which is given" and "This is my blood, which is poured out." He names and designates the bequest when he says "for the forgiveness of sins." And he appoints the heirs when he says, "for you and for many," that is, for those who accept and believe the promise of the testator.

Luther's insight here is that a testament involves promises which become operational only after the death of the person who made those promises in the first place. The liturgy of the eucharist thus makes three vitally important points:

1 It affirms the promises of grace and forgiveness.
2 It identifies those to whom those promises are made.
3 It declares the death of the one who made those promises.

The eucharist thus dramatically proclaims that the promises of grace and forgiveness are now in effect. It is "a promise of the forgiveness of sins made to us by God, and such a promise as has been confirmed by the death of the son of God." By proclaiming the death of Christ, the community of faith affirms that the precious promises of forgiveness and eternal life are now effective for those with faith. As Luther himself puts this point:

> So you see that what we call the mass is a promise of the forgiveness of sins made to us by God, and such a promise that has been confirmed by the death of the Son of God. For the only difference between a promise and a testament is that the testament involves the death of the one who makes it . . . Now God made a testament. Therefore it was necessary that God should die. But God could not die unless he became a human being. Thus the incarnation and the death of Christ are both included explicitly in this one word, "testament."

The Eucharist: The Question of the Real Presence

What happens at the eucharist? In what way, if any, do the eucharistic bread and wine change as a result of being used in this service? A number of approaches to the question have been explored during the centuries, of which the following are of especial importance.

Transubstantiation

This doctrine, formally defined by the Fourth Lateran Council (1215), rests upon Aristotelian foundations – specifically, on Aristotle's distinction between "substance" and "accident." The *substance* of something is its essential nature, whereas its *accidents* are its outward appearances (for example, its color, shape, smell, and so forth). The theory of transubstantiation affirms that the accidents of the bread and wine (their outward appearance, taste, smell, and so forth) remain unchanged at the moment of consecration, while their substance changes from that of bread and wine to that of the body and blood of Jesus Christ.

This approach was heavily criticized by Protestant theologians, especially at the time of the Reformation, for introducing Aristotelian ideas into Christian theology. It was not until 1551 that the Council of Trent finally set forth the positive position of the Roman Catholic church in the "Decree on the Most Holy Sacrament of the Eucharist." Up to this point, Trent had merely criticized the reformers, without putting forth a coherent alternative position. This deficiency was now remedied. The Decree opens with a strong affirmation of the real substantial presence of Christ: "After the consecration of the bread and wine, our Lord Jesus Christ is truly, really and substantially contained in the venerable sacrament of the holy eucharist under the appearance of those physical things." The Council vigorously defended both the doctrine and the terminology of transubstantiation. "By the consecration of the bread and wine a change is brought about of the whole substance of the bread into the substance of the body of Christ and of the whole substance of the wine into the blood of Christ. This change the holy catholic church properly and appropriately calls transubstantiation."

In more recent times, the idea of transubstantiation has been reworked by Roman Catholic theologians, such as Edward Schillebeeckx. Two such reworkings are of especial importance. The notion of *transsignification* expresses the idea that consecration is primarily concerned with the *change of meaning* of the bread and the wine. The related notion of *transfinalization* expresses the idea that consecration alters the end or purpose of the bread and wine. Both these notions rest upon the assumption that the identity of the bread and wine cannot be isolated from their context or use – an idea which finds expression in the writings of Zwingli.

What makes the bread at a communion service different from any other bread? If it is not the body of Christ, what is it? Zwingli answers this question with an analogy. Consider a queen's ring, he suggests. Now consider that ring in two quite different contexts. In the first context, the ring is merely present. Perhaps you can imagine a ring lying on a table. It has no associations. Now imagine that ring transferred to a new context. It is placed on the finger of a queen, as a gift from her king. It now has personal associations, deriving from its connection with him – such as his authority, power, and majesty. Its value is now far greater than that of the gold of which it is made. These associations arise through transfer from the original context to the new context: The ring itself remains completely unchanged.

So it is with the communion bread, Zwingli argues. The bread and the ring are both unchanged in themselves, while their signification alters dramatically. The signification – in other words, the associations of the object – can change, without any difference in the nature of the object itself. Zwingli suggests that exactly the same process can be seen with the bread and the wine. In their ordinary everyday context, they are plain bread and wine, with no especial associations. But when they are moved into a new context, they take on new and important associations. When they are placed at the center of a worshipping community, and when the story of the last night of the life of Christ is retold, they become powerful reminders of the foundational events of the Christian faith. It is their context which gives them this meaning; they remain unchanged in themselves.

Consubstantiation

This view, especially associated with Martin Luther, insists upon the simultaneous presence of both bread and the body of Christ at one and the same time. There is no change in substance; the substance of both bread and the body of Christ are present together. The doctrine of transubstantiation seemed to Luther to be an absurdity, an attempt to rationalize a mystery. For Luther, the crucial point was that Christ was really present at the eucharist – not some particular theory as to how he was present. He deploys an image borrowed from Origen to make his point: If iron is placed in a fire and heated, it glows – and in that glowing iron, both the iron and heat are present. Why not use some simple everyday analogy such as this to illustrate the mystery of the presence of Christ at the eucharist, instead of rationalizing it using some scholastic subtlety?

> For my part, if I cannot fathom how the bread is the body of Christ, yet I will take my reason captive to the obedience of Christ, and clinging simply to his words, firmly believe not only that the body of Christ is in the bread, but that the bread is the body of Christ. My warrant for this is the words which say: "He took bread, and when he had given thanks, he broke it and said, 'Take, eat, this (that is, this bread, which he had taken and broken) is my body.'" (1 Corinthians 11: 23–4)

It is not the doctrine of transubstantiation which is to be believed, but simply that Christ really is present at the eucharist. This fact is more important than any theory or explanation.

A Real Absence: Memorialism

This understanding of the nature of the eucharist is especially associated with Zwingli. The eucharist is "a memorial of the suffering of Christ, and not a sacrifice." For reasons which we shall explore below, Zwingli insists that the words "this is my body" cannot be taken literally, thus eliminating any idea of the "real presence of Christ" at the eucharist. Just as a man, on setting off on a long journey from home, might give his wife his ring to remember him by until his return, so Christ leaves his church a token to remember him by until the day on which he should return in glory.

But what of the words "this is my body" (Matthew 26: 26), which had been the cornerstone of traditional Catholic views of the real presence, and which Luther had seized upon in his defense of the real presence? Zwingli argued that "there are innumerable passages in Scripture where the word 'is' means 'signifies.'" The question that must therefore be addressed is

> whether Christ's words in Matthew 26, "This is my body" can also be taken metaphorically or *in tropice*. It has already become clear enough that in this context the word "is" cannot be taken literally. Hence it follows that it must be taken metaphorically or figuratively. In the words "This is my body," the word "this" means the bread, and the word "body" means the body which was put to death for us. Therefore the word "is" cannot be taken literally, for the bread is not the body.

The Controversy over Infant Baptism

The second major sacrament which is virtually universally recognized throughout Christianity is baptism. Perhaps the most important controversy to center upon this sacrament is whether it is legitimate to baptize infants – and if so, what theological justification may be provided for the practice. It is not clear whether the early church baptized infants. The New Testament includes no specific references to the baptism of infants. However, it does not explicitly forbid the practice, and there are also a number of passages which could be interpreted as condoning it – for example, references to the baptizing of entire households (which would probably have included infants) – at several points (Acts 16: 15, 33; 1 Corinthians 1: 16). Paul treats baptism as a spiritual counterpart to circumcision (Colossians 2: 11–12), suggesting that the parallel may extend to its application to infants.

The practice of baptizing infant members of Christian parents – often referred to as *paedobaptism* – appears to have been a response to a number of pressures. It is possible that the parallel with the Jewish rite of circumcision led Christians to devise an equivalent rite of passage for Christian infants. More generally, there seems to have been a pastoral need for Christian parents to celebrate the birth of a child within a believing household. Infant baptism may well have had its origins partly in response to this concern. However, it must be stressed that there is genuine uncertainty concerning both the historical origins and the social or theological causes of the practice.

What can be said is that the practice had become normal, if not universal, by the second or third century, and, as we shall see, would exercise considerable influence over a major theological debate – the Pelagian controversy (pp. 444–5). In the second century, Origen treated infant baptism as a universal practice, which he justified on the basis of a universal human need for the grace of Christ. A similar argument would later be deployed by Augustine: In that Christ is the savior of all, it follows that all – including infants – require redemption, which baptism confers, at least in part. Opposition to the practice can be seen in the writings of Tertullian, who argued that the baptism of children should be deferred until such time as they "know Christ."

In more recent times, infant baptism has been subjected to intense negative scrutiny in the writings of Karl Barth, who directs three major lines of criticism against the practice, as follows.

1   It is without biblical foundation. All the evidence points to infant baptism having become the norm in the post-apostolic period, not the period of the New Testament itself.

2 The practice of infant baptism has led to the disastrous assumption that individuals are Christians as a result of their birth. Barth argues, in terms which remind many of Bonhoeffer's idea of "cheap grace," that infant baptism devalues the grace of God, and reduces Christianity to a purely social phenomenon.

3 The practice of infant baptism weakens the central link between baptism and Christian discipleship. Baptism is a witness to the grace of God, and marks the beginning of the human response to this grace. In that infants cannot meaningfully make this response, the theological meaning of baptism is obscured.

While all of Barth's arguments can be countered, they are an impressive witness to a continuing unease within the mainstream churches over the potential abuse of the practice of infant baptism.

Three major approaches to the question of infant baptism can be discerned within the Christian tradition. In what follows, we shall consider these individually.

Infant Baptism Remits the Guilt of Original Sin

This position owes its origins to Cyprian of Carthage, who declared that infant baptism procured remission of both sinful acts and original sin. The final steps in the theological justification of the practice are due to Augustine of Hippo, in responding to the issues surrounding the Pelagian controversy. Had not the creed laid down that there was "one baptism for the forgiveness of sins"? It therefore followed that infant baptism remitted original sin.

This raised a question of potential difficulty. If original sin was remitted by baptism, why did the infants in question behave in a sinful manner in later life? Augustine met this objection by distinguishing between the *guilt* and the *disease* of original sin (see pp. 373–4). Baptism remitted the guilt of original sin, but did nothing to get rid of its effects, which could only be eliminated by the continuing work of grace within the believer.

One major implication of this approach relates to the fate of those who die without being baptized. What happens to those who die without having been baptized, whether in infancy or later in life? If baptism remits the guilt of original sin, people who die without being baptized remain guilty. So what happens to them? Augustine's position demands that such people cannot be saved. Augustine himself certainly held to this belief, and argued forcefully that unbaptized infants were condemned to eternal damnation. However, he conceded that such infants would not have as unpleasant a time in hell as those who lived to adulthood, and committed actual sins. Considerations such as these considerably increased apprehension over the idea of hell, as we shall see later (pp. 474–5).

Nevertheless, Augustine's position was modified in the light of popular pressure, apparently based upon a belief that his doctrine was unjust. Peter Lombard argued that unbaptized infants received only "the penalty of being condemned" and do not receive the more painful "penalty of the senses." Although they are condemned, that condemnation does not include the experience of the physical pain of hell. This idea is often referred to as "limbo," although this has never become part of the official teaching of any Christian body. It is reflected in Dante's description of hell, which we shall consider later (p. 473).

Infant Baptism is Grounded in the Covenant between God and the Church

Earlier, we noted how many theologians interpret sacraments as concerned with the *affirmation of belonging to a community* (see pp. 436–8). A series of Protestant writers have sought to justify the practice of infant baptism by seeing it as a sign of the covenant between God and his people. The baptism of infants inside the church is regarded as a direct counterpart to the Jewish rite of circumcision.

The origins of this approach are to be found with Zwingli. Zwingli regarded the idea of "original guilt" with considerable skepticism. How could an infant be said to be guilty of anything? Guilt implied a degree of moral responsibility which was quite lacking in infants. By rejecting the Augustinian notion of "original guilt," Zwingli found himself temporarily without any justification for the practice of infant baptism – a practice which he regarded as justified, on the basis of the New Testament. So how was this practice to be justified theoretically?

Zwingli found his answer in the Old Testament, which stipulated that male infants born within the bounds of Israel should have an outward sign of their membership of the people of God. The outward sign in question was circumcision – that is, the removal of the foreskin. Infant baptism was thus to be seen as analogous to circumcision – a sign of belonging to a covenant community (see p. 437). Zwingli argued that the more inclusive and gentle character of Christianity was publicly affirmed by infant baptism. The more *inclusive* character of Christianity was affirmed by the baptism of both male and female infants; Judaism, in contrast, recognized only the marking of male infants. The more *gentle* character of the gospel was publicly demonstrated by the absence of pain or the shedding of blood in the sacrament. Christ suffered – in being circumcised himself, in addition to his death on the cross – in order that his people need not suffer in this manner.

Infant Baptism is Unjustified

The rise of the radical Reformation in the sixteenth century, and subsequently of Baptist churches in England during the seventeenth century, witnessed a rejection of the traditional practice of baptizing infants. Baptism was to be administered only when an individual showed signs of grace, repentance, or faith. The silence of the New Testament on the matter is to be taken as indicating that there is no biblical warrant for infant baptism whatsoever.

In part, this position rests upon a particular understanding of the function of sacraments in general, and baptism in particular. A long-standing debate within the Christian tradition centers on whether sacraments are *causative* or *declarative* (see pp. 434–5). In other words, does baptism cause forgiveness of sin? Or does it signify or declare that this forgiveness has already taken place? The practice of "believer's baptism" rests upon the assumption that baptism represents the public declaration of faith upon the part of a converted individual. Conversion has already occurred; baptism represents the public declaration that this has taken place. There are parallels between this position and that of Zwingli, noted above; the essential difference between Zwingli's view and this Baptist position is that the event which baptism publicly declares is interpreted differently. Zwingli understands the event in question to be *birth into a believing community*; Baptist writers understand it to be *the dawn of a personal faith in the life of an individual*.

This position is set out succinctly by Benajah Harvey Carroll (1843–1914), a leading figure in Southern Baptist life in the state of Texas. For baptism to be valid, Carroll argued, four requirements must be met:

1 The proper *authority* – that is, the church – must administer the sacrament.
2 The proper *subject* – that is, the penitent believer – must receive the sacrament. Carroll insists that conversion precedes baptism.
3 The proper *act* must be performed: Baptism is by total immersion in water.

4 The proper *design* must be affirmed: Baptism is symbolic, and can in no way be understood to effect the conversion of the individual who is thus baptized.

This represents a slight development of the criteria laid down by James Robinson Graves (1820–93), probably the most significant intellectual force in the early period of the Southern Baptist Convention. Graves had identified three essential characteristics of baptism: The proper subject (a believing Christian); a proper mode, which is total immersion and baptism in the name of the Trinity; and a proper administrator, who must be "an immersed believer, acting under the authority of a gospel church."

We have now considered the major theological aspects of the life of the Christian church, including the question of how the church and its sacraments relate to the gospel. However, a cluster of new questions now await us. How does the Christian community relate to other communities outside the Christian faith? This question has become of considerable importance, as western society acknowledges its multicultural nature. How does the Christian church understand its relationship to non-Christian religions? We shall consider such issues in the following chapter.

Questions for Chapter 14

1 "A sacrament is a sign of divine things." Why was this early definition so inadequate?

2 Name the seven sacraments recognized by the medieval church.

3 Identify the three criteria used by the reformers to reduce the number of the sacraments from seven to two.

4 On what grounds did Zwingli reject the idea of "a real presence" of Christ in the eucharist?

5 Give a brief summary of the main arguments for and against the baptism of infants. Does it make any difference to the infant concerned?

15

Christianity and the World Religions

The modern western world is acutely aware of a plurality of cultures within its midst. As British theologian Lesslie Newbigin remarks:

> It has become a commonplace to say that we live in a pluralist society – not merely a society which is in fact plural in the variety of cultures, religions and lifestyles which it embraces, but pluralist in the sense that this plurality is celebrated as a thing to be approved and cherished.

Newbigin here makes an important distinction between pluralism as a fact of life, and pluralism as an ideology – that is, the belief that pluralism is to be encouraged and desired, and that normative claims to truth are to be censured as imperialist and divisive (an important aspect of the postmodern worldview). Our concern here is with the former.

Western Pluralism and the Question of the Religions

The Christian proclamation has always taken place in a pluralist world, in competition with rival religious and intellectual convictions. The emergence of the gospel within the matrix of Judaism; the expansion of the gospel in a Hellenistic milieu; the early Christian expansion in pagan Rome; the establishment of the *Mar Thoma* church in south-eastern India – all of these are examples of situations in which Christian apologists and theologians, not to mention ordinary Christian believers, have been aware that there are alternatives to Christianity on offer, and have had to make appropriate responses.

It is quite possible that this insight may have been lost to most British and American Christians of the late nineteenth or early twentieth centuries, trapped in a contented and lazy parochialism. For such people, pluralism might have meant little more than a variety of forms of Protestantism, while "different religions" would probably have been understood to refer simply to the age-old tension between Protestantism and Roman Catholicism.

Yet immigration from the Indian subcontinent has changed things irreversibly within Britain, with Hinduism and Islam becoming foci of identity for ethnic minorities, just as France has been shaken by the new presence of Islam through emigration from its former north African colonies. The western seaboard of the United States and Canada and many cities in Australia have experienced an influx of peoples of eastern faiths, especially those originating from a Chinese context. As a result, western theologians (who still seem to dominate global discussion of such issues) have at long last become aware of and begun to address issues which are routine facts of everyday life for Christians in many parts of the world. The result is that providing a theological account of the relation of Christianity to other religions has become of major significance in the modern world.

Two fundamentally different styles of approach to the religions may be adopted, each of which can be readily discerned in modern western academia.

1 The *detached* approach, which seeks to give an account of the religions, Christianity included, from the standpoint of philosophy or the social sciences, or from a loosely "religious" perspective (as in many modern American "faculties of religion"). An excellent example of this approach may be found in Anthony Giddens's highly influential textbook, *Sociology*, which approaches religious matters from a sociological standpoint. His approach is instructive; for example, he gives four illustrations of what religion is *not*, in order to indicate the extent to which western cultural bias can creep into thinking about religions. According to Giddens, religion is *not*:

(a)   to be identified with *monotheism*;
(b)   to be identified with *moral prescriptions*;
(c)   necessarily concerned with explanations of the world;
(d)   to be identified with the supernatural.

Giddens's comments in relation to the too-easy identification of religion with monotheism are of considerable interest:

> Religion should not be identified with monotheism (belief in one God). Nietzsche's thesis of the "death of God" was strongly ethnocentric, relating only to western religious ideas. Most religions involve many deities . . . In certain religions, there are no gods at all.

Giddens's concern is simply to document the phenomenon of religion, without imposing a restrictive interpretive framework upon it.

2 A *committed* approach, which seeks to give an account of the origins and functions of religions from an explicitly Christian perspective. It is this approach which particularly concerns us in this volume, dealing as it does with a specifically *Christian* theology, rather than theories about religion in general. However, the importance of the question of religions in modern culture is such it is entirely proper to open this discussion by considering some "detached" approaches to the world religions, before moving on to consider more explicitly Christian approaches.

Approaches to Religions

In what follows, we shall consider a number of major approaches to the religions of the world. Only one such approach – that of Karl Barth and Dietrich Bonhoeffer – can be regarded as explicitly Christian in its orientation. It is included here on account of its impact upon the "death of God" or the "secular meaning of the gospel" movements which emerged in the United States during the 1960s and early 1970s. We begin by considering the views which emerged at the time of the Enlightenment.

The Enlightenment: Religions as a Corruption of the Original Religion of Nature

The Enlightenment witnessed the birth of the idea that religion was fundamentally a corruption of a primeval rational worldview, engineered by priests as a means of enhancing and preserving their positions within society. This approach is illustrated in the title of Matthew Tindal's highly influential work, *Christianity as Old as Creation, or, The Gospel a Republication of the Religion of Nature* (1730). On the basis of the foundational Enlightenment assumption of the rationality of reality, and the ability of human beings to uncover and apprehend this rationality, it was argued that whatever lay behind the various world religions was ultimately rational in character, and thus capable of being uncovered, described, and analyzed by human reason.

The idea of a universal rational religion was, however, at odds with the diversity of the world religions. As European knowledge of these religions deepened, through the growth of the genre of "voyager literature," and through the increasing availability of Chinese, Indian, Persian, and Vedic religious writings, it became increasingly clear that the notion of a universal religion of reason faced difficulties when confronted with the evidence of the astonishing variety of human religious beliefs and practices. Many Enlightenment writers, perhaps more concerned with championing reason than with wrestling with the empirical evidence, developed a theory of religion which accounted for this diversity, at least in part.

In his *True Intellectual System of the Universe* (1678), Ralph Cudworth argued that all religions were ultimately based upon a common ethical monotheism – a simple religion of nature, basically ethical in character, and devoid of all the arbitrary doctrines and religious rites of Christianity or Judaism. The primordial rational religion of nature had become corrupted through its early interpreters. The theory which gained an especially wide hearing was that the various world religions were little more than the inventions of cultic leaders or priests, whose main motivation was the preservation of their own interests and status. The Roman historian Tacitus had suggested that Moses invented the Jewish religious rites as a means of ensuring religious cohesion after the expulsion from Egypt; many writers of the early Enlightenment developed this notion, arguing that the variety of human religious rites and practices were simply human inventions in response to specific historical situations, now firmly in the past. The way was open to the recovery of the universal primordial religion of nature, which would put an end to the religious squabbles of humanity.

The idea of "superstition" emerged as significant at this term, often becoming pejoratively synonymous with "religion." In his *Natural History of Superstition* (1709), John Trenchard developed the idea of the inherent credulity of humanity, which permitted natural monotheism to degenerate into the various religious traditions of humanity. The enthusiasm with which this idea was received can be judged from the comments of the *Independent Whig* (December 31, 1720), to the effect that "the peculiar Foible of Mankind is Superstition, or an intrinsick and pannick Fear of invisible and unknown Beings."

For Trenchard, the religions represented the triumph of superstition over reason. By eliminating such superstitious beliefs and rites, a return to the universal and simple religion of nature could be achieved. A similar idea was developed during the French Enlightenment by

Paul Henri Thiry, Baron d'Holbach, who argued that religion was little
more than a form of pathological disorder. The French Revolution
seemed set to eliminate this disorder; its total failure to do so raised
awkward questions for the general Enlightenment approach to religions. For this reason, the approach adopted by Ludwig Feuerbach
seemed to offer new possibilities for those disaffected from the
European religious situation at the time.

Ludwig Feuerbach: Religion as an Objectification of Human Feeling

In the foreword to the first edition of his *Essence of Christianity* (1841),
Feuerbach states that the "purpose of this work is to show that the
supernatural mysteries of religion are based upon quite simple natural
truths." The leading idea of the work is deceptively simple: Human
beings have created their own gods and religions, which embody their
own idealized conception of their aspirations, needs, and fears. We
have already considered some aspects of Feuerbach's approach (see
pp. 199–200); it now demands to be treated in more detail.

It is not correct to suggest that Feuerbach merely reduces the divine
to the natural. The permanent significance of Feuerbach's work lies in
its detailed analysis of the means by which religious concepts arise
within the human consciousness. The thesis that human beings create
the gods in their own image is but the conclusion of a radical and
penetrating critique of concept-formation in religion, based on the
Hegelian concepts of "self-alienation" and "self-objectification."

The Hegelian analysis of consciousness requires that there be a
formal relation of subject to object. The concept of "consciousness"
cannot be isolated as an abstract idea, in that it is necessarily linked
with an object: To be "conscious" is to be conscious *of something*.
Human consciousness of feelings, such as fear or love, leads to their
objectification and thus to externalization of these feelings. Divine
predicates are thus recognized to be human predicates.

> Consciousness of God is human self-consciousness; knowledge of
> God is human self-knowledge. By the God you know the human,
> and conversely, by the human, you know the God. The two are
> one. . . . What an earlier religion took to be objective, is later re-
> cognized to be subjective; what formerly was taken to be God, and
> worshipped as such, is now recognized to be something human.
> What was earlier religion is later taken to be idolatry: humans are
> seen to have adored their own nature. Humans objectified them-
> selves but failed to recognize themselves as this object. The later

religion takes this step; every advance in religion is therefore a deepening in self-knowledge.

It is obvious that Feuerbach tends to use the terms "Christianity" and "religion" interchangeably throughout *The Essence of Christianity*, thus glossing over the fact that his theory has some difficulty in accounting for non-theistic religions. Nevertheless, it is clear that his reduction of Christian theology to anthropology is of considerable significance.

The most important epistemological analysis in *The Essence of Christianity* is concerned with the role of feeling in the process of religious concept-formation, and has important consequences for the "religious feeling"-centered approach of Schleiermacher and the later liberal tradition. For Feuerbach, Christian theology has tended to interpret the externalized image of "feeling" or self-consciousness as a wholly other, absolute essence, whereas it is in fact it is a "self-feeling feeling": human religious feelings or experience cannot be interpreted as an awareness of God, but only as a misunderstood self-awareness. "If feeling is the essential instrumentality or organ of religion, then God's nature is nothing other than an expression of the nature of feeling. . . . The divine essence, which is comprehended by feeling, is actually nothing other than the essence of feeling, enraptured and delighted with itself – nothing but self-intoxicated, self-contented feeling."

Important though Feuerbach's analysis may have been, it was overshadowed by that of Karl Marx, to which we may now turn.

Karl Marx: Religion as the Product of Socio-Economic Alienation

In his 1844 political and economic manuscripts, Marx develops an approach to religion which rests upon ideas demonstrably due to Feuerbach. Religion has no real independent existence. It is a reflection of the material world, and is derived from the social needs and hopes of human beings (see pp. 89–92). "The religious world is but the reflex of the real world." Marx argues that "religion is just the imaginary sun which seems to humans to revolve around themselves until they realize that they themselves are the center of their own revolution." In other words, God is simply a projection of human concerns. Human beings "look for a superhuman being in the fantasy reality of heaven, and find nothing there but their own reflection."

Yet the human nature which generates religious ideas is *alienated*. The notion of alienation is of central importance to Marx's account of the origins of religious belief. "Humans make religion; religion does not make humans. Religion is the self-consciousness and self-esteem of people who either have not found themselves or who have already lost themselves again." Religion is the product of social and economic alienation. It arises from that alienation, and at the same time encourages that alienation by a form of spiritual intoxication which renders the masses incapable of recognizing their situation and doing something about it. Religion is a comfort, which enables people to tolerate their economic alienation. If there were no such alienation, there would be no need for religion. The division of labor and the existence of private property introduce alienation and estrangement into the economic and social orders.

Materialism affirms that events in the material world bring about corresponding changes in the intellectual world. Religion is thus the result of a certain set of social and economic conditions. Change those conditions, so that economic alienation is eliminated, and religion will cease to exist. It will no longer serve any useful function. Unjust social conditions produce religion, and are in turn supported by religion. "The struggle against religion is therefore indirectly a struggle against *the world* of which religion is the spiritual fragrance."

Marx thus argues that religion will continue to exist as long as it meets a need in the life of alienated people. "The religious reflex of the real world can . . . only then vanish when the practical relations of everyday life offer to humanity none but perfectly intelligible and reasonable relations with regard to other human beings and to nature." Feuerbach had argued that religion was the projection of human needs, an expression of the "uttered sorrow of the soul." Marx agrees with this interpretation. However, his point is more radical. It is not enough to explain how religion arises on account of sorrow and injustice. By changing that world, the causes of religion can be removed. It is important to note that Marx regards Feuerbach as correct in his analysis of the origins of religion, even if as having failed to discern how an understanding of those origins might lead to its eventual elimination. It is this insight which underlies his often quoted eleventh thesis on Feuerbach: "The philosophers have only interpreted the world, in various ways; the point, however, is to change it."

Sigmund Freud: Religion as Wish-Fulfillment

The basic ideas associated with Feuerbach and Marx found new life in the writings of the psychoanalyst Sigmund Freud. In fact, it is probably fair to say that the "projection" or "wish-fulfillment" theory is best known today in its Freudian variant, rather than in Feuerbach's original version. The most powerful statement of Freud's approach may be found in *The Future of an Illusion* (1927), which develops a strongly reductionist approach to religion.

For Freud, religious ideas are "illusions, fulfillments of the oldest, strongest and most urgent wishes of humanity." Religion represents the perpetuation in adult life of a piece of infantile behavior, being little more than an immature response to the awareness of helplessness, by going back to one's childhood experiences of paternal care: "My father will protect me; he is in control." Belief in a personal God is thus little more than an infantile delusion. Religion is wishful thinking, an illusion, which can easily degenerate into a pathological disorder.

Emile Durkheim: Religion and Ritual

In his *Elementary Forms of the Religious Life* (1912), Durkheim explored the relation between religion and the institutions of society in general. The case study upon which most of his ideas are grounded is that of totemism in Australian aboriginal societies. For Durkheim, totemism represents the "elementary form of the religious life." The totem was originally an animal or plant which was regarded as having especial symbolic significance for a people. It was thus treated as sacred – that is, as being set apart from the routine aspects of human life.

The reason for this, according to Durkheim, is that the totem comes to represent values which are central to society itself. As a result, it comes to be a symbol of the group. The reverence with which the totem is treated is, in reality, reverence for the group itself and its undergirding values. The true object of worship is thus not the totem, but society itself. The ceremony and ritual which attend this worship are seen as reflections of the need for social cohesion. The special religious ceremonies which are associated with birth, marriage, and death are to be regarded as a reaffirmation of group solidarity at moments of cultural importance. Thus funeral rites demonstrate that the values of a society will outlive the death of any of its individual members.

Despite the development of a scientific worldview, Durkheim believes that religion will continue to play an important role in the future, in view of its providing social cohesion for societies (a point we noted in relation to the sacraments, pp. 436–8). The emergence of "civil religion" in the United States, centering upon the person of the president or the symbol of the Stars and Stripes, could be seen as confirmation of this approach, as could the emergence of an atheist "state religion" in the former Soviet Union under Lenin and Stalin.

Karl Barth and Dietrich Bonhoeffer: Religion as a Human Invention

A final approach of considerable importance has its origins within Christianity, and specifically within the dialectical theology of Karl Barth. This approach develops the idea that "religion" is a purely human construction, often an act of defiance in the face of God. Religion is here seen as an upward search for God on the part of humanity. This contrasts sharply with God's self-revelation, which exposes religion as a human fabrication.

Barth, it will be recalled, received his theological education within German liberal Protestantism. The "culture Protestantism" of the period laid considerable emphasis upon the importance of human religiosity. In a lecture of 1916, entitled "The Righteousness of God," Barth declared that human religiosity was little more than a Tower of Babel – a purely human construction, erected in defiance of God. There is a radical discontinuity between God's self-revelation to humanity, which leads to faith, and humanity's search for God, which leads to religion. Barth is thus able to endorse criticisms of religion along the lines of Feuerbach and Marx, precisely because he believes these to be directed against the human invention of religion. Religion, for Barth, is an obstacle which must be eliminated if God is to be discerned in Christ. At its worst, it is idolatrous, in that it involves people worshipping a human construction.

Many writers have tried to summarize Barth's view on religion in the phrase "the abolition of religion." It is certainly true that the standard English translation of section 17 of the *Church Dogmatics*, volume 1, part 2, is entitled "The Revelation of God as the Abolition of Religion." This English phrase is, however, profoundly misleading and needs careful explanation. It must be remembered that Barth wrote in German, not English. The German word translated by "abolition" is *Aufhebung*, a term with a long and distinguished history of use within the German philosophical tradition, especially within Hegelianism. It is ambiguous, and possesses two root meanings: "to remove" and "to exalt."

It is certainly true that in his early writings Barth adopts a very negative attitude toward religion, understood as a human invention. Yet Barth is here stressing the natural human tendency to form concepts of God, and to seek justification in relation to them. He is not criticizing other *religions* but *religion* in general. Barth sees the phenomenon of "religion" at work in Christianity as much as anywhere else; cultural values intrude into the gospel, and become merged with it. Barth's intense anxiety about this development was particularly focused upon the German church struggle of the 1930s, in which he believed that Germanic ideals were becoming incorporated into Christian faith.

However, Barth's attitude mellowed in his later period. He came increasingly to see the need for religion this side of eternity. "Religion" comes to mean more "human institutions" or "modes of worship," rather than "a human attempt to determine what God is like." Barth's references to the "abolition" of religion do not make sense, in that he insists that "religion" will continue until the end of time, as a necessary prop or support to faith. Rather, Barth's concern is to emphasize that, by the grace of God, this "religion" is transcended and surpassed by God. It is something neutral, not negative.

This is most emphatically *not* what Dietrich Bonhoeffer thought. Bonhoeffer's most significant contribution to modern theology is generally regarded to be his analysis of the cultural situation within which Christ is to be proclaimed in the modern world. On April 5, 1945, Bonhoeffer was arrested by the Gestapo for his alleged involvement in a plot against Adolf Hitler. During the eighteen months of his imprisonment at Berlin's Tegel prison, he wrote his celebrated *Letters and Papers from Prison*, in which he reflected on the question of the identity of Jesus Christ in a "world come of age," a time of "no religion at all." He argued passionately for a "religionless Christianity."

This powerful phrase has often been misunderstood. Bonhoeffer directed his criticisms against forms of Christianity based on the assumption that human beings were naturally religious – an assumption that Bonhoeffer regarded as untenable, given the new godless situation. A "religionless Christianity" is a faith which is based not upon the untenable and discredited notion of "natural human religiosity," but upon God's self-revelation in Christ. An appeal to culture, to metaphysics, or to religion was thus to be avoided, in that these were inherently implausible in the new secular world, and inevitably led to distorted understandings of God (there are strong affinities between Barth and Bonhoeffer here). The crucified Christ provided us with a model of God appropriate for the modern world – a God who "allows himself to be pushed out of the world and on to the cross." These ideas, especially as they related to the new secularism and the need to ground theology elsewhere than religion or metaphysics, were to prove seminal to post-war German Christology, and had a deep impact upon many writers in the United States during the 1960s.

There were, however, obvious confusions here. Bonhoeffer's phrase "a religionless Christianity" and Barth's phrase "the abolition of religion" were taken by many more radical writers of the period to mean the end of any corporate Christian life, or an abandoning of traditional Christian ideas. These misunderstandings can be seen in influential popular works of the 1960s, such as John Robinson's *Honest to God* and the "death of God" movement.

Having dealt with one Christian approach to the question of religion in general, we may now move on to examine specifically Christian approaches to other religions.

Christianity and other Religious Traditions: Three Theological Approaches

Christianity is but one world religious tradition among a host of others. So how does it relate to other religious traditions? The question is not modern; it has been asked throughout Christian history. Initially the question concerned Christianity's relationship with Judaism, from whose matrix it emerged in the period AD 30–60. And as it expanded, it encountered other religious beliefs and practices, such as classical paganism. As it became established in India in the fifth century, it encountered the diverse native Indian cultural movements which western scholars of religion have misleadingly grouped together and termed "Hinduism." Arab Christianity has long learned to co-exist with Islam in the eastern Mediterranean.

In the modern period, the question of the relation of Christianity to other religious traditions has assumed a new importance in western academic theology, partly on account of the rise of multiculturalism in western society. As will become clear, three main approaches have gained currency. However, it will be helpful to begin by considering the idea of "religion" itself.

A naïve view of religion might be that it is an outlook on life which believes in, or worships, a supreme being. This outlook, characteristic of Deism and Enlightenment rationalism, is easily shown to be inadequate. Buddhism is classified as a religion by most people; yet here a belief in a supreme being is conspicuously absent. The same problem persists, no matter what definition of "religion" is offered. No unambiguously common features can be identified amongst the religions, in matters of faith or practice. Thus Edward Conze, the great scholar of Buddhism, recalled that he "once read through a collection of the lives of Roman Catholic saints, and there was not one of whom a Buddhist could fully approve. . . . They were bad Buddhists though good Christians."

There is a growing consensus that it is seriously misleading to regard the various religious traditions of the world as variations on a single theme. "There is no single essence, no one content of enlightenment or revelation, no one way of emancipation or liberation, to be found in all that plurality" (David Tracy). John B. Cobb Jr also notes the enormous difficulties confronting anyone wishing to argue that there is an "essence of religion":

> Arguments about what religion truly is are pointless. There is no such thing as religion. There are only traditions, movements, communities, peoples, beliefs, and practices that have features that are associated by many people with what they mean by religion.

Cobb stresses that the assumption that religion has an essence has bedeviled and seriously misled recent discussion of the relation of the religious traditions of the world. For example, he points out that both Buddhism and Confucianism have "religious" elements – but that does not necessarily mean that they can be categorized as "religions." Many "religions" are better understood as cultural movements with religious components.

The idea of some universal notion of religion, of which individual religions are subsets, appears to have emerged at the time of the Enlightenment. To use a biological analogy, the assumption that there is a genus of religion, of which individual religions are species, is a very western idea, without any real parallel outside western culture – except on the part of those who have been educated in the west, and uncritically absorbed its presuppositions.

What, then, of Christian approaches to understanding the relation between Christianity and other religious traditions? In what way can such traditions be understood, within the context of the Christian belief in the universal saving will of God, made known through Jesus Christ? It must be stressed that Christian theology is concerned with evaluating other religious traditions *from the perspective of Christianity itself*. Such reflection is not addressed to, or intended to gain approval from, members of other religious traditions, or their secular observers.

Three broad approaches can be identified: *exclusivism*, which holds that only those who hear and respond to the Christian gospel may be saved; *inclusivism*, which argues that, although Christianity represents the normative revelation of God, salvation is nonetheless possible for those who belong to other religious traditions; and *pluralism*, which holds that all the religious traditions of humanity are equally valid paths to the same core of religious reality. We shall consider these individually.

The Exclusivist Approach

Perhaps the most influential statement of this position may be found in the writings of Hendrik Kraemer (1888–1965), especially his *Christian Message in a Non-Christian World* (1938). Kraemer emphasized that "God has revealed *the* Way and *the* Truth and *the* Life in Jesus Christ, and wills this to be known throughout the world." This revelation is *sui generis*; it is in a category of its own, and cannot be set alongside the ideas of revelation found in other religious traditions.

At this point, a certain breadth of opinion can be discerned within this approach. Kraemer himself seems to suggest that there is real knowledge of God outside Christ when he speaks of God shining through "in a broken, troubled way, in reason, in nature and in history." The question is whether such knowledge is only available through Christ, or whether Christ provides the only framework by which such knowledge may be discerned and interpreted elsewhere.

Some exclusivists (such as Karl Barth) adopt the position that there is no knowledge of God to be had apart from Christ; others (such as Kraemer) allow that God's self-revelation occurs in many ways and places – but insist that this revelation can only be interpreted correctly, and known for what it really is, in the light of the definitive revelation of God in Christ. (There are important parallels here with the debate over natural and revealed knowledge of God.)

What, then, of those who have not heard the gospel of Christ? What happens to them? Are not exclusivists denying salvation to those who have not heard of Christ – or, who having heard of him, choose to reject him? This criticism is frequently levelled against exclusivism by its critics. Thus John Hick, arguing from a pluralist perspective, suggests that the doctrine that salvation is only possible through Christ is inconsistent with belief in the universal saving will of God. That this is not, in fact, the case is readily demonstrated by considering the view of Karl Barth, easily the most sophisticated of twentieth-century defenders of this position.

Barth declares that salvation is only possible through Christ. He nevertheless insists on the ultimate eschatological victory of grace over unbelief – that is, at the end of history (a point we considered earlier, in connection with his doctrine of election, pp. 400–2). Eventually, God's grace will triumph completely, and all will come to faith in Christ. This is the only way to salvation – but it is a way that, through the grace of God, is effective for all. For Barth, the particularity of God's revelation through Christ is not contradicted by the universality of salvation.

The Inclusivist Approach

The most significant advocate of this model is the leading Jesuit writer Karl Rahner. In the fifth volume of his *Theological Investigations*, Rahner develops four theses, setting out the view, not merely that individual non-Christians may be saved, but that the non-Christian religious traditions in general may have access to the saving grace of God in Christ.

1   Christianity is the absolute religion, founded on the unique event of the self-revelation of God in Christ. But this revelation took place at a specific point in history. Those who lived before this point, or who have yet to hear about this event, would thus seem to be excluded from salvation – which is contrary to the saving will of God.
2   For this reason, despite their errors and shortcomings, non-Christian religious traditions are valid and capable of mediating the saving grace of God, until the gospel is made known to their members. After the gospel has been proclaimed to the adherents of such non-Christian religious traditions, they are no longer legitimate, from the standpoint of Christian theology.
3   The faithful adherent of a non-Christian religious tradition is thus to be regarded as an "anonymous Christian."
4   Other religious traditions will not be displaced by Christianity. Religious pluralism will continue to be a feature of human existence.

We may explore the first three theses in more detail. It will be clear that Rahner strongly affirms the principle that salvation may only be had through Christ, as he is interpreted by the Christian tradition. "Christianity understands itself as the absolute religion, intended for all people, which cannot recognize any other religion beside itself as of equal right." Yet Rahner supplements this with an emphasis upon the universal saving will of God: God wishes that all shall be saved, even though not all know Christ. "Somehow all people must be able to be members of the church."

For this reason, Rahner argues that saving grace must be available outside the bounds of the church – and hence in other religious traditions. He vigorously opposes those who adopt too-neat solutions, insisting that *either* a religious tradition comes from God *or* that it is an inauthentic and purely human invention. Where Kraemer argued that non-Christian religious traditions were little more than self-justifying human constructions, Rahner argues that such traditions may well include elements of truth.

Rahner justifies this suggestion by considering the relation between the Old and New Testaments. Although the Old Testament, strictly speaking, represents the outlook of a non-Christian religion (Judaism), Christians are able to read it and discern within it elements which continue to be valid. The Old Testament is evaluated in the light of the New, and, as a result, certain practices (such as dietary laws) are discarded as unacceptable, while others (such as the moral law) are retained. The same approach can and should, Rahner argues, be adopted in the case of other religions.

The saving grace of God is thus available through non-Christian religious traditions, despite their shortcomings. Many of their adherents, Rahner argues, have thus accepted that grace, without being fully aware of what it is. It is for this reason that Rahner introduces the term "anonymous Christians," to refer to those who have experienced divine grace without necessarily knowing it.

This term has been heavily criticized. For example, John Hick has suggested that it is paternalist, offering "honorary status granted unilaterally to people who have not expressed any desire for it." Nevertheless, Rahner's intention is to allow for the real effects of divine grace in the lives of those who belong to non-Christian traditions. Full access to truth about God (as it is understood within the Christian tradition) is not a necessary precondition for access to the saving grace of God.

Rahner does not allow that Christianity and other religious traditions may be treated as equal, or that they are particular instances of a common encounter with God. For Rahner, Christianity and Christ have an exclusive status, denied to other religious traditions. The question is: Can other religious traditions give access to the same saving grace as that offered by Christianity? Rahner's approach allows him to suggest that the beliefs of non-Christian religious traditions are not necessarily true, while allowing that they may, nevertheless, mediate the grace of God by the lifestyles which they evoke – such as a selfless love of one's neighbor.

The Pluralist Approach

The most significant exponent of a pluralist approach to religious traditions is John Hick (b. 1922). In his *God and the Universe of Faiths* (1973), Hick argued for a need to move away from a Christ-centered to a God-centered approach. Describing this change as a "Copernican Revolution," Hick declared that it was necessary to move away from "the dogma that Christianity is at the centre to the realization that it is

God who is at the centre, and that all religions. . . . including our own, serve and revolve around him."

Developing this approach, Hick suggests that the aspect of God's nature of central importance to the question of other faiths was his universal saving will. If God wishes everyone to be saved, it is inconceivable that the divine self-revelation should be effected in such a way that only a small portion of humanity could be saved. In fact, as we have seen, this is not a necessary feature of either exclusivist or inclusivist approaches. However, Hick draws the conclusion that it is necessary to recognize that all religions lead to the same God. Christians have no special access to God, who is universally available through all religious traditions.

This suggestion is not without its problems. For example, it is fairly clear that the religious traditions of the world are radically different in their beliefs and practices. Hick deals with this point by suggesting that such differences must be interpreted in terms of "both–and" rather than "either–or." They should be understood as complementary, rather than contradictory, insights into the one divine reality. This reality lies at the heart of all the religions; yet "their differing experiences of that reality, interacting over the centuries with the different thought-forms of different cultures, have led to increasing differentiation and contrasting elaboration." (This idea is very similar to the "universal rational religion of nature," propounded by Deist writers, which became corrupted through time.) Equally, Hick has difficulties with those non-theistic religious traditions, such as Advaitin Hinduism or Theravada Buddhism, which have no place for a god.

These difficulties relate to observed features of religious traditions. In other words, the beliefs of non-Christian religions make it difficult to accept that they are all speaking of the same God. But a more fundamental theological worry remains: Is Hick actually talking about the Christian God at all? A central Christian conviction – that God is revealed definitively in Jesus Christ – has to be set to one side to allow Hick to proceed. Hick argues that he is merely adopting a *theo*centric, rather than a *Christo*centric approach. Yet the Christian insistence that God is known normatively through Christ implies that authentically Christian knowledge of God is derived through Christ. For a number of critics, Hick's desertion of Christ as a reference point means abandoning any claim to speak from a *Christian* perspective.

The debate over the Christian understanding of the relation of Christianity to other religious traditions will continue for some considerable time, fueled by the rise of multiculturalism in western society. The three options outlined above are likely to continue to be represented in Christian writing on the matter for some time to come.

Our attention now turns to the final aspect of Christian theology, traditionally known as "the last things," or, more technically, as *eschatology*.

Questions for Chapter 15

1 How would you define a "religion"?

2 Why was Dietrich Bonhoeffer so attracted to the idea of a "religionless Christianity"?

3 Do all religions lead to God?

4 How helpful and persuasive do you find Karl Rahner's idea of an "anonymous Christian"?

5 Why have ideas such as the resurrection and divinity of Christ proved to be such a hindrance to inter-faith dialogue? Is there a case for their elimination, in order to make such a dialogue more fruitful?

16

Last Things: The Christian Hope

In earlier discussions of the resurrection and the doctrine of salvation, we touched upon aspects of eschatology – that is, the Christian understanding of the "last things." The term "eschatology" comes from the Greek term *ta eschata*, "the last things," and relates to such matters as the Christian expectations of resurrection and judgment. In the concluding chapter of this work, we shall deal with this subject in more detail.

Several major aspects of this topic have already been covered elsewhere in this volume. In particular, the following discussions should be noted:

1 The debate over the resurrection of Jesus Christ, and its theological implications (pp. 328–36).
2 The rediscovery of the eschatological aspect of the New Testament concept of the "kingdom of God" in the late nineteenth century (pp. 320–1).
3 The eschatological dimensions of the Christian doctrine of salvation (pp. 340–1).

In the broadest sense of the term, "eschatology" is "discourse about the end." The "end" in question may refer to an individual's existence, or to the closing of the present age. A characteristic Christian belief, of decisive importance in this context, is that time is linear, not cyclical. History had a beginning; it will one day come to an end. "Eschatology" deals with a network of beliefs relating to the end of life and history, whether of an individual or of the world in general. It has unquestionably stimulated and contributed extensively to some of the most creative and fantastic movements within Christianity.

Developments in the Doctrine of the Last Things

It is generally thought that the most important developments relating to Christian understanding of the "last things" have taken place during the period since the Enlightenment. In what follows, we shall briefly consider the New Testament foundations for eschatology, before moving on to consider their more recent interpretations.

The New Testament

The New Testament is saturated with the belief that something new has happened in the history of humanity, in and through the life and death of Jesus Christ, and above all through his resurrection from the dead. The theme of *hope* predominates, even in the face of death. The New Testament brings together a cluster of eschatological beliefs, of which the following are the most important.

1 *The parousia* Jesus Christ is expected to return, bringing history to its close. At his "coming" or "appearance," Christ will usher in the "last day," and bring the world to judgment (1 Thessalonians 4: 16). Some New Testament writings appear to expect this return of Christ to take place during the lifetime of those who were witnesses to the resurrection (1 and 2 Thessalonians appear to fall into this category); others tend to treat the *parousia* as something future, with present implications (the Fourth Gospel being a particularly important case in point).

2 *The resurrection* The New Testament proclaims the reality of the resurrection of Christ. As we noted earlier (pp. 328–36), the resurrection is enormously significant Christologically. However, the New Testament affirms that the resurrection does more than provide insights concerning the identity and significance of Jesus, important though these may be. It also declares that, through faith, the believer will share in Christ's resurrection. The resurrection of Christ is both the ground and the anticipation of the resurrection of believers.

3 *The kingdom of God* Especially in the preaching of Jesus, the idea of the "kingdom of God" assumes a major role in New Testament expectations concerning the future. This kingdom is seen as something transformative and renewing, breaking into human history in order to redeem it from its present inadequacies. The interpretation of the concept is complex, and we shall return to consider some approaches shortly (pp. 469–72).

Augustine: The Two Cities

One of the most influential reworkings of the corporate dimension of the eschatological ideas of the New Testament is that of Augustine of Hippo, found in his *City of God*. This work was written in a context which could easily be described as "apocalyptic" – the destruction of the great city of Rome, and the collapse of the Roman Empire. A central theme of the work is the relation between two cities – the "city of God" and the "secular city" or "the city of the world." The complexities of the Christian life, especially its political aspects, are due to the dialectic between these two cities.

Believers live "in this intermediate period," separating the incarnation of Christ from his final return in glory. The church is to be seen as in exile in the "city of the world." It is in the world, yet not of the world. There is a strong eschatological tension between the present reality, in which the church is exiled in the world, and somehow obliged to maintain its distinctive ethos in the midst of a disbelieving world, and the future hope, in which the church will be delivered from the world, and finally allowed to share in the glory of God. It will be clear that Augustine has no time for the Donatist idea of the church as a body of saints (pp. 408–9). For Augustine, the church shares in the fallen character of the world, and therefore includes the pure and the impure, saints and sinners. Only at the last day will this tension finally be resolved.

Yet alongside this corporate understanding of eschatology, Augustine shows an awareness of the individualist dimensions of the Christian hope. This is especially clear in his discussion of the tension between what human nature presently is, and what it finally will be. Believers are saved, purified, and perfected – yet in hope (*in spe*) but not in reality (*in re*). Salvation is something that is inaugurated in the life of the believer, but which will only find its completion at the end of history. This idea is developed by Martin Luther, as noted earlier (pp. 382–7).

Augustine is thus able to offer Christians hope, as they contemplate the sinful nature of their lives, and wonder how this is to be reconciled with the gospel imperatives to be holy, like God. For Augustine, believers are able to reach out in hope, beyond their present condition. This is not a spurious or invented hope, but a sure and certain hope which is grounded in the resurrection of Christ.

Augustine is aware of the fact that the word "end" has two meanings. The "end" can mean "either the ceasing to be of what was, or the perfecting of what was begun." Eternal life is to be seen as the state in which our love of God, begun in this life, is finally brought to its completion and consummation, through union with the object of that love. Eternal life is the "reward that makes perfect," to which the Christian has looked forward throughout the life of faith.

The Middle Ages: Joachim of Fiore and Dante Aligheri

Augustine had proposed a relatively simple schematization of Christian history, which treated the period of the church as that era separating the coming (or "advent") and returning (or "second coming") of Christ. However, this failed to satisfy his later interpreters. Joachim of Fiore (c.1132–1202) developed a more speculative approach to history, with a strongly eschatological orientation, based upon the model of the Trinity. According to Joachim, universal history could be divided into three eras:

1 The age of the Father, which corresponds to the Old Testament dispensation.
2 The age of the Son, which corresponds to the New Testament dispensation, including the church.
3 The age of the Spirit, which would witness the rise of new religious movements, leading to the reform and renewal of the church, and the final establishment of peace and unity on earth.

What gave Joachim's views a particular urgency was the precise dating of these periods. Each age, he argued, consisted of forty-two generations of thirty years each. As a result, the "age of the Son" was due to end in 1260, to be followed immediately by the radical new "age of the Spirit." In this may be seen anticipated many of the millenarian movements of our own day.

A more poetic approach to eschatological issues is associated with the Tuscan poet Dante Aligheri (1265–1321). Dante, based in the city of Florence, wrote the *Divine Comedy* in order both to give poetic expression to the Christian hope, and to make comments on the life of both the church and city of Florence of his own day. The poem is set in the year 1300, and describes how Dante is led into the depths of the earth by the pagan Roman poet Virgil, who will act as his guide through hell and purgatory.

We shall consider aspects of Dante's vision of hell, purgatory, and paradise in due course. However, the work is an important representation of the medieval worldview, in which the souls of the departed were understood to pass through a series of purifying and cleansing processes, before being enabled to catch a glimpse of the vision of God – the ultimate goal of the Christian life.

The Enlightenment: Eschatology as Superstition

The intensely rationalist atmosphere of the Enlightenment (pp. 81–6) led to criticism of the Christian doctrine of the last things as ignorant superstition, devoid of any real basis in life. Particular criticism was directed against the idea of hell. The strongly utilitarian outlook of the later Enlightenment resulted in a growing belief that eternal punishment served no useful purpose. Feuerbach argued that the idea of "heaven" or "eternal life" was simply a projection of a human longing after immortality, without any objective basis.

A more sustained critique of the Christian doctrine of hope was found in the writings of Karl Marx (pp. 89–92). Marx argued that religion in general sought to comfort those undergoing suffering in the present through persuading them of the joy of an afterlife. By doing so, it distracted them from the task of transforming the present world so that suffering could be eliminated. In many ways, Marxism may be regarded as a secularized Christian eschatology, with "the revolution" as a secularized counterpart to "heaven."

Related developments can be discerned within nineteenth-century liberalism (pp. 92–6). The idea of a cataclysmic end of history was set to one side, in favor of a doctrine of hope which was grounded in the gradual evolution of humanity towards moral and societal perfection. The Darwinian theory of natural selection, as expressed in popular versions of the theory of evolution, seemed to point to human history, like all of human life, moving upward toward higher and more sophisticated forms. Eschatology came to be relegated to the status of a theological curiosity. The notion of the "kingdom of God," shorn of its New Testament apocalyptic associations, was viewed (for example, by Albrecht Ritschl) as a static realm of moral values, toward which society was steadily advancing through a process of continuous evolution.

The Rediscovery of Eschatology

This approach was largely discredited by two developments. In the first place, in the closing decade of the nineteenth century Johannes Weiss and Albert Schweitzer rediscovered the apocalyptic character of the preaching of Jesus, and argued forcefully that the "kingdom of God" was an eschatological notion (pp. 320–1). Jesus was not to be seen as the moral educator of humanity, but as the proclaimer of the imminent coming of the eschatological kingdom of God.

It must be stressed that not all New Testament scholars have agreed with the findings of Weiss and Schweitzer. For example, the British

New Testament scholar C. H. Dodd argued that eschatology should not be seen as something totally oriented toward the unknown future, but as something which had been realized in the coming of Jesus. Three general positions have subsequently emerged:

1 *Futurist*: The kingdom of God is something which remains in the future, and will intervene disruptively in the midst of human history (Weiss).
2 *Inaugurated*: The kingdom of God has begun to exercise its influence within human history, although its full realization and fulfillment lie in the future.
3 *Realized*: The kingdom of God has already been realized in the coming of Jesus.

The second development concerns a general collapse in confidence in human civilization as a means of bringing the kingdom of God to fulfillment. World War I was an especially traumatic episode in this respect. The Holocaust, the development of nuclear weapons and the threat of nuclear war, and the continuing threat to the destruction of the environment through human exploitation of its resources, have all raised doubts concerning the credibility of the vision of liberal humanist forms of Christianity.

But what was to be done with the idea of eschatology? One approach, which attracted considerable attention during the 1950s and early 1960s, was due to the Marburg New Testament scholar Rudolf Bultmann.

Demythologization: Rudolf Bultmann

Bultmann's controversial program of "demythologization" (pp. 330–1) proved to be especially significant in relation to beliefs concerning the end of history. Bultmann argued that such beliefs were "myths," which required to be interpreted existentially. The New Testament relates "stories" concerning remote and inaccessible times and places (such as "in the beginning" or "in heaven"), and involving supernatural agents or events. Bultmann declares that these stories possess an underlying existential meaning, which can be perceived and appropriated by a suitable process of interpretation.

Perhaps the most important of these is the eschatological myth of the imminent end of the world through direct divine intervention, leading to judgment and subsequent reward or retribution. This insight is of central importance to our narrative, in that it allows Bultmann to deal with Schweitzer's demonstration of the "thoroughgoing eschatological conditioning" of the New Testament by a comprehensive process of demythologization. For Bultmann, this "myth," and others like it, may be reinterpreted existentially.

Thus, in the case of the eschatological myth, the recognition that history has not, in fact, come to an end does not necessarily invalidate the myth: Interpreted existentially, the "myth" refers to the here and now of human existence – the fact that human beings must face the reality of their own death, and are thus forced to make existential decisions. The "judgment" in question is not some future event of *divine* judgment, to take place at the end of the world, but the present event of *our own judgment of ourselves*, based upon our knowledge of what God has done in Christ.

Bultmann argues that precisely this sort of demythologizing may be found in the Fourth Gospel, written toward the end of the first century, when the early eschatological expectations of the Christian community were fading. "Judgment" is interpreted by Bultmann to refer to the moment of existential crisis, as human beings are confronted with the divine *kerygma* addressed to them. The "realized eschatology" of the Fourth Gospel arises through the fact that the redactor of the gospel has realized that the *parousia* is not some future event, but one which has already taken place, in the confrontation of the believer with the *kerygma*:

> To the "Now" of the coming of the Revealer, there corresponds exactly the "Now" of the proclamation of the word as an historical fact, the "Now" of the present, of the moment. . . . This "Now" of being addressed at a specific moment is the eschatological "Now," because in it the decision is made between life and death. It is the hour which is coming, and, in being addressed, now is . . . Therefore it is not true that the *parousia*, expected by others as an event occuring in time, is now denied or transformed by John into a process within the soul, an experience. Rather, John opens the reader's eyes: the *parousia* has already occurred!

Bultmann thus regards the Fourth Gospel as partially reinterpreting the eschatological myth in terms of its significance for human existence. Christ is not a past phenomenon, but the ever-present word of God, expressing not a general truth, but a concrete proclamation addressed to us, demanding an existential decision on our part. For Bultmann, the eschatological process became an event in the history of the world, and becomes an event once more in contemporary Christian proclamation.

But such approaches failed to satisfy many critics, who felt that Bultmann had abandoned too many of the central features of the

Christian doctrine of hope. For example, Bultmann's notion of eschatology is purely individualist; the biblical notion is clearly corporate. Another approach began to emerge in the later 1960s, which seemed to many to offer far more than Bultmann's truncated version of hope.

The Theology of Hope: Jürgen Moltmann

Jürgen Moltmann's *Theology of Hope* created a considerable impact on its publication. Moltmann here draws on the insights of Ernst Bloch's remarkable work, *Philosophy of Hope*. Bloch's neo-Marxist analysis of human experience is based on the belief that all human culture is moved by a passionate hope for the future that transcends all the alienation of the present. Bloch saw himself as standing in direct line to the biblical idea of revolutionary apocalyptic hope. Where Bultmann sought to make eschatology acceptable through demythologization, Bloch defended it by pointing to the vigorous social critique and prophetic vision of social transformation which accompanied the ideas in their original scriptural contexts.

Building on such insights, Moltmann argued the need for the rediscovery of the corporate conception of hope as a central motivating factor in Christian life and thought. Eschatology needed to be rescued from its position as "a harmless little chapter at the conclusion of a Christian dogmatics" (Karl Barth) and given pride of place. Where Anselm of Canterbury declared "I believe, in order that I may understand," Moltmann had "I hope, in order that I may understand." The "hope" in question is not personal, individual, or existential, but a corporate vision of the renewal of a lost and fallen humanity through the graceful action of a loving and redeeming God.

Dispensationalism

Dispensationalism is a movement within contemporary evangelicalism which lays especial emphasis upon the eschatological aspects of the Christian faith, and has achieved considerable influence within a popular American Christian subculture. The term "dispensationalism" reflects the belief that the history of salvation is divided into a number of periods. The origins of the movement lie with John Nelson Darby (1800–82), who was especially associated with the Plymouth Brethren, although its later developments are associated with C. I. Scofield (1843–1921), whose *Scofield Reference Bible* (1909) secured a wide hearing for its ideas in North America.

Two central and characteristic notions within dispensationalism are those of "the rapture" and "the tribulation." The former concerns the believer's expectation of being "caught up in the clouds" to meet Christ at the time of his return (1 Thessalonians 4: 15–17). The latter is grounded in the prophetic visions of the book of Daniel (Daniel 9: 24–27) and is understood as a seven-year period of divine judgment upon the world. Dispensationalist writers remain divided as to whether the rapture is to be understood as *pre-tribulational* (in which believers are enabled to escape the pain of the tribulation) or *post-tribulational* (in which believers must endure the tribulation, in the assurance that they will subsequently be united with Christ.

The Last Things

In the remainder of this chapter, we shall consider aspects of Christian teaching concerning the "last things," concentrating upon the ideas of hell, purgatory, and heaven. It should be noted that there is some reluctance to deal with these issues in many theological circles. One reason for this was put forward by Erasmus in the early sixteenth century. Commenting on the enthusiasm with which certain Paris theologians wrote about hell, Erasmus remarked that they had evidently been there themselves!

Hell

Interest in hell reached a climax during the Middle Ages, with artists of the period taking, one assumes, a certain delight in portraying the righteous watching sinners being tormented by burning and other means of torture. The most graphic portrayal of the medieval view of hell is that of Dante, in the first of the three books of his *Divine Comedy*. Dante portrays hell as nine circles at the center of the earth, within which Satan dwells. On the gate, Dante notices the inscription "Abandon hope, all ye who enter here!"

The first circle of hell is populated by those who have died without being baptized, and virtuous pagans. (This circle corresponds to the idea of "limbo" noted earlier at p. 445). Dante declares that it is this circle which was visited by Christ during his "descent into hell" between the time of the crucifixion and the resurrection. There is no torment of any kind in this circle. As Dante advances further into hell, he discovers those who are guilty of increasingly serious sins. The second circle is populated by the lustful, the third by the gluttonous, the fourth by the miserly, and the fifth by the wrathful. These circles, taken together, constitute "upper hell." At no point does Dante refer to fire in this part of hell. Dante then draws upon Greco-Roman mythology in suggesting that the River Styx divides "upper hell" from "lower hell." Now we encounter fire for the first time. The sixth circle is populated by heretics, the seventh by the violent, the eighth by fraudsters (including several popes), and the ninth by traitors.

This static medieval view of hell was unquestionably of major influence at the time, and continues to be of importance into the modern period. It may be found clearly stated in Jonathan Edwards' famous sermon "Sinners in the Hands of an Angry God," preached on July 8, 1741:

> It would be dreadful to suffer this fierceness and wrath of Almighty God for one moment; but you must suffer it for all eternity. There will be no end to this exquisite horrible misery . . . You will know that you must wear out long ages, millions of millions of ages, in wrestling and conflicting with this almighty merciless vengeance.

However, the very idea of hell has been subjected to increasing criticisms, of which the following should be noted.

1 Its existence is seen as a contradiction of the Christian assertion of the final victory of God over evil. This criticism is especially associated with the patristic writer Origen, whose doctrine of universal restoration ultimately rests upon an affirmation of the final and total triumph of God over evil. In the modern period, the philosopher Leibniz identified this consideration as a major difficulty with the doctrine of hell:

> It seems strange that, even in the great future of eternity, evil must triumph over good, under the supreme authority of the one who is the sovereign good. After all, there will be many who are called, and yet few who are chosen or saved.

2 The notion of vindictive justice seemed unChristian to many writers, especially in the light of many New Testament passages speaking of the compassion of God. A number of writers, especially during the nineteenth century, found it difficult to reconcile the idea of a loving God with the notion of the continuing vindictive or retributive punishment of sinners. The main difficulty was that there seemed to be no point to the suffering of the condemned.

While answers may be given to these objections, there has been a perceptible loss of interest in the idea of hell in both popular and more academic Christian circles. Evangelistic preaching now seems to concentrate upon the positive affirmation of the love of God, rather than on the negative implications of the rejection of that love. One response to this within evangelical circles has been the development of a doctrine of conditional immortality, to which we may now turn.

Since the early 1980s, a growing internal debate has developed within evangelicalism concerning a network of eschatological issues, centering on the issue of immortality. Responding to criticisms of the doctrine of hell made during the modern period, a number of evangelical scholars have developed the doctrine of "conditional immortality." An example of this may be found in Philip Edgcumbe Hughes' *The True Image* (1989). Hughes argues that humanity has been created with the *potential* for immortality:

> Immortality or deathlessness is not inherent in the constitution of humanity as a corporeal–spiritual creature; though, formed in the image of God, the potential was there. That potential, which was forfeited through sin, has been restored and actualized through Christ.

Hughes argues that the essence of salvation is the actualization of the potential for immortality, which is conditional upon a response to the gospel. Those who do not respond do not enter into immortality.

It therefore follows that no division is necessary between the good and the evil, the believing and the unbelieving, after death. Augustine asserted that "after the resurrection, when the final universal judgment has been completed, there will be two kingdoms, each with its own distinct boundaries, the one Christ's, the other the devil's." Hughes argues that there will only be one. "When Christ fills all in all . . . how is it conceivable that there can be a section or realm of creation that does not belong to this fulness, and by its very presence contradicts it?"

This trend toward "conditionalism" or "conditional immortality" has met with considerable resistance within evangelicalism, with distinguished writers such as James I. Packer opposing it on the grounds of logical inconsistency and a lack of adequate scriptural foundation. It is a debate which is set to continue, and perhaps extend further into the Christian community.

Purgatory

One of the major differences between Protestant and Roman Catholic understandings of the "last things" relates to the question of purgatory. Purgatory is perhaps best understood as an intermediate stage, in which those who have died in a state of grace are given an opportunity to purge themselves of the guilt of their sins before finally entering heaven. The idea does not have explicit scriptural warrant, although a passage in 2 Maccabees 12: 39–45 (regarded as apocryphal, and hence as lacking in authority, by Protestant writers) speaks of Judas Maccabeus making "propitiation for those who had died, in order that they might be released from their sin."

The idea was developed during the patristic period. Clement of Alexandria and Origen both taught that those who had died without time to perform works of penance would be "purified through fire" in the next life. The practice of praying for the dead – which became widespread in the eastern church in the first four centuries – exercised a major impact upon theological development, and provides an excellent case study of the manner in which liturgy influences theology. What was the point of praying for the dead, it was asked, if those prayers could not alter the state in which they existed? Similar views are found in Augustine, who taught the need for purification from the sins of the present life, before entering the joys of the next. Thomas Aquinas drew a distinction between the guilt and punishment of sin. The guilt of sin may be removed immediately after death; however, the punishment of that sin remains to be borne in purgatory.

The idea of purgatory was rejected by the reformers during the sixteenth century. Two major lines of criticism were directed against it. First, it was held to lack any substantial scriptural foundations. Second, it was inconsistent with the doctrine of justification by faith, which declared that an individual could be put "right with God" through faith, thus establishing a relationship which obviated the need for purgatory. Having dispensed with the idea of purgatory, the reformers saw no pressing reason to retain the practice of prayer for the dead, which was henceforth omitted from Protestant liturgies. Both the concept of purgatory and the practice of praying for the dead continue to find acceptance within Roman Catholicism.

Heaven

The Christian conception of heaven is essentially that of the eschatological realization of the presence and power of God, and the final elimination of sin. The most helpful way of considering it is to regard it as a consummation of the Christian doctrine of salvation, in which the presence, penalty, and power of sin have all been finally eliminated, and the total presence of God in individuals and the community of faith has been achieved (see pp. 340–1).

It should be noted that the New Testament parables of heaven are strongly communal in nature; for example, heaven is portrayed as a banquet, as a wedding feast, or as a city – the new Jerusalem. Individualist interpretations of heaven or eternal life are also excluded on account of the Christian understanding of God as Trinity. Eternal life is thus not a projection of an individual human existence, but is rather to be seen as sharing, with the redeemed community as a whole, in the community of a loving God.

One aspect of the Christian expectation of heaven merits especial attention: the beatific vision. The Christian is finally granted a full vision of the God who has up to this point been known only in part. This vision of God in the full splendor of the divine majesty has been a constant theme of much Christian theology, especially during the Middle Ages. Dante's *Divine Comedy* concludes with the poet finally capturing a glimpse of God,

> the love which moves the sun and the other stars.

The anticipation of the wonder and glory of this vision was seen as a powerful incentive to keep going in the Christian life.

Christian theology can never capture that vision of God. But it can at least challenge us to think more deeply about God, and whet our appetites for what is yet to come – a fitting note on which to end this introduction to its themes.

Questions for Chapter 16

1 Explore the way in which one of the following ideas is used in the New Testament: heaven; resurrection; eternal life. You will find it helpful to use a concordance.

2 Give a brief summary of the way in which either Rudolf Bultmann or Wolfhart Pannenberg interpreted the resurrection. (You will need to turn back to chapter 10 to find some of the material you require for this answer.)

3 Study the following list of terms encountered in this chapter: age of the spirit; demythologization; the rapture; the tribulation; the two cities. With which of the following writers or movements would you associate each of them: Augustine of Hippo; Rudolf Bultmann; dispensationalism; Joachim of Fiore? (Note that two of the terms are linked with one of the writers or movements.)

4 Why is it increasingly unfashionable to speak of "hell" in many (but not all) Christian circles today?

5 Will all go to heaven? (To answer this question, you will need to draw on some of the material presented in chapter 11.)

For Further Reading

The following works are recommended on the basis of their proven useful-
ness to students studying Christian theology. However, students and teachers
should feel at total liberty to supplement or replace them with others, on the
basis of local availability or personal preference.

Landmarks

The first four chapters of this work deal with Christian history and historical
theology. The following work is especially recommended as an introduction
to the various aspects of this field.

Pelikan, Jaroslav, *The Christian Tradition: A History of the Development of
Doctrine* 5 vols (Chicago: University of Chicago Press, 1989). The five
volumes of this excellent study are arranged as follows: 1, *The Emergence
of the Catholic Tradition* (100–600); 2, *The Spirit of Eastern Christendom*
(600–1700); 3, *The Growth of Medieval Theology* (600–1300); 4, *Reformation of
Church and Dogma* (1300–1700); 5, *Christian Doctrine and Modern Culture*
(since 1700).

Chapter 1   The Patristic Period

Bettenson, Henry, *Documents of the Christian Church* 2nd edn (Oxford: Oxford
University Press, 1963).
Chadwick, Henry, *The Early Church* (London/New York: Pelican, 1964).
Comby, Jean, *How to Read Church History* vol. 1 (London: SCM Press, 1985).
Daniélou, Jean, and Marrou, Henri, *The Christian Centuries* vol. 1 (London:
Darton, Longman and Todd, 1964).

Frend, W. H. C., *The Rise of Christianity* (Philadelphia: Fortress Press, 1984).

Hazlett, Ian (ed.), *Early Christianity: Origins and Evolution to AD 600* (London: SPCK, 1991).

Jedin, Herbert, and Dolan, John (eds), *A Handbook of Church History* vol. 1 (London: Burns & Oates, 1965).

Kelly, J. N. D., *Early Christian Doctrines* 4th edn (London: A & C Black, 1968).

van der Meer, F., and Mohrmann, Christine, *Atlas of the Early Christian World* (London: Nelson, 1959).

Stevenson, J., *A New Eusebius: Documents Illustrating the History of the Church to AD 337* revised edn (London: SPCK, 1987).

——, *Creeds, Councils and Controversies: Documents Illustrating the History of the Church, 337–461* revised edn (London: SPCK, 1987).

Chapter 2   The Medieval and Renaissance Periods

Burke, Peter, *The Italian Renaissance: Culture and Society in Italy* revised edition (Oxford: Polity Press, 1986).

Coplestone, Frederick, *A History of Medieval Philosophy* (London: University of Notre Dame Press, 1990).

Gilson, Etienne, *The Spirit of Medieval Philosophy* (London: Sheed & Ward, 1936).

Grassi, E., *Rhetoric as Philosophy: The Humanist Tradition* (University Park, Pa.: University of Pennsylvania Press, 1980).

Grossmann, Maria, *Humanism at Wittenberg 1485–1517* (Nieuwkoop: Nijhoff, 1975).

Herrin, Judith, *The Formation of Christendom* (Princeton: Princeton University Press, 1987).

Levi, A. H. T., "The Breakdown of Scholasticism and the Significance of Evangelical Humanism," in *The Philosophical Assessment of Theology*, ed. G. R. Hughes (Georgetown, 1987), pp. 101–28.

Nauert, Charles G., "The Clash of Humanists and Scholastics: An Approach to Pre-Reformation Controversies," *Sixteenth Century Journal* 4 (1973), pp. 1–18.

Oberman, Heiko A., *The Harvest of Medieval Theology* (Cambridge, MA: Harvard University Press, 1963).

——, *Masters of the Reformation* (Cambridge, UK: Cambridge University Press, 1981).

Overfield, J. H., *Humanism and Scholasticism in Late Medieval Germany* (Princeton: Princeton University Press, 1984).

Pieper, J., *Scholasticism* (London: Faber, 1961).

Spitz, Lewis W., *The Religious Renaissance of the German Humanists* (Cambridge, MA: Harvard University Press, 1963).

Chapter 3   The Reformation and Post-Reformation Periods

Bossy, John, *Christianity in the West* (Oxford: Oxford University Press, 1985).

Cameron, Euan, *The European Reformation* (Oxford: Oxford University Press, 1991).

Chadwick, Owen, *The Reformation* (Pelican History of the Church, vol. 4; London, Pelican, 1976).

Elton, G. R. (ed.), *The Reformation 1520–1559* (New Cambridge Modern History, vol. 2, 2nd edn; Cambridge, UK: Cambridge University Press, 1990).

George, Timothy, *The Theology of the Reformers* (Nashville, Tenn.: Abingdon, 1988).

McGrath, Alister E., *Reformation Thought* 2nd edn (Oxford/Cambridge, MA: Blackwell, 1993).

Muller, Richard A., *Post-Reformation Reformed Dogmatics* (Grand Rapids: Baker, 1987).

Noll, Mark A., *Confessions and Catechisms of the Reformation* (Grand Rapids: Eerdmans, 1991).

Ozment, Steven E., *The Age of Reform 1250–1550* (New Haven/London: Yale University Press, 1980).

Preus, Robert, *The Inspiration of Scripture: A Study of the Seventeenth Century Lutheran Dogmaticians* (London: Oliver & Boyd, 1955).

Reardon, B. M. G., *Religious Thought in the Reformation* (London: Longmans, 1981).

Scharlemann, Robert P., *Thomas Aquinas and John Gerhard* (New Haven: Yale University Press, 1964).

Spitz, Lewis W., *The Protestant Reformation 1517–1559* (New York: Scribners, 1986).

Chapter 4   The Modern Period

Blumhofer, Judith L., and Carpenter, Joel A., *Twentieth Century Evangelicalism: A Guide to the Sources* (New York: Garland Publishing, 1990).

Bonino, José Miguel, *Christians and Marxists: The Mutual Challenge to Revolution* (Grand Rapids: Eerdmans, 1976).

Bottomore, Tom (ed.), *A Dictionary of Marxist Thought* (Oxford: Blackwell, 1983).

Brown, Robert McAfee, *Theology in a New Key: Responding to Liberation Themes* (Philadelphia: Westminster Press, 1978).

Carr, Anne E., *Transforming Grace: Christian Tradition and the Experience of Women* (San Francisco: Harper & Row, 1988).

Cragg, G. R., *Reason and Authority in the Eighteenth Century* (Cambridge, UK: Cambridge University Press, 1964).

Daly, Mary, *Beyond God the Father: Toward a Philosophy of Women's Liberation* (Boston: Beacon Press, 1973).

Dyson, A. O., "Theological Legacies of the Enlightenment: England and Germany," in *England and Germany: Studies in Theological Diplomacy*, ed. S. W. Sykes (Frankfurt/Berne: Verlag Peter Lang, 1982), pp. 45–62.

Flew, A., *Hume's Philosophy of Belief: A Study of His First Inquiry* (New York: Humanities Press, 1961).

Frei, Hans, *The Eclipse of Biblical Narrative: A Study in Eighteenth and Nineteenth Century Biblical Hermeneutics* (New Haven/London: Yale University Press, 1977).

Gay, Peter, *The Enlightenment, an Interpretation* 2 vols (Wildwood House: London, 1973).

Hampson, Daphne, *Theology and Feminism* (Oxford: Blackwell, 1990).

Hutchison, William R., *The Modernist Impulse in American Protestantism* (New York: Oxford University Press, 1982).

Lindbeck, George A., *The Nature of Doctrine: Religion and Theology in a Post-liberal Age* (Philadelphia: Fortress Press, 1984).

McGrath, Alister E., "The Enlightenment," in *The History of Christian Theology I: The Science of Theology*, ed. P. D. L. Avis (Eerdmans: Grand Rapids, 1986), pp. 206–29.

Marsden, George, *Fundamentalism and American Culture: The Shaping of Twentieth Century Evangelicalism 1870–1925* (New York: Oxford University Press, 1980).

Oden, Thomas C., *After Modernity . . . What? Agenda for Theology* (Grand Rapids: Zondervan, 1990).

Placher, William C., *Unapologetic Theology: A Christian Voice in a Pluralistic Conversation* (Louisville: Westminster/John Knox Press, 1989).

Reardon, B. M. G., *Liberal Protestantism* (Stanford, CA: Stanford University Press, 1968).

——, *Roman Catholic Modernism* (Stanford, CA: Stanford University Press, 1970).

——, *Religion in the Age of Romanticism* (Cambridge, UK: Cambridge University Press, 1985).

Ruether, Rosemary Radford, *Sexism and God-Talk* (Boston: Beacon Press, 1983).

Stephenson, A. M. G., *The Rise and Decline of English Modernism* (London: SPCK, 1984).

Taylor, Mark C., *Erring: A Postmodern A/Theology* (Chicago: University of Chicago Press, 1984).

Thiemann, Ronald E., *Revelation and Theology: The Gospel as Narrated Promise* (Notre Dame: University of Notre Dame Press, 1985).

Trevor-Roper, H. R., "The Religious Origins of the Enlightenment," in *Religion, The Reformation and Social Change* (London: Macmillan, 1967), pp. 193–236.

Vidler, A. R., *The Modernist Movement in the Roman Church* (Cambridge, UK: Cambridge University Press, 1934).

Wellek, René, "The Concept of Romanticism in Literary History," in *Concepts of Criticism* (New Haven/London: Yale University Press, 1963), pp. 128–221.

Chapter 5   Getting Started: Preliminaries

Barbour, Ian G., *Myths, Models and Paradigms* (London: SCM Press, 1974).

Battles, Ford Lewis, "God Was Accommodating Himself to Human Capacity," *Interpretation* 31 (1977), pp. 19–38.

Bauer, Walter, *Orthodoxy and Heresy in Earliest Christianity* (Philadelphia: Westminster Press, 1971).

Berkhof, Hendricus, *Christian Faith* (Grand Rapids: Eerdmans, 1979), pp. 1–6; 41–5.

Braaten, Carl E., "Prolegomena to Christian Dogmatics," in C. E. Braaten and R. W. Jenson (eds), *Christian Dogmatics* 2 vols (Philadelphia: Fortress Press, 1984), vol. 1, pp. 5–78.

Chadwick, Henry, "The Circle and the Ellipse," in *History* and *Thought of the Early Church* (London: Variorum, 1982).

Clouser, R. A., *The Myth of Religious Neutrality* (Notre Dame: University of Notre Dame Press, 1991).

Frend, W. H. C., "Heresy and Schism as Social and National Movements," *Studies in Church History* 9 (1972), pp. 37–56.

Hesse, Mary B. *Models and Analogies in Science* (Notre Dame: University of Notre Dame Press, 1966).

Hick, John, *Faith and Knowledge* (Ithaca: Cornell University Press, 1966), pp. 11–31.

Hooykaas, R., *Religion and the Rise of Modern Science* (Edinburgh: Scottish Academic Press, 1972).

McFague, Sally, *Metaphorical Theology* (Philadelphia: Fortress Press, 1983).

Macquarrie, John, *Principles of Christian Theology* (London: SCM Press, 1966), pp. 1–36.

Pannenberg, Wolfhart, *Theology and the Philosophy of Science* (London: Darton, Longman and Todd, 1976), pp. 3–22.

Ramsey, Ian T. *Christian Discourse: Some Logical Explorations* (London: Oxford University Press, 1965).

Scharlemann, Robert, "Theological Models and Their Construction," *Journal of Religion* (1973), pp. 65–82.

Soskice, Janet Martin, *Metaphor and Religious Language* (Oxford: Clarendon Press, 1985).

Weber, Otto, *Foundations of Dogmatics* 2 vols (Grand Rapids: Eerdmans, 1981), pp. 38–62.

Chapter 6   The Sources of Theology

Abraham, William J., *The Divine Inspiration of Holy Scripture* (Oxford: Oxford University Press, 1981).

Barr, James, "Revelation through History in the Old Testament and in Modern Theology," *Interpretation* 17 (1963), pp. 193–205.

Barth, Karl, and Brunner, Emil, *Natural Theology* (London: SCM Press, 1947).

Berkouwer, G. C. *General Revelation* (Grand Rapids: Eerdmans, 1955).

Butler, Diana, "God's Visible Glory: The Beauty of Nature in the Thought of John Calvin and Jonathan Edwards," *Westminster Theological Journal* 52 (1990), pp. 13–26.

Davies, W. D., "Canon and Christology," in *The Glory of Christ in the New Testament*, ed. L. D. Hurst and N. T. Wright (Oxford: Clarendon Press, 1987), pp. 19–36.

Dowey, E. A., *The Knowledge of God in Calvin's Theology* (New York: Columbia University Press, 1952).

Downing, F. Gerald, *Has Christianity a Revelation?* (Philadelphia: Westminster Press, 1964).

Dulles, Avery, *Models of Revelation* (Dublin: Gill & Macmillan, 1983).

Ebeling, Gerhard, *The Word of God and Tradition* (Philadelphia: Westminster Press, 1968.)

Farley, Edward, and Hodgson, Peter, "Scripture and Tradition," in *Christian Theology*, ed. P. Hodgson and R. King (Philadelphia: Fortress Press, 1982), pp. 35–61.

France, Richard T., "The Worship of Jesus: A Neglected Factor in Christological Debate?", in *Christ as Lord*, ed. H. H. Rowdon (Leicester: Inter-Varsity Press, 1982), pp. 17–36.

Frei, Hans, *The Eclipse of Biblical Narrative* (New Haven: Yale University Press, 1974).

Hauerwas, Stanley, and Jones, L. Gregory (eds), *Why Narrative? Readings in Narrative Theology* (Grand Rapids: Eerdmans, 1990).

van Huyssteen, Wentzel, *Theology and the Justification of Faith* (Grand Rapids: Eerdmans, 1989).

Lehmann, P., "Barth and Brunner: The Dilemma of the Protestant Mind," *Journal of Religion* 20 (1940), pp. 124–40.

Lindbeck, George, *The Nature of Doctrine* (Philadelphia: Fortress Press, 1984).

McGrath, Alister E., "Theology and Experience: Reflections on Cognitive and Experiential Approaches to Theology," *European Journal of Theology* 2 (1993), pp. 65–74.

Metzger, Bruce M., *The New Testament Canon* (Oxford: Oxford University Press, 1987).

Morgan, Robert, *Biblical Interpretation* (Oxford: Oxford University Press, 1988).

Niehbuhr, H. Richard, *The Meaning of Revelation* (New York: Macmillan, 1941).

Oberman, Heiko A., "Quod vadis, Petre? Tradition from Irenaeus to Humani Generis," *Scottish Journal of Theology* 16 (1963), pp. 225–55.

O'Donovan, Joan E. "Man in the Image of God: The Disagreement between Barth and Brunner Reconsidered," *Scottish Journal of Theology* 39 (1986), pp. 433–59.

Pelikan, Jaroslav, *The Vindication of Tradition* (New Haven: Yale University Press, 1984).

Stroup, George, "Revelation," *Christian Theology*, ed. P. Hodgson and R. King (Philadelphia: Fortress Press, 1982), pp. 88–114.

Swinburne, Richard G., *Faith and Reason* (Oxford: Clarendon Press, 1981).

Thiselton, Anthony C., *New Horizons in Hermeneutics* (Grand Rapids: Zondervan, 1992).

Tremblath, K. R., *Evangelical Theories of Biblical Inspiration* (Oxford: Oxford University Press, 1988).

Wainwright, Geoffrey, *Doxology: The Praise of God in Worship, Doctrine and Life* (New York: Oxford University Press, 1980).

Williams, D. D., "Brunner and Barth on Philosophy," *Journal of Religion* 27 (1947), pp. 241–54.

Wolterstorff, Nicolas, *Reason within the Bounds of Religion* 2nd edn (Grand Rapids: Eerdmans, 1984).

Chapter 7 The Doctrine of God

Barbour, Ian G., *Issues in Science and Religion* (New York: Harper & Row, 1971).

——, *Religion in an Age of Science* vol. 1 (San Francisco: Harper & Row, 1990).

Brümmer, Vincent, *Speaking of A Personal God: An Essay in Philosophical Theology* (Cambridge, UK: Cambridge University Press, 1992).

Brunner, Emil, *Truth as Encounter* (London: SCM Press, 1964).

Buber, Martin, *I and Thou* (New York: Scribners, 1970).

Burrell, David B., "The Spirit and the Christian Life," in *Christian Theology*, ed. P. Hodgson and R. King (Philadelphia: Fortress Press, 1982), pp. 248–73.

Bynum, C. W., *Jesus as Mother: Studies in the Spirituality of the High Middle Ages* (Berkeley/Los Angeles: University of California Press, 1982).

Congar, Yves, *I Believe in the Holy Spirit* 3 vols (New York: Seabury Press, 1983).

Dawe, D. G., "A Fresh Look at the Kenotic Christology," *Scottish Journal of Theology* 15 (1962), pp. 337–49.

Edwards, Rem B., "The Pagan Dogma of the Absolute Unchangeableness of God," *Religious Studies* 14 (1975), pp. 305–13.

Gilkey, Langdon, "God," in *Christian Theology*, ed. P. Hodgson and R. King (Philadelphia: Fortress Press, 1982), pp. 62–87.

Griffin, D. R., *God, Power and Evil: A Process Theodicy* (Philadelphia: Westminster, 1976).

Hendry, G. S., *Theology of Nature* (Philadelphia: Westminster Press, 1980).

Jenson, Robert W., "The Triune God," in *Christian Dogmatics* 2 vols, ed. C. E. Braaten and R. W. Jenson (Philadelphia: Fortress Press, 1984), vol. 1, pp. 83–191.

Johnson, E. A., "The Incomprehensibility of God and the Image of God as Male and Female," *Theological Studies* 45 (1984), pp. 441–65.

Katz, Steven T., "Dialogue and Revelation in the Thought of Martin Buber," *Religious Studies* 14 (1975), pp. 57–68.

Lee, Jung Yung, *God Suffers for Us: A Systematic Inquiry into a Concept of Divine Passibility* (The Hague: Nijhoff, 1974).

McFague, Sally, *Models of God* (Philadelphia: Fortress Press, 1987), pp. 91–180.

McGrath, Alister E., *Luther's Theology of the Cross* (Oxford: Blackwell, 1985).

McWilliams, W., "Divine Suffering in Contemporary Theology," *Scottish*

Journal of Theology 33 (1980), pp. 35–54.

Moltmann, Jürgen, *The Crucified God* (Philadelphia: Westminster Press, 1974).

Nash, Ronald H., *The Concept of God* (Grand Rapids: Zondervan, 1983).

Pannenberg, Wolfhart, "The Appropriation of the Philosophical Concept of God as a Dogmatic Problem of Early Christian Theology," in *Basic Questions in Theology*, vol. 2 (London: SCM Press, 1971), pp. 119–83.

Pollard, T. E., "The Impassibility of God," *Scottish Journal of Theology* 8 (1955), pp. 353–64.

Chapter 8   The Doctrine of the Trinity

Bracken, J., "The Holy Trinity as a Community of Divine Persons," *Heythrop Journal* 15 (1974), pp. 166–82; 257–70.

Brown, David, *The Divine Trinity* (London: Duckworth, 1985).

Congar, Yves, *I Believe in the Holy Spirit* 3 vols (New York: Seabury Press, 1983).

Gunton, Colin E., *The Promise of Trinitarian Theology* (Edinburgh: Clark, 1991).

Hendry, G. S., *The Holy Spirit in Christian Theology* (Philadelphia: Westminster Press, 1956).

Heron, A. I. C., *The Holy Spirit* (Philadelphia: Westminster Press, 1983).

Hill, W. J., *The Three-Personed God: The Trinity as the Mystery of Salvation* (Washington, DC: Catholic University of America Press, 1983).

Jenson, Robert W., *The Triune Identity: God According to the Gospel* (Philadelphia: Fortress Press, 1982).

——, "The Triune Identity," in *Christian Dogmatics* 2 vols, ed. C. E. Braaten and R. W. Jenson (Philadelphia: Fortress Press, 1984), vol. 1, pp. 83–191.

Lossky, Vladimir, "The Procession of the Holy Spirit in Orthodox Trinitarian Theology," in *In the Image and Likeness of God* (New York: St Vladimir's Press, 1974), pp. 71–96.

Macquarrie, John, *Principles of Christian Theology* (London: SCM Press, 1966).

Sears, R., "Trinitarian Love as Ground of the Church," *Theological Studies* 37 (1976), pp. 652–79.

Tavard, George, *Vision of the Trinity* (Washington, DC: Catholic University of America Press, 1981).

Torrance, Thomas F., "Towards an Ecumenical Consensus on the Trinity," *Theologische Zeitschrift* 31 (1975), pp. 337–50.

Wainwright, A. W., *The Trinity in the New Testament* (London: SPCK, 1969).

Williams, R. D., "Barth on the Triune God," in *Karl Barth: Studies of His Theological Method*, ed. S. W. Sykes (Oxford: Oxford University Press, 1979), pp. 147–93.

Zizoulas, J. D., *Being as Communion: Studies in Personhood and the Church* (London: Darton, Longman and Todd, 1985).

Chapter 9   The Doctrine of the Person of Christ

Baillie, D. M., *God was in Christ: An Essay in Incarnation and Atonement* (London: Faber & Faber, 1956).

Cullmann, Oscar, *The Christology of the New Testament* (London: SCM Press, 1959).

Dorner, J. A., *History of the Development of the Doctrine of the Person of Christ* 4 vols (Edinburgh: Clark, 1869–91).

Dunn, J. D. G., *Christology in the Making* (London: SCM Press, 1980).

Frend, W. H. C., *The Rise of the Monophysite Movement* (Cambridge, UK: Cambridge University Press, 1979).

Fuller, R. H., *The Foundations of New Testament Christology* (London: Collins, 1969).

Grillmeier, Aloys, *Christ in Christian Tradition* 2nd edn (London: Mowbrays, 1975).

Hahn, F., *The Titles of Jesus in Christology* (London: Lutterworth, 1969).

Kelly, J. N. D., *Early Christian Doctrines* 4th edn (London: A & C Black, 1968).

Lonergan, Bernard, *The Way to Nicea* (London: Darton, Longman and Todd, 1976).

Marshall, I. Howard, *The Origins of New Testament Christology* 2nd edn (Leicester: Inter-Varsity Press, 1992).

Moule, C. F. D., *The Origin of Christology* (Cambridge: Cambridge University Press, 1977).

Sellers, Robert V., *The Council of Chalcedon* (London: SPCK, 1961).

Sobrino, Jon, *Christology at the Crossroads* (London: SCM Press, 1978).

Williams, Rowan, *Arius: Heresy and Tradition* (London: Darton, Longman and Todd, 1987).

Chapter 10   Faith and History: A New Christological Agenda

Carnley, Peter, *The Structure of Resurrection Belief* (Oxford: Clarendon Press, 1987).

Harvey, Van A., *The Historian and the Believer* (London: SCM Press, 1976).

Jansen, J. F., *The Resurrection of Christ in New Testament Theology* (Philadelphia: Westminster Press, 1980).

Käsemann, Ernst, "Blind Alleys in the Jesus of History Controversy," in *New Testament Questions of Today* (London: SCM Press, 1969), pp. 23–66.

Michalson, Gordon E., *Lessing's Ugly Ditch: A Study of Theology and History* (University Park: Pennsylvania State University Press, 1985).

Perkins, Pheme, *Resurrection: New Testament Witness and Contemporary Reflection* (New York: Doubleday, 1984).

Peters, Ted, "The Use of Analogy in Historical Method," *Catholic Biblical Quarterly* 35 (1973), pp. 474–82.

Robinson, James M., *A New Quest for the Historical Jesus* (London: SCM Press, 1959).

Rumscheidt, H. M., *Revelation and Theology: An Analysis of the Barth–Harnack Correspondence of 1923* (Cambridge, UK: Cambridge University Press, 1972).

Schweitzer, Albert, *The Quest of the Historical Jesus* (London: Black, 1911).

Chapter 11 The Doctrine of Salvation in Christ

Aulén, Gustaf, *Christus Victor: An Historical Survey of the Three Main Types of the Idea of the Atonement* (London: SPCK, 1970).

Baillie, D. M., *God was in Christ: An Essay in Incarnation and Atonement* (London: Faber & Faber, 1956).

Daly, R. L., *The Origins of the Christian Doctrine of Sacrifice* (London: Darton, Longman and Todd, 1978).

Dillistone, F. W., *The Christian Understanding of Atonement* (London: SCM Press, 1984).

Fiddes, Paul, *Past Event and Present Salvation* (London: Darton, Longman and Todd, 1989).

Franks, Robert S., *The Work of Christ: A Historical Study* (London/New York: Nelson, 1962).

Gunton, Colin E., *The Actuality of Atonement* (Edinburgh: Clark, 1988).

MacCulloch, J. A., *The Harrowing of Hell* (Edinburgh: Clark, 1930).

McGrath, Alister E., "The Moral Theory of the Atonement," *Scottish Journal of Theology* 38 (1985), pp. 205–20.

Morris, Leon, *The Apostolic Preaching of the Cross* (Leicester: Inter-Varsity Press, 1965).

Rashdall, Hastings, *The Idea of Atonement in Christian Theology* (London: Macmillan, 1919).

Swinburne, Richard, *Responsibility and Atonement* (Oxford: Clarendon Press, 1989).

Sykes, S. W. (ed.), *Sacrifice and Redemption* (Cambridge, UK: Cambridge University Press, 1991).

White, Vernon, *Atonement and Incarnation* (Cambridge, UK: Cambridge University Press, 1990).

Wiederkehr, Dietrich, *Belief in Redemption: Concepts of Salvation from the New Testament to the Present Time* (London: SPCK, 1979).

Chapter 12 The Doctrines of Human Nature, Sin, and Grace

Donfried, K. P., "Justification and Last Judgement in Paul," *Zeitschrift für Neutestamentlichen Wissenschaft* 67 (1976), 90–110.

Dunn, J. D. G., "The New Perspective on Paul," *Bulletin of the John Rylands Library* 65 (1983), 95–122.

Haight, R., *The Experience and Language of Grace* (Mahwah, NJ: Paulist Press, 1979).

Hartt, Julian N., "Creation and Providence," in *Christian Theology*, ed. P. Hodgson and R. King (Philadelphia: Fortress Press, 1982), pp. 115–40.

Hefner, Philip J., "Creation," in *Christian Dogmatics* 2 vols, ed. C. E. Braaten and R. W. Jenson (Philadelphia: Fortress Press, 1984), vol. 1, pp. 269–357.

Kelsey, David H., "Human Being," in *Christian Theology*, ed. P. Hodgson and R. King (Philadelphia: Fortress Press, 1982), pp. 141–67.

Küng, Hans, *Justification* (London: Burnes & Oates, 1963).

McGrath, Alister E., *Iustitia Dei: A History of the Christian Doctrine of Justification* 2 vols (Cambridge: Cambridge University Press, 1986).

Sanders, E. P., *Paul and Palestinian Judaism* (London: SCM Press, 1977).

——, *Paul, The Law, and the Jewish People* (London: SCM Press, 1983).

Sponheim, Paul R., "Sin and Evil," in *Christian Dogmatics* 2 vols, ed. C. E. Braaten and R. W. Jenson (Philadelphia: Fortress Press, 1984), vol. 1, pp. 363–463.

Stendahl, K., *Paul among Jews and Gentiles* (Philadelphia: Fortress Press, 1976).

Toon, Peter, *Justification and Sanctification* (Westchester, Ill.: Crossway, 1983).

Williams, N. P., *The Ideas of the Fall and Original Sin* (London: Longmans, 1927).

Williams, R. R., "Sin and Evil," in *Christian Theology*, ed. P. Hodgson and R. King (Philadelphia: Fortress Press, 1982), pp. 168–95.

Chapter 13 The Doctrine of the Church

Aulén, Gustaf, *Reformation and Catholicity* (Philadelphia: Fortress Press, 1961).

Campenhausen, Hans von, *Ecclesiastical Authority and Spiritual Power in the Church of the First Three Centuries* (Stanford: Stanford University Press, 1969).

Dulles, Avery, *Models of the Church* (Dublin: Gill & Macmillan, 1976).

Hefner, Philip J., "The Church," in *Christian Dogmatics* 2 vols, ed. C. E. Braaten and R. W. Jenson (Philadelphia: Fortress Press, 1984), vol. 2, pp. 183–247.

Hodgson, Peter, "The Church," in *Christian Theology*, ed. P. Hodgson and R. King (Philadelphia: Fortress Press, 1982), pp. 223–47.

Küng, Hans, *The Church* (New York/London: Sheed & Ward, 1968).

Moltmann, Jürgen, *The Church in the Power of the Spirit* (New York: Harper & Row, 1977).

Pannenberg, Wolfhart, *Theology and the Kingdom of God* (Philadelphia: Westminster Press, 1969).

Schillebeeckx, Edward (ed.), *The Church and Mankind* (New York: Paulist Press, 1965).

Schmidt, Karl L., *The Church* (London: Black, 1950).

Segundo, Juan Luis, *The Community Called Church* (Maryknoll, NY: Orbis Books, 1978).

Willis, Geoffrey G., *Saint Augustine and the Donatist Controversy* (London: SPCK, 1950).

Chapter 14 The Doctrine of the Sacraments

Aland, Kurt, *Did the Early Church Baptize Infants?* (Philadelphia: Westminster Press, 1963).

Avis, P. D. L., *The Church in the Theology of the Reformers* (Basingstoke: Marshall Pickering, 1980).

Barth, Karl, *The Teaching of the Church Regarding Baptism* (London: SCM Press, 1948).

Beasley-Murray, G. R., *Baptism in the New Testament* (Grand Rapids: Eerdmans, 1962).

Clark, Francis, *Eucharistic Sacrifice and the Reformation* (London: Darton, Longman and Todd, 1960).

Fisher, J. D. C., *Christian Initiation: Baptism in the Medieval West* (London: SPCK, 1965).

Gerrish, Brian A., "Gospel and Eucharist: John Calvin on the Lord's Supper," in *The Old Protestantism and the New* (Edinburgh: Clark, 1982), pp. 106–17.

Hall, Basil, "*Hoc est corpus meum*: The Centrality of the Real Presence for Luther," in *Luther: Theologian for Catholics and Protestants*, ed. George Yule (Edinburgh: Clark, 1985), pp. 112–44.

Jenson, Robert W., *Visible Words* (Philadelphia: Fortress Press, 1978).

Jeremias, Joachim, *Infant Baptism in the First Four Centuries* (Philadelphia: Fortress Press, 1962).

——, *The Eucharistic Words of Jesus* (Philadelphia: Fortress Press, 1977).

Kavanagh, Aidan, *The Shape of Baptism* (New York: Pueblo Publishing, 1978).

Lampe, G. W. H., *The Seal of the Spirit* 2nd edn (London: SPCK, 1967).

Leeming, Bernard, *Principles of Sacramental Theology* (Westminster, Md.: Newman Press, 1960).

Riley, Hugh M., *Christian Initiation* (Washington, DC: Catholic University of America Press, 1974).

Schillebeeckx, Edward, "Transubstantiation, Transfinalization, Transsignification," *Worship* 40 (1966), pp. 324–38.

Steinmetz, David C., "Scripture and the Lord's Supper in Luther's Theology," in *Luther in Context* (Bloomington, Ind.: Indiana University Press, 1986), pp. 72–84.

Chapter 15 Christianity and the World Religions

Cobb, John B., *Christ in a Pluralistic Age* (Philadelphia: Westminster Press, 1975).

——, "The Religions," in *Christian Theology*, ed. P. Hodgson and R. King (Philadelphia: Fortress Press, 1982), pp. 299–322.

D'Costa, Gavin, *Theology and Religious Pluralism* (Oxford: Blackwell, 1986).

—— (ed.), *Christian Uniqueness Reconsidered: The Myth of a Pluralistic Theology of Religions* (Maryknoll, NY: Orbis Books, 1990).

Hick, John, *An Interpretation of Religion* (London: Macmillan, 1989).

——, and Knitter, Paul (eds), *The Myth of Christian Uniqueness* (Maryknoll, NY: Orbis Books, 1987).

Knitter, Paul, *No Other Name? A Critical Study of Christian Attitudes towards the World Religions* (Maryknoll, NY: Orbis Books, 1985).

Kraemer, Hendrik, *The Christian Message in a Non-Christian World* (London: Harpers, 1938).

Smith, Wilfred Cantwell, *Towards a World Theology* (London: Macmillan, 1981).

Whitehead, Alfred North, *Religion in the Making* (Cambridge: Cambridge University Press, 1926).

Chapter 16 Last Things: The Christian Hope

Baillie, John M., *And the Life Everlasting* (London: Oxford University Press, 1934).

Bratten, Carl E., "The Kingdom of God and the Life Everlasting," in *Christian Theology*, ed. P. Hodgson and R. King (Philadelphia: Fortress Press, 1982), pp. 274–98.

Bultmann, Rudolf, *History and Eschatology* (Edinburgh: Scottish Academic Press, 1957).

Cullmann, Oscar, *Christ and Time* (London: SCM Press, 1962).

MacCulloch, J. A., *The Harrowing of Hell* (Edinburgh: Clark, 1930).

Martin, James, *The Last Judgement in Protestant Theology* (Edinburgh: Oliver & Boyd, 1963).

Minear, Paul, *Christian Hope and the Second Coming* (Philadelphia: Fortress Press, 1974).

Moltmann, Jürgen, *Theology of Hope: On the Ground and the Implications of a Christian Eschatology* (New York: Harper & Row, 1967).

Niehbuhr, H. Richard, *The Kingdom of God in America* (New York: Harper & Row, 1959).

Robinson, J. A. T., *In the End God* (London: Collins, 1968).

Sanders, John, *No Other Name: An Investigation into the Destiny of the Unevangelized* (Grand Rapids: Eerdmans, 1992).

Schwarz, Hans, *On the Way to the Future: A Christian View of Eschatology* (Minneapolis: Augsburg Publishing House, 1979).

Stendahl, Krister (ed.), *Immortality and Resurrection* (New York: Macmillan, 1965).

Glossary of Theological Terms

What follows is a brief discussion of a series of terms that the reader is likely to encounter in the course of reading.

adiaphora
Literally, "matters of indifference." Beliefs or practices which the sixteenth-century Reformers regarded as being tolerable, in that they were neither explicitly rejected nor stipulated by Scripture. For example, what ministers wore at church services was often regarded as a "matter of indifference." The concept is of importance in that it allowed the sixteenth-century reformers to adopt a pragmatic approach to many beliefs and practices, thus avoiding unnecessary confrontation.

Alexandrian school
A patristic school of thought, especially associated with the city of Alexandria in Egypt, noted for its Christology (which placed emphasis upon the divinity of Christ) and its method of biblical interpretation (which employed allegorical methods of exegesis). A rival approach in both areas was associated with Antioch. See pp. 18–19; 287–9.

Anabaptism
A term derived from the Greek word for "re-baptizer," and used to refer to the radical wing of the sixteenth-century Reformation, based on thinkers such as Menno Simons or Balthasar Hubmaier. See p. 61.

analogy of being (*analogia entis*)
The theory, especially associated with Thomas Aquinas, that there exists a correspondence or analogy between the created order and God, as a result of the divine creatorship. The idea gives theoretical justification to the practice of drawing conclusions concerning God from the known objects and relationships of the natural order. See pp. 135–6.

analogy of faith (*analogia fidei*)
The theory, especially associated with Karl Barth, which holds that any correspondence between the created order and God is only established on the basis of the self-revelation of God. See pp. 135–6.

Anglicanism
A branch of theology especially associated with the churches historically derived from the Church of England. In the past, characteristic emphases have included the recognition of the relation between liturgy and theology, and an emphasis upon the importance of the doctrine of the incarnation.

anthropomorphism
The tendency to ascribe human features (such as hands or arms) or other human characteristics to God. See p. 140.

Antiochene school
A patristic school of thought, especially associated with the city of Antioch in modern-day Turkey, noted for its Christology (which placed emphasis upon the humanity of Christ) and its method of biblical interpretation (which employed literal methods of exegesis). A rival approach in both areas was associated with Alexandria. See pp. 18–19; 289–91.

anti-Pelagian writings
The writings of Augustine relating to the Pelagian controversy, in which he defended his views on grace and justification. See "Pelagianism."

apophatic
A term used to refer to a particular style of theology, which stressed that God cannot be known in terms of human categories. Apophatic (which derives from the Greek *apophasis*, "negation" or "denial") approaches to theology are especially associated with the monastic tradition of the Eastern Orthodox church.

apostolic era
The period of the Christian church, regarded as definitive by many, bounded by the resurrection of Jesus Christ (*c.*AD 35) and the death of the last Apostle (*c.*AD 90?). The ideas and practices of this period were widely regarded as normative, at least in some sense or to some degree, in many church circles.

appropriation
A term relating to the doctrine of the Trinity, which affirms that while all three persons of the Trinity are active in all the outward actions of the Trinity, it is appropriate to think of each of those actions as being the particular work of one of the persons. Thus it is *appropriate* to think of creation as the work of the Father, or redemption as the work of the Son, despite the fact that all three persons are present and active in both these works. See pp. 254–5.

Arianism

A major early Christological heresy, which treated Jesus Christ as the supreme of God's creatures, and denied his divine status. The Arian controversy was of major importance in the development of Christology during the fourth century. See pp. 283–7.

atonement

A term originally coined by William Tyndale to translate the Latin term *reconciliatio*, which has since come to have the developed meaning of "the work of Christ" or "the benefits of Christ gained for believers by his death and resurrection." See pp. 341–60.

Augustinianism

A term used in two major senses. First, it refers to the views of Augustine of Hippo concerning the doctrine of salvation, in which the need for divine grace is stressed. In this sense, the term is the antithesis of Pelagianism. Second, it is used to refer to the body of opinion within the Augustinian order during the Middle Ages, irrespective of whether these views derive from Augustine or not.

Barthian

An adjective used to describe the theological outlook of the Swiss theologian Karl Barth (1886–1968), noted chiefly for its emphasis upon the priority of revelation and its focus upon Jesus Christ. The terms "neo-orthodoxy" and "dialectical theology" are also used in this connection. See pp. 98–100.

Black theology

A movement in North American theology which became especially significant in the late 1960s, which emphasized the importance and distinctiveness of the religious experience of black people. See pp. 107–9.

Calvinism

An ambiguous term, used with two quite distinct meanings. First, it refers to the religious ideas of religious bodies (such as the Reformed church) and individuals (such as Theodore Beza) who were profoundly influenced by John Calvin, or by documents written by him. Second, it refers to the religious ideas of John Calvin himself. Although the first sense is by far the more common, there is a growing recognition that the term is misleading. See pp. 60–1.

Cappadocian fathers

A term used to refer collectively to three major Greek-speaking writers of the patristic period: Basil of Caesarea, Gregory of Nazianzen, and Gregory of Nyssa, all of whom date from the late fourth century. "Cappadocia" designates an area in Asia Minor (modern-day Turkey), in which these writers were based.

catechism
A popular manual of Christian doctrine, usually in the form of question and answer, intended for religious instruction.

Chalcedonian definition
The formal declaration at the Council of Chalcedon that Jesus Christ was to be regarded as both human and divine.

charisma, charismatic
A set of terms especially associated with the gifts of the Holy Spirit. In medieval theology, the term "charisma" is used to designate a spiritual gift, conferred upon individuals by the grace of God. Since the early twentieth century, the term "charismatic" has come to refer to styles of theology and worship which place particular emphasis upon the immediate presence and experience of the Holy Spirit.

Christology
The section of Christian theology dealing with the identity of Jesus Christ, particularly the question of the relation of his human and divine natures.

circumincession
See *perichoresis*.

confession
Although the term refers primarily to the admission of sin, it acquired a rather different technical sense in the sixteenth century – that of a document which embodies the principles of faith of a Protestant church. Thus the Augsburg Confession (1530) embodies the ideas of early Lutheranism, and the First Helvetic Confession (1536) those of the early Reformed church. The term "Confessionalism" is often used to refer to the hardening of religious attitudes in the later sixteenth century, as the Lutheran and Reformed churches became involved in a struggle for power, especially in Germany. The term "Confessional" is often used to refer to a church which defines itself with reference to such a document. Confessions (which define denominations) should be distinguished from creeds (which transcend denominational boundaries).

consubstantiation
A term used to refer to the theory of the real presence, especially associated with Martin Luther, which holds that the substance of the eucharistic bread and wine are given together with the substance of the body and blood of Christ. See pp. 441–2.

creed
A formal definition or summary of the Christian faith, held in common by all Christians. The most important are those generally known as the "Apostles' creed" and the "Nicene creed." See pp. 17–18.

Deism

A term used to refer to the views of a group of English writers, especially during the seventeenth century, the rationalism of which anticipated many of the ideas of the Enlightenment. The term is often used to refer to a view of God which recognizes the divine creatorship, yet which rejects the notion of a continuing divine involvement with the world. See pp. 184–5.

demythologization

An approach to theology especially associated with the German theologian Ruldolf Bultmann (1884–1976) and his followers, which rests upon the belief that the New Testament worldview is "mythological." In order for it to be understood within, or applied to, the modern situation, it is necessary that the mythological elements should be eliminated. See pp. 330–1.

dialectical theology

A term used to refer to the early views of the Swiss theologian Karl Barth (1886–1968), which emphasized the "dialectic" between God and humanity. See pp. 98–100.

dispensationalism

A Protestant movement, especially associated with North America, placing emphasis upon the various divine "dispensations" with humanity, and stressing the importance of eschatology. See pp. 472–3.

Docetism

An early Christological heresy, which treated Jesus Christ as a purely divine being who only had the "appearance" of being human. See p. 149.

Donatism

A movement, centering upon Roman North Africa in the fourth century, which developed a rigorist view of the church and sacraments. See pp. 407–10.

Ebionitism

An early Christological heresy, which treated Jesus Christ as a purely human figure, although recognizing that he was endowed with particular charismatic gifts which distinguished him from other humans. See p. 149.

ecclesiology

The section of Christian theology dealing with the theory of the church. See pp. 405–26.

eucharist

The term used in the present volume to refer to the sacrament variously known as "the mass," "the Lord's supper," and "holy communion."

Enlightenment, The
A term used since the nineteenth century to refer to the emphasis upon human reason and autonomy characteristic of much of western European and North American thought during the eighteenth century. See pp. 78–86 for a detailed analysis.

eschatology
The section of Christian theology dealing with the "last things," especially the ideas of resurrection, hell, and eternal life.

evangelical
A term initially used to refer to the nascent reforming movements, especially in Germany and Switzerland, in the 1510s and 1520s. The term was later replaced by "Protestant" in the aftermath of the Diet of Speyer. In modern times, the term has come to be used of a major movement, especially in English-language theology, which places especial emphasis upon the supreme authority of Scripture and the atoning death of Christ. See pp. 110–13.

exegesis
The science of textual interpretation, usually referring specifically to the Bible. The term "biblical exegesis" basically means "the process of interpreting the Bible." The specific techniques employed in the exegesis of Scripture are usually referred to as "hermeneutics."

exemplarism
A particular approach to the atonement, which stresses the moral or religious example set to believers by Jesus Christ. See pp. 355–60.

fathers
An alternative term for "patristic writers."

feminism
A major movement in western theology since the 1960s, which lays particular emphasis upon the importance of women's experience, and has directed criticism against the patriarchalism of Christianity. See pp. 100–2.

Five Ways, the
A standard term for the five "arguments for the existence of God" especially associated with Thomas Aquinas. See pp. 132–5.

Fourth Gospel
A term used to refer to the Gospel according to John. The term highlights the distinctive literary and theological character of this gospel, which sets it apart from the common structures of the first three gospels, usually known as the synoptic gospels.

fundamentalism
A form of American Protestant Christianity which lays especial emphasis upon the authority of an inerrant Bible. See pp. 112–13.

Gnosticism
A movement placing especial emphasis upon a contrast between the material and spiritual realms, which became of major importance during the second century. Its most characteristic doctrines include redemption apart from the material world, a dualist worldview which held that different gods were responsible for creation and redemption, and an emphasis upon the importance of "knowledge" (*gnosis*) in salvation. See pp. 15–16.

hermeneutics
The principles underlying the interpretation, or exegesis, of a text, particularly of Scripture.

historical Jesus
A term used, especially during the nineteenth century, to refer to the real historical person of Jesus of Nazareth, as opposed to the Christian interpretation of that person, especially as presented in the New Testament and the creeds. See pp. 316–27.

homoousion
A Greek term, literally meaning "of the same substance," which came to be used extensively during the fourth century to designate the mainstream Christological belief that Jesus Christ was "of the same substance as God." The term was polemical, being directed against the Arian view that Christ was "of similar substance" (*homoiousion*) to God. See pp. 18; 250.

humanism
A complex movement, linked with the European Renaissance. At the heart of the movement lay not (as the modern sense of the word might suggest) a set of secular or secularizing ideas but a new interest in the cultural achievements of antiquity. These were seen as a major resource for the renewal of European culture and Christianity during the period of the Renaissance. See pp. 37–42.

hypostatic union
The doctrine of the union of divine and human natures in Jesus Christ, without confusion of their respective substances. See pp. 287–9.

incarnation
A term used to refer to the assumption of human nature by God, in the person of Jesus Christ. See pp. 304–8. The term "incarnationalism" is often used to refer to theological approaches (such as those of late nineteenth-century Anglicanism) which lay especial emphasis upon God's becoming human.

justification by faith, doctrine of
The section of Christian theology dealing with how the individual sinner is able to enter into fellowship with God. The doctrine was to prove to be of major significance at the time of the Reformation.

kenoticism
A form of Christology which lays emphasis upon Christ's "laying aside" of certain divine attributes in the incarnation, or his "emptying himself" of at least some divine attributes, especially omniscience or omnipotence.

kerygma
A term used, especially by Rudolf Bultmann (1884–1976) and his followers, to refer to the essential message or proclamation of the New Testament concerning the significance of Jesus Christ. See pp. 324–5.

liberal Protestantism
A movement, especially associated with nineteenth-century Germany, which stressed the continuity between religion and culture. See pp. 92–6.

liberation theology
Although the term could designate any theological movement laying emphasis upon the liberating impact of the gospel, it has come to refer to a movement which developed in Latin America in the late 1960s, which stressed the role of political action and oriented itself toward the goal of political liberation from poverty and oppression. See pp. 105–7.

limited atonement
An approach to the doctrine of the atonement, especially associated with Calvinist writers, which holds that Christ's death is only effective for those who have been elected to salvation.

liturgy
The written text of public services, especially of the eucharist.

Lutheranism
The religious ideas associated with Martin Luther, particularly as expressed in the Lesser Catechism (1529) and the Augsburg Confession (1530). A series of internal disagreements within Lutheranism after Luther's death (1546) between hardliners (the so-called "Gnesio-Lutherans" or "Flacianists") and moderates ("Philippists"), led to their resolution by the Formula of Concord (1577), which is usually regarded as the authoritative statement of Lutheran theology.

magisterial Reformation
A term used to refer to the Lutheran and Reformed wings of the Reformation, as opposed to the radical wing (Anabaptism).

modalism
A Trinitarian heresy, which treats the three persons of the Trinity as different "modes" of the Godhead. A typical modalist approach is to regard God as active as Father in creation, as Son in redemption, and as Spirit in sanctification.

neo-orthodoxy
A term used to designate the general position of Karl Barth (1886–1968), especially the manner in which he drew upon the theological concerns of the period of Reformed orthodoxy. See pp. 98–100.

nominalism
Strictly speaking, the theory of knowledge opposed to realism. The term is, however, still used occasionally to refer to the *via moderna*. See pp. 34–5.

ontological argument
A form of argument for the existence of God especially associated with the scholastic theologian Anselm of Canterbury. See pp. 130–2.

orthodoxy
A term used in a number of senses, of which the following are the most important: Orthodoxy in the sense of "right belief," as opposed to heresy (see pp. 145–9); orthodoxy in the sense of a movement within Protestantism, especially in the late sixteenth and early seventeenth centuries, which laid emphasis upon need for doctrinal definition (see pp. 68–71).

parousia
A Greek term, which literally means "coming" or "arrival," used to refer to the second coming of Christ. The notion of the parousia is an important aspect of Christian understandings of the "last things." See p. 466.

patristic
An adjective used to refer to the first centuries in the history of the church, following the writing of the New Testament (the "patristic period"), or scholars writing during this period (the "patristic writers"). For many writers, the period thus designated seems to be *c*.100–451 (in other words, the period between the completion of the last of the New Testament writings and the Council of Chalcedon).

Pelagianism
An understanding of how humans are able to merit their salvation which is diametrically opposed to that of Augustine of Hippo, placing considerable emphasis upon the role of human works and playing down the idea of divine grace.

perichoresis
A term relating to the doctrine of the Trinity, often also referred to by the Latin term *circumincession*. The basic notion is that all three persons of the

Trinity mutually share in the life of the others, so that none is isolated or detached from the actions of the others.

Pietism
An approach to Christianity, especially associated with German writers in the seventeenth century, which places an emphasis upon the personal appropriation of faith, and the need for holiness in Christian living. The movement is perhaps best known within the English-language world in the form of Methodism. See pp. 73–4.

postliberalism
A theological movement, especially associated with Duke University and Yale Divinity School in the 1980s, which criticized the liberal reliance upon human experience, and reclaimed the notion of community tradition as a controlling influence in theology. See pp. 102–5.

postmodernism
A general cultural development, especially in North America, which resulted from the general collapse in confidence of the universal rational principles of the Enlightenment.

Protestantism
A term used in the aftermath of the Diet of Speyer (1529) to designate those who "protested" against the practices and beliefs of the Roman Catholic church. Prior to 1529, such individuals and groups had referred to themselves as "evangelicals."

radical Reformation
A term used with increasing frequency to refer to the Anabaptist movement – in other words, the wing of the Reformation which went beyond what Luther and Zwingli envisaged.

Reformed
A term used to refer to a tradition of theology which draws inspiration from the writings of John Calvin (1510–64) and his successors (see pp. 68–72). The term is generally used in preference to "Calvinist."

Sabellianism
An early trinitarian heresy, which treated the three persons of the Trinity as different historical manifestations of the one God. See pp. 256–7.

sacrament
In purely historical terms, a church service or rite which was held to have been instituted by Jesus Christ himself. Although Roman Catholic theology and church practice recognize seven such sacraments (baptism, confirmation, eucharist, marriage, ordination, penance, and unction), Protestant theologians generally argue that only two (baptism and eucharist) were to be found in the New Testament itself. See pp. 427–47.

schism
A deliberate break with the unity of the church, condemned vigorously by influential writers of the early church, such as Cyprian and Augustine. See pp. 408–9.

scholasticism
A particular approach to Christian theology, associated especially with the Middle Ages, which lays emphasis upon the rational justification and systematic presentation of Christian theology. See pp. 32–6.

Scotism
The scholastic philosophy associated with Duns Scotus.

Scripture principle
The theory, especially associated with Reformed theologians, that the practices and beliefs of the church should be grounded in Scripture. Nothing that could not be demonstrated to be grounded in Scripture could be regarded as binding upon the believer. The phrase *sola scriptura*, "by Scripture alone," summarizes this principle.

Septuagint
The Greek translation of the Old Testament, dating from the third century BC. The abbreviation LXX is generally used to refer to this text.

Sermon on the Mount
The standard way of referring to Christ's moral and pastoral teaching in the specific form which it takes in chapters 5–7 of Matthew's gospel.

soteriology
The section of Christian theology dealing with the doctrine of salvation (Greek: *soteria*).

synoptic gospels
A term used to refer to the first three gospels (Matthew, Mark, and Luke). The term (derived from the Greek word *synopsis*, "summary") refers to the way in which the three gospels can be seen as providing similar "summaries" of the life, death, and resurrection of Jesus Christ.

synoptic problem
The scholarly question of how the three synoptic gospels relate to each other. Perhaps the most common approach to the issue is the "two source" theory, which claims that Matthew and Luke used Mark as a source, while also drawing upon a second source (usually known as "Q"). Other possibilities exist: For example, the Grisebach hypothesis treats Matthew as having been written first, followed by Luke and then Mark.

theodicy
A term coined by Leibnitz to refer to a theoretical justification of the goodness of God in the face of the presence of evil in the world.

Thomism, *via Thomae*
The scholastic philosophy associated with Thomas Aquinas.

transubstantiation
The medieval doctrine according to which the bread and the wine are transformed into the body and blood of Christ in the eucharist, while retaining their outward appearance.

Trinity
The distinctively Christian doctrine of God, which reflects the complexity of the Christian experience of God. The doctrine is usually summarized in maxims such as "three persons, one God." See pp. 247–69.

two natures, doctrine of
A term generally used to refer to the doctrine of the two natures, human and divine, of Jesus Christ. Related terms include "Chalcedonian definition" and "hypostatic union."

Vulgate
The Latin translation of the Bible, largely deriving from Jerome, upon which medieval theology was largely based. Strictly speaking, "Vulgate" designates Jerome's translation of the Old Testament (except the Psalms, which was taken from the Gallican Psalter); the apocryphal works (except Wisdom, Ecclesiastes, I and II Maccabees, and Baruch, which were taken from the Old Latin Version); and all the New Testament. The recognition of its many inaccuracies was of fundamental importance to the Reformation.

Zwinglianism
The term is used generally to refer to the thought of Huldrych Zwingli, but is often used to refer specifically to his views on the sacraments, especially on the "real presence" (which for Zwingli was more of a "real absence").

Index